POETRY AND POLITICS
IN THE ENGLISH RENAISSANCE

D0544196

POETRY AND POLITICS IN THE ENGLISH RENAISSANCE

Revised Edition

DAVID NORBROOK

OXFORD
UNIVERSITY PRESS

OXFORD

UNIVERSITY PRESS

Great Clarendon Street, Oxford OX2 6DP

Oxford University Press is a department of the University of Oxford.
It furthers the University's objective of excellence in research, scholarship,
and education by publishing worldwide in

Oxford New York

Auckland Bangkok Buenos Aires Cape Town Chennai
Dar es Salaam Delhi Hong Kong Istanbul Karachi Kolkata
Kuala Lumpur Madrid Melbourne Mexico City Mumbai Nairobi
São Paulo Shanghai Singapore Taipei Tokyo Toronto

Oxford is a registered trade mark of Oxford University Press
in the UK and certain other countries

Published in the United States
by Oxford University Press Inc., New York

British Library Cataloguing in Publication Data

Data available

Library of Congress Cataloging in Publication Data

Data available

ISBN 0-19-924718-8
ISBN 0-19-924719-6 (pbk.)

1 3 5 7 9 10 8 6 4 2

Typeset in Ehrhardt MT
by SNP Best-set Typesetter Ltd., Hong Kong
Printed in Great Britain
on acid-free paper by
Biddles Ltd,
Giuldford and King's Lynn

Contents

Preface and Acknowledgements to the
Revised Edition

SINCE *Poetry and Politics in the English Renaissance* was published in 1984, it has become widely used by readers in search of an overview and a coherent narrative of the relations between poetry and politics in the years up to the Civil War. It is reissued now in the belief that the map then provided is still serviceable in its broad outlines, although an abundance of new research has provided sharper delineation and modified the contours. I have pointed to this new material (or as much of it as I have been able to assimilate) in footnotes, but have left the bulk of the text as it was in 1984. The major exceptions are slight changes in Chapters 7 and 8 to fine-tune my presentation of the relations between Jonson and the Spenserians; new material on the contexts of the Parliament of 1614 to incorporate some more recent research; and some added pages in Chapter 9 to try to make a fuller connection with my later work on George Wither. The book was something more than a reference guide; it was also a polemic, some of whose targets are scarcely current now, though others remain very much with us. The polemical aims help to explain the book's inclusions and omissions, and to rewrite from scratch would lose the argumentative structure. At the same time, I hope that in a number of ways the book will be found timely today. When it was published, 'revisionism' in the study of early modern politics was at its height and the line I took was consciously going against the grain of current work; by now, the tide has significantly changed. The 'new historicism' was also beginning its ascendancy with a very sharp reaction against the kinds of enquiry into authorship and agency with which my book was concerned; now, however, the balance between different approaches is starting to look more equal, and all kinds of rapprochement are taking place between different kinds of historical scholarship. I have added an Afterword which tries to situate the book in its original polemical context, to survey more recent work in the area, and to make some suggestions for further research. Also added to the new edition are a chronological table and a brief guide to further reading.

My thanks are due first of all to Sophie Goldsworthy for making possible this new edition. Funding for research assistance was provided by the College of Arts and Humanities of the University of Maryland, and I thank Mandi Chapman for her hard work in checking and correcting. In revisiting some of this material after a long absence I have been able to learn a great deal from my colleagues at the University of Maryland, with special thanks to Ralph Bauer, Kent Cartwright, Jane Donaworth, Neil Fraistat, Marshall Grossman, Donna Hamilton, Gary Hamilton, Ted Leinwand, and Bill Sherman. James Holstun provided helpful comments on the

Afterword. I am grateful to Gordon Campbell, Emrys Jones, and others who helped me to spot errors in the earlier edition. I have even less excuse for any remaining errors than I had in 1984.

Sharon Achinstein helped me with every kind of criticism, advice, help, and encouragement.

D. N.

Acknowledgements 1984

THIS book began life as an Oxford D.Phil. thesis on 'Panegyric of the Monarch and its Social Context under Elizabeth I and James I', submitted in 1978. I am indebted to my supervisors, John Buxton and Penry Williams, for their constant help and encouragement. I began postgraduate work at Balliol College, Oxford, and I would like to take this opportunity of paying tribute to the then Master, Christopher Hill, whose writings provided the initial impulse for this project. A research fellowship at Magdalen College, Oxford, helped me with much of the preliminary work which has now gone into the book, and I am very grateful to the President and Fellows for the privilege of a long period of uninterrupted research. A grant of sabbatical leave from the College and from the University enabled me to complete the first draft of the book. Several generations of undergraduates from Magdalen and some other colleges may have delayed the completion of this project but they have also greatly helped me by asking central questions and by resisting obfuscation. A work of synthesis like this is essentially the product of many people, and inevitably incurs more intellectual debts than it is possible adequately to acknowledge in footnotes or elsewhere, but I have done my best.

Many people have kindly read and commented on sections of the book or the whole typescript: I must thank Simon Adams, John Creaser, Patricia Duncker, Joanna Hodge, Emrys Jones, John King, John Pitcher, Kevin Sharpe, Nigel Smith, Penry Williams, Blair Worden, and Henry Woudhuysen. Errors and misjudgements are, of course, all my own work. I have learned a lot from discussions with Paul Hamilton, Bernard O'Donoghue, and Bob White. My parents have provided much support and encouragement. I am grateful for help with my research to the staff of the libraries of Magdalen College, of the English and Modern History Faculties, and of the Taylorian Institution in Oxford; of the British Library; and of the Folger Shakespeare Library, Washington. I have been very fortunate to be able to draw on the resources of the Bodleian Library for most of my research and I am grateful to the staff there for much help and for coping so valiantly with my handwriting.

D. N.

Chronology

1509	Death of Henry VII, accession of Henry VIII	
1512		Erasmus, *De copia*
1513		More writes *History of Richard III* Machiavelli, *The Prince* written; probably also working on drafts of *Discourses on Livy*
1515	Wolsey made Lord Chancellor	First printed edition of Tacitus' recently 'discovered' *Annals*
1516		More, *Utopia* Erasmus, New Testament in Latin
1517	Luther proclaims his theses against the church	
1518		Cambridge dispute between humanists and critics
1521	Burning of Luther's writings Henry VIII declared Defender of the Faith	1521–3 Skelton, 'Speak, Parrot' and other satires against Wolsey written
1522		Vives, *Instruction of a Christian Woman*, trans. R. Hyrde
1524		Tyndale works on English translation of Bible
1526		Copies of Tyndale's New Testament on sale in England, suppressed
1528		Tyndale, *Obedience of a Christian Man*
1529	More made Lord Chancellor	More, *Dialogue Concerning Heresies*
1530	Henry VIII initiates divorce	Tyndale's Old Testament published in Antwerp

1531		Sir Thomas Elyot, *The Boke Named the Gouernour* Machiavelli, *Discorsi* printed
1532		Machiavelli, *Il principe* printed ?*The Plowman's Tale* printed
1533	Henry VIII marries Anne Boleyn Pope excommunicates Henry VIII	
1534	Act of Supremacy establishing king as head of church in England and in Ireland More sent to Tower	
1535	More beheaded	
1536	Anne Boleyn beheaded, Wyatt imprisoned Northern Rebellion	Tyndale executed in Netherlands Wyatt, 'Mine Own John Poyntz' written possibly now, possibly 1541
1537		Cranmer, *The Institution of a Christian Man*
1538	Cromwell initiates programme of iconoclasm	John Bale, *King John*
1539		Publication of Coverdale's Great Bible—copy placed in every church
1540	Henry VIII marries Anne of Cleves; marriage annulled; marries Catherine Howard Cromwell beheaded	
1541	Abolition of all shrines ordered Henry VIII declared king of Ireland	
1542	Catherine Howard executed Wyatt imprisoned	
1543	Henry VIII marries Katherine Parr Access to vernacular Bible forbidden to men of lower sort and women below rank of gentlewoman	
1544	English liturgy introduced	
1545	Arrest of Anne Askew Council of Trent, beginning of Counter-	Sir Thomas Elyot, *Defence of Good Women*

	Reformation	Princess (later Queen) Elizabeth presents translation of Marguerite of Navarre, *Mirror of the Sinful Soul*, to Queen Katherine Parr ?Bale, *The Image of Both Churches*
1546		*First Examinacyon of Anne Askewe*
1547	Henry VIII dies, succeeded by Edward VI War with Scotland Book of Homilies Priests ordered to buy Erasmus' *Paraphrases*	Earl of Surrey executed for treason Katherine Parr, *The Lamentation of a Sinner* 'Vox populi vox Dei'
1548	Feast of Corpus Christi abolished	Shepherd, *John Bon and Mast Person* Princess Elizabeth, trans. of Marguerite de Navarre, *Godly Meditation*, ed. Bale Bale, *Illustrium maioris Britanniae scriptorum . . . summarium* ?La Boétie, *Discours de la servitude volontaire*
1549	Book of Common Prayer introduced Kett's rebellion Somerset ousted from power	Crowley, *The Voyce of the Laste Trumpet*
1550		Crowley (ed.), *Piers Plowman* Crowley, *The Way to Wealth*
1551		Anne, Margaret, and Jane Seymour, *Hecatodistichon* (elegies for Marguerite of Navarre) More, *Utopia*, trans. R. Robinson
1552	Revised Book of Common Prayer Somerset beheaded	
1553	Death of Edward VI, who has named Protestant Lady Jane Grey as successor and declared Mary and Elizabeth illegitimate. Lady Jane, put on throne by her father-in-law, the Duke of Northumberland, deposed after brief reign, subsequently executed. Mary Tudor takes throne Return to Catholicism, Mary relinquishes title of Supreme Head	Thomas Wilson, *The Arte of Rhetorique* *Pierce the Ploughmans Crede* reprinted

1554	Failed rebellion by Sir Thomas Wyatt, son of the poet Mary marries Philip II of Spain Parliament restores Catholicism	?*Mirror for Magistrates* suppressed
1555	Latimer and Ridley burned at stake	
1556		Foxe, *Christus triumphans*
1557		*Tottel's Miscellany* More, *English Works* Stationers' Company given monopoly of printing
1558	Death of Mary, accession of Elizabeth I	Knox, *First Blast of the Trumpet against the Monstrous Regiment of Women*
1559	Acts of Supremacy and Uniformity renounce Papal supremacy New Book of Common Prayer First Roman *Index librorum prohibitorum*	*Mirror for Magistrates*
1560		Geneva Bible Anne Lock, sonnets in translation of Calvin's sermons on Hezekiah
1561		Sackville and Norton, *Gorboduc* acted Hoby, translation of Castiglione, *The Book of the Courtier*
1562	John Hawkins, first slaving voyage to Guinea	Sternhold and Hopkins, *The Whole Book of Psalms*
1563	Parliament urges Elizabeth to marry and declare a successor Thirty-Nine Articles	Foxe, *Acts and Monuments* Barnabe Googe, *Eglogs, Epytaphes, and Sonettes*
1565		*Gorboduc* printed
1566	Controversy over ecclesiastical vestments	
1567	Mary Stuart abdicates in favour of James VI Revolt of the Netherlands against Philip II	

1568	Mary Stuart flees to England, Commissioners debate her case and casket letters	
1569	Rebellion of Earls of Northumberland and Westmoreland in name of Mary Stuart	
1570	Pope excommunicates Elizabeth	
1571		Foxe's *Acts and Monuments* to be displayed in every church
1572	Puritans campaign for religious reforms in Parliament St Bartholomew's Day massacre, Paris	
1575	Leicester entertains Elizabeth at Kenilworth	
1576	Puritans campaign for church reform in Parliament	Opening of The Theatre, London's first professional playhouse Thomas Drant, *Praesul*
1577	Archbishop Grindal placed under house arrest	Sidney, 'Discourse of Irish Affairs' Buchanan, *Baptistes* printed *Memoires de l'estat de France sous Charles neufiesme*: first printing of La Boétie, *Discours de la servitude volontaire*
1578		Holinshed, *Chronicles*, 1st edn. Work begins on Catholic Douai Bible Sidney, 'The Lady of May' ?Puttenham, 'Partheniades'
1579	Union of Utrecht: foundation of Dutch Republic Public uproar over proposal for marriage of Elizabeth to Duke of Alençon; negotiations delayed	Languet, *Vindiciae contra tyrannos* Buchanan, *De jure regni* Spenser, *Shepheardes Calender*
1580	Lord Grey appointed Lord Deputy of Ireland; Spenser becomes his secretary; Grey's forces massacre enemies at Smerwick, Ireland	John Lyly, *Euphues and his England* Sidney begins work on *Arcadia*

1581	Parliament introduces strong anti-Catholic legislation	
	The Fortress of Perfect Beauty staged at court	
	Marriage treaty signed between Elizabeth and Anjou	
1582	Lord Grey recalled from Ireland	Mulcaster, *The Elementarie*
		Buchanan, *Rerum Scoticarum historia*
1583	John Whitgift made Archbishop of Canterbury	Sir Thomas Smith, *De republica Anglorum*
1584	William of Orange assassinated	
	Bond of Association to defend Elizabeth	
1585	Elizabeth is offered sovereignty of Netherlands, declines but sends English troops under Leicester	
1586	Mary Stuart placed on trial	
	Sir Philip Sidney killed in Netherlands	
	New censorship restrictions	
1587	Mary Stuart executed	Holinshed, *Chronicles*, 2nd edn.
1588	Spanish Armada defeated	
	Marprelate tracts against bishops	
1589	Henry III of France assassinated; Henry of Navarre fights for succession	Anne Dowriche, *The French History*
		Puttenham, *Arte of English Poesie*
1590		Sidney, *Arcadia* (revised version ed. Sanford and Greville)
		Spenser, *The Faerie Queene*, Books I–III
		Ralegh visits Spenser at Kilcolman
1591		Spenser, *Complaints*
1592		Ralegh imprisoned for seducing a royal waiting-woman; ?writes 'The Ocean to Cynthia'
1593	Henry of Navarre becomes a Catholic	Sidney, *Arcadia* (composite version ed. Countess of Pembroke)
		Chapman, *Hymnus in Cynthiam*

1594	Henry IV crowned King of France Henry O'Neill, Earl of Tyrone, rises against Elizabeth I Trial of Lopez, the Queen's Jewish physician	Hooker, *Laws of Ecclesiastical Polity*
1595	Controversy over predestination at Cambridge. Elizabeth forbids publication of Whitgift's Calvinist Lambeth Articles. Ralegh sets sail to find El Dorado	Spenser, *Amoretti and Epithalamion*, *Colin Clouts Come Home Againe*; ?*View of the Present State of Ireland* written ?–1601 Greville, 'Letter to an Honourable Lady'
1596	Rebellion in Munster, Ireland Essex takes Cadiz	Spenser, *The Faerie Queene*, Books IV–VI, *Prothalamion*
1597		Bacon, *Essays*
1598	Spenser's castle at Kilcolman destroyed Edict of Nantes grants toleration to French Protestants	
1599	Essex appointed Lord Lieutenant of Ireland Bishops' ban on satires	Mary Sidney presents Psalms to Elizabeth Hayward, *Life of Henry IV* Contarini, *The Commonwealth and Government of Venice*, trans. Lewkenor
1600		Jonson, *Cynthia's Revels*
1601	Essex stages *coup d'état*, is executed	Performance of *Richard II* sponsored by Essex's supporters Jonson, *Poetaster*
1603	Elizabeth dies; succession of James VI and I. Ralegh imprisoned for high treason	Jonson questioned by Council over *Sejanus* Daniel, *A Panegyrike Congratulatorie*
1604	Hampton Court Conference to settle church Richard Bancroft appointed Archbishop of Canterbury –1610 first Parliament of James I	Drayton, *The Owle* Daniel, *Vision of the Twelve Goddesses*
1605	Gunpowder Plot	Daniel, *Philotas* printed Jonson, *Sejanus* printed Jonson, *Masque of Blacknesse*

1606

The Plowman's Tale reprinted
Drayton, *Pastorals*
Daniel, *The Queen's Arcadia*

1607   Earls of Tyrone and Tyrconnel flee from   Richard Niccols, *The Cuckow*
Ulster
Jamestown settlement, Virginia

1608   Plantation of Ulster begins
Protestant Union in Germany

1609   Truce between Spain and Netherlands

1610   Debates in Parliament over impositions   Daniel, *Tethys' Festival*
Jonson, *The Alchemist*
?Greville begins life of Sidney

1611   George Abbot appointed Archbishop of   Jonson, *Oberon*
Canterbury   Duplessis-Mornay, *Mysterie of*
Arbella Stuart escapes from Tower   *Iniquitie*
Authorized Version of the Bible

1612   Death of Salisbury, contest for   Drayton, *Poly-Olbion*, Part I
succession as Secretary of State   Wither, *Prince Henries Obsequies*
Death of Prince Henry

1613   Princess Elizabeth marries Frederick,   Chapman, *Masque of the Middle*
Elector Palatine   *Temple and Lincoln's Inn*
Sir Thomas Overbury poisoned   Browne, *Britannia's Pastorals*
Countess of Essex obtains divorce   Wither, *Epithalamia, Abuses Stript*
and Whipt

1614   Marriage of Somerset to Countess of   Ralegh, *History of the World* called
Essex   in
'Addled Parliament'; Wither, Hoskyns,   Sir Arthur Gorges, translation of
and others imprisoned   Lucan
Brooke, *The Ghost of Richard III*
Browne, *The Shepheards Pipe*
Wither, *A Satyre*
Selden, *Titles of Honour*

1615

Camden, *Annales rerum Anglicarum*
Wither, *The Shepherds Hunting, Fidelia*

1616   Trial and conviction of Earl and   James VI and I, *Works*
Countess of Somerset   Jonson, *Works, The Vision of Delight*
Rise to favour of George Villiers   Browne, *Britannia's Pastorals*, Part
II

		William Goddard, *A Satirycall Dialogue*
		Thomas Scott, *Philomythie*
1617	Ralegh, voyage to Guyana	
	James I visits Scotland	
1618	Revolt in Bohemia marks beginning of	Jonson, *Pleasure Reconciled to Virtue*
	Thirty Years War	Masque at Cole-Orton
	Synod of Dort	Daniel, *The Collection of the Historie of*
	Ralegh executed	*England*
	'Book of Sports' issued	
1619	Frederick V elected King of Bohemia	Wither, *A Preparation to the Psalter*
		Fletcher and Massinger, *Sir John van*
		Olden Barnavelt
		Weckherlin, *Oden und Gesänge*
1620	Frederick and Elizabeth driven into exile	Jonson, *News from the New World, Pan's*
	Voyage of *Mayflower* to New England	*Anniversary*
		Scott, *Vox populi*
		Wither, *Exercises upon the Firste Psalme*
1621	James I's third Parliament: Commons	Wither, *The Songs of the Old Testament*,
	attacks monopolies, impeaches Bacon;	*Wither's Motto*
	Sandys and Selden arrested	Wither arrested
		Jonson, *The Gypsies Metamorphosed*
1622		Whitehall Banqueting House
		completed
		Drayton, *Poly-Olbion*, Part II
		Wither, *Faire-Virtue*
		First English printings of serial
		newsbooks
		Jonson, *The Masque of Augurs*
1623	Charles and Buckingham journey to	Wither, *Hymnes and Songs of the*
	Spain, return campaigning for war	*Church*
	against Spain	
1624	James I's fourth Parliament	Jonson, *Neptune's Triumph for the Return*
	George Abbot, *A Treatise of the*	*of Albion*
	Perpetuall Visibility and Succession of	John Reynolds, *Vox coeli*
	the True Church printed	Middleton, *A Game at Chess* performed
		Browne works on *Britannia's*
		Pastorals, Part III
		Wither, *The Schollers Purgatory*
1625	Death of James I, accession of Charles I	

First Parliament of Charles I
Charles marries Henrietta Maria
War with Spain

1626   Second Parliament of Charles I   Jonson, *The Staple of News* performed
        Impeachment of Buckingham; Charles
        dissolves Parliament, orders forced loan

1627   Buckingham leads expedition to Île de   Thomas May, translation of Lucan
        Rhé   Drayton, *The Battle of Agincourt*
                                                          Phineas Fletcher, *Locustae*

1628   Third Parliament of Charles I. Petition   Wither, *Britain's Remembrancer*
        of Right
        Buckingham assassinated by John Felton

1629   Parliament dissolved, Selden imprisoned   Hobbes, translation of Thucydides
                                                          Milton, 'On the Morning of Christ's
                                                          Nativity'

1630   Drayton, *The Muses Elizium*

1631   Jonson/Jones, *Love's Triumph, Chloridia*

1632   Gustavus Adolphus killed in battle   Townshend, *Tempe Restor'd*
                                                          ?Milton, *Arcades*
                                                          Quarles, *The Shepherd's Oracles* written

1633   Declaration of Sports reissued   Herbert, *The Temple*
        Charles I visits Scotland; entertainments   Donne, *Poems*
        by Jonson at Welbeck, Drummond at   Prynne, *Histrio-Mastix*
        Edinburgh   Spenser, *View of the Present State
        Laud appointed Archbishop of   of Ireland* printed
        Canterbury
        Lady Eleanor Davies fined and
        imprisoned

1634   Writs for ship money   Shirley, *Triumph of Peace*
                                                          Carew, *Coelum Britannicum*
                                                          Jonson, *A Tale of a Tub* published
                                                          Jonson, *Love's Welcome at Bolsover*
                                                          Milton, *A Maske Presented at Ludlow
                                                          Castle*

1635   Davenant, *The Temple of Love*
                                                          Mure, *The Joy of Teares*

1636   Wither (trans.), Nemesius, *The
                                                          Nature of Man*

1637	Riots at Edinburgh against new prayer book	Death of Ben Jonson; Davenant emerges as poet laureate
	Star Chamber decree: new censorship laws	Masque at Skipton featuring Comus
	Trials of Burton, Prynne, and Bastwicke	Milton, *A Maske* printed
	Conflicts over ship money	
1638	Scottish National Covenant; Scottish General Assembly votes to abolish episcopacy	Davenant, *Britannia triumphans*
		Jonsonus Virbius; *Justa Edovardo King*
		Drummond, 'Irene'
1639	War with Scots, ended with Pacification of Berwick	
1640	'Short Parliament' meets and is quickly dissolved	Cokayne, masque at Bretby
	Scots invade England	
	'Long Parliament' assembles, Laud impeached	
1641	Triennial Bill	Milton, *Of Reformation*
	Strafford beheaded	Wither, *Haleluiah: or Britain's Second Remembrancer*
1642	Charles leaves London, raises standard against Parliament at Nottingham	

Introduction 1984[1]

SOME of the greatest English Renaissance poets were politicians, and all of them tried to influence public affairs through their writings. The rhetorician George Puttenham declared that poets had been the first lawgivers and the first politicians. Sir Philip Sidney believed that writing could be as politically important as practical statecraft: the poet could create images of political virtue which would be imitated in future ages, and could 'feign' a whole commonwealth, like Sir Thomas More in the *Utopia*. Ben Jonson agreed that the poet could 'feign a Commonwealth'. These facts have long been known, but much modern criticism has given a distorted picture of the political complexion of Renaissance poetry. In their anxiety to avoid projecting an anachronistic liberalism on to the period, critics have instead attributed to Renaissance poets a conservatism which is sometimes equally anachronistic. Nineteenth-century 'Whigs' and radicals had regarded English history as a steady progression towards enlightenment, and had seen the great poets as prophets of social and religious reform. The founding fathers of modern academic criticism, T. S. Eliot and F. R. Leavis, briskly dismissed the 'Whig' tradition, whose optimism had come to appear very hollow in the aftermath of the First World War. In their reading of seventeenth-century poetry Leavis and his disciples were very much concerned to counter Marxist interpretations, which had inherited some of the old radical language—a language that was to become disastrously compromised by the rise of Stalinism. The merit of the writings of Leavis and L. C. Knights was a refusal to accept the glib simplifications that contented some of their 'progressive' adversaries. But they had to produce some simplifications of their own, for the evidence in fact made it very difficult to write political radicalism completely out of the Renaissance poetic tradition. That tradition had culminated in Milton, whose uncompromising republicanism places his views even today outside the conventional framework of political discussion in England. Eliot and Leavis did not flinch from a drastic solution: Milton must be declared to have been a bad poet, and 'dislodged' from the canon.

The argument about Milton was not, of course, conducted in directly political terms. On the contrary, it was frequently argued that the poet's true function was to

---

[1] For fuller discussion of these issues see *Afterword*, below. Mention should be made of the following reviews: Richard Helgerson, *Studies in English Literature*, 26 (1986); Christopher Hill, *Note and Queries*, 33 (1986), 226–7; Frank Kermode, *Times Literary Supplement*, 18 January 1985, 65–6, reprinted in *The Uses of Error* (1989), 142–50; John N. King, *Huntington Library Quarterly*, 49 (1986), 277–80; Katharine Eisaman Maus, *Western Humanities Review*, 39 (1985), 369–71; Ivan Roots, *Literature and History*, 12 (1986); Peter L. Rudnytsky, *Renaissance Quarterly*, 40 (1987), 153–5; Kevin Sharpe, *History*, 71 (1986), 241–3; Daniel Woolf, *Queen's Quarterly*, 94 (1987), 145–7; Blair Worden, *London Review of Books*, 7:4 (1985), 13–14.

transcend politics, to reach, as L. C. Knights put it, a 'pre-political' area.[2] Leavis and his followers therefore tended to prefer either private, lyric poetry, or public verse which had a strong personal voice; the explicitly public forms of epic and political allegory fell from critical favour. Allegory was seen as marking a dissociation, a split between form and content, between public rhetoric and individual voice. The true poetic unity was 'organic' or 'symbolic', reflecting an indissoluble union between tradition and individual talent. And here political considerations became explicit: how could such a harmonious union of individual and society be achieved except in a traditionalist 'organic society' where the individual was part of a wider community? The poets Leavis and Knights brought to the fore were for the most part Anglicans who had rejected Puritan arguments and were, or seemed to be, committed to tradition: Donne, Jonson, Herbert. Banished from this new canon of traditionalists were not only Milton but also several other poets who were suspected of radical tendencies and whose poetry was held to be flawed by rhetoric: Greville, Sidney, Spenser. The effect of these exclusions, however, was a serious distortion of literary history. The important continuities from earlier 'prophetic' poets through to Milton were completely obscured. The narrowly English frame of reference of Leavisite criticism obscured the internationalist outlook of many Renaissance poets: it is impossible to understand the political concerns of Spenser or Milton without paying attention to European as well as national events.

It proved to be impossible in the long term to sustain such a radical revision of the canon. The next major phase of Renaissance criticism took a different course and led in some ways to a better political understanding. Partly under the influence of Aby Warburg and the formidable scholars who founded the Warburg Institute, literary critics began to take a new interest in rhetoric, iconography, and political allegory. The most imaginative of the Warburg scholars, Frances Yates, pioneered the study of prophetic and apocalyptic traditions in art and poetry; all subsequent work on Renaissance political poetry is greatly in her debt. Her increasing interest in magic and occultism, however, led perhaps to an overemphasis on mystical cults of monarchy at the expense of more critical and rationalistic elements in Renaissance political thought. Literary critics tended to seize on the more conservative aspects of iconographical scholarship, and on the central role of the court in patronizing the arts and in determining symbolic meanings, on the idea of works of art as arcane mysteries accessible only to a narrow elite.[3] Whereas the Leavisite critics had exalted sincerity above rhetoric, the new historically based criticism tended to go to the opposite extreme, to urge that any notion of authenticity was completely irrelevant to Renaissance court art. Poets and painters, it was pointed out, were not isolated individuals in this period, they were artificers who had a job to do; and given the domi-

---

[2] On the politics of Leavis and his followers see Francis Mulhern, *The Moment of* Scrutiny (London, 1979); L. C. Knights, *Further Explorations* (Stanford, Calif., 1965), 32; see also the same author's *Public Voices: Literature and Politics with Special Reference to the Seventeenth Century* (London, 1971).
[3] On the connection between social elitism and Neoplatonic symbolism see D. J. Gordon, 'Roles and Mysteries', in Stephen Orgel (ed.), *The Renaissance Imagination* (Berkeley and Los Angeles, 1975), 3–23.

nance of the court in the Renaissance patronage system, very often that job was to praise the monarch. Jonson's masques, which had been regarded by earlier critics as embarrassingly sycophantic, were praised for their iconographical erudition, and it was argued that only an anachronistic liberal sentimentality could find their effusive panegyrics in any way troublesome. Because of this new emphasis on the poet as voice of the patron's ideas rather than an intellectual innovator, the political explication of poetic allegories proved ultimately to be a rather predictable business: it was not to be expected that poets would criticize their patrons or oppose official policies.

Analysis thus tended to move from political content to artistic form; in fact, Renaissance poetry seemed to show that artistic forms could resolve political problems. Florentine Neoplatonist theory argued that apparently antagonistic ideologies could be reconciled, that certain arcane mythical images veiled transcendent, universal truths, though these could be understood only by a courtly elite. Artists could embody such truths in the forms of their works, forming complex numerical patterns which reconciled disharmonies. These theories were seized on by numerological critics who devoted immense effort to showing that even an apparently rambling and 'romantic' work like *The Faerie Queene* conformed to rigid mathematical laws: the structure of the poem thus embodied the poet's conviction that the state and the universe were all patterned on just and divinely ordained principles.[4] All the virtuous females in the poem were read as images of Queen Elizabeth in her capacity as personal reconciler of political disputes. The new historical scholarship helped our general understanding of Renaissance poetry, but it did not give a complete account either of *The Faerie Queene*'s formal idiosyncrasies or of the political influences on Spenser's thought. This line of historical criticism tended to stop short at points where history became politically contentious. Numerological and mythological criticism reached their height in the post–Second World War period which saw a general reaction against historicism and political ideologies, a search for timeless archetypal and mythical patterns, and even the best historical criticism of the period tended to flatten out tensions and contradictions in the poetry into a mandarin formalism. In a seminal essay Frank Kermode did try to counter archetypal readings by an insistence on Spenser's engagement with history, and he drew attention to the important influence of apocalyptic ideas on *The Faerie Queene*. But he was anxious to show that Spenser was not too 'extreme': Kermode was deeply suspicious of large-scale schemes of historical explanation, a hostility that extended into his work on narrative structure. He linked radical Protestant apocalyptic thought with the idealist historical patterns adopted by Yeats and Lawrence; but this comparison itself evaded history by failing to recognize the very different historical contexts of sixteenth-century Protestantism and twentieth-century reactionary ideology. His reading of Spenser subordinates the apocalyptic element in the poem to courtly celebration: *The Faerie Queene*, he says, celebrates Elizabeth's accession and the Elizabethan church settlement as an unrepeatable interruption of the normal processes of history, 'a phase of no temporal cycle but a once-for-all historical event, like the Incarnation itself'. The

---

[4] See especially Alastair Fowler, *Spenser and the Numbers of Time* (London, 1964)

poem engages with history only in so far as it celebrates the queen as a living embodiment of transcendent truths.[5]

Leavisite criticism had tended to see Renaissance England as a unified organic community whose poets defended tradition against political and economic changes; in more recent historical criticism the Tudor and Stuart courts have been seen as the centres of English cultural life, and critics of the court, by extension, as inherently inimical to culture. In both cases the nation tends to be seen as a unified work of art: political dissension is regarded as a negative force which shatters that unity. In conservative, hierarchical societies where social roles are kept very distinct, public symbolism will tend to be sharply and clearly defined; hence the claim of some poets and critics that such societies are a particularly secure basis for the production of poetry.[6] The further implication is that the uncertainties of liberal pluralism erode artistic production: hence the flirtation of such influential twentieth-century poets as Yeats and Pound with fascist ideas. As Walter Benjamin pointed out, fascist leaders and ideologues tried to aestheticize politics, to turn the state into a spectacular work of art in order to legitimize their power.[7] This process was already in evidence in the Renaissance: the Medici princes exploited elaborate pageantry and spectacle to gain the people's affection. Faced with such phenomena, radical politicians from the sixteenth century down to the present day have sometimes despaired of art altogether, viewing it as a mere instrument for the domination of a corrupt prince or ruling class. As Hazlitt wrote in a moment of pessimism:

The cause of the people is . . . but little calculated as a subject for poetry: it admits of rhetoric, which goes into argument and explanation, but it presents no immediate or distinct images to the mind. . . . The language of poetry naturally falls in with the language of power . . . [The imagination] is a monopolising faculty, which seeks the greatest quantity of present excitement by inequality and disproportion; [the understanding] is a distributive faculty, which seeks the greatest quantity of ultimate good, by justice and proportion. The one is an aristocratical, the other a republican faculty. The principle of poetry is a very anti-levelling princi-

    [5] Frank Kermode, 'Spenser and the Allegorists', in *Shakespeare, Spenser, Donne* (London, 1971), 16, 22; cf. his *The Sense of an Ending: Studies in the Theory of Fiction* (New York, 1967), 29.

    [6] The antithesis between the modern, fragmented 'Gesellschaft' and the traditional, unified 'Gemeinschaft' can be traced back to the Romantic period. Compare the comment by A. W. Schlegel that in Shakespeare's time 'the distinction of ranks was as yet strongly marked: a state of things ardently to be desired by the dramatic poet': *Lectures on Dramatic Art and Literature*, trans. J. Black, ed. A. J. W. Morrison (London, 1846), 349.

    [7] Walter Benjamin, 'The Work of Art in the Age of Mechanical Reproduction', in *Illuminations*, ed. Hannah Arendt, trans. H. Zohn (London, 1970), 244. I have adapted the phrase 'aestheticization of politics' from Benjamin but shall be using it in a more general sense. Benjamin's work on images and politics forms an interesting contrast to the approach of the Warburg school. Benjamin's label is of course anachronistic; but the kinds of aestheticization against which he protested had long-term roots in nineteenth-century idealizations of the Italian Renaissance, notably Jacob Burckhardt's analysis of 'the state as a work of art'. Though often seen in current histories of Renaissance scholarship as celebrating modern individuality, Burckhardt was an ambivalent celebrator of Renaissance despotisms, reacting sharply against the vision of earlier historians like J. C. L. de Sismondi, who were still in touch with a republican, civic humanist tradition. Debates between republican and courtly models of political culture were intensely lively in the early modern period, and to that extent it is not anachronistic to see 20th-century debates as recapitulating many themes of earlier disputes. See David Norbrook, 'Life and Death of Renaissance Man', *Raritan*, 8:4 (Spring, 1989), 89–110.

ple. . . . Wrong dressed out in pride, pomp, and circumstance, has more attraction than abstract right.[8]

Renaissance political poetry, and its reception by modern critics, would seem to bear out Hazlitt's analysis. But what gives the period an unusual interest is that some of the most original political poets were aware of the problem Hazlitt describes, and from the *Utopia* through to *Comus* their works reveal a number of attempts to redress apparent imbalances between imagination and rhetoric, between might and right. Already in the early sixteenth century Machiavelli had criticized those who took unity and harmony as the sole criteria of political well-being. In his *Discourses*, written to challenge the ideology propagated by supporters of the Medici, he argued that dissension and disorder, the inevitable concomitants of popular participation in government, could in some circumstances be sources of strength rather than weakness. The Roman republic had owed its political dynamism to its mixed constitution which included popular participation; the search for complete order and harmony might lead merely to stagnation.[9] Machiavelli was, it is true, unusual in adopting these arguments, and most of his contemporaries laid much more emphasis on the priority of order. As so many modern critics have pointed out, it was generally believed that too much liberty was a bad thing; what has been less often recognized is that for some Renaissance writers there could be such a thing as too much order. It was also being argued in the sixteenth century that authoritarianism led to artistic as well as political stagnation, that the imagination was in the long run more likely to be weakened than strengthened by conditions of rigid and inflexible hierarchy. Art that can imagine nothing beyond the existing political order is extremely limited; and an art that projects its visions of harmony and reconciliation into the future, in a prophetic, utopian spirit, is very different from an art that simply glorifies its own patrons. Most of the major Renaissance poets were at one time or another in the service of powerful monarchs, and their language of necessity fell in with the language of power; but far from regarding this process as 'natural', they developed elaborate strategies to try to preserve a degree of independence for their writing. It may be questioned how far they succeeded; but the process gives an unusual interest and complexity to their writing. To understand their poetry, however, it is essential to relate it to other forms of political discourse: in Benjamin's phrase, to politicize aesthetics.

To attempt to politicize the sphere of the aesthetic is to risk the accusation of reductionism. Certainly one should not deny the distinctions between poetry and other forms of discourse. But in the Renaissance these distinctions were by no means as absolute as they became in Romantic theory: as long as so many poets were actively involved in public affairs, the similarities between poetry and rhetoric were felt to be as significant as the differences. And a rigid antithesis between political and aesthetic

---

[8] *The Complete Works of William Hazlitt*, ed. P. Howe, 21 vols (London, 1930), iv.214–15. Cf. Marilyn Butler, *Romantics, Rebels and Reactionaries: English Literature and its Background 1760–1830* (Oxford, 1981), 167.

[9] Machiavelli, *Discourses*, 1.2–5.

spheres is itself reductive. The claim that poetry should 'transcend' politics implies that the political sphere is irredeemably fallen, that art alone can redeem us from its contagion: thus all political activity, of whatever kind, is reduced to the same degraded status. The issue is not so much why one should politicize poetry as why critics have for so long been trying to depoliticize it. The quest for a transcendence of politics in fact ends up by reducing poetry itself. Those traditionalist writers— Shakespeare, Jonson, Hooker—whom Leavisite critics considered able to reach a 'pre-political' area were often praised in terms which implied they had also reached a pre-verbal level, that their writings gave unmediated access to the inner personality. But poetry can never be entirely 'redeemed' from language; and it cannot be 'redeemed' from the political assumptions encoded in all systems of signification. From religious rituals to conventional sexual roles, such systems postulate particular power relations as part of the natural order, and hence as not open to political negotiation; such claims should not be taken at face value.[10] Our conventional notion of the 'political' itself involves certain assumptions about those institutions which are open to question and those which are not: for example, only relatively recently has it become widely acknowledged that sexual roles are 'political' precisely because the power relations they embody have been challenged. Religious disputes in the Renaissance period so often seem to have centred on 'forms' rather than theological 'content' because it was recognized that the traditional forms legitimized hierarchical power structures in the church. These liturgical debates may seem abstruse in the present ecumenical age, but the continuing controversy over the role of women in religious ritual raises comparable issues of power and authority. Similarly, poetic forms and conventions may have political implications which go deeper than the author's explicit allegiances. It is certainly true that Jonson's poems of praise are not as overly polemical as Bale's dramas; this does not mean, however, that these texts completely transcend political issues. Moreover, in the cases of Hooker and Jonson the adoption of an apparently non-rhetorical position may itself be part of a rhetorical strategy. Concentrating on the sincere personality which is held to underlie the texts obstructs proper recognition of their role in the sphere of public discourse.

A new awareness of the fundamentally political character of forms, of rhetoric, has led to a shift in much recent criticism away from the analysis of political content as conventionally defined towards epistemological issues, towards the politics of the sign. The Leavisite critics regarded the poetic symbol as an almost sacramental union of sign and thing signified: the author's personality was fully present in an authentic poem. 'Poststructuralist' critics take issue with this idea that there is a stable relationship between self and symbol: the self, they argue, is a construct with no meaning outside language, and linguistic signifiers are markers of absence: meaning and consciousness are never sacramentally 'present' in them. Iconographically trained critics were confident that symbols had definite, verifiable meanings: post-

---

[10] See Michel Foucault, 'The Order of Discourse', in Robert Young (ed.), *Untying the Text: A PostStructuralist Reader* (Boston, 1981), 48–78. I must emphasize that I am using the term 'poststructuralist' very generally; my concern is with the application of certain approaches to Renaissance texts, not with the full complexities of the original theories.

structuralists argue that such a confident move from signifier to signified does violence to the complexity of the play of signifiers and is hence inherently authoritarian. The radicalism of texts is now located not in their overt political content but in their subversion of the conventional processes of signification. Thus Jonathan Goldberg can describe *The Faerie Queene* as 'revolutionary' because of the text's preoccupation with the processes by which meaning is produced.[11] Goldberg is of course using the word 'revolutionary' in an epistemological sense, without making any assumptions about Spenser's conscious political intentions: the text itself is radical because it allows readers to participate in the production of meanings rather than providing them with a fully formed content.

Recent critical theory has opened up new ways of analysing the relationships between texts and power which go beyond simply lining up poets according to their explicit political views. These new lines of enquiry will need to be taken further. But in some cases the assault on traditional modes of explication has been pushed so far that the methodology undermines political analysis rather than aiding it. As Frank Lentricchia has pointed out, there is a danger that a 'new formalism' may emerge which, for all its self-dramatizing radical rhetoric, effectively 'transcends' politics as completely as the old.[12] There is, of course, a major philosophical difference between the idea that there is no unifying authorial presence in *The Faerie Queene* and the idea that the author impartially presents both sides of every question; but both theories divert our attention away from Spenser's specific ideological allegiances. Like the New Critics, many poststructuralists are extremely hostile to the project of reconstructing authorial intention. Such a reconstruction can only be hypothetical and I do not believe that it can offer a complete and authoritative guide to interpretation: but if, as so often in the Renaissance period, authorial intention has a substantial and under-acknowledged political element, to ignore the intention is effectively to depoliticize.[13] Many recent Marxist critics have become so anxious to avoid the crude didacticism of older theorists that they have accepted the poststructuralist tenet according to which the most radical text is that which most effectively resists a single determinate interpretation. They have argued as strongly as Leavis ever did that the

---

[11] Jonathan Goldberg, *Endlesse Worke: Spenser and the Structures of Discourse* (Baltimore, 1981), 137 n. 7. Goldberg quickly adds that the 'revolution' the text 'glimpses' is a purely linguistic one and is in any case completely impossible.

[12] Frank Lentricchia, *After the New Criticism* (Chicago, 1980), 180. It should be said that my 1984 survey omitted the figure of William Empson, a great critic and close reader who was also keenly interested in history and politics.

[13] It is impossible to give an adequate discussion here of the complex question of literary intention. It has been much discussed in relation to political as well as literary texts by Quentin Skinner; see, for example, 'Hermeneutics and the Role of History', *New Literary History*, 7 (1975–6), 209–32. Alastair Fowler makes a strong case for intentionalism in 'The Selection of Literary Constructs', ibid. 39–55; but on the limitations of the best-known intentionalist critic, E. D. Hirsch, see Lentricchia, 'E. D. Hirsch: The Hermeneutics of Innocence', in *After the New Criticism*, 257–80. Some of Skinner's essays have been collected, along with a series of critiques and Skinner's reply, in James Tully (ed.), *Meaning and Context: Quentin Skinner and his Critics* (Princeton, 1988); on pragmatics and criticism see Sandy Petrey, *Speech Acts and Literary Theory* (New York, 1990). Skinner, in Tully (ed.), *Meaning and Context*, 269–70, distinguishes his position from that of Hirsch, who insists that the author's determining will is the ultimate guide to a text's meaning; Skinner's concern is not with the meaning but with the illocutionary act.

lyrics of Donne and Marvell are valuable because they do not force the reader to take sides, and that Milton should be expunged from the literary canon because of his texts' insistent moves towards closure.[14] The continuing challenge to the 'Whig' view of history has extended to the realm of metre: Antony Easthope has acutely pointed out the strongly linear, teleological movement of the iambic pentameter metre popularized by sixteenth-century humanists and has argued, echoing a Leavisite concern, that the poetry of the old feudal order embodied a much more positive sense of community.[15] The ghost of the old 'dissociation of sensibility' reappears: for Leavis it was the dissociated Puritans who tried to restore the old unity of being, while now the Puritans are seen as denying the radical split in human subjectivity in their impossible search for an imaginary self-presence.

The new shift from the political to the epistemological has revived some older sociological ideas. The notion of the 'organic community' reappears in a new guise in the idea that the 'carnivalesque' discourse of the medieval order permitted a free play of signifiers, a movement beyond narrowly individual subjectivity, which was suppressed by the new bourgeois order. Literary critics seem particularly susceptible to the charm of an era before the curse of mass literacy. The writings of Mikhail Bakhtin, Marshall McLuhan, and Walter J. Ong have given renewed authority to the argument that the best features of Renaissance literature derived not from intellectually innovative currents but from residual elements of the old 'oral' culture. In Spenser, Father Ong has argued, that residue is still strong enough to give his poetry an 'oral' character despite his professed commitment to the new Protestant culture; but in Milton's more narrowly individualistic poetry Puritan radicalism has finally suppressed this traditional source of energy.[16] The interest in communal rituals which worked against the emergence of the individual subject has produced a continuing fascination with the culture of Renaissance courts, which were, as one historian has noted, paradises for structuralists.[17] Courtiers had of necessity to rid themselves of any notion of the autonomous self, to become living allegories. Such an environment, critics have argued, was the best site for poetic composition. There has been a continued fascination with Jonson's masques, those triumphs of dissimulation. The courtly aesthetic scorned art which yielded up its meanings too easily to the vulgar and preferred esoteric texts, complex labyrinths to be contemplated rather than explicated; such an emphasis is more congenial to poststructuralists than didactic theories of literature.[18] There is indeed a certain continuity in the work of one of the most eminent Renaissance critics, Frank Kermode, who has moved from

---

[14] Catherine Belsey, *Critical Practice* (London, 1980), 98; Antony Easthope, 'Towards the Autonomous Subject in Poetry: Milton "On his Blindness"', in Francis Barker et al. (eds.), *1642: Literature and Power in the Seventeenth Century* (Colchester, 1981), 301–14, and id., *Poetry as Discourse* (London, 1983), 160–3.

[15] Easthope, *Poetry as Discourse*, 70 ff., 78 ff.

[16] Walter J. Ong, 'Oral Residue in Tudor Prose Style', *Publications of the Modern Language Association of America*, 80 (1965), 145; cf. Marshall McLuhan, *The Gutenberg Galaxy: The Making of Typographic Man* (London, 1962), and Mikhail Bakhtin, *Rabelais and his World*, trans. Helene Iswolsky (Cambridge, Mass., 1968).

[17] Lauro Martines, *Power and Imagination: City-States in Renaissance Italy* (London, 1979), 317 ff.

[18] Daniel Javitch, *Poetry and Courtliness in Renaissance England* (Princeton, 1978).

his earlier interest in Neoplatonic images to a sympathetic (though not uncritical) exposition of current theories of the infinite plurality of meanings. His work on the Renaissance revealed profound doubts about the validity of attempts to find coherent meanings either in fictive narratives or in the course of history as interpreted by apocalyptic or progressive theories. In his recent writings these doubts have been voiced with increasing insistence, approaching the all-embracing scepticism of some deconstructionists. 'World and book, it may be, are hopelessly plural, endlessly disappointing; we stand alone before them, aware of their arbitrariness and impenetrability.'[19] Such scepticism may be justifiable as a resistance to naively optimistic or crudely all-embracing theories of history; but a refusal to find meanings can itself become a limiting dogma, inhibiting a full understanding of the past, and, perhaps, the production of effective political poetry in the present. In one of his early books, *Romantic Image*, Kermode forcefully criticized the Symbolist aesthetic which placed above literary texts the notice: 'No road through to action.'[20] A quarter of a century later the notice is still there.

There are interesting parallels between the reactions against teleology in literary theory and in historiography. The high point of Victorian liberal historiography, S. R. Gardiner's *History of England*, traced the origins of the Civil War back to the start of the seventeenth century. He was working during the heyday of the Victorian novel and his own project displayed an immense confidence in the power of narrative to reveal important truths. Many modern historians regard such long-term explanations as unnecessary or meaningless: denying that the Civil War represented any major conflict of principles or classes, they search for explanations in ever more minute temporal and geographical units. And the closer the behaviour of local communities over short periods is scrutinized, the harder it becomes to detect the old large concepts like 'Puritanism' and 'liberty'. Liberal historiography at times embodied a Hegelian evolutionism in which concepts like 'liberty' developed in harmony with the progress of Spirit. To such historical 'realism' revisionist historians have responded with an emphatic nominalism. They have argued that anachronistic terms like 'progressive' and 'conservative' are irrelevant to the study of Renaissance political thought.[21] A comparable assault on teleology has been made by anti-Hegelian and 'anti-humanist' theorists like Althusser and Foucault.[22] Admittedly British and American historians have so far been less radical in their assault on conventional teleological theories; they have appealed to empirical evidence rather than

---

[19] Frank Kermode, *The Genesis of Secrecy: On the Interpretation of Narrative* (Cambridge, 1979), 145; quoted by Goldberg, *Endlesse Worke: Spenser and the Structures of Discourse*, p. xii. On Kermode's critical premisses see Lentricchia, *After the New Criticism*, 31 ff.

[20] Frank Kermode, *Romantic Image* (London, 1957), 161.

[21] See, for example, Conrad Russell's introduction to *The Origins of the English Civil War* (London, 1973), 5–6. For a different approach see Lawrence Stone, *The Causes of the English Revolution 1529–1642* (London, 1972). For fuller discussion of the historiographical issues see the 'Afterword' below.

[22] For an ambitious interpretation of the Renaissance influenced by Althusser's idea of different levels of temporality which follow autonomous courses see Perry Anderson, *Lineages of the Absolutist State* (London, 1974), 421 ff. Anderson has noted elsewhere the massive political pessimism that underlies much recent anti-teleological writing: *Considerations on Western Marxism* (London, 1976), 88–92.

to theories of discourse and have tended to assume that every political text must have a definitive meaning governed by authorial intention. They have defended narrative history, albeit sometimes of a narrowly political kind, against the anti-humanist critique of all kinds of discourse which place the individual subject at the centre of the historical process. But the revisionist historians share with Foucault and his disciples an emphasis on the radical discontinuity between Renaissance political consciousness and modern liberal or radical ideas. Arguing that there was an overwhelming consensus on fundamental ideological questions in the sixteenth and earlier seventeenth centuries, many recent historians have fixed their attention on the forms rather than the ideological content of political discourse. Political arguments in the period are held to have reflected personal rivalries in the struggle for position within the court patronage system, and much emphasis has been placed on the role of aristocratic patrons in determining political consciousness.[23] Many recent literary critics have endorsed this view of the Renaissance, concentrating not on ideological issues but on the struggle for personal advancement.

The revisionist historians have certainly brought into the light a great deal of important evidence and have provided a corrective to some conventional oversimplifications. But literary criticism, as I have tried to show, has been engaged in its own process of revaluation and revision since the 1920s, and by this time critics are likely to err in the direction of overemphasizing, rather than underemphasizing, the gulf between past and present. Historians are perhaps inevitably concerned with the common denominators of political thought; but major poets are already in some sense exceptional, and I believe that to try to interpret their texts by reference to the commonplaces of the age can be extremely misleading. If the more conventional writers throughout the period took the existence of the traditional social hierarchies and political institutions for granted, as part of the order of nature, there were a few who asked rather more searching questions. In recent years some excellent scholars and critics have been exploring the more innovative currents of political and religious thought in the English Renaissance. My main aim is to make these discoveries more widely available and to try to shape them into a broad overview of the period. Such an overview must of course be partial and provisional; I am painfully aware of many topics which deserve much fuller and more systematic treatment than I have been able to give them. The main focus of the book is on the period from 1578 to 1637, and the first two, essentially introductory, chapters have to cover a great deal of ground in a fairly summary way. Literary history always faces the problem of generalizing about a large body of texts without becoming critically banal. My comments have often had to be very brief, suggesting a general context in which a political reading can best be made rather than spelling out the details of such a reading. I have also had to be selective politically: in emphasizing the more innovative currents of thought, which link More with Milton, I have inevitably given less prominence to the undoubtedly powerful continuance of traditional ideas. The literature of the period

---

[23] See the collection of essays edited by Kevin Sharpe, *Faction and Parliament: Essays on Early Stuart History* (Oxford, 1978).

between More and Milton certainly does not show a steady, purposive march to liberal enlightenment. Radical potential in particular ideas or symbols might be latent for many years and become realized only at moments of crisis, as in the occasional outbursts of apocalyptic fervour. But only the continued presence of such radical potential can explain what conservatives felt it necessary to react against. Parliament is not perhaps the right place to look for radical ideas: traditionalism, and a hostility to abstract ideas as dangerous foreign inventions, have been consistent features of British political life from the seventeenth century to the present day. There were a number of reasons, however, why poets in the Renaissance period should have failed to conform to the dominant patterns of thought. Both their literary interests and their careers placed them in contact with radically different political traditions. The act of writing became for them a means of moving away from received ideas and experimenting with new political values, of 'feigning commonwealths'. This process need not always have had radical intentions. Even if, as some scholars argue, More outlined the communist republic of Utopia only as an enormous Aunt Sally to be demolished by ridicule, the fact remains that he was playing with ideas which were far removed from his everyday experience, and hence bringing them slightly closer to the threshold of acceptable discourse. (Sidney recognized this utopian element in writing by classing More's work as a poem.) The conscious intentions of some poets may in fact have been less conservative than has often been assumed. More's independence from received ideas was facilitated by the fact that he was writing not for a patron but for the growing European audience for printed books. As John Danby put it, Renaissance England had a 'mixed' literary economy in which aristocratic patronage was being supplemented by production for the market, and some writers were beginning to earn their living by writing pamphlets and plays.[24] Most poets, it is true, continued to rely on some form of patronage. But despite More's general strictures on aristocratic conservatism, a number of noble patrons in the period were more receptive to new ideas than most of the popular audience for printed books; and poets could try to mould their patrons' opinions instead of simply becoming their mouthpieces. Although it is not possible in the period before 1640 to find an equivalent of Milton's plea for liberty of printing in *Areopagitica*, there were currents of discontent with the prevailing methods of controlling and licensing the diffusion of opinion. Writers' receptiveness to new ideas did, of course, have clear limits. They were prepared to question many features of the traditional social and ecclesiastical hierarchies which seemed to them to be irrational and to block the access to power of an educated elite. But they were very critical too of the traditional pursuits of the lower orders: true rationality could be the prerogative only of a very limited social group. The *Utopia* itself owes its speculative communism more to a negative desire to discipline the lower orders than to a positive sense of common humanity. This rationalist elitism emerges clearly in Spenser's writings on Ireland, which proposed a radical break with traditional political solutions by what would have amounted to a cultural

---

[24] John F. Danby, *Elizabethan and Jacobean Poets: Studies in Sidney, Shakespeare, Beaumont and Fletcher* (London, 1965), 16.

revolution in which Irish popular traditions gave way to the complete dominance of a literate minority. The 'humanism' of many English Renaissance writers failed to recognize women as fully human: like the lower orders, women were often felt to be inherently irrational. A full feminist reading would need to extend the concept of the 'political' further than I have done here and would bring out the limitations of even the most imaginative of the male writers. It can be said, however, that these limitations are all the more visible because Renaissance poets engaged themselves in political affairs to a degree unusual in later English poetry; without necessarily endorsing all their political priorities, it is still possible to learn something from the way they set about trying to unify poetic and political concerns.

Two major intellectual influences encouraged sixteenth- and seventeenth-century poets to pose new political questions: humanism and the Reformation. The recovery of classical texts and the attempt to set them in a precise historical context inevitably sharpened awareness of the discrepancies between classical political forms and English traditions. Humanist literary analysis tended to reject medieval theories of multiple allegorization and insist on the recovery of authorial intention; such a technique, today regarded by some theorists as inherently reactionary, provided a critical perspective on the humanists' own society. A representative sixteenth-century edition of Euripides praises the dramatist's political wisdom and refers the reader to a speech in *The Suppliant Women* which celebrates the Athenian constitution; a marginal note reads 'Praise of Democracy'.[25] Such annotations would provoke thought in an imaginative reader; this may have been the case with Milton, who set the speech in question at the head of *Areopagitica*. Literary historians have sometimes regarded the ideals of humanism as inimical to those of the Reformation, and regarded radical Protestantism as hostile to literary culture. But it was the application of humanist methods of exegesis to the Bible that provided the rationale for the Protestant critique of ecclesiastical tradition, for a decisive and unprecedented break with the past. The prophetic books and the Gospels provided a sanction for social criticism; and their style and rhetoric challenged conventional notions of literary decorum. The apocalyptic view of history which the mid-century reformers derived from Revelation may appear bizarre to modern critics but it was based on a coherent logic of interpretation. The conviction that the life of society as a whole as well as of each individual was soon to come to an end, that judgement was at hand, provided a powerful stimulus for religious and social reform. It could also sanction a new kind of prophetic poetry; the reformers developed a literary theory which deeply influenced Milton and which had more in common with Shelley's *Defence of Poetry* than with courtly neoclassicism. Rather than seeing the existing state as a well-ordered work of art, they tended to see history as a carefully structured divine drama which was not yet quite complete; its imminent conclusion would be heralded by major religious and political reforms.

[25] *Euripidis tragoediae*, ed. Gulielmus Xylandrus (Basel, 1558), 5, 423–5; see discussion and reproduction in David Norbrook, *Writing the English Republic: Poetry, Rhetoric and Politics 1627–1660* (Cambridge, 1999), 125–9.

If the reformers politicized aesthetics, the major Elizabethan poets would appear to have aestheticized politics. They celebrated the universe as a vast masque or pageant and their writings are full of descriptions of courtly tournaments. Monarchy, hierarchy, and inequality are presented in their writings as parts of a mystical order of nature, transcending rational questioning. It has normally been assumed by critics that this apparently complacent conservatism was the natural ideology of Renaissance poets, so that what needs to be explained is how Milton, who owed so much to the Elizabethans, emerged as a radical. It would be equally valid to turn the question round and ask why the relative radicalism of the earlier sixteenth century developed into such a rigid conservatism. In fact the orthodox exhortations about order and degree would not have been necessary had the principle of hierarchy not been coming under question. Conservative Protestants like Hooker were attempting to give a new positive force, a mellow lustre, to the word 'tradition' precisely because it had normally been used in a pejorative sense in decades of Protestant propaganda. Elizabethan texts like the *Arcadia* and *The Faerie Queene* which are often seen as embodying the hierarchical world-view in fact reveal signs of strain. Both works were never completed, and their labyrinthine complexities and irregularities reflect difficult tensions between courtly forms and less conservative content.

The *Arcadia* (which will be classed here, following Sidney's definition, as a work of poetry) reveals a certain anxiety about the aestheticization of politics. Spenser's epic certainly has its courtly elements, and it presents recurrent epiphanies in which moral and political conflicts are reconciled in artistic harmony, culminating in the vision on Mount Acidale, where courtesy becomes a symbol of a social order in which beauty and morality are united. But such visions are elusive: Spenser is constantly alert to the dangers of the false resolution, by facile fantasies of timeless aesthetic harmony, of problems which can be solved only by great effort over a long period of time. This does not mean, however, that the poem undercuts any search for closure; but its structure is apocalyptic, prophetic, rather than merely panegyrical. Spenser, like most major Elizabethan poets, was influenced by apocalyptic ideas and was committed to English intervention in the decisive religious wars on the Continent. Such sympathies placed English Protestants in close contact with Continental co-religionists whose religious and political views were often radical and anti-traditionalist; hence the conservative queen tended to be suspicious of this faction. Spenser and his allies were increasingly bitter because they believed their views were censored and misrepresented by conservative courtiers. Many subsequent critics have complied with this process by turning Spenser into an unreflective mouthpiece of official policies. His most notorious disagreement with official policy came over the Irish question. Critics anxious to present Spenser as a contemplative Neoplatonist or a genial Anglican have tended to feel that Ficino or Hooker are better guides to what Spenser really thought than Spenser himself; for his *View of the Present State of Ireland* is a radically original work by Elizabethan standards, advocating a complete break with traditional policies and owing as much to Machiavelli as to more conservative writers. His hostility to the native Irish is not an accidental blemish but a structural component of his political thought, which combined humanist distaste for popular culture with a strong enthusiasm for the energetic diffusion of Protestant English 'civility', both within the queen's Irish realm and in the New World. As confidence in Britain's imperial destiny has wavered, critics have become understandably reluctant to accept the expansionist drive behind Spenser's didacticism. But recent criticism has tended not to confront this element in Spenser's thought but to claim instead that his heart cannot have been in it. It has been widely argued that the later books of *The Faerie Queene* reflect an increasing disillusion with political action, a retreat into quietism. The familiar moral can then be drawn that poets should not meddle in politics. While acknowledging the bitterness of some later parts of the poem, I do not believe that he began *The Faerie Queene* as a naive idealist and suddenly realized after 1590 that politics could be an unpleasant business. Like other former members of the Sidney–Leicester circle, however, he was politically uneasy in the 1590s; this unease is most visible in the poetry of Fulke Greville, where an impulse towards radical speculation is constantly held in check by a mechanism of self-censorship. Greville was greatly alarmed when the fictitious rebellion in one of his plays turned into reality in Essex's attempted *coup d'état*.

The emergence of Ben Jonson as leading court poet under James I marks a decisive political shift. The current admirers of Jonson's masques have perhaps been too willing to take his words at face value, to assume that all his critics were ignorant fanatics. In fact Jonson owed his precedence at court to his rejection of sixteenth-century traditions of prophetic poetry, which had become tainted with implications of political subversiveness. Jonson's courtly classicism was extremely influential and helped to move a younger generation of poets in the direction of a revisionist, high-church Anglicanism; in the political reaction after the Civil War it was to be Jonson who offered Dryden and Pope a model of cultural conservatism. In the sixteenth century intellectuals had frequently looked to the highly urbanized, advanced Protestant culture of the Netherlands for inspiration; in the earlier seventeenth century the aristocratic, ritualized culture of Spain began to exercise an attraction for some young poets.[26] Prince Charles's enthusiasm for Spanish artistic achievement was clearly related to his marked distaste for the unseemly dissension of republican forms of government. The Caroline religious reaction can be seen as an attempt to aestheticize politics, to transform the realm into a work of art as harmonious as the landscapes painted on masque backcloths. But these cultural shifts encountered some resistance. Already in the reign of James I a number of poets had challenged Jonson's literary dictatorship, taking Spenser as their chief model. They constituted a kind of poetic 'opposition', and, though neglected by literary historians, they form an important link between Elizabethan politics and the young Milton. In Milton's early poetry we can see the latent radicalism of the Protestant prophetic tradition emerging with a new clarity and energy. *Comus* and *Lycidas* oppose the

---

[26]   On Spain and the Netherlands as rival political models on the eve of the Civil War see the letter from the Earl of Dorset to the Earl of Middlesex in the autumn of 1639 quoted by Charles J. Phillips, *History of the Sackville Family*, 2 vols. (London, 1930), i.333–4.

Caroline aestheticization of politics: the voice of apocalyptic prophecy threatens to destroy the artistic framework. Milton's implicit claim in his early work is that the central tradition of English poetry is not Jonson's conservative neoclassicism but a long line of radical prophets. There is an intense apocalyptic and utopian excitement not far beneath the surface of his early works, which were written on the threshold of an unprecedented period of political speculation and experimentation. Some critics have seen the Puritan revolution as a drastic interruption of the natural course of English poetry; but it could be argued that the apocalyptic excitement of the 1640s released tensions which had been building up over many years. As more conservative (or realistic) writers had long recognized, radical political ideas were not deeply enough rooted in English society as a whole to be able to establish a secure position. But for a time it seemed possible not just to feign a 'reformed' commonwealth but to build it.

1. *The* Utopia *and Radical Humanism*

IN the second book of Sir Thomas More's *Utopia*, Raphael Hythlodaeus enthusias-tically describes life in a communist republic in which there is no money and private property, where all political and religious offices are elective and there is no heredi-tary aristocracy, where meals are eaten in common and labour is communal, where luxury and idleness are unknown. More's persona in the dialogue listens to the description of Utopia politely but sceptically:

many things came to my mind which seemed very absurdly established in the customs and laws of the people described—not only in their method of waging war, their ceremonies and reli-gion, as well as their other institutions, but most of all in that feature which is the principal foundation of their whole structure. I mean their common life and subsistence—without any exchange of money. This latter alone utterly overthrows all the nobility, magnificence, splen-dor, and majesty which are, in the estimation of the common people (*ut publica est opinio*), the true glories and ornaments of the commonwealth. (p. 245)[1]

The constitution of Utopia certainly contradicts the common sense ('publica opinio') of More's age. Utopia tolerates many religions and subsidises priests, but there is no one state religion: the state's basis is essentially secular, and great value is attached to participation in public life, which is the right of every male citizen. Fully to lead the good life is to participate in Utopian politics. The Utopians' assumptions about public life were not, however, widely shared in sixteenth-century England. The concepts of 'politics' as an autonomous area of activity, and of political philoso-phy as distinct from moral philosophy, scarcely existed.

The low valuation of the public life implicit in such usages can be traced back to the early Middle Ages.[2] In *The City of God* St Augustine had drawn a sharp distinc-tion between the earthly city of Rome, the focus of worldly ideals, and the heavenly city of the New Jerusalem. All earthly cities were no more than shadows of the eter-nal city, and the life of contemplating heavenly things was therefore inherently superior to the active political life. Civic affairs, in the view of many medieval writers, belonged to an inferior order of time, the 'saeculum', and were subject to the unpredictable rule of Fortune; the heavenly city existed in the superior tem-

---

[1] Page numbers in parentheses refer to the translation in the Yale edition of *The Complete Works of St. Thomas More*, vol. iv, ed. Edward Surtz, SJ, and J. H. Hexter (New Haven, 1965). I have used this trans-lation for ease of reference but Paul Turner's version (Harmondsworth, 1965) is much less ponderous. See also the parallel-text edition by George M. Logan, Robert M. Adams, and Clarence H. Miller (Cambridge, 1995).

[2] In the following paragraph and throughout this chapter I draw heavily on J. G. A. Pocock, *The Machiavellian Moment: Florentine Political Thought and the Atlantic Republican Tradition* (Princeton, 1975), 9–48.

poral order of 'aeternitas'. Such virtue and legitimacy as the secular order possessed came down from above, as a grace, rather than being conferred by the activity of the people. Some theorists conferred a privileged kind of immortality on the dignity of the royal office, which was held to exist in 'aevum', an intermediate area between the secular and the eternal. But this somewhat mystical concept still implied the inferiority of purely secular political orders.

In the essentially hierarchical world-view which still governed the 'common sense' of More's England, participation in public life was a privilege rather than a civic right. The social hierarchy was held to be an earthly shadow of the hierarchical order which God had ordained amongst the angels: social inequalities were not only desirable but had a mystical aura. Wealth and magnificence were important as the outward signs of social rank. Even if an individual prince or nobleman was corrupt, the honour that was paid to the symbols of office would serve to reinforce the hierarchical order that bound together heaven and earth. The commonplace analogy between the prince and God insisted that the highest kind of rule was personal rule in which subjects owed allegiance to an individual rather than to an impersonal state; the prince's personal household served as the bureaucracy of the nation. The English monarch, of course, periodically consulted a partly elected Parliament, and was expected to abide by custom in many areas of decision-making; but there remained a mystical residue in medieval constitutional theory. There is no such residue in Utopia: there is no divinely ordained hereditary monarch to mediate between the secular and eternal realms. And whereas medieval constitutional theory revered custom and precedent, Utopian laws are based on reason rather than tradition and are drafted so as to be immediately intelligible to all citizens.

The political ideas of the Utopians are so remote from the realities of sixteenth-century England that many critics have argued that More cannot have been advancing them for serious consideration. The work is cast in a dialogue form in which Hythlodaeus' enthusiasm for communism is balanced against the scepticism and caution of More's persona. This caution is reflected in the serpentine syntax of the book's penultimate sentence, which most English translators have had to cut into several sentences, including those quoted above. This one Latin period enacts More's oscillation between his reluctance to challenge received ideas, his awareness that these received ideas are current amongst the masses and hence perhaps suspect, and his fear of arousing Hythlodaeus' censure for his timidity: he ends this sentence in which he has said how much absurdity he finds in Utopian institutions by praising the Utopians to Hythlodaeus and taking him in to dinner, reserving the right, however, to discuss Utopia further on a later occasion and perhaps to raise his doubts. More's caution often comes to the fore in the dialogues in Book I; the description of Utopia in Book II is enlivened by a number of humorous touches, such as the Utopians' unorthodox methods of rearing chickens (p. 115), which seem to undermine the seriousness of the praise of their political institutions. Many critics have pointed to flaws in Hythlodaeus' character: he is a restless, dissatisfied individual who has said farewell to his parents and family and can therefore be regarded as rootless and irresponsible, unlikely to gain the approval of More the family man.[3]

Such interpretations direct our attention away from political issues towards More's literary skill, from ideas to the characters who express them. The trouble with a narrowly literary approach, however, is that it tends to neutralize some of the most powerful, and influential, passages in the book. Hythlodaeus eloquently denounces indiscriminate enclosures, which mean that in England sheep are eating men (p. 67), and claims that the existing social order is 'a kind of conspiracy of the rich, who are aiming at their own interests under the name and title of the commonwealth' (p. 241). The force of such statements is blunted by one of the editors of the standard edition, who argues that imaginative literature, as opposed to political rhetoric, sees both sides of every question, and therefore assumes that More's real message is that 'a man should view his private goods not as his own but as common to all, at least to the extent of sharing possessions with the indigent'.[4] If More intended such a bland and anodyne message it is difficult to see why he went to the trouble of imagining his fictitious commonwealth in such detail. It is probable that he wrote Book II with its description of Utopian institutions first and only later added the framing and qualifying dialogue in Book I. And the process of imagining new situations, of breaking with traditional frames of reference, seems to have been important to More at the time he wrote the *Utopia*. Hythlodaeus criticizes More for his inability to envisage any political order outside the conventional world of kings and courts. The 'balance' involved in More's syntax looks to Raphael like a failure of nerve, of imagination: he has 'no picture (*imago*) at all, or else a false one, of the situation I mean' (p. 107). As Emrys Jones puts it, in Utopia 'kings are both menacingly present, sinister looming shadows, and at the same time exhilaratingly absent—absent, that is, to the imagination that dares to project a future without them'.[5]

To say that More took the Utopian ideal seriously is not to argue for a purely 'political' reading which ignores 'literary', linguistic issues. Historians of political thought are becoming increasingly aware of the need to relate the content of political theories to the discursive forms in which they are produced, to particular kinds of linguistic and conceptual framework.[6] Critics have found it hard to square the ideals

---

[3] The critical reception of the *Utopia* has followed a characteristic course. The first full-length study, which appeared (in German) late in the 19th century, was a Marxist analysis which took the Utopian idea seriously: Karl Kautsky, *Thomas More and his Utopia*, trans. H. J. Stenning (New York, 1927). Many if not most of the 20th-century studies have been explicitly revisionist, ranging from attempts to show that the *Utopia* was a prophetic warning against godless communism to 'comic' readings which emphasize light-hearted irony. For a clever ironic reading see Andrew D. Weiner, 'Raphael's Eutopia and More's *Utopia*: Christian Humanism and the Limits of Reason', *Huntington Library Quarterly*, 39 (1975–6), 1–27.

[4] Surtz, edn. cit., p. cxlii. On the dichotomy between Surtz's 'literary' reading of the *Utopia* and Hexter's 'political' reading, see Quentin Skinner, 'More's *Utopia*', *Past and Present*, 38 (1967), 153–68.

[5] Emrys Jones, 'Commoners and Kings: Book One of More's *Utopia*', in P. L. Heyworth (ed.), *Medieval Studies for J. A. W. Bennett* (Oxford, 1981), 255–72 (271–2).

[6] This concern with language is shared by Pocock, *The Machiavellian Moment*, and Quentin Skinner, whose *The Foundations of Modern Political Thought*, 2 vols. (Cambridge, 1978) is the fruit of much theoretical reflection as well as empirical research. My debt to this book will be obvious throughout the present study.

of Utopia with the personality of More the good Catholic; but the *Utopia*, more than some of his other writings, belongs to a particular discourse, that of radical humanism, which carried with it some distinctive standpoints and values. A central feature of Renaissance humanism was that political and rhetorical experimentation were closely associated. The recurrent verbal games and rhetorical paradoxes in the *Utopia* are not opposed to the political satire but are integral parts of the process of undermining older forms of political discourse. Humanism had originated in the study of classical rhetoric, an art which had been disparaged by conservatives since the time of Plato because it implied a pragmatic, nominalistic attitude to language and truth. Rhetoricians had to recognize that the issues they were dealing with were relative rather than absolute, concrete and practical rather than eternal and philosophical. They had to have a large stock of techniques of argument and figures of speech that could be adjusted to different situations. Rhetoricians taught the art of sophistic disputation, of arguing on both sides of the question (*in utramque partem*).[7] With the decline of democracy in ancient Athens, and again with the collapse of the Roman republic, rhetoric came under suspicion: it could only provoke dissension and disorder unless it was properly controlled, and unity and order were now the prime political values. Under the Roman empire rhetoric became increasingly a 'literary' rather than political art, providing techniques for adorning poetic compositions and ceremonial prose with figures of speech. Italian humanists tried to restore rhetoric to its political function, at the same time as they reaffirmed the dignity of the active, political life: 'It is better to will the good than to know the truth,' declared Petrarch.[8] And this entailed a revaluation of rhetoric, a renewed emphasis on its political role.

Rather than a piece of realistic characterization, a transcendent epiphany of human nature, the dispute between More and Hythlodaeus needs to be seen as a classic humanist disputation in which both sides of a question are given extensive treatment. This does not necessarily mean that there is a completely impartial balance. For the humanists' very willingness to stand apart from obvious conclusions was itself a powerful solvent of traditional political prejudices. They revived the ancient debate between philosophy and rhetoric (a debate which has recently been renewed by Derrida and the poststructuralists).[9] The humanists accused their adversaries, the scholastic philosophers, of reifying abstractions by seeking universal truths outside any particular linguistic embodiment. Scholastic commentators tended to abstract the ideas of Aristotle from their historical and linguistic contexts, forming them into a general system. Humanists argued that this process was inherently reductive and was symptomatic of a lack of imagination, of an inability to cope with the complex

[7] On this aspect of rhetoric see Joel Altman, *The Tudor Play of Mind: Rhetorical Inquiry and the Development of Elizabethan Drama* (Berkeley and Los Angeles, 1978), 31–63, 68–71.

[8] Quoted by Hanna H. Gray, 'Renaissance Humanism: The Pursuit of Eloquence', *Journal of the History of Ideas*, 24 (1963), 497–514 (501), citing Petrarch, *De sui ipsius et multorum ignorantia*, trans. Hans Nachod in Ernst Cassirer, Paul Oscar Kristeller, and John Herman Randall, Jr. (eds.), *The Renaissance Philosophy of Man* (Chicago, 1948), 47–133 (105).

[9] The convergences between some humanist rhetorical theories and Derrida's ideas are illustrated by Terence Cave in *The Cornucopian Text: Problems of Writing in the French Renaissance* (Oxford, 1979), 3–18

play of rhetorical tropes to be found in all interesting texts. The humanists' characterization of their opponents as reactionary 'dunces' was of course unjust: scholastic philosophy formed the basis of an important school of radical political thought, while humanist concern with language could easily degenerate into a sterile and pedantic formalism. But the insistence on the rhetorical rather than philosophical approach to language could encourage a critical attitude towards received ideas, an awareness of the rhetorical basis of notions that seemed to common sense, to 'publica opinio', to be natural and eternal verities. Pico della Mirandola's *Oration on the Dignity of Man* presented man as an essentially rhetorical creature, capable of adopting an infinite variety of disguises rather than possessing one unvaried and natural essence. In questioning abstract systematization, the humanists emphasized the need to set texts in their historical context; and their historical scholarship made them increasingly aware of the discrepancies between medieval and classical conceptions of human nature. And an ideological break, a shift towards a more secular and individualistic world-view, was precisely what was demanded in the mercantile city-states which had broken out of the feudal orbit. A leading authority on humanism has described it as 'the ideological superstructure of a specifically capitalist culture'.[10]

But humanism was Protean in its political character. The career of the first great humanist scholar and poet, Petrarch, illustrates the fluidity of humanist political discourse. As a young man he had been impressed by the austere values of the Roman republic, which he celebrated in his neo-Latin poem *Africa*. His interest in classical republicanism was not merely antiquarian. In 1347 the adventurer Cola di Rienzo started a *coup d'état* in Rome and tried to revive the republic, unearthing an inscription which, he claimed, proved that power resided with the people. He made a bungled attempt to liquidate the Roman aristocracy. Textual criticism could thus justify social revolution. For a time Petrarch was enthusiastic about Rienzo's coup and the idea was even floated that he and Rienzo might become joint leaders of the city. The dream of power was never far from the minds of many humanists. Though Rienzo's project soon failed, the cult of the Roman republic was taken up elsewhere, most notably in Florence and Venice whose institutions seemed close enough to those of the classical era to make the project of emulating the old republican virtues in practice seem feasible. Petrarch realized, however, that the immediate future of republicanism was insecure: the fourteenth century had seen the extinction of representative government in many of the major city-states, and political power and discussion were confined in the new absolutist 'signorie' to aristocratic rulers and small circles of advisers. Even the surviving republics gradually became more aristocratic and conservative in their social character, so that the differences between *signorie* and republics were less significant in practice than in theory. But there was still a sense of outrage in republican Florence when Petrarch accepted an invitation to

[10] R. R. Bolgar, *The Classical Heritage and its Beneficiaries*, rev. edn. (Cambridge, 1973), 246. On the social bases of humanism cf. Perry Anderson, *Lineages of the Absolutist State* (London, 1974), 148 ff., 420 ff., and Lauro Martines, *Power and Imagination: City-States in Renaissance Italy* (London, 1979), 277 ff.

attend the Visconti court at Milan, the most powerful of the *signorie*. Petrarch was to spend a considerable part of his life at the courts of princes.

His justifications of his political stance were to become characteristic of the more conservative currents in humanism. Literary culture, it was argued, should transcend politics. A despot who showed favour to a humanist was honouring letters in his person; princes would be far less likely to become corrupt if they had a learned adviser. Even while appearing to flatter the prince the humanist could indicate to him the virtues that he ought to possess—the strategy that became known as instructing by praise, 'laudando praecipere'. Petrarch continued to claim that he was no partisan, that in praising virtue wherever he found it, in republics or monarchies, he was indicating his political independence. But this very stance of autonomy indicated an acceptance of some conservative assumptions: the courtly humanist wanted to belong to an intellectual aristocracy whose values mirrored the traditional aristocratic disdain for practical and mercantile activities. The contemplative life came to be valued above the active life. Such traits have led some historians to characterize humanists as, in Gramsci's phrase, 'organic intellectuals' of the signorial era, reinforcing rather than challenging the values of the ruling class.[11] Such a label would perhaps be an oversimplification in the case of Petrarch; as will be seen, the restless self-consciousness of his poetry was to appeal to sixteenth-century reformers who found in him a spiritual ancestor. But it is true that in the fourteenth and fifteenth centuries Petrarch's immediate influence strengthened conservative currents of thought. Italian humanists often failed to develop the critical potential of their methods of study; their ambitious intellectual programmes tended to degenerate into pedantry, with the ability to parrot Greek and Latin commonplaces becoming a badge of entry into the ruling class. Humanist political writing placed more and more emphasis on the princely virtues of magnificence and conspicuous consumption. Republican theorists who remained faithful to more austere values argued that excessive desire for wealth was a source of political corruption: a tyrant could buy off the political community by offering riches instead of liberty. And indeed many 'quattrocento' princes suppressed the rhetoric of public political discussion but tried to compensate for this change by turning their states into works of art, theatres for the display of their princely glory. The image of the ideal city in late fourteenth-century art, and the public architecture of the period, is magnificent but authoritarian in character: vast palaces are separated by huge public spaces whose function is the display of princely authority.[12] It could be said that such a political order appealed to the imagination; but not to the sceptical, innovative imagination posited by Hythlodaeus: instead, traditional social hierarchies were given a new gloss and

---

[11] Antonio Gramsci, *Il Risorgimento* (Turin, 1949), 24–5; G. Petronio qualifies Gramsci's view in 'Storicità della lirica politica', *Studi petrarcheschi*, 7 (1961), 247–64.

[12] Martines, *Power and Imagination*, 378 ff.; Skinner, *The Foundations of Modern Political Thought*, i.113 ff.; on the tendency of humanist intellectual methods to ossify into intellectual and social conformism cf. Anthony Grafton and Lisa Jardine, *From Humanism to the Humanities* (London, 1986), ch. 1; Bolgar, *The Classical Heritage*, 333–6; Françoise Waquet, *Latin or the Empire of the Sign: From the Sixteenth to the Twentieth Centuries*, trans. John Howe (London, 2001).

presented as beautiful images of a divine order. In reality, of course, this wealth had often been acquired by commerce rather than by traditional aristocratic means, but the investment in courtly spectacle was a means of trying to shake off this contagion.

More was familiar with the 'mirrors for princes' literature; but he would also have known of the recent political crises that had led to brief resurgences of radical republicanism. In 1494 Charles VIII of France invaded Italy, precipitating a long series of battles in which France and the Empire battled for domination of the peninsula, ending in the mid-sixteenth century with the establishment of Spanish hegemony and the reinforcement of conservative social tendencies. But the immediate effect of the invasion in Florence was to bring down the rule of the Medici; the republic was restored, and Savonarola initiated a brief period of radical religious and social reform. His austere republicanism had a powerful influence even on contemplative Neoplatonists like Pico della Mirandola; and John Colet, a pioneer of humanism and a close friend of More, may have heard his sermons. In his translation of a biography of Pico More judiciously suppressed a reference to the controversial Savonarola, which implies that he knew of his ideas.[13] At the time he was working on the *Utopia* More was in close contact with Erasmus, who had spent several years in Italy; he had published an energetic satire of the most magnificent of all contemporary Italian princes, who happened also to be the Pope, Julius II. Erasmus said that Julius was a Caesar who lacked his Brutus: an attempted anti-Papal rebellion in Rome had failed in 1511.[14] Erasmus shared the general humanist irreverence for medieval tradition. Though he accepted the institution of hereditary monarchy in practice, and wrote a treatise on the virtues required by an ideal king, his defence of the institution was somewhat negative: 'the thing is so established that it is impossible to root it out.' Hereditary rule seemed to him to be irrational: 'If anyone is to be a coachman he learns the art, spends care and thought; but, for anyone to be a king, we think it is enough for him to be born.'[15] He and More collaborated in translations of Lucian's dialogues, including a speech in praise of tyrannicide. Both men's writings abound in theatrical metaphors: the idea of the king as image of God is exposed as a mere rhetorical trope, a mystifying illusion which is passed off as natural. In his *History of Richard III*, which he probably began about 1513 as a warning against Henry VIII's authoritarian tendencies, More describes the people's response to the usurping ruler's feigned refusal of the crown:

they said that these matters bee Kynges games, as it were stage playes, and for the more part plaied vpon scafoldes. In which pore men be but yᵉ lokers on. And thei yᵗ wise be, wil medle no

---

[13] Stanford E. Lehmberg, 'Sir Thomas More's Life of Pico della Mirandola', *Studies in the Renaissance*, 3 (1956), 70–1; cf. Dominic Baker-Smith, *Thomas More and Plato's Voyage* (Cardiff, 1978), 13–15. On interest in Savonarola in England see James K. McConica, *English Humanists and Reformation Politics under Henry VIII and Edward VI* (Oxford, 1965), 65, 71, 100–1.

[14] Roland H. Bainton, *Erasmus of Christendom* (London, 1969), 104; Skinner, *The Foundations of Modern Political Thought*, i.142–3.

[15] *Erasmus on his Times: A Shortened Version of the* Adages *of Erasmus*, ed. Margaret Mann Phillips (Cambridge, 1967), 40. Bolgar, *The Classical Heritage*, 299, points out that Erasmus was attracted to Greek culture by its democratic ambience.

farther. For they that sometyme step vp and playe wᵗ them, when they cannot play their partes, they disorder the play & do themself no good.[16]

In the *Utopia* More presents a similarly critical view of court life in another dramatic analogy. It is necessary, says More's persona, to temper philosophical advice with courtly compliment. A humanist who walked into a palace and urged the necessity of austere social reforms would be like someone who dressed up as a philosopher and rushed on stage during a comedy by Plautus in which 'the household slaves are making trivial jokes at one another' (p. 99). The analogy is not flattering to monarchs; its relevance to the *Utopia* becomes all the more obvious when one examines the play which More imagines the dramatic philosopher as quoting. In the pseudo-Senecan *Octavia* (ll. 377–435), Seneca, anxious about the emperor's deterioration into tyranny, soliloquizes nostalgically about the Golden Age before injustice and inequality reigned, and expresses the wish that the old world might be destroyed and a new world reborn.

In attacking courtly magnificence and servility More was rejecting the increasingly courtly ethos of recent political writing, and recalling humanism to older ideals: in Quentin Skinner's phrase, the *Utopia* is 'by far the most radical critique of humanism written by a humanist'.[17] But his Utopia undeniably has a somewhat abstract and unreal quality. Humanist ideals seem to present an impossible choice: the impulse towards the active, political life will lead to excessive compromise while the ideals of radical rationalism seem impossibly remote. In practice, of course, More was to accept the arguments for entering public life, but he was unusually keenly aware of the difficulties. The dilemma posed in the *Utopia* bears specifically on More's England but it reflects the general position of radical humanism in the early sixteenth century. The general effect of the foreign invasions of Italy was to undermine the political viability of small republics like Florence: in 1512 the Medici returned to power with Spanish aid. About the time More was working on the *Utopia*, two very different authors were offering sharply contrasting responses to the Italian situation. In his *Book of the Courtier*, Castiglione blandly ignored the scale of the crisis: the humanist must accept the need to serve princes, and if they became tyrannical—well, very probably they would not.[18] In *The Prince*, Machiavelli, temporarily despairing of the viability of the old city-states, called for a resolutely active prince who would scorn the conventional moralizing of the mirrors for princes and be bold enough to break radically with moral and political traditions, republican as well as monarchical: no less drastic solution would suffice. Savonarola's limitation had been that, though a prophet, he was unarmed. Venice was the only surviving example of a strong and stable republic: the future seemed to lie with the ideals of courtly magnificence. Republican theory in Italy became increasingly abstract and utopian: More's *Utopia* was translated into Italian before an English version appeared.

---

[16] More, *The History of Richard III*, ed. Richard S. Sylvester, in *The Complete Works of St. Thomas More*, vol. ii (New Haven, 1963), 81.

[17] Skinner, *The Foundations of Modern Political Thought*, i.256.

[18] Martines, *Power and Imagination*, 460–5.

If republican theorists in Italy seemed to be going against the grain of the historical process, the situation of the radical humanist in England was even more difficult.
It may have been his sense of the extreme disparity between humanist ideals and the
English situation that pushed More into the further speculative radicalism of imagining a realm not only without kings but also without money. Humanism had in practice provided an ideological rationale for economic individualism even as it professed
to scorn worldly wealth; More turns the cutting edge of humanist critical analysis
against its own social basis. But in fact Utopian communism is more a negative, anti-
traditional phenomenon than a warmly realized positive ideal, and it is significantly
qualified: More draws back from some of the logical consequences of his argument.
In Book II he turns upside down a host of traditional aristocratic ideals. What the
Utopians object to is the irrationality involved in accumulating wealth: people value
gold for its external appearance, but like all conspicuous wealth it has no practical
function or intrinsic value. It is because money is a symbol of honour and magnificence—which More equates with the sin of pride—and because it stimulates an
appetite for irrational pleasures that it is condemned. Money, like language, is a
system of arbitrary signs which only the ignorant consider to be natural. The
Utopians are not Stoics and they value pleasure, but their pleasures are simple and
normally serve some kind of practical function: they would have been acceptable to
the thrifty merchants of Antwerp, where More sets his dialogue.[19] More's communism is a way of criticizing the aristocratic belief that work is degrading. The condemnation of enclosures in Book I is linked with the general attack on aristocratic
traditions: because the ruling class pursue such frivolous pleasures, they cannot provide useful employment for the poor who have been displaced from the countryside
and who either ape their superiors in the pursuit of idle pleasures or foment rebellion. If Utopia lacks an aristocracy, however, on close examination it does prove to
have at least a potential ruling class: the intelligentsia are exempt from the manual
labour in which all other citizens participate. Utopia is a paradise for humanists. And
the Utopians do in fact have slaves who do some of the menial work: this heightens
the resemblance between the island and a classical city-state. The Utopians'
communism does not extend to the family unit: they are organized into families with
strict patriarchal authority. If the Utopians can produce as many goods as other societies even though their working hours are shorter, this is largely because all women
too are engaged in the work, whereas, according to Hythlodaeus, in Europe they are
'idle'; and yet Utopian women are still apparently expected to do all the cooking and
look after children. Like many later thinkers, More found it much easier to imagine
a society in which all men were equal with one another than one in which men were
equal with women. Despite all these limitations, however, More's imagination certainly ranged far beyond the conventional boundaries of political thought.

---

[19] In 1622 the Puritan propagandist Thomas Scott described the Protestant Netherlands, a centre of
trade and religious liberty, as the living fulfilment of More's Utopia: *The Belgicke Pismire* (London, 1622),
90. On Utopia as a reflection of advanced middle-class ideals see the different interpretations by Kautsky,
Thomas More and his Utopia, and Russell A. Ames, *Citizen Thomas More and his Utopia* (Princeton, 1949).

When More's persona suggests that communism is all right in theory but would never work in practice, Hythlodaeus replies that the existence of Utopia proves that it can work; but of course the name Utopia means 'nowhere'. The name indicates More's wry acceptance of the difficulty of establishing humanist ideas, let alone egalitarianism, in England. In practice the English humanists needed the support of the monarchy. The Florentine republicans had rejected the old legend that their city was founded by a mythical prince and had argued that it had come into being through the collective decisions of its citizens.[20] Utopia, however, was definitely created by one man, Utopos, who had the isthmus linking Utopia to the mainland cut through to turn it into an island and who trained and civilized the original inhabitants. The dependence of the Utopian ideal on a strong ruler reflects More's own sense of dependence on the monarchy. Henry VIII needed increasingly large numbers of diplomats and administrators well versed in the new classical and rhetorical learning, and he overruled the conservatism of the academic establishments in Oxford and Cambridge and endowed new chairs in classical learning.[21] The institution of monarchy might be irrational in itself, but the monarch alone had the power to cut through reactionary opposition to change.[22] A strong central government could help to introduce the degree of labour discipline and social control which More advocated in the *Utopia*. One of the issues discussed in the first book is the danger of popular rebellion: Hythlodaeus travelled to England just after a major peasant uprising, and he advocates social reforms as means of keeping the people contented. If courts were often unsympathetic to humanist ideals, the people seemed still more so. English humanism appeared an alien growth with no roots in the English social order; Hythlodaeus often uses the metaphor of pulling up established institutions by the roots (pp. 86/21, 98/25, 242/2, 244/8). Given this precariousness, the humanists had to seek the powerful ally of the monarchy. Renaissance humanism could be critical of the established order, but the emphasis on the virtues of the active life, the need to get results, encouraged a belief in practical compromise. It was better to do something than to stand on the sidelines. More entered the royal service soon after completing the *Utopia*.

But he was well aware of the dangers of compromise. The old prejudice against rhetoric had had some validity; the politically conscious humanist who used his eloquence to gain advancement could too easily become a shifty Proteus, able so easily to argue on both sides of a question that he lost sight of any deeper ideals. In Book I More portrays the difficulty of getting new ideas accepted at court, the insidious temptations towards excessive compromise. There are some enlightened patrons in England, such as Cardinal Morton, but they cannot shake off the many flatterers who are content to mirror whatever someone of high rank happens to think at a given moment. In such conditions it is hard to achieve fruitful discussion. More did not

[20] Pocock, *The Machiavellian Moment*, 52.

[21] Joan Simon, *Education and Society in Tudor England* (Cambridge, 1966), 63 ff., 84 5.

[22] On the latent authoritarianism in much utopian writing, which lessened the difference between More's view and the monarch's, see Marie Louise Berneri, *Journey through Utopia* (London, 1950).

cast the *Utopia* in the form of an address to a monarch; instead, he had it published in Antwerp, one of the leading centres of European commerce, including the rapidly expanding book trade. In this cosmopolitan environment, where the snobberies of English society could be forgotten and where news was constantly arriving from foreign lands, it seemed possible to achieve a detached and critical view of traditional institutions.

But in order to reach the international audience of humanists More had to write in Latin; he believed that he would find more kindred spirits amongst Continental humanists with no knowledge of his native tongue than in England. Renaissance humanists liked to write to each other in a purified classical Latin because both the vernacular and medieval Latin were considered to be shot through with barbarisms, terms reflecting the feudal social order and its values rather than classical rationalism and austerity. Erasmus criticized the tendency to reproduce artificial social distinctions in grammar by splitting the second person into differing familiar and reverential forms—'tu' and 'vos', 'thou' and 'ye'. By writing in classical Latin one could escape from some contemporary social pressures and recreate a different scale of values: in writing the *Utopia* More left the English monarchy and became a citizen in the republic of humanist letters.[23] The pressure of the medieval vocabulary of honour and reverence on More's relatively austere Latin style can be seen by comparing the Latin of the *Utopia* with Robinson's translation of 1551. Throughout the book More has been ironically undermining the vocabulary of honour and public glory, so that there is strong irony in his persona's final repudiation of Hythlodaeus' arguments: 'una re funditus euertitur omnis nobilitas, magnificentia, splendor, maiestas' (p. 244/19–20). But Robinson tends to sprinkle his description of Utopia with conventional terms of honour and magnificence to express his enthusiasm; he scatters the word 'gorgious' liberally throughout his translation. The result is that More's final worry that communism would destroy 'all nobility, magnificence, worship, honour, and majesty' (note how Robinson adds a word to the catalogue) comes to seem not so much ironic as a genuine anxiety.[24] The Latin medium enables More to establish a more complete distance from the received opinions he wants to challenge, but only at the expense of greatly limiting his national audience.

There is a further level of linguistic alienation: the name Utopia is of course not Latin but Greek, and Hythlodaeus believes that the Utopians must be descended from the Greeks because they take to the language so easily. He gives them most of the works of Plato, his favourite author (p. 87), to read; the *Republic* was, of course,

---

[23] On Latin composition as an escape from conventional political and religious values, cf. Fred J. Nichols's introduction to *An Anthology of Neo-Latin Poetry* (New Haven, 1979), 6 ff. Nichols notes that Christian humanists often abandoned Christian concepts when writing in Latin and explored important issues from a non-Christian, if not necessarily an explicitly pagan, viewpoint.

[24] *Utopia*, ed. John Warrington (London, 1951), 135, 56, 62; James Binder, 'More's *Utopia* in English: A Note on Translation', *Modern Language Notes*, 62 (1947), 370–6. On More's revision of conventional evaluative terms see J. H. Hexter, 'The Loom of Language and the Fabric of Imperatives: The Case of *Il principe* and *Utopia*', *American Historical Review*, 69 (1964), 945–68. David Weil Baker, *Divulging Utopia: Radical Humanism in Sixteenth-Century England* (Amherst, Mass., 1999), ch. 4, offers a more complex analysis of Robinson's translation in the context of the politics of the Edwardian 'commonwealth's men'.

one of the main sources for More's ideas about Utopian communism. But few readers of the *Utopia* in England would have had much familiarity with the *Republic*: in 1516 lectureships in Greek were only just being established at Oxford and Cambridge and there was no English translation of any of Plato's works in print. More makes the Utopians admire another of his favourite writers, Lucian, whose witty, sceptical dialogues offended the conventionally minded. He declares in his prefatory letter that Hythlodaeus' Latin is not as good as his Greek, and he tries to give the Latin style of the *Utopia* something of the texture of Lucian's Greek, with much playing on words and a general avoidance of stiffly formal vocabulary.[25] But had he actually written in Greek his audience would have been much smaller. Utopia is an impossible world created in a defunct language, apparently lacking roots in the linguistic and social forms of Tudor England; the book's very radicalism seems to deprive it of practical efficacy.

The split between the ideas embodied in Utopia and the realities of Henry's court is an acute form of an opposition that was familiar to many Renaissance humanists. Montaigne wrote of his friend La Boétie that had he had the choice he would have been born in Venice rather than France, but that he accepted his duty to abide by the traditions of his native land: he was a kind of inner exile.[26] The values of courtly magnificence seem to gain ascendancy over humanist radicalism in English poetry later in the century. Not until the 1650s did Italian republican ideas become a central political ideology in England, and then only for a very brief period. But some political theorists saw England as having a 'mixed constitution', with elements of democracy as well as aristocracy and monarchy. England did have an important parliament, and though it generated an ideology of constitutional tradition that was more empirical and less theoretical than Italian humanist republicanism, the parliamentary tradition did affirm, and with increasing vigour, the dignity of the active, political life.[27] The political structure of Utopia seems to have been influenced by humanist theories of the mixed government: in terms of constitutional forms, England was not quite so remote from Utopia as Hythlodaeus assumed.[28]

[25] On More's Latin style see Marie Delcourt's edition, *L'Utopie* (Paris, 1936), 28 ff., 213–16.
[26] Montaigne, 'Of Friendship,' in *Essays*, i.28; *The Complete Essays of Montaigne*, trans. Donald Frame (Stanford, Calif., 1958), 144.
[27] Pocock, *The Machiavellian Moment*, 338 ff. Studies since 1984 have tilted the emphasis much further towards the influence of civic humanism in early modern England. Patrick Collinson has written of Elizabethan England as a 'monarchical republic' in which 'citizens were concealed within subjects': *Elizabethan Essays* (London, 1994), 31 ff., 19; for further development of Pocock's paradigm see Markku Peltonen, *Classical Humanism and Republicanism in English Political Thought 1570–1640* (Cambridge, 1995), 1–17 and *passim*.
[28] Z. S. Fink, *The Classical Republicans: An Essay in the Recovery of a Pattern of Thought in Seventeenth-Century England* (Evanston, Ill., 1945), 21–2. The *Utopia* exercised its most direct contemporary influence on the Spanish humanist Vasco de Quiroga who set up communities modelled on More's book for Indians in Latin America: Silvio Zavala, *Sir Thomas More in New Spain: A Utopian Adventure of the Renaissance* (London, 1955). On the influence of More's communism on later Spanish political thought see Gerald Brenan, *The Spanish Labyrinth*, 2nd edn. (Cambridge, 1950), 45, 341–5.

2. The Reformation and Prophetic Poetry

WHEN More advises Hythlodaeus in Book I of the *Utopia* to be cautious in expressing his ideas openly, the indignant reply is that

if all the things which by the perverse morals of men have come to seem odd are to be dropped as unusual and absurd, we must dissemble almost all the doctrines of Christ. Yet He forbade us to dissemble them to the extent that what He had whispered in the ears of His disciples He commanded to be preached openly from the housetops. (p. 101)

Hythlodaeus presents himself as a prophet with the right to preach in public. Though More sympathized with the ideals he attributed to Hythlodaeus, he was himself extremely cautious about assuming the role of a prophet. In writing the *Utopia* in Latin he was escaping from the debased values of the ignorant aristocracy but was also making sure that he could not be accused of stirring up popular unrest. The communism More envisages is imposed from above by an enlightened humanistic leader, and is hence uncontaminated by the ignorance and prejudice of the common people. But prophetic voices of increasing vehemence were being heard throughout Europe. Savonarola had appealed to the authority of Scripture as well as to Florentine republican traditions, and his apocalyptic fervour was to make Protestants regard him as one of their own. The year after the *Utopia* was published, Luther began the public dispute with the Papacy that led to the schism in the Western church. More himself feared that religious reformation was more likely to produce violence and disorder than constructive reform, and fiercely opposed the reformers. In 1533 he declared that he would burn the *Utopia* if this would prevent its being translated into English and perhaps causing social unrest.[1]

But by the middle of the century the cause of reform had triumphed, and Protestant prophecy, rather than humanist dialogue, became the dominant literary mode. The heyday of the prophets was the reign of Edward VI, which in some ways formed the high-water mark of the sixteenth-century Reformation. It was seen by later Puritans as 'a legendary period of freedom and truth, which, had it not been cut short, might have fulfilled millenarian dreams of a perfect Protestant kingdom'. Despite this, literary historians have paid little attention to the Edwardian 'cultural revolution'.[2] It is described as a 'drab age', an unfortunate lapse in the stately

---

[1] *The Confutation of Tyndale's Answer*, in *The Complete Works of St. Thomas More*, vol. viii, ed. Louis A. Schuster et al., 3 parts (New Haven, 1973), i.177–9.
[2] John N. King, *English Reformation Literature: The Tudor Origins of the Protestant Tradition* (Princeton, 1982) (hereafter King, *ERL*), 443, 16; on 'drab' verse and prose see C. S. Lewis, *English Literature in the Sixteenth Century Excluding Drama* (Oxford, 1954), 222–317.

progress of English poetry towards the 'golden', courtly magnificence of Sidney and Spenser. But Elizabethan poetry is in fact more heavily influenced by Edwardian ideals than is at first apparent. And the apparent gulf between 'Renaissance' and 'Reformation' is deceptive: there is a direct community between radical humanism and radical Protestantism. Though More himself might not have liked the fact, it was appropriate that the first English translation of the *Utopia* should have appeared in the reign of Edward.

The interaction between literary, political, and religious issues in mid-century texts can be illustrated by a dialogue published in 1548, *John Bon and Mast Person*.[3] The author was one 'Luke Shepherd', whose name may have been a pseudonym, combining as it does so strikingly the two main strands in Edwardian literature. 'Luke' refers us to the Gospels; and the shepherd, along with the ploughman, is a favourite persona of mid-century writers, who like to present themselves as speaking simple truths in the voice of the people.[4] A parson encounters the ploughman 'John Bon' and asks him if he is going to the Corpus Christi festivities. John feigns incomprehension: 'What saynt is copsi cursty a man or a woman?' The parson explains that Corpus Christi is a man, Christ's own self. John's reply is irreverent:

> I knowe mast parson? and na by my faye
> But me thinke it is a mad thinge that ye saye
> That it shoulde be a man howe can it come to passe
> Because ye maye hym beare within so smal a glasse[.]

The priest is alarmed: 'Nowe I maye perceyue ye loue thys newe geare.' His parishioner has become infected by the Protestant heresy. John disowns the charge with an elaborate display of humility and deference that yet returns to the original question:

> Gods forbod master, I should be of that facion
> I question wy your mashippe in waye of cumlication
> A playne man ye may se wil speake as cometh to mind
> Ye muste holde vs ascused for plowe men be but blynd
> I am an elde felowe of fifty wynter and more
> And yet in all my lyfe I knewe not this before[.]

John declares that the doctrine of 'cropsy cursty' is not in his creed, and resumes his questioning. The priest replies by appealing to the church's authority:

> Why folishe felowe, I tel the it is so
> For it was so determined by the churche longe ago[.]

John is unimpressed: he appeals to reason and common sense, not tradition. The priest warns him that this is a dangerous course:

---

[3] Luke Shepherd, *John Bon and Mast Person*, in *An Edition of Luke Shepherd's Satires*, ed. Janice Devereux (Tempe, Ariz., 2001), 50–7. Diarmid MacCullough, *Edward VI and the Protestant Reformation* (New York, 2001), 74–5, shows that the text enacts its iconoclasm: the title-page engraving of a Corpus Christi procession 'came from a traditionalist devotional tract of 1526 where the context had been one of celebration and reverence'.

[4] King, *ERL*, 253.

> To meddle muche wyth thys may brynge ye sone to wo . . .
> I maruell muche ye wyll reason so farre
> I feare if ye vse it, it wyll ye mar[.]

John has revealed that the priest's arguments rely ultimately on power and authority, not on reason; he drives off, whistling merrily.

This dialogue was probably published to coincide with Cranmer's abolition of the feast of Corpus Christi in 1548.[5] This was an event with momentous symbolic associations. The feast had been established in the fourteenth century, at the height of Catholic sacramentalism—or, in the reformed view, idolatry. The emphasis on the priest's power to transform the bread into the body of Christ at the climax of the mass was a striking symbol of a firmly hierarchical structure of ecclesiastical authority. Christ's message, his Word, had been again made flesh, a representation had become a real presence. The reverence paid to Christ's body in the Corpus Christi ritual epitomized the general emphasis on bodily as opposed to spiritual, conceptual communication in medieval religion.[6] And the body was represented in hierarchical terms: the bodily gestures of reverence reinforced the hierarchical symbolism of the social order. Many hierarchically based rituals and conventions had been adopted by the church in the period of late antiquity when Roman society was becoming stratified on an increasingly rigid basis. Just as lesser individuals in the secular order were represented in the community only by the mediation of socially superior patrons, so they needed a priest to mediate with God. In the secular order, only those of noble rank were fully entitled to a public 'person', a word which still carried something of its etymological sense of a mask, an image representing the self in the public world. The parson (a word identical with 'person') was a patron or 'pattern' (the words are etymologically the same), an image mediating between divine and human orders. And in this system of hierarchical representation, the mediator partook of something of the divine lustre of the Deity: medium and message were inseparable. As in the secular realm, so in the divine, reverence was paid not to the fallible individual who bore the public role but to the image of divinity in him. In all social transactions the exchange of messages had to be reinforced by signs reinforcing the hierarchical social forms through which they passed. John Bon pays tribute to the parson verbally—he addresses him as 'ye' while the priest responds with 'thou'. By slightly exaggerating the deferential tone, however, he manages subtly to insult the priest even while praising him. But he would certainly have been expected to reinforce his verbal tribute by bodily obeisance, and it is more difficult to bow or remove one's hat ironically than to speak ironically: the bodily gesture enacts a complete public submission.

Theologians analysed this bodily semiotic in terms of an opposition between 'natural' and 'artificial' signs. At the moment of transubstantiation the sacrament became a natural sign, partaking of that which it represented, just as a son partook of

---

[5] King, *ERL*, 258–9.
[6] Mervyn James, 'Ritual, Drama and Social Body in the Late Medieval English Town', in *Society, Politics and Culture: Studies in Early Modern England* (Cambridge, 1986), 16–47.

his father's being.[7] The status of natural signs did not extend to religious images; but the underlying concept of the natural sign undoubtedly reinforced the general reverence paid to all mediators and religious symbols, giving rise in the popular mind to all kinds of magical beliefs. Words were held to be 'artificial' signs, but in the mass they took on a natural, magical character. Since Latin had ceased to be a popular spoken language, the words of the mass had become obscure to most of the congregations, and the ornate musical settings further dissociated sound from meaning. For John Bon—or so he claims—'copsi cursty' is a meaningless jumble of sounds. His further variant 'cropsy cursty' suggests the popular superstition that magical rituals could help the crops grow: the calendar of church festivals in many cases corresponded to a more primitive pagan cyclical calendar of fertility and harvest.[8]

The reformers mounted a frontal attack on this system of 'natural signs', or, as they saw it, idolatrous confusion between sign and thing signified. They argued that sacramental signs seemed 'natural' only because of the corruption of the imagination which was always ready to draw false analogies. Religion should appeal to the mind and the spirit, not to the body. The reformers delighted in exposing Catholic claims of miraculous powers as mere rhetoric: religious images were as deceitful as rhetorical tropes, rather than being pure incarnations of a divine content. They compared medieval religious practices to play-acting: and indeed the performance of plays dramatizing religious ideas had been a regular feature of Corpus Christi festivities. Shepherd's dialogue turns this tradition against the Catholics, parodying the Corpus Christi plays and exposing priests as themselves illusionists, play-actors. The title page illustrates the spectacular Corpus Christi procession which John Bon will certainly not attend. It is not known whether this dialogue was actually performed, but the early reformers were certainly not hostile to the stage on principle: John Foxe acclaimed players, along with printers and preachers, as a 'triple bulwark against the triple crown of the pope', and his friend John Bale wrote many propaganda plays.[9] But their plays were intended as supplements to a widely available vernacular Bible, not as substitutes for it.

The reformers' attack on idolatry was a logical extension of humanist principles of textual criticism. The Italian humanist Lorenzo Valla had used his knowledge of semantic changes to expose the 'Donation of Constantine', one of the key documents on which the Roman church based its secular authority, as an anachronistic forgery. Just as huge abstract systems, based on ecclesiastical traditions, had grown up around Aristotle and other classical authors, so the truths of the Bible had, in the humanists' view, been obscured by a host of anachronistic allegorical interpretations. Both the essential simplicity of the Gospels' message and the distinctive qualities of biblical

---

[7] Nicholas Sander, *A Treatise of the Images of Christ, and of his Saints* (Louvain, 1567), sig. 164ᵛ; see also John Phillips, *The Reformation of Images: Destruction of Art in England, 1535–1660* (Berkeley and Los Angeles, 1973), ch. 1. Cf. Mary Douglas, *Natural Symbols: Explorations in Cosmology*, 2nd edn. (London, 1973).

[8] Keith Thomas, *Religion and the Decline of Magic: Studies in Popular Beliefs in Sixteenth- and Seventeenth-Century England*, rev. edn. (Harmondsworth, 1973), 71–6.

[9] King, *ERI*, 277.

language had been obscured by medieval exegetical traditions. Erasmus and other humanists called for the Bible to be made widely available in vernacular translations. Other religious images, said Erasmus, represent only Christ's body, but the Gospels give 'the living image of His holy mind'.[10] Vernacular translation constituted a kind of verbal iconoclasm, stripping away the aura of mystery that surrounded the Latin text. A favourite Protestant emblem depicted the Bible as a sword issuing out of Christ's mouth, an image conveying the sharpness and radical immediacy of the divine message in its vernacular form.[11] Conservatives—including More, who had reacted against his earlier speculative radicalism and was now defending religious images—complained that religious reform would lead to a subversive individualism: in traditional worship the individual imagination was subordinated to authorized public images which mediated divine truths, but the new emphasis on inner, spiritual authenticity would lead to a confused babel of personal visions and imaginations. When it became clear that the publication of a vernacular Bible could no longer be postponed, one conservative, Stephen Gardiner, proposed that the sword of Scripture should effectively be blunted by making the diction as elevated and obscure as possible: complex Latinisms would preserve something of the aura of the Vulgate.[12] Tyndale's translation was indeed exceptionally forceful and idiomatic, and the editors of the Authorized Version were to feel it necessary to adopt a more elevated and socially decorous linguistic register.[13] Printed Bibles were far harder to subject to social control than rituals: the message could be detached from traditional forms. In 1542 Henry VIII established an index of prohibited books, the first of its kind in Europe, to discourage the appearance of radical commentaries on Scripture, and in 1543 the reading of the Bible was restricted on a class basis.[14] But before his death Henry seems to have decided that it was better to have the vehement Protestant minority in favour of the monarchy rather than against it, and he entrusted his son's education to a group of reformers. And when the 9-year-old Edward VI came to the throne in 1547, the real power belonged to the Protector, Edward Seymour, Duke of Somerset, who believed in religious toleration. One of the first measures of the first Edwardian Parliament was the repeal of earlier censorship laws: there was greater freedom of the press under Somerset than at any time before the Civil War. Many images were removed from churches; the reign of the Word had begun.

The reformers changed the symbolic space of public worship, focusing attention on the pulpit rather than the altar and images. They also radically revised the religious conceptualization of time. Cranmer, the Archbishop of Canterbury, drama-

---

[10] King, *ERL*, 45, citing Erasmus' preface to his translation of the New Testament, from Desiderius Erasmus, *Christian Humanism and the Reformation: Selected Writings*, ed. John C. Olin (New York, 1965), 106.

[11] King, *ERL*, fig. 9.

[12] A. W. Pollard (ed.), *Records of the English Bible: The Documents Relating to the Translation and Publication of the Bible in English, 1525–1611* (Oxford, 1911), 272–4.

[13] John Carey, 'Sixteenth and Seventeenth Century Prose', in Christopher Ricks (ed.), *English Poetry and Prose 1540–1674* (London, 1970), 345–53.

[14] On censorship see D. M. Loades, 'The Press under the Early Tudors: A Study in Censorship and Sedition', *Transactions of the Cambridge Bibliographical Society*, 4 (1964–8), 29–50.

tized the break with the traditional symbolic order by systematically running down the old church calendar. In the course of 1548 each feast-day in turn was marked by the ostentatious refusal to carry out the traditional rituals, and the revised English service was gradually phased in at crucial points of the calendar.[15] Luke Shepherd's dialogue marked the final demise of the traditional Corpus Christi festivities. The reformers never tired of pointing out that many of these feast-days had been geared to older, pagan seasonal rituals. To the reformers, the idea that one time of the year was more holy than another savoured of the same kind of idolatry that assumed God to be more fully present in some images than in others. The Roman church had laid claim to a false immanence: only in the future, in the last days, would Christ be fully present on earth. 'Truth is the daughter of time' became a favourite Protestant proverb: the truth was not something whose meaning had been fixed once and for all by the ecclesiastical authorities, it had been obscured by the hierarchical masks and disguises of the Roman church and only now, as the end of time was approaching, was it being finally unveiled. Protestant writers were fond of using metaphors derived from neoclassical dramatic theory: history was not just a blind cycle governed by Fortune, it had a carefully controlled providential structure. John Foxe deliberately deferred the ending of his religious play *Christus triumphans*, leaving the figure of the Lady Ecclesia standing on the stage in her bridal costume, waiting for the arrival of her bridegroom Christ and asking how long his coming would be delayed. Foxe left the end of the text to be written by God himself: as he said in the prologue, 'it seems that all the parts of the play have been acted out, and that the scene of this world is rushing to that final "Farewell, and applaud" '.[16]

Foxe described his play as an 'apocalyptic comedy', and many Edwardian writers were especially interested in the last book of the Bible, the Apocalypse of St John. 'Apocalypse' of course means 'unveiling', 'revelation', and the book claims to shadow forth the mysteries of the last days of human time when the truth will be unveiled and falsehood unmasked. Medieval commentators tended to argue that these mysteries should not be pried into too much, and to interpret the book as a generalized moral allegory rather than a detailed vision of the future. The author of the first published English commentary on Revelation, Foxe's friend John Bale, believed that it was possible to go much further, that though the book was especially full of 'figurate speche', a rhetorically sensitive reading could unveil the hidden truths. The whole book, he claimed, had been written in one day: it was effectively an immediate transcription of the divine Voice.[17] And its message was heavily political. In one of the key passages of the book, chapter 12, St John has a vision of a woman clothed with the sun, standing above the moon and with a crown of twelve stars; she brings forth

---

[15] King, *ERL*, 150–2. On the new status of the word in worship see Ramie Targoff, *Common Prayer: The Language of Public Devotion in Early Modern England* (Chicago, 2001), ch. 1.

[16] *Two Latin Comedies by John Foxe the Martyrologist*, ed. John Hazel Smith (Ithaca, NY, 1973), 207; cf. Katharine R. Firth, *The Apocalyptic Tradition in Reformation Britain, 1530–1645* (Oxford, 1979), 212. See also Richard Bauckham, *Tudor Apocalypse: Sixteenth Century Apocalypticism, Millenarianism and the English Reformation: From John Bale to John Foxe and Thomas Brightman* (Abingdon, 1978).

[17] John Bale, *The Image of Both Churches* (London, 1550), sigs. B3ᵛ, A5ᵛ; also in *Select Works of John Bale, D.D. Bishop of Ossory*, ed. Henry Christmas (Cambridge, 1849), 261, 253–4.

a male child who, it is prophesied, will rule all nations with an iron sceptre. But she is threatened by a huge monster with seven crowned heads, who tries to devour the child; the woman escapes into the wilderness where God has made a safe place for her. Medieval exegesis normally identified the woman with the Virgin Mary, or, on a secondary level, with the church, involved in an eternal struggle with the devil. Bale politicizes the incident: the monster's seven heads represent successive stages of political corruption, the last being embodied in the Papacy. Protestants were increasingly identifying the Pope with the Antichrist denounced in Revelation. For Bale the woman who wanders in the wilderness is not Mary but the Invisible Church, the remnants of the faithful who have seen through the deceitful pretensions of the corrupt Visible Church. Her wanderings were equated by Protestants with the gradual growth of pockets of resistance to the Roman church, from small sects like the Albigensians and Waldenses, via early prophets of reform like Wycliffe and Hus, up to Luther and the current generation of reformers. Revelation prophesied the final defeat of Antichrist; and the more specifically Antichrist was identified with the Papacy, the more sanction Scripture seemed to give for political action to further the overthrow of the corrupt institution.

Protestant apocalypticism thus challenged the Augustinian distinction between secular and sacred spheres, and in so doing it gave renewed importance to the active political life. Italian humanism had denied Augustine's negative valuation of the earthly city as opposed to the city of God. Bale departed from Augustine in a slightly different way, but with not dissimilar political implications. He identified the earthly city with the corrupt Roman church, the heavenly city with the Invisible Church: 'eyther we are citeze[n]s in the new Hierusalem with Jesus Christ, or els in the old supersticious Babylon with antichrist the vicar of Satha[n].'[18] Bale agreed that the world of the spirit was superior to the secular world. But he shifted the axis from a vertical to a horizontal one: Revelation ends with a vision of the New Jerusalem descending to a transfigured earth, and the whole perspective of the book is prophetic, valuing the present only in so far as it adumbrates a future fulfilment. Bale believed that it was possible to take decisive political action in order to unmask the deceitful false church and resume the reign of the true church. Protestant exegesis opened the way for a conception of the incarnation as operating in a linear, progressive manner, as opposed to the medieval conception of a vertical hierarchical cosmos of gradated images and shadows. It is thus appropriate that Bale should have written what has been called the first English 'history play': in *King John* he politicized the struggle between good and evil that was conventionally represented in morality plays, giving the protagonists the historical identities of the English monarchy and the Papacy.

It was precisely the possible political explosiveness of the interpretation of Revelation that led to its downgrading in the Middle Ages. The book described a thousand-year reign by Christ on earth, and it was possible to read this as a sign that

---

[18] Bale, *The Image of Both Churches*, sig. A3ᵛ, *Select Works*, 252. On apocalyptic ideas and political activism cf. J. G. A. Pocock, *The Machiavellian Moment* (Princeton, 1975), 44–8, 50–1, 342–7.

all traditional political institutions would be overthrown and a completely new order be established.[19] The prophecies of the twelfth-century mystic Joachim of Fiore had fuelled not only imperial campaigns against the Papacy's power but also popular rebellions aimed at establishing egalitarian commonwealths. Savonarola had appealed to apocalyptic ideas, and in the minds of some Florentine humanists and artists the humanist rediscovery of classical culture seemed to be a secular sign of an apocalyptic religious renewal. In the *Mystic Nativity* an apocalyptic fervour informs even the courtly and contemplative art of Botticelli. In the 1520s and 1530s there were popular rebellions in Germany which drew inspiration from apocalyptic ideas. It is not surprising that the socially conservative Luther paid little attention to Revelation. But by the 1540s, with the religious divisions of Europe growing more rigid, some reformers began to fuel their arguments against the Papacy with the valuable ammunition provided by apocalyptic ideas. And in England the Reformation was not associated with popular revolt: it had been imposed from above with the consent of the monarchy. Bale found it easy to neutralize the more radically subversive implications of Revelation. Though the earlier sections of his *Image* reveal some hope of a future millennium, by the closing parts of his commentary he was setting the millennium firmly in the past, in the relatively uncorrupted period of the church before the growth of idolatry under the later Popes.[20] Bale and other 'magisterial' reformers believed that Constantine, the first Christian emperor, had exercised supreme authority over the church and that the Papacy had usurped secular authority with the forged 'Donation of Constantine'. Now godly monarchs could restore the proper relations between church and state. The English monarchy could lay particular claim to imperial authority because Constantine had been born in England. Moreover, reformers claimed that England had in the past enjoyed a particularly pure form of Christianity, introduced by Joseph of Arimathea in the first century; the English church could thus lay claim to a continuity independent of the Papacy. Bale did not hold out visionary hopes of the reign of Christ on earth; before long he would come in judgement and secular history would come to an end.

Bale was a pioneer not only in apocalyptic commentary but also in literary history; and he applied the same apocalyptic pattern to his reading of English poetry. His chronological catalogue, *Illustrium maioris Britanniae scriptorum catalogus*, was not just a history of 'literature' narrowly defined but of all kinds of writing. But Bale was convinced that all manifestations of verbal and scholarly energy were signs of radical religious views. He Protestantized the humanist opposition between arid scholasticism and lively rhetoric, equating intellectual stagnation with monkish idleness. He applied an apocalyptic structure to his chronological analysis of literary history: there was an original state of purity which was gradually corrupted by the Roman church but which was now returning with the advent of Protestantism. He took the story of British learning right back to the legendary period of the Druids, who, he

---

[19] On this tradition see Norman Cohn, *The Pursuit of the Millennium: Revolutionary Millenarians and Mystical Anarchists of the Middle Ages*, 2nd edn. (London, 1970).
[20] Firth, *The Apocalyptic Tradition*, 43.

claimed, were monotheists and closer in essentials to the true faith than the Roman church. Bale regarded ancient visionaries like Merlin as authentic prophets of the true religion.[21] Learning began to decline as the Papacy became more and more corrupt: here the literary history coincided with the apocalyptic framework, for Bale began his second book with the reign of Pope Sylvester II, who, he claimed, had unloosed Satan by magic after his thousand years of being bound in hell. From then on the worldly power of the Papacy had grown greater and greater; but it was at the moment when it was at its height that a counter-movement began. Bale opened the fourth book with the history of John Wycliffe, whose preaching and literary works heralded the Reformation. The fifth book began with Humphrey Duke of Gloucester, who was very popular with the reformers and who, according to Bale, was murdered at the instigation of the Roman church.[22] Throughout Bale's history the highest praise went to heroic individualists who caught glimpses of the truth and could see through the deceptions of those in power. He enlisted the major English poets into the company of religious prophets: Chaucer, Langland, Hoccleve, and Skelton all attacked abuses in the church and thus contributed to the triumph of the true faith.[23]

Bale's highly politicized view of literary history was shared by many Edwardian writers. Langland had an especially strong appeal for mid-century reformers: his narrative of a restless search for Truth, embodied in a simple ploughman, accorded with the apocalyptic theme of Truth in the wilderness. Although Langland himself was no Wycliffite, his poem became very popular with Lollards, and already in the late fourteenth or early fifteenth century the figure of Piers Plowman was being used to put across reforming propaganda in the anticlerical satire *Pierce the Ploughmans Crede*.[24] Langland's energetic and abrasive style, which contrasted strikingly with the more courtly diction and metre of Chaucer, seemed an appropriate medium for propaganda in favour of the wide diffusion of the simple gospel truth. Protestants of the mid-sixteenth century made no distinction between Langland and his Lollard imitators. *Pierce the Ploughmans Crede* was printed in 1553 and several works on religious and social topics were published in the Edwardian period under the ploughman persona. In 1550 Bale's close friend Robert Crowley, who was himself the author of several apocalyptic poems calling on the people to prepare for the day of judgement, published an edition of *Piers Plowman*.[25] Bale had at first attributed the poem to Wycliffe, and Crowley emphasized in his preface that it was written in the time of Wycliffe when God first opened the eyes of many to his truth. In his marginal notes he highlighted Langland's prophecies of an apocalyptic king who would restore religious purity. He regarded the more obviously Catholic elements in the

---

[21] Bale, *Illustrium maioris Britanniae scriptorum . . . summarium* (Ipswich, 1548), fos. 2ᵛ, 27ʳ.

[22] Ibid., fos. 154ᵛ, 200ʳ.

[23] Ibid., fos. 198ʳ⁻ᵛ; *Index Britanniae scriptorum: John Bale's Index of British and Other Writers*, ed. R. L. Poole and M. Bateson (Oxford, 1902), 76, 383, 448, 252–3.

[24] *Pierce the Ploughmans Crede c.1394*, ed. W. W. Skeat, Early English Text Society (London, 1867); see D. A. Lawton, 'Lollardy and the *Piers Plowman* Tradition', *Modern Language Review*, 76 (1981), 780–93.

[25] *The Vision of Pierce Plowman* (London, 1550); J. N. King, 'Robert Crowley's Edition of *Piers Plowman*: A Tudor Apocalypse', *Modern Philology*, 73 (1976), 342–52.

poem, such as praise of the Virgin Mary and references to transubstantiation, as later interpolations. Only forty years later the courtly rhetorician George Puttenham was to condemn Langland's language as too 'hard and obscure' to give pleasure, but in the mid-century archaic language, far from presenting a problem, had a special prestige because it was associated with the rugged purity of the early reformers. Later Wycliffite tracts had tried to keep as closely as possible to Wycliffe's own language. Hugh Latimer adopted the same rugged style in his 'Sermon of the Plough' to indicate that the reforms he was advocating were not just recent innovations but had a long history of religious zeal behind them.[26]

'The fine courtier', complained Thomas Wilson in 1553, 'wil talke nothing but *Chaucer*'; he objected that there was a split between 'court talke' and 'countrey speech'. Edwardian gospelling poets tended to prefer the 'countrey speech' of Langland, but there were aspects of Chaucer's work which they could admire.[27] A poem like 'The Pardoner's Tale' would appeal as an ironic revelation of ecclesiastical duplicity, and several more radical satires were widely attributed to Chaucer. *Jack Upland*, a Wycliffite satire attacking friars as disciples of Antichrist, was printed in the 1530s with an attribution to Chaucer. *The Plowman's Tale*, another Wycliffite work, was also reported to be by Chaucer. In this poem a plain ploughman overhears a dialogue between a pelican, who represents the reformers, and a griffin, representing the conservative clergy; the griffin at first takes a blandly genial tone, urging the pelican to be moderate in his demands and not counsel extremism, but when this fails he turns to violence and sets other birds of prey on the pelican; but Christ the Phoenix comes to his aid.[28] *The Plowman's Tale* is probably contemporary with *Pierce the Ploughmans Crede*, though it was revised in the sixteenth century, but another apocryphal Chaucerian poem, *The Pilgrim's Tale*, which contains attacks on bishops for suppressing the truth, was probably written in the 1530s.[29] It is hard to determine how far the ascription of poems to Chaucer reflected genuine confusion on the part of editors and how far it was a calculated device to get round the censor. John Foxe certainly had no doubt that Chaucer was 'a right Wicklevian', hiding his reforming sympathies under obscure allegories to confound the censors: 'under shadows covertly, as under a visor, he suborneth truth in such sort, as both privily she may profit the godly-minded, and yet not be espied of the crafty adversary.' Foxe thought that many people had been converted from Catholicism by reading him.[30] According to the editor's son, one edition of Chaucer's works was almost completely suppressed

---

[26] George Puttenham, *The Arte of English Poesie*, ed. Gladys D. Willcock and Alice Walker (Cambridge, 1936), 62; Robert L. Kelly, 'Hugh Latimer as Piers Plowman', *Studies in English Literature 1500–1900*, 17 (1977), 13–26.

[27] Thomas Wilson, *The Arte of Rhetorique* (London, 1553), ed. G. H. Mair (Oxford, 1909), 162, 164; King, *ERL*, 50–2, 229.

[28] *The Plowman's Tale* was included by W. W. Skeat in his edition of *The Complete Works of Geoffrey Chaucer*, 7 vols. (Oxford, 1894–7), vii.147–90; there is a modern edition of the editions of *c.*1532 and 1606 by Mary Rhinelander McCarl (New York, 1997). See Andrew N. Wawn, 'The Genesis of "The Plowman's Tale"', *Yearbook of English Studies*, 2 (1972), 21–40.

[29] *The Pilgrim's Tale* was printed in the anthology *The Court of Venus*, ed. Russell A. Fraser (Durham, NC, 1955), 82–110.

[30] Foxe, *Acts and Monuments*, ed. J. Pratt, 8 vols. (London, 1877), iv.249.

in Henry VIII's reign because of Chaucer's heretical associations.[31] More recent poets were also posthumously recruited to the Protestant cause. John Skelton had been patronized by the conservative Howard family and was hardly an unqualified admirer of the new learning; but he had vigorously attacked clerical abuses under the alliterative persona of Colin Clout, who was easily associated by reformers with Piers the Ploughman. Several Protestant satires were written in Skeltonic metre. When Spenser adopted the name of Colin Clout he was aligning himself with this tradition.[32]

Though the writers of the mid-century were especially interested in native religious traditions, they were by no means narrowly nationalistic. It was Bale's central contention that Protestantism and learning went together because the Roman church had a vested interest in ignorance, and he believed that throughout Europe the most learned men had sympathized with religious reform. Like true faith, true learning might be found anywhere in the world, and it was most likely to flourish amidst pockets of resistance to the ecclesiastical hierarchy. Foxe is perhaps best known today as the propagator of a myth of England as the 'elect nation'; but he had originally intended his *Acts and Monuments* to describe the fates of the faithful throughout Europe. Exiles from many different countries took refuge in Edwardian England. From Scotland came John Knox, who eagerly supported Somerset's attempts to carry through a dynastic union between England and Scotland. The appearance of the term 'Great Britain' in the titles of works by Bale and Crowley indicates the gospellers' support of this project. Protestant enthusiasm here reinforced humanist interests: the name 'Britannia' was more satisfyingly and authentically classical than the 'barbaric' name 'Anglia'. Anglo-Scottish union was an imaginative ideal for the mid-century gospellers long before it became a political reality.[33]

English reformers have become notorious for their prejudices against Italy, but it is not always recognized that their hostility was partly ideological, not nationalistic, and went with great admiration for some aspects of Italian literary culture. The first English history of Italy, by William Thomas, was published in the Edwardian period.[34] Many Italian humanists had criticized the corruptions of the church and

---

[31] Felix Swart, 'Chaucer and the English Reformation', *Neophilologus*, 62 (1978), 616–19, presents evidence to confirm Francis Thynne's account of the censorship, which has been doubted by some scholars. There seems to have been an unsuccessful attempt to include *The Plowman's Tale* in the 1532 edition of Chaucer; it eventually appeared in the 1542 edition.

[32] e.g. *The Image of Hypocrisy* (a religious satire, *c.*1534) and 'Vox populi vox Dei' (a protest against enclosures, *c.*1547): see Robert S. Kinsman (ed.), *John Skelton, Early Tudor Laureate: An Annotated Bibliography c.1488–1977* (Boston, 1979), 16, 19. Paul E. McLane, 'Skelton's *Colyn Cloute* and Spenser's *Shepheardes Calender*', *Studies in Philology*, 70 (1973), 141–59, ignores this tradition in arguing for Spenser's religious conservatism.

[33] Denys Hay, 'The Use of the Term "Great Britain" in the Middle Ages', *Proceedings of the Society of Antiquaries of Scotland*, 89 (1955–6), 55–66; cf. W. K. Jordan, *Edward VI: The Young King: The Protectorship of the Duke of Somerset* (London, 1968), 269–70; cf. Ch. 3 n. 63 below.

[34] William Thomas, *The Historie of Italie* (London, 1549), declares that the Italian nation 'seemeth to flourisshe in ciuilitee moste of all other at this daie' (dedication, sig. A2ʳ). Though anti-Papal in tone, the history is certainly not democratic in sympathy: popular rule is equated with a decline 'both in courtesie and chiualrie' (ibid., fo. 148ʳ).

the excessive powers gained by the Papacy, and continued to hope that a general council of the church might remedy the worst abuses and heal the religious schisms of Europe. But the conditions of general political reaction in sixteenth-century Italy limited the drive to religious reform.

The Papacy took an increasingly hard line against religious dissent; in 1542 the Roman Inquisition was founded, and repression of intellectual dissent was formalized in 1559 by the establishment of the Roman Index of Prohibited Books. When the Council eventually assembled at Trent it combined administrative reforms with a strong endorsement of an authoritarian church structure. If Italians sympathetic to reform lacked the intolerance of Calvin and his followers, they also lacked their political determination and they were reluctant to seek popular support; they tended to bow towards the pressure for reaction and accept either inner, spiritual exile or exile abroad; several Italian reformers came to Edwardian England.[35] These links with Italian culture were to be further strengthened when reformers like Bale and Foxe themselves went into exile under Mary.

English reformers could find in Italian culture rough equivalents of their own 'ploughman' tradition. Sir Thomas Elyot had established a link between the Italian 'pasquinade' satires and the plain-speaking English persona.[36] There were also affinities between the vernacular idiom of Dante's attacks on the clergy in the *Divine Comedy* and Langland's alliterative satire. English interest in Dante was encouraged by ideological debates. He had indicted the Papal usurpation of imperial authority in *De monarchia*, a work which was condemned by the Roman Inquisition after 1544 but was republished along with other anti-Papal satires by a printer in Basel, where Bale and Foxe eventually took refuge. The more zealously the Inquisition tried to control the production of books in Italy, the more enthusiastically did printers elsewhere try to meet the demand for anticlerical texts. As the propaganda war escalated, texts and parts of texts which had been reprinted by Protestants for their anti-Papal rhetoric would be placed on the Index which would then be eagerly consulted by Protestant printers for sources of fresh ideological ammunition. Foxe probably got to know the *Divine Comedy* through extracts printed by the Lutheran writer Matthias Flacius Illyricus; from this source he quoted the enthusiastic account of Dante as a proto-Protestant which appeared in his *Acts and Monuments*. It is unlikely that his acquaintance with the *Divine Comedy* went much deeper than that; but there were after all further affinities between Dante's prophetic poetry and the English prophetic tradition, affinities which Milton was to explore in greater depth. While Dante's theology was hardly Protestant, his poem did narrate an essentially personal search for salvation, mediated not by the Virgin Mary but by his own love Beatrice. The first Italian edition of the *Vita nuova* made extensive textual changes to minimize Dante's subversive individualism.[37]

---

[35] Lauro Martines, *Power and Imagination: City-States in Renaissance Italy* (London, 1979), 432–4.
[36] King, *ERL*, 379.
[37] On Dante and Protestant propaganda see Paget Toynbee, *Dante Studies* (Oxford, 1921), 109 ff., and (correcting some of Toynbee's points) Frances A. Yates, *Astraea: The Imperial Theme in the Sixteenth Century* (London, 1975), 8 ff., 39–47. Matthias Flacius Illyricus, *Catalogus testium ueritatis* (Strasbourg,

Milton was to praise Dante as a moral poet who defended chaste love and attacked clerical corruption; and he took much the same view of Petrarch. This image of Petrarch was again popularized in the Reformation period. In sixteenth-century Italy Dante's poetry was passing out of fashion for social as well as religious reasons: his vernacular idiom was considered too 'low', and Petrarch was acclaimed as the best model for correct, courtly diction. But this was a selective reading of his poetry; the reformers took a very different, though equally selective, view. They emphasized his vindication of the rights of the emperor against the corrupt Papacy. In his apocalyptic sonnets (*Canzoniere*, nos. 114, 136–8) he denounced the Anti-Pope at Avignon and predicted that a new Constantine would return to abolish such abuses. These sonnets gave authority for identifying the Pope with Antichrist and duly took their place in Protestant polemics. Sixteenth-century English poets took almost as much interest in Petrarch's political poems as in his love sonnets. It was indeed possible to make direct connections between the amatory and political poems: Petrarch made a great deal of the chastity and purity of his mistress Laura and wrote a separate *Triumph of Chastity*. Petrarch could be seen as a poet of chaste love, opposed to the corrupt lust of the Whore of Babylon.[38] The Dutch poet Jan van der Noot was to systematize this idea, publishing versions of some of Petrarch's visions of Laura with Du Bellay's visions of the transience of Rome and his own apocalyptic sonnets based on Revelation. Petrarch was thus established as a visionary poet groping towards a Protestant world-view even though he placed too much importance on worldly things. Van der Noot drew on Bale's *The Image of Both Churches* for his notes on his *Theatre for Worldlings*.[39]

English poets who are now normally thought of as the authors of courtly love lyrics were interested in Petrarch as a political poet. Wyatt adapted Petrarch's love poems in order to voice his criticisms of the insecure atmosphere of Henry VIII's court, and he lamented the fall of Cromwell's reforming regime in an adaptation of *Canzoniere*, no. 269—a poem also translated by a mid-century poet. Wyatt's sympathies with the ideals of the Reformation were so well known that *The Plowman's Tale* was sometimes ascribed to him.[40] His friend Surrey mourned him as a scholar and statesman rather than merely as a love poet, and he read Wyatt's strongly Protestant versions of the *Penitential Psalms* as a warning to princes:

> In Prynces hartes Goddes scourge yprinted depe
> Myght them awake out of their synfull slepe.

1562), 505–7, quotes from *Paradiso* ix, xviii, and xxix; his list of witnesses to the truth begins with St Peter and includes the Waldensians (424 ff.), Petrarch (308), Mantuan (568–9), and even Machiavelli (567). For further Dante references see Jackson Campbell Boswell, *Dante's Fame in England: References in Printed Books 1477–1640* (Newark, Del., 1999). William Thomas not only cited Dante in his *Historie of Italy* but published in 1551 *Principal Rules of the Italian Grammer, with a Dictionarie for the Better Vnderstandying of Boccace, Petrarcha, and Dante*: though Dante's language was by now difficult even for Italians, Thomas's book indicates an English readership ready to make the effort.

[38]   Yates, *Astraea*, 112–14.
[39]   Carl J. Rasmussen, '"Quietnesse of Minde": *A Theatre for Worldlings* as a Protestant Poetics', *Spenser Studies*, 1 (1980), 3–27. Bale praises Petrarch in *The Image of Both Churches, Select Works*, 520, 563.
[40]   Swart, 'Chaucer and the English Reformation', 618–19.

Wyatt had imitated one of the anti-courtly satires by Luigi Alamanni, a friend of Machiavelli who had fled Italy after an unsuccessful plot against the Medici. Surrey shared Wyatt's interest in Petrarch as a religious prophet; he adapted one of the anti-Papal sonnets (*Canzoniere*, no. 138) in an apocalyptic denunciation of the state of London.[41] The Hill manuscript, transcribed *c*.1553–62, indicates the strong political interest in Petrarch in the mid-century: translations of moral and religious sonnets outnumber love poems.[42]

The Edwardian period established a conception of the function of poetry, and a canon of reforming poetry, which was to remain influential until the Civil War. The old 'ploughman' tradition became overshadowed in the Elizabethan period by more courtly poetic modes, but awareness of the older tradition was preserved, especially in Puritan circles. Spenser made his poetic debut with a translation of van der Noot's apocalyptic sonnets. An English translator of a commentary on Revelation in 1589 thought it appropriate to include not only the Italian text of Petrarch's three major anti-Papal sonnets (nos. 136–8) but line-by-line English translations and verse translations by Thomas Howell.[43] In his first anti-episcopal pamphlet, *Of Reformation*, Milton appealed to a European tradition of reforming prophetic poetry: he quoted from Chaucer's description of the Friar, from *The Plowman's Tale*, from Dante, and from Petrarch's *Canzoniere*, no. 138.[44] The same sonnet was translated by Marvell's patron Sir Thomas Fairfax.[45] Milton's sonnets of the Civil War period look back to the political Petrarchism of the sixteenth century. Where Milton differs from the Edwardians, of course, is in his far superior technical control: it is a long way from the anonymous Tudor poet's

> Vengaunce must fall on thee, thow filthie whore
> Of Babilon, thow breaker of Christs fold,
> That from achorns, and from the water colde
> Arte riche become with making many poore.[46]

to Milton's

> Avenge O Lord thy slaughtered saints, whose bones
> Lie scattered on the Alpine mountains cold,
> Even them who kept thy truth so pure of old
> When all our fathers worshipped stocks and stones[.]

---

[41] *Henry Howard Earl of Surrey: Poems*, ed. Emrys Jones (Oxford, 1964), 30–1, 127–8. Recent scholarship has shown the importance of Surrey's late move towards apocalyptic Protestantism, which served as poetic inspiration to Anne Askew: Susan Brigden, 'Henry Howard, Earl of Surrey, and the "Perjured League"', *Historical Journal*, 39 (1996), 1–31, and W. A. Sessions, *Henry Howard: The Poet Earl of Surrey. A Life* (Oxford, 1999), 354–7. See below, p. 293.

[42] Kenneth Muir, 'Sonnets in the Hill Manuscript', *Proceedings of the Leeds Philosophical and Literary Society*, 6 (1944–52), 464–71. The anonymous translator of these sonnets may also have composed the translations of the apocalyptic sonnets (136–8) sometimes ascribed to Sir John Harington: *The Arundel Harington Manuscript of Tudor Poetry*, ed. Ruth Hughey, 2 vols. (Columbus, Oh., 1960), i.380–1.

[43] Lambert Daneau, *A Treatise, Touching Antichrist*, trans. J. Swan (London, 1589), 181–5.

[44] *The Complete Prose Works of John Milton*, ed. Don M. Wolfe et al., 8 vols. in 10 (New Haven, 1953–82), i.570, 579, 558–9.

[45] Bodleian MS Fairfax 40, 604.

[46] Hughey (ed.), *The Arundel Harington Manuscript*, i.380; Milton, 'On the Late Massacre in Piedmont', *The Poems of John Milton*, ed. John Carey and Alastair Fowler (London, 1968), 411.

But Milton's sense of solidarity with Protestantism throughout Europe—his poem laments a massacre of the Waldenses—and his conviction that pure faith, pure learning, and pure poetry go together, had their roots in the prophetic poetry of the sixteenth century.

The Edwardian 'gospellers' liked to present themselves as the voice of the people, as simply transcribing a text already written by the commons:

> for the come*nes* of this Lande
> hath sone this in there sande,
> plowghyng it with ther hande.
> I fonde it where I stonnde,
> And I ame but the hayne
> that wrythe new agayne
> The copy, for to see . . .
> for I a sheparde ame,
> A sory powre man[.][47]

But of course the writer of these lines was not really a simple shepherd, he was adopting a rhetorical persona. Not that literate shepherds did not exist; an eloquent annotation surviving from the year 1546 reads: 'I bout thys boke when the Testament was obberagatyd [abrograted] that shepeyerdys myght not red hit. I prey God amende that blyndnes.'[48] The Edwardians wanted to reach such people, and they scorned literary ornamentation that might obscure their reforming message. They rejected the new Italianate poetic metres and tended to use the old popular measures—alliterative verse or ballads—hence the old-fashioned impression their verse gives.[49] Experiments were even made in spelling reform in the Edwardian period; had simplified spelling been adopted relatively early in the history of the printed book the whole process of popular education would have been greatly eased.[50] But the Edwardians were aware that reaching a large public needed literary skill as well as sincerity, and they were well versed in the art of rhetoric; two important rhetorical treatises, by Thomas Wilson and Richard Sherry, were published in the reign of Edward VI.[51] Bale could switch easily from vernacular English to humanist Latin; Foxe began his chronicle of Protestant martyrs in Latin but its English version became a popular classic. Luke Shepherd's dialogue owes something to Erasmus' *Colloquies*, which were coming under suspicion in Catholic countries. While he pits

---

[47] Anon., *Vox populi, vox Dei*, in Frederick J. Furnivall (ed.), *Ballads from Manuscripts*, 2 vols. (London, 1868–72), i.130.

[48] A. G. Dickens, *The English Reformation*, rev. edn. (London, 1967), 265.

[49] On the social implications of the shift to the iambic pentameter medium see Anthony Easthope, *Poetry as Discourse* (London, 1983), 64–77.

[50] Richard Foster Jones, *The Triumph of the English Language: A Survey of Opinions Concerning the Vernacular from the Introduction of Printing to the Restoration* (Stanford, Calif., 1953), 142 ff. The poet Thomas Churchyard, who began publishing in the Edwardian period, developed an individual system of orthography.

[51] Richard Sherry, *A Treatise of Schemes and Tropes* (London, 1550), facsimile reprint ed. Herbert W. Hildebrandt (Gainsville, Fla., 1961); Wilson, *Arte of Rhetorique*. On political aspects of Wilson's treatise see David Colclough, '*Parrhesia*: The Rhetoric of Free Speech in Early Modern England', *Rhetorica*, 17 (1999), 177–212 (195–8).

the uneducated ploughman's common sense against the parson's pomposity, he is not idealizing ignorance: in other works he also satirizes the clergy's deficient Latinity. Macaronic jingles at once satirize and exemplify the way the clergy mangle classical Latin and turn it into obfuscatory nonsense.[52] The anarchic and frequently obscene learned wit of Shepherd, like the fantastic satires of Rabelais, ran counter to the increasingly influential ideals of courtly decorum propagated by writers like Castiglione. The Edwardian 'gospellers', of course, could claim classical authority for adopting a 'low' style in satire and polemic, and no doubt they would have adopted a slightly different idiom had they seen fit to write love lyrics. The extreme scurrilousness of their language of vituperation, which has discredited them amongst later literary historians, needs to be seen as a rhetorical strategy rather than a direct expression of their personalities. Bale insisted that he was attacking roles rather than individuals: the office of the Papacy had chosen to play the role of Antichrist, and it was the satanic role, not the individuals who bore it, that Bale was attacking. But newer, more restrained standards of decorum were soon to make such vehement writing appear outmoded. It cannot be claimed that the Edwardian writers were great poets: in literature as in politics, the age promised more than it performed. But it is unlikely that they would have suffered such a total eclipse if their voices had been more conservative.

For by the Elizabethan era Edwardian populism was tainted by associations with political disorder. The alarm was already being sounded in 1549 when Somerset was toppled from power. In 1550 Sir Thomas Smith complained that Somerset had surrounded himself with 'hotlings' who 'devise commonwealths as they like'. He later declared his hostility to works like Plato's *Republic* and More's *Utopia* which presented 'feigned common wealths, such as neuer was nor never shall be, vaine imaginations, phantasies of Philosophers'.[53] But Smith himself had helped to imagine commonwealths: he belonged to the school of Henrician and Edwardian humanists who have been labelled 'commonwealth men'. These writers analysed the social order in a detached and critical way: if they did not endorse More's communism, they did share his interest in social reforms that would extend rather further than simply exhorting the ruler to be more virtuous. Speaking of a 'commonwealth' rather than a 'kingdom' was not in itself a sign of radical views but it did imply a habit of mind that saw the state as an artifice that had been created by a collective agency, rather than a natural hierarchy embodied in the person of the monarch. One of the 'commonwealth men', Thomas Starkey, who was a great admirer of the Venetian republic, was perhaps the first English writer to use the word 'state' in its modern sense.[54] Conservative fears about the word 'commonwealth' were expressed by Sir

---

[52] King, *ERL*, 257, 262–70.

[53] Quoted by M. L. Bush, *The Government Policy of Protector Somerset* (London, 1975), 67; Sir Thomas Smith, *De republica Anglorum*, ed. L. Alston (Cambridge, 1906), 142.

[54] Quentin Skinner, *The Foundations of Modern Political Thought*, 2 vols. (Cambridge, 1978), i.224–8, ii.356–7; cf. Arthur B. Ferguson, *The Articulate Citizen and the English Renaissance* (Durham, NC, 1965), 250 ff. On Smith and the Edwardian radicals see Anne McLaren, 'Reading Sir Thomas Smith's *De republica Anglorum* as a Protestant Apologetic', *Historical Journal*, 42 (1999), 911–48.

Thomas Elyot in his *Boke Named the Gouernour* (1531). The term, he felt, implied that property should be in common, or at least that the commoners should gain in prosperity at the expense of the nobility and gentry. This was a terrifying prospect for Elyot, who could not imagine a universe without hereditary inequality and personal rule: the only alternative, he declared, was chaos. He chose the more neutral term 'publike weal' to translate the Latin 'res publica'.[55] But other sixteenth-century humanists were more capable of imagining political alternatives. Undaunted by More's own social anxiety, an Edwardian translator issued the first English version of the *Utopia*, and there was a new upsurge of social criticism.

Some historians have made a rigid distinction between the forward-looking, secular-minded humanism of men like Smith and the backward-looking, idealistic conservatism of reformers like the preacher Hugh Latimer and the poet Robert Crowley.[56] But there were direct continuities between 'Renaissance' and 'Reformation' ideals. Somerset had patronized Smith as well as the gospellers. Smith had suffered a spell in prison after Somerset's fall—which is one reason why he tried to dissociate himself from other controversial figures. Certainly Latimer and Crowley were more immediately concerned with religious issues than Smith. But they were painfully aware that the first stages of religious reform had raised new social problems. The church lands and property confiscated by Henry VIII had not, as the early reformers had hoped, been used to finance social reforms; instead, the property had been sold off to gain crown revenue and the beneficiaries were wealthy merchants and gentry rather than the poor. As Crowley put it, before the Reformation the problem had been fat priests, now it was fat merchants.[57] These newly enriched members of the gentry seemed to lack any sense of social responsibility. In his satire *Philargyrie of Great Britayne* (1551) Crowley pointed out that some merchants supported Protestantism because it seemed a cheaper religion than Catholicism: if one could be saved by faith alone, it did not seem necessary to devote so much energy to good works like helping the poor. His poem personified the evils of the old order in the figure of Hypocrisie, the greed and extravagance of the Roman hierarchy; but the new order was dominated by the equally unattractive figure of Philaute, self-love, who represented the acquisitive spirit that had now been given free rein by the removal of some traditional religious constraints.[58]

Yet Crowley was not unequivocally nostalgic. Like most reformers, he looked back to a time when the church had been free of corruption and saw himself as helping to restore that purity rather than building a completely new order. But this idealized

---

[55] Sir Thomas Elyot, *The Boke Named the Gouernour*, ed. H. S. Croft, 2 vols. (London, 1880), i.1–3.

[56] G. R. Elton, 'Reform and the "Commonwealth-Men" of Edward VI's Reign', in P. Clark, A. G. R. Smith, and N. Tyacke (eds.), *The English Commonwealth 1547–1640: Essays in Politics and Society* (Leicester, 1979), 23–38. Elton's article fails to take account of a substantial body of literary evidence examined by King in *ERL* and supplemented by MacCulloch, *Edward VI and the Protestant Reformation*, 122 ff.

[57] Anon., *Pyers Plowmans Exhortation unto the Lordes, Knightes and Burgoysses of the Parlyamenthouse* (London, 1550?), sigs. A1ᵛ–2ʳ; King, *ERL*, 474, accepts a possible attribution to Crowley.

[58] '*Philargyrie of Greate Britayne* by Robert Crowley', ed. John N. King, *English Literary Renaissance*, 10 (1980), 47–75 (68–71).

past was extremely remote; for the more recent past, and for many religious institutions that had been hallowed by tradition, he had no respect. Crowley did not challenge the hierarchical ordering of society: he urged each estate to labour in its vocation. But he did want to remodel the traditional social structure in a number of ways. He wanted the rural workers who made up the bulk of the population to reject all the old traditions and superstitions that had arisen from the rhythms of their labour. The abolition of many traditional feast-days would have changed the pattern of work in the countryside and cut down the amount of leisure. Crowley idealized hard work and scorned idleness; his ideal commonwealth would feel no obligation to support those who did not work. Its landscape would have borne a distinct resemblance to that of More's Utopia. Crowley also wanted to reform the upper classes; like More, he called on them to abandon their traditional idle pursuits and to educate themselves to work in the service of the community. In order to prevent idleness he suggested that they should give their surplus wealth to the poor. He did not specify at what point wealth became excessive—though Edward's government did consider a proposal to fix a maximum income—but he did make it clear that distinctions of income were not part of the order of nature. Personal property, he argued, was relative, not absolute; people were stewards, not lords, of their possessions.[59]

During Somerset's regime some attempt was made to put such ideals into practice. In the countryside illegal enclosures were causing discontent. The population had been steadily rising and there was increasing resentment against the enclosure of large areas that could have given food and employment to the dispossessed. Hythlodaeus' complaint that sheep were eating men seemed newly topical and was echoed by Thomas Becon, one of Somerset's chaplains.[60] The prophetic poem 'Vox populi, vox Dei' called for action. In 1548 a commission under the humanist John Hales was established to investigate the situation in the country; some modest measures of reform were proposed, though none was passed by Parliament. The aim of such proposals was to prevent unrest rather than to stir it up, and Somerset certainly had no intentions of introducing radical social change.[61] But the climate of impending reform did help to arouse expectations in the countryside that the government would help the poor against exploiting landlords; and in 1549 there were popular

---

[59] Robert Crowley, *The Voyce of the Laste Trumpet Blowen bi the Seventh Angel* (London, 1549), sigs. C6ʳ–7ʳ; repr. in *Select Works of Robert Crowley*, ed. J. M. Cowper, Early English Text Society, ES 15 (London, 1872), 92. On maximum incomes see W. K. Jordan, *Edward VI: The Threshold of Power: The Dominance of the Duke of Northumberland* (London, 1970), 411.

[60] Thomas Becon, 'The Jewel of Joy', in *The Catechism of Thomas Becon . . . with Other Pieces*, ed. John Ayre (Cambridge, 1844), 434: sheep 'which were created of God for the nourishment of man do now devour man'.

[61] Bush, *The Government Policy of Protector Somerset*, 41 ff., gives a detailed account of the pragmatic motives behind the agrarian reforms. However, new evidence has come to light suggesting that Somerset did indeed make major concessions to the rebels and follow a populist line, and that this was a major force behind his overthrow: Ethan Shagan, 'Protector Somerset and the 1549 Rebellions: New Sources and New Perspectives', *English Historical Review*, 144 (1999), 34–63, and MacCullough, *Edward VI and the Protestant Reformation*, 43–52; see also M. L. Bush's reply, 'Protector Somerset and the 1549 Rebellions: A Post-Revision Questioned', *English Historical Review*, 115 (2000), 103–12.

uprisings in several parts of the country. The rebels had widely differing motives. In the west they were religious conservatives protesting against the new prayer book. But the East Anglian rebels did have social and economic grievances, and they were convinced that the government would support them against their immediate superiors. The rebellions caused great alarm and were ruthlessly suppressed. The blame was placed on Somerset, who was deposed by John Dudley, Duke of Northumberland. Somerset's enemies accused him of fomenting hostility to gentlemen. Censorship restrictions were reintroduced, and though Crowley went on publishing poetry he was deeply disturbed by Somerset's fall; he and the other 'gospellers' continued to revere his memory and Foxe enshrined the myth of the 'good duke' in his *Acts and Monuments*.

Somerset's character and the nature of his regime remain controversial. Revisionist historians have done much to undermine the idea propagated by his conservative enemies, and later by liberal admirers, that he was a sincere champion of the poor: his agrarian reforms can be explained by pragmatic political considerations. The propaganda put out by his supporters was orthodox enough in content, calling for improvements in the way the existing hierarchy functioned rather than for its overthrow. Many of the rebels of 1549 were protesting against religious reform rather than gaining inspiration from it. But if the content of the gospellers' writings was orthodox, the tone and symbolism struck a new note.[62] Preachers had been calling on the people to repent for centuries, but Crowley's exhortations had an exceptional urgency because he believed that the apocalypse was approaching. He compared his prophetic voice to the sound of the seventh trumpet blown by the angel in Revelation who breaks the seventh seal, thus indicating that the end was very near. In looking back to an idealized past he was also looking forward to the future and calling for vigorous action to meet it. The truth had been obscured in the past and was only now coming to light: 'it hath pleased the almyghty and lyuyng God to open vnto vs those abhominacions, whych haue heretofore ben kept secret and hyd from vs.'[63] Those who had claimed respect for their authority had been proved to have misunderstood or actively suppressed the truth. Crowley had ridiculed the idea that private individuals must not presume to pass judgement on their superiors:

> They say we must,
> Their iudgement trust,
> And obey theyr decrees,
> Although we see,
> Them for to bee,
> Against Gods veritics.
> They say how can,
> The priuate man,

---

[62]   King, *ERL*, 80–94, argues that Bush takes his revisionist argument too far. On writing and agrarian reform see also Andrew McRae, *God Speed the Plough: The Representation of Agrarian England, 1500–1660* (Cambridge, 1996), ch. 1.

[63]   Crowley, *The Voyce of the Laste Trumpet*, *Select Works*, 53–104; *An Informacion and Peticion* (London, 1548), sig. A2ʳ, *Select Works*, 154.

> Discerne Gods veritie . . .
>   For God they say,
>   Giueth alway,
> The truth to the rulers.[64]

In the reign of Henry VIII Crowley had seriously doubted whether rulers were necessarily so godly. Under Edward, of course, the monarchy was a strong supporter of reform; and Crowley's apocalyptic rhetoric was magisterial in its emphasis, giving a central place to the role of godly king. But he did touch on some more sensitive issues. He looked back to the distant days of the early church when wealthy members of the congregation sold their property to distribute it amongst poorer members of their congregations. He argued that Christians should do even better than the pagans who had argued that all things should be in common between friends. All members of a Christian commonwealth were friends:

we are all one mans chyldren, and haue (by nature) lyke ryght to the richesse and treasures of thys worlde whereof oure natural father Adame was made Lord and Kinge. Which of you can laye for hym selfe any naturall cause whye he shoulde possesse the treasure of this wor[l]de, but y^t the same cause may be founde in hym also whome you make your slaue? By nature (therefore) you can claime no thynge but that whiche you shall gette with the swet of your faces.[65]

Language like this had been used by radical sects to justify apocalyptic egalitarianism. In his edition of *Piers Plowman* Crowley noted that 'Christ was pore' and drew attention to Langland's attacks on the wealthy.[66] Crowley was not advocating egalitarianism any more than Langland had been: like the medieval poet, he believed that '[f]or the best ben somme riche and somme beggers and pore'.[67] 'Take me not here,' insisted Crowley, 'that I shoulde go about by these wordes to perswade men to make all thynges commune . . . For I take God to wytnes I meane no such thynge.'[68] But once special attention had been drawn to Christ's pronouncements about the evils of riches, it was necessary to go to extra efforts to show that he had not meant these sayings to be taken too literally. Crowley would probably have known that John Ball had quoted from Langland's praise of the poor to justify the 1381 peasants' revolt. Langland had been so alarmed that he inserted attacks on communism in later versions of the poem, and his reluctance to be associated with subversive ideas may in fact account for his failure to put his name to the poem.[69] In the early Edwardian period radical sects like the Anabaptists were gaining ground in England. Though the easing of censorship restrictions specifically excluded the Anabaptists, the

[64] Crowley, *The Opening of the Wordes of the Prophet Joell* (London, 1567), sigs. F5^{r-v}. Though written in Henry VIII's reign, this poem was not published until Elizabeth's reign when Crowley was again losing faith in the monarch's will to reform.

[65] Crowley, *An Informacion and Peticion*, sigs. A7^v–8^r, *Select Works*, 163. Bush thinks that Somerset read this work (*The Government Policy of Protector Somerset*, 71).

[66] King, *ERL*, 332; note to *Piers Plowman*, B-text, XI, ll. 178–80.

[67] William Langland, *The Vision of William Concerning 'Piers the Plowman' and 'Richard the Redeless'*, ed. Walter W. Skeat, 2 vols. (Oxford, 1886), i.342.

[68] Crowley, *An Informacion and Peticion*, sig. A4^r, *Select Works*, 156.

[69] *The Vision of Piers Plowman*, ed. A. V. C. Schmidt (London, 1978), p. xiii.

general climate of debate and political excitement probably contributed to the spread of radical ideas. Regardless of the content of Edwardian polemic, the dissolution of traditional forms of social control, the encouragement of individual speculation and self-education, helped to undermine respect for traditional social institutions. Sir William Paget complained in 1548 that 'now every man hath liberty to do and speak at liberty without danger . . . The governor is not feared; the noblemen contempted; the gentlemen despised.'[70] Some of the East Anglian rebels had certainly been influenced by reforming ideas.

Many members of the gentry were relieved when Somerset had been removed and normality restored. In his attack on the rebels of 1549, *The Hurt of Sedicion*, Sir John Cheke thundered against any challenge to the established social order; he concentrated on the sins of the poor and had nothing to say about any possible limitations in the rich. This was to become the standard emphasis of Elizabethan statements about order and degree. Crowley's response to the rebellion was significantly different. In his pamphlet *The Way to Wealth* (1550) he began by voicing conventional ideas about the sinfulness of rebellion, reminding the peasants that it was their duty to obey established authority and rebuking them for their superstition—here he was clearly thinking of the western rebels. Crowley assumed that Catholicism led to rebellion while good Protestants would obey properly, and rebuked the clergy for failing to show enough zeal in bringing the word of God to the people. But the climax of the pamphlet came when Crowley rounded on the upper classes. The rebellion had not made him any more cautious about his demands for the rich to mend their ways: on the contrary, he satirized the way the upper classes use rebellion as an alibi for complacency:

Nowe if I should demaund of the gredie cormeraunces what thei thinke shuld be the cause of Sedition: they would saie, the paisant knaues be to welthy, prouender pricketh them. They knowe not themselues, they knowe no obedience, they regard no lawes, thei would haue no gentlemen, thei wold haue al men like themselues, they would haue al thinges commune. Thei would not haue vs maisters of that which is our owne. They wil appoint vs what rent we shal take for our groundes[.] We must not make the beste of oure owne. These are ioly felowes. Thei wil cast doune our parckes, & laie our pastures open, thei wil haue the law in their own handes, They wil play the kinges. They wyll compel the kinge to graunt theyr requestes. But as they like their fare at *the* breakefaste they had this laste somer, so let them do againe. They haue ben metely well coled, and shalbe yet better coled if they quiet not them selues. We wyll tech them to knowe theyr betters. And because they wold haue al commone, we wil leaue them nothing. And if they once stirre againe or do but once cluster togither, we wil hange them at their own dores. Shal we suffer *the* vilaines to disproue our doynges? No, we wil be lordes of our own & vse it as we shal thinke good.[71]

Crowley is repelled by the violent hysteria with which the gentry had responded to the rebellion. They have no right, he says, to rebuke the poor for disobedience, for

---

[70] Quoted by King, *ERL*, 82–3, from B. L. Beer, 'A Critique of the Protectorate: An Unpublished Letter of Sir William Paget to the Duke of Somerset', *Huntington Library Quarterly*, 34 (1971–2), 280.
[71] Crowley, *The Way to Wealth . . . A Remedy for Sedicion* (London, 1550), sigs. B2ᵛ–3ʳ; *Select Works*, 142–3.

they disobeyed the king by enforcing illegal enclosures. He concludes with a solemn warning: if they continue to oppress the common people, they will destroy themselves. If the poor remain obedient to established authority, 'be sure that God wyll fyghte for them, and so are ye ouer matched'. But if the peasants rebel and a class war breaks out, both sides will be destroyed.[72]

Such sympathy for the poor was to become markedly less apparent in Elizabethan poetry and social thought. The 1549 rebellion does seem to have marked a watershed in attitudes to popular rebellion. The traditional feudal ties that had given the nobility a sense of responsibility to their tenantry were being eroded. In the Middle Ages noblemen had sometimes been prepared to enlist the support of their tenants in rebellion against the monarchy and to protect low-born rebels against punishment. Aristocratic honour was felt to consist in loyalty to local family traditions, which might conflict with the demands of the central government. The Tudor monarchs encouraged the nobility to redefine honour in terms of service of the monarchy: they must be prepared to sacrifice their tenants' interests for the good of the state. The 'Pilgrimage of Grace' in 1536 had shown vestiges of the old pattern; but in 1549 the upper classes united against the rebels. The old complex network of reciprocal obligations was giving way to a simpler model of the social order in which unconditional obedience had to be paid to the monarch at the head of the hierarchy while at the bottom lay the fearsome, undifferentiated multitude. '[D]issidence was seen, no longer as a confrontation between an unworthy king and his nobility, but almost as a natural calamity—the shattering of polity by insensate popular forces completely alien to it.'[73]

Sidney and Spenser were to give this new, more rigidly centralized model of the social order a definitive poetic expression, informing the social hierarchy with Neoplatonic ideas of cosmic harmony. But it was to take a long time to perfect this new 'golden' poetic idiom: the literature of the 1550s and 1560s remained distinctly 'drab', and reflected the dominant disillusion of these years. Under Northumberland the pace of social and religious reform had already slowed down a little, though the change should not be exaggerated. Northumberland still patronized committed Protestants, and on Edward's death he tried to sidestep the direct line of succession and put his daughter-in-law Lady Jane Grey, rather than the Catholic Mary Tudor, on the throne. But the majority of the nobility and gentry had by now had enough of the social and political instability which seemed the inevitable consequence of excessive ideological zeal; and they rallied to Mary. Crowley, Bale, and Foxe went into exile, but many Protestants felt able to reconcile themselves to Mary's regime; order and continuity were preferable to ideological purity bought at the price of social unrest. Apocalyptic hopes gave way to a resigned acceptance of the vagaries of Fortune. Though the persecution of Protestants in Mary's reign

---

[72] *The Way to Wealth*, sig. B7ᵛ; *Select Works*, 149.
[73] Mervyn James, 'English Politics and the Concept of Honour, 1485 1642', in *Society, Politics and Culture: Studies in Early Modern England* (Cambridge, 1986), 308–415. On Tudor social thought in general see Fritz Caspari, *Humanism and the Social Order in Tudor England* (Chicago, 1954).

produced a certain amount of resistance, active opposition was confined to a small minority.[74]

The major poetic production of the 1550s, *The Mirror for Magistrates*, reflects the weary scepticism with which so many people responded to the political upheavals. The project of bringing Lydgate's *Fall of Princes* up to date originated with William Baldwin, whose life embodied the cautious pragmatism preached by his poetry: he had written masques for Edward VI, acted as an informer under Mary, and before long would be enthusiastically praising Queen Elizabeth. The tragedies of *The Mirror for Magistrates* advocate resignation before Fortune. Italian humanism and Protestant apocalyptic ideas had in different ways challenged the power of Fortune: civic activism and religious reform could decisively change the course of history and realize God's providential purpose. But in *The Mirror for Magistrates*, as in Lydgate and other medieval writers, Fortune is an inscrutable and irresistible power.[75] Although she ultimately works as an agent of God's purpose in punishing tyrants, the precise mechanisms of this process remain obscure and un-predictable. For subjects it is necessary to obey a tyrant even though there is no guarantee that God's vengeance will come swiftly; for monarchs the lesson is if anything even less consoling:

although you shall finde . . . that sum haue for their vertue been enuied and murdered, yet cease not you to be vertuous, but do your offices to the vttermost: punish sinne boldly, both in your selues and other, so shall God (whose lieutenauntes you are) eyther so mayntayne you, that no malice shall preuayle, or if it do, it shal be for your good, and to your eternall glory.[76]

What role did this world-view give the poet? A rather more limited one than that envisaged by Crowley or Bale: he could produce oblique, ironic criticisms of tyrants, perhaps, but certainly not enthusiastic prophecy addressed to the people. The tragedy of the poet Collingbourne in the *Mirror* suggests the dangers of politically committed poetry. Collingbourne had been executed under the reign of Richard III for writing a satire against the king. His ghost tells poets to beware

> that purpose to rehearce
> By any arte what Tyrantes doynges are,
> Erinnis rage is growen so fell and fearce
> That vicious actes may not be toucht in verse:
> The Muses freedoome, graunted them of elde,
> Is barde, slye reasons treasons hye are held.[77]

Collingbourne says that the only way for poets to survive is to flatter Caesar's faults,

> And whan they touch thinges which they wish amended.
> To sause them so, that fewe nede be offended.

---

[74] On the regimes of Northumberland and Mary see Robert Tittler and Jennifer Loach (eds.), *The Mid-Tudor Polity c.1540–1560* (London, 1980).

[75] James, 'English Politics and the Concept of Honour', 367–8.

[76] Baldwin's preface to *The Mirror for Magistrates*, ed. Lily B. Campbell (Cambridge, 1938), 67.

[77] Ibid. 347, 352.

Though the *Mirror* was not particularly politically controversial, it was censored by the Marian authorities and did not appear until Elizabeth's reign. In its somewhat ponderous didacticism, this work perfectly illustrates what C. S. Lewis meant by 'drabness'; but it differs from the works of Bale or Crowley in its lack of apocalyptic urgency. Drabness has become depoliticized.[78] Mary's reign did not match her predecessor's in the exploitation of the press for propaganda and original literary works. Though the period remains relatively unexplored, there seems to have been a return to more courtly modes of literature, a fashion for dream-visions and allegories; the works of Malory were reprinted but not those of Chaucer or Langland. Humanist publication certainly continued, often with a courtly flavour, with successive translations of Virgil evoking ideas of Roman Catholic empire.[79] The anthology *Tottel's Miscellany*, published in 1557, concentrates on love poetry rather than political verse and presents Wyatt, whose son had been executed in 1554 for leading a rebellion against Mary, not as a Protestant humanist but as a courtly lover. The censor changed an attack on Rome in his first satire to a generalized condemnation of irreligion.[80] The Marian censor prefers poetry to deal with eternal human truths, not transient political issues. But it is the dominant sense of political caution that makes so much 'drab' verse dull: the exuberant populism and apocalyptic excitement found in some Edwardian poetry gradually ebbs away, and there is as yet no alternative store of poetic imagery to express the visions of Neoplatonic order which inform the poetry of Sidney and Spenser. It was at this period that the future Queen Elizabeth was undergoing her education, and her own poetry is stamped by the mood of the age, expressing a wary, worldly-wise morality in pithy, gnomic form:

> The doubt of future foes, exiles my present ioy,
> And wit me warnes to shun such snares as threaten mine annoy.

[78] King, *ERL*, 414–17, is sceptical about the political allusions found in the *Mirror* by some critics, though he does note that an allusion to *Piers Plowman* in one poem would have aroused official disapproval. My 1984 discussion of this heavily ironic text draws on Campbell's reading, which has been highly influential on interpretations of the 'Elizabethan World Picture'. That reading, however, does not properly explain why the Marian authorities thought the work worth suppressing in the first place; for a challenge to Campbell's intepretation of the date and circumstances of its suppression, see Scott Campbell Lucas, 'The Suppressed Edition and the Creation of the "Orthodox" *Mirror for Magistrates*', *Renaissance Papers* (Raleigh, NC, 1994), 31–54. Andrew Hadfield, *Literature, Politics and National Identity: Reformation to Renaissance* (Cambridge, 1994), 81–107, complements Lucas in emphasizing oppositional aspects of this text, whose fascinating self-consciousness about the processes of bringing controversial history into the public sphere deserves much fuller exploration.

[79] Loades, 'The Press under the Early Tudors', 46–7. But see further Jennifer Loach, 'The Marian Establishment and the Printing Press', *English Historical Review*, 101 (1986), 135–48, who argues that the Marian regime did not differ conspicuously from its predecessors in the extent of state propaganda—though she concedes that much official printing under her reign was directed to a Continental rather than native audience. See also Donna B. Hamilton, 'Re-engineering Virgil: *The Tempest* and the Printed English *Aeneid*', in Peter Hulme and William H. Sherman (eds.), '*The Tempest*' *and its Travels* (London, 2000), 114–20 (115–16). The Marian period is ripe for re-examination, but I have not had the opportunity of properly revising the very sketchy account here given.

[80] *Tottel's Miscellany (1557–1587)*, ed. Hyder Edward Rollins, 2 vols. (Cambridge, Mass., rev. edn. 1965), ii.219. For a careful assessment of Elizabeth's views see Patrick Collinson, 'Windows in a Woman's Soul: Questions about the Religion of Elizabeth I', in *Elizabethan Essays* (London, 1994), 87–119.

For falshood now doth flow, and subiect faith doth ebbe,
Which would not be, if reason rul'd or wisdome weu'd the webbe.[81]

The upheavals of the mid-century had made Elizabeth, like many of her subjects, deeply suspicious of religious and political ideologies. Her enigmatic personality seems to have retained an underlying sympathy with the ideals of the more tolerant of the mid-century reformers; but she was acutely aware of the practical constraints on reform. Her most urgent concern was to preserve what she could from the all-engulfing power of mutability.

[81] Quoted by Puttenham, *The Arte of English Poesie*, 248. The attribution to Elizabeth is uncertain, but Puttenham would hardly have printed it in a book dedicated to the queen had he not had reason to believe that she would have approved of its sentiments. The poem was 'the most frequently anthologized of all Elizabeth's verses' in commonplace books: *Elizabeth I: Collected Works*, ed. Leah S. Marcus, Janel Mueller, and Mary Beth Rose (Chicago, 2000), 133. For an analysis persuasively bringing out the poem's multiple intersections with Elizabeth's concerns see Jennifer Summit, *Lost Property: The Woman Writer and English Literary History, 1380–1589* (Chicago, 2000).

3. The Shepheardes Calender:
Prophecy and the Court

SPENSER'S *Shepheardes Calender* marked a revolution in English poetry. The volume was a virtuoso display of the stylistic and metrical skill of this 'new poet' who assimilated and imitated a great many Continental and classical literary models. Despite these innovations, however, Spenser also paid tribute to English traditions, including the tradition of reforming, prophetic poetry. Ten years earlier he had published translations of van der Noot's apocalyptic sonnets, which had been influenced by Bale's writings. In the envoy he says to his book:

> Dare not to match thy pype with Tityrus hys style,
>   Nor with the Pilgrim that the Ploughman playde a whyle[.][1]

'Tityrus' is Chaucer; the second line seems to refer to *The Pilgrim's Tale* and *The Plowman's Tale*. Spenser's poetic persona, Colin Clout, carries similar associations with the poetry of social and religious protest. One of his protagonists is named Piers and his attack on ecclesiastical luxury evokes memories of *Piers Plowman*. That poem's contemporary editor, Robert Crowley, was still a prominent figure in London when Spenser published his eclogues. Spenser's personae are shepherds rather than ploughmen, but in the Middle Ages the two figures had similar associations. Virgil's eclogues were generally read as moral or political allegories; little attention was paid by commentators to the sensuous qualities of his poetry. Petrarch had set a precedent for allegorical eclogues which attacked political and religious abuses. His fifth eclogue had alluded favourably to Cola di Rienzo's republican coup. The tradition of allegorical eclogues was continued by the fifteenth-century poet Mantuan, whose poems became standard school textbooks and were translated into English in 1567. He was regarded by Bale and other Protestants as a prophet of the Reformation.[2] Mantuan was taken as a model by Barnabe Googe, who published in 1563 the last collection of English eclogues to appear before *The Shepheardes Calender*. A zealous Protestant, Googe revised Mantuan's poems to make the tone even more moralistic and included an allegorical denunciation of the persecution of Latimer and Ridley.[3]

---

[1] *The Works of Edmund Spenser: A Variorum Edition*, ed. Edwin Greenlaw et al., 10 vols. (Baltimore, 1932–49), vii.120. Quotations from Spenser will be taken from this edition.

[2] On the allegorical eclogue see Helen Cooper, *Pastoral: Mediaeval into Renaissance* (Ipswich, 1977), 36–46, 108–11; I am also indebted to Sukanta Chaudhuri, *Renaissance Pastoral and its English Developments* (Oxford, 1989). Bale listed Mantuan as a herald of the Reformation in *The Image of Both Churches* (*Select Works of John Bale, D.D. Bishop of Ossory*, ed. Henry Christmas (Cambridge, 1849), 521).

[3] Paul E. Parnell, 'Barnabe Googe; A Puritan in Arcadia', *Journal of English and Germanic Philology*, 60 (1961), 273–81; Barnabe Googe, *Eglogs, Epytaphes, and Sonettes* (London, 1563), sigs. Bl^r-v. Willy Maley,

Spenser likewise imitates Mantuan, but he also borrows directly from the 'plough-man' tradition.[4] In *The Plowman's Tale* the pelican attacks the luxury and vainglory of the prelates,

> That hye on horse wylleth ryde
> In glytterande golde of great aray
> Ipaynted and portred all in pride
> No co[m]men knyght may go so gaye
> Change of clothyng every day
> with golden gyrdels great and small[.] (ll. 133–8)[5]

Spenser's Thomalin makes a similar attack on the luxury of the clergy, imitating the rugged metre of older English poetry:

> They bene yclad in purple and pall,
>   so hath theyr god them blist,
> They reigne and rulen ouer all,
>   and lord it, as they list:
> Ygyrt with belts of glitterand gold. ('July', ll. 173–7)

When *The Shepheardes Calender* was published the issues of ecclesiastical pride and luxury were newly controversial. A group of religious radicals had become impatient at the slow pace of reform under the Protestant queen from whom they had hoped for so much, and had begun to turn the old anti-Catholic rhetoric against the Elizabethan hierarchy. The rhetoric of Spenser's ecclesiastical eclogues is at least superficially similar to the radicals' propaganda, and led many later Puritans to claim him as one of their own. In 1606 a group of presbyterians reissued *The Plowman's Tale* and included marginal annotations which referred to *The Shepheardes Calender*. In his anti-episcopal *Animadversions* (1641) Milton quoted from Piers's prophecy in the 'May' eclogue of an eventual return of the church to primitive purity:

> The time was once, and may againe retorne . . .
> When shepeheards had none inheritaunce,
> Ne of land, nor fee in sufferaunce. ('May', ll. 103–6)[6]

In the last days of the Commonwealth Milton's friend Henry Stubbe likewise quoted this passage to show that Spenser had prophesied the Puritan revolution.[7] Down to

---

Salvaging Spenser: Colonialism, Culture and Identity (Houndmills, 1997), 15–18, discusses Googe's Irish experiences as paralleling Spenser's.

[4] Spenser's debt to *The Plowman's Tale* is noted by Alice S. Miskimin, *The Renaissance Chaucer* (New Haven, 1975), 93, 290.

[5] *The Plowman's Tale* (London, 1532?), ed. Mary Rhinelander McCarl (New York, 1997), 72. McCarl's edition includes the 1606 printing, whose editor she identifies as Anthony Wotton, a Puritan who had been a chaplain to the Earl of Essex; she discusses Wotton's reading of Spenser through *The Plowman's Tale*, 62–3.

[6] *The Complete Prose Works of John Milton*, ed. Don M. Wolfe et al., 8 vols. in 10 (New Haven, 1953–82), i.723.

[7] Henry Stubbe, *A Light Shining out of Darknes*, 2nd edn. (London, 1659), 174–6. Stubbe emphasized the line 'For ought may happen, that hath bene beforne'. An independent like Milton, Stubbe mischie-

the nineteenth century it remained common to locate Spenser in a broadly Puritan tradition.

More recently, however, there has been a tendency to deny any connection between Spenser and Puritanism. Historians have pointed to the limitations of the old model of 'Puritanism' as some kind of autonomous entity which underwent a steady organic evolution; some authorities would argue that the word 'Puritan' is so vague and confusing that it should be abandoned or at least strictly limited.[8] Literary critics who have dissociated Spenser from Puritanism have been more often motivated by certain assumptions about the relationship between culture and politics: 'Puritan' has become a label for all those who would 'reduce' poetry to religious or political functions. If it is assumed that poetry should transcend politics, then it becomes necessary to interpret the 'moral' eclogues in a different way, as embodying, in the words of a representative critic, 'an ambivalence in which neither perspective can [lay] claim to the whole truth'. For example, the 'May' eclogue, in which Piers rebukes Palinode for his worldliness, can be read as conveying not an argument for further reform but the cautious conclusion that 'while distrust of instinct is a necessary part of caution and restraint, carried too far it may also extinguish the good in instinct'.[9] It becomes clear, however, that for this critic it is the Puritans who carry things too far; the Anglican bishops emerge as those with a far deeper insight into human nature. Thus the poem's apparent 'ambivalence' does seem to indicate that Anglicans, not Puritans, know 'the whole truth'. The reaction against the old 'Puritan' readings has reached its most extreme form in the fullest modern study of Spenser's religious allegory, by Paul McLane, who claims that 'Spenser's sympathies were entirely with the conservative party in the Established Church, and that his few deviations from Anglican doctrine were Catholic rather than Calvinistic in origin'.[10]

vously cast the presbyterians as heirs to Spenser's Palinode; he also cited Milton's translation from Dante's onslaught on the Papacy in the *Inferno*.

[8] C. H. George, 'Puritanism as History and Historiography', *Past and Present*, 41 (1968), 77–104; Paul Christianson, 'Reformers and the Church of England under Elizabeth I and the Early Stuarts', *Journal of Ecclesiastical History*, 31 (1980), 463–82.

[9] Patrick Cullen, *Spenser, Marvell, and Renaissance Pastoral* (Cambridge, Mass., 1970), 31, 32.

[10] Paul E. McLane, *Spenser's* Shepheardes Calender: *A Study in Elizabethan Allegory* (Notre Dame, Ind., 1961), 260 n. 50; McLane is summarizing the argument for another reading of Spenser as anti-Puritan, Virgil K. Whitaker, *The Religious Basis of Spenser's Thought* (Stanford, Calif., 1950). Since McLane's book is still sometimes cited as an authority on Spenser's religious views, it should be said that it is seriously misleading on many major issues of interpretation. To avoid detailed counter-arguments, the limitations of the book on religious issues can be summarized as stemming from complete unfamiliarity with, or reluctance to consider, Protestant traditions of composition and interpretation. For example, McLane argues (126) that because he admired Mantuan Spenser must have had Catholic sympathies, an argument that would have made a Catholic of John Bale. McLane often locates attacks on Puritans in odd places, such as the satire on worldly, play-going priests in *Mother Hubberds Tale* (ibid. 118–20); play-going was not normally regarded as an instantly recognizable feature of Puritans. For a more concise and reliable guide see Anthea Hume's book (below, n. 36); see also John N. King, *Spenser's Poetry and the Reformation Tradition* (Princeton, 1990), ch. 1 and appendix, 233–8. King provides valuable evidence for continuities from the mid-century. He argues strongly that Spenser, while a 'progressive Protestant', was in no sense a Puritan; he draws sharper distinctions between these categories than I would do, and in claiming that Spenser was not invoked by Puritans until the Civil War he does not mention the 1606 printing of *The Plowman's Tale*, see n. 5 above.

Modern scholarship has brought forward new evidence which does require a revision of the simpler 'Puritan' readings; but the revision need not be quite so drastic. Milton's remarks about Spenser's prophetic powers were in any case not to be taken too literally. He would have read Spenser in the same way as scholars like Bale and Foxe read Dante and Petrarch, as someone whose perspectives might have been limited by his own situation but who was able to move beyond those limits up to a point, who was alert to the need for reform, and whose poetry gained its power from its reforming spirit. In the 1570s Spenser believed that the energies of the Reformation could still be sustained within the forms of the Anglican church; by the 1640s Milton believed that such hopes were false. But the continuing power of Spenser's poetry resided, in Milton's view, not in the political compromises necessitated by his particular situation, but in the poet's commitment to the general prophetic tradition. To interpret the poem too narrowly in terms of its immediate context would be politically as well as poetically reductive. The fact that there was an Anglican bishop named Piers may indicate a secondary topical allusion in *The Shepheardes Calender*; but the name 'Piers' is primarily an allusion to a whole poetic tradition.[11] Milton, and some of Spenser's contemporaries, believed that the Elizabethan church was not a supremely wise *via media* but a provisional, and disturbingly inconsistent, arrangement which needed further modification. Spenser was clearly more disposed to compromise than the radicals, but to determine the nature of that compromise it is necessary to set *The Shepheardes Calender* both in its immediate context and in a rather longer perspective.

Many of the Edwardian reformers who had been driven into exile in Mary's reign returned to England on Elizabeth's accession with high hopes of further reformation. Their experience of Continental reformed churches had made them more than ever anxious to break with those features of the English church that had survived from the Catholic past. They were internationalist in their outlook, dissatisfied with appeals to purely English traditions and eager to bring the English Reformation more closely in line with its Continental allies. Already in Edward's reign John Hooper, one of Somerset's protégés, had protested against the retention of the traditional ecclesiastical vestments, a powerful public symbol of continuity with the old mystical hierarchy. But any hopes that Elizabeth might sweep away such vestiges of the old order were soon disappointed. Conservative in temperament, and aware that further radical changes in religion would probably provoke disorder, she resisted many of the more far-reaching reforms demanded by the exiles. Clergy who refused to wear the vestments were strictly disciplined. Before the first decade of the new reign was over, Crowley was urging passive resistance to the ecclesiastical hierarchy; the veteran gospelling poet threw in his lot with the group of dissidents who became known as 'Puritans'. In 1567 he published his prophetic poem *The Opening of the Wordes of the Prophet Joell*, which he had written towards the end of Henry VIII's reign but which now seemed relevant to the 1560s: Elizabeth's bishops, like Henry's,

---

[11] McLane, *Spenser's* Shepheardes Calender, 174–87, confidently identifies 'Piers' with Bishop John Piers, John Young's predecessor at Rochester. He argues that Piers was 'probably' very conservative and that he may have been driven to drink in his despair at Elizabeth's accession (177 and n. 4). Such an identification thus disposes of the 'Piers Plowman' tradition.

were more concerned to persecute the godly than to further the cause of reformation.[12] Foxe, though more conciliatory in temperament, was also disturbed by the
enforcement of conformity on the issue of vestments. It began to seem to some of the
protesters that the fault lay not just with the personalities of individual bishops but
with the whole institution of episcopacy. Whatever good intentions a bishop might
start with, the pomp and wealth of his office would eventually blunt his reforming
zeal. A highly articulate minority began in the 1570s to call for the English church
to abolish episcopacy and adopt the elective, presbyterian system of church order
which was becoming the norm in the 'best reformed' Calvinist churches on the
Continent. Another group abandoned the idea of a state church altogether and
formed separatist congregations.

The old conventions of anti-Catholic protest literature were adapted by the
Elizabethan radicals to attack the Anglican hierarchy. The greatest anti-episcopal
satires, the tracts attributed to 'Martin Marprelate' (1588–9), were very much in the
spirit of mid-century satirists like Luke Shepherd. 'Marprelate' pitted his own wit
and verbal energy against the 'bald writings, without sap or edge' of the bishops and
their defenders who could not even write a pentameter line correctly. He appealed
not only to Foxe but also to *Piers Plowman* and Chaucer as authorities for his position. An old 'ploughman' satire, *I Plaine Piers Which Can Not Flatter*, was reprinted
with an attribution to 'the Gransier of Martin mareprelate'.[13] Two pamphlets which
appeared closer to the publication of *The Shepheardes Calender*, both of them associated with Crowley, will help to illustrate the conventions of political rhetoric which
readers had grown to expect, and may help to situate Spenser's own rhetoric. One of
the most famous of all Puritan satires was Anthony Gilby's *Pleasaunt Dialogue*,
which was written in 1566 though the author withheld publication until some years
later; it appeared with a dedication to several eminent Puritans including Robert
Crowley and Foxe's friend Lawrence Humphrey. Like Spenser's 'May' eclogue, the
work is a dialogue between a zealous Protestant and a worldly chaplain who provides
some comic relief. Like Spenser's Palinode, Gilby's Sir Bernard Blynkarde believes
that reform must be very gradual because human nature cannot support very much
change. Using a comically inappropriate proverb, he declares that Rome cannot be
built in a day. But in fact Sir Bernard does not really want reform to progress too far.
His fear is not that human nature cannot be changed but that it can be: now that mere
soldiers and servingmen can talk so much of Scripture they are no longer so respect-
ful to their betters.[14] Arguments about human nature also motivated the campaign
against various social 'abuses', from dice-playing to stage-plays, which was reaching

[12] On Crowley's role in this early phase of the controversy see M. M. Knappen, *Tudor Puritanism: A
Chapter in the History of Idealism*, rev. edn. (Chicago, 1966), 198 ff., and John N. King, *English Reformation
Literature: The Tudor Origins of the Protestant Tradition* (Princeton, 1982) (hereafter King, *ERL*), 431–2.

[13] *The Marprelate Tracts, 1588, 1589*, ed. William Pierce (London, 1911), 414, 380; Leland H. Carlson,
Martin Marprelate, Gentleman: Master Job Throkmorton Laid Open in his Colors (San Marino, Calif., 1981),
376 n. 65. *I Plaine Piers* is not, as Carlson implies, an edition of *Piers Plowman*; but the last Elizabethan edition of that poem, published in 1561, had explained that it denounced the great wickedness of bishops
(sig. A2ʳ).

[14] Anthony Gilby, *A Pleasaunt Dialogue, betweene a Souldior of Barwicke, and an English Chaplaine*
(n.pl., 1581), sigs. E8ᵛ, C3ᵛ. Cf. Knappen, *Tudor Puritanism*, 200–3.

its height at the time *The Shepheardes Calender* appeared. The conservative view of these issues is represented by George Puttenham, whose poems will be discussed below; the fundamentalist line can be illustrated by a dialogue by Thomas Lovel to which Crowley contributed a preface in 1581. In this attack on dancing the devil's advocate is the worldly and jovial figure of Custom:

> Shall we sit dumpish, dum, and still,
>   All day like stones in street?
> With tripping toyes, and footing fine,
>   we wil eche other meet.[15]

Palinode's criticisms of dull piety are similar:

> How falles it then, we no merrier bene,
> Ylike as others, girt in gawdy greene? . . .
> Such merimake holy Saints doth queme,
> But we here sytten as drownd in a dreme. ('May', ll. 3–4, 15–16)

Though Lovel tries to enliven his dialogue by giving the figure of Custom some comic vigour, he leaves the reader in no doubt that the austere Veritie has the better arguments. Readers familiar with such dialogues would have been predisposed to assume that Spenser's Palinode was in the wrong.

Spenser did not, however, go as far as people like Lovel in criticizing traditional festivities; and the annotations to the 'May' eclogue emphasize that his targets are not the same as the presbyterians', that Palinode is a Catholic, not a high-flying Anglican. A note by 'E.K.' leaves the reader in no doubt: 'nought here spoken, as of purpose to deny fatherly rule and godly gouernaunce (as some malitiously of late haue done to the great vnreste and hinderaunce of the Churche).' Some critics have taken this disclaimer as central evidence that Spenser was deeply conservative and fiercely opposed to all manifestations of religious enthusiasm. Certainly Spenser would not have taken a post as secretary to Bishop John Young of Rochester in the late 1570s had he been a presbyterian: Young was to help to crack down on the pres-byterian movement. On the other hand, it should be pointed out that he did not stay with Young very long, seeking out the more influential patronage of the Earl of Leicester. The fact that he rejected presbyterianism does not in itself tell us much about his political outlook unless we also know why he did so.

The more conservative churchmen tended to seize on the politically subversive implications of presbyterianism, and appeal to the values of tradition and natural order. The movement, however, was hardly as subversive as its opponents claimed: in England many of its leading patrons were aristocrats. Though presbyterianism had an elective element, only a small elite would play a major part in decision-making.

---

[15] Thomas Lovel, *A Dialogue between Custom and Veritie* (London, 1581), sigs. B8^r, C2^v. Patrick Collinson cites Lovel's poem as part of a major shift in Protestant culture away from the exploitation of plays, images, and ballads for the godly cause to concerted attacks on the media themselves: 'From Iconoclasm to Iconophobia: The Cultural Impact of the Second English Reformation', in Peter Marshall (ed.), *The Impact of the English Reformation 1500–1640* (London, 1997), 278–308 (292).

The fact remained that in this system authority and legitimacy were conferred from below, rather than being handed down from above in a mystical hierarchy. Whereas the English Reformation could be seen as a blessing conferred on the grateful populace by wise monarchs and prelates, many Continental reformed churches had been made by the people, sometimes in direct opposition to their anointed sovereign. Once the principles of legitimacy and continuity had been challenged in the religious sphere, political rebellion became easier to justify. Conservatives therefore often emphasized the national symbolic and institutional traditions of the English church, those features which distinguished it from the Continental reformed churches. The emphasis on the Church of England as a *via media* between Catholic and Protestant extremes was a way of minimizing the common cause of English Protestants with their foreign co-religionists.[16] Admittedly, the Elizabethan settlement had brought the English church doctrinally close to Continental Calvinism, and this consensus was not effectively challenged until the 'Arminian' movement in the 1620s.[17] But conservatives did lay a great deal of emphasis on the need to combine purity of faith with order and hierarchy in external forms. With the effective crushing of the presbyterian movement at the end of the 1580s, the high-flying Bishop Bancroft began to make exalted claims for the divine right of episcopacy, proclaiming that bishops derived their legitimacy directly from the continuity of the apostolic succession. Earlier reformers had been prepared to accept the continuation of episcopacy in some form, but not on such mystical terms. Conservative rhetoric laid more and more emphasis on natural order, setting out the analogies between the social hierarchy, the structure of the Church of England, and the macrocosm. The classic Elizabethan panegyric of natural hierarchy was to be provided by Richard Hooker in his *Ecclesiastical Polity*, a work written with propagandist as well as philosophical intention—though his heterodox views on episcopacy and monarchy meant that the last sections of his work, had they been published at the time, would have been less pleasing to the authorities.[18] But the constant analogies between secular, ecclesiastical, and cosmic harmonies made by apologists for the church were distasteful to the presbyterian leader Thomas Cartwright, who attacked the 'insolence and intolerable conceit' of those who would justify secular institutions by analogy with God's sovereignty or the order of nature. Presbyterians themselves claimed divine authority for their system, but it was an authority based on the Bible, not on tradition or nature.[19]

[16] On this point see S. L. Adams, 'The Protestant Cause: Religious Alliance with the W. European Calvinist Communities as a Political Issue in England, 1585–1630' (unpublished D.Phil. thesis, Oxford, 1973), ch. 1. My debt to this thesis throughout the book is very strong; though in the course of his further researches Dr Adams has modified some of his views.

[17] The fundamental unity of the church is emphasized by Patrick Collinson, *The Religion of Protestants: The Church in English Society 1559–1625* (Oxford, 1982); see also his earlier *The Elizabethan Puritan Movement* (London, 1967).

[18] On the polemical element in Hooker, frequently underestimated by his literary admirers, see W. D. J. Cargill Thompson, 'The Philosopher of the "Politic Society": Richard Hooker as a Political Thinker', in W. Speed Hill (ed.), *Studies in Richard Hooker: Essays Preliminary to an Edition of his Works* (Cleveland, 1972), 3–76 (14 ff.).

[19] A. F. Scott Pearson, *Thomas Cartwright and Elizabethan Puritanism 1535–1603* (Cambridge, 1925), 14, 419–21; cf. Michael Walzer, *The Revolution of the Saints: A Study in the Origins of Radical Politics*

To reject presbyterianism, however, it was not necessary to be a deep devotee of tradition. Many members of the Church of England attached less importance than the conservatives to liturgical continuity, and shared with the presbyterians a strong sense of solidarity with Calvinists throughout Europe. Their theology was in fact more emotive and more heavily influenced by apocalyptic ideas than Calvin's own thought. They were conscious of a perpetual tension between soul and body in the individual and between pure doctrine and external forms in the outward church. For them the inner struggles of the individual and the apocalyptic struggle against Antichrist were closely connected. They viewed the English church not as a serene *via media* transcending the European struggles but as part of the international reformed community. This tendency in the Church of England has been termed 'moderate Puritanism', though these 'Puritans' would probably have rejected such a label with its implications that they were a heterodox minority: they were a very powerful force and as far as they were concerned their views were perfectly in harmony with the Thirty-Nine Articles. Many Elizabethan bishops were 'Puritans' in this very broad sense. But such men felt themselves to have much in common with the presbyterians: it is impossible to divide Elizabethan Protestantism neatly into 'moderate' and 'extreme' compartments.[20] There were, however, tensions between the presbyterians and the others. John Foxe himself was moved to denounce the 'thrice pure Puritans' when he found that his own son was coming under attack from his colleagues at Magdalen College, Oxford, for his religious lukewarmness.[21] Magdalen was Foxe's and Crowley's old college and it now had a Puritan atmosphere under the presidency of Foxe's old friend Lawrence Humphrey. But Foxe and Humphrey found the new generation of young radicals too intolerant. The grounds of their criticisms, however, were different from Bancroft's. Humphrey was no great traditionalist and disliked the enforcement of conformity over vestments. As a younger man he had held relatively radical political views, defending the right of Parliament to depose a tyrant. He had written a treatise on nobility in which he conceded that the validity of a system of hereditary aristocracy had been 'muche doubted, and cald in question of many' who believed that they 'deserue as vnprofitable members to be cutte of'. He set himself to show that the 'learned' (e.g. More?) who argued in this way were mistaken, that the nobility was in fact 'profitable' if it could be persuaded to work; but the utilitarian, unmystical premisses of his argument were as significant as the orthodox conclusion. When he used the symbolism of the cosmic order it was not, as with Elyot, to defend the need for ceremony but to emphasize that everything

(London, 1966), ch. 5. Walzer greatly exaggerates the differences between the opposed parties, which were constantly muffled by various political compromises, but critics of his book have not quite been able to establish the counterclaim that Puritanism had nothing whatever to do with the origins of radical politics. For fuller discussion of Cartwright and other critics of natural analogy in politics, see David Norbrook, 'Rhetoric, Ideology, and the Elizabethan World Picture', in Peter Mack (ed.), *Renaissance Rhetoric* (London, 1994), 140–64.

[20] On these points see especially Peter Lake, *Moderate Puritans and the Elizabethan Church* (Cambridge, 1982).

[21] V. Norskov Olsen, *John Foxe and the Elizabethan Church* (Berkeley and Los Angeles, 1973), 158–9.

in the universe worked hard.[22] The idea of an elective system of church government would not in itself have appeared monstrous or unnatural to men like Humphrey or Foxe. But they did believe that episcopacy was not the right issue to take such a divisive stand on. Was it not somewhat hysterical to imply that Elizabeth's bishops were little better than Mary's? Were not the radicals motivated more by intellectual pride than spiritual concern? The radicals felt that men like Humphrey had become unduly complacent with age. Quarrels of this kind are likely to become acrimonious, all the more so if there is a grain of truth in the charges and counter-charges. But there was not a vast ideological gulf between the presbyterians and their moderate Puritan critics: it was precisely because of the shared premises that the differences could generate acrimony. John Foxe, one of the most temperate of the Puritans, found himself caught uneasily between Cartwright and the conservative bishops. He disliked draconian measures against the presbyterians; he had no desire to see the energies of the English Reformation lapsing into an inert and heavily policed conservatism.

The political rhetoric of Spenser's ecclesiastical eclogues suggested to contemporaries that he was endorsing this tradition of low-church Protestantism, not nostalgic conservatism. The year after the poem appeared a young Oxford poet, John Dove, translated it into Latin, praising the dedicatees for being Algrinds and Pierces, not Morells or Palinodes. In his dedication he singled out Lawrence Humphrey for praise.[23] He also wrote a poem in praise of Spenser's 'Algrind', who was Edmund Grindal, Archbishop of Canterbury, and a symbol of the low-church tradition. His appointment as Archbishop in 1575 had made it seem possible that the splits between presbyterians and others could be healed, that a sense of common reforming purpose could be restored to all members of the church. Grindal's mind had been formed in the reign of Edward VI and he looked back nostalgically to that period as a golden age, before the increasingly bitter schisms in the church. Grindal gave priority to preaching (amongst the preachers he patronized was Robert Crowley) and he was not too insistent on rigid conformity in minor ceremonial matters.[24] It was Grindal who first allowed the Geneva Bible, the Puritans' favourite version, to be printed in England. The annotations to this edition were too militant for conservatives in the English church; the notes to Revelation included fierce attacks on idolatrous bishops and archbishops.[25] But the scholarship of the Geneva version was superior to its Anglican equivalent. The new Archbishop valued inner spiritual qualities more than external conformity, and therefore disliked taking a hard line against radicals whom he considered to be sincere and truly charitable. But by the same token he could be

[22] Knappen, *Tudor Puritanism*, 174–8; Lawrence Humphrey, *The Nobles or of Nobilitye* (London, 1563), sigs. b6ᵛ, i5ᵛ. On Humphrey see also Hugh Kearney, *Scholars and Gentlemen: Universities and Society in Pre-industrial Britain 1500–1700* (London, 1970), 39 ff.

[23] Leicester Bradner, 'The Latin Translations of Spenser's *Shepheardes Calender*', *Modern Philology*, 33 (1935), 21–6. Dove was not a presbyterian and in 1606 produced a defence of the established church.

[24] Patrick Collinson, *Archbishop Grindal 1519–1583: The Struggle for a Reformed Church* (London, 1979), 48, 116; on Grindal's relations with the presbyterians see especially 55, 182. Foxe had translated a sermon by Grindal into Latin: *Concio funebris in obitum . . . Ferdinandi Caesaris* (London, 1564).

[25] King, *ERI*, 420.

angry with people who seemed to be trying to martyr themselves over relatively trivial grievances. His accession to office was greeted by Thomas Drant, a minor poet
whose work Spenser knew, with a panegyric of the episcopal office. Drant attacked
the presbyterians as well as the papists; Grindal did not approve of their activities.
But measures against the presbyterians assumed a rather different character if they
were taken by a zealous reformer, rather than a reactionary disciplinarian: Grindal
was trying to make presbyterianism unnecessary by reforming the church. In his
poem Drant urged Cartwright to come home from his exile on the Continent and
join in the work of preaching the Word at home. Using a stock pastoral metaphor, he
told Cartwright that many shepherds had been lost to the wolves, that many others
were idle, and that men like him could help guard the flock if they set aside their dangerous and divisive ideas. You who dislike all bishops, said Drant, will applaud
Grindal.[26]

But if Grindal's appointment placated many Puritans, it alarmed conservatives
who feared that he would allow dissent and disorder to flourish. Only two years after
his appointment, he was suspended from office. Spenser voiced the widespread
alarm aroused by this measure in his 'July' eclogue. Grindal's suspension did indeed
herald a religious reaction; Whitgift, his successor, was to act against the presbyterians with a ruthlessness that disturbed many Protestants. In the end the reaction did
not go far enough to provoke much resistance; the essentially Calvinist religious settlement remained intact. But at the time *The Shepheardes Calender* was published
there were fears of much more thoroughgoing changes, fears for the very future of
English Protestantism. It had long seemed to advocates of a militant foreign policy
that Elizabeth was being too half-hearted in her aid to the Dutch Protestants who
were struggling against Spanish military power. The queen's social conservatism,
her reluctance to aid William of Orange and his low-born associates, seemed to be
outweighing her ideological commitment to the Protestant cause. By the late 1570s
the Spanish were gaining ground. The queen's preferred way out of this crisis was to
marry the Duke of Anjou, brother of the French king, whose support was being
sought by the more socially conservative groups amongst the Dutch rebels. The
hope was that the queen could thus use her influence to achieve a compromise settlement that would avoid excessive political or religious radicalism. Many English
Protestants, however, feared that such a compromise would amount to betraying
their co-religionists; it might also have disastrous consequences at home. According
to his later account, the young poet Fulke Greville and his friends feared that once
he had married Elizabeth the new regent would change the state religion to
Catholicism, persecute Protestants, and rule without Parliament until 'the *Ideas* of
native freedom' had been eradicated and 'our moderate form of Monarchie' had
been metamorphosed into 'a precipitate absoluteness'.[27] But public opposition to the

---

[26] Thomas Drant, *Praesul* (n.pl., 1576), 5–6. Neel Mukherjee, 'Thomas Drant's Rewriting of Horace',
Studies in English Literature 1500–1900, 40 (2000), 1–20, complicates my account of Spenser's contexts by
demonstrating that Drant was patronized by Grindal at a period in the late 1560s when he was moving
against nonconformists, and that he attacked separatists as manipulated by Papists.

[27] *A Dedication to Sir Philip Sidney*, in *The Prose Works of Fulke Greville, Lord Brooke*, ed. John Gouws
(Oxford, 1986), 32. For a full and clear account of the political contexts see Blair Worden, *The Sound of
Virtue: Philip Sidney's* Arcadia *and Elizabethan Politics* (New Haven, 1996), 75–124.

match could be dangerous; when the Puritan John Stubbs published an outspoken attack on the project he was sentenced under a sedition law introduced by Mary Tudor and his hand was cut off.

The Shepheardes Calender appeared soon after this episode and it was printed by the Puritan Hugh Singleton, who had produced Stubbs's pamphlet. Singleton had a long history of involvement with Protestant propaganda; in Mary's reign he had secretly published works by Bale and others.[28] Spenser thus symbolically linked himself with the Protestant satiric tradition. Whether he alluded in more direct ways to the marriage project in his poems is doubtful. But the general political rhetoric of his poems indicated his commitment to traditions which the French match would have threatened. Spenser's position can further be clarified by contrasting the 'May' eclogue with the poems of a conservative who did support the match, the rhetorician George Puttenham. This turbulent figure was fiercely hostile to Puritanism and was alleged to have plotted to assassinate Grindal.[29] About 1578 or 1579 Puttenham presented to the queen a series of complimentary poems, some of which praised her virginity while others strongly hinted that she should accept Anjou's offers of marriage. Although he hedged his bets, it is clear that unlike many of his contemporaries he had no strong ideological objections to the match. On the contrary, he would have welcomed some of the consequences his opponents feared. The complete extinction of Puritanism would have safeguarded the 'Merrie England' he evoked in a series of anti-Puritan poems; a realm of hierarchy and order, of traditional rituals and festivities at court and in the countryside. In the manner of Palinode or Sir Bernard Blynkarde, if somewhat more subtly, he used the inherent imperfections of human nature as an argument against any major changes. It would be impossible to remove political abuses without destroying everything of value:

> Take fro Kinges Courtes intertaynmentes,
> From Ladyes riche habillimentes . . .
> From worldlye thinges take vanitee,
> Sleit, semblant, course, order and degree:
> Princesse, yt ys as if one take awaye
> Greene wooddes from forrests, and sunne-shine fro the daye.[30]

---

[28] H. J. Byrom, 'Edmund Spenser's First Printer, Hugh Singleton', *Library*, 4th series, 14 (1933), 121–56. However, King, *Spenser's Poetry and the Reformation Tradition*, 234–6, emphasizes that Singleton's record is not specifically Puritan.

[29] George Puttenham, *The Arte of English Poesie*, ed. Gladys D. Willcock and Alice Walker (Cambridge, 1936), pp. xxxiii–xxxiv. Since this book's first appearance Puttenham has attracted much attention, and this intriguing and original figure certainly deserves a full study across the considerable body of his writings—the label of 'conservative' is inadequate for someone with such a broad, anthropological view of different literary cultures—and writing to help women to compose poetry. However, I think that the contrast with Spenser still stands, despite Jonathan Crewe's remarkable attempt to claim Spenser's authorship of the *Arte*: *Hidden Designs: The Critical Profession and Renaissance Literature* (New York, 1986), 121–9; see also Rosemary Kegl, *The Rhetoric of Concealment: Figuring Gender and Class in Renaissance Literature* (Ithaca, NY, 1994), ch. 1, and Patricia Parker, 'Motivated Rhetorics: Gender, Order, Rule', in *Literary Fat Ladies: Rhetoric, Gender, Property* (London, 1987), 97–125.

[30] George Puttenham, 'Parthemiades', in W. R. Morfill (ed.), *Ballads from Manuscripts*, ii (Hertford, 1873), 87.

'Sleit', dissimulation, was an essential part of political life, and Puritan demands for removal of corruption in public life were unrealistic. Puttenham further argued that major religious reform was in fact impossible: it was futile to try to

> Remove misterye from religion,
> From godly feare all superstition,
> Idolatrye from deepe devotion.[31]

If 'popular preachers' were allowed to operate, they would

> Pull people and theyr prince asoonder,
> From games to gaze at and miracle to woonder;
> Forbidde pesauntes theyr countrye sporte,
> Preache all trothe to the raskall sorte.

Puttenham believed that the result of increasing popular literacy, of telling the common people all the truth, would be chaos. Faced with the choice of giving the people custom or verity, he would choose custom.

Like many conservative writers in the Renaissance, Puttenham was making a clear-cut opposition; either a hierarchical society which encourages courtly poetry and dancing and rural festivities, or Puritan iconoclasm and disorder. Hierarchy nourishes culture; Puritanism is ignorantly hostile to civilized values. The idea that poetry needs to be rooted in a conservative 'organic community' has exercised a great appeal to many twentieth-century critics; but it is unlikely that Spenser would have agreed. The Reformation had accelerated the humanist campaign to replace the traditional rituals and superstitions of popular culture by a culture based firmly on literacy.[32] Scholarship and education, in their view, provided better foundations for future poetic achievement than folk-dancing. Literary and biblical scholarship were mutually reinforcing. Despite his Spartan reputation, Lawrence Humphrey was very interested in poetry: he wrote a preface for an edition of Homer and published the first major English study of the art of poetic translation, a work drawing on a wide knowledge of English as well as classical verse. He regarded Chaucer as a prophetic poet equal in stature to Dante and Petrarch.[33] Such scholarly interests may have blinded advanced Protestants to traditional community values. But the old agrarian order had not always been as naturally harmonious as Puttenham implied; he was aestheticizing politics, seeing the old order as a masque or pageant in which all social ranks willingly participated and the Puritans as spoil-sports out to stop the dance. Spenser may not have agreed with the more aggressive moralists, but his subsequent history makes it unlikely that he would have been too nostalgic over the demise of some popular recreations. In Ireland he was to advocate repressive

---

[31] Puttenham, 'Partheniades', 85.
[32] Peter Burke, *Popular Culture in Early Modern Europe* (London, 1978), chs. 8 and 9.
[33] Lawrence Humphrey, *Interpretatio linguarum* (Basel, 1559), discusses amongst other topics the art of imitation in classical poetry (e.g. 383) and recent English verse translation (517). Cf. his preface to *Copiae cornu sive oceanus enarrationum Homericarum* (Basel, 1558), and *Jesuitismi pars prima* (London, 1582).

measures to stamp out a still more conservative set of rural traditions and effect a Protestant cultural revolution.

The 'May' eclogue begins like a defence of traditional revelry against Puritan attack: Palinode's first speech might have been written by Puttenham. But the eclogue rapidly turns into a quite different kind of poem. There was a genre of lyrics evoking the simple joys of the countryside; the prefatory woodcut, the conventional associations of the month of May, and Palinode's opening speech all prepare the reader for such a poem. The reader is led to enjoy the opening scene, to 'read' it in the same way as Palinode. Piers's first speech shatters the poem's festive framework: he reads the pastoral landscape allegorically, in the tradition of the ecclesiastical eclogues of Petrarch or Mantuan.[34] Piers's attack on May-games is in the spirit of the Puritan campaign to reform popular culture; but May-games are not really at issue here. The shepherds Piers is concerned with are the ministers who need to live by higher standards than the laity. Palinode's attempts to justify his own carefree life by analogy with rural sports are fallacious; he confuses sign with thing signified, the literal with the metaphorical, country recreations with a minister's life.[35] He is effectively aestheticizing politics by appealing to ideas of Merrie England in order to justify clerical privilege. Piers keeps trying to resist Palinode's false analogies to make him reason more coherently; but Palinode's powers of argument are feeble. He greets Piers's speech in praise of primitive simplicity first with an outburst of rage, then with a rhetorical question and some dubious proverbs, and finally with an attempt to stop the argument altogether:

> nought seemeth sike strife,
> That shepheardes so witen ech others life,
> And layen her faults the world beforne,
> The while their foes done eache of hem scorne.
> Let none mislike of that may not be mended:
> So conteck soone by concord mought be ended. (ll. 158–63)

Palinode's forsaking of the traditional rugged accentual metre for smooth iambics, and the chime of 'conteck' and 'concord', indicate his complacency and glibness, his search for beauty and harmony as a means of evading rather than resolving the issue. Despairing of convincing him by rational argument, Piers resorts to telling him a story—a low level of argument according to rhetorical theory. His fable, as the note by E.K. indicates, departs from its source: the wolf of Aesop's fable who deceives the innocent kid becomes a fox. This transformation of a wolf into a fox would have recalled for many contemporaries a famous sequence of anticlerical satires.[36] In 1543 William Turner had published an attack on the Henrician bishops under the title *The*

---

[34] Cooper, *Pastoral*, 88–9, notes that English poets were especially fond of turning 'bergerie' into religious allegory.

[35] For the view that Palinode definitely has the worse of the argument, see Michael F. Dixon, 'Rhetorical Patterns and Methods of Advocacy in Spenser's *Shepheardes Calender*', *English Literary Renaissance*, 7 (1977), 131–54 (141–2).

[36] For full discussion see Anthea Hume, 'Spenser, Puritanism, and the "Maye" Eclogue', *Review of English Studies*, NS 20 (1969), 155–67, and *Edmund Spenser: Protestant Poet* (Cambridge, 1984), 21–8.

Hunting and Fyndyng Out of the Romishe Fox. Bale had taken up the fox symbolism in a pamphlet he published the same year. With the accession of Edward, Turner, like the other gospellers, sought Somerset's patronage, and he became the Protector's personal physician. Under Mary he went into exile, and he brought out a new polemic, *The Huntyng of the Romyshe Wolfe*, in which he complained that the fox had now turned into a wolf, that Catholics who had pretended to adopt the new faith were now showing their true colours. This pamphlet was reissued in the 1560s with a preface by Gilby, under the title *The Hunting of the Fox and the Wolfe*; Gilby's preface was reprinted in his own *Pleasaunt Dialogue*. Such associations clearly imply that Piers's fable has a topical meaning, that conservative bishops who prefer ritual to preaching may be Papists in disguise. Palinode's response, however, is not very promising. He complains that Piers is 'beside thy wit'; and though he recognizes that the fable is a good one, his immediate reaction is to tell it to his friend 'sir Iohn', a parson who is always short of material for his sermons. 'Sir Iohn' clearly belongs to the tradition of dull-witted conservatives who inhabited so much Protestant satire. Precisely because he is so unintelligent, it seems more than likely that he will miss the true point of the fable, will be more impressed by the colourful rhetorical images than by the allegorical meaning. Indeed, if he did recognize the proper meaning he would try to educate himself instead of padding his sermons with other people's ideas.

The informed reader, unlike 'sir Iohn', will lift the veil of allegory, will move from sign to thing signified. Spenser does not imply, however, that this is a simple and unproblematic process; on the contrary, he draws attention to the difficulties, and the political implications, of interpretation. The dispute between Piers and Palinode over the level of reality of the landscape they inhabit alerts the reader to these difficulties, which are further highlighted by the discrepancies between the 'human' and 'animal' qualities of the protagonists of the fable. Those who read this poetry simply for entertainment, who reject didacticism as Puritan pedantry, will miss the political meanings. But more complicated readings may also go astray for political reasons. No new collection of English poems before *The Shepheardes Calender* had provided such an array of aids to interpretation: a preface, general and particular arguments, woodcuts, and lengthy glosses. Yet this explanatory matter leaves many of the most puzzling passages unexplained. The debts to anticlerical satires like *The Plowman's Tale* are unmentioned. The passages most relevant to the 'May' fable come in the 'September' eclogue, where Diggon complains that the wolves are preying on the sheep and Hobbinol replies that wolves have not been seen in England since Saxon times. And yet,

> the fewer Woolues (the soth to sayne,)
> The more bene the Foxes that here remaine. (ll. 154–5)

Diggon replies that the foxes 'gang in more secrete wise', dressing themselves in sheep's clothing. Readers familiar with Turner's satires would have recognized here a warning that conservative Anglicans might really be Papists in disguise. But the note blandly ignores such issues and takes the discussion of wolves and foxes quite literally. The 'May' notes are similarly evasive: the annotator goes out of his way to deny that the poem has topical relevance, to tie down its meaning to the conflict between Protestants and Catholics. Being against Catholicism was, in Elizabethan England, little more contentious than being against sin.

Nobody has yet been able to establish the identity of 'E.K.', and the idiosyncrasy of his annotations has made some critics see him as a persona created by Spenser, a satire on pedantic commentators. It is hard to push this argument too far, for the annotations do not really reflect a consistent personality—some are rather simple-mindedly moralistic in tone, some would be genuinely helpful for a reader lacking classical education, some are blandly evasive. Even if 'E.K.' was in fact a genuine commentator, however, the publication of his significantly inadequate commentary did draw attention to the problems, and the politics, of interpretation. Readers in such an age of controversies would have been used to exercising a certain scepticism about the commentaries and annotations in printed books.[37] The Roman Inquisition, whose activities were being widely publicized by Protestants, was trying to ensure that no text could be published without clerical authorization. Commentaries and interpretations had to observe the official line; and if the text would not fit into ortho-dox interpretations then it must be doctored or cut. Authorized annotations both on religious and on secular texts, whether on Revelation or Dante and Petrarch, had to depoliticize sensitive passages, to give them blandly general rather than controver-sially particular applications. Protestants regarded such tactics with contempt: their own more rational science of interpretation, they claimed, could penetrate beneath the 'veil' of allegory and did not need to cut embarrassing passages or to appeal to sheer authority. Much Protestant satire ridiculed not only the content of Catholic theological works but the forms of the authorized texts, the heavy tomes with their prefatory apparatus guaranteeing that they had been approved by the authorities and their pedantic annotations. The humanists had always had a fondness for learned wit—the *Utopia* had been published with elaborate spurious explanatory matter—but such literary jokes had taken on a new ideological significance. Flacius, a leading chronicler of Catholic suppression of anticlerical texts, and a pioneer of Protestant theories of interpretation, had written several satires which ridiculed the Inquisition with their false imprints. One of these works was translated in the mid-century by William Baldwin and may have influenced the mock annotations in his satire *Be-ware the Cat*.[38] Under Mary Hugh Singleton printed satires with false imprints from his underground press in London. With Elizabeth's accession, restrictions on Protestant propaganda were of course greatly eased, but there was no return to the relative press freedom of Somerset's days: John Stubbs was in fact prosecuted under a law introduced by Mary, and Singleton himself nearly lost his right hand for print-ing Stubbs's pamphlet. Though Stubbs's case was far from typical, it aroused fears

---

[37] For an interesting discussion of interpretation and authority see Gabriel Josipovici, *The World and the Book: A Study of Modern Fiction* (London, 1971), ch. 2.

[38] On Flacius' influence in England see King, *ERL*, 371 ff., and on his theory of interpretation, Wilhelm Dilthey, 'The Rise of Hermeneutic', trans Fredric Jameson, *New Literary History*, 3:2 (1972), 229–44 (237–9).

about the fragility of current freedoms.[39] Before long 'Martin Marprelate' was to turn the old weapons of Protestant satire against the English bishops: in the *Epistle* a pedantic bishop intervenes in marginal notes to quell Martin's satiric fervour.

Spenser was well acquainted with Continental and English polemical traditions.[40] *The Shepheardes Calender*, of course, is a much less clear-cut case than the more explicit religious satires. The annotations are not consistently unreliable or polemical. But the volume does generate an atmosphere of scepticism and uncertainty. Not only does the 'Piers' of 'May' not seem to function on quite the same level as 'Palinode', the 'Piers' of 'October' seems to be a different figure altogether. Problems of interpretation are raised within the poems themselves. In 'September' Hobbinol complains that Diggon's speech is 'to mirke' and asks him to speak less obscurely; but when Diggon proceeds to denounce the Roman church more explicitly, to lift the veil of allegory, Hobbinol hastily retreats:

> Nowe Diggon, I see thou speakest to plaine:
> Better it were, a little to feyne,
> And cleanly couer, that cannot be cured. (ll. 136–8)

Hobbinol wants satire to be safely and blandly general. Readers of *The Shepheardes Calender*, however, are invited to criticize such evasiveness. The hints about danger do not amount to a direct protest against censorship; Spenser was not courting martyrdom, and he probably believed that the more radical Protestants were going too far in their challenge to authority. But anyone well versed in the prophetic tradition would have found it hard to make rigid and clear-cut dividing-lines between godly fervour and subversive extremism. Interpretations which tie the 'moral' eclogues down to personal allusions or to defence of a pure Church of England against Roman corruption fail to do justice to the work's prophetic character. The allusions to 'Algrind' do anchor the eclogues firmly in a particular context, functioning as a reminder that the poetry does not simply 'transcend' politics. This particularity does not, however, reduce the poem's meaning to a single conjuncture: Grindal was a recognizable representative of a whole political tradition, and by endorsing this tradition Spenser was criticizing its enemies wherever they might arise, both in the present and in the future. The poem is not just historical but also prophetic: 'The time was once, and may againe retorne.'

The moral eclogues of *The Shepheardes Calender* are in the didactic tradition of Protestant prophetic poetry; but there is another, apparently much less didactic side to the work. Colin Clout, despite his homely name, is not a plain-speaking reformer

---

[39] The fullest account of censorship in this period is now Cyndia Susan Clegg, *Press Censorship in Elizabethan England* (Cambridge, 1997), who corrects many earlier oversimplified accounts and brings out the uneven enforcement and regulatory scope of different forms of censorship; on the Stubbs affair see her ch. 6. John Wolfe, who was to publish many books by Spenser's friend Gabriel Harvey, set himself to become the Luther of printing by challenging the monopoly of the Stationers' Company (92). See Joseph Loewenstein, 'For a History of Literary Property: John Wolfe's Reformation', *English Literary Renaissance*, 18 (1988), 389–412.

[40] Timothy Cook, 'Gabriel Harvey, "Pasquill", Spenser's Lost *Dreames* and *The Faerie Queene*', *Yearbook of English Studies*, 7 (1977), 75–80.

but an 'alienate', tormented lover. In the 'August' eclogue his obsessive melancholy, mirrored in the intricate, self-reflexive form of the sestina, forms a striking contrast with the extrovert gaiety of Perigot and Willy whose antiphonal song uses an old accentual metre. Colin's sestina lacks the dense rustic diction of the moral eclogues. Myth is used in Colin's verse in a much more sophisticated way than in Googe's pastorals. Though E.K. glosses the verse in a fiercely moralistic way, the poetry is more complex than the glosses: Spenser's goddesses are not pagan superstitions to be denounced by good Protestants but subtle and elusive symbols whose meaning is as much suggested by verbal harmony as explicitly stated. The hierarchical order of gods and goddesses is used to reflect the social hierarchy; the queen is complimented in the 'April' eclogue by comparisons with Diana and the Graces. Spenser is here imitating a new kind of pastoral which was overshadowing the traditional allegorical eclogue in sixteenth-century Italy. Sannazaro's *Arcadia* (1502) had invented a new kind of pastoral landscape, drawing on hints from Virgil and from Greek pastoralists: an idyllic world whose harmony recalls the Golden Age.[41] In the *Arcadia* this world is observed by Sincero, the representative of the poet, whose brooding melancholy provides a counterpoint to the lighter passages: the portrayal of the golden world is darkened by the awareness that the poet cannot recover it. Sannazaro inserted a certain amount of political comment into the revised 1504 edition, but on the whole there is a lack of specific social comment, and the very tenuousness of the content gives Sannazaro the freedom to engage in complex metrical experiments. Pastoral is no longer an instrument to urge people to action, it is presented as an object for contemplation. Sannazaro's style is elegant and fluent, much closer to the speech of courtiers than the rustic idiom conventionally considered appropriate for pastoral.

Sannazaro's *Arcadia* provided an idealized portrait of the world of the Renaissance courtier, as the new cult of aristocratic leisure and Neoplatonic contemplation became fashionable. The reception of these courtly ideals in England had been somewhat impeded by the political upheavals of the mid-century; and, as has been seen, the Edwardian humanists had been interested in rather different aspects of Italian culture. Castiglione's *Book of the Courtier* did in fact contain enough didactic matter to attract mid-century humanists. The publication of Sir Thomas Hoby's translation may have been delayed until 1561 because the Marian censors would have disliked Castiglione's anti-ecclesiastical satire, a feature that correspondingly endeared the work to Protestants. But not until the 1570s and 1580s was there a major revival of interest in courtly poetic forms. Spenser's headmaster, Richard Mulcaster, made some interesting comments on the role of rhetoric under a monarchy in his *Elementarie*. Opponents of monarchy, he observed, claimed that eloquence could not flourish without complete liberty, that monarchy 'mastereth la[n]guage, & teacheth it to please'. But in fact 'the qualitie of our *monarchie*', which is virtuous and tolerant, 'wil admit trew speaking, wil allow trew writing'—with the important proviso that

---

[41] Cooper, *Pastoral*, 100–7. Cooper also discusses French influence; Spenser is closer to Marot than to the more courtly Ronsard (111–13, 125, 134–5, 152–3).

writers should always 'preach peace, and preserue the state'.[42] Under a monarchy the orator, the master of persuasive, 'deliberative' rhetoric, had to become a courtier and use the 'demonstrative' rhetoric of praise and blame.

The central handbook of the new courtly aesthetic in England was George Puttenham's *Arte of English Poesie*. Though the early part of this book, possibly written in the mid-century, took an exalted view of the poet as lawgiver, by the later sections he has become no more than a 'cunning Princepleaser', aiming not to stir up public discussion but to distract 'these great aspiring mynds and ambitious heads of the world' from 'seriously searching to deale in matters of state'.[43] Puttenham finds a natural conformity between poetry and courtliness because both rely on dissimulation, 'a certaine doublenesse'. All courtiers need to use the basic figure of 'Allegoria'—that is, saying one thing and meaning another.[44] Humanists had often valued rhetoric as an instrument of demystification, of revealing traditional rituals to be no more than tropes; Puttenham delights in the process of mystification. But he has also some more philosophical justifications for poetry. Books II and III deal respectively with 'ornament' and 'proportion', and each term indicates for Puttenham a political as well as poetic principle. 'Ornament' covers the different linguistic markers, from stylistic registers to rhyme-schemes, that distinguish 'high' style, appropriate to socially elevated subject matter, from 'low' style. In the *Partheniades* he had defended 'ornament', hierarchical symbolism and ritual, in the church and state; in the *Arte* he makes an analogous case for poetic 'ornament'. 'Proportion' concerned metre and poetic structure, and here again the term had political connotations. To the question posed in the *Utopia*, the question of how a society based on hereditary inequalities could be regarded as just, Renaissance defenders of aristocracy replied that justice was a question of proportion. A democracy was just only in a very crude sense, for it portioned equal shares to all regardless of merit or breeding: the governing principle was 'commutative justice' or 'arithmetical proportion'. In an aristocracy, by contrast, exceptional merit was given exceptional rewards: the principle was 'distributive justice' or 'geometrical proportion'.[45] Renaissance theorists revived the speculations of conservative ideologists in late antiquity who exalted geometrical proportion into a mystical principle governing the universe.[46] Puttenham urges his courtly poet to construct poems with intricate rhyme-schemes beyond the capacity of the vulgar, who can only grasp simple forms like couplets: *ottava rima*, for example, is clearly a 'geometrical' form as opposed to the simple, 'arithmetical', 'poulters' measure' favoured by many mid-

---

[42]   Richard Mulcaster, *The First Part of the Elementarie*, ed. E. T. Campagnac (Oxford, 1925), 272–3.

[43]   Puttenham, *The Arte of English Poesie*, 17, 308.

[44]   Ibid. 154, 186. Daniel Javitch, *Poetry and Courtliness in Renaissance England* (Princeton, 1978), makes a case for the beneficial influence of the court on Elizabethan poetry and discusses Puttenham at length (ch. 2). But he makes no mention of Puttenham's political views.

[45]   See, e.g., Sir Thomas Elyot, *The Boke Named the Gouernour*, ed. H. S. Croft, 2 vols. (London, 1880), ii.187–8.

[46]   F. D. Harvey, 'Two Kinds of Equality', *Classica et mediaevalia*, 26 (1965), 101–46; ibid. 27 (1966), 99–100; G. E. M. de Ste Croix, *The Class Struggle in the Ancient Greek World from the Archaic Age to the Arab Conquests* (London, 1981), 413–14.

century poets.[47] As for *Piers Plowman*, Puttenham dismisses the poem on grounds that are at once aesthetic, social, and political: the poet's versification is 'but loose meetre', his diction is 'harsh and obscure', and politically he is a 'malcontent'.[48] The contented courtly poet, who recognizes that society in its present state could not possibly be improved, will produce ornate and complex poems which imitate the structure of society and of the macrocosm; and the well-ordered society itself becomes a harmonious poem. In some of his eclogues Spenser moves away from traditional verse forms to experiment in new and elaborate metres.

But Spenser is a more complex poet than Puttenham because his ideological position differs from Puttenham's consistent and coherent conservatism; there are tensions between a slightly insecure insistence on order and an element of restless radicalism. We know frustratingly little about his life, but the tensions in the career of his closest friend, Gabriel Harvey, may throw some light on Spenser himself. Most critics have emphasized the differences between the two men; but while Spenser was less relentlessly secularly minded than his friend, he can hardly have failed to share in some of his intellectual interests. And Harvey's interests were unusually wide: his ambition was to establish himself as the complete humanist, a master of all the major disciplines of scholarly enquiry. He shared the utilitarian and rationalistic outlook of many humanists in the Renaissance; he consistently scorned outmoded traditions and was eager to be up to date in his thinking. He championed the new humanist historiography, attacking chroniclers like Holinshed who were content merely to catalogue events without analysing causes.[49] He was a keen student of military science, criticizing the Earl of Leicester for the old-fashioned tactics he used in his Dutch campaign.[50] He scorned the tradition-bound common law of England and took up the study of the Roman-based civil law with its basis in general principles rather than mere custom and convention. He was enthusiastic about new discoveries in science and geography, topics which were considered somewhat low and 'mechanical' in the socially conservative atmosphere of Elizabethan England. 'Industry' was one of his favourite words; his enemy Thomas Nashe mocked him for this ungentlemanly preoccupation with hard work. Harvey's rationalism extended to the arts. He had no time for the idea of art as mere social polish: the writer must serve the state. He preferred Roman valour to Greek artistic excellence, Spartan frugality and valour to Athenian idleness.[51]

But Harvey was well aware that these preferences were not widely shared in Elizabethan England: humanist rationalism still had to make headway against conservative social prejudices. We do not live in More's Utopia or in other fantastical commonwealths, he wrote, but in Smith's state.[52] Here he was echoing Smith's

---

[47] Puttenham, *The Arte of English Poesie*, 87. On the influence of numerical theories on Renaissance poetry see Alastair Fowler, *Triumphal Forms: Structural Patterns in Elizabethan Poetry* (Cambridge, 1970), *passim*.

[48] Puttenham, *The Arte of English Poesie*, 62.

[49] Virginia F. Stern, *Gabriel Harvey: His Life, Marginalia and Library* (Oxford, 1979), 152.

[50] Ibid. 162.

[51] *Gabriel Harvey's Marginalia*, ed. G. C. Moore Smith (Stratford-upon-Avon, 1913), 141, 145.

[52] Ibid. 197–8.

observation in *De republica Anglorum* that his aim was to describe the English constitution as it really was, and not, like Plato or More, to describe 'feigned common
wealths such as neuer was nor neuer shall be'.[53] Harvey's political thought amounted
to a kind of inverted Utopianism: given the contemptible way in which society was
governed, he would exploit the rules of the game so that they worked to his best
advantage. He encountered considerable prejudice in his academic career because he
was a mere ropemaker's son and increasingly rigid social distinctions were being
introduced in Elizabethan universities. Harvey responded not by proposing that
these prejudices should be changed but by dreaming of great men who had achieved
successes despite handicaps: men like Cicero, Thomas Cromwell, and, more spec-
tacularly, Tamburlaine.[54] Since the most direct way to power in a monarchy was by
means of flattery of social superiors, this was what must be done: 'he will persuade
best who best cultivates the manners and humours of princes . . . flatter, flatter.'[55] He
praised the Emperor Tiberius for his fox-like cunning, his 'political irony'; and he
was a great admirer of Machiavelli. In his marginalia he refers admiringly to a politician who got his way by crawling beneath the table like a dog and tying a chain round
his neck to show his loyalty.[56] Nashe accused Harvey of Puritan sympathies because
he detected in him the same kind of rationalism and contempt for tradition that was
to be found in Puritan circles. He did indeed respect Cartwright and dislike intem-
perate attacks on him; but Harvey was too much of a pragmatist ever to support a
political cause that might be considered socially subversive.

In principle at least, however, Harvey held that the humanist's courtly speech
should have ends beyond mere personal advancement: it was necessary to gain support for humanist ideas by sweetening the pill with a dose of flattery. Harvey was
deeply influenced by the humanist emphasis on the primacy of the active over the
contemplative life: however pure one's political principles, they have no value unless
they are put to the test. '[P]olitique Witts,' he wrote, are 'euermore jn concreto
actiuo'.[57] Literature was valuable only in so far as it encouraged and inculcated new
ideas and discoveries: 'there be honourable woorkes to doe; and notable workes to
read.'[58] His adversary Nashe scorned the idea that literature should be utilitarian, but
Harvey was a keen supporter of the French Protestant Peter Ramus in his projects for
simplifying the art of rhetoric in order to emphasize its instrumental rather than
ornamental functions. Harvey apparently considered, however, that in Elizabethan
England the best way of gaining support for new ideas was by means of writing
panegyrics of their possible patrons at court: he wrote a long poem in praise of
Queen Elizabeth and her chief adviser Burghley, and declared that 'the State
Demonstratiue' was 'not ouerlaboured at this instant'.[59] Harvey's attempts at courtly

[53] See above, Ch. 2 n. 53.   [54] *Gabriel Harvey's Marginalia*, 90–1, 109.
[55] Ibid. 202 (my translation).   [56] Ibid. 143, 90, 192.   [57] Ibid. 199.
[58] Gabriel Harvey, *Pierces Supererogation*, in *Works*, ed. A. B. Grosart, 3 vols. (n.pl., 1884), ii.103. Lisa
Jardine and Anthony Grafton, ' "Studied for Action": How Gabriel Harvey Read his Livy', *Past and
Present*, 129 (1990), 30–78, give a fascinating account of how Harvey helped Sir Philip Sidney in his reading of Livy's history, a text full of enthusiasm for the Roman republic and its civic activism.
[59] Stern, *Harvey*, 51; Harvey, *Works*, ii.199.

flattery, however, did not rocket him to power, and though Leicester did give him some patronage his modest academic and legal career fell far short of his Machiavellian daydreams. His prickly personality was certainly to blame, but it could also be argued that his innovative humanism was too militant to find a satisfactory social context in a conservative environment.

Spenser's correspondence with Harvey, which was printed in 1580, shows that the poet shared his friend's self-conscious concern with courtly advancement; the tone of the letters is obtrusively worldly and slightly dandyish, quite different from the rugged sincerity of the idealistic pastors of *The Shepheardes Calender*. It is possible to imagine Crowley's having written the deliberative 'moral' eclogues but not the demonstrative poems in which Colin Clout praises his mistress or Queen Elizabeth. In the 'October' eclogue Piers roundly declares that the place of the poet is at court, and the accompanying woodcut represents a stately palace. But Spenser's demonstrative poems are not simple flattery and have political aims beyond personal self-advancement: like Harvey, Spenser creates images of the great with the aim of trying to influence their policies. Colin Clout is implicitly criticized for allowing his amatory obsessions to distract him from putting his art in the service of the state. Like Sannazaro's Sincero, he broods on his love-melancholy and is incapable of action. But it is clear that this melancholy has also provided a stimulus to his poetic virtuosity: the shepherds admire the plangent 'August' sestina. Love may lead the despairing poet to abandon his craft but it may also act as an inspiration ('October', ll. 91–112). The implication of the overall structure of *The Shepheardes Calender*, however, is that this virtuosity must ultimately be put to didactic purposes. The English poet cannot afford to ignore the immense technical skill of courtly poets like Sannazaro; Crowley's austere plainness is no longer enough. But the courtly poet must not entirely lose sight of the values embodied in the prophetic poetic tradition.

When he published *The Shepheardes Calender* Spenser was in the service of the Earl of Leicester, the courtier who seemed to his supporters to personify a possible synthesis between the values of the Protestant Reformation and of the Renaissance court.[60] Leicester was a dazzling courtier, a collector of paintings, and a patron of pageants and plays. But he was also a consistent patron of radical Protestants, and his death in 1588 was to mark a decisive setback for the Puritan movement. He was the son of the Duke of Northumberland, the most influential politician in the latter part of Edward VI's reign, and had Northumberland's plans worked out Leicester's brother Guildford Dudley would have been consort to the Protestant queen Lady Jane Grey. Despite the old Edwardian rivalry between the Seymours and Dudleys, Leicester inherited the support of many former followers of Somerset. His links with treason against the Tudor line and Protestant radicalism made him an object of suspicion: his enemies alleged that he had used his immense influence over the queen to establish what amounted to a Puritan republic, dominated by Leicester and a

[60] Derek Wilson, *Sweet Robin: A Biography of Robert Dudley Earl of Leicester 1533–1588* (London, 1981), 309, 159–60, on the vexed question of Leicester's religious views, see 105–6, 197 ff. See also Richard C. McCoy, *The Rites of Knighthood: The Literature and Politics of Elizabethan Chivalry* (Berkeley and Los Angeles, 1989), ch. 2.

group of like-minded Puritan aristocrats, with the queen as a mere figurehead. He patronized some highly controversial figures, such as Christopher Goodman who had published a work justifying the deposition of tyrants when in exile during Mary's reign. He retained a strong sympathy with religious radicalism, though his personal life hardly accorded with Protestant ideals of godliness. If he sought fame and honour in all his actions, as the Renaissance courtier was expected to do, he was admired by many Puritans as a nobleman in search not only of 'good fame' but also of 'godlie fame'. Leicester did not only patronize Puritans; he supported some Protestants who rejected the Calvinist doctrine of predestination. His main aim was to build up a large and devoted personal following. Though his patronage did have a certain Puritan bias, he was as impatient as Grindal with radicals who seemed to court martyrdom for no good reason and who could see no difference between Mary's Catholic bishops and Elizabeth's Protestant bishops. But he refused to accept the polarization made by some conservative propagandists between evil Puritan goats and orthodox sheep, and he supported some extremely controversial figures when they were in trouble with the authorities. He shared the apocalyptic world-view that made the Puritans advocate a militant foreign policy.[61] Without the aid of Leicester and his allies the more radical currents of English Protestantism might have been effectively destroyed in Elizabeth's reign and a conservative and authoritarian state church achieved an unchallengeable authority.

Leicester was also a notable patron of letters, and Spenser sought his favour, writing a lengthy panegyric of his ancestry.[62] By 1579 he was living at Leicester House and hoping to be sent abroad on state service at the earl's recommendation. *The Shepheardes Calender* may hint at the Leicester circle's opposition to the French match. The religious eclogues are reminders of the Protestant prophetic tradition; and even some of the more courtly poems may, in a very indirect way, indicate the dangers of a sudden shift in royal policy. The blazon of Eliza in the 'April' eclogue has become one of the most famous of all the poetic images of the Virgin Queen. But retrospect has made it hard to remember that the cult of Elizabeth as maiden goddess was still a relatively new phenomenon. And Elizabeth's virginity had taken on new political connotations in the late 1570s. In the first few years of her reign it had been widely assumed that Elizabeth would marry as her sister had done. Mary Tudor's reign had intensified in Protestant circles the traditional male suspicion of political authority invested in females. By her personal choice of a marriage partner a queen who came to the throne unmarried could decisively affect the future of her realm without having to consult with Parliament. Shortly before Elizabeth's accession, radicals in England and Scotland had joined forces in denouncing what John Knox described as the 'monstrous regiment of women'. They looked back nostalgically to the days of Protector Somerset when there had been plans to unite England and

---

[61] Adams, 'The Protestant Cause', 25 ff.
[62] On Leicester's patronage see Eleanor Rosenberg, *Leicester Patron of Letters* (New York, 1955), and on his associations with Spenser and Harvey at the time of the negotiations for the French match see Henry Woudhuysen, 'Leicester's Literary Patronage: A Study of the English Court, 1578–1582' (unpublished D.Phil. thesis, Oxford, 1981).

Scotland by a marriage between Edward VI and Mary Stuart: by failing to seize this historic opportunity, England and Scotland had been left under the rule of Catholic queens. On Elizabeth's accession Knox made a rapid volte-face, declaring that though female rule remained unnatural, God had made a special exception for Elizabeth because of her piety.[63] But many Protestants feared that Elizabeth might not be zealous enough in the defence of the true religion and hoped that she would marry a Protestant like the Earl of Huntingdon (who has been termed 'the Puritan earl' because of his religious zeal) or Leicester, who quickly became established as the queen's favourite. Mulcaster had been involved in the pageants which welcomed Elizabeth to London on her accession and which strongly hinted that she should consult Parliament over the question of her marriage. Mulcaster, or whoever devised the pageants, was using demonstrative rhetoric to put across a very pointed political message. In 1562 the Inner Temple, a centre of strong Protestant opinion, staged a masque which hinted that Leicester (personified as Desire or Pallaphilos) should marry Elizabeth. A number of masques and pageants, up to the spectacular shows at Kenilworth in 1575 (in which Mulcaster also participated), presented debates between marriage and virginity which suggested that the life of Diana, the virgin goddess, was not the best model for the queen to follow.[64]

But by the late 1570s the situation had changed: Elizabeth was negotiating for a French Catholic match, and Leicester had secretly married Lettice Knollys, a member of a Puritan family which was fiercely opposed to the match. The political rhetoric of Leicester and his allies now began to change: virginity, the life of Diana, became much more attractive. At Norwich in 1578 Thomas Churchyard, a Leicester supporter, presented for the royal visit a play in which Chastity was overcome by Cupid. In *The Four Foster-Children of Desire*, a tournament staged for the French envoys in the spring of 1581 (by which time the negotiations were fading out), the imagery of Leicester's earlier pageants was transformed.[65] Leicester and his circle certainly had some part in devising the imagery and the speeches, and Sidney and his friend Fulke Greville played a prominent part in the action. In previous entertainments the demand for the queen to marry a worthy Protestant had been represented as Desire and the queen was obliquely criticized for her imperious refusal; now the foster-children of Desire, symbolizing the French suit, were compelled to admit that

[63] Arthur H. Williamson, *Scottish National Consciousness in the Age of James VI: The Apocalypse, the Union and the Shaping of Scotland's Public Culture* (Edinburgh, 1979), 11–12; cf. James E. Phillips, Jr., 'The Background of Spenser's Attitude toward Women Rulers', *Huntington Library Quarterly*, 5 (1941–2), 5–32.

[64] On the politics of early Elizabethan pageantry see Marie Axton, *The Queen's Two Bodies: Drama and the Elizabethan Succession* (London, 1977), 38–72. For careful acounts of changes in the cult of Elizabeth, and a warning against homogenizing very different periods and attitudes, see Helen Hackett, *Virgin Mother, Maiden Queen: Elizabeth I and the Cult of the Virgin Mary* (London, 1995), and Susan Frye, *Elizabeth I: The Competition for Representation* (New York, 1993); for discussion of the most extreme anti-Elizabeth viewpoints see Julia M. Walker (ed.), *Dissing Elizabeth: Negative Representations of Gloriana* (Durham, NC, 1998).

[65] Norman Council, '*O dea certe*: The Allegory of "The Fortress of Perfect Beauty"', *Huntington Library Quarterly*, 39 (1975–6), 329–42, for a fuller study of this tournament see Woudhuysen, 'Leicester's Literary Patronage', ch. 8.

the queen's perfect beauty was infinitely superior to all possible suitors. In their propaganda during the marriage negotiations the Leicester circle seem to have been reminding the queen that her image as a champion of Protestant purity, which they had done so much to create, was one of her key political assets, a source of popularity so strong that she would be foolish to repudiate it.[66]

Is Spenser using the same kind of strategy in *The Shepheardes Calender*? The 'Eliza' blazon was a seminal work in creating the image of the Virgin Queen; and Spenser consistently draws attention to the role of the poet in creating this image.[67] He transfers to Elizabeth much of the imagery traditionally associated with the Virgin Mary. She is the 'flowre of Virgins', 'without spotte', without 'mortall blemishe'. She is compared to the 'flowre Delice', which a note explicates as the 'flower of delights'; Elizabeth, like Mary, is associated with a garden of prelapsarian pleasure. Eliza unites the qualities of Venus and Diana, emulating Mary's mysteriously fruitful chastity. In the *Gaping Gulf* Stubbs had compared England to an Eden invaded by the French serpent; Spenser portrays Eliza as the protector of a garden that transcends the fallen state by uniting flowers of different seasons. The insistence on the queen's pure ancestry was of course politically pointed at a time when Catholics were branding her as illegitimate. The positioning of the blazon in the volume as a whole emphasizes Spenser's Protestant revision of the traditional ritual calendar. Spenser does not give the reader the conventional description of carefree festivities in the 'May' eclogue; instead he directs attention towards urgent religious issues. The gloss to the 'March' eclogue strikes a puritanical note in its denunciation of the pagan cult of Flora, which was seen by radical reformers as the origin of these medieval rites. But some royal officials had seen the possibility of politicizing these revels and using them as a focus for loyalty to the crown and opposition to the Roman church. In 'April' Spenser presents just such a reformed spring ritual, directed to the service of a godly ruler.[68] The *Calender* as a whole presents a progress from a state of dependence on the cyclical rhythms of the fallen world towards a prophetic vision of its transcendence.[69]

Spenser thus revises conventional Catholic images and adapts them to the cult of the godly prince; and he draws attention to the central role which the poet can play in strengthening the prestige of his ruler. He can revise and reinterpret classical mythology, for example by making his queen into a fourth Grace (another image of virginal purity). If he can help to create the royal image, he can by the same token try to change and reshape it: though he professes his complete humility, he is in fact demonstrating that he has a certain amount of power, even that he may act more responsibly than those in political power. The 'April' eclogue seems to allude to some

---

[66] Wallace T. MacCaffrey, 'The Anjou Match and the Making of Elizabethan Foreign Policy', in P. Clark et al. (eds.), *The English Commonwealth 1547–1640: Essays in Politics and Society* (Leicester, 1979), 59–75 (71).

[67] See especially the discussion by Thomas H. Cain, *Praise in* The Faerie Queene (Lincoln, Nebr., 1978), 14–24.

[68] Cooper, *Pastoral*, 194, 197–8.

[69] See, for example, Joseph Anthony Wittreich, Jr., *Visionary Poetics: Milton's Tradition and his Legacy* (San Marino, Calif., 1979), 105–16.

of the imagery with which Leicester had courted and tried to influence the queen. The Lady of the Lake had welcomed her to Kenilworth in 1575, and Spenser makes a row of 'Ladyes of the lake' praise Eliza. The Kenilworth entertainment had also presented Diana in a slightly ambiguous light, weighing the married state carefully against virginity, and traces of this attitude towards maiden goddesses may survive in the allusion to the cruel punishment of Niobe for criticizing Diana's divinity (ll. 87–90). Images of sudden and repressive violence from those in authority, dramatizing the intense gulf that separates the low-born from the noble, often occur in Spenser's poetry (as they had done in Harvey's marginalia). In 'July' Grindal's fall from favour is represented by the grotesque image of a shellfish falling on 'Algrind' from a great height and stunning him. A note to 'April' reminds us of the poet Stesichorus who was said to have been punished with the loss of his eyes for elevating his own true love above Helen of Troy. (Castiglione had alluded to this incident.[70])

This brings us to the question of why Colin Clout is absent from the 'April' eclogue, leaving Hobbinol to read out his poem. He is said to have broken his pipe because of his disappointed love for Rosalind. Spenser may here be contrasting the responsible public poet with the irresponsible poet of private amours; but some critics have suggested that there are more specific political allusions. Does Rosalind represent Elizabeth in another guise, as the queen who is now betraying Protestantism by agreeing to marry Alençon? Or, more plausibly, is Spenser throughout the sequence contrasting relationships based on power and subordination with those based on mutuality?[71]

It is certainly true that Renaissance readers would expect to find allusions to court politics in eclogues. Humanist editions of Virgil's eclogues politicized their annotations, finding more and more detailed allusions to Augustus and his court.[72] The edition of Erasmus' friend Vives reflected the relative liberalism of early sixteenth-century humanists. He read the first eclogue, in which Menalcas thanks Maecenas for the benefits he has conferred, as Virgil's thanks to Augustus for rewarding him with an estate; but he went on to add pointedly that '*Virgil* could not have . . . flattered more artificially, than by confessing to have gained liberty by his meanes, who was suspected to haue aimed at the destruction and vsurpation of the generall liberty and immunities of *Rome*'.[73] Is Colin worried that his Eliza may be jeopardizing English liberties? In the 'October' eclogue, which discusses the poet's proper

[70] Castiglione, *The Book of the Courtier*, trans. Sir Thomas Hoby, ed. W. Raleigh (London, 1900), 348.
[71] McLane, *Spenser's* Shepheardes Calender, 27–46, identifies Rosalind with Elizabeth, and also reads the 'November' elegy for 'Dido' as a symbolic elegy for the death of the Leicesterians' image of Elizabeth as Protestant queen (ibid. 47–60). For a more plausible general reading, less reliant on such particular identifications, see Louis Adrian Montrose, ' "The Perfecte Paterne of a Poete": The Poetics of Courtship in *The Shepheardes Calender*', *Texas Studies in Literature and Language*, 21 (1979), 34–67.
[72] Chaudhuri, *Renaissance Pastoral and its English Developments*, ch. 2.
[73] Juan Luis Vives, 'In allegoriam bucolicorum Vergilii', in *Opera*, 2 vols. (Basel, 1558), i.640; quoted in the translation by William Lisle, *Virgils Eclogues Translated into English* (London, 1628), 18. See Howard D. Weinbrot, *Augustus Caesar in 'Augustan' England* (Princeton, 1978), 121 and Annabel Patterson, *Pastoral and Ideology: Virgil to Valéry* (Oxford, 1988), ch. 2.

relationship to the court, Spenser does seem to indicate unease. Cuddie complains that poets are neglected at court, while Piers seems to offer praise of the warlike Leicester as an alternative, and perhaps a superior one, to praise of the queen:

> Whither thou list in fayre *Elisa* rest,
> Or if thee please in bigger notes to sing,
> Aduaunce the worthy whome shee loueth best,
> That first the white beare to the stake did bring. (ll. 45–8)

The bear with the ragged staff was the Dudley emblem. The masculine world of heroism, and of epic poetry, is contrasted with the homely pastoral world, which is suitable for the young poet, or one resting after he has 'slackt the tenor' of his string, but is not the highest poetic goal. Even within the 'April' eclogue Spenser hints at the existence of different, less exclusively courtly, forms of poetry. The uneven line-lengths and complex rhyme-scheme, reflecting the kind of metrical experimentation advocated by Puttenham, are played against the old accentual rhythms. And at the end of the central stanza, when the poet makes his personal declaration of loyalty, he quotes directly from *The Plowman's Tale*:

> To her will I offer a milkwhite Lamb:
> Shee is my goddesse plaine,
> And I her shepherds swayne,
> Albee forswonck and forswatt I am. (ll. 96–9)

At the opening of *The Plowman's Tale* the narrator describes the grotesque features of the simple countryman and prophet:

> In scrip he bare both bred & lekes
> He was forswonke & all forswat
> Men might haue sene through both his chekes
> And every wang toth & where it sat[.][74]

To readers familiar with the old prophetic tradition, the clash of discourses would have amounted to an alienation effect.

   Such hints of unease are, however, very oblique. Spenser would have been risking severe punishment had he openly criticized the match in a published work. He was equipping himself to become a court poet, and for that he would need the 'doubleness' recommended by Puttenham. His syntax at key points is strategically ambiguous:

> The flowre of Virgins, may shee florish long,
>   In princely plight. ('April', ll. 48–9)

Does the poet wish her to flourish long as a virgin or for this virgin to flourish in princely plight (which could include marriage)? The 'flowre Delice' seems to be identified with Elizabeth, but the phrase 'shall match with the fayre flowre Delice' raises the possibility of a marriage and evokes the French fleur-de-lis (a connection

---

[74] *The Plowman's Tale*, ed. McCarl, 65 (ll. 12–16).

which the annotator conspicuously refrains from making). The blazon draws on the epithalamic image of the 'Song of Songs'. Elizabeth had liked to present herself as not needing to marry an individual because she was already married to England; and this 'marriage' was taken by some panegyrists as a type of the nation's marriage to the true church. The French match would imperil these unions.[75] On the other hand, the epithalamic imagery would be appropriate if the queen did marry Alençon. Spenser says that the 'Pawnce' and the 'Cheuisaunce' will match with the 'flowre Delice'. A 'pansy' was a thought as well as a flower, and the word 'chevisaunce' does not seem to have been used as a flower name outside this poem: in 'May' it appears, and is glossed, in the normal sense of 'enterprise', often a dubious one, or 'chiefdome', or 'spoyle, or bootie'—ominous associations. Is the implication that the project of the French marriage is suspect? Spenser's garland of flowers provides an elaborate, if not impenetrable, camouflage for his private opinions. The need for court poets to keep their options open at this period is reflected in Puttenham's *Partheniades*. In some of the poems he praises her ability to reject suitors who 'bidd repulse of the great Britton Mayde', but in another he seems to be openly, indeed slightly coarsely, inviting the French king to board the royal vessel:

> None but a kinge or more maye her abourde;
> O gallant peece, well will the Lillye afoorde
> Thow strike mizzen and anker in his porte.[76]

This comparison reveals, however, that just as Puttenham was more categorical than Spenser in denouncing Puritans, so he could be much more emphatically in favour of the French match. There is a further possible connotation of 'match' which returns us to the idea of the poet as 'creating' the ruler he praises rather than passively flattering her every action. It is the poet who 'matches' one thing to another, who appropriates the prestige of classical culture and gives it to the rulers he praises in mythological disguise. Colin Clout is described as one with 'skill to make', and a note explains the Greek etymology of 'poet' as 'maker'. The genealogy that names Eliza's parents as Pan and Syrinx is not primarily historical (Henry VIII and Anne Boleyn) but mythological; and in the myth Pan did not succeed in conquering the nymph Syrinx, who was transformed into reeds, and had to content himself with making music from a reed. The allusion thus reinforces the idea that the monarch's public 'image' or 'person' is in part created by poets.[77] The words 'make' and 'match' were still interchangeable in the sixteenth century; 'make' could also mean 'mate', and the lyric that celebrated Mary as 'a maiden that is makeless' acclaimed her as both peerless and unmarried. When Colin declares that 'I will not match her with *Latonaes* seede' he is indicating that Elizabeth is incomparable and perhaps hinting at the political dangers of commenting on public affairs. But there is an undercurrent

---

[75] L. Staley Johnson, 'Elizabeth, Bride and Queen: A Study of Spenser's April Eclogue and the Metaphors of English Protestantism', *Spenser Studies*, 2 (1981), 75–91; Virginia Tufte, *The Poetry of Marriage: The Epithalamium in Europe and its Development in England* (Los Angeles, 1970), 167–78.

[76] Puttenham, 'Partheniades', 81.

[77] Cain, *Praise in The Faerie Queene*, 16–17.

of resistance to the idea of any 'match' for Elizabeth. At the time he wrote *The Shepheardes Calender* Spenser was already beginning to plan *The Faerie Queene*. The whole structure of the poem centres on a deferred marriage, on a courtship of a queen who is so ideal that the final marriage can only be an apocalyptic symbol, a transcendent fusion of history and divinity. The Protestant Virgin Queen became Spenser's ideal Muse. As wife of a French prince in increasingly close alliance with foreign powers, she would have lost this symbolic resonance, quite apart from the practical fact that a French-dominated court might have demanded a very different kind of poetry. The ideal poet presented in *The Shepheardes Calender* is a Protestant heroic poet who aspires to court favour but retains a measure of prophetic independence.

In *The Shepheardes Calender* Spenser established a political rhetoric that was to remain popular until the Civil War. The figure of the shepherd poet became associated with the kind of policies adopted by Leicester and his political heir the Earl of Essex: a militant foreign policy and at home a religious policy that was reasonably sympathetic to the more radical brethren, while not necessarily favouring all the radical demands. The first direct imitation of *The Shepheardes Calender* was produced by a poet connected with Leicester's Puritan following. Thomas Blenerhasset's *A Revelation of the True Minerva* (1582) describes how the gods and goddesses go in search of a new Minerva and find her in the English queen, to whom they yield up all their gifts.[78] The poem is sternly Calvinist in tone, containing a long digression in which the Papists plot against the queen and presenting her as a zealous evangelistic Protestant, proud of having defaced the heathen idols of the Papists. This poem is clearly aimed at Puritan readers who might have scruples about mythological verse: it is accompanied by a series of notes in which the printer explains that the gods are not idolatrous fictions but poetical names for virtuous men and women of antiquity. He points out that in calling Elizabeth a goddess the poet has biblical precedent. The gods themselves explain to a rather literal-minded Elizabeth that they are only signs for the virtues they signify. These annotations are much less subtle than Spenser's, but the aim of showing that poetry can provide moral instruction rather than merely courtly diversion is ultimately similar. These somewhat naive notes are indeed reminders that some of E.K.'s notes which appear somewhat absurd to modern readers may have had a genuinely instructive aim, directed at an audience eager for self-education.

Blenerhasset dedicated his poem to Lady Leighton, née Cecilia Knollys, the sister of Leicester's wife. Her father had Puritan sympathies and had intervened in 1579 on behalf of the presbyterian John Field. The family had incurred the queen's wrath over their hostility to the French match—Blenerhasset makes a scornful allusion to the 'fleur-de-luce'. Blenerhasset would have known Lady Leighton through his service in Guernsey under her husband Sir Thomas Leighton, a member of 'Leicester's

---

[78] Thomas Blenerhasset, *A Revelation of the True Minerva*, ed. Josephine Waters Bennett (New York, 1941), sigs. D3ʳ–4ᵛ, E2ʳ–4ᵛ, **1ᵛ; see also Ivan L. Schulze, 'Blenerhasset's *A Revelation*, Spenser's *Shepheardes Calender*, and the Kenilworth Pageants', *ELH* 11 (1944), 85–91.

Commonwealth' who maintained a presbyterian discipline on the island. Thus the poem has Puritan associations. There are many references to Spenser's pastorals and to Leicester's pageants. The Lady of the Lake and the Fairy Queen, who had appeared at Kenilworth and Woodstock in 1575, make an appearance; there is a reference to Pallaphilos, the persona representing Leicester in the 1562 Inner Temple masque; and at the end of the poem there is a description of Accession Day tournaments. Two of Lady Leighton's brothers had taken part in *The Four Foster-Children of Desire*, dramatizing their opposition to the match in symbolic form. At several points Blenerhasset alludes to *The Shepheardes Calender*, which he clearly regards as belonging to the world of Leicester's pageants. There is a pastoral interlude in which Elizabeth is celebrated in a series of lyrics cast in complex stanza forms, some derived from Spenser. The evil designs of the Papists are recorded in verses which, the printer says, observe decorum, the verse having no sense just as the Pope's devices have force: presumably the metrical virtuosity of the pastoral poems is meant by contrast to reflect the superior orderliness of Calvinist minds. It would be misleading to suggest that all Elizabethan admirers of *The Shepheardes Calender* had Puritan sympathies: some readers were content to enjoy the poem's metrical and rhetorical virtuosity. But in moments of crisis, poets who saw themselves as defending the Protestant prophetic tradition would revive Spenser's pastoral rhetoric.[79]

[79] For a reading stressing sociopolitical more than religious radicalism, see Robert Lane, *Shepheards Devices: Edmund Spenser's* Shepheardes Calender *and the Institutions of Elizabethan Society* (Athens, Ga., 1993).

4. Sidney and Political Pastoral

SPENSER dedicated *The Shepheardes Calender* to Sir Philip Sidney, a man who was acclaimed by his contemporaries as the ideal courtier, the embodiment of chivalric magnanimity and gracefulness of speech. It was especially appropriate to dedicate a pastoral work to him because Sidney himself assumed the persona of the 'shepherd knight' in tournaments at court and was the author of pastoral poetry.[1] Sidney had helped to introduce the new courtly forms of pastoral to England. He was well acquainted with Sannazaro's *Arcadia* and admired the Italian poet's gifts of verbal harmony, courtly metrical virtuosity, and purity of diction.[2] In 1578 or 1579 he wrote a pastoral entertainment, *The Lady of May*, which helped to inaugurate the cult of Elizabeth as a pastoral goddess. The relative merits of the May Lady's two suitors, a shepherd and a forester, were debated and at the end Elizabeth was praised as the true Lady of May. Sidney became so closely associated with pastoral verse that after his death in 1586 one elegist, George Whetstone, assumed that he had written *The Shepheardes Calender*, which had appeared anonymously.[3] In his *Defence of Poetry* Sidney had praised Spenser's eclogues but he had also found fault with them for being insufficiently courtly: he disliked Spenser's use of the old rugged pastoral diction, and his own pastoral verse is much more polished and courtly in metre and diction than Spenser's poetry.[4] Sidney was very conscious of his kinship with some prominent noble families and would have regarded it as beneath him to put his poetry on public sale as Spenser had done. Sidney is a courtier rather than a prophet.

Sidney's major pastoral work, the *Arcadia*, borrows its title from Sannazaro and has much in common with the atmosphere of Italian courtly pastoral. Sidney tells how two heroic princes, Musidorus and Pyrocles, arrive in Arcadia in disguise and fall in love with Pamela and Philoclea, the daughters of Duke Basilius. The princes have to disguise themselves to woo the princesses, for their father, trying to escape the effects of a threatening oracle, has retired to the country and put aside official business. Basilius delights in this abandonment of the active for the contemplative life, and takes pleasure in the joys of the countryside and in particular in pastoral entertainments. Monarchy, we are told, benefits the arts: nothing lifted up the shepherds' poetry 'to so high a key as the presence of their own

---

[1] On connections between Sidney's poems and his appearances in tournaments, see Peter Beal, 'Poems by Sir Philip Sidney: The Ottley Manuscript', *Library*, 5th series, 33 (1978), 284–95.

[2] On the influence of Sannazaro see David Kalstone, *Sidney's Poetry: Contexts and Interpretations* (Cambridge, Mass., 1965), 9–39.

[3] George Whetstone, *Sir Philip Sidney, his Honorable Life, his Valiant Death, and True Vertues* (London, 1587), sig. B2ᵛ.

[4] *The Defence of Poetry*, in *Miscellaneous Prose of Sir Philip Sidney*, ed. Katherine Duncan-Jones and Jan van Dorsten (Oxford, 1973), 112.

duke'.[5] Between the books or 'acts' of the 'Old Arcadia' there are singing contests which provide Sidney with an opportunity of displaying his own virtuosity as a poet. The leisure of Arcadia permits a high degree of metrical and stylistic experimentation, and most of the Arcadian poems adopt complex verse forms.

Sidney emphasizes the link between social rank and poetic skill: the very shepherds of Arcadia are socially superior to their counterparts elsewhere, but when they engage in singing contests with the princes they are outdone. Thus in the 'first eclogues' (pp. 58–64) the shepherd Lalus challenges Musidorus to sing of his loved one, initiating the contest in a very difficult verse form ('terza rima' with triple rhymes); Musidorus effortlessly meets every metrical challenge Lalus sets him while at the same time producing a more complex and intellectual kind of poetry, abstract and philosophical where Lalus' language is concrete and rustic. The whole exercise reveals Sidney's mastery of Italian verse forms, which he uses with an ease and grace that no previous English poet had achieved.[6] Sidney also experiments with imitations of classical metres. Humanists throughout Europe had made similar experiments, the product not of mere pedantry but of the belief that the ancient Greeks had achieved a uniquely harmonious balance between words and music in their lyric poetry, and that if poetry imitating classical metres were set to the new 'monodic' music it might be possible to regain this powerful and quasi-magical harmony.[7] In the *Arcadia* these experiments are given to the princes alone: they require an erudition beyond the abilities of the vulgar.

The *Old Arcadia* describes an aristocratic society in which love is the main preoccupation and in which contemplation is valued more than action. This is the kind of society celebrated by Castiglione and other defenders of court life. The state has become a work of art: strife and disagreement have been banished and the monarch's presence instils harmony. But having aroused certain expectations by the title *Arcadia* and the courtly atmosphere, Sidney proceeds to subvert them. It appears that the duke's attempt to turn his life into a work of art is precisely the problem: by delighting in pastoral poetry in the charmed seclusion of his rural retreat he has neglected more important political issues. Sidney has produced a critique of irresponsible absolutism by means of a critique of courtly poetic forms. The reader of courtly romance would normally expect a relaxed, associative structure without clear formal principles; the *Old Arcadia* is a masterpiece of controlled plotting. The pastoral interludes are enclosed within a main plot that is tightly and ingeniously constructed on the model of classical drama rather than the rambling romances in which so many aristocratic readers delighted. Sidney was one of the first English writers to have made a careful study of Aristotle's *Poetics*, which had been rediscovered only in the late fifteenth century but was already becoming extremely influential in Italy as the basis of neoclassical poetics. In its later developments neoclassicism became an

---

[5] *The Countess of Pembroke's Arcadia (The Old Arcadia)*, ed. Jean Robertson (Oxford, 1973), 56. References in the text are to this edition (*OA*).

[6] John Thompson, *The Founding of English Metre* (New York, 1961), 139–55.

[7] John Hollander, *The Untuning of the Sky: Ideas of Music in English Poetry 1500–1700* (Princeton, 1961), 141–3; Frances A. Yates, *The French Academies of the Sixteenth Century* (London, 1947), 36 ff.

intellectually authoritarian movement, binding the writer's freedom with rigid rules and prescriptions; and it is often regarded as having authoritarian political implications. It is true that the dominance of neoclassical theory in Italy and France coincided with periods of political absolutism.[8] Italian neoclassical drama tended to combine rigid formal unity with relatively bland and courtly subject matter. But Sidney was aware of more radical currents in classical studies. One of the few contemporary writers he singled out for commendation in *The Defence of Poetry* was the Scottish poet George Buchanan, whose neo-Latin plays reflected his radical views. Bale had praised him as a Protestant martyr in his *Summarium* but in fact he had escaped to the Continent and had returned to Scotland in the 1560s.[9] In 1567 he had supported the Protestant *coup d'état* that overthrew Mary Stuart, and had written a theoretical justification of the episode in his treatise *De jure regni*. Sidney and his circle were interested in Buchanan as much for his politics as for his poetry: at the height of the crisis over the French match Sidney's friend Daniel Rogers arranged to have the *De jure regni* surreptitiously printed in England, and he also encouraged him to complete his *History of Scotland*, which was a vindication of the people's right to overthrow tyrants.[10] Another friend of Sidney's arranged the English publication of Buchanan's *Baptistes*, a play which portrayed the grim fate reserved for the prophet who dared to speak truths that went against the interests of the establishment: in 1643 the House of Commons ordered a translation of this work as part of the campaign to justify their rebellion.[11] Like many Protestant intellectuals, Buchanan wavered in his attitude to the people. Truth had sometimes been preserved amongst the common people when the established church had been irredeemably corrupt, but on the other hand the masses were more likely than the educated to believe in superstitions and to resist new ideas. 'For the most part', he complained, 'the people like to stick to old ways and customs, and are opposed to change.'[12] They preferred fantastic plays which portrayed impossibly idealized princes to neoclassical drama in much the same way that they preferred religious rituals and processions to the pure Word of God. But the drama Buchanan most loved, that of classical Greece, had been produced in a democracy. He had translated some plays of Euripides—whose critical, rationalistic outlook was to make him Milton's favourite dramatist. Sidney may have been working on the *Defence of Poetry* during the controversy over the French match, and he may have been thinking of Buchanan's plays when he wrote that tragedy 'makes kings fear to be tyrants'.[13]

[8] Vernon A. Hall, Jr., *Renaissance Literary Criticism: A Study of its Social Content* (New York, 1945).

[9] I. D. McFarlane, *Buchanan* (London, 1981), 77; on the possible influence of Bale's John the Baptist play on Buchanan see 381–2.

[10] James E. Phillips, 'George Buchanan and the Sidney Circle', *Huntington Library Quarterly*, 12 (1948–9), 23–55. On the radical humanist politics of Buchanan's poetry see *George Buchanan: The Political Poetry*, ed. Paul J. McGinnis and Arthur H. Williamson (Edinburgh, 1995), introduction.

[11] McFarlane, *Buchanan*, 391–2; J. T. T. Brown, 'An English Translation of George Buchanan's *Baptistes*', in P. Hume Brown (ed.), *George Buchanan: Glasgow Quatercentenary Studies* (Glasgow, 1907), 61–173.

[12] Quoted by Arthur H. Williamson, *Scottish National Consciousness in the Age of James VI: The Apocalypse, the Union and the Shaping of Scotland's Public Culture* (Edinburgh, 1979), 113.

[13] Sidney, *Miscellaneous Prose*, 96.

Sidney defended poetry on fundamentally didactic grounds, arguing that it was superior to philosophy and history in moving people to action. His type of the pedantic enemy to poetry was not the Puritan—he shared the Puritans' hostility to the French match, and indeed to much popular theatre—but the philosopher; he was reviving the old quarrel between philosophy and rhetoric.

There is, however, a certain tension in the *Defence* between humanist didacticism and a rather more courtly view of poetry. Sidney's conception of the poem as a 'golden world', more richly adorned than anything to be found in nature, recalls the increasing escapism of sixteenth-century Italian court culture, the search for ideal aristocratic utopias which would transcend political crisis.[14] But Sidney's argument is not just that the 'golden world' is more beautiful than the natural world but also that, as Aristotle had put it, poetry is more philosophical than history because less dependent on contingent facts. The poetic world is a model whose very autonomy, its freedom from subjection to empirical fact, allows a detachment from traditional ideas and the free exploration of alternatives. The detached and critical cast of mind that enabled Sidney to conceive of the work of art as a 'world' was the same kind of capacity that produced the concept of the 'commonwealth' as a complex entity independent of the person of the ruler. In the *Defence* Sidney draws a distinction between different kinds of poetic idealization. Some writers, like Xenophon and Virgil, create a portrait of the ideal prince (a genre which was, of course, especially popular with courtiers). But, Sidney continues, it is also possible to feign 'a whole commonwealth, as the way of Sir Thomas More's *Utopia*'.[15] In praising not the communist ideas but the 'way' of the *Utopia* Sidney was presumably referring to More's ability to see all the evils of society as closely interrelated rather than remaining content with moral denunciations of particular 'abuses'. In the *Arcadia* Sidney presents not just an idealized prince but a whole commonwealth. At first the focus seems to be limited, as is customary in courtly romance, to the prince and his followers. But when a group of rebels unexpectedly storm his retreat Basilius is made to remember that a commonwealth is made up of more people than just the prince, that his personal well-being is not necessarily identical with the well-being of his subjects. Towards the end of the work the neighbouring monarch Euarchus arrives to remind Basilius of the need to join a Grecian alliance against the Roman threat: this episode recalls the Leicester circle's frustration at the queen's reluctance to join an anti-Habsburg alliance. Basilius' retreat is a sign of effeminacy, a fact symbolized by his falling in love with Pyrocles in his female disguise. The Leicester circle felt that Elizabeth lacked the firm decisiveness that might have been shown by a male ruler. Sidney hints that a monarchy may not necessarily be the best form of government for consulting the interests of all: under Basilius' rule '[p]ublic matters had ever been privately governed', and we are told that this is 'a notable example how great dissipations monarchal governments are subject unto' (p. 320). Sidney's 'feigned commonwealth' of Arcadia is not just a timeless idyll but a state with a complex economy and

---

[14]   Lauro Martines, *Power and Imagination: City-States in Renaissance Italy* (London, 1979), 452 ff.
[15]   Sidney, *Miscellaneous Prose*, 86.

social structure. He takes considerable pains to give historical verisimilitude to the setting in classical Greece: his feigned commonwealth must be made politically accurate. Sidney has politicized Italian courtly romance, enclosing it within a carefully organized humanist framework.[16]

The princes as well as Basilius have allowed private interests to interfere with public responsibilities. On their way to visit Pyrocles' father Euarchus, they are so enchanted by the princesses' beauty that they resolve to adopt disguises in order to enter their presence. Because they are disguised, not only does Euarchus worry about their fate but their friend Plangus, who is searching for them to tell them that the virtuous queen Erona is in danger and needs their help, is unable to find them. His despairing story is told during the first eclogues, and a bitter lament by him is sung in the second eclogues. The princes decide that they have time enough to save Erona, but this subplot darkens the work's atmosphere. Their own poems, in which they declare their love to the princesses, give a sense of confinement, almost claustrophobia: they are forced to disguise their identities and cannot speak their passion openly. Their attempt to win the princesses without their father's consent leads to political chaos: they abduct the princesses, while Basilius, in love with Pyrocles, and Gynecia, in love with Musidorus, engage in a series of devious manoeuvres which end in the duke's drinking a sleeping-potion and being feared dead. The princes are put on trial for abducting and raping the princesses and for murdering Basilius. Though they adopt their best courtly garb to gain the crowd's sympathy, the laws of Arcadia strongly reject the aristocratic double standard of sexual conduct and Euarchus, who has arrived in search of the princes and has been appointed regent, decides that the laws must sentence them to cruel deaths. Only a twist of the plot, the belated revival of the duke who has not after all been poisoned, saves the princes from their fate. Basilius arbitrarily sets aside the laws which condemned them, for though they have been innocent of trying to murder him the law still prescribes death for seducing and kidnapping princesses.

The *Old Arcadia* thus subverts the expectations aroused by its title and subjects the Italian courtly ideals of retirement, contemplation, and love to severe Protestant humanist scrutiny. It reflects the ambivalence with which the Leicester circle viewed Italian culture. In the *Defence of Poetry* Sidney argued that English literature was underdeveloped, that it had not yet acquired the rhetorical skill of classical literature, and his poetic practice shows that he felt he had nothing to learn from the mid-century 'gospelling' poets or indeed from much previous English poetry. He found the best models in Romance languages amongst the Italians. But Sidney always judged cultural issues in their political context, and he did not admire current tendencies in Italian politics. Greville was speaking for the Leicester circle when he later declared that Italy's 'excellent temper of spirits, earth and air' had 'long been smoth-

---

[16] In his excellent study *Sir Philip Sidney: Rebellion in Arcadia* (Hassocks, 1979), Richard C. McCoy gives a much fuller study of the critical issues involved than is possible here. See further Richard C. McCoy, *The Rites of Knighthood: The Literature and Politics of Elizabethan Chivalry* (Berkeley and Los Angeles, 1989), ch. 3.

ered and mowed down by the differing tyrannies of Spain and Rome'.[17] Languet warned Sidney that the Italians' 'spirits are broken by long servitude', and that 'nothing is more harmful to the intellects of free men' than the 'arts' of courtly flattery, 'which soften their manly virtue and prepare their spirits for servility'.[18] On Languet's advice Sidney confined his visit to Italy to Venice, a republic that jealously defended its political traditions. He admired Contarini's description of the laws of Venice, which was to become a key text for seventeenth-century republicans, and advised his brother Robert to study the Venetian constitution. He considered all other Italian regimes to be too servile and oligarchical.[19] The *Old Arcadia* reflects the radical humanists' suspicion of the aestheticization of politics, of the tendency of princes to compensate their subjects for the loss of liberty by spectacles and courtly festivities. Sidney certainly did not think of Elizabeth as a tyrant, and he wrote a pastoral masque for her himself. But *The Lady of May* is relatively muted in its praise of the queen. Sidney may have intended the queen to favour the forester, whose active life would contrast with the pacific and contemplative existence of the shepherd and might be taken to symbolize the more active foreign policy favoured by the Leicester circle. This allegorical interpretation is debatable; what is notable, however, is that both forester and shepherd criticize the life of the court with its 'servile flattery' and futile wooing of an evasive royal mistress. The only poem Sidney wrote in praise of Queen Elizabeth, which prefaces the masque, declares that '[y]our face hurts oft' even though 'still it doth delight'.[20] Like *The Lady of May*, the *Old Arcadia* combines courtly pastoral with a detached and critical view of monarchy.

At one point, indeed, Sidney abandons the newer, Italianate pastoral idiom and writes an eclogue under the traditional rugged persona of the plain-speaking, anti-courtly shepherd. Between the third and the fourth books, at a crucial point in the work's structure, Sidney includes a long beast-fable. The poem is a classic exposition of the radical Protestant fear of the growing power of absolute rulers. It tells how at one time the beasts were represented by a few aristocratic senators, but the baser beasts stupidly made suit to Jove:

> With neighing, bleating, braying, and barking,
> Roaring, and howling, for to have a king. (p. 256)

Jove warns them that kings will become tyrants, but the beasts are obdurate and even yield up their right to freedom of speech in their eagerness to be ruled by a monarch. The new king—Man in the allegory—begins his reign by provoking dissension in the aristocracy and wiping them out. At first the people are delighted to have lost their noble oppressors, but they learn by bitter experience that the aristocracy at least

---

[17] *A Dedication to Sir Philip Sidney*, in *The Prose Works of Fulke Greville, Lord Brooke*, ed. John Gouws (Oxford, 1986), 61.

[18] Quoted by McCoy, *Sir Philip Sidney: Rebellion in Arcadia*, 16, from James M. Osborn, *Young Philip Sidney 1572–1577* (New Haven, 1977), 208–9.

[19] *The Complete Works of Sir Philip Sidney*, ed. Albert Feuillerat, 4 vols. (Cambridge, 1912–26), iii.127.

[20] Sidney, *Miscellaneous Prose*, 22; for interpretation see Katherine Duncan-Jones, *Sir Philip Sidney: Courtier Poet* (London, 1991), 148–52.

acted as a buffer between themselves and the tyrant, who now proceeds to enslave them. The people are urged, ominously if vaguely, to 'know your strengths' (p. 259). Significantly, this is the one part of the *Arcadia* where Sidney reverts to the self-consciously archaic diction of mid-century prophetic poetry. The reciter of the poem, 'Philisides', explains that he learned it from a shepherd on Ister Bank: this is a reference to Hubert Languet, the Huguenot intellectual who was Sidney's lifelong mentor and correspondent. Languet was closely involved with international Protestant politics: he helped to draft the *Apology* with which William of Orange justified his rebellion against Philip II. With his friend Philippe Duplessis-Mornay, he is thought to have co-authored one of the most eloquent Huguenot justifications of resistance against tyranny, the *Vindiciae contra tyrannos*. The sixteenth-century theorists of resistance were not democrats: they argued that only men of rank and property had the right to resist tyranny, otherwise there would be social chaos. Sidney's Ister Bank eclogue reflects the view of these aristocratic radicals that only a strong nobility could safeguard liberty. It is possible to trace a clear line of succession, both in intellectual and familial kinship, from Sidney and his circle down to the classical republicans of the Commonwealth in the 1650s—down to Sir Philip's great-nephew Algernon Sidney.[21]

There can be little doubt that Sidney's close contacts with radical political thinkers contributed to the queen's suspicion of her young nephew. Despite his image as the ideal courtier, Sidney was not on particularly good terms with Elizabeth, who was reluctant to entrust him with important diplomatic or military duties. Even the knighthood by which he is known to posterity was conferred on him only late in his short life to enable him to carry out a minor diplomatic ceremony. The queen knew that on the Continent Sidney was regarded as an important political figure because of his family connections with the Earl of Leicester: it was not inconceivable that he might become a candidate for the throne. Negotiations began at one time for a marriage between Sidney and the sister of William of Orange: this project, if followed through, would have brought him to the centre of European Protestant politics. Elizabeth did not want this brilliant young man to have ideas above his station. The fact that he was in contact with foreign radicals does not, of course, mean that he endorsed all their ideas. He would probably have agreed with Harvey that because he was living in Smith's commonwealth rather than More's Utopia he had to adjust himself to political realities. What concerned him was to make sure that the monarchy did not step beyond the bounds traditionally allotted to it.[22]

---

[21] Blair Worden, 'Classical Republicanism and the Puritan Revolution', in Hugh Lloyd-Jones et al. (eds.), *History and Imagination: Essays in Honour of H. R. Trevor-Roper* (London, 1981), 182–200 (185–90). However, Worden has since noted that the *Arcadia* considers and rejects republican options: *The Sound of Virtue: Philip Sidney's* Arcadia *and Elizabethan Politics* (New Haven, 1996), 227–33. Lisa Jardine and Anthony Grafton, ' "Studied for Action": How Gabriel Harvey Read his Livy', *Past and Present*, 129 (1990), 30–78, demonstrate one aspect of Sidney's interest in republican texts. On Algernon Sidney's view of his Elizabethan heritage see Jonathan Scott, *Algernon Sidney and the English Republic 1623–1677* (Cambridge, 1988), 44–8.

[22] On the possible influence of Smith on Sidney see Ernest William Talbert, *The Problem of Order: Elizabethan Political Commonplaces and an Example of Shakespeare's Art* (Chapel Hill, NC, 1962), 89–97.

Sidney's political caution was intensified by an element of social fear. His generation had been deeply affected by the upheavals of 1549: Leicester as a young man had
ridden with his father the Protector to crush the rebels. Aristocratic privilege was
liable to threats from below as well as from above. Sidney completely lacks the interest of earlier generations in the social problems caused by economic changes such as
enclosures: the *Arcadia* itself was, according to legend, written in a park which had
been made by enclosing a whole village and evicting the tenants, and where Sidney
could enjoy leisure and contemplation.[23] Many members of Leicester's circle were
essentially *nouveaux riches*, despite the archaizing feudal costumes they wore at court
tournaments. Sir Henry Lee, who aided Leicester in devising entertainments for the
queen and appeared as the queen's champion in Accession Day tilts, 'belonged to the
new school of landowners, with whom landowning was a business'.[24] A great sheep-
farmer, he owed much of his wealth to enclosures. His relations with his tenants were
not particularly paternalistic. He gained a licence from the queen to make the many
serfs remaining on his lands pay large sums to buy their liberty: if they refused he had
the right to seize their lands.[25] His activities as a landlord helped to provoke an uprising in Oxfordshire in 1596. Sidney was acutely conscious that members of old landed
families looked down on his own more modest ancestry. The Earl of Oxford, a
Catholic supporter of the French match, engaged in an extremely public quarrel
with Sidney in 1579 in which he cast scorn on his lowly origins. To Oxford Sidney
was an upstart with dangerous political ideas; his antagonist responded by stiffly
insisting on his own and Leicester's good breeding. Hence his insistence on the
immense gulf between himself and Spenser the professional poet—the distance was
not quite as great as he might have liked.

Sidney's aristocratic consciousness thus affects his political outlook in complex
ways: if it makes him sympathize with noble rebels against tyrannous monarchs, it
also instils considerable social caution. This caution tempers his severe judgement of
the princes for their neglect of their duty. Some critics have argued that Sidney
means the princes to be found wanting by a rigorous Calvinist standard of morality,
that the *Arcadia* is, in the sexual sense, a puritan work.[26] There is certainly a tension
in the *Old Arcadia* between sensualism and morality. The reader is constantly put in
the position of the princes as they watch with relish an attractive female body:
Philoclea's garment, says the appreciative narrator, was light enough 'to have made
a very restrained imagination have thought what was under it' (p. 37). But having

---

[23] Noted by R. H. Tawney, *The Agrarian Problem in the Sixteenth Century* (London, 1912), 194.

[24] *Dictionary of National Biography*, 'Sir Henry Lee'.

[25] E. K. Chambers, *Sir Henry Lee: An Elizabethan Portrait* (Oxford, 1936), 43–6, 92–3, 165–8. Frances
A. Yates, *Astraea* (London, 1975), 89–108, discusses Lee's career in terms of an 'imaginative re-
feudalization' of European culture (108).

[26] Franco Marenco, *Arcadia puritana* (Bari, 1968); Andrew D. Weiner, *Sir Philip Sidney and the Poetics
of Protestantism: A Study of Contexts* (Minneapolis, 1978). An interest in representations of female beauty
was, of course, far from unknown amongst Puritans: it is interesting to study the passages from the
Arcadia transcribed by the American Puritan Seaborn Cotton (Samuel Eliot Morrison, 'The Reverend
Seaborn Cotton's Commonplace Book', *Publications of the Colonial Society of Massachusetts*, 32 (1937),
320–52 (323)).

aroused such imaginations, Sidney seems to quell them at the end by showing the disastrous consequences of the princes' self-indulgence. Though Sidney later revised the *Old Arcadia* to mitigate their guilt in abducting the princesses, in the original version they are undoubtedly guilty of this offence and the sentence of death is, though harsh, definitely legal. By the standards of the conduct of the heroes in many sixteenth-century romances, however, their behaviour has not been particularly heinous.[27] The aristocratic 'double standard' tolerated strong sexuality in young noblemen if not young women: in *Astrophel and Stella* Sidney enters sympathetically into the predicament of a courtier who wants to seduce a married lady.

Why, then, did Sidney submit his heroes to such rigorous judgements? The trial scene indicates the keen interest of Sidney and his circle in legal issues: in composing the prosecution and defence speeches Sidney draws heavily on Cicero's account of legal rhetoric in *De inventione*. The relationship of the law to sexual morality was in fact being debated in the 1570s: the Puritans were campaigning for stricter laws against sexual misconduct, drawing their precedents not only from the Old Testament but also from the laws of Greece and Rome. The Puritans did not go so far as the Arcadians in wanting to punish fornication by death, but they did want the death penalty for adultery. Such rigour was not easily compatible, however, with the traditionally more indulgent aristocratic attitude to sexual misconduct. In 1593 a proposal to have men as well as women whipped for bastardy was rejected 'for fear the penalty "might chance upon gentlemen or men of quality"'.[28] Pyrocles asks Philanax not to be too 'precise' in his judgement (p. 414): the word 'precise' was often applied to Puritans, and the topical controversy may have influenced Sidney's presentation of the issues. Shakespeare was to explore similar questions in his presentation of 'the precise Angelo' in *Measure for Measure*.[29] Like Shakespeare, Sidney dramatizes a conflict between law and equity. Euarchus is renowned for his equity, but he announces at the outset that he will set aside all considerations other than the letter of the law of Arcadia. He does this because only the prince is empowered to dispense equity, and as a mere outsider called in by the Arcadians to exercise judgement he is extremely anxious not to do anything that might imply that he wants to usurp the ducal authority. Sixteenth-century legal theory indeed normally associated equity with the monarch, who was empowered in special cases to overrule the letter of the law. In England, equity was especially associated with prerogative courts like the Star Chamber.[30] More generally, equity was associated by political theorists with

[27] John J. O'Connor, *Amadis de Gaule and its Influence on Elizabethan Literature* (New Brunswick, NJ, 1970), 204–5, notes that most English adaptations of Continental romances adopt a stricter sexual morality.

[28] Keith Thomas, 'The Puritans and Adultery: The Act of 1650 Reconsidered', in Donald H. Pennington and Keith Thomas (eds.), *Puritans and Revolutionaries: Essays in Seventeenth-Century History Presented to Christopher Hill* (Oxford, 1978), 257–82 (267).

[29] Donald J. McGinn, 'The Precise Angelo', in James G. McManaway et al. (eds.), *Joseph Quincy Adams Memorial Studies* (Washington, 1948), 129–39.

[30] Frank Kermode, '*The Faerie Queene*, I and V', in *Shakespeare, Spenser, Donne* (London, 1971), 50–7. On the Sidney circle's interest in equity, see Henry Woudhuysen, 'Leicester's Literary Patronage' (unpublished D. Phil. thesis, Oxford, 1981), 70–4.

aristocratic societies which were governed by distributive rather than commutative justice: in democracies the narrow letter of the law prevailed and all citizens were treated alike irrespective of circumstances, while in an aristocracy or monarchy there was more latitude for equity. Sidney clearly expects his readers to feel the injustice of treating noble and magnanimous princes in the same way as anyone else: where Puritanism seems to have democratic tendencies, he fears it. And what resolves the conflict is the revival of the duke, who alone is able to dispense equity and to pardon the princes. But many critics have found this ending unsatisfactorily perfunctory: the pardoning seems to partake more of 'blatant favoritism' than of equity.[31] Sidney tried to remedy this defect in revision, but it is an interesting index of the social and political tensions that affected his writing.

Without the monarch, the status of the nobility would be threatened. The plot of the *Arcadia* ultimately points this moral. The harmony of the landscape can be disturbed without warning by an armed uprising, the country houses that adorn the Arcadian countryside abruptly become islands in a 'violent flood' of rebellious 'clowns' carried 'they themselves knew not whither' (pp. 123–4). The social focus in Sidney's 'feigned commonwealth' is much narrower than in More's. Sidney does not view the social order as a naturally harmonious, organically ordered body but as a precarious union of warring elements: once the duke has withdrawn from political life the state becomes 'like a falling steeple, the parts whereof . . . were well, but the whole mass ruinous' (p. 320). In the revised *Arcadia* Sidney expands on the social motives of the rebels in order to show how contradictory they are: the peasants 'would have the Gentleme[n] destroied', the citizens 'would but have them refourmed', while the richer burgesses look down on both groups.[32] The Leicester circle had supported the Dutch rebels against Philip II, but William of Orange had been careful to emphasize that this was a rebellion with strong feudal precedents and with aristocratic leaders. When he took command in the Netherlands Leicester sided strongly with the Calvinist party because the more liberal Protestant party was led by mere merchants. He recommended that

> only the nobility of the land or other learned persons, well versed in matters of state should be appointed to the country's councils. . . . True, there are many good and trusty merchants whose services one might use, but nonetheless they will always seek profit for themselves.[33]

Leicester wanted to impose a firm and efficient central government on the different states of the Netherlands. A seventeenth-century Dutch historian reported fears that had Sidney lived he would have 'used his industry, valour, and ability in

---

[31] McCoy, *Sir Philip Sidney: Rebellion in Arcadia*, 136. Debora Shuger, 'Castigating Livy: The Rape of Lucretia and *The Old Arcadia*', *Renaissance Quarterly*, 51 (1998), 526–48, points out that Euarchus' pardoning of his son inverts the classic republican motif of Brutus's refusing to spare his monarchist children. For fuller discussion of the legal issues see R. S. White, *Natural Law in English Renaissance Literature* (Cambridge, 1996), 137–48.

[32] Sidney, *Works*, i.315 (*New Arcadia*, II, ch. 26).

[33] Quoted by Jan Albert Dop, *Eliza's Knights: Soldiers, Poets, and Puritans in the Netherlands, 1572–1586* (Alblasserdam, 1981), 164.

undermining liberty'.[34] The ambivalence with which the Sidney circle viewed rebellion emerges especially clearly in the opening sections of the *New Arcadia*, in which Musidorus finds himself involved in a class war 'betweene the gentlemen & the peasants' in Laconia: but elsewhere the Helots are viewed as not just the common people but a whole nation who have been oppressed by foreign overlords—like the Dutch in their struggle against Philip II.[35] The ambiguity is left unresolved; the episode indicates Sidney's anxiety about the difficulty of distinguishing between controlled aristocratic uprisings and social revolutions. Sidney is also aware that not all aristocratic uprisings serve the good of the state as a whole or even of all members of their own class. On Basilius' death, schemes are floated for a 'Lacedemonian' (aristocratic, Venetian) or democratic republic, while the aristocrat Timautus intrigues to gain power behind a figurehead monarch. Only 'the discoursing sort of men' favour such radical changes, which are 'a matter more in imagination than practice' (p. 321). The more active politicians are well aware that a republic, however attractive it might be in theory, could never take root in a country that 'knew no government without a prince'.

Though the *Old Arcadia* reflects the Sidney circle's suspicion of monarchs who try to turn political life into a theatre, substituting spectacle and pageantry for proper political debate, the work also reveals the importance of ceremony in maintaining social order. Sidney sometimes seems closer to Puttenham than to Languet. The wise king Euarchus stage-manages the trial of the princes effectively, clothing himself in black and sitting in the ducal judgement-seat, '[f]or Euarchus did wisely consider the people to be naturally taken with exterior shows far more than with inward consideration of the material points . . . in these pompous ceremonies he well knew a secret of government much to consist' (*OA*, 375). The princes try to manipulate the power of the imagination, dressing themselves in their most spectacular clothes in order to arouse the people's sympathy. This is clearly a dishonest attempt to disguise their failings; but they have earlier used precisely the same technique to save Basilius from the rebels. Pyrocles, still in his female disguise, climbs into the very judgement-seat in which Euarchus is later to sit, and harangues the crowd in a speech that appeals to their imagination more than their reason: necessarily so, since a fully honest and rational explanation of why he was there would make him emerge in an unfavourable light and confirm the Arcadians' suspicion that their prince is irresponsibly allowing himself to be led astray by a foreigner. He peppers his speech with rhetorical questions, which are, as the rhetorician John Hoskyns pointed out, 'very fit for a speech to many and indiscreet hearers, and therefore much used in Pirocles's oration to the seditious multitude'.[36] He reinforces his points by means of striking gestures, which display a 'sweet magnanimity' (or, in another manuscript, 'sweet imagination' (*OA*, 131)) and these gestures 'gave . . . a way unto her speach through the rugged

[34]   P. C. Hooft, cited by J. A. van Dorsten, *Poets, Patrons, and Professors: Sir Philip Sidney, Daniel Rogers, and the Leiden Humanists* (Leiden, 1962), 167.

[35]   Sidney, *Works*, i.14 (*NewArcadia*, I, ch. 2).

[36]   John Hoskins, *Directions for Speech and Style*, ed. Hoyt H. Hudson (Princeton, 1935), 33. Shuger, 'Castigating Livy', suggests the influence of Lipsius and Tacitus on Sidney's interest in political dissimulation.

wildernesse of their imaginations'.[37] In their pursuit of their loved ones the princes use somewhat Machiavellian strategies of pursuit and disguise: Musidorus callously exploits the low-born Mopsa in order to gain access to Pamela by this 'policy' (*OA*, 102), while Pyrocles is said to display a 'dangerous cunning'. But their skill in disguise is politically useful: Pyrocles plans to outwit the Helots by disguising soldiers as peasants so that the rebels will admit them to their town under the impression that they sympathize with their class war. Sidney argued in the *Defence of Poetry* that literature was more exemplary than history because it distributed rewards and punishments justly, but many critics have found the treatment of the princes at the end more indulgent than just. But Sidney may not always have thought as moralistically as he tried to do in the *Defence of Poetry*. He is known to have translated the first two books of Aristotle's *Rhetoric*, a work which takes a cynically pragmatic view of the best means of influencing an audience, notably different from the more moralistic conceptions of rhetoric and political virtue found in Cicero or Quintilian. John Hoskyns makes an interesting comment about Sidney's processes of composition:

The perfect expressing of all qualities is learned out of Aristotle's ten books of moral philosophy; but because, as Machiavel saith, perfect virtue or perfect vice is not seen in our time, which altogether is humorous and spurting, therefore the understanding of Aristotle's *Rhetoric* is the directest means of skill to describe, to move, to appease, or to prevent any motion whatsoever[.][38]

Sidney, says Hoskyns, had learned this lesson. The *Arcadia* can be seen as the product of Machiavellian rhetoric rather than moral philosophy.

Sidney seems to have decided that the first version of the *Arcadia* was not didactic enough, for soon after it was completed he began to revise it, making the conduct of the princes less devious and more exemplary. These revisions became more and more elaborate until they overshadowed the original narrative. The revised version of the *Arcadia* became a heroic romance, a celebration of Protestant magnanimity. Sidney added lengthy descriptions of chivalric combats. Humanists in the earlier sixteenth century had ridiculed romance with its glorifications of meaningless combats and adulterous loves; but Sidney tries to give romance political significance and a clear, coherent structure. Pyrocles and Musidorus do battle with political evils rather than mythical beasts: when they do meet some giants, Sidney adds the demystifying comment that they are really only 'two brothers of huge both greatnesse & force'.[39] The princes roam through Asia Minor righting wrongs and deposing tyrants, their sympathies going to 'the yong men of the bravest minds' who 'cried with lowde voice, Libertie'.[40] The political scenes seem to indicate Sidney's endorsement of the Huguenot theory of limited rebellion, though, as has been seen in the case of the Helot episode, there are hesitations and ambiguities.[41] Sidney is trying to synthesize the aristocratic cult of honour with humanist and Protestant didacticism, to produce

---

[37] Sidney, *Works*, i.318 (*NewArcadia*, II, ch. 26).   [38] Hoskins, *Directions for Speech and Style*, 41
[39] Sidney, *Works*, i.204 (*New Arcadia*, II, ch. 9).   [40] *Works*, i.200 (*New Arcadia*, II, ch. 8).
[41] Martin Bergbusch, 'Rebellion in the *New Arcadia*', *Philological Quarterly*, 53 (1974), 29–41.

a work that men like Languet or Buchanan could respect on political as well as literary grounds.[42]

But the attempt is not a complete success. The revisions are not fully integrated with the original framework. The heroic deeds of Pyrocles and Musidorus are recounted in extensive flashbacks: the princes are in fact telling the princesses of their heroic deeds in order to make their wooing more effective. The rhetorical end of these narratives may be didactic as far as the reader is concerned but it is meant to be erotic to the princesses. At the start of Book III the plot takes a new turn and the princesses are abducted, not by the princes but by the tormented aristocrat Amphialus. The centre of interest now passes to the princesses and Pyrocles and Musidorus play a relatively subordinate part from now on. Basilius comes to rescue the princesses but the siege becomes a frustrating stalemate. Amphialus tries to justify his resistance to Basilius by using some of the commonplaces of Calvinist theories of rebellion, but his motives are essentially personal and selfish, springing from a romantic obsession rather than a political objective. In analysing Amphialus' conduct, and throughout the romance, Sidney oscillates between sophisticated humanist political discourse and the clichés of chivalric romance. Battle is confined to a series of single combats, which can be described in terms borrowed from courtly tilts rather than in the language of sixteenth-century military science. The knights dress up in fantastic and colourful costumes; the field of battle becomes a 'blooddy Teniscourt' in which the 'game of death' is played; blood becomes a caparison 'decking' Amphialus' armour, which is also adorned with blood as he struggles with Musidorus: 'their blood in most places stayning the blacke, as if it would give a more lively coulour of mourninge, then blacke can doo.'[43] Violent action is blocked and displaced into spectacle; Amphialus stages a grisly mock-execution of Pamela in front of Philoclea, a sadistic 'Tragedie'.[44] The princesses are kidnapped after they have been lured into a grove on the promise of being shown pastoral 'devises'. The captivity scenes reflect Sidney's growing interest in inner spiritual qualities which make external pomp and ceremony seem emptily theatrical.

But Sidney's essentially courtly style did not offer a suitable vehicle for exploring inner states and the result is normally somewhat clumsy and external. Art is persistently associated with violence in the revised *Arcadia*. Sidney extended his portrayal of the defeat of the rebels in Book II, including a scene in which a 'poore painter' who had tried to portray the battle has both his hands chopped off. Spectacular representations of massacres were, it may be noted, in vogue in European courts of the sixteenth century, but Sidney seems exceptional in the sadistic comedy he tried to extract from scenes like that of the painter 'well skilled in wounds, but with never a hand to performe his skill'.[45] In another episode an evil king writes the sonnets of his love in the blood of his subjects and tunes them in their cries.[46] The grotesque

---

[42] On the Protestantization of the cult of honour in relation to Sidney see Mervyn James, 'English Politics and the Concept of Honour, 1485–1642', in *Society, Politics and Culture: Studies in Early Modern England* (Cambridge, 1986), 308–415 (387–91).

[43] *Works*, i.390, 392, 457 (*New Arcadia*, III, chs. 8, 18).

[44] *Works*, i.476 (*New Arcadia*, III, ch. 21).   [45] *Works*, i.313 (*New Arcadia*, II, ch. 25).

[46] *Works*, i.233 (*New Arcadia*, II, ch. 13).

juxtapositions of warfare and courtly spectacle grow more and more insistent in the later part of the revised *Arcadia*. Sidney broke off the revision before he had reached the end of the third book, possibly because he realized that the work's serious religious and political concerns, and its increasing inwardness, were becoming incompatible with the courtly framework.

The later parts of the *Arcadia* reveal a tendency which, as will be seen, becomes increasingly explicit in the later writings of Spenser and of Sidney's closest friend, Fulke Greville: the imagery of courtly ceremonial is associated with violence and imprisonment rather than delight. The claustrophobic atmosphere reflects Sidney's frustration at enforced inactivity. It has often been noted that the tournaments in the *Arcadia* are modelled on the joustings held at Queen Elizabeth's court; in Book II he portrays 'Philisides' in the costume of the shepherd knight which he had himself adopted at court, and pays tribute to Queen Helen of Corinth, who bears a resemblance to Queen Elizabeth. But the specific compliment to Elizabeth is in fact remarkably brief, in comparison with the tendency of many Elizabethan romance-writers to drop into praise of Elizabeth at the slightest provocation. The political connotations of tournaments were complex. In the Middle Ages tournaments had often been viewed with suspicion by the monarchy because they tended to foment rivalry and dissension amongst the nobility. While the aristocrats tended to stress the practical function of tournaments, monarchs anxious to discipline their often anarchic desire for personal honour preferred to turn them into spectacles, displays of courtly elegance rather than military valour.[47] The Tudor monarchs had been anxious to curb the military power of the aristocracy, and this process was effectively completed by Elizabeth when she crushed the last major Catholic uprising in 1570–1. After the Northern Rising the tilts held to commemorate the queen's Accession Day acquired a strongly Protestant colouring, and the Leicester circle were enthusiastic participants. For the old Catholic nobility the cult of aristocratic honour was associated with the old religion, but the Leicester circle saw themselves as Protestant noblemen with a firm commitment to the monarchy. There were still tensions, however: they were anxious to serve the queen on the battlefield, whereas Elizabeth was reluctant to spend money on warfare. The *Vindiciae contra tyrannos* gave an eloquent warning against the danger that monarchs would aestheticize politics, would turn real privileges into empty spectacle:

You speak of peers, notables, and officials of the crown, while I see nothing but fading names and archaic costumes like the ones they wear in tragedies. I see scarcely any remnant of ancient authority and liberty. . . . Let electors, palatines, peers, and the other notables not assume that they were created and ordained merely to appear at coronations and dress up in splendid uniforms of olden times, as though they were actors in an ancient masque playing the parts of a Roland, Oliver, Renaldo or any other great hero for a day, or as though they were staging a scene from King Arthur and the Knights of the Round Table . . . and that where the crowd has gone and Calliope has said farewell, they have played their parts in full.[48]

[47] Richard Barber, *The Knight and Chivalry* (London, 1970), 293 ff.
[48] Julian H. Franklin (trans. and ed.), *Constitutionalism and Resistance in the Sixteenth Century: Three Treatises by Hotman, Beza, and Mornay* (New York, 1969), 167, 191–2.

Sidney participated in tournaments in order to testify his loyalty, but he was more and more eager to turn tiltyard fictions into military reality. There was an element of bitter irony in his chosen persona of the 'shepherd knight': he was forced to spend his time in peaceful, contemplative pursuits because he was forbidden the opportunity to put his ideals into action. His New Year's gift to the queen in 1581 concentrated the political ambivalence of the *Arcadia* into a striking symbol: it was a jewel-encrusted whip.

In his last years Sidney seems to have turned to more explicitly Protestant literary forms: he translated parts of Duplessis-Mornay's *Of the Truth of the Christian Religion* and the *Divine Weeks and Works* of the Huguenot poet Du Bartas. His chance to serve the queen in action did not come until 1585, when Elizabeth at last gave way to circumstances—after the assassination of William of Orange, the Spanish had been gaining ground against the rebels—and allowed Leicester to lead an expedition to the Netherlands. The expedition became a Protestant crusade; the queen nearly revoked Leicester's appointment when she realized the radicalism of many of the followers he had chosen. When they arrived in the Netherlands Leicester and his allies angered the queen by seeming to go beyond their instructions. Certainly Sidney, in moments of Protestant enthusiasm, came to see the expedition as a crusade in which religious considerations were ultimately more important than service of the queen: she was 'but a means whom God useth . . . I am faithfully persuaded that if she shold withdraw her self other springes woold ryse to help this action.'[49] But Leicester's campaign was a failure, marred by tensions analogous to those which prevented Sidney from completing the *Arcadia*. Leicester and his supporters complained that they did not receive enough backing from England: their religious zeal made them rather suspect to conservatives at home. On the other hand, their military effectiveness may have been diminished by the fact that they were much more experienced in symbolic conflicts in the tiltyard than in real warfare. Fulke Greville's account of Sidney's death was almost certainly much distorted by hindsight but it does capture something of the atmosphere that surrounded the expedition; Sidney, he says, removed a crucial part of his armour so that he would not be better protected than his peers, and was thus unprotected from his fatal wound.[50] Aristocratic role and godly self formed a perfect union only in what Sidney had called 'the game of death'.

---

[49] Sidney, *Works*, iii.166.   [50] Greville, *A Dedication to Sir Philip Sidney*, 76–7.

5. The Faerie Queene *and Elizabethan Politics*

THE first part of *The Faerie Queene* was published in 1590, three years after Sidney's death. Spenser's heroic poem is the fullest poetic embodiment of the political ideals of Sidney and his circle; and it reveals the complexities and contradictions inherent in those ideals. Like Sidney, Spenser argued that poetry could convey political ideas more memorably than abstract philosophy:

For this cause is Xenophon preferred before Plato, for that the one in the exquisite depth of his iudgement, formed a Commune welth such as it should be, but the other in the person of Cyrus and the Persians fashioned a gouernement such as might best be: So much more profitable and gratious is doctrine by ensample, then by rule.[1]

Spenser's 'feigned commonwealth', Faerie Land, is not, however, a precisely imagined political entity like Sidney's Arcadia; it is a cloudier realm, more romanticized and idealized. Spenser's monarchical figures are presented with more reverence than Sidney's Basilius; the poem reveals the influence of the Italian courtly aesthetic. Spenser's Faerie Queene is presented as a mirror or image of Queen Elizabeth who is in turn imaged by other female figures—Belphoebe, Britomart, Mercilla, Medina—all of whom are emanations of the glory of the Virgin Queen.[2] Spenser's view of the universe is hierarchical: each image is inferior to the transcendent truth it images, and yet it also partakes of something of the dignity of its prototype, so that the social order becomes a mirror of the cosmic hierarchy. Like the Italian courtly writers, Spenser identifies political virtue with love rather than liberty. The quest for honour is identified with the quest for love: Arthur's quest for Gloriana is an education in love, and all Gloriana's knights are motivated by strong personal devotion to their sovereign. The basic unifying idea of the poem, as outlined in the 'Letter to Ralegh', is the series of annual feasts of the 'Order of Maidenhead' from which each year one of Gloriana's knights sets forth in search of adventure. Spenser probably derived this idea from the annual festivities of the Order of the Garter, which involved rituals of devotion to the monarch, and the annual Accession Day tilts. Courtiers like Sidney and Essex would make spectacular entries at these tilts,

---

[1] 'Letter of the Authors . . . To the Right Noble, and Valorous, Sir Walter Ralegh', in *The Works of Edmund Spenser: A Variorum Edition*, ed. Edwin Greenlaw et al., 10 vols. (Baltimore, 1932–49), i.168. On the influence of Xenophon's *Cyropaedia* on Renaissance poetry see O. B. Hardison, Jr., *The Enduring Monument: A Study of the Idea of Praise in Renaissance Literary Theory and Practice* (Chapel Hill, NC, 1962), 72 ff.

[2] On the panegyric elements see Frances A. Yates, *Astraea: The Imperial Theme in the Sixteenth Century* (London, 1975), 69–74, and *The Occult Philosophy in the Elizabethan Age* (London, 1979), 95–108; Alastair Fowler, *Spenser and the Numbers of Time* (London, 1964), 77–8; Thomas H. Cain, *Praise in* The Faerie Queene (Lincoln, Nebr., 1978); and Robin Headlam Wells, *Spenser's* Faerie Queene *and the Cult of Elizabeth* (London, 1983).

dressed in romantic costumes and making speeches in which the deeds they had performed in the queen's service that year were cast in the imagery of romance. The romantic idiom of these occasions helped to overcome male courtiers' dislike of subjecting themselves to a woman; they could see themselves as ideal knights gaining honour from the service of a distant and virtuous lady. *The Faerie Queene* enacts a process of political sublimation in which Arthur and the lesser knights subordinate their individual quests for glory to the service of the Faerie Queene who alone can confer true magnanimity. Spenser's loyalty to the monarch was rewarded in 1591 by a substantial pension of £50; he became, in effect if not in name, poet laureate.

Spenser referred to his poem as a 'pageant', and many critics have developed the analogy between *The Faerie Queene* and Renaissance court entertainments. The proem to each book arouses expectations of a form rather like a masque at the court of the Medici, culminating in a ceremonial unveiling of an image of royal power: the actual ruler would be celebrated as a living embodiment of divine virtue, whose person could reconcile all social, religious, and political conflicts.[3] But the emphasis in the poem lies on the difficulty of achieving such transcendent visions, and the images of divine monarchs are much more elusive than would be normal in a masque. The poem is full of prophecies of future ceremonies which will resolve all contradictions, most notably the marriage of Arthur and Gloriana. But these ceremonies are always deferred, and the emphasis is on the difficulty of completing the quests and the dangers of complacency. The Redcross Knight has to leave Una and fight for another six years before their wedding can take place. Guyon and the Palmer fail to transform Grill. Arthegall's victory over Grantorto is marred by the attacks of the Blatant Beast, which is still roaming at large by the end of Book V. Britomart's marriage to Arthegall is predicted but not described; and Arthur himself seems to have made little progress in his quest for Gloriana by the end of Book VI. At the centre of the dance of the Graces in that book, where one would expect an image of royal power, there is an image of Spenser's own loved one rather than of his ruler, and the poet reassumes the persona of Colin Clout, the plain-speaking Protestant prophet. Throughout the poem, moreover, there is a deep suspicion of false resolutions, of deceptive claims to transcendence: images can be deceptive rather than true mirrors of the divine, and pageants may be instruments of evil, like the masque with which Busirane abducts Amoret. The experience of reading *The Faerie Queene* is not of neat numerical patterns and political harmonies but of a constant and unpredictable

---

[3] The analogy with pageants is developed most extensively by Fowler, *Spenser and the Numbers of Time*. Arguments for the poem's essential unity, from slightly different points of view, are given by Ronald Arthur Horton, *The Unity of* The Faerie Queene (Athens, Ga., 1978), and James Nohrnberg, *The Analogy of* The Faerie Queene (Princeton, 1976). Michael Leslie, *Spenser's 'Fierce Warres and Faithfull Loves': Martial and Chivalric Symbolism in* The Faerie Queene (Cambridge, 1983), 186–95, argues that the poem reveals a corrupt chivalric order that needs reformation, pointing to the ideals of the Protestant chivalry of the Sidney circle; Richard C. McCoy, *The Rites of Knighthood: The Literature and Politics of Elizabethan Chivalry* (Berkeley and Los Angeles, 1989), 142 ff., goes further than Leslie in emphasizing the poem's scepticism about the likelihood of reformation. Richard Helgerson, 'Two Versions of Gothic', in *Forms of Nationhood: The Elizabethan Writing of England* (Chicago, 1992), ch. 1, discusses the tension between monarchical and aristocratic principles.

quest. Spenser problematizes the act of reading, discouraging his audience from taking the interpretations they are offered immediately on trust. It is the idolatrous magicians Archimago and Acrasia who encourage readers to take sign for reality, representation for thing represented; the alert reader is reminded, by a series of what amount to alienation effects, to keep experience under constant rational scrutiny.

This does not mean, however, that Spenser sets out to plunge his readers into an existential void. The enormous self-consciousness of the poem is designed to reinforce the didactic aim of fashioning a gentleman, not to undermine it. Like Sidney, he has the humanist aim of politicizing romance; and he chooses to do so by means of allegory. The details of the allegory constantly disrupt the linear movement of the narrative, thus preventing readers from surrendering themselves completely to the dream-world of romance. Spenser sets himself to 'overgo' Ariosto and all other previous authors of heroic poems from ideological as well as personal motives: his poem attempts the extraordinarily ambitious task of emulating all the major Western epics and romances, imitating their best features but simultaneously demonstrating the superior ideological perspective provided by reformed humanism. For example, the knight's battle with the dragon at the end of Book I draws on the most basic elements of popular romance, but conspicuously allegorizes the story. Humanists and reformers had been hostile to legends about dragons, and in particular to the legend of St George, but Spenser's biblical allusions make it clear that the knight's struggle foreshadows an apocalyptic battle. But the reader is not encouraged to treat the narrative simply as a transparent medium through which the content can be easily reached. There is a note of Ariostan playfulness in some of the descriptions of the dragon, such as the claim that the stream of his blood would drive a water-mill (I.xi.22). Like Ariosto, Spenser distances himself from medieval romance conventions and draws attention to his own poetic wit and creativity. But Spenser turns this playfulness to an ideological end foreign to Ariosto. He returns the reader to asking questions about the Protestant meaning of the narrative. The direct juxtaposition of biblical references (e.g. the waters of Silo and Jordan, I.xi.30) with allusions to prosaically secular phenomena (the waters of Bath) prevents readers either from moving directly from sign to thing signified or from reading the story as a story and forgetting the allegory. The narrator offers the reader several different interpretations of events (I.xi.36) but does not give an easy answer: at the same time, the search for answers is presented as a moral imperative. Learning to read Spenser's poem is not just a means towards the further end of moral and political education, it is part of the process. The Spenserian stanza itself embodies the process of revaluing the conventions of previous heroic poems. Spenser's stanza overgoes by one line the eight-line stanza favoured by Ariosto and Tasso. The self-enfolding dispersion of the rhymes reinforces the effect of self-conscious analysis rather than unreflective narrative movement, while the final alexandrine permits a further moment of reflection before moving to the next stanza. Spenser's archaic diction gives a note of dignity called for in heroic poetry, but it also draws attention prominently to the linguistic medium and warns the reader to be alert for allegorical references. The archaic spelling further calls attention to multiple meanings. *The Faerie Queene* is very much a poem of the new age of the printed book, for before that time no poet could have exercised sufficient control over the process of reproduction of his texts to permit such precise nuances in visual effect.[4] Down to the details of form and presentation, *The Faerie Queene* is innovative more than conservative.

But Spenser was celebrating in his poem a ruler who, if no extreme reactionary, was certainly wary about political and religious change; and his personal situation limited his openness to new ideas in some respects. There are therefore recurrent tensions in the poem between conservative defensiveness and more radical elements. It is impossible in a single chapter to attempt a full political reading of the poem; it seems best to try to indicate some of the significant tensions in three particular areas: the treatment of female rulers, the religious allegory of Book I, and the political allegory of Books V and VI. It is appropriate to begin with Spenser's praise of Queen Elizabeth, long recognized as one of the central political concerns of the poem. The quest for virtue as embodied in an ideal female figure had of course been a central feature of romance poetry. Spenser politicized this theme: his Muse is not Beatrice or Laura but Gloriana, an image of political as well as private virtue. In the first Proem Spenser directly dissociates himself from a more recent poet, Tasso, who had invoked the Virgin Mary: Spenser's Muse is a Protestant Virgin Queen who becomes associated with the woman clothed with the sun in Revelation. In thus politicizing his Muse, however, Spenser faced a number of ideological problems; and his achievement in naturalizing the cult of the Virgin Queen has tended to obscure some of the difficulties which lay in his way. In some respects Spenser's praise of idealized female figures reflected the humanist revaluation of woman's traditional role; his name was often invoked by champions of women. But it would be unwise to identify every virtuous woman in the poem directly with Queen Elizabeth: this would be precisely the kind of uncritical reading Spenser was trying to discourage. Despite the general celebration of female rulers, his poem does hint at the problems some radical humanists and Protestants had believed to inhere in giving supreme power to a woman. Though theoretically in favour of educating women, male humanists were only too willing to accept the notion that females were less rational than men; a woman in power would therefore be likely to oppose enlightened reform. When Spenser began work on *The Faerie Queene*, the idealization of Elizabeth as Virgin Queen had only recently begun to gather momentum after a long period when many courtiers hoped she would marry a worthy Protestant. Both in her lifetime and in retrospect the cult of Elizabeth was often, in effect, a cult of Elizabeth imagined as following the advice of firm Protestants; and courtiers like Leicester and Essex sometimes thought that she did not pay enough attention to their counsels. In the following century the Puritan Lucy Hutchinson wrote that 'the felicity of her reigne was the effect of her submission to her masculine and wise Councellors'.[6]

---

[4] Walter J. Ong, *Interfaces of the Word: Studies in the Evolution of Consciousness and Culture* (Ithaca, NY, 1977), 189 ff., emphasizes elements of continuity from the oral tradition in Spenser's style, but does not consider the interface between style and political standpoint.

[5] Cain, *Praise in* The Faerie Queene, 44–8.

[6] Lucy Hutchinson, *Memoirs of the Life of Colonel Hutchinson*, ed. James Sutherland (London, 1973), 48. After a detailed analysis of Elizabeth's various marriage negotiations, Susan Doran comes to the con-

Confronted with such attitudes, Elizabeth did not attempt to undermine an already somewhat precarious political position by seeming to challenge the whole patriarchal order. She took no action to change the position of women in general; she did not particularly encourage female education.[7] In her public appearances she prudently presented herself as an exception to the general rules about male superiority. ⌈'I know I have the body of a weak and feeble woman,' she declared in her famous Tilbury speech, 'but I have the heart and stomach of a king, and of a king of England too.'⌉[8] In another speech she declared that she could lay claim to only two of the four traditional kingly virtues, justice and temperance; the other two, prudence and magnanimity, could be exercised only by men.[9] Some Renaissance writers, such as the poet Tasso, did argue that in their capacity as rulers, women were entitled to exercise some traditionally masculine virtues such as courage, but this courtly concession did not in any way imply a general improvement in woman's status: 'The princess is, as it were, a man by virtue of her birth, and hence the masculine standard of morality applies to her.'[10] Elizabeth was anxious to conform to general norms of natural hierarchy, and courtly propagandists emphasized that her rule was indeed natural rather than a divinely ordained exception. The first full-length reply to Knox's treatise against female rule, by John Aylmer, conceded that under an elective system of government rule by males would be more natural, but Aylmer argued that under a hereditary system, where the prince was 'prouided of God by lineall succession', it was necessary to accept the legitimate heir whether male or female. Elizabeth's rule is natural, then, not because rule by women is natural in itself but because of the principle of legitimacy and hereditary succession.[11]

What were Spenser's views on these issues? The evidence in *The Faerie Queene* is complex and apparently contradictory; he was exploring the implications of different views without necessarily beginning from a fixed position. It can certainly be

clusion that she did indeed show herself ready to bow to the wishes of the Council and public opinion rather than divide the nation: *Monarchy and Matrimony: The Courtships of Elizabeth I* (London, 1996), 210–18.

[7] On Elizabeth's acceptance of conventional female roles see Allison Heisch, 'Queen Elizabeth I and the Persistence of Patriarchy', *Feminist Review*, 4 (1980), 45–56. See further Susan Bassnett, *Elizabeth I: A Feminist Perspective* (Oxford, 1988); Helen Hackett, *Virgin Mother, Maiden Queen: Elizabeth I and the Cult of the Virgin Mary* (London, 1995); Susan Frye, *Elizabeth I: The Competition for Representation* (New York, 1993).

[8] From the famous speech at Tilbury in 1588: *Elizabeth I: Collected Works*, ed. Leah S. Marcus, Janel Mueller, and Mary Beth Rose (Chicago, 2000), 326.

[9] From a speech to Parliament, 24 Nov. 1586: *Collected Works*, 198.

[10] Ian Maclean, *The Renaissance Notion of Woman: A Study in the Fortunes of Scholasticism and Medical Science in European Intellectual Life* (Cambridge, 1980), 62, summarizing Tasso, *Discorso della virtù feminile e donnesca* (1582).

[11] John Aylmer, *A Harborowe for Faithfull and Trewe Subiectes* (Strasbourg, 1559), sig. H4ᵛ. A. N. McLaren has argued for a more complex reading: in countering Knox, Aylmer was pushed into arguing that England was a mixed polity in which the monarchy was only one of the three estates that met in Parliament, and that worries about female rule need be the less because the monarch was always constrained by the Council—a position with which Lucy Hutchinson would have been happy. See A. N. McLaren, *Political Culture in the Reign of Elizabeth I: Queen and Commonwealth? 1558–1585* (Cambridge, 1999), 59–6; see also James E. Phillips, Jr., 'The Background of Spenser's Attitude toward Women Rulers', *Huntington Library Quarterly*, 5 (1941–2), 5–32, and Constance Jordan, 'Woman's Rule in Sixteenth-Century British Political Thought', *Renaissance Quarterly*, 40 (1987), 421–51.

pointed out that he includes at key moments in his poem images which invert the normal relations between male and female: in the Garden of Adonis episode it is Venus who has priority over her lover, and Form, traditionally masculine, is made female while Matter is masculine. In the Temple of Isis the goddess dominates the male crocodile. There are two images of hermaphrodites. Alastair Fowler has suggested that these images, in a poem addressed to a female ruler, formed a kind of compensation for the traditional symbolic order. Spenser may have been drawing on Neoplatonic theory in which the highest kind of unity is not just a prosaic mean between extremes but a more dynamic and paradoxical kind of coincidence of opposites. In a male-dominated world, giving priority to the female seems paradoxical, but it is precisely such paradoxes which can stimulate the reader into a meditation on the mysteries of the universe. All the images of Queen Elizabeth involve various kinds of mystical coincidence of opposites: they combine the qualities of Venus and Diana, of Mars and Minerva, of men and women.[12] Spenser even transfers to Elizabeth some attributes traditionally belonging to the Virgin Mary, thus associating the Virgin Queen with fertility and natural life-giving processes rather than merely negative chastity.[13]

But if one tries to translate these mystical images back into more prosaic terms, one seems to find an endorsement more than a questioning of the general principle of female subordination. Spenser's treatment of the virgin-queen figure is not uniformly reverent. After all, before Spenser gave her a courtly apotheosis, the Fairy Queen of folklore was not a dignified and transcendent figure but a mischievous, black-faced trickster. Some peasant rebels in the early sixteenth century had claimed to be led by the Queen of Fairies.[14] Before Spenser began work on his poem, attempts had been made to introduce her to royal pageantry. But in her first fully documented appearance, at Woodstock in 1575, she still had some of her traditional attributes; she praised the queen but was certainly not identified with her. Elizabeth's presence turned her black face white.[15] In the 1570s the female figures in entertainments associated with Leicester were still sometimes viewed with a certain detachment. Josephine Waters Bennett has argued that at an early stage of composition, when he was most directly imitating Ariosto, Spenser intended to view the Faerie Queene in a relatively light and humorous way.[16] One of the significant epiphanies of Book I, when Arthur recounts his vision of Gloriana (I.ix.13–15), is derived from Chaucer's tale of Sir Thopas; the erotic physicality of the dream is difficult to reconcile with Platonic transcendence. This allusion should perhaps be seen as a characteristic Spenserian alienation effect rather than a residue from an early stage of composition,

---

[12]   Alastair Fowler, 'Emanations of Glory: Neoplatonic Order in Spenser's *Faerie Queene*', in Judith M. Kennedy and James A. Reither (eds.), *A Theatre for Spenserians* (Toronto, 1973), 53–82.

[13]   Wells, *Spenser's* Faerie Queene *and the Cult of Elizabeth*, 14–21.

[14]   Keith Thomas, *Religion and the Decline of Magic: Studies in Popular Beliefs in Sixteenth- and Seventeenth-Century England*, rev. edn. (Harmondsworth, 1973), 732.

[15]   Yates, *Astraea*, 94–8.

[16]   Josephine Waters Bennett, *The Evolution of* The Faerie Queene (Chicago, 1942), 47 ff.; but see Henry Woudhuysen, 'Leicester's Literary Patronage' (unpublished D.Phil. thesis, Oxford, 1981), 217 ff.

but in either case it momentarily undermines a simple identification between faerie legend and the historical Elizabeth.

In the entertainments of the 1570s, as has been seen, the female figures had sometimes been presented in an obliquely critical light. At Kenilworth in 1575 the Lady of the Lake had been somewhat overshadowed by the figure of King Arthur, a symbol of the military glory to which Leicester was then aspiring. It is highly unlikely that Spenser ever intended Arthur as a direct representation of Leicester in his role of suitor to the queen. But the earl's 'courting' of Elizabeth in pageants was as much symbolic as realistic; he was urging the queen to respect the body of strong Protestant opinion he claimed to represent. Spenser does make a symbolic courtship between an activist hero and an apparently passive ruler the central theme of his poem. Had he ever finished it he would have had to face the embarrassing question of how to handle Gloriana's marriage with Arthur: for once the Faerie Queene was married she would lose her political supremacy, a state to which Elizabeth had clung against all the importunities of Leicester and other suitors.

Spenser represents the queen's unmarried state in the figure of Belphoebe, her 'private' as opposed to 'public' person. He borrowed the name from Ralegh, whose prefatory sonnet compared Spenser to Petrarch: Elizabeth was his Laura.[17] It has been seen that sixteenth-century Protestants sometimes regarded Petrarch as a prophet of opposition to the Papacy, a poet celebrating chaste love rather than the corrupt Whore of Babylon. As a young man Spenser had translated Jan van der Noot's Protestantized Petrarchan poems. Belphoebe is an emanation of Diana, the goddess of the moon; the lunar imagery could also be given apocalyptic associations. Dante and other critics of the Papacy had associated the Pope with the sun, the Emperor with the moon, and later royal antagonists of the Papacy had sometimes used similar imagery. Chapman draws on these traditions in his *Hymnus in Cynthiam* (1594): the queen is urged to

> set thy Christall, and Imperiall throne,
> (Girt in thy chast, and neuer-loosing zone)
> Gainst Europs Sunne directly opposit,
> And giue him darknesse, that doth threat thy light.[18]

But Spenser is concerned not so much with the public associations of the Diana figure as with the personal relationship between monarch and courtier. Elizabeth skilfully exploited the language of love poetry to overcome the unease felt by many male courtiers at being subordinate to a woman. The fiction that courtiers were Platonic lovers was maintained with remarkable consistency: the queen became furious if any of her favourite courtiers got married or was guilty of sexual misconduct. The queen's favourites adapted themselves to this situation and praised her with poems of their own or their clients' composition. But there were undercurrents of unease. The language of Petrarchan love poetry implied an absolute gulf between

---

[17] On the Petrarchan cult of Elizabeth see Leonard Forster, *The Icy Fire: Five Studies in European Petrarchism* (Cambridge, 1969), 122–47.

[18] *The Poems of George Chapman*, ed. Phyllis Brooks Bartlett (New York, 1941), 33.

virtuous mistress and humble suitor, a state of complete subjection. Elizabeth's cult of courtly love actualized a metaphor that was always latent in monarchical systems of government: relations between individual and authority were not those of citizen and state but those of a subject, a dependent, to a single individual whose favour had to be 'courted'. As the French radical Étienne de La Boétie put it, 'it is hard to believe that there is anything of common wealth in a country where everything belongs to one master'; in Sidney's Arcadia '[p]ublic matters had ever been privately governed'.[19] Momentous decisions could hinge on which courtier happened to be in or out of favour, sometimes for apparently arbitrary reasons.

Spenser explores the relationship between courtier and sovereign in the story of Timias and Belphoebe. And he points out in the preface that the figure of Timias alludes to Sir Walter Ralegh, whose relationship with the queen did indeed exemplify in a particularly pure form the utter dependency of courtly client on the royal patron. Spenser places much emphasis on Timias' lowly status as a squire because Ralegh, unlike the great noblemen who are sometimes 'shadowed' in *The Faerie Queene*, was of relatively humble origins and owed his privileged status at court solely to the queen's favour. Ralegh's vulnerability was dramatically illustrated after Part I of *The Faerie Queene* had been published: in 1592 he incurred the queen's disfavour for marrying one of her waiting-women and was thrown into the Tower. Ralegh voiced his discontent in a long poem, 'The Ocean to Cynthia'; he vented his long-suppressed frustration at having to abase himself before a woman whose judgement he considered often inferior to his own:

> Yet will shee bee a wooman for a fashion . . .
> So hath perfection, which begatt her minde,
> Added therto a change of fantasye
> And left her the affections of her kynde.[20]

Ralegh was an advocate of an interventionist foreign policy and was frequently impatient at what he considered to be the queen's vacillation, her reluctance to follow the advice of men of action: 'her majesty', he later complained, 'did all by halves.' He protested at the arbitrary way favour was distributed at court: her favourites were an 'ellect', chosen by processes as inscrutable as the Calvinist Deity's election of redeemed souls.[21]

Spenser could not, of course, voice his friend's criticisms in a poem for public consumption, but in Book IV, published in 1596, he hinted delicately at the incident. Belphoebe grows jealous when she sees Timias apparently embracing Amoret but Arthur eventually effects a reconciliation. There is no direct criticism of Belphoebe. But the episode, coming in the book of Friendship, does illustrate the difficulty of establishing a secure relationship where the balance of power is enormously unequal. La Boétie argued that a tyrant (a term which for him included all absolute rulers)

---

[19] Étienne de La Boétie, *Anti-Dictator: The* Discours sur la servitude volontaire *of Étienne de La Boétie*, trans. Harry Kurtz (New York, 1942), 4; Sidney, *Old Arcadia*, 320.

[20] *The Poems of Sir Walter Ralegh*, ed. Agnes M. C. Latham (London, 1951), 32.

[21] Ralegh, *Works*, 8 vols. (Oxford, 1839), viii.246; *Poems*, 37.

'finds himself already beyond the pale of friendship, which receives its real suste-
nance from . . . equality'.[22]

At several points in *The Faerie Queene* the gulf between virgin ruler and humble
subject is viewed with a certain amount of fear or resentment. Spenser's Diana,
Belphoebe's prototype, takes on some of the attributes of the cruel Diana of early
Elizabethan entertainments when the queen was still being urged to marry. There is
a passing reference (IV.vii.30) to Diana's cruel punishment of Niobe (already cited by
Spenser in *The Shepheardes Calender*). In the *Mutabilitie Cantos* Diana seems to over-
react to the voyeuristic Actaeon's intrusion by defacing the landscape and turning it
into a wilderness. The Diana–Actaeon myth was regularly taken by Renaissance
mythographers to symbolize the dire fate of subjects who pry into mysteries of state.
The queen's punishment of slanderous poets is more directly represented at V.ix.25
in the image of Malfont with his tongue nailed to a post. For Spenser, as for Gabriel
Harvey, the monarch is a remote figure, capable of sudden and apparently arbitrary
assertions of authority which arouse resentment—but also ecstatic, self-abasing
devotion. At other times Spenser treats Belphoebe or Diana with a certain irreverent
humour. In her first encounter with Braggadochio (II.iii) Belphoebe is put in a rather
unseemly position, and it has been suggested that this is another episode composed
at an early period of composition, before Spenser's virgin goddesses became such
ideal figures.[23]

The most highly developed image of the synthesis of Diana and Venus is
Britomart, who is both a chaste warrior and a woman destined to bear children. Like
many Elizabethan writers, Spenser enjoys portraying an active woman who can take
the initiative and who in fact displays more competence than the male characters
around her. On one level this Amazonian figure is an image of Queen Elizabeth; but
Spenser did not draw attention to the analogy in the 'Letter to Ralegh', perhaps
because of the marked differences. Britomart is in love and wants to marry. Her
chastity is not the self-contained virtue of Belphoebe but a quality compatible with
Amoret's married state. Though Britomart's marriage to Arthegall is to produce the
Tudor line, her decision to get married contrasts strikingly with Elizabeth's firm virginity. Admittedly, Elizabeth was regarded as being married to the realm, but
Britomart's courtship is decidedly less abstract. It is noteworthy that the person
Britomart falls in love with is Arthegall, the 'Salvage Knight', who in Book V represents a militant Protestant foreign policy. The narrative of Book V shows how female
qualities can temper male violence; but it is made clear that Britomart's feminine
virtues must ultimately be complemented by and subordinated to the traditional
male qualities. In the legal allegory the female characters are associated with equity,
the men with the rigours of the law. In the Temple of Isis the goddess of equity is represented subduing the grotesque crocodile which images male violence. But in the
end the male principle triumphs. Britomart herself condemns Arthegall for his
'vnmanly maske' when, yielding to sentimental pity, he allows the aggressive virago
Radigund to conquer him and dress him in woman's clothes. Britomart overthrows

[22] La Boétie, *Anti-Dictator*, 51.   [23] Bennett, *The Evolution of* The Faerie Queene, 49–50.

Radigund's commonwealth of separatist feminists and restores male rule; and she is prepared in the end to subordinate herself to Arthegall. Similarly, another image of female equity, Mercilla, exemplifies the need to temper the rigours of the law but in the end she accords with the harsh advice of her male counsellors. The allegory of law and equity in Book V would seem also to indicate Spenser's view that female rulers can only be a divinely ordained exception rather than a general principle.[24]

Spenser's praise of Elizabeth, then, is not unqualified and confronts some of the problems raised by woman rulers. And his panegyric of the leading monarchical figure, Gloriana, is placed in perspective in Book I. The Redcross Knight, when he sees the New Jerusalem, becomes aware that heavenly glory is infinitely more important than the secular order. The hermit gives an answer that is more in the spirit of Renaissance humanism than of medieval monasticism; he argues that the active life is extremely important and that the knight should continue to serve Gloriana. But this is because her cause is a godly one: the knight must, like Leicester, seek not just 'good fame' but also 'godlie fame'.[25] Book I serves as a kind of extended prologue to the whole poem, setting secular values in a wider context; and it is becoming increasingly clear that the book owes an important debt to the Protestant prophetic tradition. Revelation is a generic model for Book I.[26] In the House of Holiness Fidelia presents the Redcross Knight with a book, warning him that it can be properly understood only by faith: this seems to be Revelation. The central plot structure of Book I is clearly indebted to the themes of apocalyptic church history. The Redcross Knight is faced with a choice between two women, the simple and innocent Una and the seductive and corrupt Duessa. The choice between the Invisible Church and the corrupt Visible Church had been presented in similar terms in Bale's *Image of Both Churches*, and he and Foxe had developed this imagery in their plays and in Foxe's preface to the *Acts and Monuments*. Both Bale and Foxe had adapted the structure of the morality play to express their apocalyptic ideas. In *King John* Bale shows how the monarch is deceived by the Papacy into betraying the wandering widow England just as the Redcross Knight is led astray by Duessa and Archimago and abandons Una. Foxe's 'apocalyptic comedy' *Christus triumphans* has a similar structure, with the representatives of the Papacy, Pseudamnus and Pornapolis, corresponding to Spenser's Archimago and Duessa. In the basic structure of the young hero's straying into temptation and eventually following good counsel and returning to the fold Spenser,

[24] James E. Phillips, Jr., 'The Woman Ruler in Spenser's *Faerie Queene*', *Huntington Library Quarterly*, 5 (1941–2), 211–34. See also Thomas Roche, Jr., *The Kindly Flame: A Study of the Third and Fourth Books of Spenser's* Faerie Queene (Princeton, 1964), 114–16.
[25] One Elizabethan annotator, John Dixon, identified the Redcross Knight with Leicester: *The First Commentary on* The Faerie Queene, ed. Graham Hough (Chichester, 1964), 2, note to I.i.2.
[26] The pioneering study by John E. Hankins, 'Spenser and the Revelation of St John', *Publications of the Modern Language Association of America*, 60 (1945), 364–81, has been developed by Frank Kermode, 'Spenser and the Allegorists' and '*The Faerie Queene*, I and V', in *Shakespeare, Spenser, Donne* (London, 1971), 12–59, and by Joseph A. Wittreich, *Visionary Poetics* (San Marino, Calif., 1979), 54–78. In his desire to show the differences between Spenser and Milton, Wittreich arguably exaggerates the former's conservatism. See further John N. King, *Spenser's Poetry and the Reformation Tradition* (Princeton, 1990).

like Bale, is Protestantizing popular drama—St George and the dragon were regular characters in mummers' plays.

Book I is less courtly in tone than the later books. Spenser constantly emphasizes Una's simplicity: she is more sober and simply dressed than Venus or Diana. The book's values are essentially dualistic: virtue is humble, and is characteristically to be found wandering far from palaces—the word 'wandering' is constantly repeated, emphasizing Una's status as woman wandering in the wilderness. This image of virtue as a female figure in the wilderness of the world was especially popular with Puritans and was to be taken up by Milton in *Comus*. The poetic force of Book I comes from Spenser's vivid presentation of the recurrent temptations of idolatry, which is closely associated here as in Book II with female sexuality and with courtly splendour and magnificence. However enthusiastically Spenser may hymn female virtue, throughout the poem there is an undercurrent of fear of women. There was a pronounced anti-female element in much Protestant propaganda: the evil of Roman idolatry was symbolized by the figure of the Whore of Babylon, and the imagery and ornamentation of the churches, which, in the Protestant view, tempted the faithful to lapse into idolatry, were compared to lascivious women using cosmetics to seduce upright men. Idolatry was described as 'spiritual fornication'; Calvinist rationalism tended to equate the irrational with what were seen as the feminine elements in the personality. Fear of idolatry and fear of women were closely associated for Fulke Greville:

> Mans superstition hath thy truths entomb'd,
> His Atheisme againe her pomps defaceth,
> That sensuall vnsatiable vaste wombe
> Of thy seene Church, thy vnseene Church disgraceth[.][27]

The control of sexuality is an essential precondition of religious reformation, just as it is the necessary basis for political civility: Duessa must be unveiled, the Bower of Bliss completely destroyed.[28] Una, the embodiment of religious purity, is relatively sexless. She finally triumphs at a feast which seems 'but bare and plaine', far from the 'proud luxurious pompe' of the modern world (I.xii.14).

Her fiancé, the Redcross Knight, is said to spring from the blood of kings, but he has been brought up by a ploughman—a word redolent with literary associations in the sixteenth century—and Spenser establishes the etymological link between the name George and the land. Redcross compares himself to a pilgrim (I.x.64–6). The 'Letter to Ralegh' presents him as a 'clownishe younge man' characterized by humble 'rusticity'. Thus Spenser links his hero with the prophetic tradition of *The Plowman's Tale* and *The Pilgrim's Tale*. At the corresponding point in Book VI, which is carefully balanced structurally with Book I, Spenser introduces himself in

---

[27] Greville, 'Caelica', no. 109, in *Poems and Dramas of Fulke Greville First Lord Brooke*, ed. Geoffrey Bullough, 2 vols. (Edinburgh, 1939), i. 153 ll. 13–16.
[28] Stephen Greenblatt, 'To Fashion a Gentleman: Spenser and the Destruction of the Bower of Bliss', in *Renaissance Self-Fashioning from More to Shakespeare* (Chicago, 1980), 157–92 (170–4, 188–91).

his humble persona of Colin Clout. Beneath Spenser's iambic metre there can still be heard the harsher beat of the old alliterative satires.[29]

By the end of the book Una's wanderings seem to be over and she has been betrothed to the Redcross Knight. As one Elizabethan annotator of the poem realized, this event signified, on one level, the accession of Queen Elizabeth, who claimed that she considered herself married to her realm.[30] Spenser probably knew of the pageants which greeted Elizabeth's entry to London in 1559, of which his schoolmaster Mulcaster had written a description; at one point the figure of Protestant Truth had presented the queen with a Bible. Her personal motto was 'semper eadem' so that it was appropriate to praise her for her unity and singleness: Gabriel Harvey and Thomas Drant had already praised her as Una.[31] But it would be wrong to press the identification of Una in Book I with Elizabeth too far. The attempts of an older school of critics to identify every event in Book I with the fortunes of the Tudor dynasty have been rightly rejected in more recent criticism; it is clear that no one level of interpretation will account for all the facts. On the other hand, to reject a political level completely would be to ignore the whole impetus of Protestant hermeneutics in Spenser's age. Commentaries on Revelation were urgently concerned to link general spiritual qualities with their institutional embodiments. The tendency in exegesis was towards increasing particularity: as the world neared its end, the correspondences between John's prophecies and the facts of history became clearer and clearer. But commentators like Bale did make a distinction between the roles described in Revelation and the individuals or institutions that came to embody them: as the Roman church became corrupt, so it began to assume the role of Antichrist. Protestant panegyrists hailed one ruler after another as the Emperor of the Last Days who would lead the decisive battle against Antichrist; but there was always a provisional element in such identifications, and if one ruler failed to live up to his promise, the apocalyptic hopes would soon be transferred to another. What was certain was that one day the role would be filled. Any identification between Elizabeth and the woman clothed with the sun must similarly be tentative and provisional: indeed, the author of one pamphlet who pushed the identification further than usual did so in a very cautious manner, as if afraid of being accused of blasphemy.[32] Foxe and the other

---

[29]   Spenser, *Works*, i.169. Cf. Judith H. Anderson, *The Growth of a Personal Voice:* Piers Plowman *and* The Faerie Queene (New Haven, 1976). Anderson does not discuss politics.

[30]   *The First Commentary on* The Faerie Queene, ed. Hough, 11 (note to I.xii.40), 9 (headnote to I.xii).

[31]   C. Bowie Millican, 'Spenser's and Drant's Poetic Names for Elizabeth: Tanaquil, Gloria, and Una', *Huntington Library Quarterly*, 2 (1938–9), 251–63; Yates, *Astraea*, 65. Cain, *Praise in* The Faerie Queene, 58–83, equates Una with Elizabeth in all the major epiphanies of the book.

[32]   E. Hellwis, *A Maruell Deciphered* (London, 1589), 5, noted by Richard Bauckham, *Tudor Apocalypse: Sixteenth Century Apocalypticism, Millenarianism and the English Reformation: From John Bale to John Foxe and Thomas Brightman* (Abingdon, 1978), 128–9, 179–80. Bauckham and other scholars have shown that Yates exaggerated Foxe's enthusiasm for Elizabeth (cf. *Astraea*, 42–50, 69–72). But Bauckham does show that one apocalyptic treatise, James Sandford's translation of a commentary on Revelation by Giacomo Brocardo (1582), associates Elizabeth very strongly with apocalyptic hopes; Sandford had links with Leicester so that Spenser could have known of this work. But Brocardo was a pre-millennialist, hoping for a future redeemed state on earth, a belief which conservatives considered politically subversive (Bauckham, *Tudor Apocalypse*, 218–21).

gospellers had greeted Elizabeth's accession with high apocalyptic hopes, but Crowley and Foxe had since become somewhat disillusioned. Foxe's concerns had always been internationalist rather than narrowly nationalistic, despite his modern reputation as the celebrator of the 'elect nation', and his last work had been a commentary on Revelation which did not include extensive panegyrics of Elizabeth.[33]

Foxe's allegorical drama *Christus triumphans* provides an interesting analogue for Book I of *The Faerie Queene*. Though Foxe's play contains some local allusions—one scene is set in Oxford—the overall framework is much wider in scope. Foxe takes the story of the Invisible Church from the days of Adam and Eve to the approach of the apocalypse, and he deals with the fortunes of the faithful in Africa and Asia as well as Europe. Book I, while rather more local and dynastic in emphasis, retains a similarly broad scope. Una's encounter with the satyrs (I.vi) may allude to the survival of the true faith amongst ignorant but pious outsiders like the Waldensians—a theme dear to Protestant writers.[34] Una's parents are Adam and Eve: like Foxe, Spenser goes back to the beginning of time. The betrothal ceremony is a simple ritual performed without a priest, symbolizing the purity of prelapsarian religion before it was corrupted by priestly hierarchies.[35] The allegory looks back to the beginning of time and forward to its end. The Redcross Knight's final defeat of the dragon is described in densely apocalyptic imagery which adumbrates the final defeat of Antichrist. The celebrations for the betrothal of Una and the Redcross Knight draw heavily on the epithalamic imagery of the Song of Solomon, which was popular with apocalyptic writers because it was held to prophesy the final union of Christ with his church. *Christus triumphans* ends with Ecclesia dressing herself in her bridal garments ready for the approach of her heavenly husband. Spenser's Una is also left waiting at the end of Book I. She is waiting for the return of Redcross, who must go off for six years to serve Gloriana. On the historical level this probably refers to the six years of Mary's reign which had to elapse before the true faith finally triumphed under Elizabeth. But the fact that Spenser defers the description of Una's marriage, and presents her as waiting for a future event, throws the emphasis on the persistent difficulty of making the truth prevail rather than on the fact that it has triumphed under Elizabeth.[36]

It has sometimes been argued that Book I adopts an essentially conservative theological position, defending a traditionalist 'Christian humanism' against Calvinism. Spenser's poem glorifies the active life and explicitly refers to 'free will' (I.x.19); Calvinist predestinarianism, it is alleged, would have undermined any commitment

---

[33] For a full discussion see V. N. Olsen, *John Foxe and the Elizabethan Church* (Berkeley and Los Angeles, 1973), 40 ff.

[34] Kermode, '*The Faerie Queene*, I and V', 48.

[35] James McAuley, 'The Form of Una's Marriage Ceremony in "The Faerie Queene"', *Notes and Queries*, 219 (1974), 410–11. The ceremony is a betrothal rather than a marriage.

[36] Most of Dixon's annotations to I.xi–xii are generally apocalyptic rather than specifically referring to Elizabeth: 'Una . . . or wyffe of y⁰ Lambe of god' (I.xii.7); Dixon identifies Redcross, for whom Una must wait, with 'Christe ye bridgrome of [God's] Church re: 19:7'. One Puritan annotator indignantly rejected Spenser's allegory as Papist: see Stephen Orgel, 'Margins of Truth', in Andrew Murphy (ed.), *The Renaissance Text: Theory, Editing, Textuality* (Manchester, 2000), 91–107 (99–107).

to political activism.[37] But the political rhetoric of Book I is the defence of reformed Christianity against idolatry rather than a defence of medieval Christendom against zealous Protestants. The Elizabethan church was not yet torn by the controversies between Calvinists and Arminians that were to cause its collapse a generation later. The Lambeth Articles of 1595 reaffirmed the hierarchy's commitment to fundamentally Calvinist positions. It is true that there were dissenting views; the queen herself was no Calvinist, and Spenser may, like Harvey, have been influenced by the revisionist theologian Peter Baro who rejected Calvinist predestinarianism. But whatever private reservations Spenser may have had, it would have been wise to maintain at least a strategic ambiguity, an openness to Calvinist interpretations, in a public poem. Calvinist readers in the seventeenth century, such as Phineas Fletcher, seem to have read the poem as defending their beliefs rather than conducting a frontal assault on them. The idea that Calvinist beliefs, particularly as modified by apocalyptic currents of thought, produced a state of paralytic inaction scarcely fits the facts of sixteenth-century history: it was precisely the political activism of the German and Dutch Calvinists that made them suspect to conservatives in the English hierarchy. Since the Council of Trent had made a belief in free will a characteristic of orthodox doctrine, the more militant Protestants were the more eager to go to the opposite extreme and to accuse those who fudged the issue of strengthening the Papist cause. In the Netherlands the Calvinist party accused the more tolerant Erasmians of lack of zeal in the struggle; and when he went to the Netherlands Leicester firmly backed the Calvinists. Like Leicester, Spenser believed that the fortunes of English Protestantism were inextricably bound up with those of Continental reformed churches, and when he took up the story of Elizabeth's reign in Book V he allegorized Leicester's Calvinist expedition as a triumph of Protestant honour. To understand how Spenser's political ideals were translated into concrete terms it is necessary to take a closer look at the topical allegory of Book V.

Of course, this book is not exclusively concerned with topical issues, and it has become unfashionable to pay close attention to Spenser's political allegory. Before turning to directly historical topics it is necessary to consider some other issues. The greater part of Book V deals with general legal theory (a topic in which, incidentally, Harvey and other followers of Leicester took a great interest). Arthegall's quest is to restore her rightful lands to Irene; this is a topical reference to Ireland but also, perhaps, a more general legal allusion. The French absolutist philosopher Bodin used the term *eirene* to describe the highest kind of justice, a fusion of democratic 'arithmetical proportion' and aristocratic 'geometrical proportion' to produce a 'harmonical proportion'. The monarchy embodied this principle of justice because it

---

[37] See Virgil K. Whitaker, *The Religious Basis of Spenser's Thought* (Stanford, Calif., 1950). Wells, *Spenser's* Faerie Queene *and the Cult of Elizabeth*, 34–47. But see King, *Spenser's Poetry and the Reformation Tradition*, 58–65, for the House of Holiness as revising Catholic imagery and stressing the primacy of Faith. King however recognizes that Spenser's imagery is open to differing religious interpretations, as does Darryl J. Gless, *Interpretation and Theology in Spenser* (Cambridge, 1994). Carol V. Kaske, *Spenser and Biblical Poetics* (Ithaca, 1999), relating the poem to Biblical hermeneutics in Spenser's Cambridge, argues that after deliberately confounding clear-cut interpretative responses the poem finally tends towards a religious conservatism—or defence of indeterminacy—close to Elizabeth's.

mediated between the interests of aristocracy and people. This 'harmonical proportion' was, in Bodin's view, the secret of the construction of the whole universe: Form
and Matter could only be held together by this mediating principle. The cosmos represented a combination of arithmetical proportion (the regular movement of the
spheres) and geometrical proportion (the irregular movement of the planets).[38] In
Book V Spenser shows how the monarch can embody in her person a transcendent
fusion of Law and Equity.[39] If his poem itself is seen as a kind of cosmos structured
on numerological principles, it can be said to embody the principles of monarchical
order in its form.

A further caution against exclusively topical interpretations of Book V is provided
by the 'Letter to Ralegh', in which Spenser emphasized that he was not directly concerned in his poem with topical issues, other than general praise of the queen: he was
dealing with private virtues, with Arthur's education before he became a king.
Spenser claimed that when he had completed the present poem he would embark on
a second twelve-book epic celebrating Arthur's public virtues and, through them,
the victories of Elizabeth's troops. A similar claim is made before Redcross's struggle with the dragon (i.xi.7). By refraining in *The Faerie Queene* from direct descriptions of warfare, by concentrating on inner rather than external conflict, Spenser was
better able to maintain his complimentary structure. As a woman Elizabeth could not
lead troops in battle, and she disliked spending her meagre resources on expensive
campaigns; she also disliked delegating too much authority to commanders whose
reliability she doubted. By concentrating on private rather than public virtues
Spenser was able to blur traditional distinctions between masculine and feminine
spheres of influence. The sun was conventionally associated with the active life and
with males, the moon with the contemplative life and with females; Spenser at various points associates Gloriana, Britomart, and Una, all of whom represent aspects of
the queen's public person, with the sun, while Belphoebe is of course a lunar figure.

Spenser's general preference for describing internal conflict rather than deeds of
arms places him in a humanistic tradition that goes back to More and Erasmus and
looks forward to Milton's attack on

> Wars, hitherto the only argument
> Heroic deemed[.][40]

But in the later sixteenth century many humanists considered vigilance against the
Habsburgs to be an essential condition for the defence of their values; moral virtue

---

[38] Jean Bodin, *The Six Bookes of a Common Weale*, trans. Richard Knolles (London, 1606), 755 ff.,
792–4. On the influence of Bodin on Book V see H. S. V. Jones, 'Spenser's Defence of Lord Grey',
University of Illinois Studies in Language and Literature, 5 (1919), 50 ff., and on Spenser's number symbolism, Jerry Leath Mills, 'Spenser and the Numbers of History: A Note on the British and Elfin Chronicles
in *The Faerie Queene*', *Philological Quarterly*, 55 (1976), 281–7.

[39] Many accounts of the structure of Book V have been given, none of them quite consistent with the
others: see, e.g., James E. Phillips, Jr., 'Renaissance Concepts of Justice and the Structure of *The Faerie
Queene*, Book V', *Huntington Library Quarterly*, 33 (1969–70), 103–20; cf. Horton, *The Unity of 'The
Faerie Queene*', 124–37.

[40] *Paradise Lost*, ix.28–9, in *The Poems of John Milton*, ed. John Carey and Alastair Fowler (London,
1968).

in the abstract had to be seen in its political context. There is a general movement in *The Faerie Queene* from private to public virtues which culminates in Books V and VI. Whatever the general concerns of Book V, its central quest, Arthegall's mission to free Irene, has clear topical meanings. Spenser's discussion of justice is not blandly general but raises some sensitive topical issues. In his manual for aspiring court poets George Puttenham told the story of a 'great clerk' who

presented king *Antiochus* with a booke treating all of iustice, the king that time lying at the siege of a towne, who lookt vpon the title of the booke, and cast it to him againe: saying, what a diuell tellest thou to me of iustice, now thou seest me vse force and do the best I can to bereeue mine enimie of his towne?[41]

Puttenham obligingly shifted his printed opinions on the Dutch war to accord with a change in government policy. But Spenser draws attention in Book V to some extremely controversial episodes at home and abroad. Spenser's public image in the 1590s was of a poet sympathetic to the cause of the Earl of Essex, an increasingly controversial figure who eventually rebelled against the queen. Already by the early seventeenth century, admirers of Essex were propagating the myth of Spenser not as a court panegyrist but as an exile from court, championed in his poverty by Essex alone. Milton inherited this view of Spenser, which helps to explain why he could find this monarchist poet such an inspiring example.

The attitude of the Leicester and Essex circles to the issues Spenser allegorizes in Book V can be illustrated by the discussion of foreign affairs in Fulke Greville's *Life of Sidney*. This work was written after Elizabeth's death and no doubt hindsight distorted Greville's view of the way Sidney had thought; but his book does give us an idea of the opinions Spenser would have heard aired at Leicester House or Essex House. Greville admired Sidney for his political imagination: where more timid ministers limited their horizons to local issues, Sidney could see that English politics needed to take account of the whole European scene and that vigilant action abroad as well as at home was necessary to ensure the triumph of religious reform. Much of Europe seemed to Greville to be sunk in political lethargy, with only two vital, dynamic forces. At one extreme there was Spain, which together with its Austrian allies was seeking the domination of Europe. The vitality of the Habsburg powers was almost paradoxical, a sign of satanic aid, for Spain was an absolute monarchy and Greville saw tyranny as essentially a stultifying, enervating force, robbing the people of the energy they showed under a parliamentary monarchy where traditional liberties were preserved. But at the moment the Habsburg tyranny seemed to be triumphing throughout Europe: Italy and Germany, fractured into petty princedoms, had been slowly infiltrated into this 'passive bondage' and the princes, having enslaved their people, in turn became the puppets of the Spanish or Austrians. In France there was a danger of a similar process unless vigorous aid to anti-Spanish forces encouraged them to 'shake off a chargeable and servile yoke of mountebank

---

[41] George Puttenham, *The Arte of English Poesie*, ed. Gladys D. Willcock and Alice Walker (Cambridge, 1936), 267.

holiness'. The only large state which had not been gripped by the 'fatal passiveness' of absolutism was the Netherlands, which gained its vigour from liberty, Protestant religion, and also from the 'true philosophers' stone of traffic' which turns base metal into gold and makes wars profitable.[42] Throughout the *Life of Sidney*, Greville associates commodity exchange with vigour, the antithesis of absolutist stagnation; France allows its natural riches to lie 'barren' at home whereas the Netherlands possess the 'mysteries' that 'multiply native wealth'.[43] Like many later observers, Greville thus established a link between Protestantism and capitalism. Greville was no democrat, but there was a tension between his social conservatism and his admiration of Dutch industry and efficiency. The struggle between the reactionary tyranny of the Counter-Reformation and the vitality promoted by religious reform was an epochal conflict in which England must take sides.

The pattern underlying Greville's view of foreign policy was in the end apocalyptic: England must ally with the reformed nations to defeat Antichrist. But Greville, like other supporters of Leicester and Essex, was aware of the complexities of the political scene and was not advocating a simple crusade of Protestants against all Catholics. He praised Elizabeth for taking the wise course of defensive wars, constant pinpricks which prevented the Habsburg powers from building up their military resources and at the same time encouraged the forces for liberty and religious reform in the countries aided. Rather than alienating all Catholics it was essential to seek support from the many liberal Catholics who disliked the authoritarianism of the Counter-Reformation. Even after Henry IV became a Catholic, Essex continued to urge Elizabeth to support him because he was a strong opponent of the Habsburg powers; Spenser stressed the importance of continued support for the French in the 'Burbon' episode (v.xi.44–5), which may have been revised at the last minute to support Essex's campaign for an alliance with France in 1596.[44] The Essex circle's interest in Venice reflected their hope that the Venetians, who also disliked the influence of the Jesuits and the Spaniards, might eventually become Protestants and thus start to swing the balance of power in Italy. Essex also hoped that English Catholics could be persuaded to overcome their sense of allegiance to Rome. In 1596 Anthony Copley, a Catholic loyal to the queen, published a parody of Book I of *The Faerie Queene* in which he expressed English Catholics' loyalty to their monarch.[45] Greville praised Elizabeth's wars as 'victorious, enriching and ballancing': the queen was not pursuing warfare for its own sake but shrewdly judging the best way at a particular

[42] Greville, *A Dedication to Sir Philip Sidney*, in *The Prose Works of Fulke Greville, Lord Brooke*, ed. John Gouws (Oxford, 1986), 48–53, 57–8, 85.

[43] Ibid. 34; for this analysis of the opposing blocs in Europe cf. J. V. Polišensky, *The Thirty Years' War*, trans. Robert Evans (London, 1971), chs. 1–2.

[44] Bennett, *The Evolution of 'The Faerie Queene'*, 201–5.

[45] Anthony Copley, *A Fig for Fortune* (London, 1596); Henry Constable, a poet in the Sidney circle, tried to keep open links between French Catholics and the English court after his conversion (see my D.Phil. thesis, 'Panegyric of the Monarch and its Social Context under Elizabeth I and James I' (Oxford, 1978), hereafter 'PM', 98–9). On analogies between the Eliza cult and liberal Catholic monarchism in France see Yates, *Astraea*, 80–7. But Protestants who tried to court liberal Catholic support were not necessarily aiming at a bland synthesis between the two faiths: such alliances could be seen as tactical, as steps towards the eventual bringing of enlightened Papists into the fold.

moment of advancing her cause, whether by diplomacy or by a carefully planned and limited military intervention.[46] But the long-term aim was not just a static balance of power but a decisive forward movement, a diminution of the power of the forces of Antichrist. It is just such a complex synthesis of peace and war that Spenser represents in the figure of Britomart, who has attributes of the peaceful deity Pallas but also of the aggressive Mars; her name indicates that the arts of war are as important as the arts of peace. Arthegall's long-term aim is Irene, peace; but it is a peace that can only result from a complete reformation of religion and politics and must therefore be prepared for by vigorous action. Britomart must marry the militant Arthegall.

When writing the *Life of Sidney* Greville was preoccupied with the evils of James's pacific foreign policy; in retrospect he celebrated Elizabeth as a militant 'she-David'.[47] In her lifetime, however, he may have been slightly less enthusiastic. Many members of the Essex circle would have echoed Ralegh's comment that the queen did things 'by halves', that she did not follow through the necessary policies vigorously enough. Sidney had long been impatient at what seemed to be her unnecessary vacillations. It is true that by the late 1580s she had been forced into war, and in 1588 the Spanish Armada had been scattered. But this victory was not seen at the time as the decisive turning point it seems in retrospect: the English had had more than their share of luck, and as the Armada was preparing to sail Elizabeth had been trying to negotiate peace with the Spanish: she was anxious to curtail expensive military expeditions. Spenser allegorizes the defeat of the Armada in the episode of the Souldan (v.viii.28–44), but he does not place it at a decisive turning point in the action. Essex and his circle continued to feel that they had to fight an uphill battle to keep the English war effort at its most effective. Sidney had effectively declared Essex his military heir by bequeathing him his sword, and Essex sealed the association by marrying Sidney's widow. Like Sidney, he played a prominent role in Accession Day tilts, constantly emphasizing the need for Protestant militancy. But in the 1590s court pageantry became increasingly the scene of political rivalry, with Essex's supporters satirizing their great rival Sir Robert Cecil. They believed that Cecil was frustrating Essex's military efforts by failing to ensure that he was properly supplied, and even that he was intriguing for a Spanish succession. The patronage system in the 1590s became increasingly polarized, and eventually Essex and a handful of his supporters, believing that they had been unjustly excluded from political influence, attempted a *coup d'état*.[48]

---

[46] Greville, *A Dedication to Sir Philip Sidney*, 127. The caution which tempered Greville's apocalyptic world-view helps to explain why he patronized the more conservative historian Camden and drew on his writings: see Mark L. Caldwell, 'Sources and Analogues of *The Life of Sidney*', *Studies in Philology*, 74 (1977), 279–300.

[47] Greville, *A Dedication to Sir Philip Sidney*, 98.

[48] In this section I draw heavily on S. L. Adams, 'The Protestant Cause' (unpublished D.Phil. thesis, Oxford, 1973). In his more recent work Adams has expressed scepticism about the significance of faction: see Simon Adams, 'Favourites and Factions at the Elizabethan Court', in John Guy (ed.), *The Tudor Monarchy* (London, 1997), 253–74. I presented a fuller account of the public poetry of the period in 'PM', ch. 3, and fuller documentation of some points will be found there. For more recent discussions of Essex's role see Mervyn James, 'At a Crossroads of the Political Culture: The Essex Revolt, 1601', in *Society, Politics and Culture: Studies in Early Modern England* (Cambridge, 1986), 416–65, McCoy, *The Rites of*

Essex's rebellion was not a coherently planned political revolution, and historians have tended to emphasize its personal rather than ideological character: a group of malcontents were trying to grab more pickings from the court patronage system. But there had always been in Essex's circle an unusually high number of people with relatively radical political views. It is possible to trace intellectual, and indeed family, continuities from the Essex circle back to the mid-century and forward to the Jacobean 'opposition' and the republicans of the 1650s. Essex's advocacy of a militant foreign policy was doubtless influenced by the hopes of recovering his tottering financial fortunes by the spoils of war; but there were ideological factors behind the particular kind of campaigns he called for. He seems to have been influenced by the apocalyptic world-view that underlay Greville's vision of European politics: it was essential to aid Protestants throughout Europe, and Essex was anxious to seal political alliances, based on a common resistance to the Counter-Reformation powers, with the Huguenots and the Dutch. This would have involved England in expensive long-term commitments on the Continent; the queen, however, preferred to limit the war as far as possible, and to concentrate on naval raids which were economical and avoided compromising ideological commitments and alliances.

Essex's commitment to ideologically based campaigns placed him in some potentially embarrassing political company. His advocacy of the Huguenot cause put him at odds with conservatives like Bishop Richard Bancroft, a scourge of the Puritans, who complained that the French Protestants were rebelling against their anointed king and hence against the order of nature. Essex welcomed to England a Spanish exile, Antonio Pérez, who had participated in a rebellion against Philip II. Pérez wrote a justification of the rebellion, drawing on Roman republican ideas, which the government allowed to be published for circulation abroad but considered too politically sensitive to be translated into English. Another anti-Spanish work, possibly by Pérez, was published with a dedication to Fulke Greville and circulated in manuscript despite being suppressed.[49] Essex's interest in Venetian affairs also served to make him politically suspect: Bancroft complained in 1593 that 'the world now a dayes, is set all vpon liberty' and that travellers from Venice were extolling its republican constitution.[50] In 1599 a translation of Contarini's description of Venice, which Sir Philip Sidney had sought out during his journey to Italy, was published with poems of commendation by members of the Essex circle. Maurice Kyffin praised a system

> Where all corrupt means to aspire are curbd,
> And Officers for vertues worth elected.[51]

Knighthood, ch. 4, and Paul E. J. Hammer, *The Polarisation of Elizabethan Politics: The Political Career of Robert Devereux, 2nd Earl of Essex, 1585–1597* (Cambridge, 1999).

[49] See Gustav Ungerer, *A Spaniard in Elizabethan England: The Correspondence of Antonio Pérez's Exile*, 2 vols. (London, 1974–6), i.208 ff., Paul E. J. Hammer, 'The Earl of Essex, Fulke Greville, and the Employment of Scholars', *Studies in Philology*, 91 (1994), 167–80 (173).

[50] R. Bancroft, *A Survey of the Pretended Holy Discipline* (London, 1593), 7.

[51] M. Kyffin, commendatory poem to *The Commonwealth and Gouernment of Venice*, trans. Lewes Lewkenor (London, 1599). The volume was dedicated to the Countess of Warwick, Leicester's sister-in-

—conditions which, according to Essex's supporters, did not apply in England at the time. Cecil was accused of corrupting the system of political patronage by demanding massive bribes. The Venetian system was acclaimed by its admirers for the way it had overcome the problems of corruption. It was also admired for its political stability. The problem of transition of power in a hereditary monarchy when the line had died out was of course an urgent one in the 1590s. Some Puritans urged the queen to declare a successor, and *Gorboduc*, with its call for rulers to consult Parliament in determining the succession, was reprinted in 1590. But the queen insisted that the succession was a 'mystery of state' which subjects must not be allowed to discuss. In such a political context, some members of Essex's circle do seem to have been toying with republican ideas, or at least wishing that there were more constitutional constraints on the monarch.[52] Contarini's book was to become a favourite work of republican theorists in the seventeenth century.

Essex's support for an apocalyptic foreign policy made him popular with Protestant radicals, and here again his political connections did not endear him to conservatives. John Penry, who was accused of writing the 'Marprelate' tracts, appealed to Essex on his arrest, and there were rumours that the earl had written the pamphlets himself. Penry, being of low birth, made a convenient scapegoat and was executed (on a different charge), but the more likely author of the tracts was Job Throckmorton, a respectable member of the gentry.[53] His career illustrates the difficulty of making clear-cut distinctions between the loyalist members of the Leicester and Essex circles and subversive, extremist presbyterians. He had passionate views about foreign policy: he had been arrested after a bitter speech in the 1587 Parliament in which he warned that the Protestant cause in Europe was being betrayed and spoke so vehemently against the rulers who were persecuting the godly that he was held to have discredited monarchy.[54] 'Marprelate' displayed a similar concern for the unity of European Protestantism and offered to address his works in Latin to a Continental audience.[55] Leicester might not have approved of the vehemence of Throckmorton's language in Parliament but he would have endorsed his apocalyptic vision of foreign policy. But Leicester died in 1588 and several of his allies in

law. The commendatory poems seem to have been written some years before the book was published. Another contributor, Henry Helmes, had taken the leading role in a Gray's Inn masque of 1595, written by Pérez's friend—or lover—Francis Davison to plead Essex's loyalty to the queen (Ungerer, *A Spaniard in Elizabethan England*, i.194; Norbrook, 'PM', 106). Markku Peltonen, *Classical Humanism and Republicanism in English Political Thought 1570–1640* (Cambridge, 1995), 102–18, argues in detail that Lewkenor's translation was designed to draw attention to Venice's republican solutions to problems that beset England in the 1590s; Howard Erskine-Hill, *Poetry and the Realm of Politics: Shakespeare to Dryden* (Oxford, 1996), 115–26, discusses Spenser in relation to English interest in Italian republics; and Andrew Hadfield cites the sonnet on Contarini in posing the question 'Was Spenser a Republican?', *English*, 47 (1998), 169–82.

[52] On the debate of some fairly radical ideas in the drama of the 1590s, see Marie Axton, *The Queen's Two Bodies: Drama and the Elizabethan Succession* (London, 1977), 88 ff.

[53] See the full discussion by Leland H. Carlson, *Martin Marprelate, Gentleman: Master Job Throkmorton Laid Open in his Colors* (San Marino, Calif., 1981).

[54] J. E. Neale, *Elizabeth I and her Parliaments 1584–1601* (London, 1957), 169–73.

[55] *The Marprelate Tracts, 1588, 1589*, ed. William Pierce (London, 1911), 404.

'Leicester's Commonwealth' died soon afterwards, thus removing much of the protection radicals had previously enjoyed. It became much easier for John Whitgift,
who had succeeded Grindal as Archbishop of Canterbury in 1583, to carry through
his policy of cracking down on dissidents. In 1592 Sidney's old ally Philippe
Duplessis-Mornay visited England and expressed astonishment at the political climate he found there—why was the queen devoting so much energy to persecuting
Protestants when there was still great danger from the Catholic enemy? Essex lacked
the broad political base Leicester had enjoyed, which helps to explain why his political career was so unstable; and he prudently kept on good terms with Whitgift. But
he remained an especially popular figure with Puritans.

In the 1590s Spenser several times expressed his commitment to Essex as the heir
of the political traditions of Sidney and Leicester, even though this put him on controversial ground. In 'The Teares of the Muses' he lamented the loss to learning
caused by the deaths of so many members of Leicester's circle; it had equally been a
political loss. In 1591 his satire *Mother Hubberds Tale*, which contained spirited
attacks on Burghley and Cecil, was called in by the authorities. In 1593 George Peele
described Spenser as one of many victims of 'Courts disdaine, the enemie to Arte'.[56]
Peele was an Essex supporter who wrote poems and pageants glorifying Protestant
chivalry in a Spenserian manner. Spenser was not an exclusive partisan of Essex: he
was a close friend of Sir Walter Ralegh whom the earl and his Puritan friends
regarded as a wicked atheist.[57] But Ralegh did support a militant foreign policy; and
Spenser did not share Ralegh's friendship with Cecil, the earl's most consistent
adversary. In 1596 he publicly endorsed one of the earl's propaganda campaigns.
Essex was trying to persuade the queen to join a triple alliance with Henry IV and the
Dutch against the Spanish; he and his allies feared that Cecil's influence was preventing the queen from giving the anti-Habsburg forces enough support. The year
1596 was the queen's 'grand climacteric', her sixty-third year, and excited prophecies
of great political changes were circulating. Essex himself was attracting great
apocalyptic hopes: George Gifford, who had been a close friend of Sidney, published
in 1596 a commentary on Revelation with a dedication to Essex which envisaged the
earl as the rider on a white horse who was prophesied as winning great victories
against Antichrist.[58] Essex did take part in a successful naval expedition against
Cadiz; but, as his friends had feared, while he was away Cecil finally managed
to achieve the coveted and influential post of Secretary. And Essex was unable to
obtain the propaganda advantage he had expected from the expedition; the public

[56] New evidence that the *Complaints* volume of 1591 was indeed called in is given by Richard S.
Peterson, 'Laurel Crown and Ape's Tail: New Light on Spenser's Career from Sir Thomas Gresham',
Spenser Studies, 12 (1998), 1–35. George Peele, 'The Honour of the Garter', in *The Life and Minor Works
of George Peele*, ed. David H. Horne (New Haven, 1952), 247.

[57] Spenser may have shared Ralegh's interest in the occult and Hermeticist ideas of people like
Giordano Bruno: see Yates, *The Occult Philosophy in the Elizabethan Age*, 95–108. But note the qualifica-
tions to Yates's arguments given by Andrew D. Weiner, 'Expelling the Beast: Bruno's Adventures in
England', *Modern Philology*, 78 (1980–1), 1–13.

[58] Gifford's dedication is reprinted by Bauckham, *Tudor Apocalypse*, 353–8. On the context see further
Norbrook, 'PM', 107–10.

celebrations he had planned to sponsor in honour of his return were restricted by the queen's opposition. Fearing that the official account of the expedition would not give him enough prominence, Essex prepared a version of his own, with Fulke Greville's aid; but the account was suppressed. In this political context, Spenser's publication in the autumn of 1596 of his *Prothalamion* with its praise of the Cadiz expedition marked a clear declaration of political alignment—though Spenser's praise was tempered by a discreet note of warning against hubris.[59] About the same time Spenser composed a complimentary sonnet for the translation of Contarini. And Book V of *The Faerie Queene*, also published in 1596, amounted to a sustained defence of the Leicester–Essex foreign policy, looking back over the past ten or fifteen years and looking forward to possible future victories.

In the 'Letter to Ralegh' Spenser had declared that he set his poem in the days of King Arthur partly because his subject would then be 'furthest from the daunger of enuy, and suspition of [the] present time' (*Works*, i.167). But in Book V he allegorized political events which had aroused a great deal of envy and suspicion in the minds of the queen and her more conservative advisers. In the description of Mercilla's palace (v.ix.25–6) Spenser tells how the seditious poet Bonfont has had his tongue nailed to a post and been renamed Malfont. The grotesque image of censorship is too disturbing to reflect complete credit on the monarch; and the question of censorship was one that had much exercised the Leicester and Essex circles as they saw their own exploits described as evil rather than heroic by their opponents. The 'Belge' episode was recognized by a contemporary annotator to be an allegorization of Leicester's expedition to the Netherlands.[60] This had been a highly controversial episode. Soon after Book V was published, the queen's most trusted adviser, Burghley, commissioned an official history of the reign from William Camden and offered him access to state papers. Camden's view of the Dutch campaign was rather different from Spenser's. For Camden, as for many observers, Leicester's campaign had been a disaster caused by his overweening pride and military incompetence.[61] Camden's hostility to Leicester was sharpened by his general hostility to Puritanism and its sympathizers. Though Camden's history was not completed and published until the following reign, his views probably reflected those of Burghley and his son Robert Cecil, both of whom favoured a cautious and pacific foreign policy and disliked apocalyptic enthusiasm. The queen herself had been extremely reluctant to intervene in the Netherlands: the Dutch, she thought, had excessively radical religious views and they were subverting the order of nature by rebelling against their

[59] Alastair Fowler, *Conceitful Thought: The Interpretation of English Renaissance Poems* (Edinburgh, 1975), 82–3.
[60] Anon., 'MS Notes to Spenser's *Faerie Queene*', *Notes and Queries*, 202 (1957), 509–15 (512–13); A. Fowler, 'Oxford and London Marginalia to the *Faerie Queene*', *Notes and Queries*, 206 (1961), 416–19 (416–17).
[61] William Camden, *The History of the Most Renowned and Victorious Princess Elizabeth, Late Queen of England*, ed. Wallace T. MacCaffrey (Chicago, 1970), 214–19, 303–5. Burghley had refused permission to the poet Giles Fletcher to gain access to state papers for a history of Elizabeth's reign; Fletcher was a staunch supporter of a militant foreign policy, and his sons the 'Spenserian' poets Giles and Phineas inherited from him a fierce hostility to the *regnum Cecilianum*: *The English Works of Giles Fletcher the Elder*, ed. Lloyd E. Berry (Madison, 1964), 383, 44–6.

sovereign, and Elizabeth did not want to encourage her subjects to have too much contact with such people. Leicester and his allies had been urging since the 1570s that England should help the Dutch, but they met with hostility from conservatives like Whitgift, who argued that Elizabeth should not help the Dutch rebels because it would be unnatural for the head of one body politic to assist the feet of another.[62] Eventually the military situation became so desperate that the rebels' defeat seemed likely and in 1585 the queen was persuaded to intervene. Three days after she agreed to help the Dutch, Antwerp, the largest city in the Netherlands, fell to the Spanish. The terms in which Elizabeth justified her aid were strictly limited: she stressed the legal sanctions for such intervention and declared that she was motivated by the traditional friendship between the two peoples rather than by any religious ideology. She refused to accept a Dutch offer of sovereignty. Justification could be found even in the absolutist Bodin for certain limited interventions by a neighbouring monarch against a tyrant.[63] What was important for Elizabeth was to make it clear that she did not consider that the defence of the reformed religion could serve on its own as a valid justification for rebellion.

Leicester's campaign seemed to justify all the worst fears of his enemies. Elizabeth contemplated replacing Leicester by another commander when she found how many Puritans he had included on his strength. When he arrived in the Netherlands he sided with the militant Calvinist faction, and alienated the more tolerant and Erastian magistrates. His sense of mission was heightened by pageants which hailed him in apocalyptic terms as the nation's deliverer. In one of the pageants he was likened to King Arthur.[64] This glorification of a subject disturbed the queen. Descriptions of the Dutch pageants were excised from the 1587 edition of Holinshed's *Chronicles*—one of the first operations of new and more rigid censorship restrictions which Whitgift, taking advantage of Leicester's absence, had helped to push through.[65] The earl's campaign did not live up to his champions' hopes, and his campaign did not achieve its aims. His enemies blamed Leicester's vanity and incompetence.[66] But he and his supporters could justifiably have claimed that had the queen followed their advice much earlier Antwerp might never have been lost and the map of this part of Europe might have looked very different. Leicester was eventually allowed to set off only when the military situation was at its worst. Before he departed he voiced his fears that the queen's irresolution was demoralizing his expedition and that she would end up by making the Protestant cause look like a mere 'show' or 'scarecrow'. That is precisely what did happen.[67]

---

[62] Quoted by Adams, 'The Protestant Cause', 60.

[63] Quentin Skinner, *The Foundations of Modern Political Thought*, 2 vols. (Cambridge, 1978), ii.286.

[64] R. C. Strong and J. A. van Dorsten, *Leicester's Triumph* (Leiden, 1964), 47–8.

[65] Eleanor Rosenberg, *Leicester Patron of Letters* (New York, 1955), 94–5. Descriptions of the pageants did, however, appear in later editions of Stow's *Annals*. Cyndia Susan Clegg, *Press Censorship in Elizabethan England* (Cambridge, 1997), 159–61, suggests that the removal of these sections was a counter to some earlier excisions that favoured Leicester, thus revealing the ability of opposing factions to influence censorship rather than a uniform policy.

[66] Cf. the criticisms cited by Jan Albert Dop, *Eliza's Knights* (Alblasserdam, 1981). Gabriel Harvey criticized the Earl's tactics (above, Ch. 3 n. 50).

[67] Adams, 'The Protestant Cause', 48.

Spenser's handling of this controversial episode in *The Faerie Queene* clearly endorses the views of Leicester's supporters. He gives considerable prominence to the Dutch campaign, which Merlin prophesies at the climax of his genealogy of Elizabeth (III.iii.49):

> Then shall a royall virgin raine, which shall
> Stretch her white rod ouer the *Belgicke* shore,
> And the great Castle smite so sore with all,
> That it shall make him shake, and shortly learne to fall.

In Revelation 12:5 the woman clothed with the sun bears a child who will rule all nations with a rod of iron, and this child is often identified by the commentators with the Emperor Constantine in his role as true head of the church. In the pageant for Leicester at The Hague in 1587 Constantine was shown presiding over a battle between the English and Spanish troops.[68] Spenser's prophecy emphasizes the apocalyptic character of the conflict in the Netherlands. Merlin begins by emphasizing the peace and civility which the reign of the Tudors will bring; but the climax of his prophecy is a description of the Dutch war. In Book V Spenser allegorizes the Dutch campaign, using imagery that is strikingly similar to the pageants for Leicester. Spenser presents the Lady Belge as a widow whose second husband tyrannizes over her. The pageants at Haarlem had presented the Netherlands as a widow who appealed to the earl to restore her former felicity. The implication was that the widow's first husband had been a Duke of Burgundy and that the English ruler was to reassume the benevolent rule he had exercised.[69] Spenser diplomatically makes Arthur refuse the sovereignty as Elizabeth had done, but he goes on to make Arthur act in a way that Elizabeth might not have altogether approved. The widow in *The Faerie Queene* has five surviving sons, representing the free provinces. Five cherubs appear on a medal struck by the Dutch in 1587 to commemorate Leicester's mission; Leicester attends an enthroned Elizabeth who tramples the Beast of the Apocalypse under her feet. On the reverse, the Pope and his followers were shown falling to Hell. This medal, perhaps struck without the queen's approval, was unusual in depicting Elizabeth in an actively apocalyptic role, and placed more emphasis on the ideological character of the conflict than she normally thought desirable.[70] Spenser lays great stress on Arthur's apocalyptic role. Not only does he defeat Geryoneo and restore her dominion to the Lady Belge—an essentially legalistic account of the incident—but he also destroys the giant's idol, which is clearly identified with Catholic religious practices. The campaign is thus presented as a religious war rather than merely a limited secular alliance.[71] Arthur's destruction of the idol and its beast is parallel to Redcross's struggle against the apocalyptic dragon.

Leicester's campaign had, of course, ended very differently, with the military

---

[68] Strong and van Dorsten, *Leicester's Triumph*, 46–7.   [69] Ibid. 65.

[70] Bauckham, *Tudor Apocalypse*, 128–9; cf. Roy C. Strong, *Portraits of Queen Elizabeth I* (Oxford, 1963), 138 f.

[71] Douglas A. Northrop, 'Spenser's Defence of Elizabeth', *University of Toronto Quarterly*, 38 (1969), 227–94 (282).

situation still critical. The account of Arthur's expedition in Book V takes Leicester's mission as its starting point but is not restricted to one phase of what English Protestants saw as a long struggle. When Spenser published Book V, the war against the Spanish was going much better. But Antwerp remained unconquered, the Spanish were still fighting; the situation still did not justify Spenser's description of the decisive overthrow of Geryoneo. Clearly the Geryoneo episode is prophetic, looking forward to a victory that has not yet been fully accomplished. Geryoneo's castle is given such enormous significance that it can hardly represent a city less important than Antwerp: Arthur's victory means the end of Spanish domination and of Catholic worship in the Netherlands. And since the fall of Antwerp was often linked in Elizabethan writing with the fall of Jerusalem, its liberation has apocalyptic overtones.[72] In publishing Book V Spenser was endorsing Essex's campaign for further vigorous action in the Netherlands; to do so he risked making a prophecy which had not yet been fulfilled. Antwerp was never retaken. But by giving the Dutch campaign such prominence in a poem about Queen Elizabeth Spenser helped to strengthen the English conviction that the Dutch were their natural allies. The queen is said to have become worried in the last days of her reign that her subjects' close contacts with the Netherlands were infecting them with republican sympathies: they spoke of England as a 'state', a relatively new word in political discourse, rather than as a monarchy in which loyalty was owed to a personal ruler.[73] In the following reign, when James was cautiously trying to shift his subjects' attention from the Protestant Netherlands to Spain, English writers borrowed Spenser's terminology to stress their special admiration for the Netherlands. In his play *The Whore of Babylon* (*c.*1605), a dramatization of Elizabeth's reign which utilized Spenser's 'faerie' imagery, Thomas Dekker made a character praise the Dutch as

> the nation,
> With whome our Faries enterchange commerce,
> And by negotiation growne so like vs,
> That halfe of them are Fayries.[74]

Leicester had hurried back from the Netherlands in order to take part in the trial of Mary Stuart, an event which he and his supporters had long hoped for.[75] In her imprisonment Mary had continued to intrigue with foreign Catholics and the Puritans were convinced that her presence was a danger to the state; she represented

[72] S. M. Pratt, 'Antwerp and the Elizabethan Mind', *Modern Language Quarterly*, 24 (1963), 53–60. An Elizabethan annotator of *The Faerie Queene* (Anon., 'Ms Notes to Spenser's *Faerie Queene*', 512–13) identified Arthur both with Leicester and with Essex: Arthur represented the role of apocalyptic hero, and Leicester and Essex were those who had played that role most energetically. But see Bennett, *The Evolution of* The Faerie Queene, 190–1.

[73] G. N. Clark, 'The Birth of the Dutch Republic', *Proceedings of the British Academy*, 32 (1946), 189–217 (195, 213–17); Skinner, *The Foundations of Modern Political Thought*, ii.352 ff.

[74] *The Dramatic Works of Thomas Dekker*, ed. Fredson Bowers, 4 vols. (Cambridge, 1955–61), ii.526.

[75] The following paragraphs are based on James Emerson Phillips, *Images of a Queen: Mary Stuart in Sixteenth Century Literature* (Berkeley and Los Angeles, 1964), see also Norbrook, 'PM', 79–82. For an interesting discussion of the politics of Duessa's trial see Jonathan Goldberg, *James I and the Politics of Literature: Jonson, Shakespeare, Donne, and their Contemporaries* (Baltimore, 1983), 1–6.

one part of the universal attempt by the Habsburg powers and their allies and the Roman church to suppress the Protestant heresy, and she must be executed before she caused more unrest. Elizabeth, however, disliked the vehemence of the Puritan campaign against Mary, who was, after all, her cousin and a legitimate monarch; Elizabeth did not want to give any encouragement to the idea that monarchs could be deposed if they were idolatrous. The leading theorist and propagandist of the *coup d'état* that had deposed Mary had been George Buchanan, whose views on limited monarchy made him suspect to Elizabeth though he was admired by the Leicester circle. Spenser knew and admired Buchanan's radical *History of Scotland*. By 1586–7 Elizabeth had come to see that Mary was a permanent danger to her authority and agreed to put her on trial. Here again, as with the Dutch campaign, Elizabeth was belatedly following a course Leicester had long been urging. But she was still reluctant to sanction overt irreverence towards monarchs. Some anti-Marian sections of Buchanan's *History* appeared in the 1587 edition of Holinshed's *Chronicles*; but some other attacks on Mary were censored along with the descriptions of the Dutch pageants. Elizabeth publicly disowned the responsibility for Mary's execution, putting the blame on her subordinates. Soon after the execution, propaganda against Mary began to be played down. After all, her son James Stuart was Elizabeth's likely successor. The publication of the attack on Mary in the 1596 *Faerie Queene* was therefore not directly in line with government propaganda policies: James was extremely angry because he assumed that the poem had been published with official approval, and an English agent in Edinburgh had to explain that *The Faerie Queene* had not received a royal licence.

Spenser may thus have embarrassed Elizabeth; but of course he embarrassed James still more, and the queen took a certain pleasure in teasing the Scottish king in his impatience to assume the English throne. Spenser keeps his portrayal of Duessa-Mary relatively restrained. The Puritans emphasized her religious impiety, seeing her as part of an international Catholic conspiracy which must be resisted on ideological grounds. Elizabeth refused to introduce religious issues to her trial and concentrated on the charge of treason. Spenser follows the official line in his trial scene—though of course by naming her Duessa he is in fact implicitly linking her with the Roman Church. Spenser praises Mercilla-Elizabeth for her transcendent Mercy. Her reluctance to condemn Duessa—the kind of hesitation that Puritans denounced as womanly weakness—is seen as a manifestation of equity, a branch of the law which was closely associated with the power of the monarch. In the Temple of Isis episode Britomart too is associated with equity, while the crocodile is identified with Arthegall, the harsh and ruthless knight of justice, and perhaps also with the irreverent and unchivalrous campaign of the Puritans against Mary.[76] It is Britomart who comes to Arthegall's rescue when his incompetence has led to his being imprisoned by the Amazon Radigund. Many critics have noted that Arthegall,

[76] René Graziani, 'Elizabeth at Isis Church', *Publications of the Modern Language Association of America*, 79 (1964), 376–89. On equity see Kermode, '*The Faerie Queene*, I and V', 50–8. The issues raised by Mary's trial were similar to those raised by the trial of the princes in the *Arcadia* (see Ch. 4, above).

who frequently resorts to cunning or, through his servant Talus, to brute force, is an unattractive hero who seems to belong to the world of Machiavelli rather than to a chivalric romance.

But while Britomart and Mercilla may be more romantic than Arthegall, it is not clear that Spenser comes down unequivocally on their side. As in Sidney's *Arcadia*, the relations between equity, social class, and royal power cause some unease. Arthegall is killed because, yielding to sentiment, he has spared Radigund's life when he could have killed her—precisely the kind of fault to which Elizabeth was liable as long as she continued to spare Mary. In the allegory of Book V it is made clear that women ought in general to be subject to men even though there may be certain divinely sanctioned exceptions like Elizabeth. Britomart herself will eventually marry Arthegall, the 'salvage knight': her womanly qualities may become dangerous without strong male guidance. Despite all Mercilla's vacillations, she does eventually sanction Duessa's execution. In *Horestes*, a play performed before the queen in 1567, John Pickering had voiced the views of those who wanted Mary to be executed, suggesting that the monarch should be able to put the claims of Justice above the ties of Nature.[77] This is the choice that lies before Mercilla, and in the end justice triumphs. It is true that Spenser presents the decision in an extraordinarily oblique way that suggests a certain unease or embarrassment.[78] Some critics have felt that this indicates Spenser's natural humanitarianism triumphing over the cruel demands of politics. But Book V is often a cruel book, and it is equally possible that Spenser's evasiveness derives from the fact that he is praising the queen for a policy about which he and his supporters had been considerably more enthusiastic than Elizabeth herself. The debate between law and equity could be given a transcendental, philosophical colouring, with equity being seen as a divine and monarchical principle; but Spenser would have known that classical rhetoricians took a more cynically pragmatic view of the difference between law and equity. One praised equity and mercy if one's case was weak, adherence to the letter of the law if it was strong. Both on pragmatic grounds of reason of state and on ideological grounds of Mary's false religion, she had to be executed; Spenser is prepared, however, to allow the queen to indulge in some slightly crocodile-like tears. The iconography of Mercilla's court suggests that Spenser may have meant it to represent Parliament.[79] The Parliament of 1586–7 had seen a Puritan campaign for radical reform of the church, possibly with Leicester's backing, and a number of very outspoken attacks on Catholic monarchs which disturbed the queen. The allegorical core of Book V portrays a predominantly Puritan Parliament approving the execution of a reigning monarch.

From Mercilla's court Arthur sets off for the Netherlands while Arthegall goes to restore to Irene the lands Grantorto has taken from her. Spenser's allegorization of Elizabethan policies in Ireland remains one of the most controversial parts of the poem. The actual combat with Grantorto is described briefly, and after a few stanzas

[77] Phillips, *Images of a Queen*, 46–9.   [78] Cain, *Praise in* The Faerie Queene, 141–6.
[79] Douglas A. Northrop, 'Mercilla's Court as Parliament', *Huntington Library Quarterly*, 36 (1972–3), 153–8.

describing his severe execution of justice in Irene's realm Arthegall is called back to the Faerie court. But the issues raised by the English 'reformation' of Ireland are central to the poem as a whole and are confronted with increasing frequency as the poem's scope widens from private to public issues. Book VI further explores the problems of 'reformation' and 'civility', and the *Mutabilitie Cantos* return to the Irish question. Few critics are now willing to endorse the views of an earlier generation of Spenser critics who, faced with accusations from Irish nationalists that Spenser was an apologist for imperialism, replied that this was precisely what he was and that his writings offered useful tips on ways of putting down native risings.[80] More often it seems to be assumed that Spenser's poem transcends the problem. But the subjugation of Ireland was a major concern of Spenser's political imagination and became a preoccupation of many seventeenth-century poets.

The contrast between English policies in Ireland and their support for rebellion in the Netherlands presented a difficulty for defenders of Elizabeth's justice. If it was right for Elizabeth to aid her co-religionists in the Netherlands, why was it wrong for Philip II to aid Catholics in Ireland? This problem was so obvious that John Hoskyns presented it as a stock topic for discussion in a treatise on rhetoric.[81] Burghley is said to have believed that the English treated the Irish more cruelly than the Spanish treated the Dutch. Arthegall in his role as deliverer of Irene represents the kind of strategy adopted by Spenser's patron Arthur Lord Grey, who had aroused much criticism because of his savagely repressive tactics. Contestants in Accession Day tilts sometimes adopted the personae of Irish knights, and Captain Thomas Lee, cousin of the queen's champion Sir Henry Lee, had himself painted in an Irish costume. But there was little that was romantic about the English conduct of the Irish campaign. Earlier in the century, however, different tactics had been attempted. Humanists in the reign of Henry VIII believed that Ireland was badly in need of reform, but they thought that reform could be achieved peacefully. The English monarchy had lost much of the limited control it had once enjoyed over Ireland. The first Norman occupation had not been fully followed through; the nobles gradually became assimilated into the native Irish culture, and only in the dwindling fortified area of the Pale was the nobility reasonably Anglicized. Outside this area the social structure was effectively pre-feudal: there was a nomadic warrior caste, not bound firmly to the land and passing on power and property by election rather than heredity. There were few towns. The Catholic church in Ireland seemed from the stand-

[80]   Spenser, *A View of the Present State of Ireland*, ed. W. L. Renwick, 2nd edn. (Oxford, 1970), 212–13. Cf. the view of Émile Legouis, *Spenser* (London, 1926), 22–3: 'To purify Ireland from its evils, Spenser would not have hesitated to exterminate the natives. Do not imagine, however, that he utters such ideas with the passion and vehemence of a fanatic . . . The thoroughness of his politics was not at all extraordinary for the time, but they seldom found such a gentlemanly, courteous expression.' Contrast Karl Marx's denunciation of 'Elizabeth's arse-kissing poet' in his notes on earlier Irish history: *The Ethnological Notebooks of Karl Marx*, ed. Lawrence Krader (Assen, 1972), 305. Since the first edition of this book there has been a major resurgence of interest in Spenser and Ireland; for a concise overview see Andrew Hadfield, *Edmund Spenser's Irish Experience: Wilde Fruit and Salvage Soyl* (Oxford, 1997).
[81]   John Hoskins, *Directions for Speech and Style*, ed. Hoyt H. Hudson (Princeton, 1935), 20: 'comparison of things different . . . is most commendable when there seems to be great affinity in the matter conferred, as in the King of Spain's assisting the Irish, the Queen of England's aiding the Netherlands.'

point of Renaissance humanists exceptionally backward and barbarous. But many humanists hoped that a gradual improvement would be possible. In 1541 Henry VIII made Ireland a kingdom in its own right, with its own Parliament and a degree of political independence. It seemed possible that under this political solution the different cultures in the island would be able to develop on reasonably friendly terms.[82] There was as yet no clearly defined Irish nationalism based on language or religion; the Irish bards wrote poems in praise of particular chiefs but not of the Irish nation, while the 'Old English' ruling class, which had been established in Ireland for many years, felt itself to have much in common with Gaelic speakers as well as with the English speakers on the other island.

The Reformation, and the danger that England's enemies would exploit Catholic sentiment in Ireland to undermine Tudor authority, helped to harden English feeling against Irish traditions. The more militant Protestants argued that severe measures were essential to keep Ireland in order. They tended to view Ireland less as a kingdom with its own traditions than as a backward wilderness on much the same level as North America. The Catholic populace were viewed as little more civilized than American Indians. What was necessary was to establish English colonies, to bring Ireland into civility by suppressing idolatry and introducing an English ruling class that would not lapse into sympathy with the indigenous inhabitants.[83] There were, of course, differences between Ireland and America: the English had no doubt that Ireland was part of Elizabeth's sovereign territory, and their establishment of colonies was therefore not viewed as territorial expansion. But the most enthusiastic advocates of the policy of colonization tended to come from the circle of firm Protestants who also favoured overseas expansion. Sir Henry Sidney, father of Sir Philip, had taken a hard line as Viceroy of Ireland; Walter Devereux, Earl of Essex, father of Elizabeth's favourite Robert, made an unsuccessful attempt to establish a colony in Ulster. Spenser went to Ireland in the service of Sidney's successor Lord Grey, who had close dynastic ties with the Protestant aristocracy: his father had been a strong supporter of Somerset, and the young Lord Grey was one of Leicester's followers. He was a patron of letters as well as a soldier: he helped George Gascoigne and the historian Raphael Holinshed.[84] And in going to Ireland Spenser was following in the path of a number of Tudor poets. A play on the state of Ireland had been staged at Edward VI's court, and John Bale, appointed Bishop of Ossory in Edward's reign, had his violently anti-Papal plays staged in the streets of Kilkenny. Barnabe Googe and Thomas Churchyard also served in Ireland. Spenser considered it his responsibility as a Protestant humanist to put his literary skill in the service of the

---

[82] On humanist policies see Brendan Bradshaw, *The Irish Constitutional Revolution of the Sixteenth Century* (Cambridge, 1979), 49 ff. Sir Thomas Lee's portrait is a very striking example of the congruence of civic humanist, chivalric, and Irish discourses: its motto patterned his proposed mediation with O'Neill after Livy's Gaius Mucius Scaevola. See Hiram Morgan, 'Tom Lee: The Posing Peacemaker', in Brendan Bradshaw, Andrew Hadfield, and Willy Maley (eds.), *Representing Ireland: Literature and the Origins of Conflict, 1534–1660* (Cambridge, 1993), 132–65 (141–3). See further pp. 299–302 below.

[83] Nicholas Canny, *The Elizabethan Conquest of Ireland: A Pattern Established 1565–76* (Hassocks, 1976), 123 ff.

[84] For information on Grey I am indebted to an unpublished paper by Belinda McKay.

cause of political reformation. And he endorsed the hard line of men like Bale and Grey rather than the more conciliatory policies of earlier humanists.

Spenser's *View of the Present State of Ireland* was written about 1595 as a critique of what he considered to be the weak and vacillating policies pursued by the administration over the reformation of Ireland. At the beginning of the work he rejects the idea that the 1541 Act of the Irish Parliament making Ireland a kingdom gave Henry VIII any legal rights that he did not already enjoy: he ruled Ireland by right of conquest and therefore in no way required the consent of the people. Spenser's spokesman Irenius argues that the 1541 Act made matters worse: before, the Irish had been absolutely bound to the king's obedience, but now they consider themselves to be 'tyed but with tenures' (*Works*, ix.52).[85] Only unpardonable weakness on the part of the English government could have allowed the native Irish to get the idea that they had rights. The difference between English policy in Ireland and Spanish policy in the Netherlands is, as far as Spenser is concerned, that Philip is acting as a tyrant in denying the traditional rights of the Dutch people, so that limited intervention by another head of state is justified, whereas Elizabeth rules Ireland by conquest and cannot be a tyrant because the people have no rights for her to deny.[86] Spenser presents Philip II, who was intervening to aid the Irish, as 'Grantorto', the perpetrator of a legal 'tort'. The language here is legalistic: again, as in his treatment of the trial of Duessa, Spenser cautiously steers clear of directly ideological, religious justification of war against Catholics. But his attitude to the Irish question is closer to that of the more zealous, 'new English' Protestant settlers than to the queen's own political caution. At the end of Book V Spenser comes close to criticizing Elizabeth by showing how Arthegall's services go unrewarded at court. In the *View of the Present State of Ireland* he amplifies these criticisms. Grey had been criticized for his excessive brutality; but, says Spenser, though his 'platformes' were 'blodye' (*Works*, ix.159), they offered the only realistic means of achieving ultimate peace—the 'Irene' of his allegory. Elizabeth seemed to be dithering over Ireland as she had done over the Netherlands; in each case the Protestant cause was endangered.

Spenser makes only passing reference in the *View* to religious issues, but this does not mean that he considered them unimportant. Like many English Protestants, he

---

[85] Nicholas Canny has shown that Spenser's views are close to those of the hard-line Protestants: 'Edmund Spenser and the Development of an Anglo-Irish Identity', *Yearbook of English Studies*, 13 (1983), 1–19. Jean R. Brink, 'Constructing the *View of the Present State of Ireland*', *Spenser Studies*, 11 (1990), 203–28, and 'Appropriating the Author of *The Faerie Queene*: The Attribution of the *View of the Present State of Ireland* and *A Brief Note of Ireland* to Edmund Spenser', in Peter E. Medine and Joseph Wittreich (eds.), *Sounding of Things Done: Essays in Early Modern Literature in Honor of S. K. Heninger Jr.* (Newark, Del., 1997), 93–136, questions the attribution of this treatise to Spenser, citing the lack of ascription to Spenser before the edition by Sir James Ware in 1633. She notes that no edition has yet dated and collated the extant manuscripts—more than twenty survive—and that we cannot be clear whether Ware was deliberately cutting offensive matter or drawing on a manuscript with different readings from those that survive. I remain unpersuaded that Ware's attribution is false, but it has been helpful to be reminded of the need for more textual work. The *View* will be edited by Nicholas Canny and Elizabeth Fowler for the forthcoming Oxford edition; there is an edition of the 1633 text ed. Andrew Hadfield and Willy Maley (Oxford, 1997).

[86] Cf. Northrop, 'Spenser's Defence of Elizabeth', 280.

believed that it was impossible to reform religion properly until social stability had been obtained; as Machiavelli had pointed out, prophets never prevailed unless they were armed.[87] The kind of religious settlement he envisages is Grindalian: he condemns the English clergy for their idleness and calls for men whose zeal will match their Catholic opponents, who will preach eloquently and set an example by their lives. He praises the recently founded Trinity College, Dublin, which had a strongly Puritan character (*Works*, ix.136–42).[88] Like Grindal, Spenser has no time for Puritans who are 'too nice': irresponsible and untimely iconoclasm under Irish conditions will only alienate the people still further rather than drawing them to the reformed church (*Works*, ix.223).[89] But there are definite limits to Spenser's tolerance. The Irish, he says, have been taught to 'drinke of that Cupp of fornicacion with which the purple Harlott . . . made all nacions drunken'. They 'lye weltringe in suche spirituall darkenes harde by hell mouthe even readye to fall in yf god happelie helpe not' (*Works*, ix.137). When the *View* was published in 1633, at a time when government policy towards Catholics was more conciliatory, extensive cuts had to be made (*Works*, ix.519–23). Spenser's contempt for idolatry and irrationality hardens his humanist scorn for popular culture, leading him to speak of the Irish problem with clinical ruthlessness: the corrupt branches must be pruned and foul moss scraped away, the aim must be to turn the island to good use, to prescribe a proper diet like a good physician, to frame the land anew in the forge (*Works*, ix.146–8). At present Elizabeth's policy of alternating between severe and conciliatory governors is as if the same patient were treated by two physicians, the one advocating strict purgation of the body, the other pampering the patient (*Works*, ix.163). The best solution is a short, sharp shock, a ruthless war of attrition which, if pursued without any wavering, will make the Irish surrender within a year. Only then will it be possible to move to further reform of the social structure and of religion; and only by giving sufficient power to the English commander can Elizabeth achieve this end. Spenser wanted her to give these powers to Essex, 'vppon whom', he wrote, 'the ey of all Englande is fixed and our laste hopes now rest' (*Works*, ix.228); 'Great *Englands* glory and the Worlds wide wonder', as he described him in *Prothalamion* (l. 146). Leicester's expedition to the Netherlands must have seemed to Spenser to have failed because the queen had been indecisive and had not given enough backing; the same thing must not be allowed to happen to Essex. Spenser's criticisms of past policies and his praise of the increasingly controversial Essex may account for the fact that when the *View* was entered for publication in 1598 it was not granted a licence.

---

[87] Canny emphasizes the Machiavellian character of Spenser's treatise: 'Edmund Spenser and the Development of an Anglo-Irish Identity', 6–7.

[88] Hugh Kearney, *Scholars and Gentlemen: Universities and Society in Pre-industrial Britain 1500–1700* (London, 1970), 66–70.

[89] Cf. the condemnation of iconoclasm in *The Faerie Queene*, VI.xii.23–5. According to Ben Jonson the Blatant Beast represented the Puritans. Since Lord Grey, Arthegall's prototype, was a patron of Puritans, Spenser was presumably attacking irreverence amongst the lower orders, which was condemned as strongly by socially respectable Puritans as by high churchmen. Jones, 'Spenser's Defence of Lord Grey', argues that Spenser advocated religious tolerance and did not hold strong religious views, but the passages from the *View* quoted below are far from conciliatory.

Behind the praise of Elizabeth in Book V of *The Faerie Queene* is a view of her policies sufficiently critical to be liable to censorship.[90]

It is with a sigh of relief that Spenser turns in the Proem to Book VI from Justice
to Courtesy, and critics sometimes write of Book VI as if the cruel atmosphere of
Book V had passed. Here Spenser writes of the need to complement the rigour of the
law by courteous speech and conduct, and holds up the poet as the guide to gracious
conduct. Courtesy, a divine grace handed down from above, surpasses justice as holiness surpasses the more earth-bound and calculating virtue of temperance. But we
are not long into Book VI before it becomes clear that the concerns of the previous
book have not disappeared. By stanza 23 Calidore has dispatched a churl by cleaving
his head asunder to the chin; the carcass, a 'lumpe of sin', blocks the door. When
Calidore fights Crudor, the knight's sides gush forth blood like a purple lake (VI.i.37).
In canto iii Serena is given a gory wound and Turpine wounds Calepine till the blood
gushes forth like a well gushing out of a hill (VI.iii.50). The Salvage Man avenges this
attack by laying about him until he is 'steeming red' with the blood of Turpine's servants. Arthur deals with one of Turpine's henchmen until he lies in a 'wyde bloudie
lake' which steams about him (VI.vii.15). Courtesy, it turns out, needs to be supplemented by violence in the chaotic landscape of Book VI in which brigands and
wicked churls are constant menaces. This setting has much in common with the Irish
landscape Spenser would have known, where brigands would suddenly emerge from
forests, and where Spenser saw an old woman drinking the blood that seeped from an
executed traitor's head and smearing her face and breast with it (*Works*, ix.112). It
was frequently alleged that the Irish practised cannibalism, so that the cannibals of
canto vii would have seemed compatible with an Irish atmosphere.[91] Such a landscape needs to be disciplined by violence as well as by courtesy, and the lower orders
receive small shrift in Book VI. The Blatant Beast, the nightmare, many-headed
monster of Book VI, has associations not only with the Beast of Revelation but also
with the 'many-headed monster', the common people.[92] The social morality of Book
VI is extremely rigid: noble birth is frequently exalted. The Salvage Man seems to be
an exemplar of primitive virtue but in reality he, like all the virtuous characters, has
noble blood. This insistence on nobility, like the violence, is a generic feature of the
romances Spenser is imitating in Book VI, but it seems also to reflect an increasing

---

[90]   I put this more tentatively than in the first edition: Brink, 'Constructing the *View of the Present State
of Ireland*', has initiated a debate over whether the *View* was in fact subjected to censorship. The
Stationers' Register entry merely defers publication until further authority is received, and it is possible
that the refusal of a licence sprang from rivalry between stationers. But the tract's criticisms of Elizabeth,
and idealization of Essex, would have been highly sensitive in print. As Paul Hammer has shown, the
boundary line between manuscript circulation to a select circle and the leaking of such material into print
was a difficult one: 'The Uses of Scholarship: The Secretariat of Robert Devereux, Second Earl of Essex,
c.1585–1601', *English Historical Review*, 109 (1994), 26–51.

[91]   Canny, *The Elizabethan Conquest of Ireland*, 126.

[92]   Paul D. Green, 'Spenser and the Masses: Social Commentary in *The Faerie Queene*', *Journal of the
History of Ideas*, 35 (1974), 389–406; cf. Christopher Hill, *Change and Continuity in Seventeenth-Century
England* (London, 1974), 181–204. Hill suggests that one reason for the gradual increase in usage of
'animal' as opposed to 'beast' at the turn of the century was the reaction of conservatives against
apocalyptic language: *Antichrist in Seventeenth-Century England* (London, 1971), 40.

rigidity in Spenser's social thought. As defender of a bastion of English culture in a threatening milieu, he identifies very strongly with the ruling elite in his anxiety to differentiate himself from the idolatrous Catholic masses. In Book V Spenser had described with approval the violent overthrow of an egalitarian giant. He would have been aware of the heightened fears of social disorder in England in the 1590s following a series of bad harvests.

Into this savage land comes Calidore, the smooth-tongued courtier who has yet to learn the full realities of life far from the comforts of the city. He thinks he has found a safe pastoral retreat when he meets Pastorella, but his courtesy is of no help when the brigands assault the village and kidnap Pastorella and other villagers. This is the climax of a series of episodes throughout the book where characters enjoying repose are suddenly interrupted: in Book VI as in Book I, whose structure Spenser is here echoing, it is dangerous to be too relaxed. Spenser's version of pastoral is thus as strenuous as Sidney's: courtiers who want to escape from their political obligations may put themselves and others in danger. Calidore can only redeem the situation by wearing weapons under his pastoral disguise and assaulting the brigands. Spenser is hostile to the 'churls' below but also shows the possible limitations of a narrowly courtly perspective: those who live at the frontiers know that the courtier's arts are not enough to maintain order.[93]

At the climax of Book VI Spenser reintroduces his old pastoral persona of Colin Clout. The name conjures up the associations of prophetic, anti-courtly poetry. The Colin Clout of *The Shepheardes Calender* had represented a modification of the older prophetic tradition, introducing a new, Italianate formal sophistication, and the Colin of Book VI is the Colin of the earlier eclogues, presiding over a dance of the Graces, a mythological epiphany drawing on Neoplatonic imagery. The virtue that Colin's vision embodies is courtesy, a virtue that had little place in the world of Langland and his imitators. But this courtesy is of a paradoxically uncourtly nature: the appearance of the courtier Calidore interrupts the poet's vision, and at the centre of the dance stands not an image of Queen Elizabeth but the figure of the poet's own love. Spenser signals the fact that he is reversing expectations where the reader would anticipate an image of Elizabeth in a stately palace by saying that the 'lasse' excels Ariadne's crown, one of Elizabeth's personal emblems.[94] In *Amoretti*, the sonnet sequence portraying his courtship of his second wife in the 1590s, Spenser apologizes to the queen for delaying his work on his epic to praise his own personal fulfilment (sonnets xxxiii, lxxx). In *Colin Clouts Come Home Againe* (written 1591–5) Spenser suggests that Colin can find inspiration only when he is away from court. In canto x Spenser apologizes directly to the queen for celebrating this relationship of mutual love as opposed to the courtly relationship of service and adoration which the queen expected of her panegyrists.

But in Book VI Spenser is not simply retreating from the public world into a

---

[93] On Book VI as a critique of courtly values see Daniel Javitch, *Poetry and Courtliness in Renaissance England* (Princeton, 1978), ch. 5.
[94] Gerald Snare, 'Spenser's Fourth Grace', *Journal of the Warburg and Courtauld Institutes*, 34 (1971), 350–5; cf. Cain, *Praise in* The Faerie Queene, 160–1.

private realm of the imagination: for him the function of the imagination remains essentially political, the poet is engaged in feigning a commonwealth. Sir Walter Ralegh, annotating his copy of *The Faerie Queene*, identified himself with the intruding Calidore, Spenser with Colin; he would have been thinking of the visits he paid to Spenser in Ireland.[95] Spenser would not have thought of the sixth book as being set exclusively in Ireland: 'Faerie Land' is a more general region. But the settlement of Ireland was a particular instance of the general process of political and cultural reformation which he was celebrating in his poem. (The colonization of America would be another example.[96]) To claim that the Acidale vision 'transcends' politics would be to miss the point: for Spenser the poet's imaginative visions can be justified only if they can be translated into political action. Colin's vision is of a kind of grace that is the common source of political and aesthetic harmony. The Graces, Colin explains, represent 'Ciuility' and 'friendly offices'—the civil virtues described by Cicero in *De officiis*, one of the humanists' favourite political works. In another important work, *De inventione*, Cicero had emphasized the importance of eloquence in producing civil order: organized society only became possible, he argued, when people could be persuaded that their primitive state of violent competition was not in anyone's interest and that working hard for the common good benefited all. Renaissance humanists contrasted Hercules the representative of brute force with Hercules Gallicus, who prevailed by means of eloquence rather than violence: he was depicted leading the people after him by golden chains attached to their ears. He resembled Orpheus, whose skill in drawing the beasts after him was also interpreted as an allegory of the power of eloquence in taming that wild beast the multitude.[97] Spenser regarded the Irish masses as not much superior to beasts, but he did hope that poetry could help to bring them to order by instilling in them a proper love of the monarchy (*Works*, ix.124–7). He complained in the *View* that their bards did not instruct young people in 'morall discipline' but wrote panegyrics of 'suche lewde persones as live . . . lawleslye and licentiouslye vppon stealthes and spoiles'—that is, they wrote heroic poems in praise of their chieftains. The Irish bards at this stage had little sense of national loyalty and generally confined their political interests to the defence of particular patrons and vilification of their enemies. But they were beginning to show some signs of a national consciousness, and Spenser complained that their poems tended 'for the moste parte to the hurte of the Englishe or mayntenaunce of theire owne lewd libertie'.[98] He had no doubt that poetry had an enormous influence on young people: 'evill thinges beinge decte and suborned with the gaye attire of good-

[95] On the common political concerns of Books V and VI see Horton, *The Unity of* The Faerie Queene, 76–99, and on the geographical setting, 30–3, 119–23 (he errs, however, in assuming that Elizabeth ruled Scotland). On Spenser and Ireland see also Greenblatt, 'To Fashion a Gentleman', 179, 184–8.

[96] On the common interest in Irish and American colonization in Spenser's early circle, see Lisa Jardine, 'Encountering Ireland: Gabriel Harvey, Edmund Spenser, and English Colonial Ventures', in Bradshaw, Hadfield, and Maley (eds.), *Representing Ireland*, 60–75.

[97] On Hercules and Orpheus in Book VI see Cain, *Praise in* The Faerie Queene, 169–71.

[98] Cf. Brendan Bradshaw, 'Native Reaction to the Westward Enterprise: A Case-Study in Gaelic Ideology', in K. R. Andrews et al. (eds.), *The Westward Enterprise: English Activities in Ireland, the Atlantic, and America, 1480–1650* (Liverpool, 1979), 65–80 (76).

lye wordes maye easelye deceaue and Carrye awaie the affeccion of a yonge minde' (*Works*, ix.125). Both the form and the content of Irish poetry must therefore be 'reformed'. Bards must be compelled to stop singing of liberty and to sing instead of the glories of English rule. For such poetry to carry conviction it must, however, outdo the old bardic verse not only in political content but also in harmony of language. The bards sprinkled their verse with 'some prettie flowers of theire owne naturall devise which gaue good grace and Comlinesse vnto them'; but, like Acrasia in the Bower of Bliss, they misused Beauty, making it an incentive to political disorder. What was needed was to show that superior political sentiments could be made even more beautiful: the poets' skill, previously 'abused to the gracinge of wickednes and vice', could 'with good vsage serue to beautifye and adorne vertue' (*Works*, ix.127). Colin Clout's vision of the Graces is in part a vision of the beautiful poetry which will help to persuade all inhabitants of Ireland that their best interests are served by English rule.

Spenser believed that poetry could not only help to bring the Irish to civility but could also provide inspiration for the English colonists. Orpheus could not only tame the beasts but also draw the trees after him, transforming the landscape. Poetry could enact a similar transformation, not literally but by prophetic vision, by imagining the world as it might be and encouraging people to remake it. On Elizabethan progresses this process of transformation could be made actual: landscape artists would prepare the way for the queen's advent by smoothing out blemishes, adorning statues, even digging whole lakes.[99] The transformed landscape symbolized the civility which good rule produced. Such transformations were of course more difficult in Ireland. The south-east of England was sufficiently temperate and well cultivated for it to be possible without too great a stretch of the imagination to present it as an Arcadia inhabited by classical deities. The Irish landscape, in Spenser's opinion, was more like Scythia: the herdsmen drove their cattle from place to place without having settled homesteads. They could thus easily be diverted into warlike activities, whereas settled husbandry 'is moste ennemye to warr' (*Works*, ix.216). The sword must give way to the ploughshare. Poetry could help to inspire the colonists in the long-term aim of transforming the island's agriculture. In the Mount Acidale incident, and more directly in *Colin Clouts Come Home Againe* and the *Mutabilitie Cantos*, Spenser imagines the Irish landscape as transformed into a prelapsarian order, peopled by the deities of classical mythology rather than by savage kerns. He enacts a process of imaginative colonization, the development of a genre of Irish Georgics which will celebrate the Pax Anglicana when a definitive military victory has been won. Many Renaissance Englishmen took Virgil's description of the origins of Rome as a model for their own expansionist activities: Sir John Davies, watching the new settlement of Londonderry being built, quoted from Virgil's description of the new colony of Carthage under construction.[100]

[99] Bruce R. Smith, 'Landscape with Figures: The Three Realms of Queen Elizabeth's Country-House Revels', *Renaissance Drama*, NS 8 (1977), 57–115.
[100] Cyril Falls, *The Birth of Ulster* (London, 1936), 19). Davies quoted from *Aeneid*, 1.422: 'Instant ardentoo Tyrii'. On Spenser and Renaissance interpretations of Virgil see Michael O'Connell, *Mirror and*

Had Spenser been a more courtly poet he might have praised Elizabeth's rule of her Irish domains by claiming that the idea of her beauty transformed the landscape into harmony. But Spenser's vision had a harsh Machiavellian realism: rather than aestheticizing politics, he politicized aesthetics. He had no illusion about the power of art to transform the world unless it was aided by political action. Poetic prophecy could certainly inspire people to action by holding a utopian vision before them, but perfect harmony lay in the future rather than the present. He introduced a reminder of violence even into the vision of the Graces by his allusion to the bloody battle between the Centaurs and the Lapiths (VI.x.13). In the long term, intellectual labour, 'all sciences and those which are Called liberall artes', would be the best instruments of Ireland's 'reformation' (*Works*, ix.216); but in the short term the arts of war had to have precedence. Ireland was one of those areas which the Puritans described as the 'dark corners of the land': economically and socially backward in comparison with the urban centres, and hence more superstitious and in urgent need of religious reformation.[101] Such areas had to be secured by military means before they could be properly civilized. Spenser, like many Elizabethans, thought that Ireland in the sixteenth century was in much the same stage of historical development as Britain had been before the Roman conquest, or at the time of the Saxon kings (*Works*, ix.180, 202).[102] Spenser sets *The Faerie Queene* in the time between the decline of Roman rule and the triumph of the Saxons. Considered in relation to England, the setting provides a contrast: Merlin can prophesy the order and civility that will one day be established by Elizabeth. But the poem's present mirrors the state of Ireland as seen by Spenser: a region so culturally backward that it must be forcibly propelled into the sixteenth century. The other 'dark corners of the land' had at least been secured physically: the defeat of the rebellion of 1570–1 had finally pacified the North, and the Council for the Marches of Wales had established good order. But Ireland remained to be pacified, and the arts of war were essential. Colin's vision of the Graces is a transitory one and must remain so unless Calidore can tear himself away from it and return to his quest. Spenser's vision of a 'reformed' Ireland, like his vision of a liberated Netherlands, was in 1596 no more than a prophecy in which hope was mingled with considerable trepidation. Arthegall and Calidore are struggling against slander and there is little sign that the court will appreciate their efforts. In 1595 a major rebellion under Tyrone had broken out in Ulster, and by 1598 the fighting had spread to Munster and Spenser's house was destroyed by rebels. Once again the English cause seemed to have suffered for lack of firm tactics. Spenser returned to London and died soon afterwards. Elizabeth appointed Essex to lead an English expedition; before he departed he arranged Spenser's funeral. The expedi-

Veil: The Historical Dimension of Spenser's Faerie Queene (Chapel Hill, NC, 1977), 23 ff. Thomas Blenerhasset, author of the *Revelation of the True Minerva*, published a work advocating settlement in Ulster in 1610.

[101]   Christopher Hill, 'Puritans and "the Dark Corners of the Land"', in *Change and Continuity in Seventeenth-Century England*, 3–47.

[102]   The comparison between the English settlers and the Romans in Britain was a common one: see Canny, *The Elizabethan Conquest of Ireland*, 128–30.

tion proved a disaster. Once again Essex and his followers complained that they were not receiving enough support from home, that political manipulation at court—the slander of the 'blatant beast'—was undermining the project's success. When he returned to plead his case Essex burst into the queen's chamber unannounced and greatly alarmed her; he was banished from court in disgrace. Eventually, furious at what they considered to be the injustice of their treatment, Essex and his followers staged their unsuccessful *coup d'état* and the earl was executed. His successor in Ireland, Mountjoy, had more success in defeating the rebels. But tensions between the settlers and the Irish remained and flared up again in the 1640s. Not until Cromwell's campaign of 1650 was Spenser's policy of crushing all opposition in a year by adopting ruthless tactics finally carried through.

> The Irish are ashamed
> To see themselves in one year tamed

wrote Marvell in his 'Horatian Ode' commemorating Cromwell's campaign.[103] Cromwell duly recognized Spenser's contribution to 'the reduction of the Irish to civility' by restoring some lands to his grandson. Now Ireland was well and truly 'reformed' on an English model: by 1685 little more than 20 per cent of the land in Ireland was in Catholic hands.[104]

All the frustrations that the Leicester circle had felt over the years—in connection with the French match, intervention in the Netherlands, the fate of Mary Stuart, the campaigns of the 1590s—accumulate in the *View* and in the darker passages of the later books of *The Faerie Queene*. Like many Puritans of his own age and Whigs of a later age, Spenser is critical of authoritarianism and intolerance in England and on the Continent but his tolerance disappears when it comes to the Celtic peoples of the north and west of Britain. His humanism can be narrow and repressive when compared with the more open humanism of the early sixteenth century. By moving to Ireland this son of a London journeyman had been able to acquire a castle and a large estate; his imagination could spare no sympathy for those who might threaten this personal progress. But he would probably have justified his position in more elevated terms. Vigilant action in Ireland could help to safeguard political and intellectual progress throughout Europe. Ireland was a potential weak link in the chain of anti-Habsburg powers that extended from the north of Europe down to Italy; if a Spanish foothold were established in Ireland the struggle to safeguard this alliance, and to

---

[103] I am assuming that the 'Horatian Ode', like the *View of the Present State of Ireland*, is an expression of Protestant Machiavellianism rather than, as is sometimes argued, an oblique satire of Cromwell. Cf. Blair Worden, 'Classical Republicanism and the Puritan Revolution', in Hugh Lloyd-Jones et al. (eds.), *History and Imagination: Essays in Honour of H. R. Trevor-Roper* (London, 1981), 182–200 (197–8) and my *Writing the English Republic: Poetry, Rhetoric and Politics 1627–1660* (Cambridge, 1999), ch. 6. Debora Shuger, 'Irishmen, Aristocrats and Other White Barbarians', *Renaissance Quarterly*, 50 (1997), 494–525, stresses the social radicalism of the *View*. Peltonen, *Classical Humanism and Republicanism in English Political Thought*, 75–102, points to a work closely parallel to the *View*, Richard Beacon's *Solon his Follie* (Oxford, 1594; ed. Clare Carroll and Vincent Carey, Binghamton, NY, 1996), as the fullest Elizabethan appropriation of Machiavellian republicanism.
[104] Ruth Dudley Edwards, *An Atlas of Irish History* (London, 1973), 165.

extend it to the New World, might be disastrously weakened. The alternative to war would in the long run be a stagnant and authoritarian peace; the peace he envisages arising from the struggles in Ireland would be fertile and energetic. For Spenser, then, there could be no validity in a direct comparison between Philip's treatment of the Dutch and the English treatment of the Irish. Vacillation only compounded the agonies of European warfare; decisive action, a resolute short-cut in the historical progress, might help to bring about an apocalyptic reversal. But of course the real effect of draconian measures against the Irish was to compound the problem, to heighten religious and political bigotry on both sides. Irish poetry was not to be 'reformed' in the way Spenser had hoped. Poets certainly began to turn from celebrating the deeds of particular local chieftains to more general concerns; but instead of praising the benefits of English civility they sang the glories of the Counter-Reformation and expressed a growing sense of linguistic and national identity. Instead of giving their verse the kind of rhetorical polish and ornamentation Spenser had advocated, they began to turn from the traditional highly formal syllabic metre to a more popular accentual metre which appealed to a wider audience.[105] A less draconian approach to the Irish problem than that advocated by Spenser and eventually adopted by Cromwell might have weakened the extreme polarizations on cultural, linguistic, and religious lines that divide the land today. But in the face of a desperate military situation, Spenser could see no alternative. It might seem that for a committed Protestant there was in fact no alternative. But fifty years later some Levellers, faced with an equally grim military situation, refused to fight in Ireland, declaring that it was not for England to impose a tyranny on the Irish. Spenser's courtly ambitions and his long residence in Ireland had, however, taken him a long way from the more democratic elements in the radical Protestant tradition, and he would surely have treated the popular Protestantism of the Levellers with as much scorn as the popular Catholicism of the Irish. In fact the section of Book V in which Arthegall and Talus crush a levelling giant was reprinted as an anti-Leveller pamphlet in 1648.[106]

Some critics have argued that the poetic decline sometimes visible in Book V and perhaps parts of Book VI was caused by his hardening political attitudes.[107] But while some parts of Book V are extremely uninspired, there is no evidence of a steady decline. Some of the best, as well as some of the weakest, poetry appears towards the end of *The Faerie Queene*. It is impossible to deduce Spenser's spiritual history from his poetry, but his imagination does seem to have been stimulated as much as weakened by political adversity. The mood of the later sections of the poem fluctuates between deep pessimism and visionary exaltation. What seems to have been the very

---

[105] Bradshaw, 'Native Reaction to the Westward Enterprise', 76; cf. Nicholas Canny, 'The Formation of the Irish Mind: Religion, Politics, and Gaelic Irish Literature 1580–1750', *Past and Present*, 95 (1982), 91–116.

[106] *The Fairie Leveller: or, King Charles his Leveller Described in Queen Elizabeth's Dayes* (London, 1648). Reprinted by John N. King, '*The Faerie Leveller*: A 1648 Royalist Reading of *The Faerie Queene*, v.ii.29–54', *Huntington Library Quarterly*, 48 (1984–5), 297–308.

[107] See especially O'Connell, *Mirror and Veil*, 130 ff.

last part of the poem Spenser wrote, the *Mutabilitie Cantos*, may have postdated the disaster in which Spenser's house and possibly many of his manuscripts were destroyed; and yet the tone of these cantos is one of almost Olympian assurance and gaiety. The episode of Faunus and Diana is a mythological explanation of how the Arlo Hill area has become a wilderness peopled by wolves and thieves. The cause is *'Dianaes* spights': the virgin queen has cruelly punished not only Faunus, who has spied on her, but also the surrounding landscape. The related myth of Actaeon and Diana was commonly used by Renaissance mythographers to symbolize the dire fate awaiting subjects who defied the royal will and pried into mysteries of state. After Essex's return from Ireland in disgrace, Ben Jonson alluded to his intrusion into the royal bedchamber under the myth of Diana and Actaeon in his play *Cynthia's Revels*. Essex, on Jonson's firmly loyal reading of the situation, had presumed too far on the royal favour. Spenser presents the plight of Faunus more sympathetically. He has broken the mystical taboo that forbids direct contemplation of the divine queen: yet at several points in the poem (most notably in the incident of Braggadochio and Belphoebe, II.iii) the reader has been put in the position of the person who wants to break the taboo.[108] On one level the Faunus–Diana episode can be taken as an allegory of the queen's relationship with Ireland. This interpretation should not be pressed too far: this light Ovidian myth has its own independent interest, and had Spenser intended Faunus as a direct representation of the rebellious Tyrone he would doubtless have taken him more seriously. But on a rather more general level the episode presents an image of the desolation caused in Ireland by an act of the royal will. The last stanza of canto vi emerges with tremendous force after the previously comic tone, the eruption of all the suppressed discontent with the virgin queen that has run through the poem.[109]

Mutabilitie is the other character who breaks the royal taboo: she enters the sphere of Cynthia, thus questioning the idea that she is constant and unchanging. Here Spenser is challenging one of the most common themes of Elizabethan panegyric, which had celebrated the queen as an immortal moon. Traditionally, all beneath the moon was thought to be imperfect while everything above it was perfect. The moon could be seen to change every month, and was thus often associated with the allegedly feminine qualities of inconstancy and fickleness. Court poets of course claimed that Elizabeth was a special kind of moon, being absolutely constant and immortal, embodying a mystical paradox that was not accessible to the vulgar multitude. But it was hard altogether to exclude the more sinister associations of the moon. In classical mythology she was associated not only with the virtuous Diana but also with the sinister witch Hecate. In *Endimion* Lyly contrasts Cynthia's heavenly attributes with her more inconstant aspects, her dark phase, when she walks the earth as the scheming Tellus.[110] In a public poem Ralegh roundly declared that 'Eternitie in hir oft chaunge she beares', but in 'The Ocean to Cynthia' he is not so sure: though

[108] Angus Fletcher, *Allegory: The Theory of a Symbolic Mode* (Ithaca, NY, 1964), 272.
[109] Cain, *Praise in The Faerie Queene*, 182.
[110] Axton, *The Queen's Two Bodies*, 71–2; cf. Greville, 'Caelica', no. 55, in *Poems and Dramas*, i.106.

his 'harts desire' makes him want to believe in the immortality of the Virgin Queen, 'strong reason' tells him that all things must change.[111]

Spenser's Cynthia is unable to resist Mutabilitie. In the 1590s anxiety about the queen's mutability reached its height as people were forced to contemplate the imminent possibility of her death and a change of government which was hard to imagine after such a long reign. Chapman expressed his anxiety in the *Hymnus in Cynthiam* (1593), where he imagines the chaos that would be caused if the moon withdrew her light from the world. Like the *Mutabilitie Cantos*, the *Hymnus in Cynthiam* is in two parts, one dealing with Cynthia's earthly embodiment as Diana the chaste huntress, the other with her cosmic role as the moon.[112] When Mutabilitie threatens to strike Cynthia the world is darkened, as in Chapman's poem.

Spenser's portrayal of Cynthia thus hinted at some Elizabethan political anxieties. Mutabilitie, Cynthia's adversary, herself has some attributes in common with the moon-goddess, and she has been described as a 'demonic parody' of Elizabeth.[113] Fortune was commonly represented as an arbitrary and irrational tyrant, dispensing her favours capriciously. Since she was sometimes depicted as blindfolded, she could also be associated with the god of love. She thus became a negative image of the prince in Neoplatonic ideology, who was the image of virtue with whom subjects were linked by love, the personal embodiment of the strengths of the state. Republicans, however, tended to regard the rule of one individual, who might be fickle and inefficient, as an unnecessary subjection to the power of Fortune: a rational republic could challenge this power. Machiavelli was impatient with those who resigned themselves to Fortune: she was a woman, he declared, and needed a strong man to take her in hand by decisive action. The defeat of republican ideas and the growth of absolutism in the later sixteenth century led to an increasing pessimism about the possibility of overcoming Fortune: Montaigne declared that 'Fortune, not wisdom, rules the life of man'.[114]

Elizabethan courtiers frequently viewed Elizabeth as the personification of Fortune, and though they generally accepted the need to submit to her power they had moments of impatience and self-assertion. Sir Walter Ralegh complained in 'The Ocean to Cynthia' at the arbitrary way merit was rewarded at court, reflecting the sovereign's whim rather than merit: having lost favour he has no option but to 'geue fortune way'. In another poem, which he showed to the queen, he complained that Fortune had conquered his love: had she seen with wisdom's eyes his love would have lasted for ever, but she was blind. His only consolation was that the goddess, who ruled the earth and earthly things, could conquer even kings.[115] In the 1590s the

[111]   Ralegh, *Poems*, 11, 31.
[112]   Chapman, *Poems*, 31–45; on the political allegory see Raymond B. Waddington, *The Mind's Empire: Myth and Form in George Chapman's Narrative Poems* (Baltimore, 1974), 72–91.
[113]   See William Blissett, 'Spenser's Mutabilitie', in Millar MacLure and F. W. Watt (eds.), *Essays in English Literature from the Renaissance to the Victorian Age Presented to A. S. Woodhouse* (Toronto, 1964), 26–42.
[114]   This very simplified summary is based on Skinner, *The Foundations of Modern Political Thought*, i.95–8, 119–22, ii.278–84, and J. G. A. Pocock, *The Machiavellian Moment* (Princeton, 1975), 38 ff., 156–69.
[115]   Ralegh, *Poems*, 42; Walter Oakeshott, *The Queen and the Poet* (London, 1960), 154.

Earl of Essex addressed several poems to Elizabeth in which compliment was over-shadowed by complaints at the arbitrary way she treated him:

> She useth the aduantage tyme and fortune gave,
> Of worth and power to gett the libertie;
> Earth, Sea, Heaven, Hell, are subject unto lawes,
> But I, poore I, must suffer and knowe noe cause.[116]

In one indignant letter he complained, 'What, cannot princes err? Cannot subjects receive wrong? Is an earthly power or authority infinite?' He complained that the queen seemed to be seeking an 'infinite absoluteness'.[117] His invasion of the royal bedchamber was a misjudged attempt at a display of Machiavellian 'virtù', trying to force Fortune, to frighten the woman-ruler into taking his side.

The conventional celebrations of Elizabeth as the unchanging moon, transcending Fortune, had a hollow ring to them by the late 1590s, and scarcely masked the political anxiety they were designed to conceal. A Legend of Constancy that tried to include panegyric of the queen was in danger either of degenerating into empty flattery or of becoming politically controversial. In the *Mutabilitie Cantos* Spenser faces this challenge directly. Instead of denying that the queen is mutable, he concedes the fact. But this does not mean that he is criticizing her: instead, he relates this mutability to the order of the entire universe. If Elizabeth must change, so must the whole of God's creation, and so her dignity is not impaired by the admission. Elizabeth of course knew perfectly well that she was mortal; indeed, mutability was something of an obsession with her. She had never been strongly influenced by the optimism of Renaissance republicanism or by Protestant apocalyptic thought. The pessimistic resignation to Fortune advocated by the Neo-Stoics would have appealed to her: in 1593 she translated Boethius' *Consolation of Philosophy*, which advocates resignation in the face of Fortune's power. She composed a reply to the poem in which Ralegh lamented Fortune's effects:

> Fortune I grant sometimes doth conquer kings,
> And rules and raignes on earth and earthlie things,
> But never thinke that fortune can beare sway,
> If vertue watche and will her not obay.[118]

In her youth Elizabeth had translated part of Petrarch's *Triumph of Eternity*, in which, as in the *Mutabilitie Cantos*, the poet despairingly contemplates the power of change but has a vision of eternity:

> Amazed to see, nought vnder heavens cope
> steddie and fast, thus to my self I spake
> Advise the well: on whome doth hang thie hope,
> On god (said I) that promyse never brake

---

[116] Steven W. May, *The Elizabethan Courtier Poets: The Poems and their Contexts* (Columbia, Mo., 1991), 254.

[117] W. B. Devereux (ed.), *Lives and Letters of the Devereux, Earls of Essex*, 2 vols. (London, 1853), i.501–2.

[118] May, *The Elizabethan Courtier Poets*, 319.

> With those that trust in hym. But now I know
> how earst the fickle world abvsed me . . .
> Whyle deeper yet my searching mynd I cast
> a world all new even then it seemed me
> in never chaunging and ever lyving age.[119]

In presenting the power of Mutabilitie, then, Spenser may be not diminishing Elizabeth's status but rather paying her a particularly subtle compliment: through Ralegh if through no one else he would have known something of her literary and philosophical interests. But the poem does not necessarily endorse Elizabeth's conservative world-view of resignation to the power of Fortune. In the late sixteenth century Neo-Stoic philosophy was gaining in popularity as people disillusioned by years of political strife looked above all for stability; confidence in the possibility of overcoming Fortune was waning.[120] Theories of the inevitable decay of the world were gaining ground. Spenser himself sometimes inclined to the view that the world was declining (e.g. Proem to Book V). But he was not advocating political quietism or passivity. The *View of the Present State of Ireland* is almost unique amongst Elizabethan political treatises in advocating, not a mere defence and consolidation of the status quo, but radical innovation, a conscious and ruthless process of social transformation. Spenser makes the cautious Eudoxus oppose Irenius' proposal to 'beginne all as it weare anewe and to alter the whole forme of the governement', warning that 'all inovacion is perillous'; but Ireneus replies that if the state is unstable change may be essential (*Works*, ix.147). He outlines his proposal for a radical reformation of the body politic, in which an energetic military commander will seize the moment and change the course of Irish history. Spenser gives Machiavelli's *Discourses* as his authority for giving Essex exceptional powers (*Works*, ix.229). The *Mutabilitie Cantos* present change as a menacing but also a beautiful phenomenon; the secular order, and hence also political activity, are not irredeemably tainted just because they change. Spenser draws a distinction between change, which is inevitable, and decay: though constantly changing, the earth is still fertile. This distinction between change and decay can be found in Bodin and Lipsius but it was also compatible with an essentially apocalyptic world-view. It was to be the starting point of George Hakewill in his challenge to theories of cosmic decline, *An Apologie . . . of the Power and Providence of God* (1627). Hakewill's book stands between the writings of the many late sixteenth-century Protestants who drew pessimistic conclusions from Revelation, assuming that decline would precede the apocalypse, and the mounting optimism of a new generation of Puritans who thought that a millennial renewal was at hand. Hakewill cites the poetry of Spenser and Sidney as one example of the continuing creativity of man and nature. For Spenser as for Hakewill the apocalypse is still a distant event;

---

[119] *The Arundel Harington Manuscript of Tudor Poetry*, ed. Ruth Hughey, 2 vols. (Columbus, Oh., 1960), i.360–1.
[120] The following paragraph is based on Victor Harris, *All Coherence Gone* (Chicago, 1949), 55–6, 72, 100–20.

Spenser longs for 'that Sabaoths sight' but is prepared to accept the instability of the intervening period.[121]

One of the sources of the *Mutabilitie Cantos* is the last book of Ovid's *Metamorphoses*. Ovid ends his description of universal change with a panegyric of the Roman imperial dynasty succeeded by a declaration that his verse will live forever; the juxtaposition seems to imply that Ovid has a rather better chance of immortality than his prince. Spenser refrains from staking his own claims to immortality, but he knew well enough that his poetry would outlive Elizabeth.[122] And so would the political causes he had celebrated; for the Gloriana of the poem is a symbol, Spenser's personal reshaping of an image created by the Leicester and Essex circles. The image of Gloriana had never corresponded exactly to the reality and by the 1590s the disparity was striking. She had not done as much as she could have done to secure the political triumphs Spenser prophesied; there would need to be further developments in the future. Spenser's Gloriana would outlive, as a political symbol, the ageing queen; for, as he had stated to Ralegh, Elizabeth was only his 'particular' intention.

[121] On Hakewill see further Ch. 10 n. 25 below.
[122] Michael Holahan, '*Iamque opus exegi*: Ovid's Changes and Spenser's Brief Epic of Mutabilitie', *English Literary Renaissance*, 6 (1976), 244–70 (252–4).

6. *Voluntary Servitude:*
Fulke Greville and the Arts of Power

'[I]T pleased God, in this decrepit age of the world, not to restore the image of her ancient vigour in him otherwise than as in a lightning before death.'[1] Fulke Greville spent his life in mourning for Sir Philip Sidney; and for him Sidney represented a unique combination of aristocratic magnanimity and Protestant integrity, heroic action and literary intelligence. Both Sidney and Spenser had attempted in different ways to achieve synthesis in their lives and writings, to reconcile a courtly, Neoplatonic aesthetic with the demands of a Protestant conscience. But their works had embodied the tensions inherent in such a synthesis; and in Greville's writings these tensions are pushed to breaking point, resulting in a despairing self-censorship. The critical subtexts of the *Arcadia* and *The Faerie Queene* become explicit. Elizabethan court poetry presented the social order as a harmonious microcosm of the universal hierarchy, united by love of the prince. The state became a decorous work of art with the monarch at the centre. Greville agrees that the state is a work of art, but for him it is a glittering façade covering dissimulation and corruption, a specious substitute for lost liberties. His writings enact a steady process of iconoclasm; praise of the monarch as image of God develops into a sweeping denunciation of all secular honour as idolatry; and the art of poetry itself becomes suspect.

Greville began his poetic career by writing love sonnets in emulation of Sidney's. He continued to add to the *Caelica* sequence all through his life, but the later poems reflect his increasing political disillusionment. Two of the poems, nos. 55 and 81, refer directly to Queen Elizabeth; they are given structurally important positions, immediately before poems associated with Sidney which are placed halfway and three-quarters of the way through the sequence.[2] The other ladies addressed in the

---

[1] *A Dedication to Sir Philip Sidney*, in *The Prose Works of Fulke Greville, Lord Brooke*, ed. John Gouws (Oxford, 1986), 23. The first printed edition, published in 1652 long after Greville's death, was entitled *The Life of the Renowned Sir Philip Sidney*. The work is more mixed than the term *Life* implies, however, and Gouws prefers the 'Dedication' title which is found in two of the four surviving manuscripts. This title likewise, however, gives a rather misleading impression of a text whose status was always problematic, and in my text I continue to refer to the *Life of Sidney*. For discussion of the text see Victor Skretkowicz, 'Greville's *Life of Sidney*: The Hertford Manuscript', *English Manuscript Studies 1100–1700*, 3 (1992), 102–36, and John Gouws, 'Fulke Greville's *A Dedication to Sir Philip Sidney* and the Protocols of Textual Scholarship', *English Manuscript Studies 1100–1700*, 6 (1997), 114–39. I am particularly indebted to Ronald A. Rebholz, *The Life of Fulke Greville: First Lord Brooke* (Oxford, 1971); see also Joan Rees, *Fulke Greville, Lord Brooke, 1554–1628: A Critical Biography* (London, 1971), and Richard Waswo, *The Fatal Mirror: Themes and Techniques in the Poetry of Fulke Greville* (Charlottesville, Va., 1972).
[2] On the placing of poems associated with Sidney see B. J. Sokol, 'Numerology in Fulke Greville's *Caelica*', *Notes and Queries*, 225 (1980), 327–9. These proportions are obscured by Geoffrey Bullough's

sequence cannot be directly identified with the queen; but the idea of love was highly politicized in Renaissance poetry, and the relationship between lover and mistress serves Greville as a political metaphor. There is no evidence that he was ever passionately attracted to a woman, and a strong possibility that he was homosexual. But the conventions of love poetry enabled him to explore, and denounce, the psychological mechanisms by which a ruler can exploit the weaknesses of her subjects.

In the later parts of the *Arcadia* Sidney himself had taken an increasingly sombre view of love; there is a gulf between inner devotion and the externals of social convention, which are increasingly seen as potentially deceitful. Images of imprisonment and torment become more and more frequent. This analysis of imprisoned love found its way into the poetry of his brother Sir Robert Sidney, and here again there were political undertones. Sir Robert found it extremely difficult to gain advancement at court; he spent most of the 1590s in semi-exile, commanding an English garrison in the Netherlands. It is likely that the suspicion with which the queen and Burghley had regarded Sir Philip extended to his brother. Sir Robert's secretary described Burghley as 'Saturn', the god of melancholy; and Sidney was one of many courtiers in the 1590s who adopted a stance of despairing melancholy. This courtly fashion was to some extent a mere social game, but it could take on political connotations. Essex had poetry and music written for him which publicized his despair at his unjust treatment by his enemies; Greville may have written some of these poems.[3] The figure of the melancholy malcontent who peoples so much Jacobean drama was already a reality at the Elizabethan court. Sir Robert Sidney's love poems, probably written about 1596–8, are wintry and melancholy in their atmosphere, and full of images of violence and imprisonment.[4] Love amputates the poet's limbs, it is a canker eating away his bowels. These poems are in no sense directly political but they share their imagery of winter and twilight with Ralegh's explicitly political 'The Ocean to Cynthia', and some verbal echoes suggest that Sidney knew Ralegh's poem. *Caelica* has much in common with Ralegh's and Sidney's poems, but Greville in some respects goes much further in his critical scrutiny of courtly devotion. In *The Faerie Queene* Spenser had hinted at the difficulties underlying relationships like that between Timias and Belphoebe; Greville presents all such 'courtship' as a kind of idolatry. In 1581 a Puritan chaplain, Robert Wright, had condemned the cult of Elizabeth as 'idolatry'; Greville seems, at times, to have agreed.[5]

And yet in the *Life of Sidney* Greville idealized Elizabeth, taking her as a model for

renumbering of the poems in his edition: *Poems and Dramas of Fulke Greville First Lord Brooke*, 2 vols. (Edinburgh, 1939), i.73–153. I have retained Bullough's numbering in citation for ease of reference. For further discussion of numerology see Tom W. N. Parker, *Proportional Form in the Sonnets of the Sidney Circle* (Oxford, 1998), 109.

[3] *Historical Manuscripts Commission: Report on the Manuscripts of Lord De L'Isle and Dudley*, ii, ed. C. L. Kingsford (London, 1934), 123; Roy Strong, *The English Icon: Elizabethan & Jacobean Portraiture* (London, 1969), 352–4; Lillian M. Ruff and D. Arnold Wilson, 'The Madrigal, the Lute Song and Elizabethan Politics', *Past and Present*, 44 (1969), 3–51 (39).

[4] *The Poems of Robert Sidney*, ed. P. J. Croft (Oxford, 1984).

[5] Roy Strong, *The Cult of Elizabeth: Elizabethan Portraiture and Pageantry* (London, 1977), 125–6.

all monarchs to follow. The *Life*, however, was written after the queen's death, when Greville was using Elizabeth as an antitype to the corrupt rule of James. In her life-time, Greville, like many members of the Sidney and Essex circles, was less uncriti-cal; his relations with the queen were difficult, for she constantly intervened to prevent him from undertaking foreign missions which might have placed him in dubious political company. Her judgement that Greville had subversive tendencies was a shrewd one: if it is a little exaggerated to compare him, as one critic has done, with Lenin, he is certainly one of the most radical Elizabethan poets in his constant denunciation of tyranny and inequality.

> Tyrants! Why swell you thus against your Makers?
> Is rays 'd Equalitie so soone growne wilde? . . .
> No People, No. Question these Thrones of Tyrants;
> Reuiue your old equalities of Nature;
> Authority is more than that she maketh . . .
> Then let them stirre, and teare away this veyle
> Of pride from Power; that our great Lord may see
> Vnmiracled, his owne Humanity.[6]

Greville was not himself inciting rebellion: the counsellor in his play *Mustapha* who calls for resistance to tyranny abruptly checks himself and decides to save the estab-lished order. But this very abruptness is characteristic of Greville's writing: radical sentiments keep emerging, apparently almost against the author's will, and have to be repressed. Greville was frightened of rebellion precisely because the whole traditional structure of power and authority seemed to him to be fragile, almost illusory: the people obeyed only because of a kind of conjuring trick by which rulers made themselves appear all-powerful. In a speech to Parliament at a time of eco-nomic hardship in the 1590s he declared that '[i]f the feet knew their strength as we know their oppression, they would not bear as they do.'[7] Greville constantly returns to the idea that the conventional symbolism of authority is a kind of arbitrary stage-play:

> People are superstitious, caught with showes:
> To power why doe they else their freedome giue,
> But that in others pompe these *shadowes* liue?[8]

At the crisis of both tragedies the 'mysteries of Empire' are 'dissolued' and the people suddenly realize that they can take power into their own hands. The Chorus in *Mustapha* compare the people to a blind Samson who suddenly becomes aware of his powers: let them

> gather in againe those strengths they gaue away;
> And so plucke downe that *Sampsons* post, on which our *Sultans* stay.[9]

---

[6] Greville, *Mustapha*, v.ii.1-2, v.iii.92-4, IV.iii.205-7; *Poems and Dramas*, ii.126, 131, 120; cf. Una Ellis-Fermor, *The Jacobean Drama: An Interpretation*, 4th edn. (London, 1958), 197.
[7] Rebholz, *Life of Fulke Greville*, 92.   [8] *Alaham*, III.iii.89-91; *Poems and Dramas*, ii.184.
[9] *Mustapha*, IV, Chorus 123-4; *Poems and Dramas*, ii.125.

The general phenomenon of obedience to a dazzling but heavily outnumbered minority makes the differences between monarchy and tyranny appear relatively insignificant in comparison. In his treatise on monarchy Greville explored the difference between good kings and tyrants and came to the conclusion that there was in practice very little difference: both had to use the 'arts' of power, to dazzle the people into obedience. Tyrants were admittedly able to use powers of coercion which constitutional rulers denied themselves, but even these powers would not be enough to overrule the massive numerical majority of the people were there not some strange psychological mechanism by which subjects actually co-operated in subjection. In the *Life of Sidney* Greville wrote that the people of France were 'voluntary slaves' in the choice of 'passive bondage'.[10]

Greville's analysis of the psychology of obedience has striking similarities with one of the most famous or notorious of radical texts in the sixteenth century, Étienne de La Boétie's *Discours de la servitude volontaire*. Like Greville, La Boétie was concerned not so much with the specific differences between tyrants and good kings, the conventional matter of political theory, as with the general phenomenon of obedience by the majority to one man or to a small ruling elite. The similarities between Greville's thought and La Boétie's need not indicate direct influence; both men drew on common sources, Seneca, Tacitus, and probably Machiavelli. Their writings illustrate the general situation of radical humanism confronted with an overwhelmingly conservative political universe. But Greville does often seem to be groping, very obscurely, towards some unusually original ideas on which La Boétie's more clear-cut writings provide a valuable gloss. The *Discours* was in any case well known amongst French Protestants, with whom the Sidney and Essex circles were in close contact. La Boétie's close friend Montaigne had praised the work highly in his *Essays* and originally intended to publish the work as a tribute to his friend, who had died in 1563. But he became alarmed when the Huguenots got hold of a copy and issued it as propaganda for their rebellion against Henry III; Montaigne had more respect for custom and tradition than La Boétie, who had himself in any case become a loyal servant of the crown, and he claimed that his friend would never have countenanced rebellion. But in suppressing the work he was calling attention to it. He substituted some of his friend's love poems, but given the politicization of love in much Renaissance poetry—including Greville's—this amounted to 'a displacement out of politics into an erotic realm of the question of *servitude volontaire*'.[11] Greville's attention may well have been attracted by the elegiac aspect of Montaigne's writings: several recent critics have argued that Montaigne's later work involved repeated attempts to regain contact with the living voice of his late friend, just as Greville tried to address Sidney directly after his death (the *Life of Sidney* really constituted a 'Dedication' of his collected works to Sir Philip). Greville would not have been able

---

[10] Greville, *A Dedication to Sir Philip Sidney*, 58.

[11] Jeffrey Mehlman, 'La Boétie's Montaigne', *Oxford Literary Review*, 4:1 (Autumn 1979), 45–61 (48). The *Discours* was first printed in full in *Memoires de l'estat de France sous Charles IV* (Middelburg, 1577), iii.160 ff.; the collection also included Hotman's *Franco-Gallia*, one of the best-known justifications of Protestant resistance.

to dismiss La Boétie's radical potential as decisively as Montaigne, for he sympathized with the Huguenot rebellion Montaigne had condemned, and he seems to have had a reputation for taking a radical view of French politics. In 1589 he was praised in an English volume of epigrams which enthusiastically celebrated the assassination of Henry III by a Catholic fanatic. This volume took irreverent pleasure in the death of an anointed king and the rarity of surviving copies has led to speculation that it may have been censored.[12] Greville served for a time in Henry of Navarre's Huguenot armies; and he was a close friend of Anthony Bacon, who knew Montaigne well.

La Boétie's analysis of political power starts from rationalistic and egalitarian premisses: human beings are all made from the same mould, and social inequalities are artificial impositions on the natural state.[13] If this is so, then why are tyranny and inequality so widespread? La Boétie probably wrote his treatise in 1548 or 1549, after a rebellion in south-west France against the increasing power of the state—a rebellion comparable in some respects with the English risings of 1549. What puzzles La Boétie is not why the people rebel but why they so seldom do so. One of his explanations is the tyranny of tradition: nature has less power over the mind than custom, which can make people accept irrational institutions as if they were natural.[14]

The second main cause of voluntary servitude can be summarized as the propensity of the imagination to corruption. La Boétie lists the many different ways in which tyrants make the people lose their natural desire for liberty and become corrupt and effeminate. Courtly ceremonial, stage-plays, religious rituals, myths of divine monarchy and divine healing: all these dazzling displays act as a kind of drug, they appeal to the imagination rather than the reason and are difficult to resist. The result is that the people lose not only liberty but the very desire for liberty which in La Boétie's view is naturally implanted in everyone.[15] Desire itself becomes perverted: and this corruption poisons all social relations. Towards the end of the treatise La Boétie launches into an extensive discussion of love and friendship. True friendship is possible only between equals; tyrants can never know love, only lust and fear. But each tyrant is surrounded by a group of dependants who glitter with his reflected light, producing in their dependants in turn the psychology of dependence and 'voluntary servitude': every local official is himself a petty monarch. La Boétie

[12] Hoyt H. Hudson, 'An Oxford Epigram-Book of 1589', *Huntington Library Quarterly*, 2 (1938–9), 213–17. For a link between Greville and La Boétie apparently made by a contemporary, William Drummond, see below, Ch. 10 n. 115.

[13] For a short introduction to La Boétie's thought see Nannerl O. Keohane, 'The Radical Humanism of Étienne de La Boétie', *Journal of the History of Ideas*, 38 (1977), 119–30. For a full and extremely subtle reading of the Discourse see the essay by Claude Lefort entitled 'Le Nom d'Un' in Miguel Abensour (ed.), *Le Discours de la servitude volontaire: La Boétie et la question du politique* (Paris, 1976), 247–307. The contributors to this volume assimilate La Boétie to the elegiac social thought of the Frankfurt School rather than the militant liberalism seen in Harry Kurtz's introduction to his wartime translation, *Anti-Dictator* (New York, 1942). There are more recent translations by Malcolm Smith (Egham, 1988) and by David Lewis Schaefer (ed.), *Freedom over Servitude: Montaigne, La Boétie, and 'On Voluntary Servitude'* (Westport, Conn., 1998), 189–222; Schaefer assembles arguments for attributing the *Discours* to Montaigne himself.

[14] *Discours*, ed. Abensour, 133; *Anti-Dictator*, 26.   [15] *Discours*, 137–48; *Anti-Dictator*, 29–39.

describes this hierarchy of corruption as a network or as a golden chain: the latter image, derived ultimately from Homer, was of course very popular in the Renaissance, but for La Boétie what counts is not the gold but the fact that it is still a chain.[16]

If the people could only see through their imaginative delusions they could easily overthrow tyranny: La Boétie compares it to a huge statue which would topple down from its own weight if the base were shaken.[17] If this so seldom happens, it is because the common people can be too easily mystified: La Boétie is scathing about their ignorance and their willingness to be deluded. Despite his claims about natural equality, it is clear that in fact he believes that some people definitely constitute an elite. But he does give reasons for the quiescence of the common people: it is not that they are naturally inferior but that tyrants can more easily exploit them. Their mental horizons are narrow, they gain their knowledge only from everyday experience: and precisely what seems 'natural' on the basis of custom and 'common sense' is really unjust and unnatural. It is in the interest of tyrants to prevent people from breaking out of their limited traditional worlds. For most people the idea of liberty becomes almost literally unthinkable, tyrants remove the 'freedom of action, of speech, and almost of thought'. The lower orders have no memory of a better state to guide them, they cannot 'recall the things of the past in order to judge those of the future, and compare both with their present condition'. Only the educated few have access to a kind of memory which tyrants cannot completely eradicate: the memory of liberty that is preserved in books. The literate can imagine liberty and feel it in their minds, they can almost taste it: and this is the first step to making it a reality again. That is why tyrants need an apparatus of censorship: as long as opposition is atomized, as long as the lovers of liberty have no contact with each other, their ideal remains without effect because they do not know each other ('sentrecongnoistre'). They remain isolated in their imaginations, 'tous singuliers en leurs fantasies': the individual imagination can only become a redeeming force when it is shared with others.[18]

The relationship between lover and mistress in *Caelica* conforms to La Boétie's analysis of 'voluntary servitude'. Greville's world is one of 'hurt imaginations' (no. 100, l. 12), in which desire is distorted by specious inequalities.[19] Greville's increasingly severe Protestantism makes him even less optimistic than La Boétie about the prospect of breaking out of this bondage, but he shares with the French writer an

---

[16] *Discours*, 150–64; *Anti-Dictator*, 41–54.

[17] *Discours*, 116–17; *Anti-Dictator*, 13 (the first part of the *Discours* to be printed, in the Huguenot volume *Reveille matin des Francois* (1574), ended with this provocative simile).

[18] *Discours*, 134–5; *Anti-Dictator*, 26–7 (I have paraphrased where Kurtz's translation is inadequate).

[19] References in parentheses are to the numbers of the poems in the *Caelica* sequence above. Thom Gunn gives an excellent analysis in the introduction to *Selected Poems of Fulke Greville* (London, 1968). Concluding a new historicist analysis of the love sonnet, Arthur F. Marotti, '"Love is not Love": Elizabethan Sonnet Sequences and the Social Order', *ELH* 49 (1982), 396–428 (419–21), argues that Greville turned from the form because it was no longer a means to self-advancement, which implies a more pragmatic reading of the earlier poems than my own. See also Elaine Y. L. Ho, 'Fulke Greville's *Caelica* and the Calvinist Self', *Studies in English Literature 1500–1900*, 32 (1992), 35–57.

intense nostalgia for a natural state before current inequalities which to some extent works against his demand for resignation. Only in the first few poems in the *Caelica* sequence does Greville follow the orthodox conventions of Neoplatonic flattery, transferring the language of religious devotion to a 'saint' who is as worthy of adoration as a religious image. Even here, however, the woman is praised in not altogether attractive terms: the conventional idea of love as a wound is expressed with exceptional violence in the image of his passion as a dog devouring his bowels (no. 2). The lady's worth is a rod with which to whip his senses (no. 34). She arouses fear as much as love, and her honour and chastity are associated with coldness and ruthlessness: honour is the 'frozen Art' with which Myra tyrannizes Cupid's 'Kingdome of desire'. Cupid heads and feathers his shafts with fear (no. 27, ll. 7, 8, 14).

Petrarchan lovers had traditionally suffered both hope and anxiety, fire and ice, but in Greville's poems the accent on fear is unusually strong. Those who seek love must pass the 'Monarchy of Feare' (no. 59, l. 2). The poet tells Cupid that

> feare and lust in you are so confounded,
> As your hot fire beares water still in it. (no. 20, ll. 7–8)

The lady seems to relish inspiring fear and anxiety in her lover, and this leads to a questioning of her motives: may not honour and chastity be a mere mask for frigidity or promiscuity? The mistress, like a Renaissance monarch, claims to inspire love in her subjects; but she seems in fact to be following Machiavelli's counsels and aiming to inspire fear as well. The professed moral rigour of her rule may mask fickleness and inconstancy, a refusal to be loyal to her most devoted admirer. English writers sometimes commented on the superior moral virtue of northern ladies to the inconstant dames of the south; Queen Elizabeth benefited from this idea, being praised, as in Greville's fifty-fifth poem, as the Northern Star, fixed and constant. But he cynically observes in poem no. 11 that the vaunted virtue of northern ladies is merely a product of frigidity, '[f]eare keeping lust there very long at gaze'. When kindled by the fire of lust, they will be all the more insatiable and inconstant to their loyal admirers. While in *Caelica* no. 55 he says that those who think that the moon changes are merely deceived by their sense, in no. 64 he brings out the implication of the lunar image that was kept discreetly veiled by panegyrists of Elizabeth: Caelica turns a beautiful face on her admirers but he is now in a position to see the inconstant, dark side of the moon. The lady becomes a cunning tyrant, increasing the lover's abject dependence with a mask of honour which conceals her desire while increasing his. Such 'entisinge deniralls', Greville wrote elsewhere, have been figured by poets in the myth of Endymion and Diana.[20] In poem no. 74 a naive lover, failing to understand the rules of the game, is deterred by the lady's pretence of unwillingness from taking the sexual opportunity she has offered him. But on the whole the ladies in the sequence seem to prefer tormenting the lovers to granting their demands. From time to time the lover expresses his desire to renounce the mistress's tyranny: if she can be

---

[20] Greville, *A Letter to an Honorable Lady*, in *The Prose Works of Fulke Greville, Lord Brooke*, ed. Gouws, 142.

inconstant, so can he. His devotion has been an illusion, his worship of her has been mere idolatry, which is presented in increasingly explicit terms as the central human sin. Love is merely 'false lust disguised with deuotion' (no. 36, l. 12). The very idea that devotion to a mortal, and in particular to a member of the female sex, can in any way have a religious value emerges as blasphemous nonsense.

The Neoplatonic conception of the political world held together by love thus emerges as a deceitful disguise behind which the true relationships are those of domination and exploitation. The hierarchy is held together by fear rather than love, and its basis is irrational rather than a manifestation of cosmic order: the lady's favourites are chosen by an arbitrary grace rather than merit. The political analogies are made explicit in poem no. 30: Greville looks back to a time when his relations with Myra were based on good will and complains that she is now flattered by false friends and does not choose her followers on the basis of worthiness. The change parallels that from the republic, when the senators chose their governors and the people were free, to the empire, when legions gave power by 'bought voices' and worth was ignored. Interestingly, Greville reveals a much more favourable attitude to the Roman republic in this aside than he does when trying to set out his official views in the *Treatise of Monarchy*.[21] In poem no. 77 Greville traces the decline from a traditional order, in which many different social groups enjoyed distinct rights and privileges, to the present when tyrants are trying to 'enthrall Mens hearts' and undermine all traditional bastions of liberty, such as 'Church, Law, Custome, Peoples gouernment'. The poem resembles Sidney's beast-fable in the *Arcadia*, warning of the need for the nobility to preserve their traditional rights. In the old constitutional order 'love' meant a relationship between equals and based on a clear idea of mutual obligation, but 'time, and selfenesse' turn '[l]oue into complements' and sincere language degenerates into courtly flattery. In poem no. 49 Greville says that we praise princes 'for the good they neuer had'. At several points in the sequence Greville expresses nostalgia for a lost paradise in which love was pure and mutual:

> Beauty then neither net, nor made by art,
> Words out of thoughts brought forth, and not forgotten. (no. 44, ll. 6–7)

But Greville holds out little hope of reviving this golden age. Like La Boétie, he believes that most people have ceased even to desire liberty. They will their servitude, and make idols of their own desires. Greville's political analysis sharpens the relevance of a text that was very popular with Puritans: 'the imaginacion of mans heart *is* euil, *euen* fro[m] his youth' (Genesis 8: 21).[22] In poem no. 42 a lover tries to embrace his inconstant lady but finds himself instead holding on to his own desire:

> This Cloud straight makes a stream, in whose smooth face,
> While I the Image of my selfe did glasse,

---

[21] Greville, *A Treatise of Monarchy*, stanzas 614 ff., in *The Remains: Being Poems of Monarchy and Religon*, ed. G. A. Wilkes (Oxford, 1965), 189 ff.; cf. D. R. Woolf, *The Idea of History in Early Stuart England: Erudition, Ideology, and 'the Light of Truth' from the Accession of James I to the Civil War* (Toronto, 1990), 175–7.

[22] Quoted from the Geneva translation of 1560, fo. 4ᵛ.

> Thought Shadowes I, for beautie did embrace,
> Till streame and all except the cold did passe;
>   Yet faith held fast, like foyles where stones be set,
>   To make toyes deare, and fooles more fond to get.

The chill of chastity and narcissism is in some ways more attractive, because less threatening to the ego, than the fire of sexual passion. The tyrannical mistress would not be able to exercise such sway unless the lover himself desired his own enslavement; and she may fear the lover as much as he fears her (see no. 65). Because she is obsessed with honour, which depends on external validation rather than inner purity, she can never be self-sufficient. Both mistress and servant in this fallen world live in a state of perpetual insecurity from which they are unable to escape. The *Caelica* sequence reflects Greville's increasing disillusion with the aristocratic cult of honour and magnificence, which he was eventually to assault explicitly in his *Inquisition upon Fame and Honour*. Like La Boétie, Greville regarded the corruption inherent in the relations between monarch and courtier as extending down the social hierarchy; he too satirized the conventional 'chain of being' image. Titles of honour and ornaments of office are 'Powers golden fetter' with which wise kings 'adorne' their courtiers and compensate them for their lack of liberty; they are *'subiections gilded blisse'* (*Caelica*, no. 92, l. 9). Bought off by the monarchy, the nobility serve in turn to gull the people into believing that their external splendour implies inner worth:

> For place a Coronet on whom you will,
> You straight see all great in him, but his *Ill*. (no. 92, ll. 23–4)

The aristocracy is the 'luster wherin powre is magnified' and thus serves to command that 'tame wilde beast' the people, who are easily taken by 'faire shadowes of authoritie' (*Treatise of Monarchy*, stanzas 350, 332). Greville shares the conventional scorn of radical humanists for the gullibility of the people who are so easily dazzled by external show.

Greville came to see external social roles as hollow façades, alienations of the essential inner self. Compounds involving the word 'self' appear frequently in *Caelica* as in much Puritan writing. But if the façade of social appearances is normally deceptive, the inner self is also treacherous and paradoxical, and here Greville's Protestantism complicates his humanist individualism. The lover rebels against the mistress's demand that he abandon all 'selfe-nesse', but it becomes clear that the idol he adores is as much a projection of his own desires as an objective phenomenon. To maintain his subjectivity he has to subject himself. His dilemma resembles Ralegh's in 'The Ocean's Love to Cynthia': he struggles against 'the gentell chaynes of love' but does not really want his mistress to 'vntye' them.[23] The more the lover tries to escape external limitations and assert himself, the more problematic his self appears to be; he has a

---

[23]   *The Poems of Sir Walter Ralegh*, ed. Agnes M. C. Latham (London, 1951), 37.

> . . . double heart that loueth it selfe best,
> Yet can make selfe-loue beare the name of friend[.] (no. 67, ll. 7–8)

Sidney had advised the poet to 'look in thy heart and write', but Greville believed that

> when each of vs, in his owne heart lookes,
> He findes the God there, farre vnlike his Bookes.[24]

Only divine grace could ultimately resolve this dilemma, liberating the will from its perpetual bondage.

Greville's critical scrutiny of the cult of the female ruler was sharpened by a streak of misogyny. But because he was analysing the relations between ruler and subject in general, rather than Elizabethan conditions in particular, it was possible for him to reverse the sexual roles, as he did in his *Letter to an Honourable Lady* (*c.*1595). Here he still affirms the male's general superiority but takes a slightly more sympathetic viewpoint towards the woman, who is married to a tyrannical husband and thus becomes a symbol of the plight of the subject under a tyranny. The techniques used by an evil husband to bully his wife resemble the 'arts' of tyranny; government consists in making equality unequal, bringing freedom into subjection. Like Machiavelli, Greville argues that since we live in a fallen world, those who have a knowledge of evil will be better able to gain domination than the pure and innocent. The husband, or tyrant, gains his sway by a cunning alternation of hope and fear, just like the mistress in *Caelica*: subjects give away their rights for fear of losing them, but hope makes them worship false idols. In each case, they 'forsake the true flesh, to catch at the reflexion of shaddowes'. Again like the mistress in *Caelica*, the husband will find that the more skilfully he can exploit a virtuous admirer, the more bored he will become with her: he will desire change, and conceive 'idolatrouse longinge after strange, and uglie Images' of sin.[25] The husband/tyrant is less virtuous than the wife/subject, and is thus no more than a play-actor: 'exorbitancie of passions do manie times (like players upon stages) represent the office of a Kinge, in the person of a begger.' The powerful nostalgia for a golden age in which love was sincere and equal, which pervaded *Caelica*, is found again in the 'Letter': it was a time of 'true golden freedome', which has been replaced by the 'guilt, or painted fetters' of social inequalities. Tyrants have 'sinned against the true equalities of love, to take priviledge in the false sanctuaries of place, person, sexe, or time'.[26]

But Greville does not think such inequalities can now be remedied. He advises the lady to take a course that amounts to passive resistance. Certainly she must abandon any attempt to please or flatter him: where their relations are really governed by fear and domination, it would be mere mystification to claim that they involve love. She should no more dissimulate in order to please her husband than subjects should compromise themselves to please the prince who will make us 'like the little flies, apt to covet after the flatteringe light wherin we burne'. The image of moths being

---

[24] *Mustapha*, 'Chorus Sacerdotum', ll. 23–4; *Poems and Dramas*, ii 137
[25] Greville, *A Letter to an Honorable Lady*, 157, 140.   [26] Ibid. 167, 157, 140.

attracted to a flame had been used as a metaphor for the effects of tyranny by La Boétie, who gave one of Petrarch's sonnets (*Canzoniere*, no. 19) as his source.[27] Greville goes on to say that it would be futile for the lady to try to 'master' her husband, to rebel against his authority. He quotes the example of Sejanus' rebellion against the Emperor Tiberius—a topic Jonson was to dramatize shortly after Essex's rebellion. If there is no peace to be gained by trust of superiors, says Greville, there is no honour in strife against them. Moreover, in the case of the husband–wife relationship there is an additional factor: Greville insists that though the wife may excel the husband in some points, women are naturally inferior overall.[28] Divorce would be the domestic equivalent of rebellion against a tyrant in the political world, and Greville condemns both courses equally strongly.

But here again he is touching on sensitive ground. Traditionalists strongly opposed divorce on the grounds that if such an important bond could be severed the whole principle of order and degree would be threatened. But some more radical reformers tended to support divorce and remarriage. If they tended to equate irrationality and idolatry with female qualities, they were prepared to admit that pious and learned women could exist, and they emphasized that marriage should be a matter of rational choice rather than a mere arranged transaction. If this made them especially severe on adultery, it made them also prepared to sanction the dissolution of a marriage if it was failing to achieve its aims. In the Edwardian period plans had been made for an extensive reform of canon law which would permit certain kinds of divorce; Foxe reprinted these plans in 1571.[29] Milton, when writing his divorce tracts, was to take one of his major precedents from the Edwardian period. The Elizabethan age, however, saw a reaction on this issue and divorce remained difficult. Greville yet again counsels submission. The lady must draw the sap down to her roots and wait till the spring comes.[30] But the atmosphere of his writing is autumnal, and he leaves little to hope for.

In the end all of Greville's writings come down on the side of obedience and resignation. But, as La Boétie had pointed out, writing was itself a political act, helping to renew, at least inwardly, images of former liberty. It is not surprising that for Greville the act of writing was problematic. He kept touching on ideas more radical than those to which he was officially committed; he constantly revived the dreams of freedom and equality which his political caution made him regard as dangerous and delusory. Greville had great difficulty in casting his ideas in a final shape and in deciding on his relationship to his audience. After his love poems he embarked on the composition of closet dramas, plays which toyed with the idea of rebellion against tyrants even though they eventually rejected it. The closet drama was an essentially private form, and could be regarded as more politically responsible than the public

[27]   Greville, *A Letter to an Honorable Lady*, 147; La Boétie, *Discours*, 162, La Boétie, *Anti-Dictator*, 52; on the image as applied to Queen Elizabeth cf. Leonard Forster, *The Icy Fire: Five Studies in European Petrarchism* (Cambridge, 1969), 131–2.
[28]   Greville, *A Letter to an Honorable Lady*, 165, 145.
[29]   A. G. Dickens, *The English Reformation*, rev. edn. (London, 1967), 344–5.
[30]   Greville, *A Letter to an Honorable Lady*, 159.

theatre. Whereas seditious views expressed in public might stir up public disorder, a neoclassical verse drama was unlikely to inflame the multitude. But the dramatic form also made it possible to explore some radical ideas without publicly committing oneself to them. Thus it had been possible for Buchanan's *Baptistes* to be publicly printed in England while the *De jure regni*, of which it constituted the 'poetical draft', was banned. Interestingly, one early manuscript of Greville's *Mustapha* was bound up with the first English translation from the *De jure regni*.[31] Greville indeed was very sensitive to the accusation that his plays might be considered politically subversive. After Essex's rebellion he burned his play about Antony and Cleopatra, fearing that it would be misconstrued as a topical allegory. He decided to turn some of the choruses which contained general reflections into more abstract and orthodox political treatises. The first and longest treatise, that on Monarchy, was orthodox in doctrine, arguing that monarchy was the best form of government and comparing it favourably with aristocracy and democracy. But when Greville came to revise the poem some years later, he was disturbed by what he found: it seemed to him that it might 'cast scandal upon the sacred foundations of monarchy'.[32] He tried to save the situation by a series of formal strategies. First he recast the poem in a higher and more courtly style, apparently fearing that the poem's reductive and iconoclastic tone scarcely harmonized with its orthodox content. But he did not feel at home with the new style, and decided instead to 'take away all opinion of seriousness' from the poem by using 'that hypocritical figure ironia'. He then decided that such a strategy would again seem to take an insufficiently reverent view of monarchy. Finally, he left the treatise in such a state that his descriptions of the artifices of power could be applied equally to kings or tyrants, leaving it to the reader to decide what conclusions to draw. His argument that good kings and tyrants used very similar political strategies, and his powerful nostalgia for a golden age before monarchy was established, combined to suggest that all monarchy was at best a corrupt manifestation of the Fall. And if monarchical authority was not a divine gift, part of a natural cosmic order, but a corrupt secular artifice, then it might seem to follow that the people, who were at least no more corrupt than their ruler, had some inherent right to share in the process of government.[33] Sometimes he seems to be rejecting the 'descending' theory of authority: if the people are the 'makers' of tyrants, then they can also unmake them. The radical ambivalence of this treatise disturbed the censors in the 1630s when Greville's collected works were published, and it was suppressed.

Greville's writings not only analyse the phenomenon of voluntary servitude, in some ways they exemplify it. Greville frequently tried to break out of conventional patterns of thought and share his ideas with others. But not only external censorship but also inner inhibitions prevented him from reaching a large audience. Greville frequently uses images of confinement when describing his own writings. In the *Life of Sidney* he tells how the queen's distrust of him made him 'contract my thoughts from

---

[31] I. D. McFarlane, *Buchanan* (London, 1981), 387. On radical ideas in the drama see J. W. Lever, *The Tragedy of State* (London, 1971), 7 9. See also below, p. 191 n. 61.

[32] Greville, *A Dedication to Sir Philip Sidney*, 91.

[33] Ibid. 91–2; J. G. A. Pocock, *The Machiavellian Moment* (Princeton, 1975), 352–3.

those larger, but wandering, horizons' of foreign service and 'bound my prospect within the safe limits of duty'. In the same way, when describing his revisions of his tragedies, he explains that as a young man he 'ventured upon this spreading ocean of images' but wandered 'beyond proportion'.[34] Sidney had spoken of the poet's disdaining to be tied to the subjection of Nature but freely ranging within the zodiac of his wit; Greville subjected his imagination. There was a clear parallel here with the political caution that made Greville reconcile himself to the queen's will. Sidney had been less patient: in Greville's words, his 'industry, judgement and affections perchance seemed too great for the cautious wisdoms of little monarchies to be safe in'.[35] But Sidney's life and writing had been cut short: his curtailed promise became for Greville a symbol of the impossibility of breaking free of conventional bonds. He highlighted the incompleteness of the *Arcadia* by publishing his friend's book in its truncated final form, breaking off in mid-sentence. He emphasized and imitated this incompleteness in the *Life*: 'I will cut off his actions—as God did his life—in the midst'.[36] Greville's own writings are fissured by ellipses, by abrupt transitions, by sudden curtailments of dangerous lines of thought. The stylistic contortions of the *Life* can partly be accounted for by the tension between different levels of political discourse, from apocalyptic fervour to the cautious pragmatism of William Camden, one of his major sources. His poetry is so compressed that the sense is often obscure. His long prose sentences lack the architectonic balance of Sidney's periods, turning into syntactic labyrinths in which the sequence of ideas is hard to follow. It is as if Greville is half-reluctant to communicate his meaning to the reader: in La Boétie's terms, instead of sharing his imagination with others he remains singular in his fantasy. The voice of radical humanism has lapsed into a self-protective stutter.

Greville's style could be accurately described as 'obscure and melancholy': this was how another member of the Essex circle, Antonio Pérez, characterized his own style, and however idiosyncratic Greville may be, his writings are in many ways characteristic of a particular kind of political discourse in the 1590s.[37] Throughout Europe, in the later sixteenth century, writers were turning away from the elaborate 'Ciceronian' style, a style associated with public debate and oratory, and turning to 'silver Latin' writers like Seneca and Tacitus. These men were writing at a time when the Senate had lost its real political power and important decisions were taken in private by the emperor and his associates. Thus the 'Tacitist' movement had marked,

---

[34] Greville, *A Dedication to Sir Philip Sidney*, 89, 90.   [35] Ibid. 24.   [36] Ibid. 76.

[37] On Pérez in relation to Lipsius and Tacitus see Gustav Ungerer, *A Spaniard in Elizabethan England: The Correspondence of Antonio Pérez's Exile*, 2 vols. (London, 1974–6), ii.350–57, 371–7 ('obscurum & melancholicum', 325); on 'Tacitism' see Peter Burke, 'Tacitism', in T. A. Dorey (ed.), *Tacitus* (London, 1969), 149–71 and Pocock, *The Machiavellian Moment*, 351–7; on stylistic changes cf. Morris W. Croll, *Style, Rhetoric and Rhythm*, ed. J. Max Patrick et al. (Princeton, 1966), chs. 1 and 3. See further Alan R. Bradford, 'Stuart Absolutism and the "Utility" of Tacitus', *Huntington Library Quarterly* 46 (1983), 127–55; J. H. M. Salmon, 'Seneca and Tacitus in Jacobean England', in Linda Levy Peck (ed.), *The Mental World of the Stuart Court* (Cambridge, 1991), 169–88; Richard Tuck, *Philosophy and Government in England 1572–1651* (Cambridge, 1993), 39–119; Peter Burke, 'Tacitism, Scepticism, and Reason of State', in J. H. Burns (ed.), *The Cambridge History of Political Thought 1450–1700* (Cambridge, 1991), 479–98. On Greville and Lipsius, see Adriana McCrea, *Constant Minds: Political Virtue and the Lipsian Paradigm in England, 1584–1650* (Toronto, 1997), ch. 3.

though ambiguous, political connotations. Tacitism was in some ways a disguised Machiavellianism; and Machiavelli's own political writings were decidedly ambiguous. Educated in the spirit of republican humanism, he had despaired of the political infighting that allowed the Medici to suppress the republic with the help of foreign aid. Perhaps only a really decisive prince could finally liberate Italy from foreign domination, and he described this figure in *The Prince*. But if Machiavelli rejected the pious moralism of orthodox republicanism, he also challenged conventional ideas of political legitimacy, admiring resolute 'new men' who were bold enough to challenge fortune and convention. As the *Discourses* later made clear, he never lost his admiration for classical republicanism. Towards the end of the sixteenth century, however, an increasing number of conservative theorists throughout Europe began to take an interest in Machiavelli's writings. They argued that the tactics employed by Machiavelli's prince could be employed by legitimate rulers anxious to restore political order in the face of the disastrous series of religious wars. But Machiavelli's rationalistic analysis of political artifice did not easily harmonize with a public discourse in which it was still obligatory to speak of rulers as semi-divine images of God, in harmony with a natural order. Thus Machiavellian ideas tended to be adopted under a classical disguise, in the form of commentaries on Tacitus. The Roman historian's analysis of the triumph of the emperors over republican liberties provided a detailed account of successful techniques of political manipulation. Tacitus had republican sympathies, but he believed that the political elite had been so corrupted by imperial machinations that there was no hope of restoring the republic. His histories could be taken by theorists of 'reason of state' as detached and impartial analyses of the techniques necessary to maintain political order. The most influential commentator on Tacitus in the later sixteenth century, Justus Lipsius, was an admirer of Machiavelli and a theorist of reason of state. But Lipsius and other Tacitists warned that the artifices of power were 'mysteries of state' which should be revealed only to the few: if widely publicized they would shock the multitude who were still accustomed to idealizing the ruler as a sacramental image of God.

Tacitist discourse was, then, potentially dangerous: commentaries on Tacitus had a Machiavellian subtext and *The Prince* could be said to have a republican subtext. The study of Tacitus could help to nourish the very spirit of opposition it was designed to quell. La Boétie quoted Tacitus' analysis of the ways the emperors reconciled the multitude to their loss of liberty by providing them with public spectacles and games. In England, it was the restless members of the Sidney and Essex circles who popularized the study of Tacitus and Machiavelli. Sir Philip Sidney had urged his brother to study Tacitus, and as Sir Robert's heavily annotated copy has survived we know that he followed the advice. 'Princes', reads a characteristically double-edged annotation, 'may please the people with some shows of their ancient liberties.'[38] Greville's poetry is full of references to princes who tempt man to 'throw his libertie away', to exchange 'reall things' for mere 'glorious shadowes' like a dog

---

[38] Quoted by Blair Worden, 'Classical Republicanism and the Puritan Revolution', in Hugh Lloyd-Jones et al. (eds.), *History and Imagination: Essays in Honour of H. R. Trevor-Roper* (London, 1981), 182–200 (185–7).

who drops his bone to bite at his reflection in the water (*Caelica*, no. 78). The first English translation of Tacitus contained a preface probably written by Essex himself; one of the translators, Henry Cuffe, helped to plan the rebellion. Pérez had drawn on Tacitus' histories to provide ideological justification for the Aragonese rebellion against Philip II. In 1599 Sir John Hayward dedicated to Essex his Tacitean *Life of Henry IV*, which was alleged by the authorities to justify the deposition of evil rulers. The Sidney and Essex circles also took an informed interest in Machiavelli, as is shown by Spenser's *View of the Present State of Ireland*. Like so many writings associated with Essex, the *View* may have been censored.[39]

The political ambivalence of Greville's writings is characteristic of sixteenth-century Tacitism. He supported some of the arguments of the theorists of reason of state. Though he condemned traditional social roles as vain and idolatrous, he also justified their retention, though on grounds not of reverence for tradition but of practical utility. He was made more cautious by each new political disappointment—the death of Sidney, the collapse of Essex's more ambitious projects, and eventually the rebellion itself. He denied that Essex had acted with treasonable intent; and he clearly believed that he would not have been justified in forcing the queen's hand in an unconstitutional manoeuvre. Such actions risked precipitating the very development they opposed, making the monarchy lose patience with traditional constraints on its power. Only caution and prudence could safeguard the precarious political balance that still allowed England more liberties than many other European countries.

But though he rejected radical action, Greville was painfully apprehensive that the English monarchy might before long follow the general European trend and become 'metamorphosed' into a 'precipitate absoluteness'.[40] Towards the end of his life this fear led to an uncharacteristic move towards marginally more open political statement: he chose a young radical scholar, Isaac Dorislaus, to inaugurate a new history lectureship at Cambridge. The first two lectures caused a sensation and the series was suspended.[41] The political tensions of the Jacobean and Caroline periods made Elizabeth's reign seem in retrospect to have been a golden age. But Greville's writings of the 1590s suggest that he and other members of the Essex circle were not so certain at the time. Essex was campaigning for the succession of the Scottish king, who had been educated by the radical humanist George Buchanan and who, it was hoped, might listen to the earl's viewpoint more sympathetically than Elizabeth. But if Greville shared in these high hopes for James's reign, they were quickly disappointed.

[39] On Greville's close links with Essex just before the rebellion, see Paul E. J. Hammer, 'The Earl of Essex, Fulke Greville, and the Employment of Scholars', *Studies in Philology*, 91 (1994), 167–80. Hammer speaks of Essex as receiving 'tutorial-like' instruction on Tacitus from his scholarly associates: 'The Uses of Scholarship: The Secretariat of Robert Devereux, Second Earl of Essex, c.1585–1601', *English Historical Review*, 109 (1994), 26–51 (49). On censorship in the late 1590s see also Richard A. McCabe, '"Right Puisante and Terrible Priests": The Role of the Anglican Church in Elizabethan State Censorship', in Andrew Hadfield (ed.), *Literature and Censorship in Renaissance England* (Houndmills, 2001), 75–94.

[40] Greville, *A Dedication to Sir Philip Sidney*, 32.

[41] Rebholz, *Life of Fulke Greville*, 293–302.

7. Jonson and the Jacobean Peace, 1603–1616

WITHIN a few years of James VI and I's accession to the throne, Ben Jonson had become established as the leading court poet. Though he was never officially created laureate, he was on close personal terms with the king and was the regular author of court masques from 1605 to the end of the reign. As Spenser had celebrated Elizabeth in his epic, so Jonson celebrated James in his poems and masques. But his political stance marked a significant break with the major Tudor traditions of public poetry. Spenser had inherited from mid-century gospellers the idea of the poet as a prophet, celebrating the achievements of the Reformation and satirizing ecclesiastical abuses. Jonson reacted against this Protestant prophetic tradition in the most emphatic possible way: in the 1590s he became converted to Catholicism. The satire of Papal enormities and the fear of idolatry that ran through Spenser's poetry gave way to satires of the excesses of radical Protestants. Jonson never attempted to present himself as a prophetic poet; his stance was that of a detached and ironic observer of human affairs rather than a visionary who laid claim to special prophetic insights.

Sidney and Spenser had been brought up to believe that there was an international conspiracy by Catholic rulers to stamp out Protestantism and that free humanist enquiry was also threatened by Catholicism; the causes of humanism and of reformed religion were identical. Jonson questioned this belief. He was much more worried by the bigotry and dogmatism of radical Protestantism. In religious and political outlook he was influenced by his teacher at Westminster School, William Camden.[1] As has been seen, Camden disliked Puritan apocalyptic enthusiasm, hated the Earl of Leicester, and did not share Spenser's view of the Dutch campaign as an epochal struggle between good and evil. If Jonson ever saw the Dutch struggle in apocalyptic terms, he seems to have been disillusioned by the experience of going there as a soldier in the 1590s. The grim realities of sixteenth-century warfare were very different from the chivalric ideals of the Accession Day tilts. An attentive observer of Dutch politics would also soon have realized that the political issues were far more complex than many Englishmen believed: while the Calvinists were ardent believers in continuing the war against Antichrist, many members of the urban oligarchies were unsympathetic to Calvinist dogmatism and fanaticism; their Protestantism retained an Erasmian belief in free will. This group provided the basis for what became known as the 'Arminian' faction in the seventeenth century; the Arminians tended to favour peace with Spain and disliked Calvinist predestinarianism. It is significant that Jonson returned to the Church of England in the second

---

[1] Hugh R. Trevor-Roper, *Queen Elizabeth's First Historian: William Camden and the Beginnings of English 'Civil History'* (London, 1971).

decade of James's reign when Arminian ideas were flourishing in the Netherlands and were beginning to gain ground in the Church of England. In his later years Jonson was associated with the 'Great Tew' group of liberal Protestants who drew inspiration from Erasmus and the Arminians.[2] In the 1590s, however, it was difficult for such views to find a hearing in the English church; in 1595 Archbishop Whitgift declared predestination to be an essential part of the official doctrine. Possibly influenced by Lipsius' example, Jonson seems to have decided that only Catholicism could offer a firm point of stability in a world that seemed to be the victim of an infinitely proliferating series of religious schisms and ideological conflicts.[3]

For the subject of a Protestant ruler, of course, a change of religion produced an inevitable conflict of loyalties. But Jonson aligned himself with the moderate Catholics who disliked Jesuit fanaticism and were willing to affirm their loyalty to the English crown. In 1605 he willingly served as a government spy against the Gunpowder conspirators. For all his loyalty to the crown, however, he found himself alienated from the political symbolism of the Elizabethan period. He found the Protestant chivalry of the Elizabethan court distasteful both because of the aversion to war he had learned in the Netherlands and because of its associations with apocalyptic enthusiasm. He disliked Spenser's archaic language and was irreverent about many admired figures of Elizabethan public life, such as Sir Philip Sidney. He tried to gain favour at court with his play *Cynthia's Revels*, but his presentation of the queen and her court was slightly lacking in the mythical fervour normally expected in devotees of the monarch. He had aroused much criticism by bringing on a character representing Elizabeth to resolve the action in one of his comedies, *Every Man out of his Humour*: to involve the queen in a realistic comedy was felt to be indecorous. Jonson's sceptical temper found the whole cult of the Fairy Queen somewhat absurd: in *The Alchemist* he was to present belief in fairies as the whimsical fantasy of a foolish London clerk.[4]

Jonson's alienation from the court quickly ended when James came to the throne. The new king found the ambitious poet's views and personality congenial. A shrewd tactician, James had set himself on a gradual course of stabilizing Scottish politics by diminishing the authority of both Catholic and Protestant militants and restoring the prestige of the monarchy, which had become seriously undermined in a long

---

[2] For some pertinent comments on Jonson's religious views see Graham Bradshaw, 'Three Poems Ben Jonson Did Not Write: A Note on Jonson's Christian Humanism', *ELH*, 47 (1980), 484–99.

[3] On Lipsius' influence on Jonson's style see Wesley Trimpi, 'Jonson and the Neo-Latin Authorities for the Plain Style', *Publications of the Modern Language Association of America*, 77 (1962), 21–6; on his political ideas, Quentin Skinner, *The Foundations of Modern Political Thought*, 2 vols. (Cambridge, 1978), ii.278–83; see also Morris Croll, *Style, Rhetoric, and Rhythm*, ed. J. Max Patrick et al. (Princeton, 1966), chs. 1 and 3. See also Robert C. Evans, *Jonson, Lipsius, and the Politics of Renaissance Stoicism* (Wakefield, NH, 1992), Adriana McCrea, *Constant Minds: Political Virtue and the Lipsian Paradigm in England 1584–1650* (Toronto, 1997), ch. 4, and Blair Worden, 'Ben Jonson among the Historians', in Kevin Sharpe and Peter Lake (eds.), *Culture and Politics in Early Stuart England* (London, 1994), 67–90.

[4] On Jonson's distaste for Elizabethan symbolism see Frances Yates's (rather too solemn) discussion in *Shakespeare's Last Plays: A New Approach* (London, 1975), 109–26; on the general shift towards a courtly classicism see R. Malcolm Smuts, *Court Culture and the Origins of a Royalist Tradition in Early Stuart England* (Philadelphia, 1987), ch. 4.

series of factional disputes. In recent years the most critical opposition had come from the presbyterians, who had disputed the monarch's right to intervene in clerical affairs and were prepared to subject the king to lectures on his duties. Reacting against Buchanan's lectures about limited monarchy and the rights of the people, James laid more and more emphasis on the glories and the divine character of hereditary kingship. The reaction was not complete: despite his exalted rhetoric, James's political practice, both in Scotland and in England, tended to be prudently constitutional. And he remained faithful, for most of his life at least, to his youthful Calvinism. But he was deeply suspicious of the subversive potential of radical Protestantism. And even before he came to England he had started to use the drama to reinforce his cult of kingship. Despite a chronic lack of financial resources, he had begun to stage occasional court masques—he wrote one of them himself—and a troupe of English actors was developing into a royal theatre company. Violent attacks on stage-plays by the presbyterians strengthened his resolve to defend the theatre as a symbol of royal authority.[5] On his arrival at the English court, with its much greater resources, he was quick to take over the patronage of the Lord Chamberlain's Men and to sponsor masques at court. He was determined to extend his role as royal mediator between Protestant and Catholic extremes to the European political stage, and in Jonson he found someone sympathetic to these ideals and able to dramatize them on the court stage.

But it was to take some time for Jonson to establish his position at court. On James's accession it would have seemed likely to many observers that the role of leading court poet would be filled by Samuel Daniel, who was widely seen on Spenser's death as the most eminent living poet. He wrote a *Panegyrike* for presentation to the king on his way south to London in 1603, and was commissioned to write one of the first Jacobean masques, *The Vision of the Twelve Goddesses*, as part of the first season of court revels. But Daniel was not temperamentally well equipped for the role of laureate. He had inherited from the Sidney and Essex circles a certain distrust of courtly luxury and spectacle. He had served as tutor to the young William Herbert, Earl of Pembroke, the nephew of Sir Philip Sidney, and in the 1590s he was strongly influenced by Fulke Greville. While Greville was working on his closet dramas Daniel had been writing a political play, *Philotas*, which revealed a comparable preoccupation with tyranny. The play showed Alexander the Great unjustly putting to death a worthy favourite; Cecil became convinced that this was a seditious defence of Essex. Whether or not this was a just accusation, Daniel's hostility to pomp and ceremony was too deep-rooted to make him a very effective court poet. In his critical treatise *A Defence of Ryme* Daniel had adopted a severely Spartan view of culture and society. It was, he said, 'vnlearned *Rome*' in its austere early days that had laid the foundations of the Roman state, whereas 'eloquent *Rome*' fell into disorder and allowed a collapse 'from the glory of a common-wealth' to an absolutist empire.

[5] Arthur Melville Clark, *Murder under Trust; or, The Topical* Macbeth *and Other Jacobean Matters* (Edinburgh, 1981), 127–78. See further James Shapiro, '*The Scot's Tragedy* and the Politics of Popular Drama', *English Literary Renaissance*, 23 (1993), 428–49 (434–6).

'Eloquence and gay wordes', he said, were merely 'the garnish of a nice time, the Ornaments that doe but decke the house of a State', a superstructure that was useless without a secure base.[6] In his *Panegyrike* Daniel praised the frugal Henry VII and urged James to avoid luxury. One of his sources was James's own treatise on kingship, *Basilicon Doron*; but it soon became clear that James preferred dispensing money to saving it. Daniel's masque revealed a similar anxiety about courtly luxury; though elaborate scenery was provided by Inigo Jones, Daniel took care that spectacle should not obscure the verbal content.[7]

Dismissing—for the time being at any rate—such inhibitions about spectacle, Jonson was convinced that he would be able to outdo Daniel, who was an old rival, in the art of the masque. He took an interest in the court masques that winter; he and his friend Sir John Roe were expelled from one masque for disorderly behaviour. Perhaps Jonson had pointed out that he could do better.[8] He certainly made every effort to attract the royal family's attention: in the first two years of the reign he wrote two royal entertainments, a civic pageant, and some pageants for the king's state entry to London in March 1604. Jonson published his contributions to the royal entry separately from his collaborators Dekker and Middleton: he was eager to show his unique ability to fashion new kinds of courtly compliment out of his mythological erudition. It was Jonson who was commissioned to write the major court masque for January 1605, and this was such a success that Jonson became the regular masque-writer. Insofar as Daniel did gain patronage, it was at the court of Queen Anne, which became an alternative patronage centre. Bitter about his failure to receive royal patronage, in 1605 he complained that the Muses no longer flourished under the new reign.[9]

But Jonson's muse flourished. The masques gave him an unrivalled opportunity to exercise political influence, to put his art in the service of the state. In his *Discoveries* he wrote that a poet 'can faine a *Common-wealth*'; he was perhaps echoing Sidney's description of More.[10] But the values of Jonson's ideal commonwealth are very different from those of Utopia, or indeed of Sidney's *Arcadia*. More had despised the ideal of magnificence: Sidney and Spenser valued it but insisted that it must be kept under control and must be combined with Protestant virtue. The Jacobean masque glorified conspicuous consumption on an unprecedented scale. The Privy Council, alarmed at James's extravagance, had suggested that there should be no repetition of the first year's round of extravagant masques: Elizabeth

---

[6] Daniel, *A Defence of Ryme*, in *Poems and A Defence of Ryme*, ed. Arthur Colby Sprague (Cambridge, Mass., 1930), 144–5. On Daniel and the shift in culture under James I, see Curtis Perry, *The Making of Jacobean Culture: James I and the Renegotiation of Elizabethan Literary Practice* (Cambridge, 1997), 25–6 and *passim*.

[7] Daniel's masque, *The Vision of the Twelve Goddesses*, has been edited by Joan Rees in T. J. B. Spencer et al. (eds.), *A Book of Masques in Honour of Allardyce Nicoll* (Cambridge, 1967), 17–42.

[8] Roe's poem on this occasion is printed in *Ben Jonson*, ed. C. H. Herford and Percy and Evelyn Simpson, 11 vols. (Oxford, 1925–52) (hereafter *H&S*), xi.371.

[9] Preface to *Philotas*, in *The Complete Works in Verse and Prose of Samuel Daniel*, ed. Alexander B. Grosart, 5 vols. (London, 1885–96), iii.102.

[10] *H&S*, viii.595.

had spent so much money only on very exceptional occasions.[11] But James seems to have considered regular masques to be essential to his conception of the dignity of monarchy.

Jonson's idealization of magnificence was combined with a strong hostility to the frugal values of the City. In his masque *Love Restored* he presented critics of the masques' extravagance as mean-spirited misers. In the sixteenth century trade and commerce had expanded enormously, and Jonson frequently satirized the narrowly acquisitive values which seemed to him to be becoming dominant in London. Only a society which valued honour and nobility could avoid being dominated by the values of the market-place.[12] Jonson pointedly set *Volpone* in the mercantile republic of Venice, a city whose constitution was idealized by republicans, and showed that its vaunted claims for superior justice were spurious: everyone in the city was out for financial gain.[13] In *The Alchemist* the three conspirators, Face, Subtle, and Doll Common, form a contract to share out the proceeds of their trickery, but because their 'republic' of shared interests has no basis in nature or tradition it quickly disintegrates. It is Doll Common, the whore who is ready for everything, who refers to herself as a 'republic'—literally, the 'public thing'—and the pun indicates Jonson's low opinion of an egalitarian commonwealth.[14] Jonson often spoke of hereditary nobility with scorn, but in fact he had much more respect for titles and traditions than the early sixteenth-century humanists. Jonson's disdain for republics harmonized with James's views. The king disliked the traditional Puritan admiration for the Dutch; in 1620 he declared that the English were becoming 'too republicanising', and he considered the dignity and majesty of the Spanish court as a more suitable model for the English to emulate.[15] His desire for closer ties with the old Spanish enemy culminated in the negotiations for Charles to marry a Spanish princess in the 1620s; Inigo Jones built the stately new Banqueting House for the masques which were planned to celebrate the dynastic link between the Stuarts and the House of Habsburg.

Though Jonson admired aristocratic dignity, he insisted that the nobility must abandon their traditional concern with military glory and pursue the arts of peace. Here he was returning to a theme often sounded by the earlier humanists but neglected in the militant atmosphere of the later sixteenth century. Leicester and

---

[11] *Historical Manuscripts Commission. Calendar of the Manuscripts of the Most Hon. the Marquess of Salisbury, Preserved at Hatfield House* xvi, ed. M. S. Giuseppi (London, 1933), 388–9.

[12] On this topic see L. C. Knights, *Drama and Society in the Age of Jonson* (London, 1937); but Knights's approach to Jonson is rather too moralistic, see also the review by Alick West, 'Ben Jonson Was No Sentimentalist', *Left Review*, 8 (Sept. 1937), 468–75. Isabel Rivers, *The Poetry of Conservatism 1600–1745: A Study of Poets and Public Affairs from Jonson to Pope* (Cambridge, 1973), ch. 2, gives a general survey of Jonson's political views. Julie Sanders, *Jonson's Theatrical Republics* (Houndmills, 1998) offers a stimulating riposte to my anti-republican readings and an ambitious attempt to link older interpretations of Jonson's communalism with newer republican discourses.

[13] Daniel C. Boughner, 'Lewkenor and *Volpone*', *Notes and Queries*, 207 (1962), 124–30.

[14] *The Alchemist*, I.i.110; *H&S*, v.299.

[15] Simon Adams, 'Spain or the Netherlands? The Dilemmas of Early Stuart Foreign Policy', in Howard Tomlinson (ed.), *Before the English Civil War: Essays on Early Stuart Politics and Government* (New York, 1983), 79–101; *Calendar of State Papers . . . Venice, 1619–21*, 490 (*troppo republicanti*).

Essex had sometimes allowed their desire for military glory to interfere with their loyalty to the monarch: Jonson insisted that peace and service of the monarch were more glorious than war. Under Elizabeth the dominant form of panegyric had been the tournament with its glorification of military values: under James the tournament was eclipsed by the masque. The harmony of the music and poetry symbolized the peace and harmony which James was trying to promote throughout Europe. Rather than venturing abroad on irresponsible military ventures, the nobility should pursue the arts of peace under the guidance of their sovereign. The masque form drama-tized this dependence of the nobility on the monarch: all the participants had to act out a formal pattern that centred on the ruler. This pre-eminence of the king was highlighted by the perspective stage, which Jones devised so that the lines of sight converged on the monarch.[16] Jones borrowed many of his ideas for royal entertain-ments from the absolutist court of the Medici at Florence. Jonson used optical effects as a symbol of royal power in an epigram of 1613:

> Except your Gratious Eye as through a Glass
> made prospectiue, behould hym, hee must pa<s>e
> still that same little poynte hee was; but when
> your Royal Eye which still creat[t]es new men
> shall looke, & on hyme soe, then arte's a lyer
> yf from a little sparke hee rise not fier.[17]

The prince is the creator of his subject's public roles, the architect of the 'theatre' of the court. His activity is thus directly parallel to the poet's activity: the state is the prince's work of art.[18] Jonson is particularly fond of drawing analogies between poets and princes, an analogy which Spenser and Sidney had used less often. It seemed especially appropriate because James was himself a poet and had had himself crowned with laurel on the model of Petrarch's 'coronation'.[19] After his arrival in England James dropped this public role as poet-prince, though he continued to write some poems, and Jonson strongly hinted that he would like to receive the laureateship.[20] More generally, the analogy between poet and prince indicates how firmly Jonson's conception of the well-being of the state was centred on the monarchy: he was much more completely the court poet than Spenser had been.

This does not mean that Jonson was an uncritical mouthpiece of royal policy. He developed a knack of praising the king without compromising his own integrity by

---

[16] Stephen Orgel and Roy Strong, *Inigo Jones: Theatre of the Stuart Court*, 2 vols. (London, 1973), i.1–14.

[17] *H&S*, viii.383.

[18] Ernst H. Kantorowicz, 'The Sovereignty of the Artist: A Note on Legal Maxims and Renaissance Theories of Art', in *Selected Studies* (New York, 1965), 352–65.

[19] On James's poetic career see Helena Mennie Shire, *Song, Dance and Poetry of the Court of Scotland under King James VI* (Cambridge, 1969) and Rhodes Dunlap, 'King James's Own Masque', *Philological Quarterly*, 41 (1962), 249–56.

[20] Jonson made his friend John Selden include an account of the coronation of poets in the 1631 edi-tion of his *Titles of Honour*, *H&S*, xi.383–4.

adapting James's favourite political metaphors and subtly varying them.[21] These strategies were so oblique that it is questionable whether the king noticed anything more than flattery; but at several points in the reign Jonson found himself in trouble for what were considered to be openly offensive statements in his plays. In 1605 he was imprisoned along with Marston and Chapman because of some passages in their jointly written play *Eastward Ho!* which were taken to be attacking James and his Scottish favourites. His troubles with the authorities had begun almost as soon as James came to the throne: the Earl of Northampton took exception to his play *Sejanus* and he was called before the Council. The play has several points in common with the political dramas of Greville and Daniel. It shows how Tiberius uses both direct censorship and cunning dissimulation to destroy liberty and instil an atmosphere of terror and suspicion. Northampton, one of the king's most unpopular councillors, evidently feared that the play could be taken as a satire on his own love of political intrigue. Jonson constantly equates princes with play-actors: 'Rarely dissembled,' exclaims one of the characters about Tiberius' actions, and his friend replies, 'Prince-like, to the life.'[22]

But Jonson's attitude to play-acting is slightly different from Greville's or Daniel's. He portrays Tiberius' Machiavellian cunning with a certain amount of sardonic relish: as in his comedies, this is a world largely divided into fools and knaves, and however pure the virtuous characters may be they are not as dramatically interesting as the dissemblers. Jonson draws his story mainly from Tacitus' *Annals*, and his virtuous characters voice the stock criticisms of imperial tyranny. But his reading of Tacitus is a 'Machiavellian' one, revealing an admiration for cunning strokes of political manipulation. Jonson was christened 'Monsieur Machiauell' by his rival Dekker and he was certainly familiar both with the Florentine's writings and with Lipsius' 'Machiavellian' Tacitism.[23]

The tone of *Sejanus* has something in common with one of the most Machiavellian of all Renaissance handbooks to court life, Lorenzo Ducci's *Ars aulica*, which appeared in Italy shortly before Jonson wrote his play and was translated a few years later with a dedication to Jonson's patron, the Earl of Pembroke, and his brother. Ducci's treatise is a satire on political corruption, but throughout the book he never lets his ironic mask slip, and the effect is highly disturbing: the reader is left without any positive moral guidelines and is made to feel rather naive and unworldly when confronted with the cool assurance with which Ducci's narrator gives his Machiavellian prescriptions. His central assumption is that the aim of the courtier will always be to seek his own personal advantage. But, he says, the best way to achieve this end will be to give the impression that he is serving the prince

[21] Jonathan Goldberg, *James I and the Politics of Literature: Jonson, Shakespeare, Donne, and their Contemporaries* (Baltimore, 1983), 120 ff.; the most ingenious example of this strategy, in *The Gypsies Metamorphosed*, is analysed by Dale B. J. Randall, *Jonson's Gypsies Unmasked: Background and Theme of The Gypsies Metamorphos'd* (Durham, NC, 1975).

[22] *Sejanus*, I.395; *H&S*, iv.368. See also Worden, 'Ben Jonson among the Historians', 76–89.

[23] See Daniel Boughner, 'Jonson's Use of Lipsius in *Sejanus*', *Modern Language Notes*, 73 (1958), 247–55, and *The Devil's Disciple: Ben Jonson's Debt to Machiavelli* (New York, 1968).

disinterestedly, for only in this way will he gain lasting favour. The best courtier will therefore be the most skilful dissimulator. Ducci summarizes with relish Tacitus' story of how Sejanus flung himself in front of some falling rocks to protect the Emperor. For Ducci this act is an example not of heroism but of masterly dissimulation: nobody could have imagined that such an act proceeded from anything but disinterested loyalty, but Ducci is sure that his hero had time in the split second before the rocks hit him to calculate that he would advance his long-term interests better by risking injury and saving his master than by running away like the other imperial servants.[24] Jonson relates this incident in *Sejanus*, and the atmosphere of his play is rather similar: Tiberius, the supreme master of cunning dissimulation, gains a certain amount of admiration. The virtuous characters are rather dull—Arruntius bitterly describes himself and his fellow republicans as 'good-dull-noble lookers on'.[25] It is Tiberius, whether on or off stage, who initiates the most important actions in the play; and his ability as a dissembler, an actor, to some extent undermines the audience's moral disapproval.

Jonson does not abandon moral considerations altogether; he is not holding up Tiberius for our approval. The criticisms of tyranny still have considerable force, and Jonson gives more explicit moral guidelines than Ducci. But Jonson's play does differ in its moral balance from the political dramas of Greville and Daniel. Both the latter poets make sharp distinctions between inner virtue and external appearance. Greville in particular takes as his ideal a spiritual purity which may be invisible except to the eye of faith. He is so contemptuous of mere external actions, as opposed to inner faith, that all public roles and values come to seem no more than empty play-acting in his writings. Jonson, by contrast, was rather suspicious of claims to inner purity: any attempt to achieve absolute purity in a fallen world seemed to him potentially hypocritical. It seemed to him more honest to acknowledge that all secular activity involved some kind of moral compromise. Jonson said that his fellow poet William Drummond was 'too good and simple': moral idealism was no good without a realistic awareness of corruption.[26] One reason for the Puritans' hostility to the public stage was their belief that actors in external disguises could not be expected to represent inner purity. Greville and Daniel shared this attitude in differing degrees. Jonson was the first major English public poet to have made a living as a playwright, and his hostility to Puritanism was, it could be said, professional. But it was consistent with his general reverence for ritual and ceremony. Jonson had none of Daniel's scruples about turning the court into a theatre.

And yet Jonson also produced a large body of non-dramatic verse in which he expressed his scorn of courtiers and courtly spectacles. In his poem 'To Sir Robert Wroth', published in *The Forest* (1616), Jonson praises Sir Robert for staying

[24] Lorenzo Ducci, *Ars aulica or the Courtiers Arte*, trans. E. Blount (London, 1607), 27, 33–5, 97–8, 108, 269–70; cf. *Sejanus*, IV.47–60; *H&S*, iv.420. Ducci was an anti-Spanish Tacitist: see Giorgio Spini, 'Historiography: The Art of History in the Italian Counter Reformation', in Eric Cochrane (ed.), *The Late Italian Renaissance 1525–1630* (London, 1970), 91–133 (119–20).

[25] *Sejanus*, III.16; *H&S*, iv.393.   [26] *H&S*, i.148.

in the country rather than going to watch court masques, 'the short brauerie of the night'.[27] Several of the poems in *The Forest* are addressed to members of the Sidney family: the second poem, 'To Penshurst', to Sir Philip's brother Robert Sidney, Viscount Lisle, the fifteenth to his son Sir William Sidney, and the twelfth to Sir Philip's daughter, the Countess of Rutland. Sir Robert Wroth was married to Sir Robert Sidney's daughter Mary. Jonson dedicated his 'Epigrams', which were published along with *The Forest*, to the Earl of Pembroke, the son of Sir Philip Sidney's sister Mary. Pembroke gave Jonson an annual allowance. By making public his many links with the Sidney dynasty, Jonson was establishing himself as an heir of the Elizabethan tradition of public poetry. Sidney's relations with the court, as has been seen, had not been altogether easy. His brother Robert felt that he had never received the direct recognition he deserved. In 'To Penshurst' Jonson contrasts the relative modesty of Sidney's country seat with the 'proud, ambitious heaps' of the 'prodigy-houses' which other members of the nobility were building to display their wealth. Some of these houses, such as Sir Robert Cecil's, were built with the aid of large pensions from the Spanish; Sir Robert Sidney, true to Elizabethan tradition, had refused a Spanish pension.[28] Sir Robert Wroth came from a family with strong Puritan traditions. The Earl of Pembroke became a leader of the anti-Spanish group at court; he has been described as the head of a parliamentary and Puritan 'opposition'.[29]

But *The Forest* is not really an anti-courtly volume. Jonson certainly values the Sidney and Herbert families for their tradition of proud independence, their refusal to become servile courtiers. But this does not necessarily mean that he supports the tradition of Protestant militancy with which they were also associated. Throughout *The Forest* the emphasis is on peaceful activities; Sidney and Wroth devote their energies to cultivating the land, whose fertility Jonson constantly emphasizes. Imagery of natural growth runs through the volume. The one reference to Sir Philip Sidney alludes not to his restless Protestant internationalism but to a tree planted at his birth and now flourishing under the Stuart peace.[30] The cultivation of plants is associated with the rearing of the family; Jonson is fond of developing the stock analogy between a dynasty and a tree. He asks Lady Aubigny to

> raise a noble stemme, to giue the fame,
> To CLIFTON's bloud, that is deny'd their name.

[27] Ibid., viii.96, l. 10.

[28] Ibid. 96, l. 101; J. C. A. Rathmell, 'Jonson, Lord Lisle, and Penshurst', *English Literary Renaissance*, 1 (1971), 250–60; Lawrence Stone, *Family and Fortune: Studies in Aristocratic Finance in the Sixteenth and Seventeenth Centuries* (Oxford, 1973), 57–8.

[29] Margot Heinemann, *Puritanism and Theatre: Thomas Middleton and Opposition Drama under the Early Stuarts* (Cambridge, 1980), 264–79. Pembroke's influence may have something to do with the fact that Jonson did not satirize moderate Puritans who remained in the established church: his attacks are directed at separatists, whom moderate Puritans detested. On Pembroke as a literary patron see Michael Brennan, *Literary Patronage in the English Renaissance: The Pembroke Family* (London, 1988), chs. 6–8.

[30] 'To Penshurst', ll. 13–14; *H&S*, viii.94. On the imagery of cosmic order in this poem, including the presentation of James's visit to the house as a type of the Second Coming, see Alastair Fowler, 'The Locality of Jonson's *To Penshurst*', in *Conceitful Thought: The Interpretation of English Renaissance Poems* (Edinburgh, 1975), 114–34.

> Grow, grow, faire tree, and as thy branches shoote,
> Heare, what the *Muses* sing about thy roote.[31]

The emphasis is on the positive aspects of growth and continuity; Jonson's satirical allusions to social abuses are only secondary. The poems give the sense of a nation which, whatever its faults, is essentially harmonious and well ordered and reflects credit on its governors. Clarendon wrote of Pembroke that he 'lived many years about the Court before in it, and never by it'. Pembroke's very independence helped to strengthen public confidence in the monarchy, making 'the Court itself better esteemed and more reverenced in the country'.[32] Clarendon was referring to the earl's later years when he had become established as a political leader; but when *The Forest* was published Pembroke had in any case not yet assumed a major political role. Jonson got to know him when he was very much the courtier rather than the Protestant politician; he took part in many masques and himself wrote some love poetry. His private life was far from puritanical, and he had two illegitimate children by Sir Robert Wroth's wife Lady Mary.[33] In this period of relative political calm, before the outbreak of the Thirty Years War, the heirs of the Elizabethan anti-Spanish tradition were reasonably content to settle into a peaceful and relatively inactive public role. Sir Robert Sidney had moments of frustration with courts and court life, and seems to have flirted with republican ideas, but he regularly made an appearance at court in his most spectacular clothing; there was no polarization between 'court' and 'country'.[34]

One of the arts of peace which the Sidney and Herbert families now pursued was poetry. The Earl of Pembroke, Sir Robert Sidney, his daughter Mary, and the Countess of Rutland all wrote poetry themselves, and patronized poets. The title of the collection links poetry with the general pattern of organic growth. 'Sylva' was the Latin term for a collection of varied raw materials or writings, a 'forest' of different poems.[35] Jonson's fondness for using arboreal metaphors for poetic composition reflects his rejection of the idea of poetry as prophecy: Spenser and his seventeenth-century imitators regularly compared poetry to music, or water, or light, implying that it was divinely inspired, a gift rather than just an art, flowing irresistibly through the poet who was its medium. Such language was of course figurative: Spenser knew that poetry needed conscious shaping. But he tried to give his verse a musical quality,

[31]   *H&S*, viii.119, ll. 97–100.

[32]   Edward Hyde, Earl of Clarendon, *The History of the Rebellion and Civil Wars in England*, ed. W. Dunn Macray (Oxford, 1888), i.71.

[33]   *The Poems English and Latin of Edward, Lord Herbert of Cherbury*, ed. G. C. Moore Smith (Oxford, 1923), 42; Brennan, *Literary Patronage in the English Renaissance: The Pembroke Family*, 156–7.

[34]   On Sir Robert Sidney see Blair Worden, 'Classical Republicanism and the Puritan Revolution', in Hugh Lloyd-Jones et al. (eds.), *History and Imagination: Essays in Honour of H. R. Trevor-Roper* (London, 1981), 182–200 (185–7).

[35]   Alastair Fowler, 'The *Silva* Tradition in Jonson's *The Forrest*', in Maynard Mack and George deForest Lord (eds.), *Poetic Traditions of the English Renaissance* (New Haven, 1982), 163–80; on Jonson's organic imagery see also Richard S. Peterson, *Imitation and Praise in the Poems of Ben Jonson* (New Haven, 1981), 10, 30, 102–10.

to make it flow as smoothly as possible. Jonson roundly declared that 'Spencers stan-zaes pleased him not, nor his matter', and he certainly tried to achieve rather differ-ent effects.[36] He ridiculed 'Womens-*Poets*' who had 'a kind of tuneing, and riming fall, in what they write'.[37] The implication is that sense is masculine, harmony of verse feminine: the poet should not allow verbal beauty to override the meaning. He complained that King James, whose taste had been formed by Italian poets and their French and English imitators, sang verses instead of reading them. He disliked sonnets because their rhyme-scheme was too artificial: couplets, he said, were the bravest kind of verse.[38] Jonson did not like poetry that tried to achieve some kind of special prophetic status by deviating too far from everyday speech. He never adopted the persona of the poet as visionary shepherd which Spenser had made central to English public poetry.

Jonson has been described as a poet of the 'plain style', but this description is slightly misleading. He disliked obtrusive artifice but he did believe that poetry should be polished, that it should have a smooth texture; he thought that Donne went too far in his reaction against ornamental courtly verse and became unnecessarily harsh and obscure.[39] His poetry is always carefully finished and formally organized, and even a relatively 'plain' poem like 'To Penshurst' proves on closer examination to have a complex numerological structure. But Jonson aimed to naturalize the artifice of his poetry, to give an impression of directness and colloquial energy. The verbal texture of a poem, he said, should be 'like a Table, upon which you may runne your finger without rubs, and your nayle cannot find a joynt; not horrid, rough, wrinckled, gaping, or chapt'.[40] The wood has been polished until it is smooth, but the polishing can never entirely remove its organic texture. Art and nature collaborate harmo-niously; the poet does not lay claim to a privileged kind of knowledge but unobtru-sively formalizes the natural processes of speech and thought, going with the grain of the language. Jonson has been praised for the 'rooted and racy Englishness' of his style.[41] This sense of rootedness reflects the fact that his political and social ideals were not so radical that they could not find some concrete embodiment in English social and religious traditions. More's classicism had in some ways been rootless because he was dissatisfied with the established order in England; Jonson found faults in particular individuals but believed that the principle of social hierarchy and monarchy was perfectly sound.

His conservatism was not simply backward-looking: his organic imagery has strongly positive associations, reflecting a belief that intellectual and political progress was being made. He was a great admirer of Bacon. One of his favourite writers was the sixteenth-century humanist Vives, a friend of More and Erasmus, who used the imagery of natural growth to indicate the possibility of making new discoveries:

[36] *H&S*, i.132. This remark should of course be taken with a grain of salt since Jonson was fond of teasing William Drummond, a great admirer of Spenser.
[37] Ibid., viii.585.   [38] Ibid., i.148, 132.
[39] 'Done for not keeping of accent deserved hanging', ibid., i.133.   [40] Ibid., viii.626.
[41] F. R. Leavis, *Revaluation: Tradition and Development in English Poetry* (London, 1936), 17.

Nature is not yet so effete and exhausted as to be unable to bring forth, in our times, results comparable to those of earlier ages. She always remains equal to herself, and not rarely . . . comes forward more strongly and powerful than in the past, as if mustering together all her forces.[42]

Vives praised Aristotle because he dared 'to pluck up by the root the received opinions of his predecessors'; Jonson endorsed the view that new advances could be made and that the ancients should not be idolized. His conservatism was in some ways radical: some of his contemporaries feared that James was trying to increase royal power illegitimately and looked back nostalgically to Elizabethan institutions, whereas Jonson believed that a strong monarchy was essential and was prepared to risk antagonizing some people by helping to glorify it in innovative masques. Whatever short-term controversies might ensue, in the long term a strongly authoritative monarchy would be the best means of holding in check some of the more undesirable aspects of economic and religious individualism.

It was appropriate, then, that he should model himself on Horace, in whom the austerity of some earlier Latin writers had given way to delicate irony with a courtly tone. Jonson found Horace 'the best master, both of vertue, and wisdome'. He was such a good judge of causes and reasons 'not because he thought so; but because he knew so, out of use and experience'. Horace had no time for utopian speculation, he concentrated on what was concretely possible. He gently satirized poets who had high vatic pretensions, representing himself as a plain man who preferred to cultivate his rural estate. But he was also, as Jonson recalled, 'in high favour with the Emperour', and his poetry celebrated the peace which the imperial regime had brought to a countryside formerly ravaged by civil war.[43]

Jonson's celebration of the rural life in 'To Penshurst' and 'To Sir Robert Wroth' was enormously influential in the Stuart period. He was 'feigning a commonwealth' in these poems just as much as in his masques, and the ideal he portrayed was one which reflected the political priorities of the Stuart monarchs. James and Charles were anxious for the nobility not to spend too much time in the city and to maintain their traditional function of maintaining order and dispensing hospitality in the country. James's attention had been drawn to problems in the countryside by a series of risings against enclosures in 1607. In 1612 there were riots on the Earl of Pembroke's estate. In 1614 James issued a proclamation calling on the nobility to return to the countryside and warning that if they did not do so there would be more trouble from the 'levellers', as the rebels now called themselves. He also wrote a poem on the subject. Jonson and Jones ended their 1616 masque *The Vision of Delight* with a scene depicting the pleasures of the countryside, and thereafter court masques

[42] Juan Luis Vives, *On Education: A Translation of the* De tradendis disciplinis *of Juan Luis Vives*, with an introduction by Foster Watson (Cambridge, 1913), 8–9; cf. *H&S*, viii.567. For a fuller analysis of complexities in Jonson's poetic ideology see Don E. Wayne, *Penshurst: The Semiotics of Place and the Poetics of History* (Madison, 1984).

[43] *H&S*, viii.642–3. For an interesting survey of Horace's reputation as a court poet see Howard D. Weinbrot, *Augustus Caesar in 'Augustan' England* (Princeton, 1978).

frequently ended with a rural vista.[44] 'To Sir Robert Wroth' anticipates another important theme of Stuart poetry by describing the joys of revelry in the countryside: Comus presides over festivities in which country folk join with their master and mistress. Comus made his appearance in Jonson's 1618 masque *Pleasure Reconciled to Virtue*, in which Hercules put an end to the drunken and unseemly revelry of the 'belly-god' and his followers but proceeded to take part in a more decorous dance with the court masquers. This masque probably alluded on one allegorical level to a recent controversy over country sports.[45] Puritans in Lancashire had complained to King James that the traditional Sunday revels in this backward area of the country were disrupting church services. Puritans regarded rural sports as relics of paganism which should be kept completely separate from religious affairs and, if possible, abolished altogether. They were particularly anxious that the Sabbath should be kept holy. But the association of the church year with the agrarian calendar with its intervals of revelry was a deep-rooted part of rural existence, and James concluded that to take excessive measures against rural sports would drive people away from church. In 1618 he issued a proclamation in which he ordered that Sabbath revelry should not be allowed to become disorderly but forbade the Puritans to stamp out harmless recreations. In *Pleasure Reconciled to Virtue* Jonson dramatized the distinction between lawless and excessive revelry, symbolized by Comus, and legitimate revelry sanctioned by the authorities. Jonson's allegory associated the illegitimate, licentious revelry with the old religion, and sour hostility to revels with Puritanism: the ideal was a mean between these extremes.

Jonson had by now returned to the Church of England. Measures like the issuing of the proclamation on sports showed that the English church could be regarded as itself a guardian of tradition; though the king remained a defender of Calvinist orthodoxy, more liberal currents of theological opinion were tolerated in the church. There were practical political reasons for trying to hold in check the radicalism of the Puritans in the countryside: it was widely believed that the traditional ceremonies helped to keep the people contented, whereas, as James's proclamation noted, if they were forbidden their traditional pleasures they would utter 'idle and discontented speaches' in alehouses. Puttenham had warned that Puritanism might provoke rebellion by trying to preach 'all trothe' to the 'raskall sorte'.[46] Similar views were expressed by Jonson's last major patron, the Earl of Newcastle, in a letter to the young Charles II. He advised the young king not to spend too much time on divinity or moral philosophy, which teaches 'Philosophicall Worlds & Utopias. Schollars hath made and fansied to themselues such worlds as neuer was is or shall be.' He warned that people who were too Bible-mad might provoke civil war. Rather than encouraging people to spend too much time reading the Bible, he should ensure that

---

[44] *The Poems of King James VI*, ed. J. Craigie, 2 vols. (Edinburgh, 1955–8), ii.178. On this topic see Leah Sinanoglou Marcus, *The Politics of Mirth: Jonson, Herrick, Milton, Marvell, and the Defense of Old Holiday Pastimes* (Chicago, 1986), 67–76.

[45] Marcus, *The Politics of Mirth*, ch. 4.   [46] See above, Ch. 3 n. 31.

ceremony was maintained, for ceremony had a powerful though irrational effect in preserving order and degree: 'euen the wisest though he know it & not accustomed to it, shall shake of his wisdome & shake for fear of it, for this is the mist is cast before vs and maskers [i.e. confuses] the Common Wealth.'[47] Newcastle elaborated on these points in a treatise written for Charles after the Restoration: he praised King James for his defence of rural sports which kept the people in 'harmles action'. He regretted that the Bible had ever been translated into English so that every weaver or chambermaid could read it. But Newcastle recognized that it was impossible to go back to the medieval order; in any case, he considered that the Roman church had overdone the emphasis on ceremony, turning religion into 'pupett playes' and thus making it ridiculous to the people. The Church of England had achieved an appropriate *via media*—precisely the conclusion of Jonson in *Pleasure Reconciled to Virtue*.[48] Thus Jonson's activities as deviser of court masques and as poet of the retired life were not incompatible: in both cases he was celebrating a society which attached due importance to ceremonial as a means of maintaining reverence for the social hierarchy.

The very title of *The Forest* has courtly associations. Strictly speaking an area could be a forest whether or not it had any trees: the term defined an area which was outside, 'foris', the normal common law and subject directly to a special forest law. The initial purpose of a forest was to allow the monarch to hunt freely and without interruption: in the words of an Elizabethan treatise, the protection of wild beasts in forests 'is for the delight and pleasure of the King onely, and his nobles, and for no other end nor purpose'.[49] Some of the early Norman kings had aroused resentment by extending the boundaries of royal forests too far, but a compromise had been reached under Henry III by which the monarchy undertook not to go beyond traditional limits. The royal forests could thus become a symbol of the political balance established by Magna Carta. Jonson alludes to James's love of hunting in the royal forests in 'To Sir Robert Wroth', and the motto of that poem, and of the whole collection, might have come from Pope's 'Windsor Forest': 'Peace and Plenty tell, a STUART reigns.'[50] The Earl of Pembroke was Chief Justice of the royal forests south of the Trent. Sir Robert Wroth had particularly close connections with the royal forests.[51] His house at Enfield was situated between Waltham or Epping Forest to the east and Enfield Chase, which had a status analogous to forests though within the common law, to the west. To the north lay the prodigy-house of Theobalds, whose estates provided excellent hunting; James was a regular visitor and in 1607 Sir Robert

[47] British Library Harl. MS 6988, fos. 111–12.

[48] S. Arthur Strong (ed.), *A Catalogue of Letters and Other Historical Documents Exhibited in the Library at Welbeck* (London, 1903), 227, 188 ff.

[49] J. Manwood, *A Treatise and Discourse of the Lawes of the Forrest* (London, 1598), 3; see George Hammersley, 'The Revival of the Forest Laws under Charles I', *History*, 45 (1960), 85–102.

[50] See E. Thompson, *Whigs and Hunters: The Origin of the Black Act* (London, 1975), 27–54, 278–94.

[51] For information about Wroth see W. C. Waller, 'An Extinct County Family: Wroth of Loughton Hall', *Essex Archaeological Society Transactions*, NS 8 (1900–3), 145–81; I wrote without the benefit of Martin Elsky's much fuller discussion in 'Microhistory and Cultural Geography: Ben Jonson's "To Sir Robert Wroth" and the Absorption of Local Community in the Commonwealth', *Renaissance Quarterly*, 53 (2000), 500–28.

Cecil handed the house over to James in a ceremony for which Jonson wrote an entertainment. James frequently visited Sir Robert Wroth and Jonson alludes to the times
when the king 'makes thy house his court' on his hunting expeditions (l. 24). Wroth
was in fact much more dependent on the court for his way of life than Jonson's poem
implies. At the time the poem was written Wroth was still living in his house at
Enfield, but he was petitioning the king for help in improving his larger property at
Loughton. He assured the king that he would make the house stately enough to give
him a ceremonious reception on his visits. Wroth used the mediation of his wife who
seems to have been on closer personal terms with the queen. Lady Mary frequently
appeared at court and participated in several of Jonson's masques; the poet wrote an
epigram in praise of her masque costumes. Despite the condemnation of masquing
at the start of 'To Sir Robert Wroth', Jonson knew perfectly well that Sir Robert's
style of life could not be maintained without some contact with the court. After her
husband's death Lady Mary published a long romance which contains a description
of a royal visit to a country residence. The king in her fiction loves the forest, which
he calls his garden, and the noblemen who live there dress up as foresters in order
to entertain him, thus becoming 'Courtly Forresters, and civill wild-men'.[52] Lady
Mary describes a visit to a country house in which a young man dressed as a forester
gives a speech of welcome to the king. This incident perhaps reveals the kind of
entertainment Sir Robert Wroth provided for the king. The rhetoric of the Wroth
poem is not, then, directly anti-courtly; on the contrary, like Jonson's patron
Pembroke, it has the effect of making 'the Court itself better esteemed and more reverenced in the country'. The government had in fact used the independent reputation of Wroth's father in 1604 to gain support for their measures: by asking him to
put forward a controversial bill they could neutralize any prejudice against royal officials. Bacon supported this tactic of having motions proposed by 'some grave and
discreet gentlemen of the country, such as have least relation to the court'.[53]

Jonson's presentation of Wroth's austere self-sufficiency is, then, somewhat idealized. How accurate is his portrayal of Wroth as the benevolent landlord dispensing
hospitality to his peasants? Jonson and his disciples depicted the English countryside
as an ideal organic community in which rich and poor lived together in harmony and
charity. This image was set against an image of the city as corrupted by wealth and by
Puritanism. But the enclosures of the fifteenth and sixteenth century had transformed the English landscape in a way that was hardly 'organic'.[54] Traditional rural
social relations had not been eradicated, however, and Jonson's portrayal of Wroth,
though undoubtedly idealized, may have had an element of truth. Forest laws had
originated to defend royal privileges, but they were not enforced very rigidly and it
had become customary for local people to graze animals on forest land and chases

[52] Lady Mary Wroth, *The First Part of the Countess of Montgomery's Urania*, ed. Josephine Roberts
(Binghamton, NY, 1995), 344.
[53] Nicholas Tyacke, 'Wroth, Cecil and the Parliamentary Session of 1604', *Bulletin of the Institute of
Historical Research*, 50 (1977), 120–5 (124 n. 2), citing *The Letters and the Life of Francis Bacon*, ed.
J. Spedding, 7 vols. (London, 1861–74), vii.146.
[54] Raymond Williams, *The Country and the City* (London, 1973), 22 ff.

without undue harassment. Wroth's father took an interest in preserving traditional rights. In 1603, when the king was visiting Theobalds, his household officers came face to face with a group of women from Enfield who told them that local custom did not allow any outsider to remove wood from Enfield Chase. Sir Robert Wroth senior seems to have helped to give the women's case a fair hearing and half the wood was given to them, the other half to Theobalds. The women of the area were apparently very active, for in 1617 'a showre of shrewes' protested so vigorously against further enclosures around Theobalds that work was halted for a time.[55]

But the young Sir Robert was subject to social pressures that worked against respect for traditional rural standards of fair behaviour. Someone living so close to Theobalds was bound to feel the need to keep up with the massive scale of the conspicuous consumption indulged in by Cecil and the king. Despite local resistance, Cecil did his best to push through enclosures around his new property at Hatfield; one satire irreverently termed him 'Robin the encloser of Hatfield Wood'.[56] Sir Robert felt the need to keep up appearances in order to gain the king's favour; he overspent so drastically that, according to one contemporary, he died in debt to the tune of £23,000. His court contacts gave him valuable grants of land, and he was described on his death as 'a great commaunder or rather by the Kings favor an intruder in Waltham forrest'.[57] In the light of this accusation Jonson's portrait of Sir Robert seems somewhat over-idealized. Perhaps he intended his poem as a tactful hint, a reminder to Sir Robert that he could derive more real satisfaction from a traditional rural existence than from frenzied gambling on court favour. Jonson gave a similar message to Sir Robert Sidney in 'To Penshurst': Sir Edward Sackville's prodigy-house at nearby Knole provided a tempting model for emulation, but Sidney was better off living a less extravagant and less insecure existence.

In the case of the Wroth poem, however, Jonson's advice may seem rather disingenuous given that he was simultaneously urging Lady Mary to take part in masques at court—where she established the friendship with Pembroke that led to their later affair. Jonson told Drummond that he had disliked Wroth, who was unworthy of his wife. In the preface to the 'Epigrams' Jonson said that if he had praised anyone who did not deserve praise he hoped he would be forgiven on the grounds that the poems were good pictures even if they were bad likenesses.[58] The theory of demonstrative rhetoric assumed that somebody who was offered an idealized portrait would try to emulate the image and might thereby become a better person. But if Jonson intended to offer Wroth advice his method in this case was so oblique as to be almost unnoticeable. Wroth had every reason to be pleased with the flattering picture of his life that

[55] D. O. Parr, 'Protestant Gentlemen: The Wroths of Durants Arbour, Enfield, and Loughton, Essex', *Edmonton Hundred Historical Society Occasional Papers*, NS 25 (1973), 20; *The Victoria History of the Counties of England: Essex*, ii, ed. William Page and J. Horace Round (London, 1907), 619.

[56] *The Victoria History of the Counties of England: Hertfordshire*, iii, ed. William Page (London, 1912), 100. For satires against Cecil on this and other issues see Pauline Croft, 'The Reputation of Robert Cecil: Libels, Political Opinion, and Popular Awareness in the Early Seventeenth Century', *Transactions of the Royal Historical Society*, 6 (1991), 43–69.

[57] *The Letters of John Chamberlain*, ed. N. E. McClure, 2 vols. (Philadelphia, 1939), i.520.

[58] *H&S*, i.142, viii.26.

Jonson had disseminated. As moral advice to the ruling class, Jonson's poetry is mild indeed when compared with the denunciations of enclosures in mid-Tudor prophetic poetry. But Jonson had low expectations of humanity and regarded those with high expectations as naive. He shared with Horace a scepticism sometimes verging on cynicism. At the end of his second Epode, the model for the Wroth poem and one of Jonson's favourite poems—he translated it himself—Horace suddenly reveals that the idyllic portrait he has been drawing of the country life which the poem has presented is really no more than the self-indulgent fantasy of a financier who cannot bear in practice to give up his wealthy urban existence. Jonson's scepticism about human motives means that it is slightly misleading to portray him as a strenuously moralistic defender of an old organic community against the emergent capitalism. Jonson disliked many of the social changes he saw around him, but he had no great faith in the possibility of preventing them, since they were caused by the greed that he saw as a central and ineradicable human quality. The monarchy was adopting policies which were in some respects socially conservative and helped to preserve some features of the old rural order, but it was also engaged in enclosures and lent its support to some highly dubious commercial enterprises. In his book *Drama and Society in the Age of Jonson* L. C. Knights describes the unscrupulous activities of the London financier Sir William Cokayne, who caused a disaster in the English wool trade by establishing a personal monopoly and proceeding to manage it incompetently. Jonson satirized such unscrupulous financiers in his plays. But he was also a personal friend of Cokayne's and had close connections with the group Cokayne drank with at the Mitre Tavern. In 1616, when the full scale of the economic disaster he had helped to precipitate was becoming apparent, Cokayne tried to placate the king by staging an extravagant banquet for him. The masque or entertainment staged on this occasion was written by Ben Jonson, who had apparently managed to overcome his moral objections to commercial corruption.[59]

The Forest was published in 1616 as one part of Jonson's collected works, along with his plays and masques. This publication had established him as the leading literary figure of the age. In the same year he was awarded an annual pension and effectively recognized as laureate. He abandoned the public stage for some years and devoted much of his energy to his activity as the leading masque-writer, casting in dramatic form the political ideas that the king had definitively expressed in his collected works, which also appeared in 1616.[60] The masques published in Jonson's 1616 folio ended with *The Golden Age Restored*, in which Astraea descends again to earth to usher in the age of peace and plenty. In this new golden age presided over by

[59] Knights, *Drama and Society in the Age of Jonson*, 87, 135, 211; *H&S*, i.87; N. W. Bawcutt, 'Ben Jonson and Drunken Hamburgers: An Entertainment for King James', *Notes and Queries*, 242 (1997), 92–4; for another example of Jonson's involvement in celebrating commercial innovation, see James Knowles, 'Jonson's Entertainment at Britain's Burse', in Martin Butler (ed.), *Re-presenting Ben Jonson: Text, History, Performance* (Houndmills, 1999), 14–51. On the shady financial dealings of some of Jonson's drinking companions, see Menna Prestwich, *Cranfield: Politics and Profits under the Early Stuarts* (Oxford, 1966), 97–106.

[60] On the publication of the two men's collected writings see Graham Parry, *The Golden Age Restor'd: The Culture of the Stuart Court, 1603–42* (Manchester, 1981), 52.

James, poetry and the other arts flourish; Chaucer, Gower, Lydgate, and Spenser appear to pay tribute to the new order. Jonson was thus confidently declaring his own position in the succession of English court poets (there is no Langland in his canon). As will be seen in the next chapter, however, by 1616 there already were distinct strains involved in defending a courtly golden age.

8. The Spenserians and King James, 1603–1616

IN the 1590s the gap between Spenser's political ideals and Elizabethan realities had been becoming increasingly apparent. In *Mother Hubberds Tale* Spenser had attacked the growing political influence of Sir Robert Cecil, who was considered by his enemies to have achieved his control over the patronage system by bribery and corruption. Cecil was also accused by Essex's supporters of lacking faith in the anti-Spanish foreign policy, and towards the end of the reign there were rumours that he was intriguing for a Spanish succession. Essex's supporters placed their hope for the future in the accession of James VI of Scotland, who, it was hoped, would remove Cecil and adopt a more sympathetic attitude to the Puritans. The state of poetry as well as the state of the realm seemed to many poets to be corrupt by the 1590s. There was a vogue for Ovidian love poetry which more moralistic writers found alarming, a dereliction of the poet's public duty of writing didactic verse that could serve the cause of religion. In 1595 Josuah Sylvester published the first instalment of his translation of Du Bartas's *Divine Weeks and Works*, a poem which was to gain enormous popularity in England. Du Bartas Protestantized the courtly poetic of the sixteenth century, adapting a highly rhetorical style with stylized poetic diction to religious topics. In dedicating a new instalment to Essex, Sylvester called on Spenser, Daniel, and Drayton to 'wean our wanton Ile From *Ouids* heires' by writing divine poetry.[1] Spenser's verse had always adopted a moral standpoint that was reasonably acceptable to a Puritan audience, but younger men like Nashe, Marston, and Donne went out of their way to offend the susceptibilities of earnest readers.[2] Several English poets hoped that James would help to reform English poetry. Gabriel Harvey was a great admirer of his poems.[3] The king had translated Du Bartas's *Uranie* and sponsored a Scottish translation of the *Divine Weeks and Works*. He had paid tribute to Sidney in an elegy which was printed at the beginning of the volume produced by Cambridge University. Might not his accession usher in a new age in which those who admired Sidney's political ideals and poetic achievement would be patronized by an enlightened king?[4]

---

[1] Josuah Sylvester, *The Second Weeke; or, Childhood of the World* (London, 1598), sig. A5ᵛ. On hopes for religious verse see James Doelman, *King James I and the Religious Culture of England* (Woodbridge, 2000), ch. 2.

[2] See David Perkins, 'Issues and Motivations in the Nashe–Harvey Quarrel', *Philological Quarterly*, 39 (1960), 224–33.

[3] Virginia F. Stern, *Gabriel Harvey: His Life, Marginalia and Library* (Oxford, 1979), 126, 223.

[4] Tourneur's satire *The Transformed Metamorphosis* (1600) seems to prophesy such a reformation: *The Works of Cyril Tourneur*, ed. Allardyce Nicoll (London, 1930), 51–75; David Norbrook, 'Panegyric of the Monarch and its Social Context under Elizabeth I and James I' (unpublished D.Phil. thesis, Oxford, 1978), 122–4.

These political and poetic hopes were unrealistic, given not only the huge number of suitors but James's own political caution in his new kingdom. Far from dismissing Cecil, who had been conducting his own secret negotiations for James's succession, the new king relied heavily on his political advice. He continued the negotiations for peace with Spain which Cecil had initiated and maintained a pacific foreign policy. He gave high honours to several members of the conservative Howard family and aroused great suspicion because of the favour he showed to Henry Howard, Earl of Northampton, whose Catholicism and rumoured disloyalty had excluded him from office in Elizabeth's reign. Ben Jonson had a personal feud with Northampton but he did admire James's policy of European peace. Not all Jacobean poets took the same view. Fulke Greville, who had fallen from office under the new regime, voiced the political disillusionment of the survivors from the Essex circle in his *Life of Sidney*. This work incorporated material which Greville had intended to use in a history of Elizabeth's reign but Cecil, fearing that he would give the work the wrong kind of bias, refused him access to the state papers. It was the more cautious William Camden who produced the definitive history of the reign. In the *Life of Sidney* Greville idealized his friend as the last representative of a heroic age of austere Protestant militancy which had now given way to luxury and cowardice. His friend Samuel Daniel warned that while peace could be a good it could also lead to corruption: peace must be armed—an idea Spenser had symbolized in the figure of Britomart. An unarmed peace, on the other hand,

> letts her Armors rust, and shipps to rott
> And makes mens worth and honor be forgott.

Under the inefficient administration of Charles Howard, Earl of Nottingham, the navy was indeed rotting.[5]

In the view of his critics James was no more successful at reforming poetry than at reforming corruption in public life. The new king did, of course, give enormous influence to one poet, Ben Jonson. But Jonson had many rivals who felt themselves to be unjustly excluded from favour. Spenser had never written court masques or pageants, and Elizabeth had refrained from showing special favour to one particular poet; in fact she was not an active patron of poetry. The more favour James showed to Jonson, however, the more jealousy he aroused in other poets. As has been seen, Samuel Daniel had been shouldered out of his initial prominent position by Jonson's skill in courtly poetry; Jonson recorded that 'Daniel was at Jealousies with him'. Of another prominent poet, Michael Drayton, Jonson declared that 'Drayton feared him, and he esteemed not of him'.[6] Drayton had apparently visited James in

---

[5] *Samuel Daniel: The Brotherton Manuscript. A Study in Authorship*, ed. John Pitcher (Leeds, 1981), 136. On Daniel and other historians see D. R. Woolf, *The Idea of History in Early Stuart England: Erudition, Ideology, and 'the Light of Truth' from the Accession of James I to the Civil War* (Toronto, 1990). For a more recent analysis of James's early years, emphasizing his early links with the Essex faction, see Leed Barroll, 'Assessing "Cultural Influence": James I as Patron of the Arts', *Shakespeare Studies*, 29 (2001), 132–62.

[6] *Ben Jonson*, ed. C. H. Herford and Percy and Evelyn Simpson, 11 vols. Oxford, 1925–52 (hereafter *H&S*), i.136.

Scotland before his accession and obtained promises of favour, and he had such high expectations of the new reign that he rushed into print with a panegyric of James and was widely censured for not showing enough respect for Elizabeth's memory. But James did not keep whatever promises he had had made, and by 1606 Drayton was attacking him and Cecil in his *Pastorals*. Drayton had published a bitter satire on the 'regnum Cecilianum', *The Owle*, at the start of the reign in the apparent hope that James would remove a man he considered as a symbol of the corruption and greed that was affecting society at all levels. Drayton was not a Puritan and may have had Catholic leanings, but he was hostile to James and his advisers on moral grounds.[7] In his *Pastorals* Drayton praised a small group of poets, including Samuel Daniel, who in his opinion had escaped corruption—and who were out of favour with the Jacobean court. In an elegy for Sir Philip Sidney Drayton complained that since his day English poetry had withered under a 'cold Northerne breath'; Sidney is borne aloft,

> Laughing even Kings and their delights to scorne,
> And all those Sots that them doe Deifie.[8]

Drayton's idealization of Sidney as an anti-courtly hero resembles Greville's comment that his friend's talents were too great for 'little monarchies'.[9] Giles Fletcher senior, who had been an Essex supporter, had visited James in Scotland and had apparently, like Drayton, received promises of support which were subsequently not kept; Fletcher's son Phineas criticized this ingratitude and attacked Cecil in a series of eclogues he was writing in the early years of the reign.[10]

Thus before James had been long on the English throne there had emerged a group of poets who were alienated from the court and sometimes used the traditional symbolism of Protestant pastoral to voice their discontent. They could almost be described as constituting a poetic 'opposition'. In this period, of course, it is misleading to speak of a formal 'opposition' based on a coherent ideology.[11] The political system discouraged the emergence of ideological polarization: there might be opposing factions at court but they were often motivated by personal rather than political disagreements. Political discord was felt to be a symptom of disorder and corruption, something that might be expected in democracies but from which the

---

[7] On Drayton see Richard F. Hardin, *Michael Drayton and the Passing of Elizabethan England* (Lawrence, Kan., 1973), Bernard H. Newdigate, *Michael Drayton and his Circle*, 2nd edn. (Oxford, 1961), and Jean F. Brink, *Michael Drayton Revisited* (Boston, 1990).

[8] *The Works of Michael Drayton*, ed. J. William Hebel, Kathleen Tillotson, and Bernard H. Newdigate, 2nd edn., 5 vols. (Oxford, 1961), ii.548, 549.

[9] *A Dedication to Sir Philip Sidney*, in *The Prose Works of Fulke Greville, Lord Brooke*, ed. John Gouws (Oxford, 1986), 24 (above, Ch. 6 n. 35).

[10] Giles and Phineas Fletcher, *Poetical Works*, ed. Frederick S. Boas, 2 vols. (Cambridge, 1908–9), ii.173–222; Lloyd E. Berry, 'Phineas Fletcher's Account of his Father', *Journal of English and Germanic Philology*, 60 (1961), 258–67.

[11] The most emphatic counter-statements to the traditional 'Whig' view that there was an established Jacobean opposition have come from Kevin Sharpe (see his introduction to *Faction and Parliament: Essays on Early Stuart History* (Oxford, 1978)), and Conrad Russell, *Parliaments and English Politics 1621–1629* (Oxford, 1979).

more dignified political system under a monarchy should be immune. Participation in public discussion in Parliaments was a concession from the monarch, which had been established as a convention but which still depended ultimately on his grace and favour. Samuel Daniel praised King James for permitting a greater freedom of political discourse than was necessary under a monarchy; writing a full and objective political history was 'a liberty proper onely to Common-wealths, and neuer permitted to Kingdomes, but vnder good Princes'.[12] The monarch's responsibility was to consult with those best qualified to give advice and then to decide impartially, rather than to side with any one faction. Factions that were out of office tended to concentrate their attention not so much on their opponents' ideas as on their moral character: they must be displaced because they were personally inadequate. And yet, when all these qualifications have been made, it still seems to be possible to detect certain areas of ideological conflict in Jacobean political life. Parliamentarians might unite in agreeing that their freedom of speech was not unlimited, but they could still differ over the definition of those limits. For example, the king considered foreign policy to be a 'mystery of state' which Parliaments could discuss only as a special privilege; but some Parliamentarians seem to have considered that they had a right to discuss certain crucial international issues. Foreign policy raised important ideological questions: should it be governed by pragmatism or by Protestant principle?[13]

Analysis of the poetic 'opposition' raises similar difficulties. The poets who will be described in this chapter as 'Spenserians'—Greville, Daniel, Drayton, the Fletchers, and the younger pastoralists, William Browne and George Wither—were in varying degrees critical of dominant tendencies at court. But they were by no means a monolithic, ideologically coherent group. The first and most basic thing that divided them from Jonson, James's leading panegyrist, was that he was in favour and they were not. At the times when he was not on good terms with the king, especially in James's later years and the reign of Charles, Jonson can be found imitating some of the Spenserians' political rhetoric. But when this has been said it needs to be added that the reason Jonson enjoyed such high favour, especially in the earlier parts of James's reign, was at least partly ideological: as a Catholic, and then a high-church Anglican, he had no sympathy with the tradition of low-church Protestantism with which Spenser was associated. Jonson's silences are as significant as the topics he chose to write about: Continental politics, Princess Elizabeth, overseas colonization, and evangelical activities did not inspire him with the same enthusiasm as the

---

[12] Daniel, preface to *The Collection of the Historie of England*, *The Complete Works in Verse and Prose of Samuel Daniel*, ed. Alexander B. Grosart, 5 vols. (London, 1885–96), iv.78.

[13] Some of the more extreme statements of the 'revisionist' historians are questioned by J. H. Hexter, 'Power Struggle, Parliament, and Liberty in Early Stuart England', *Journal of Modern History*, 50 (1978), 1–50; by Theodore K. Rabb and Derek Hirst, 'Revisionism Revised: Two Perspectives on Early Stuart Parliamentary History', *Past and Present*, 92 (1981), 55–78 and 79–99; and, with reference to foreign policy, by Simon Adams, 'Spain or the Netherlands? The Dilemmas of Early Stuart Foreign Policy', in Howard Tomlinson (ed.), *Before the English Civil War: Essays on Early Stuart Politics and Government* (New York, 1983), 79–101. Since 1984 such questions have been extensively developed: see, for example, Richard Cust and Ann Hughes (eds.), *Conflict in Early Stuart England: Studies in Religion and Politics 1603–1642* (London, 1989) and Johann P. Sommerville, *Royalists and Patriots: Politics and Ideology in England 1603–1640*, 2nd edn. (London, 1999).

Spenserians. Jonson was rather alarmed by the increase in public discussion of political issues in James's reign. Several of the Spenserians, however, took a rather different attitude to mysteries of state and can be found supporting those in Parliament and in London who were trying to extend the limits of public debate or at least to prevent what they regarded as their restriction. Wither, the Spenserian with whom Jonson fell out most violently, was the most ideological of these poets, the most enthusiastic about reaching a wide popular audience with his political rhetoric. At the other extreme, Samuel Daniel distrusted public dissension and apocalyptic fervour but censured the Jacobean court on moral grounds; his quarrel with Jonson was personal more than ideological, though even here there may have been an element of theoretical disagreement. Fulke Greville is exceptionally hard to classify, for while he was jealous of traditional liberties and deeply suspicious of possible illegitimate increases in the royal prerogative, he hated 'popularity' and was so cautious that in his political practice he differed little from more orthodox figures.

What these poets did have in common was an admiration for the great figures of Elizabethan literature, for Sidney and Spenser; and this admiration took on a political colouring, given that the new regime had rejected the Elizabethan ideals of Protestant chivalry. Cecil, Spenser's great enemy, was still in office; Phineas Fletcher and several other poets propagated the myth that Spenser had died in poverty because of Cecil's hostility, and he became a symbol of proud poetic and political independence.[14] Jonson, as has been seen, lacked this poetic and political nostalgia. The same applies to John Donne, who became a prominent figure in the second half of James's reign: his Catholic upbringing had estranged him from Elizabethan public symbolism. His public poetry, with its extravagant imagery of worship and self-abasement, has nothing in common with the Protestant pastoralism favoured by the Spenserians.[15]

[14] Fletcher and Fletcher, *Poetical Works*, ii.16; cf. *The Collected Poems of Joseph Hall*, ed. Arnold Davenport (Liverpool, 1949), 123, and the poem by John Lane (a friend of Giles Fletcher senior and of Milton's father) discussed in *The Works of Edmund Spenser: A Variorum Edition*, ed. Edwin Greenlaw et al., 10 vols. (Baltimore, 1932–49), v.325. An indispensable aid for the study of Spenser's reputation is W. Wells (ed.), 'Spenser Allusions in the Sixteenth and Seventeenth Centuries', *Studies in Philology*, Special Supplements, vols. 68 (1971) and 69 (1972).

[15] Donne received poor attention in my first edition, down to my mistakenly making him a bishop; the fact that he did not receive such advancement prompted my attempt at a more nuanced account of Donne in 'The Monarchy of Wit and the Republic of Letters: Donne's Politics', in Katharine Maus and Elizabeth Harvey (eds.), *Soliciting Interpretation: Literary Theory and Seventeenth-Century English Poetry* (Chicago, 1990), 3–36. On courtly imagery in Donne see John Carey, *John Donne: Life, Mind and Art* (London, 1990), 113 ff., and Jonathan Goldberg, *James I and the Politics of Literature: Jonson, Shakespeare, Donne, and their Contemporaries* (Baltimore, 1983), 210–19. Arthur F. Marotti, *John Donne, Coterie Poet* (Madison, 1986), 183–95, draws attention to critical and satirical elements in his Jacobean writings, though seeing them as part of a highly conservative coterie; for more emphasis on a critical public role see especially Annabel Patterson, 'All Donne', in Maus and Harvey (eds.), *Soliciting Interpretation*, 37–67, and '*Quod oportet* versus *quod convenit*: John Donne, Kingsman', in *Reading between the Lines* (Madison, 1993), 160–209. Dennis Flynn, *John Donne and the Ancient Catholic Nobility* (Bloomington, Ind., 1995), counters Carey's view of Donne's careerism with an emphasis on his continuing links with Catholic circles. In a series of studies Jeanne Shami has likewise provided a corrective to court-centred readings; see, for example, 'Anti-Catholicism in the Sermons of John Donne', in Lori Ann Ferrell and Peter McCullough (eds.), *The English Sermon Revised: Religion, Literature and History 1600–1750* (Manchester,

Jonson's high ceremonial style was, of course, mainly confined to his masques, and in his non-dramatic verse he favoured a 'plain style'. But his dislike of prophetic radicalism was implicit in this style. His aim was to naturalize poetic artifice, to embody, in a richly matured form, a wisdom based on practical experience. Generalizations about the Spenserians' style are hazardous, for they varied from each other and adopted different kinds of idiom on different occasions. But they all attempted at times to achieve a poetic strain which Jonson normally denied himself. And the language of prophetic poetry had to differ conspicuously from everyday language, for its aim was to move beyond normal experience.[16] Drayton's friend Henry Reynolds was scornful of poetry that merely taught 'Morall doctrine': this could be conveyed just as well in prose. (Jonson tended to compose initial drafts of his poems in prose.) Reynolds believed that poetry could convey hidden mysteries, secrets of the natural world and its divine principles which had been lost since the early days of the world. This kind of wisdom was much superior to anything that could be found in pagan moral philosophers. He even wished that Spenser had been 'a little freer of his fiction, and not so close riuetted to his Morall'; but presumably he would have approved of passages like the *Mutabilitie Cantos* and the description of the Garden of Adonis. Poetry, said Reynolds, should present 'golden fictions'; most modern poetry seemed to him to consist either of versified morality, or worse still, of 'base seruile fawning at the heeles of worldly wealth and greatnesse'.[17] Another friend of Drayton's, William Drummond, was making a similar point when he complained that Donne did not soar high enough in his poetry; he and his school were abstracting poetry into '*Metaphysical* Ideas, and *Scholastical* Quiddities'.[18] The Spenserian poets tended to adopt a style which drew attention to its own artifice and thus highlighted the inability of language fully to embody transcendent truths: where Jonson's verse gives the impression that ideals can be organically embodied in existing institutions and linguistic formulations, Spenserian verse constantly confesses its inadequacy. Phineas Fletcher addresses God as a remote and mysterious being 'Whose breadth no feet, no lines, no chains, no eyes survey': poetic feet and poetic lines are also inadequate, and Fletcher gives his poem a flowing syntax which finds it hard to reach a definite resolution. Wither describes his poems as '*Raptures*' patterned on David and other biblical prophets, and modulates from visionary elevation to a 'plain style' that is radically different from Jonson's, constantly calling attention to the processes of writing, to the time-lag between representation and inner inspiration. Wither's 'loose' poetics can sound startlingly modern for those used to mak-

2000), 136–66; for a very different view see Debora Shuger, 'Absolutist Theology: The Sermons of John Donne', ibid. 115–35.

[16] There is a useful general study of the Spenserians, from the stylistic rather than political viewpoint, by Joan Grundy, *The Spenserian Poets* (London, 1969). On the differences between Jonson and the Spenserians see especially the excellent study by Ina Schabert, *Die Lyrik der Spenserianer* (Tübingen, 1977), 16ff.

[17] Henry Reynolds, 'Mythomystes', in J. E. Spingarn (ed.), *Critical Essays of the Seventeenth Century*, 3 vols. (Oxford, 1908–9), i.144–78 (163, 147, 155). On Reynolds see Mary Hobbs, 'Drayton's "Most Dearely-Loved Friend Henery Reynolds Esq:"', *Review of English Studies*, 96 (1973), 414–27.

[18] William Drummond, *Works*, ed. J. Sage and T. Ruddiman (Edinburgh, 1711), 143.

ing adjustment for the conventions of Renaissance writing, and has evoked a comparison with Whitman. Fletcher and the other Spenserians frequently associate God and poetic inspiration with images of light and water, infinite and indeterminate essences; they do not share Jonson's fondness for imagery of organic growth. They recognized his poetic merits but they speak of his poetry in distinctive terms. Browne praised Drayton for his visionary and emotional qualities, his 'soul-raping strains', Brooke for the flowing clarity of his inspiration, and in general valued poetry for its emotional rather than purely rational qualities. Jonson, on the other hand, he praised as 'judicious', 'well knowing', 'exact'.[19]

The Spenserians' idea of poetry as revealing transcendent truths lent itself to the expression of an apocalyptic world-view: though not yet fully understood, the truth would be unveiled in the future, and a glimpse of it might even be granted to prophetic poets. Spenser had dramatized this idea in his presentation of Una wandering in the wilderness, and similar figures appear in much Spenserian poetry. In *The Faerie Queene* masques and pageants are sometimes symbols of a false claim to immanence, an attempt to trap in the here and now a transcendent divine quality. Daniel and Greville are said to have exchanged letters on the need to 'reform' court masques.[20] It is impossible to know exactly what they said, but it is possible to infer from the opinions they expressed elsewhere that they disliked the enormous extravagance of Jonsonian masques and also perhaps had doubts about the ideology they expressed, the glorification of the monarch as a living embodiment of divine qualities. Such language was conventional up to a certain point, but in the Jacobean masques it had reached an unprecedented scale. In the preface to his play *The Queen's Arcadia* (which had the significant alternative title *Arcadia Reformed*) Daniel declared that it was not his intention to show

> In lowder stile the hidden mysteries,
> And arts of Thrones

and made some comments which apparently referred slightingly to the new perspective stage, which Jonson and Jones had recently introduced in *The Masque of Blacknesse*.[21] Daniel may have been suggesting that Jonson's praise of King James was becoming too loud.

The first major revival of Spenserian poetry took place in the period 1612–14, and it coincided with, and was to some extent stimulated by, a series of political changes. In 1610 Henry IV of France was assassinated, an event which aroused great alarm in England and the expectation that James might now be persuaded to play a more positive role in the struggle against the Habsburg powers. In the absence of a clear lead

[19] Fletcher and Fletcher, *Poetical Works*, ii.322; William Browne, *Poems*, ed. G. Goodwin, 2 vols. (London, 1894), i.239–40; George Wither, *Britain's Remembrancer* (n.pl., 1628; Spenser Society reprint, Manchester, 1880), fo. 138ᵛ; Thomas O. Calhoun, 'George Wither: Origins and Consequences of a Loose Poetics', *Texas Studies in Literature and Language*, 16 (1974), 263–79 (278).

[20] Joan Rees, *Fulke Greville, Lord Brooke, 1554–1628: A Critical Biography* (London, 1971), 201.

[21] Daniel, *Works*, iii.214; see further my article 'The Reformation of the Masque', in David Lindley (ed.), *The Court Masque* (Manchester, 1984), 94–110.

from James it had been Henry IV who had shown most enthusiasm for taking a stand against Spanish military power; but it seemed likely that after his death France would move closer to Spain, and Protestants feared a new move by the Habsburg powers to exploit their weakness. German Protestant princes had formed an Evangelical Union with which James was persuaded to make an alliance. He also agreed to a marriage between his daughter Elizabeth and Prince Frederick V of the Palatinate, the most militant Calvinist power in Europe. Salisbury's death in 1612 opened the way to a political realignment at court and several former Essex supporters hoped that the new Secretary would be an advocate of a more activist foreign policy. In 1611 Philippe Duplessis-Mornay, who had advocated close links between English and Continental Protestants since the days of Sidney, dedicated to James a treatise on the evils of the Papacy and urged him to mount a vigorous campaign against Rome.[22]

Phineas Fletcher inserted extensive references to these political changes, drawing on Duplessis-Mornay's *Mysterie of Iniquitie*, in his apocalyptic allegory of the Gunpowder Plot, *The Locusts, or Apollyonists*. Though his subject is national his poem has a European scope: he shows how the Jesuits are trying to increase their political influence throughout Europe, from the Netherlands to Russia. He praises the Venetians for their resistance to Spanish influence: Fletcher was one of those who hoped that they might be persuaded to become Protestants. All those who dislike political and religious authoritarianism seem to him to be potential Protestants; and he assumes that poetry flourishes best under conditions of religious and political liberty. In a remarkably early example of British Philhellenism, he praises Ancient Greece and laments that now the Muses are slaves because of the Turkish occupation—there had recently been a Greek revolt against the Turks but it had collapsed. In Britain, by contrast, the Muses flourish under a learned king: in this poem Fletcher reverts to the old ideal of James as the ideal Protestant poet-king, defending the faith with pen rather than the sword.[23] James had published a series of theological works warning of the dangers to royal authority presented by Catholic fanatics.

But the implication of Fletcher's poem is that the sword has to be held in reserve because the Jesuits are constantly conspiring and will gain easy victories where courts are complacent. James insisted on the evils of war and had no intention of imitating the militaristic Henry IV. Duplessis-Mornay's dedication of the *Mysterie of Iniquitie* had upset him because it seemed to imply the legitimacy of an ideological war against the Catholics: James wrote to Mornay to insist that he did not agree with such a policy.[24] The English translation of this book was dedicated not to James but to his elder son Prince Henry, who was believed to be more sympathetic to a militant, or at least a vigilant, foreign policy. Fletcher dedicated his poem to Henry rather than

[22] Philippe Duplessis-Mornay, *Le Mystere d'iniquité* (Saumur, 1611), trans. Samson Lennard, *The Mysterie of Iniquitie* (London, 1612). This work included a discussion, with quotations, of Dante's attacks on the clergy in *De monarchia*, *Purgatorio*, xvi, and *Paradiso* ix, xvii, and xxix: see Paget Toynbee, *Dante Studies* (Oxford, 1921) (above, Ch. 2 n. 37).

[23] Fletcher and Fletcher, *Poetical Works*, i.155; on the sources see 311–12.

[24] S. L. Adams, 'The Protestant Cause: Religious Alliance with the W. European Calvinist Communities as a Political Issue in England, 1585–1630' (unpublished D.Phil. thesis, Oxford, 1973), 157.

James. In another poem on the Gunpowder Plot, by Francis Herring, a conspirator makes the point that it is essential to kill Henry as well as James or a terrible revenge will be taken on the Catholic powers: the slightly tactless implication is that Henry will be much more politically effective than his father ever was.[25] Several works dedicated to him expressed apocalyptic hopes that he might marshal a decisive Protestant victory. There were rumours that after his sister's marriage he planned to go to Germany and fight alongside the Protestant princes. Attempts were being made to mould him into a new Protestant leader on the model of Leicester, Sidney, and Essex: one elegist was to adapt a poem about Sidney to mourn the prince.[26]

For present purposes Henry's private political views are not particularly material; what counts is the public image which many writers combined to create and which Henry up to a point endorsed. He had exalted ideas of monarchy and patronized artists and architects who could express the ideals of princely magnificence in spectacular forms; but he insisted that splendour should be accompanied by readiness for action, and should not degenerate into the effeminacy and unnecessary luxury which critics found in James's court. Though his name made many people compare him to Henry VIII, his self-conscious piety made him more reminiscent of Edward VI. In the year of his installation a Puritan publisher issued an edition of Sir John Cheke's elegy for Edward, which had hinted that the young king devoted rather too much time to courtly revelry towards the end of his reign.[27] Henry did take an interest in revels but he made sure that they could be harmonized with Protestant zeal. His father preferred masques to tournaments but Henry loved the tiltyard, and the barriers with which he celebrated his approaching installation as Prince of Wales revived the atmosphere of the Elizabethan Accession Day tilts. Henry was presented as a knight who would revive the decaying spirit of chivalry. He chose the name of Moeliades, an anagram of 'miles a deo': Henry was a Protestant soldier. The verses for this occasion were provided by Ben Jonson, who seems to have had doubts about the warlike advice that was being given to Henry: his friend Sir Robert Cotton had presented him with a treatise on the virtues of peace. Jonson reminded the prince of the dangers of irresponsible militancy and urged him to obey his father.[28] Jonson did try to gain favour at Henry's court, having perhaps become somewhat disillusioned with the licence James permitted; but though his entertainments for Henry reflected the prince's specific preoccupations, he regularly struck a note of caution. In *Oberon* (1611), he uncharacteristically drew on Spenserian 'faerie' mythology: the prince

[25] Francis Herring, *Popish Pietie*, trans. A.P. (London, 1610), sigs. B2^v–3^r; this is a translation of *Pietas pontificia* (London, 1606); another translation, by John Vicars, was refused a licence in the 1630s.

[26] *The Poems of Sir Arthur Gorges*, ed. Helen Estabrook Sandison (Oxford, 1953), 117, 181–2, 238. On Henry's public image see J. W. Williamson, *The Myth of the Conqueror: Prince Henry Stuart: A Study of 17th Century Personation* (New York, 1978). For more recent studies see Roy Strong, *Henry Prince of Wales and England's Lost Renaissance* (London, 1986) and T. V. Wilks, 'The Court Culture of Prince Henry and his Circle, 1603–1613' (unpublished D.Phil. thesis, University of Oxford, 1988).

[27] Sir John Cheke, *A Royal Elegie Briefly Describing the Vertuous Reigne and Happy Death of King Edward the Sixth* (London, 1610). The volume was dedicated to Viscountess Lisle, the wife of Sir Robert Sidney, and the publisher also praised her daughter Lady Mary Wroth.

[28] On Jonson's relations with Henry see Williamson, *Myth of the Conqueror*, 75–102.

was identified with the Fairy King Oberon. Jonson may perhaps have been hinting at the defects of James's court: a group of satyrs explained that they had left their old master Bacchus, the god of disorderly revelry, and come to serve Oberon.[29] But Jonson did not have major ideological objections to James's rule, and here he emphasizes that the prince must pay tribute to his father, who is celebrated as a god over kings.

Under Henry's influence, other masque-writers gave a different emphasis to the form. To some extent his court continued the patronage of Queen Anne, whose household had welcomed many former members of the old Essex circle. It was Samuel Daniel, a favourite writer of the queen's, who wrote the masque for Henry's installation, and he did so in a conscious critique of the over-hyperbolical conventions of James's masques.[30] The masques for Princess Elizabeth's wedding, in whose production Henry seems to have had considerable influence, introduced some new poets to court. Jonson was out of the country at the time of the marriage. The four Inns of Court between them staged two masques; this was the first time that the lawyers had paid this tribute to a member of the new royal house. One of the masques, written by George Chapman, glorified projects of colonization in the New World, a topic which aroused Henry's enthusiasm, particularly as it was a means of resisting Spanish power in the part of the world from which they drew their chief financial strength. Other masques and pageants at this time celebrated Protestant militancy. A draft has survived of a masque for Elizabeth's wedding which would have glorified the marriage as a means towards the apocalyptic reunion of Protestants throughout the world; the central figure of the masque was the figure of Aletheia, the apocalyptic Truth. The internationalist vision of this masque project contrasts strikingly with Jonson's celebration in his masques of England's splendid isolation, standing above the conflicts that beset the rest of Europe.[31] In his masque Chapman makes a speaker declare that the Britons are no longer, as Virgil had suggested, in the *Georgics*, divided from the world: the Palatine match had brought Britain into the mainstream of European Protestant politics. The figure of Protestant Truth also began to reappear in civic pageants at this time.

But by 1613 such apocalyptic enthusiasm was taking on a rather strained and desperate note, for the unexpected death of Prince Henry in November 1612 had removed the leading focus of Puritan hopes. There were fears that the marriage would be abandoned now that its most enthusiastic advocate was dead; in fact the

[29]   Cf. Williamson's discussion of this masque, Williamson, *Myth of the Conqueror*, 95–102.

[30]   On the queen's masques see Barbara K. Lewalski, *Writing Women in Jacobean England* (Cambridge, Mass., 1993), ch. 1, and Leeds Barroll, *Anna of Denmark, Queen of England: A Cultural Biography* (Philadelphia, 2001), ch. 4; on Daniel's relations with Henry see *The Brotherton Manuscript*, ed. Pitcher, 26–35, 93–4, and ' "In those figures which they seeme": Samuel Daniel's *Tethys' Festival*', in Lindley (ed.), *The Court Masque*, 33–46. Strong claims that if Henry had lived, 'the art of festival in Stuart England would have taken a very different course from that which ended in the sterility of the self-adulatory masques of the Caroline age': *Henry Prince of Wales and England's Lost Renaissance*, 139. See further Tristan Marshall, *Theatre of Empire: Great Britain on the London Stages under James VI and I* (Manchester, 2000), ch. 3.

[31]   See David Norbrook, '*The Masque of Truth*: Court Entertainments and International Protestant Politics in the Early Stuart Period', *The Seventeenth Century*, 1 (1986), 81–110.

wedding went ahead but the rejoicings were overshadowed by mourning for Henry. There was an unprecedented outbreak of public grief, and innumerable elegies were published in which Henry was praised as a model of godliness: several elegists noted his preference for warlike pursuits as opposed to 'the gaudy show Of ceremonies'.[32] Henry's death, following soon after Salisbury's, left a lack of serious political opposition to the king's new favourite Robert Carr, Viscount Rochester, and to the Howards with whom he was allying himself. The Howards did not constitute a coherent political bloc, but their enemies feared that they were conspiring together to persecute Puritans and improve the lot of Catholics. Northampton was especially hated because of his alleged pro-Spanish bias: contemporary opinion was summed up by the epitaph

> Here lyes my Lord of Northampton, his Maiestie's erwigg,
> Wth a Papisticall bald crowne, & a Protestant perewigg.[33]

An even more succinct satirist wrote of the Howards:

> when *they* are great
> they emprison & beat[.]

The fear that a pro-Spanish faction was coming to dominate the court increased when it was revealed that Rochester was to marry the Earl of Suffolk's daughter Frances. This marriage constituted a particularly bitter blow to those who idealized the great days of the Elizabethans, for Frances was married to the young Earl of Essex. Now the family name was being dishonoured by a particularly sordid divorce case. George Abbot, the recently appointed Archbishop of Canterbury, had grave doubts about the legitimacy of the divorce. The wedding festivities of 1614 did not arouse the same degree of public enthusiasm as Elizabeth's wedding the previous year. The Inns of Court initially planned to collaborate on a joint masque but in the end only Gray's Inn staged a masque, sponsored by Sir Francis Bacon who was anxious for court favour; the other Inns dropped out of the project, possibly because of their dislike of the marriage.[34] Only after strong pressure from the king did the City provide a wedding masque. The most enthusiastic praise of the marriage came from people who were anxious at all costs to gain favour with the newly rising faction at court, such as Bacon and John Donne, who even offered to publish a prose defence of the divorce. George Chapman published a somewhat embarrassed poem in praise of the marriage in an attempt to rescue his desperate financial state—his hopes of advancement from Henry had come to nothing and he had not yet been paid for his masque for Princess Elizabeth.[35] The atmosphere for the festivities of 1614 was in

---

[32] *The Complete Works of John Webster*, ed. F. L. Lucas, 4 vols. (London, 1927), iii.277.

[33] *The Dr. Farmer Chetham Manuscript*, ed. A. B. Grosart, 2 vols., Chetham Society (Manchester, 1873), ii.198; the other epigram quoted is an annotation in a Folger Shakespeare Library copy of Fulke Greville's *Workes* (London, 1633) (*Alaham*, 3); see below, Ch. 10 n. 115.

[34] E. A. J. Honigmann (ed.), *The Masque of Flowers*, in T. J. B. Spencer et al. (eds.), *A Book of Masques in Honour of Allardyce Nicoll* (Cambridge, 1967), 149–78 (152–3).

[35] Chapman, 'Andromeda liberata', in *The Poems of George Chapman*, ed. Phyllis Brooks Bartlett (New York, 1941), 301–35.

general an uneasy one, and the widespread hostility to the dominant groups at court contributed to the political tensions that disrupted the Parliament held that summer. There were rumours that the government planned to manipulate the Parliament and members responded by behaviour that made it completely unmanageable.[36] Fears that the English court was being dominated by Catholic sympathizers were heightened by reports that war was about to break out on the Continent. It was believed that James had been lulled into complacency by his pro-Spanish councillors and was doing nothing to prevent a planned Catholic attack on the Protestant states in Germany.[37]

Jonson and the Spenserians responded to these events in rather different ways. Jonson does not seem to have shared in the extreme mourning for Henry's death. Though he seems by this time to have returned to the Church of England he did not like the militant apocalyptic fervour that was expressed in so many of the elegies. His friend Richard Corbett revealed the attitude of many anti-Puritan observers in a satire that ridiculed the elegists for Henry, many of whom were of low social status: what did the grief of a cobbler or a Geneva bridegroom matter, and what right had such people to express their opinions about matters far above their understandings?[38] Jonson, who was travelling on the Continent at the time, had not written an epithalamium for Princess Elizabeth, but he did celebrate the Somerset marriage in a masque and in verses for the attendant barriers. Jonson was being somewhat inconsistent in doing so, for he had already celebrated Frances Howard's first marriage in a masque, *Hymenaei*, which contained mystical praise of the marriage bond. When the first masque was staged the Puritans had been campaigning for a number of reforms including relaxation of restrictions against divorce—a reform first formulated in Edward VI's reign—but the high-church party had been firmly opposed to any erosion in the traditional status of marriage. Such principles could be easily overruled, however, when it was a matter of pleasing the king's new favourite. There were, however, less cynical reasons for defending the new marriage: Frances Howard's marriage had been arranged when she was very young and it had become for her an imprisonment. The campaign of opposition to the match revealed the British public in a mood of self-righteousness which Jonson found unattractive. The misogyny that often lay behind Puritan insistence on strict female virtue could be felt in the many denunciations of Frances Howard's wantonness. As for Somerset, though he aroused much jealousy he was no monster and there is testimony to his character from George Chapman and Samuel Daniel even after his fall. Jonson saw it as his function to strengthen unity at court and respect for established institutions, and he rallied behind the king and his favourite. His masque and barriers do, how-

---

[36] These rumours were exaggerated: see Linda Levy Peck, *Northampton: Patronage and Policy at the Court of James I* (London, 1982), 205–10. For a fuller analysis of the politics and culture of 1614, which I have not been able to consult, see Stephen Clucas and Rosalind Davies (eds.), *1614: Year of Crisis. Studies in Jacobean History and Literature* (Aldershot, 2002).

[37] See, e.g., *Historical Manuscripts Commission. Report on the Manuscripts of the Marquess of Downshire Preserved at Easthampstead Park, Berks.*, iv, ed. A. B. Hind (London, 1940), 425, 514.

[38] *The Poems of Richard Corbett*, ed. J. A. W. Bennett and H. R. Trevor-Roper (Oxford, 1955), 8–10.

ever, rather conspicuously abstain from direct praise of the couple; and as we shall see, there are signs that by the summer of 1614 his loyalty to the official line was under severe strain.[39]

Where Jonson's responses were somewhat evasive, however, the Spenserians responded to the crisis by a strong affirmation of Elizabethan poetic and political traditions. The years 1613–14 saw a revival of pastoral poetry; and in adopting the persona of the plain-speaking shepherds the Spenserians were indicating their dissatisfaction with contemporary events. In 1614 the Elizabethan anthology *England's Helicon* was reprinted with additional poems by Christopher Brooke and William Browne and the new motto:

> The Courts of Kings heare no such straines,
> As daily lull the Rusticke Swaines.[40]

This might also be taken as the motto of Browne's long poem *Britannia's Pastorals*, of which the first part appeared in November 1613. In a commendatory poem Michael Drayton, who was described by a contemporary as '[o]ur still reviving Spencer', praised Browne for redeeming the world of pastoral which, he said, was 'utterly neglected' today.[41] Neither Donne nor Jonson was fond of the pastoral convention, partly because of its prophetic associations. Browne's originality in *Britannia's Pastorals* lies in the connections he makes between the symbolic figure of the shepherd as Protestant prophet and the celebration of the English countryside. Throughout the poem the country is associated with moral purity, the court with corruption. Browne's poem owes a lot to Drayton's *Poly-Olbion*, of which the first part had been published in 1612. This was an extremely ambitious project to mythologize the English countryside, to present an imaginative vision of its history and geography. Drayton was thus following Spenser's lead in *Colin Clouts Come Home Againe*. Like Browne, Drayton praised the country for its associations with moral virtue; he paid little attention to cities and the court. He celebrated the martial glories of the past, and dedicated the poem not to James but to Prince Henry, who was portrayed on the title page in full armour.

Drayton's poem contained few direct political allusions, but Browne explicitly linked his praise of the countryside with a commitment to Protestant politics. In cantos 4 and 5 of Book I Browne tells the story of Aletheia, the embodiment of

---

[39] Jonson may have inserted satirical references to the divorce in revisions to *Epicoene*, though the case is hard to prove: Thomas Kranidas, 'Possible Revisions or Additions in Jonson's *Epicoene*', *Anglia*, 83 (1965), 451–3. For a new discussion of the whole episode, emphasizing misogynistic elements in contemporary criticisms, see David Lindley, *The Trials of Frances Howard: Fact and Fiction at the Court of King James* (London, 1993); for the wave of manuscript satires see James L. Sanderson, 'Poems on an Affair of State', *Review of English Studies*, 17 (1966), 57–61.

[40] *England's Helicon 1600, 1614*, ed. Hyder Edward Rollins, 2 vols. (Cambridge, Mass., 1935), ii.9. For more on the 1614 *England's Helicon* see Jane Tylus, 'Jacobean Poetry and Lyric Disappointment', in Maus and Harvey (eds.), *Soliciting Interpretation*, 174–98 (183); on the Spenserians at this period see Michelle O'Callaghan, *The 'Shepheards Nation': Jacobean Spenserians and Early Stuart Political Culture, 1612–1625* (Oxford, 2000), chs. 1–2, and '"Now thou may'st speak freely": Entering the Public Sphere in 1614', in Clucas and Davies (eds.), *1614: A Year of Crisis*.

[41] Newdigate, *Michael Drayton and his Circle*, 199; Browne, *Poems*, i.10.

Protestant Truth. Like the woman in the wilderness, and Spenser's Una, she wanders alone through a desolate landscape. She is refused admission at an abbey and is shut out from court because Adulation is a privileged guest there. Did Browne know that it had been planned to celebrate Elizabeth's wedding with a masque of Aletheia? Certainly there are allusions in the poem to recent history: at one point Browne reprints his own elegy for Prince Henry, and there is a lengthy description of the Vale of Woe where various Protestant heroes are lamenting. The fate of the second Earl of Essex is pathetically described: this would have been especially topical just before the remarriage of his son's wife to the king's favourite. Sir Walter Ralegh makes an appearance; he had been in prison since the start of James's reign, and was in a black mood after Henry's death had removed his hopes of imminent release. (Ralegh's appearance in the poem may be said to have constituted some pre-publicity for his *History of the World*, whose publication in 1614 was to be swiftly halted by King James.) Browne dedicated the first part of the poem to Edward Lord Zouche, who was known as a strong Protestant and an enemy of Northampton. The idealization of country life in Browne and Drayton may seem to have much in common with Jonson's praise of Penshurst and Sir Robert Wroth—indeed, Drayton praises Waltham Forest in *Poly-Olbion*—but Jonson's political rhetoric is significantly different. Where Browne and Drayton praise the countryside as the site of rural simplicity and also as a place where martial virtue can be nourished, far from the luxury of courts, Jonson celebrates the common commitment of court and countryside to a traditional order of ritual and revelry, and praises the country as an image of the king's peace.[42] Browne associates the countryside both with political liberty and with poetic inspiration, and the very formlessness of *Britannia's Pastorals* becomes a symbol of imaginative freedom as opposed to courtly restraint—hence its later appeal to the young Keats and the Leigh Hunt circle. The somewhat incongruous association between 'faerie' mythology and political radicalism which was to be a feature of English political traditions down to Shelley's *Queen Mab* and beyond was already emerging in the Jacobean period.[43]

Political comment still forms a subordinate element in Book I of *Britannia's Pastorals*: Part II, published in 1616, was to contain more explicit satire. But Browne's next pastoral work, *The Shepheards Pipe* (1614), formed a kind of poetic manifesto with strong political undertones.[44] The seventh eclogue glanced at the Somerset marriage in denouncing the unfaithful 'Phillis'. The volume included not only eclogues by Browne but also poems by his friends John Davies of Hereford,

---

[42] For contrasting representations of the 'country' and the country house in Jonson and the Spenserians see Annabel Patterson, *Pastoral and Ideology: Virgil to Valéry* (Oxford, 1988), 143–4, Richard Helgerson, *Forms of Nationhood: The Elizabethan Writing of England* (Chicago, 1992), 107–47, and O'Callaghan, *The 'Shepheards Nation'*, 44–8, 104–7.

[43] Jeffrey N. Cox, *Poetry and Politics in the Cockney School: Keats, Shelley, Hunt and their Circle* (Cambridge, 1999), 75, 99, 126.

[44] Browne, *Poems*, ii.77–164; James Doelman (ed.), *Early Stuart Pastoral* (Toronto, 1999), includes editions of *The Shepheards Pipe* and Wither's *The Shepherds Hunting*, and the latter is also available in William B. Hunter, Jr. (ed.), *The English Spenserians: The Poetry of Giles Fletcher, George Wither, Michael Drayton, Phineas Fletcher, and Henry More* (Salt Lake City, 1977).

Christopher Brooke, and George Wither. Though most of these poems have a festive flavour, all three friends had strong and controversial political interests. Davies was patronized by the Earl of Northumberland, who had been imprisoned in the Tower for his alleged complicity in the Gunpowder Plot; in 1609 he had addressed to his patron a poem which implied that James was 'Upon the *Rack* of Conscience bound' for this unjust imprisonment. The poem was censored, he tartly commented in a manuscript version, by the 'p[re]cisenesse of the chaplaines allowed to allow Books'.[45] Wither, the addressee of Browne's opening eclogue, was himself in prison by the time the volume was entered in the Stationers' Register. Wither had made his poetic debut with a series of elegies for Prince Henry and an epithalamium for Princess Elizabeth, in both of which he voiced a fierce Protestant patriotism. Early in 1613 he published a long satire, *Abuses Stript and Whipt*, which achieved an enormous popular success. One reason for the poem's fame—or notoriety—was a series of veiled attacks on corruption in high places; some passages were widely taken to refer to Salisbury and Northampton. Wither's poem stands in the tradition of Protestant satires on abuses that went back to Robert Crowley in the sixteenth century. Wither gives no sign of direct acquaintance with Crowley's poetry, but he probably knew *Piers Plowman*—Drayton had drawn heavily on the poem in his *Legend of Cromwell* (1607).[46] William Browne was interested in medieval poetry and published a poem by Hoccleve in *The Shepheards Pipe*. Wither made no attempt to imitate the stylized diction of some of the older prophetic poetry; he wrote in flowing couplets which aimed to reach the widest possible readership. But he saw himself, like Crowley, as a man whose poetic gifts gave him an obligation to speak out and denounce abuses even at the risk of arousing the disapprobation of those in authority. Like Crowley, Wither was no man of the people—he came from a respectable country family—but he was always ready to vindicate his 'ancient-vsed *Hampshire Dialect*' against the fashions of court and town. He took the unusual step of dedicating *Abuses Stript and Whipt* to himself, declaring that a 'common *Mecænas*' would hardly be pleased with his 'free speech'.[47] In fact Wither took the precaution of including complimentary addresses to various leading courtiers, all of them people known for their strong Protestantism. But Wither never tried to make demonstrative rhetoric into a serious poetic art. Jonson's masques and his poems to his patrons adopt a stance of moral independence but they rely on his sense of intimacy with the monarch and his other patrons, a knowledge of their interests and character. The address is primarily to them, and the reader is involved at a certain distance, overhearing Jonson's conversation with a wise and noble courtier. Wither's dedicatory addresses are often frankly pragmatic, appeals for favour without any great measure of personal involvement; his poetry addresses the common reader, the person who may not read much poetry but who has a general interest in moral and political

[45] Stephen Clucas, '"Noble Virtue in Extremes": Henry Percy, Ninth Earl of Northumberland, Patronage and the Politics of Stoic Consolation', *Renaissance Studies*, 9 (1995), 266–91 (273–80).

[46] Drayton, *Works*, v.172–3.

[47] George Wither, *Juvenilia*, 3 vols., Spenser Society (Manchester, 1871), i, sig. A3ʳ, 9 (I cite original pagination).

matters. Jonson's constant satire of Puritans and ignorant citizens defines his audience as an erudite and conservative one; Wither, while declaring that he is not himself a Puritan, refuses to attack them:

> Who are so much tearm'd *Puritans* as they
> That feare God most?[48]

Wither's poetry was considered to be politically inflammatory, and in 1614 he was
arrested.[49] The timing of his arrest is significant: elections were being held, in an
atmosphere of great suspicion, for the Parliament which was to assemble that spring.
Wither's imprisonment seems to have been arranged by Northampton, who had opposed the summoning of the Parliament in case it led to demonstrations of hostility
to pro-Spanish courtiers and who had been attacked in Wither's poem. He seems to
have felt that Wither should be discouraged from making further political trouble at
such a sensitive period. From his prison Wither composed *A Satyre*, in which he
appealed to the king, insisting that he could not have known of his imprisonment,
which he blamed on corrupt courtiers. In later writings he continued to claim the
king's favour; as will be seen, by the end of the reign he had certainly gained it. Even
if his praise of James was sincere, however, Wither was constitutionally incapable of
advancing praise to someone in power without an immediate counter-move. If the
king's judgement is good, it is hard to see why

> each fleering *Parasite* is bold
> Thy Royall brow vndaunted to behold:
> And euery *Temporizer* strikes a string,
> That's Musicke for the hearing of a King?[50]

Wither was not released until some time after the end of the Parliament, when
several MPs arrested for provocative behaviour during the sitting had already been
set free.

Wither's imprisonment became the occasion for a manifestation of political discontent by a group of his friends. In his eclogue in *The Shepheards Pipe* Christopher
Brooke attributed to Browne the sentiment that

> Thought hath no prison and the minde is free
> Vnder the greatest king and tyrannie

and Browne replied to Brooke that 'thou canst give more to kings than kings to
thee'.[51] Wither reaffirmed this group identity when he reprinted his contributions to
The Shepheards Pipe in 1615 with some further eclogues, *The Shepherds Hunting*.
Browne's eclogue served as publicity for Brooke's poem *The Ghost of Richard III*, a
sententious denunciation of tyranny, which was entered in the Stationers' Register
the day before *The Shepheards Pipe*. In the tradition of More's Tacitean satire,

---

[48]   George Wither, *Juvenilia*, i.276.
[49]   Allan Pritchard, '*Abuses Stript and Whipt* and Wither's Imprisonment', *Review of English Studies*, NS
14 (1963), 337–45.
[50]   Wither, *Juvenilia*, iii, sig. Dd7ʳ.   [51]   Browne, *Poems*, ii.147.

Brooke presented Richard as a master-dissimulator who used flattering clergy to bolster his power. Richard resolved to

> in thine owne power, still be free,
> And what seemes best, thinke absolutely well . . .
> Nor bound thy selfe, being a boundlesse *King* . . .

he must become 'absolute instated'.[52] The poem's fear of tyranny is very close to language Brooke was using in Parliament. He had joined in the attack on the government's unpopular 'impositions', taxes on trade, from early in the session. The king, he insisted, had no absolute power to make any laws to the prejudice of his subjects: if the king could 'impose by his absolute Power, then no man [would be] certain what he hath, for it shall be subject to the King's pleasure'.[53]

The connections between poetry and politics here are especially striking. The 1614 Parliament was in fact an unusually literary body. It has gone down in history as the 'Addled Parliament', a chaotic failure that was eventually dissolved without passing any legislation. For revisionists, the angry words spoken by some MPs against the government stayed well within an ideological consensus, and can often be ascribed to manipulation by patrons like Northampton. The worries about an 'absolute' king are not to be taken as reflecting a constitutional conflict, for on some revisionist definitions the term was taken in the very restricted sense of a monarch who claimed the right to make laws without consulting anybody else; James was cautious about making such claims. But the debates in Parliament constantly compared the current monarchy with earlier English periods and with Continental states, revealing a recurrent fear that elements of popular consent at one stage inherent in the English constitution were being eroded.[54] Brooke's speeches and his poetry reveal such fears of a slowly emergent absolutism. He certainly did not believe that there was no difference between James I and Richard III, but the cartoon-like villainy of his tyrant offered a warning about what might happen if Parliament were not vigilant. It is quite true that the political allegiances of 1614 are bewilderingly complex; in bringing together literary and historical perspectives, however, it is possible to see the Parliament's failure as marking a significant moment in the emergence of a political public sphere.

The friendship between Brooke and the Spenserian poets brought together different but overlapping literary worlds. Brooke had shown no previous poetic ambitions, and his closest literary friendship was with John Donne, no admirer of Spenser. Amongst those who contributed commendatory verse to his *Ghost of*

---

[52] Christopher Brooke, *The Ghost of Richard III* (London, 1614), sigs. G2ᵛ–3ʳ; *The Complete Poems of Christopher Brooke*, ed. Alexander B. Grosart, in *Miscellanies of the Fuller Worthies' Library*, iv (Blackburn, 1872), 161. See O'Callaghan, *The 'Shepheards Nation'*, ch. 2, and ' "Talking Politics": Tyranny, Parliament, and Christopher Brooke's *The Ghost of Richard III* (1614)', *Historical Journal*, 41 (1998), 97–120, and James Doelman, 'Born with Teeth: Christopher Brooke's *The Ghost of Richard III*', *The Seventeenth Century*, 14 (1999), 115–29.

[53] *Wentworth Papers 1597–1628*, ed. J. P. Cooper, London, Camden Society, 4th series, 12 (1973), 67; Maia Jansson (ed.), *Proceedings in Parliament 1614 (House of Commons)*, *Memoirs of the American Philosophical Society*, 172 (Philadelphia, 1988), 95 (passage in brackets added).

[54] For differing views see Glenn Burgess, *Absolute Monarchy and the Stuart Constitution* (New Haven, 1996), ch. 1, and Sommerville, *Royalists and Patriots*, 224–65.

Richard III were Jonson and Chapman, both of whom, like Donne, had recently written in praise of the Somerset marriage. There are signs, however, that in 1614 Jonson was feeling the strain of his role as panegyrist of the Somerset marriage, and was keen to embrace non-courtly worlds. He had been travelling abroad with the son of Sir Walter Ralegh and had helped Sir Walter in compiling and publishing his *History of the World*, which was recalled by James after its publication in 1614 for presenting the divine punishment of monarchs too sympathetically. Jonson's contacts with the Inns of Court were particularly close at this time; he addressed a warm poem to his friend John Selden's *Titles of Honour* in which for the first time he acknowledged that he had been 'deceiv'd' and had 'prais'd some names too much'. He hailed Selden as a 'Monarch in Letters!' and praised him for dedicating his book to 'no great Name' but his fellow lawyer Edward Heyward.[55] Selden and Heyward had both contributed commendatory poems to *Britannia's Pastorals* and Selden had also provided notes for Browne's poem and for Drayton's *Poly-Olbion*; Selden may have been the 'Jockie' of Browne's *The Shepheards Pipe*.[56] Though Selden's profound scholarship refrained from any clear polemics, his work was to provide grounding for criticisms of royal policy in Parliament, and he would himself later become an active Parliamentarian. Members of the Inns of Court were playing a leading role in the emergence of a series of literary clubs which met at taverns near the bookselling centre of Paul's Churchyard. Wither and Browne allegorized convivial gatherings at the Devil and St Dunstan in their pastorals; Jonson wrote a series of rules for gatherings at the tavern's 'Apollo Room'. Donne, Brooke, and Jonson were members of another group that met at the Mermaid Tavern.[57] These clubs brought together figures with Parliamentary, legal, and courtly connections across a broad range of political sympathies: the wit John Hoskyns was on friendly terms with Northampton. Brooke collaborated with Hoskyns and others on the notorious *jeu d'esprit* 'The Parliament Fart', which was not calculated to inspire political ideals, while Hoskyns has been credited as the inventor of English nonsense verse on the basis which emerged from the literary games of the 'Sireniacs'.[58]

Such apparently 'pure' poetry may seem a long way from concrete engagement with the political world. The distance from nonsense to Parliament, however, is perhaps never entirely unbridgeable, and at this period the clubs provided a bridge. These clubs anticipate in increasingly articulate and institutionalized form the phenomenon Jürgen Habermas describes as a 'literary public sphere', and whose origins

[55]   Anna R. Beer, *Sir Walter Ralegh and his Readers in the Seventeenth Century: Speaking to the People* (Houndmills, 1997), 31–5; Cyndia Susan Clegg, *Press Censorship in Jacobean England* (Cambridge, 2001), 96 ff.; David Riggs, *Ben Jonson: A Life* (Cambridge, Mass., 1989), 192 ff.; *H&S*, ii.158–61, ll. 21, 65–9.

[56]   Anne Lake Prescott, 'Marginal Discourse: Drayton's Muse and Selden's "Story"', *Studies in Philology*, 88 (1991), 307–28; O'Callaghan, *The 'Shepheards Nation'*, 42.

[57]   I. A. Shapiro, 'The "Mermaid Club"', *Modern Language Review*, 45 (1950), 6–17; Pascal Brioist, '"Que de choses avons nous vues et vécues à la Sirène"', in Dominique Julia (ed.), *Culture et société dans l'Europe moderne et contemporaine* (Florence, 1992), 89–132; O'Callaghan, *The 'Shepheards Nation'*, 37–9.

[58]   Noel Malcolm, *The Origins of English Nonsense* (London, 1997), 5–17. For Hoskyns I follow throughout Baird W. Whitlock, *John Hoskyns, Serjeant-at-Law* (Washington, 1982); see also David Norbrook, 'Rhetoric, Ideology, and the Elizabethan World Picture', in Peter Mack (ed.), *Renaissance Rhetoric* (London, 1994), 140–64 (147–58).

he locates in Parisian *salons* and English coffee-houses of the later seventeenth century. For Habermas, such a literary public sphere is a precondition for a political public sphere, where debate would be relatively independent of the patronage structures of court and other institutions. The members of these Jacobean clubs did have some strong patronage ties and professional affiliations which cut across their sense of solidarity, and in that sense the Habermasian model does not fully apply. On the other hand, it can be argued that their political significance ultimately overshadowed their role as a literary forum.[59] Their rhetorical play was designed to sharpen the wits of members who would go on to present arguments as lawyers or as MPs; in the humanist tradition of arguing *in utramque partem*, it was recognized that arguing a paradoxical or absurd case was excellent training quite beside the pleasure it provided. Hoskyns took the process of rhetorical education seriously: he had composed a rhetorical treatise for a young friend, Robert Harley, who was to become a leading Puritan MP. For the figure of 'division' he offered the following example: 'All men exclaim upon these exactions. Nobles, gentlemen, commonalty, poor, rich, scholar, merchants, peasants, young, old, wise, ignorant, high, low, and all cry out upon the hard impositions of these burdens.'[60] When Hoskyns campaigned against impositions in 1614 he had a rich rhetorical storehouse to draw on. Training in rhetoric kept club members constantly aware of classical rhetorical and political traditions. Hoskyns drew heavily on Lipsius and was a great admirer of Tacitus. Brooke consciously patterned his *Ghost of Richard III* on the ornate, ironic rhetoric of Seneca. Davies of Hereford had recently praised Greville's *Mustapha*, which was circulating in manuscript along with Buchanan's still-proscribed *De jure regni*. In praising Brooke's poem, Jonson would have recalled that he himself had composed a play about Richard late in the previous reign, at a time when Richard was often invoked as a parallel to Cecil.[61]

Classical analogies were constantly to the fore in contemporary responses to the 1614 Parliament, even if they have been played down by later historians. They brought with them a strong anxiety about the way monarchical power may limit free speech and historical enquiry—an anxiety that may have led them on occasion to exaggerate the perils in which they stood. From the classical tradition, early modern scholars could find several words for free speech, including the Greek *parrhesia*, which could take on strongly positive connotations as a boldness in the face of political intimidation. The *locus classicus* for the recurrent hostility between absolutism

[59] Jürgen Habermas, *The Structural Transformation of the Public Sphere: An Inquiry into a Category of Bourgeois Society*, trans. Thomas Burger with Frederick Lawrence (Cambridge, Mass., 1989), 27 ff.; Brioist, ' "Que de choses avons nous vues et vécues à la Sirène" ', 127. See further below, pp. 287–8.

[60] Whitlock, *John Hoskyns, Serjeant-at-Law*, 138–9; John Hoskins, *Directions for Speech and Style*, ed. Hoyt H. Hudson (Princeton, 1935), 31.

[61] John Davies of Hereford, *Complete Works*, ed. A. B. Grosart, 2 vols. (Edinburgh, 1878), ii.k.53, praises *Mustapha* 'as it is written, not printed'. The Folger manuscript, Folger Shakespeare Library V.b.223, is bound up with the first English translation of Buchanan's *De jure regni*, and was said by Israel Gollancz to have been written out by Davies (*Athenaeum*, 19 Jan. 1907, 78–9), though later scholars have not agreed. On Jonson see Blair Worden, 'Ben Jonson among the Historians', in Kevin Sharpe and Peter Lake (eds.), *Culture and Politics in Early Stuart England* (London, 1994), 67–90 (76).

and free speech was Tacitus' account of how Sejanus had suppressed the historian Cremutius Cordus. Jonson had dramatized the episode in his *Sejanus* and been called in question by Northampton.[62] A significant publication of 1614 was Sir Arthur Gorges's translation of Lucan's *Pharsalia*, an epic written in the shadow of Tacitus which returns again and again to the theme of stifled voices and suppressed memories of freedom. Sir Walter Ralegh contributed a commendatory poem in which he warned that being a truth-teller at court might lead to death, just as in Lucan's time.[63] Sir Henry Wotton, disturbed at Northampton's attempts to muzzle criticism through the Star Chamber charge of *scandalum magnatum* (defaming a peer), drew a parallel with Cremutius Cordus.[64] As the Parliament proceeded, warnings about the dangers of excessive royal power became increasingly daring. Sir Edwin Sandys, with whom Brooke was closely aligned, quoted some lines of Juvenal (*Satires*, 10.112–13) which warned that few kings go to the grave without bloodshed, and made a speech which declared that monarchy was originally elective and that monarchs were accountable to the people. He was called before the Council for his speeches, though no charges were made. Hoskyns was one of several MPs delegated by Sandys to consult the chronicles for precedents, and his brief would have included a study of the reign of Richard III. Hoskyns and his friends used the library of Sir Robert Cotton, whose attempt to revive a Society of Antiquaries in 1614 was halted under royal disfavour.[65]

The MPs' onslaughts extended to the church. Richard Neile, a high-church bishop who was to become a strong ally of Archbishop Laud, led the way in refusing a request from the Commons to the Lords for a consultation over impositions; Hoskyns responded with the provocative warning that if the bishops went too far they would be overthrown: 'Scotland and Germany have swept away greater miters than his.'[66] Brooke's poem was calculated to fuel in turn the anxieties of those suspicious of the clergy's political role: in his Paul's Cross sermon, Dr Shaw tries to cover up the king's tyranny with a mixture of 'clouted Creame' and 'spleeneful Venome'.

---

[62] David Colclough, '*Parrhesia*: The Rhetoric of Free Speech in Early Modern England', *Rhetorica*, 17 (1999), 177–212; Worden, 'Ben Jonson among the Historians', 78–9.

[63] David Norbrook, 'Lucan, Thomas May, and the Creation of a Republican Literary Culture', in Sharpe and Lake (eds.), *Culture and Politics in Early Stuart England*, 45–66 (51–4). The translation was dedicated to the Countess of Bedford, who was associated with politics critical of the Howards and Buckingham: Lewalski, *Writing Women in Jacobean England*, 117. In the wake of the Overbury scandal a correspondent spoke of divisions at court between the 'domus Julia' and the 'Pompeiana familia', 'which is the aggregation of good patriots': *Historical Manuscripts Commission Report on the Manuscripts of the Marquess of Downshire Preserved at Easthampstead Park, Berkshire*, v, ed. G. Dyfnallt Owen (London, 1988), 284.

[64] *Life and Letters of Sir Henry Wotton*, ed. Logan Pearsall Smith, 2 vols. (Oxford, 1907), ii.23.

[65] Doelman, *Early Stuart Pastoral*, 65, suggests that the 'Neddy' of Browne's third eclogue could be Sir Edwin Sandys; O'Callaghan, *The 'Shepheards Nation'*, suggests Sir Edward Phelips. On Sandys's political views see Noel Malcolm, 'Hobbes, Sandys, and the Virginia Company', *Historical Journal*, 24 (1981), 297–321, and on his leading role in the 1614 Parliament, Theodore K. Rabb, *Jacobean Gentleman: Sir Edwin Sandys, 1561–1629* (Princeton, 1998), ch. 7; on the Juvenal allusion see 193 and Jansson (ed.), *Proceedings in Parliament 1614*, 316; on the historical research, ibid., 225–6, 306–7, and Kevin Sharpe, *Sir Robert Cotton, 1586–1631: History and Politics in Early Modern England* (Oxford, 1979), 36, 162–3.

[66] Jansson (ed.), *Proceedings in Parliament 1614*, 341.

Brooke was here closely following Sir Thomas More. The deeper anxiety behind the Shaw episode is that here, contrary to the normal fiction that the king is being led astray by bad advisers, it is the king who is using the clergy more than they are using him. Hoskyns followed up his attack on the bishops with a reference to a 'sermon at Paul's Cross in R.3.'—surely a glance at More, perhaps via Brooke. Hoskyns's provocativeness led to his being thrown in jail, whence he advised his son sardonically on the dangers of political rhetoric:

> Keepe [your tongue] in thral whilst thou art free:
> Imprison it or it will thee.[67]

As a concerned participant in this session, Wotton was torn between worries about Northampton's conduct and worries that there was some justice in the earl's suspicion that the Commons was becoming subversive. One of those arrested, Christopher Neville, attacked Neile and other bishops as those who 'to please the King . . . care not what they say to hurt the country', being 'their masters' spaniels but their country's wolves': the implied opposition between the personal interests of the king and the interests of the country as a whole was bold indeed. Wotton dismissed his speech as a mere rhetorical exercise: Neville was 'a young gentleman fresh from the school, who having gathered together divers Latin sentences against kings, bound them up in a long speech, and interlarded them with certain Ciceronian exclamations'. Perhaps, then, Northampton was being paranoid about what were only verbal gestures. There were indeed allegations that he had paid Hoskyns and other MPs to disrupt Parliament, so that their apparent independence was merely a reflection of a traditional clientage system. And yet Wotton was not confident that what he had heard in Parliament could be so easily dismissed as irrelevant to the political future. He commented that such speeches were 'better being in a Senate of Venice where the treaters are perpetual princes, than when those that speak so irreverently are so soon to return (where they should remember) to the natural capacity of subjects'. Wotton had recently returned from Venice and he was in a good position to assess the balance of monarchical and political elements in the English constitution. Hoskyns and his allies, he felt, were pushing their demands for the right to speak out so far that they were undermining the constraints a monarchical government must necessarily place upon public oratory. James had termed Southampton and his supporters in the previous Parliament the 'thirty doges'.[68] Hoskyns's case was to be taken

---

[67] Brooke, *The Ghost of Richard III*, sig. F2^r, ed. Grosart, 97; Sir Thomas More, *The History of Richard III*, ed. Richard S. Sylvester, in *The Complete Works of St. Thomas More*, ii (New Haven, 1963), 66–8; Jansson (ed.), *Proceedings in Parliament 1614*, 419–20, 353 n. 42 (Jansson declares herself unable to locate the sermon referred to, but this seems a likely candidate); Whitlock, *John Hoskyns, Serjeant-at-Law*, 469. Hoskyns's poem circulated widely in manuscript, attracting some readers with Puritan sympathies: David Colclough, ' "The Muses Recreation": John Hoskyns and the Manuscript Culture of the Seventeenth Century', *Huntington Library Quarterly*, 61 (2000), 369–400 (386–9).

[68] Jansson (ed.), *Proceedings in Parliament 1614*, 419–20; *Life and Letters of Sir Henry Wotton*, ii.37–8; Neil Cuddy, 'The Conflicting Loyalties of a "Vulger Counselor": The Third Earl of Southampton, 1597–1624', in John Morrill et al. (eds.), *Public Duty and Private Conscience in Seventeenth-Century England: Essays Presented to G. E. Aylmer* (Oxford, 1993), 121–50 (138).

up at the very beginning of the 1621 Parliament, as a threat to the principle of free speech for Members. In itself that principle was a strictly limited one, and neither the MPs nor the extra-parliamentary poets were arguing for a universal and unconditional right to free speech. Nonetheless, the impassioned invocation of different kinds of concept of freedom from different historical eras and different contexts did produce a sense of solidarity amongst different writers and public figures which could work against the tendency to division and compartmentalization inherent in the patronage system.[69]

Northampton's harsh actions against oppositional speech stemmed from his belief that it was necessary to defend monarchy against tendencies that threatened it. In the 1614 Parliament he lamented the diffusion of 'new opinions' when 'the scum are sent out of the university'. The classical parallel for oratory he preferred was Menenius Agrippa's use of a fable of the discontented body politic to quell a popular rebellion. He compared the House of Commons to a theatre: a place for demonstrative rather than deliberative rhetoric, for the king's views to be applauded rather than subjected to critical scrutiny. Northampton here anticipated the views of Hobbes and Newcastle that humanist scholarship instilled a cult of liberty incompatible with monarchical government. There was 'never any thing so deerly bought', Hobbes complained, 'as these Western parts have bought the learning of the Greek and Latine tongues . . . the *Universities* have been to this nation, as the wooden horse was to the Trojans'.[70]

On the Habermasian model, the public sphere responded to a growth in economic relationships which gained increasing autonomy from the crown. The events of 1614 offer a striking example of the intersections between economics, politics, and literary history. Brooke and Sandys were strongly involved with trading interests, Sandys being a leading champion of the Virginia Company. At the same time, they were suspicious of the crown's attempts to find an accommodation with the large trading companies which would permit their privileged status and limit dependence on Parliament; Sandys was at the head of a series of parliamentary assaults on monopolies culminating in the Statute of Monopolies. Most of the writers under discussion here had links of some kind with trading companies, though as so often in this period their particular interests sometimes pulled them in different directions. There was a common involvement in colonial expansion in Ireland and the New World. Brooke had helped to arrange the finances for Chapman's masque for Princess Elizabeth, which celebrated colonization in the New World, and in 1622 he published a poem in praise of the Virginia settlement. Wither was also an enthusiastic supporter of the Virginia enterprise, and he took an interest in a colonial project closer to home:

---

[69] Christopher Thompson, *The Debate on Free Speech in the House of Commons in February 1621* (Orsett, 1985); David Colclough, '"Better Becoming a Senate of Venice": Freedom of Speech and the Addled Parliament', in Clucas and Davies (eds.), *1614: Year of Crisis*; Dr Colclough is working on a fuller study of freedom of speech in early Stuart England. See further below, pp. 307–13.

[70] Peck, *Northampton: Patronage and Policy at the Court of James I*, 179, 183; Elizabeth Read Foster (ed.), *Proceedings in Parliament, 1610*, 2 vols. (New Haven, 1966), i.79; Thomas Hobbes, *Behemoth; or, The Long Parliament*, ed. Ferdinand Tönnies (1889), reprint, ed. Stephen Holmes (Chicago, 1990), 40.

before publishing his first poems he had apparently been in Londonderry. He was patronized by Sir Thomas Ridgeway, a political ally of Sandys. Wither seems also to have had family links with the Merchant Adventurers, the company which supervised the wool trade. This company's fate was under scrutiny in the 1614 Parliament, with a proposal to dissolve the Merchant Adventurers and found a new body controlled by Alderman William Cokayne—for which Jonson was to write a masque (above, Ch. 7 n. 59). Brooke strongly attacked this proposal: though it could be presented as an attack on a traditional monopoly, it also had overtones of court clientage which made it suspect to its critics. A number of Spenserians had links with the Merchant Adventurers. In the Elizabethan period Essex had recommended Sylvester for a post in one of their Continental stations and he was at last rescued from financial ruin after Henry's death by a post at Middelburg. Giles Fletcher senior was a member of the company. William Ferrar, who composed commendatory verses to *Britannia's Pastorals* and was addressed by Wither in *The Shepherds Hunting*, came from a family closely associated with the company and with Sandys. In 1614 Brooke introduced a bill calling for sumptuary legislation; such legislation appealed to Puritans who disliked personal vanity but also had the more practical aim of protecting the wool trade. Browne and another contributor, John Davies of Hereford, both attacked sartorial extravagance in their eclogues. If classical pastoral rested on a split between labour and poetic contemplation, this new model pastoral had a practical interest in wool production.[71]

Many years later Milton, in *Areopagitica*, was to make a connection between monopolies in the wool trade and the licensing of books: 'Truth and understanding are not such wares as to be monopoliz'd and traded in by tickets and statutes, and standards. We must not think to make a staple commodity of all the knowledge in the Land, to mark and licence it like our broad cloath, and our wooll packs.'[72] As will be seen in the next chapter, Wither, in many ways the most radical of the Spenserians, was to anticipate Milton in extending his critique of economic monopolies to the sphere of literary production. His poetic individualism in the end worked against that fidelity to the stylized conventions of pastoral which can still be found in Spenser, and that Milton was to retain in *Lycidas*. In a note to *The Shepherds Hunting*, he acknowledges that he is 'erring from the true nature of an *Eglogue*' in speaking so much in his own person rather than adopting a conventional persona. He declares

---

[71] On Brooke's different patronage connections see Menna Prestwich, *Cranfield: Politics and Profits under the Early Stuarts* (Oxford, 1966), 141; Christopher Brooke, *A Poem on the Late Massacre in Virginia* (London, 1622). I consulted this poem (not included in Grosart's edition) in a transcript in the Folger Shakespeare Library; on Wither, see Cyril Falls, *The Birth of Ulster* (London, 1936), 223; Anthony Wither's letter of September 1614, 'I send you here the picture of his mind that is one of my own tribe and name . . . it got him out of prison', looks like a reference to *A Satyre* (*Historical Manuscripts Commission Report on the Manuscripts of the Marquess of Downshire*, iv.516); Josuah Sylvester (trans.), *The Divine Weeks and Works of Guillaume de Saluste Sieur du Bartas*, ed. Susan Snyder, 2 vols. (Oxford, 1979), i.14–15, 27–8; Joan Kent, 'Attitudes of Members of the House of Commons to the Regulation of "Personal Conduct" in Late Elizabethan and Early Stuart England', *Bulletin of the Institute of Historical Research*, 46 (1973), 41–71 (44, 50–1).

[72] *The Complete Prose Works of John Milton*, ed. Don M. Wolfe et al., 8 vols. in 10 (New Haven, 1953–82), ii.535–6.

that one of his models is the Psalms of David; and increasingly in his later poems he abandons courtly and Italianate forms and turns directly to Protestant prophecy in a direct and colloquial style. In the first eclogue of *The Shepherds Hunting*, Wither has Browne draw attention to the fact that he is invoking 'our true *Pan*', a 'power, that we neglect in other layes'. Wither habitually writes in tetrameter or pentameter couplets which tend to be diffuse, like Browne's, in order to give an effect of personal spontaneity, quite different from Jonson's more restrained and disciplined couplets. In some ways Wither is returning to the older traditions of the 'gospellers' who tried to use immediately accessible verse forms, but he has a much more elevated conception of the dignity of poetry. In the fourth eclogue of *The Shepherds Hunting* he says that poetry can help the mind to transcend earthly imprisonment and find consolation in the joys of nature and in contemplation of the divine. Poetry is not just a carefully polished articulation of moral truths, but can offer by its harmony an adumbration of heavenly music.[73]

After his release Wither declared to King James that he would write no more satires for a time and would turn to panegyrics of virtue. But not long after the tumult of 1614 had died down a new crisis began and the other Spenserians returned to satire. In 1615 it began to be rumoured that Frances Howard had arranged for Sir Thomas Overbury, a friend of Somerset's who had opposed the marriage, to be murdered. He was poisoned and died a slow and agonizing death. She and her husband were put on trial the following year and were found guilty of murder. Browne and Brooke both contributed to a collection of elegies for Overbury in 1616, and Davies of Hereford published his own elegy with a dedication to Pembroke.[74] Drayton revised his satire *The Owle* for the 1619 edition of his collected poems to include an allusion to the Overbury affair. He also dropped a sonnet to James I from this edition. *The Owle* provided a model for two new satires by Thomas Scot and William Goddard which scathingly attacked the court in the aftermath of the Overbury affair. In Goddard's fable, the owl complains that the navy is being neglected, that too much money is being spent on extravagant houses, and that murders committed by the great go unpunished (the death sentence on the Earl and Countess was never carried out). With a daring glance at James's relations with his favourites, he attacks the 'plumy peacocks pride | To striue to lie by's sou'raigne Princes side'. Still more provocatively, the nobles, rejecting the conventional distinction between the king and his corrupt advisers, retort to the king that 'from your selfe sprange firste this faults abuse', a 'peremptory answer' which so incenses him that a civil war breaks out, and the owl is able to escape because of this 'Civill strife'.[75] The second book of

---

[73] Wither, *Juvenilia*, ii, sig. Ii5ʳ.

[74] O'Callaghan, *The 'Shepheards Nation'*, 106–7. *Sir Thomas Ouerburie his Wife with New Elegies* (London, 1616), sigs. ¶4ʳ⁻ᵛ, ¶6ʳ⁻7ʳ; Davies, *A Select Second Husband for Sir Thomas Overburies Wife* (London, 1616).

[75] Thomas Scot, *Philomythie or Philomythologie* (London, 1616), 26–9 (cf. Margot Heinemann, *Puritanism and Theatre: Thomas Middleton and Opposition Drama under the Early Stuarts* (Cambridge, 1980), 113–14); William Goddard, 'A Morall Satire Intituled the Owles Araygnement', in *A Satiryicall Dialogue* (n.pl., 1616), sigs. F2ʳ ff.; see further 'Afterword', below, at n. 128 and Alastair Bellany, *The Politics of Court Scandal in Early Modern England: News Culture and the Overbury Affair, 1603–1660*

Browne's *Britannia's Pastorals*, also published in 1616, reflects the dominant disillusion with the court: the tone is more satirical and Browne attacks the neglect of the
navy and other abuses. The tone of the poem can be indicated by quoting the marginalia of a contemporary reader: 'Great men have not such rest as clowns'; 'Poor
labour to feed the luxury of the rich'; 'Parasites are enlightened by the beams of
kings'.[76] Browne dedicated the second book to the Earl of Pembroke, who was beginning to emerge as a political leader rather than just a literary patron. By 1619 attacks
on courts were becoming so widespread that one writer was commissioned to answer
'the perverse petulancie of many *Poets*, which laid so many odious aspersions vpon
Courts, as if no vertue had in them any residence'.[77]

There was, of course, a notable exception to this pattern: Ben Jonson, who was by
now committed to his role as leading court poet. This involved him in an awkward
reversal in moral judgements. While abstaining from the bitter attacks on Somerset,
he found himself by the 1616 masque committed to defending a realignment of court
politics in which the king had decided that his favourite should be dropped. By 1615
a new favourite, George Villiers, had been brought forward by Pembroke and his supporters in an attempt to counter Somerset's influence, and the balance of power had
already been shifting in his direction when the murder scandal was revealed. In *The
Golden Age Restored* Jonson had to make sense of this volte-face, and he did so, interestingly, in a muted invocation of Elizabethan symbolism: the figure of Astraea, so
often associated with Elizabeth, descends to administer justice—though her power
is pointedly subordinated to that of Jove/James. Jonson presented Somerset and his
supporters as law-breakers and rebels, thus sidestepping the difficult fact that the
king himself had been strongly behind their ascendancy. Henceforward Jonson
dropped Somerset and made no further reference to him.[78]

This response may be contrasted with that of his old rival Samuel Daniel, who
kept in contact with Somerset but voiced his extreme shock at recent events in an
epistle to the Countess of Bedford.[79] This leading patron had appeared in many
Jacobean masques but had now withdrawn from court for reasons of health and
finance. Daniel tells her that she is better off in her retired state, and uses the imagery
of masques to reveal the corruption that has overtaken court life:

> you may with an vndeuided brest
> Inioy the blessings wch your peace imparts
> And be spectator of the roles they act
> Who personate vppon this stage of Court,

(Cambridge, 2002), 178–9. Goddard's *A Mastif Whelp* (1615) is dedicated to a group of members of the
Inner Temple.

[76] *The Works of John Milton*, ed. Frank A. Patterson et al., 20 vols. (New York, 1931–40), xviii.339. For
rejection of the ascription of these marginalia to Milton, see John T. Shawcross, entry in William B.
Hunter et al. (eds.), *A Milton Encyclopaedia*, 9 vols. (Lewisburg, Pa., 1978–83), v.74.

[77] 'A.D.B.', *The Court of the Most Illustrious and Magnificent James, the First* (London, 1619), dedication to the Duke of Buckingham.

[78] Martin Butler and David Lindley, 'Restoring Astraea: Jonson's Masque for the Fall of Somerset',
ELH 61 (1994), 807–27 (819–21).

[79] *Samuel Daniel: The Brotherton Manuscript*, 63–5.

> And note wth what poore cuning they compact
> All their disguisings . . .
>   howe
> Appearing not in their owne visages
> They all weare masks, and onlie are in shew.

Daniel says that the court has no room to display her virtue, 'wch th'open plaines illustrate, not a wood'. The court is as dark as the Wood of Error at the start of *The Faerie Queene*; virtue, for Daniel, can best be found in the open country far from court. The Spenserian revival of 1613–14 had expressed similar views. Daniel associates the court both with masques and with a dark and deceitful forest. It is possible that he may be glancing at his old rival Ben Jonson, whose *The Forest* had just appeared in his collected works.[80] For a poet who had identified himself as firmly with the court as Jonson, it was becoming a little difficult to maintain credibility as a moral authority.

---

[80] *Samuel Daniel: The Brotherton Manuscript*, 148, ll. 67–72, 80–2; Lindley, *The Trials of Frances Howard*, 162. For an overview of Jonson's relations with the court see Martin Butler, ' "Servant, but not Salve": Ben Jonson at the Jacobean Court', *Proceedings of the British Academy*, 90 (1995), 65–93.

9. Crisis and Reaction, 1617–1628

IN the last part of King James's reign the European peace which he had worked so hard to defend was shattered. The crisis was provoked by a rebellion of the Bohemian Estates against their new Habsburg ruler, King Ferdinand. Bohemia had long traditions of parliamentary government and of religious liberty; it had early fought for independence of the Roman hierarchy under the leadership of Jan Hus, who had drawn inspiration from Wycliffe. Ferdinand had set out to impose religious and political orthodoxy and met with mounting opposition from Protestants and liberal Catholics. They declared that the throne was elective and not hereditary, as Ferdinand maintained; and in September 1619 they offered the crown to Prince Frederick of the Palatinate. This proposal delighted the Protestant leadership of the Palatinate, who had long been campaigning for a militant anti-Habsburg alliance. Frederick's election might help to shift the political balance in the Holy Roman Empire away from the Habsburgs; it was even hoped that Frederick might one day be elected emperor. The prospect of a Protestant emperor was intoxicating for those brought up in the apocalyptic tradition: the political balance of power throughout Europe would be transformed and a decisive confrontation between Pope and emperor, the ultimate defeat of Antichrist, could be envisaged.

Such hopes were quickly dashed. Ferdinand was made emperor and the Habsburg powers began decisive countermoves; in November 1620 Frederick's forces were disastrously defeated at the White Mountain, outside Prague, and the Habsburgs were free to carry through their policies of orthodoxy and order in Bohemia. Spanish armies invaded the Palatinate and Elizabeth fled to The Hague, where she and her husband began to maintain a court in exile. The conflict began to escalate: the Dutch truce with the Spanish expired in 1621 and a European war was under way. There was enormous interest in these events in England, both because of general sympathy with the cause of Continental Protestantism and because Frederick was married to Princess Elizabeth, whose wedding had aroused so much enthusiasm. Elizabeth seems to have played an active part in sponsoring propaganda for her cause in England. The German poet Georg Rudolf Weckherlin, who had translated several poems by the English Spenserians and had been in England at the time of Elizabeth's wedding, now returned to England to try to encourage support for her cause. The Puritan exile Thomas Scott published a series of enormously popular pamphlets in which he presented a series of Puritan heroes, including Queen Elizabeth, Essex, Ralegh, and Prince Henry, as advocating active support for

Frederick and Elizabeth.[1] The old foreign policy of the Essex faction was being revived: indeed, one of Essex's old allies, the Earl of Southampton, wanted to recruit a force of British volunteers. An apocalyptic treatise which had been dedicated to Essex in 1597 was reprinted because of its relevance to the new crisis.[2]

James disliked this enthusiasm for Protestant militancy and was determined to do his best to achieve a diplomatic solution to the problem by negotiations with Spain. He kept Britain out of the Thirty Years War, which involved central Europe in agonizingly protracted carnage. Without necessarily endorsing their militancy, however, it is necessary to try to understand the motives of those who advocated intervention. The issue was not just one of pacifism versus militancy but also of choices between different military options and diplomatic alignments which raised important ideological questions.[3] There was much indiscriminate sabre-rattling from Puritans, but the better informed made a case for a strategy based on diversionary war. An alliance should be made with the Netherlands, where there were already some well-trained British troops, to keep Spanish armies tied down in the Spanish Netherlands. And a British fleet should attack the sources of Spanish financial strength by a campaign in the West Indies. A decisive British intervention might on a very optimistic reading of the situation have swung the balance against the Habsburgs and ensured a rapid resolution of the crisis. But James had allowed the navy's strength to decline disastrously, and he had no desire to be involved in an alliance with the Dutch against Spain. Any policy of protracted war would require financing from Parliament which might place unacceptable constraints on his power. James had a general dislike of political and religious radicalism; he did not desire English social relations to be contaminated by excessively close contact with the Dutch republicans. He wanted instead to strengthen ties with Spain where the principles of order and degree were more firmly maintained. Drayton noted the shift in alignment in chronicling the strange things he had seen in his lifetime:

> This Kings faire Entrance, and our Peace with *Spaine*,
> We and the *Dutch* at length our Selves to sever;
> Thus the World doth, and evermore shall Reele[.][4]

In 1617 Bacon advised James to tell his ambassador in Spain that he wanted the Spanish match to counter a creeping disposition 'to make popular estates and leagues

---

[1] Leonard Forster, *Georg Rudolf Weckherlin: Zur Kenntnis seines Lebens in England* (Basel, 1944), 51 ff.; on the literary aspects of Scott's works see Margot Heinemann, *Puritanism and Theatre: Thomas Middleton and Opposition Drama under the Early Stuarts* (Cambridge, 1980), 155–8.

[2] 'T.L.', *Babylon is Fallen* (London, 1620) (I owe this reference to Dr S. L. Adams). On the intense public debates in newsbooks, pamphlets, manuscripts, and sermons, and the government's attempts to restrict them, see Thomas Cogswell, *The Blessed Revolution: English Politics and the Coming of War, 1621–1624* (Cambridge, 1989), 20–35, 281–307.

[3] The following discussion is based on Simon Adams, 'Spain or the Netherlands? The Dilemmas of Early Stuart Foreign Policy', in Howard Tomlinson (ed.), *Before the English Civil War: Essays on Early Stuart Politics and Government* (New York, 1983), 79–101 (95 ff.).

[4] The *Works of Michael Draykon*, ed. J. William Hebel et al., 2nd edn., 5 vols. (Oxford, 1961) ii.336.

to the disadvantage of monarchies'.[5] In 1620 there were rumours that the Spanish ambassador was trying to involve him in an international league against republics. To support Frederick would be to support the Bohemians in what could be regarded as rebellion against their hereditary monarch, and James had no desire to justify elective against hereditary monarchy. He stopped Southampton's plan to involve himself with a volunteer force, suspicious of the rumoured republican sympathies of this former participant in Essex's rebellion. He would not allow Elizabeth, who might have become a focus for political opposition, to return to England. He introduced strict censorship measures to restrict public discussion of the Bohemian crisis and pressed ahead with plans to build an elaborate new Banqueting House at Whitehall in which masques could be staged to celebrate the forthcoming marriage between the Stuarts and the Habsburgs. While his more militant subjects spoke enthusiastically of a war to defeat the Papal Antichrist, James hedged on the question of whether the Pope really was Antichrist.

The Spenserians responded to the Bohemian crisis by reviving memories of the warlike days of Queen Elizabeth. As in the previous crisis years of 1613–14, the most belligerent reaction came from George Wither. He believed it to be a Protestant poet's duty to speak out in times of political crisis, and in 1621 he brought out a lengthy satire, *Wither's Motto*. Whatever else may be said about his poetic voice, it was certainly loud, and Wither's poem gained a wide hearing; printers vied with each other to pirate copies and according to Wither over 30,000 were sold. His poem was felt to contravene the ban on public political discussion and in June 1621 he was arrested. As in 1614, his arrest may have had something to do with the volatile political climate during a session of Parliament; Wither was arrested soon after James had dissolved the first session of the 1621 Parliament, when the Commons had made a ringing call for war against Spain. Shortly before Wither's arrest Sir Edwin Sandys, who had been a leading opposition spokesman, was imprisoned along with Wither's friend John Selden. Wither was not released until well after Parliament had been dissolved under dramatic circumstances: the Commons had issued a Protestation denying the king's right to imprison MPs, upon which he dissolved Parliament, tearing the Protestation from the *Commons Journal*. Wither claimed that the publication of his poem had nothing to do with the assembling of this Parliament, and that it did not violate the proclamation against public discussion of the Palatinate crisis. But such protestations were somewhat disingenuous: when Wither said that there was no need for the Spanish ambassador to bring him to his knees for his impudence he was in fact implying that the king was rashly letting the Spanish determine what English people could publish. He attacked Hispanized courtiers who deceived the king and made dark warnings about the state of Protestantism in England. He was a great admirer of Princess Elizabeth, who may have helped to prevent his being imprisoned in 1613,

---

[5] *The Letters and the Life of Francis Bacon*, ed. J. Spedding, 7 vols. (London, 1861–74), vi.159, cited by S. L. Adams, 'Foreign Policy and the Parliaments of 1621 and 1624', in Kevin Sharpe (ed.), *Faction and Parliament: Essays on Early Stuart History* (Oxford, 1978), 139–72 (141).

and his poem, while not specifically calling for military support of the Bohemian cause, would have helped to create a climate of opinion favourable to apocalyptic fears and expectations. In his *Faire-Virtue* (1622) he celebrates a type of ideal female virtue who has attributes of Elizabeth, notably her worthiness to be 'the *German Empresse*'.[6]

The publication of *Wither's Motto* brought Wither into head-on collision with Ben Jonson, who pilloried him as 'Chronomastix' in his masque *Time Vindicated* (1623), parodying his ambling and diffuse iambic couplets. For Jonson, Wither's verse was a symptom of a disturbing new phenomenon, the production of news and public opinion as a commodity. In his masque *News from the New World Discovered in the Moon*, Jonson had attacked the popularity of news-sheets describing events in the Continental wars. James was trying in vain to forbid the import of these embryo newspapers; Jonson continued his satire of the news-gatherers in *The Staple of News* (1626).[7] Jonson accused Wither of seeking fame not at court but amongst the ignorant citizens whose complacency and ignorance he flattered when he should have been rebuking it. Jonson did not believe that the common people were capable of holding informed opinions on complex political issues; foreign policy was a mystery of state whose discussion should be confined to the king and his advisers. Jonson's attack on Wither certainly revealed his insight into changes in social relations: the tone of poems like *Abuses Stript and Whipt* and *Wither's Motto* is something new, the tone that was much later to become familiar in popular journalism. Wither is turning prophecy into a commodity; he has an eye for a growing market, addressing his readers in a tone of jaunty familiarity and appealing to their prejudices. He holds his audience by constantly hinting that he knows more than he has yet revealed; there is a teasing, insinuating, provocative flavour to his verse that infuriated Jonson. Typical of his method is his claim that he has not '*taxt (directly) any one by name*'—which of course sets the reader searching for indirect allusions.[8] Though posterity has tended to follow Jonson in his contempt for Wither, there is clear evidence that his verse struck a contemporary nerve: *Abuses Stript and Whipt* went through five editions in its first year, and *Wither's Motto* at least seven. Wither replied to Jonson's attacks in a later poem, *Britain's Remembrancer*, which he published from the Netherlands in 1628. He criticized 'frothy' masques and painted a satirical portrait of Jonson's young followers, the 'tribe of Ben', whose obscene verses were published while censors forbade Wither to speak out.[9]

---

[6] George Wither, *Juvenilia*, 3 vols., Spenser Society (Manchester, 1871), iii, sig. A6ᵛ; Cyndia Susan Clegg, *Press Censorship in Jacobean England* (Cambridge, 2001), 184–5; Michelle O'Callaghan, *The 'Shepheards Nation': Jacobean Spenserians and Early Stuart Political Culture, 1612–1625* (Oxford, 2000), 211–15.

[7] See Donald F. McKenzie, '"The Staple of News" and the Late Plays', in William Blissett, Julian Patrick, and R. W. Van Fossen (eds.), *A Celebration of Ben Jonson* (Toronto, 1973), 83–128. On the newsbooks of this period see Clegg, *Press Censorship in Jacobean England*, 171–2, Sheila Lambert, 'Coranto Printing in England: The First Newsbooks', *Journal of Newspaper and Periodical History*, 8 (1992), 1–33.

[8] Wither, *Juvenilia*, ii, sig. Dd6ᵛ.

[9] George Wither, *Britain's Remembrancer* (n.pl., 1628; Spenser Society reprint, Manchester, 1880), fos. 88ᵛ, 205ʳ, 245ᵛ.

Other Spenserian poets renewed the sense of common purpose they had shown in 1614. It was probably at this time that Drayton composed an eclogue, *The Shepheards Sirena*, which is very close in theme and symbolism to the 1614 eclogues, and may glance at the fate of Elizabeth. Drayton had read and admired *Wither's Motto* before publication, and Wither praised the second part of *Poly-Olbion* when it appeared in 1622. Drayton's personal religious views seem to have been rather conservative and the poem contains a denunciation of Puritan iconoclasm and a catalogue of saints. It has even been suggested that Drayton wrote the second part in anticipation of a Spanish alliance and toleration of Catholics.[10] But though no Puritan he was strongly patriotic and Part II contains a catalogue of English military victories and a panegyric of Ralegh, who had been executed after pressure from the Spanish ambassador. Drayton seems to have favoured war against Spain after the outbreak of the Bohemian crisis, for nationalistic if not for ideological reasons, and the commendatory verses to *Poly-Olbion* were contributed by people who advocated military action. To the commendatory verse by Drayton's old friends Browne and Wither was added a poem by John Reynolds, who had recently written an anti-Spanish satire on the model of Scott's *Vox populi*. Reynolds suppressed his book for fear of censorship and when it was eventually published in 1624 he was arrested. The book appeared with the false imprint of 'Elisium', linking the cause of Princess Elizabeth with the golden age of Protestant politics under Queen Elizabeth. Scott had made Essex speak of the Elizabethan 'faerie land'. In Reynolds's book Queen Elizabeth declared that Charles should never marry a Spaniard and that he would do better to marry an English milkmaid, a solution to the problem which does not seem to have been widely advocated. Reynolds also referred to the plans being made to build a sumptuous Catholic chapel for the Infanta, alleging that Inigo Jones was going to receive a knighthood for his services to the Catholic cause, and complained that too much time and money was being wasted on plays and masques.[11]

Both Reynolds and Drayton were patronized by Sir Edward Sackville, a supporter of war in defence of the Palatine cause. In 1621–2 Drayton addressed a verse epistle to George Sandys, brother of the imprisoned MP, in which he said that English poetry was in crisis because the people did not listen to their prophets. He emphasized that poetry could move people to martial endeavours and reminded Sandys that King James had refused to patronize his verse. The implication was that James's reign had corrupted the English people by introducing them to the ways of courtly luxury. He compared English poetry to the woman wandering in the wilderness and said that it would have to emigrate to Virginia where Sandys was now living. Wither had prophesied in *Wither's Motto* that the true church might have to take refuge

---

[10] Paul Gerhard Buchloh, *Michael Drayton: Barde und Historiker, Politiker und Prophet* (Neumünster, 1964), 57.

[11] John Reynolds, *Vox coeli* ('Elisium' [London?], 1624), 45–6; see Jerry H. Bryant, 'John Reynolds of Exeter and his Canon', *Library*, 5th series, 15 (1960), 105–17; 'John Reynolds of Exeter and his Canon: A Footnote', ibid. 18 (1963), 299–303. Cf. Heinemann, *Puritanism and Theatre*, 281–2, Cogswell, *The Blessed Revolution*, 289–91, Clegg, *Press Censorship in Jacobean England*, 174–5, emphasizing Reynolds's explicit criticisms of James.

there.[12] George Herbert, a young poet who had close links with the Sandys and Ferrar families, voiced similar sentiments in 'The Church Militant', a poem possibly written about this time.[13] Many conservatives did not share the Spenserians' enthusiasm for Virginia; Jonson took a highly sceptical view of the possibilities of colonization. Sir Edwin Sandys's enemies alleged that he was trying to create a radical Protestant republic in the colony; the charge has no foundation but is a reminder that enthusiasm for the colonies could be taken as a sign of radical views. The young Thomas Hobbes seems to have been an associate of Sandys and to have suppressed this aspect of his past when he had adopted firmly absolutist views.[14]

William Browne said to Drayton in 1622 that poets should

> raise our *Muse* againe,
> In this her *Crisis*,[15]

and about 1624 he resumed work on *Britannia's Pastorals*, which he had abandoned after 1616. As a client of the Earl of Pembroke, a leading supporter of Princess Elizabeth, Browne was in a position to hear of the debates about war policy in the Parliament of that year. In Book III of *Britannia's Pastorals* he paid tribute to the days of Elizabethan naval glory under Drake and Grenville. In the 1624 Parliament Sir Benjamin Rudyerd, a close political associate of Pembroke's, called for a widening of the campaign against the Spanish by diversionary measures including naval strikes in the West Indies; Browne's poem endorsed this policy.[16] He also attacked the Spanish ambassador, Gondomar. Browne did not publish Book III, probably because of the risks he would have run. By now, however, the wave of public opposition to a Spanish alliance was gaining so much support in high places that systematic suppression of such views was impossible. Gondomar was satirized in Middleton's apocalyptic satire *A Game at Chess*, which had enough court protection, possibly from Pembroke, to be given repeated performances.[17] Vituperative anti-Spanish

---

[12] Drayton, *Works*, iii.206–8.

[13] Wither, *Juvenilia*, iii, sigs. D3ᵛ–4ʳ; *The Works of George Herbert*, ed. F. E. Hutchinson (Oxford, 1941), 196, ll. 235–6, 546–7. For readings of Herbert in the context of the mainly Calvinist Jacobean church, see Ilona Bell, ' "Setting Foot into Divinity": George Herbert and the English Reformation', *Modern Language Quarterly*, 38 (1977), 219–41; Christopher Hodgkins, *Authority, Church, and Society in George Herbert: Return to the Middle Way* (Columbia, Mo., 1993), Daniel W. Doerksen, 'The Laudian Interpretation of George Herbert', *Literature and History*, 3rd series, 3 (1994), 36–54, and Elizabeth Clarke, *Theory and Theology in George Herbert's Poetry: 'Divinitie, and Poesie, Met'* (Oxford, 1997).

[14] Noel Malcolm, 'Hobbes, Sandys, and the Virginia Company', *Historical Journal*, 24 (1981), 297–321. Cogswell, *The Blessed Revolution*, 148, aligns Sandys with a group of patriot MPs who were described by a contemporary as 'our Tribuni plebis'.

[15] Drayton, *Works*, iv.393, ll. 17–18.

[16] On the background see Joan Ozark Holmer, 'Internal Evidence for Dating William Browne's "Britannia's Pastorals", Book III', *Papers of the Bibliographical Society of America*, 70 (1976), 347–64, and Cedric C. Brown and Margherita Piva, 'William Browne, Marino, France, and the Third Book of *Britannia's Pastorals*', *Review of English Studies*, 29 (1978), 385–404.

[17] On the intense public debates in newsbooks, pamphlets, manuscripts, and sermons, and the government's attempts to suppress them, see further Cogswell, *The Blessed Revolution*, 20–35, and Clegg, *Press Censorship in Jacobean England*, 161–96. Cogswell is sceptical of Heinemann's claim in *Puritanism and Theatre* that Pembroke was the leading patron of *A Game at Chess*, partly because he differs from Simon Adams's analysis of Pembroke's political weight at this time (154 ff.; see further his 'Thomas Middleton

satires circulated widely in manuscript and the custom arose of placing them under the monument in St Paul's of the epigrammatist John Owen, who had been patronized by Prince Henry. The king became so incensed at the circulation of these irreverent satires that in late 1622 or early 1623 he composed a poem of his own in reply. The people, he declared, must not pry into the mysteries of kingship but must either submit to their monarch or else be 'puld vp like stinkinge weeds'. James criticized the Magna Carta, which, he said, had sprung up from an unjust rebellion, and warned that he had no need to take advice even from his own council and would summon Parliament only if and when it pleased him.[18]

But in opposing these subversive outbursts James was also involved in an internal court conflict with his own son and his favourite, the Duke of Buckingham. Charles had become impatient with the protracted negotiations and in February 1623 he and Buckingham set off for Spain in disguise. Finding that they could get no further in their negotiations, they returned feeling slighted and called for war with Spain. For a period Charles and Buckingham were in harmony with the Puritans in their demand for militant intervention on the Continent, and they made common cause in the 1624 Parliament with figures like Southampton and Sandys; their support made it easier to circulate anti-Spanish propaganda. But they still had ideological objections to the idea of an essentially religious alliance; Charles's grievances against Spain were not confessional in their origin. Buckingham determined to force through an alliance with France, which inevitably diluted the religious content of the campaign against the Spanish. Many Puritans were unhappy about a war against Spain if it was conducted in alliance with France, and their unease grew when a Huguenot rebellion broke out and the British government became involved in sending a fleet to suppress foreign Protestants. Some of Buckingham's opponents distrusted him so much that they would have preferred an alliance with Spain if Buckingham could be removed from power to an alliance with France controlled by Buckingham. It remained very unclear who was politically in control: it is now widely believed that James was still determined on a Spanish alliance and was using Buckingham to put pressure on Spain.[19] But in March 1625 James died, and Charles came to the throne committed to war. As many Puritans had feared, however, war conducted by Buckingham with an ill-prepared navy and half-hearted French help did not go well; in 1626 France made a separate peace with Spain. War was now declared with France but it went no better. In 1628 Buckingham was assassinated;

---

and the Court in 1624: *A Game at Chess* in Context', *Huntington Library Quarterly*, 48 (1984), 273–88). Cogswell sees the play as representing a conscious propaganda strategy by Charles and Buckingham, a claim also made by Jerzy Limon, *Dangerous Matter: English Drama and Politics 1623/24* (Cambridge, 1986), 98. But if this was so, as Cogswell notes, it was a striking departure from Charles's deep suspicion of stirring up public discussion at other points of his career. Margot Heinemann, 'Drama and Opposition in the 1620s: Middleton and Massinger', in J. R. Mulryne and Margaret Shewring (eds.), *Theatre and Government under the Early Stuarts* (Cambridge, 1993), 237–65 (247–8), notes that Buckingham signally failed to protect Drayton's friend John Reynolds, who was imprisoned for two years from July 1624 for his *Vox coeli*.

[18] *Poems of James VI*, ii.182–91.
[19] See the analysis by Adams, 'Spain or the Netherlands?', 97–9.

Charles now made peace with France and Spain, and in the 1630s he returned to his father's pro-Spanish bias.

The Spenserians showed enthusiasm for the initial warlike phase of Charles's reign. The prince had indeed shown favour to Wither and Drayton in his father's lifetime, and Drayton seems never to have hated Charles as he did James. In 1627 he rallied anti-French sentiment in his *Battle of Agincourt*; Drayton and several other poets were now able to publish satires that would have been liable to censorship under the previous reign. The Norfolk poet Ralph Knevett published a work in praise of military discipline and began work on a continuation of *The Faerie Queene* which would take Spenser's historical allegory down to the present day. Knevett took it for granted that Spenser's 'Faerie Land' included the fortunes of Protestantism throughout Europe, not just in England, and his eighth book describes the heroism of Gustavus Adolphus of Sweden who became the major Protestant leader in the 1630s. Knevett described the exploits of English soldiers who had fought in Germany and the Netherlands, but given the small scale of English intervention he found it necessary to make a Swede the hero of the book. He made King James the hero of his seventh book, but he comes out rather badly by comparison, as someone vulnerable to the temptations of courtly luxury and effeminacy. By the time Knevett had finished the supplement, Charles had reverted to a pro-Spanish policy and the poem was never published.[20]

In the 1620s, then, the Spenserians frequently found themselves in opposition to royal policy. Spenser was for them a symbol of the poet's proud independence of the court. In 1620 a monument to Spenser was finally erected in Westminster Abbey and Browne wrote an Ode to Drayton in which he declared that

> I, that serve the lovely Graces,
> Spurn at that dross which most adore;
> And titles hate like painted faces . . .
> And if my Muse to Spenser's glory come,
> No king shall own my verses for his tomb.

Browne also scorns the 'mushroom favourite'.[21] Titles and favourites were arousing particular animosity at this time because of the activities of Buckingham, the king's favourite. By the 1620s Buckingham was widely hated as embodying most of the ills of the nation, and his assassination in 1628 was hailed as the sign of a new beginning. Buckingham's stance on foreign policy was inconsistent: he supported the Spanish alliance until the voyage to Spain, returned as an advocate of war and formed a loose alliance with Puritan leaders, but worked against Puritan interests in other ways; he seemed to his enemies to be a political weathercock whose views could not be trusted. But the objections to Buckingham were social as much as ideological: he was held responsible for undermining the social structure by debasing titles of honour. He encouraged the king to sell first of all the lesser honours and eventually some of the

---

[20] Knevett's *Supplement of the Faery Queene*, now in the University Library, Cambridge, has been edited by Andrew Lavender (Ph.D. thesis, New York University, 1955).
[21] William Browne, *Poems*, ed. G. Goodwin, 2 vols. (London, 1894), ii.210–13.

highest titles in the social hierarchy. This gained the king revenue, but only at the expense of arousing the hostility of noble families who felt that their titles were being degraded. Buckingham and the king aroused further animosity by bullying various wealthy or noble families into forming marriage alliances with the extensive Villiers clan. The Earl of Berkshire was said to have committed suicide at the prospect of his daughter's marrying Buckingham's unattractive brother Christopher.[22]

A hostile elegist recalled the way Buckingham had had himself painted:

> Antwerpian Rubens' best skill made him soare,
> Ravish't by heavenly powers, unto the skie,
> Opening and ready him to deifie
> In a bright blisfull pallace, fayrie ile.
> Naught but illusion were wee.[23]

The word 'illusion' catches the source of a great deal of the hostility Buckingham aroused. Buckingham's political career seemed to be governed by opportunism and pliability, rather than any deep-rooted principles. He had been responsible for the creation of a large number of noblemen whose titles seemed to his critics no more than illusions: Buckingham owed his own elevation merely to the favour of a king who 'moulded' him 'Platonically to his owne *Idea*'.[24] He was no intellectual and could not compare with Leicester, Essex, or Prince Henry as a patron of poets. As a tactful panegyrist put it, 'as the less he was favoured by the Muses, he was the more by the Graces'.[25] He loved easy elegance in clothing and deportment, and his main contribution as a patron of the arts was to the visual arts. He was much impressed by the Spanish and Italian art he saw on his Spanish journey and tried to import many paintings.[26] As the elegist pointed out, he also commissioned a large canvas from Rubens, who came from Antwerp, the capital of the Spanish Netherlands. Rubens was a diplomat as well as an artist and used his influence with Charles and Buckingham and their advisers to try to dispose the English government better towards Spain. Buckingham's artistic tastes made him ideologically suspect. It is perhaps worth noting that Rubens was not impressed by Buckingham, whom he found capricious and arrogant. His enemies were particularly prone to associate him with illusion because he loved spectacular masques, which lacked the lasting value of Rubens's canvases but had an immediate if short-lived appeal. He had first brought himself to the king's favour by his skill in dancing in a masque.

Buckingham's taste in masques, however, was rather superficial; he liked irreverent farce or expensive spectacle but took little interest in the literary qualities of masques. Ben Jonson wrote only one masque for him, *The Gypsies Metamorphosed*, which presented the favourite and his relations as rapacious gypsies. It has been

---

[22] *The Diary of Sir Simonds D'Ewes (1622–1624)*, ed. Elisabeth Bourcier (Paris, 1974), 159.

[23] F. W. Fairholt (ed.), *Poems and Songs Relating to George Villiers, Duke of Buckingham* Percy Society, (London, 1850), 70.

[24] Sir Henry Wotton, *Reliquiae Wottonianae* (London, 1651), 4.

[25] Ibid. 20.

[26] Richard Ollard, *The Image of the King: Charles I and Charles II* (London, 1979), 31, describes Buckingham as 'a court masque in himself'.

plausibly suggested that the masque contained a double irony, making Buckingham and his cronies condemn themselves light-heartedly for faults of which Jonson himself believed them guilty.[27] Jonson satirized Buckingham's taste for riotous and farcical masques in the antimasque to *The Masque of Augurs* (1622). He was not invited to participate in the festivities that were planned to welcome the Spanish Infanta to England; it was Inigo Jones, the master of visual spectacle, who was put in charge. Jonson was angry at being excluded and wrote an 'Epistle Answering to One that Asked to be Sealed of the Tribe of Ben' in which he voiced his annoyance. Jonson attacked Jones as the man who 'guides the Motions, and directs the beares', a scathing allusion to the vulgarity of the spectacles he expected Jones to devise. Jonson's exclusion from favour seems to have put him in an unusually militant mood, for he declared that while he hoped the negotiations in Spain would go well,

> if, for honour, we must draw the Sword,
> And force back that, which will not be restor'd,
> I have a body, yet, that spirit drawes
> To live, or fall a Carkasse in the cause.[28]

Jonson's leading patron, the Earl of Pembroke, opposed the Spanish match. But the operative word in this poem is 'for honour'. Jonson does not seem to have had ideological objections to the Spanish match but disliked the reckless and irresponsible way Buckingham was handling the negotiations, which were becoming unnecessarily humiliating to national pride. It was widely believed that Charles was following Buckingham's lead. As one of the 'animated *Porc'lane*' of the court, the favourite was too shallow to be capable of defending his country's honour. If war became necessary Jonson would support it, but for dynastic rather than ideological reasons, to defend the honour of England and the House of Stuart. Jonson objected more to the preeminence given to Jones in arranging the festivities to welcome the Infanta than to the fact that the marriage would probably take place. When Charles and Buckingham returned, now in a fiercely belligerent mood—a shift that seemed to indicate how shallow and rootless their responses were—Jonson was again asked to collaborate with Inigo Jones on a masque and in *Neptune's Triumph for the Return of Albion* (1624) he voiced the new anti-Spanish mood, but the result was that the masque was cancelled, James being anxious to keep his options open. The masque was presented in a revised form the following year, but Jonson wrote no more court masques until after Buckingham's death; the favourite staged a series of spectacular entertainments but no texts have survived to indicate any literary merit. After Buckingham's death Jonson was accused of having written a poem urging his assassination.

Jonson's relations with Buckingham were, then, somewhat strained; but several of his young disciples, the 'Tribe of Ben', were on better terms with him. Robert

---

[27] Dale B. J. Randall, *Jonson's Gypsies Unmasked: Background and Theme of* The Gypsies Metamorphos'd (Durham, NC, 1975). See also James Knowles, 'The "Running Masque" Recovered: A Masque for the Marquess of Buckingham', *English Manuscript Studies 1100–1700*, 8 (1999), 79–135.

[28] *Ben Jonson*, ed. C. H. Herford and Percy and Evelyn Simpson, 11 vols. (Oxford, 1925–52), viii.219, ll. 50, 39–42, and 53.

Herrick served as a chaplain on the Cadiz expedition. Thomas Carew was a close personal friend and helped to find Christopher Villiers a wife. But though these poets admired Jonson and took him rather than the Spenserians as their model, they were less committed to the art of poetry than their master. Their verse has a light, amateurish quality suitable to their social milieu. Carew specialized in light pornography, arousing so much Puritan indignation that his poems were named in a petition to the Long Parliament as one of the abuses of the commonwealth.[29] Carew retained something of Jonson's abrasiveness; most of the poetry associated with Buckingham, however, tended towards blandness, a polish that excluded serious commitment. Sir Henry Wotton said that Buckingham's early career ran 'as smoothly as a numerous Verse', and his panegyrists adopted an appropriately smooth and flattering note.[30] After he and Charles had returned from Spain, one of Buckingham's clients urged English poets to write panegyrics of this really rather absurd exploit as a triumph of heroic virtue.[31] One of the many poems on the Spanish journey, by Edmund Waller, helps to illustrate the kind of verse that was thought to be agreeable to Buckingham, though it may have been written some time later. Waller chose to describe an incident just when Charles and the favourite were about to return to England; a storm blew up as the prince was being transferred in a small boat from one ship to the shore and his life was in danger. Waller makes this incident a sign of the prince's heroic magnanimity and of the power of love: he maintains his self-control because he has been smitten by love for his bride-to-be, Henrietta Maria of France. The episode is described with the dramatic contrasts of a baroque painting; the central contrast is that between the superbly self-controlled prince and the cowardly sailors around him.[32]

It is interesting to compare this presentation of the incident with the version reported by the Puritan diarist Sir Simonds D'Ewes, who attributed the near-disaster to the fact that God was angry with Charles for not leaving Spain more quickly and had therefore raised a storm. He said that when Charles should have fallen on his knees to give thanks to God for his deliverance he simply asked whether there was any meat for supper. D'Ewes doubted whether Charles's self-control during the storm was due to magnanimity or even to stupidity or simply to ignorance: he did not know how much danger he was in. It was feared that Charles had not properly rewarded the man who threw a line to his boat to save him. All the while, Buckingham skulked on shore and 'his bumm made buttons'.[33] Comparison of D'Ewes's version of this incident with Waller's reveals what would today be called a

---

[29] But for a sympathetic contextual reading see John Kerrigan, 'Thomas Carew', in *On Shakespeare and Early Modern Literature* (Oxford, 2001), 152–80.   [30] Wotton, *Reliquiae Wottonianae*, 9.

[31] Edmund Bolton, in Bodleian MS Tanner 73, fos. 418–21. Bolton reminded Buckingham a few years later of the part poets and artists could play in bolstering up his image: *Calendar of State Papers, Domestic Series, Addenda 1625–1649*, 129.

[32] *The Poems of Edmund Waller*, ed. G. Thorn Drury, 2 vols. (London, 1905), i.1–7.

[33] *The Diary of Sir Simonds D'Ewes*, 156–8. D'Ewes was a close friend and former pupil of Henry Reynolds, who may have been Drayton's friend, though the identity has been challenged: contrast Mary Hobbs, 'Drayton's "Most Dearely-Loved Friend Henery Reynolds Esq:"', *Review of English Studies*, 96 (1973), 414–27, and Frances Teague, *Bathsua Makin, Woman of Learning* (Lewisburg Pa., 1998), 15.

credibility gap of quite enormous proportions. James's suspicion that reverence for monarchy was being disastrously undermined in Jacobean England would perhaps have been confirmed had he been able to read D'Ewes's ideas on popular rebellion.

The political unrest in the last years of James's reign was intensified by the effects of a major economic depression. There was a slump in the wool trade throughout Europe, and the English trade was having to go through a major readjustment caused by shifts in demand for clothes. But though the recession was not wholly the government's responsibility, it was widely blamed on James's support for Alderman Cokayne's disastrous monopoly over the new Merchant Adventurers' Company, and certainly the king had not handled the problem very competently. In the 1620s there was considerable popular unrest; far from lecturing the rebels on the virtues of order and degree, D'Ewes said that the reports of their action 'at first raised a rumour of a hoped for rebellion'. A little earlier he had declared that if the English people had not altogether lost their spirits they would have rebelled. A member of the gentry, D'Ewes was not advocating a class war but hoped that popular discontent could be used to put political pressure on the government. But his notions of political order clearly differed from King James's; in his circle it was muttered that 'all his actions did tend to an absolute monarchye'.[34]

Henry Reynolds was perhaps thinking of the poems addressed to Buckingham when he spoke of modern poets' tendency to 'base servile fawning' (above, Ch. 8 n. 17). Praise of a patron was a recognized feature of Renaissance poetry but Buckingham does seem to have demanded a humiliatingly high price in flattery for any favour he granted. The period when George Herbert was seeking court advancement coincided with Buckingham's irresistible rise, and it is not surprising that he eventually abandoned the glittering career which his ancestry and education held out for him and dedicated his life and his muse to religion—a course in which Pembroke aided him. Drayton's friend Sir Henry Goodere, in debt and anxious to rescue his fortunes, wrote an effusive panegyric of Buckingham's undignified Spanish jaunt.[35] In a verse letter to William Jeffreys Drayton complained that the Muses' springs were being defiled by 'a sort of swine'.[36] He did not identify them, but in the second part of *Poly-Olbion* (1622) he complained that too much poetry was being written for circulation in manuscript instead of being published. The corruption of poetry consisted partly in the tendency of poets to abandon large-scale themes and confine themselves to courtly compliment addressed to a small coterie.[37] Drayton told Jeffreys that he was not violating the ban on discussing the Palatinate and other public matters:

> In this with State, I hope I doe not deale,
> This onely tends the Muses common-weale.[38]

---

[34] *The Diary of Sir Simonds D'Ewes*, 58–9, 64.
[35] *Calendar of State Papers, Domestic Series, 1623–25*, 147, 427, 556. For a different view of Herbert's religious poetry, as continuing courtliness in a new context, see Michael Schoenfelt, *Prayer and Power: George Herbert and Renaissance Courtship* (Chicago, 1991), and for a further social interpretation, Cristina Malcolmson, *Heart-Work: George Herbert and the Protestant Ethic* (Stanford Calif., 1999).
[36] Drayton, *Works*, iii.238.   [37] Ibid., iv.421–2.   [38] Ibid., iii.238, ll. 23–4.

But for the Spenserians the health of poetry was closely connected to the health of society. The inflation of language in court poetry was a reflection of the inflation of honours which was undermining the social structure. In a letter to William Browne Drayton complained that the island was being polluted by a 'rude ribauld crew Of base Plebeians'; in his ode to Drayton Browne criticized 'mushroom favourites'. Wither too attacked favourites in *Wither's Motto*.[39] In 1625 Christopher Brooke wrote an elegy for one of Pembroke's allies, Lord Belfast, in which he bitterly attacked the sale of honours. Brooke anticipated that his poem would get in trouble with the censor and inserted a note saying that if the allusions were considered too offensive cuts should be made to make them sound as if they were not really topical comments but merely conventional generalizations.[40] This note is a very interesting indication of the constraints under which poets were operating at the time. Despite Brooke's readiness to make cuts, the censor did not pass the poem, to which Wither had contributed commendatory verse. The German poet Weckherlin adapted one of the visions from Spenser's *Ruines of Time* (ll. 491–504) in a sonnet attacking Buckingham; when he was considering publishing the poem in the 1630s a friend advised him that it would be extremely imprudent.[41] After the favourite's death, Charles would still not hear of any public criticism of Buckingham, which gave court poetry a peculiarly unreal flavour. For Buckingham's assassin, John Felton, had been acclaimed in a series of powerful elegies and satires which hailed his act not as ungodly sedition but as a heroic liberation of the realm. This disconcertingly eloquent poetry again and again contrasted its own boldness and honesty with the specious flattery countenanced at court, illustrating how far the nation's political crisis was felt to have been also a crisis of language and poetry.[42]

Hostility to Buckingham united the Spenserians with Jonson. But in the case of Browne and Wither at least, conservative social objections to his ascendancy were combined with ideological factors, and though they used the language of order and hierarchy their position was not quite as conservative as it might seem. In the 1620s what has been termed an 'aristocratic opposition' emerged to counter Buckingham's influence.[43] It united people who were divided on other issues, from the Earl of

---

[39] Ibid. 210, ll. 70–1; Wither, *Juvenilia*, iii, sig. E1ʳ.

[40] *The Complete Poems of Christopher Brooke*, ed. Alexander B. Grosart, in *Miscellanies of the Fuller Worthies' Library*, iv (Blackburn, 1872), 213, 223–4; see further O'Callaghan, *The 'Shepheards Nation'*, 201–3.

[41] Forster, *Weckherlin*, 83, 113.

[42] For discussion of the Felton elegies see Alastair Bellany, '"Rayling Rhymes and Vaunting Verse": Libellous Politics in Early Stuart England', in Kevin Sharpe and Peter Lake (eds.), *Culture and Politics in Early Stuart England* (London, 1994), 285–310 (304–9), David Norbrook, *Writing the English Republic: Poetry, Rhetoric and Politics 1627–1660* (Cambridge, 1999), 52–8, and James Holstun, *Ehud's Dagger: Class Struggle in the English Revolution* (London, 2000), 177–86. The only extensive collection of the elegies on Buckingham and Felton remains Fairholt (ed.), *Poems and Songs Relating to George Villiers, Duke of Buckingham*, 36–78.

[43] Mervyn James, 'English Politics and the Concept of Honour, 1485–1642', in *Society, Politics and Culture: Studies in Early Modern England* (Cambridge, 1986), 308–415 (406 ff.); for special reference to Drayton, see Richard C. McCoy, 'Old English Honour in an Evil Time: Aristocratic Principle in the 1620s', in R. Malcolm Smuts (ed.), *The Stuart Court and Europe: Essays in Politics and Political Culture* (Cambridge, 1996), 133–55.

Arundel, a member of the Howard dynasty, to the anti-Spanish Earls of Essex and Southampton. These aristocrats complained that traditional noble privileges were being undermined and called for the revival of some old rights of the House of Lords. Arundel's hostility to Buckingham was personal rather than ideological; he favoured alignment with Spain, a country renowned for its reverence towards noble birth, and one of his objections to Buckingham was that his irresponsible conduct tended to undermine the good that might come of closer contacts with Spain. Jonson, who praised Arundel in *The Gypsies Metamorphosed*, seems to have taken a similar view. Other members of the aristocratic opposition, however, had a strong ideological hostility to Spain. Since the humiliation of his divorce the Earl of Essex had spent much of his time retired from court and took the first opportunity of fighting in defence of the Palatinate. Like Leicester and Essex in the previous reign, he had Protestantized the traditional cult of honour, uniting 'good fame' with 'godly fame'. Honour thus became not just something handed down by virtue of the length of one's family tree or arbitrarily conferred by a favourite but something that had to be earned by struggle. Essex's title was not in fact a very old one.[44]

A tension could arise between older ideas of honour and degree and Protestant ideals. Admittedly Essex himself and other Puritan noblemen were not particularly aware of it, but a more thoughtful observer like Fulke Greville felt the difficulties. Greville denounced the pro-Spanish and pacific courtiers of James's reign in the language of a conservative denouncing 'new men' who lacked the true independence of aristocrats: they were 'children of favour and chance'. And yet these ' "creatures" of the king' included the Howards, members of the oldest noble family in the land: Greville conceded that some Jacobean courtiers had 'a pedigree of fleshly kindred'. The Howards regarded advocates of an alliance with the Dutch as debasing traditional social values and thought that alliance with Spain was more fitting for an aristocracy. Thus Greville was using the rhetoric of social conservatives to mount a Puritan attack on a conservative court. Eventually his awareness of this tension led him to denounce the ideals of honour and magnanimity as mere idolatry and to advocate an ideal of inner spiritual purity.[45] Few other Jacobean writers were driven to such drastic conclusions, and Greville himself, it may be noted, accepted a peerage in 1621. But when the Spenserians use the rhetoric of honour and degree they often seem to be thinking in terms of a spiritual aristocracy of poets who disdain the titles

[44] Kevin Sharpe, 'The Earl of Arundel, his Circle, and the Opposition to the Duke of Buckingham, 1618–1628', in Sharpe (ed.), *Faction and Parliament*, 209–44; on the contrasting views of Southampton and his allies see Neil Cuddy, 'The Conflicting Loyalties of a "Vulger Counselor": The Third Earl of Southampton, 1597–1624', in John Morrill et al. (eds.), *Public Duty and Private Conscience in Seventeenth-Century England: Essays Presented to G. E. Aylmer* (Oxford, 1993), 121–50, who argues (148) that the king's inflation of honours was 'probably in deliberate response to aristocratic republicanism among the lay peers'. On the continuing association of Essex with Elizabethan chivalry, see J. S. A. Adamson, 'Chivalry and Political Culture in Early Stuart England', in Sharpe and Lake (eds.), *Culture and Politics in Early Stuart England*, 161–97 (167), and William Hunt, 'Civic Chivalry and the English Civil War', in Anthony Grafton and Ann Blair (eds.), *The Transmission of Culture in Early Modern England* (Philadelphia, 1990), 204–37 (232–3).

[45] James, 'English Politics and the Concept of Honour', 396 ff.; *A Dedication to Sir Philip Sidney*, in *The Prose Works of Fulke Greville, Lord Brooke*, ed. John Gouws (Oxford, 1986), 6–7.

given by the monarchy. Jonson was fond of comparing the poet to a prince, 'creating' great public figures through his courtly artifice; the Spenserians tended to identify the poet with the nobleman who proudly disdains to serve at court.

The atmosphere of disorder and irreverence in the last years of James's reign perhaps helps to explain why the king began to favour the views of a small but increasingly influential 'Arminian' group in the church who argued that Calvinist theology inevitably led to political subversiveness. James had himself remained faithful to his Calvinist upbringing, and the Gunpowder Plot in 1605 had been a graphic reminder that Catholicism could still be seen as a threat to monarchical authority. In 1609 he had appointed George Abbot, a firm Calvinist, as Archbishop of Canterbury, and he had sided with the Calvinists against the Arminians at the time of the international Synod of Dort in 1618; he had been persuaded that Arminianism represented a threat to civil order in the Netherlands and should be resisted. At the same time, he recognized the argument that hierarchy in the church contributed to political order, and he did not favour Puritan calls for a drastic reduction in the traditional ceremonial of the English church. He gave some favour to a group of divines, notably Lancelot Andrewes, who favoured a much more ritually based form of worship and were strongly critical of Calvinist theology. James preferred such criticisms to remain muted, however, and by encouraging some latitude in the enforcement of ritual observances he kept the Jacobean church a broad one, with conformity to some of the ordinances disliked by Puritans not necessarily being taken as a betrayal of Calvinist theology. With the political volatility of the later years of the reign, however, he became more open to the argument that years of neglect of ritual and good order in the English church had led to a general atmosphere of social irreverence, and that respect for hierarchy and discipline in the church could only be restored by a theological shift.[46] Abbot had lost some of his influence after accidentally killing a gamekeeper when hunting (at the home of Browne's patron Lord Zouche), and Calvinists began to be alarmed at the prospect of a reversal in the doctrine of the church as officially sanctioned since the Elizabethan period.

In abstract theological terms the debate between Calvinists and Arminians was abstruse and raised enormously complex philosophical issues. But it aroused deep passions amongst the laity because it had direct political connotations. The ecclesiastical wing of the English Arminians, unlike their Dutch counterparts, combined their hostility to predestinarianism with a belief in episcopacy by divine right; they wanted more emphasis to be placed in ritual and less on preaching. This change in emphasis was symbolically expressed by their fixing the altar in one place and railing it off, giving it more prominence than the pulpit. This change gave much more

---

[46] Nicholas Tyacke, 'Puritanism, Arminianism and Counter-Revolution', in Conrad Russell (ed.), *The Origins of the English Civil War* (London, 1973), 119–43, developed in his *Anti-Calvinists: The Rise of English Arminianism c.1590–1640* (Oxford, 1987); Kenneth Fincham and Peter Lake, 'The Ecclesiastical Policy of King James I', *Journal of British Studies*, 24 (1985), 169–207, and 'The Ecclesiastical Policies of James I and Charles I', in Kenneth Fincham (ed.), *The Early Stuart Church, 1603–1642* (Houndmills, 1993), 23–50. For the view that questions of discipline rather than doctrine were paramount in the change of direction under Charles and Laud, see Julian Davies, *The Caroline Captivity of the Church: Charles I and the Remoulding of Anglicanism, 1625–1641* (Oxford, 1992).

mystical authority to the priest in his sacramental role and to the ecclesiastical hierarchy. One of the foremost young Arminians, William Laud, had declared that there was a direct continuity in the ecclesiastical hierarchy from the early days of the Roman church to the present day. He thus seemed to be undermining a central distinction between Protestantism and Catholicism. As early as 1603 Abbot had taken issue with Laud's views in a treatise denying Laud's proposition that the true church had always been visible. Abbot reaffirmed the views of Foxe and Bale, that the true church of the faithful had existed from the beginning of time and had no necessary connection with ecclesiastical institutions; in the Middle Ages the godly had been a minority, an Invisible Church despised by the true visible Roman church. Abbot identified the true church with the woman in the wilderness, and quoted from a list of authorities which had become orthodox in Protestant apocalyptic writing, including a number of poets: Dante, Petrarch, Mantuan, and Chaucer. Abbot quoted at length from *The Plowman's Tale* (ll. 373–88), which he attributed to Chaucer, and commented:

This and a hundred times as much, he expresseth in a simple plough mans person; as euidently inferring, that the husbandman & meanest country body of that time, by the reading and hearing of the Word of God, could tell what was right and religious, and what other wise.[47]

Abbot's treatise against Laud's views was published in 1624. The logic of his argument was that the Church of England was merely one part of a universal Protestant church and that English foreign policy must therefore take account of the need to help co-religionists elsewhere. He was a consistent champion of Frederick and Elizabeth and an advocate of military intervention against the Habsburgs. Abbot, like many English Calvinists, suspected the Dutch Arminians because they seemed to have an unduly conciliatory attitude to the Habsburgs; in a time of political crisis it seemed essential to rally round predestinarian Calvinism in order to maintain unity against the Spanish threat. In their play *Sir John van Olden Barnavelt* (1619), Fletcher and Massinger had expressed the common English view of Arminianism as little more than Popery in disguise.[48] The conjunction of moves in England towards an alignment with Spain and the rise of Arminianism aroused very deep fears.

Soon after he came to the throne, it became clear that Charles was going to favour the Arminians. He seems, like his father in his last years, to have been receptive to the argument that political unrest and irreverence were on the increase in England and that renewed emphasis on ritual and hierarchy in religion would help to restore good order. He had experienced the striking contrast between the atmosphere of the Spanish court with its gravity and majesty and the political tumult that he found on his return to England. To some extent Charles modelled his political style on the Spanish monarchy: whereas his father had been garrulous and ungainly, Charles,

---

[47] George Abbot, *A Treatise of the Perpetuall Visibility and Succession of the True Church in All Ages* (London, 1624), 79–80, 54, 69–71. Laud strongly disliked his book, though it was arguably by no means as hostile to existing ecclesiastical institutions as he implied: Anthony Milton, *Catholic and Reformed: The Roman and Protestant Churches in English Protestant Thought 1600–1640* (Cambridge, 1995), 301–3.

[48] Heinemann, *Puritanism and Theatre*, 203–5.

besides being naturally shy, believed that too many words impaired the royal dignity; he preferred a posture of silent majesty. The imposition of Arminianism thus became associated in many English people's minds with the dangers of absolutism and Popery. These fears were strengthened by the number of high political offices given to members of the Arminian clergy, which aroused memories of clerical sway over the monarch before the Reformation. William Laud had by 1626 been promised the succession to the Archbishopric of Canterbury, and he effectively became chief minister.[49]

These political associations were to some extent accidental rather than being intrinsic to Arminianism. The Dutch Calvinists were presbyterians; and Calvinism had long been rejected by radical sects who disliked its austerity and tight organizational discipline. Arminianism did not necessarily entail political authoritarianism; in the Netherlands it was associated with a liberal, Erasmian tradition. The most striking example of the political complexities is the case of George Wither, whose poetry in the last part of James's reign was closely caught up with these religious reversals. So far we have seen him as an oppositional figure, imprisoned during the successive Parliaments of 1614 and 1621. By 1624, however, he found himself under attack from some of his former followers as a defender of monopoly and superstition; it has been argued that his writings were a means of furthering the cause of the new high churchmen.[50] The reversal is indeed striking, but it was not so absolute as it might seem, and reflects the extreme complexity of the contending political forces in the last years of James's reign.

Several of Wither's political allies of 1614 had been anti-Calvinist in theology. Sir Edwin Sandys won the attention of the leading Dutch Arminian, and republican, Hugo Grotius for his views; his brother George later translated a tragedy by Grotius. To John Selden, another critic of Calvinism, Wither dedicated in 1635 a treatise vindicating the freedom of the will. Christopher Brooke's brother Samuel was also an Arminian. This group was politically by no means absolutist in sympathy, and during the Civil War was to emerge either as Parliamentarian or as advocating a strongly constitutionalist royalism.[51] This theological stance, together with an emphasis on political compromise, made the group less hostile than Calvinists to some of the traditional external forms of religion, which might work in the active process of finding

---

[49] Peter W. Thomas, 'Charles I of England: The Tragedy of Absolutism', in A. G. Dickens (ed.), *The Courts of Europe: Politics, Patronage and Royalty 1400–1800* (London, 1977), 190–211; for a general study of his court see R. Malcolm Smuts, *Court Culture and the Origins of a Royalist Tradition in Early Stuart England* (Philadelphia, 1987), chs. 8–9. The extent to which Charles's religious views were swayed by Laud or were his own has been much debated by historians: for the latter view see especially Kevin Sharpe, *The Personal Rule of Charles I* (New Haven, 1992), 284 ff.

[50] Clegg, *Press Censorship in Jacobean England*, 49.

[51] On Sandys's religious views see Malcolm, 'Hobbes, Sandys, and the Virginia Company', 309–13, and Theodore K. Rabb, *Jacobean Gentleman: Sir Edwin Sandys, 1561–1629* (Princeton, 1998), 21–46; on broader aspects of the Erasmian tradition see Hugh Trevor-Roper, *Religion, the Reformation, and Social Change* (London, 1967), 24 ff., and on Laudianism and Arminianism, *Catholics, Anglican and Puritans* (London, 1987), ch. 2 (on Sandys in relation to Grotius and the Great Tew circle, 195–8). On Wither's translation of Nemesius see Charles S. Hensley, *The Later Career of George Wither* (The Hague, 1969), 80–9.

salvation. This meant that there was a certain overlap of views with figures like Andrewes, who was a friend of Sandys and to whom Wither may have addressed a poem. The friends shared an interest in church music of some ornateness: Wither provided settings for some of his hymns by Orlando Gibbons, the royal organist.[52]

As has been seen, already in 1614 Wither was turning from secular poetic models to the Psalms of David, and in the ensuing years he dedicated himself to a major new translation of the Psalms. This was a project he shared with many members of his circle: both Sir Edwin Sandys and his brother George published psalm translations.[53] What gave Wither's religious verse a more distinctly Arminian cast was his desire to experiment with hymns for use in church service, to modulate his prophetic voice into ceremonial forms. Spenserian poetry, and Wither's in particular, often sought a transcendent Spirit beyond set forms; here he was deliberately restricting his scope. He was also going against a Calvinist tradition which disapproved of the use in religious service of verse without a direct scriptural sanction. And at some stage he conceived for himself the remarkable ambition of effectively becoming the church's poet laureate, with his psalms and hymns becoming the official versions. These plans must have been in progress before the upheavals of the king's last years: the first instalment of psalms appeared in 1619. When he presented a trial selection of hymns for approval in 1621/2, it was dedicated in the first place to Abbot, whom Wither had praised in *Abuses Stript and Whipt*; Wither declared himself willing to change any elements that were found offensive. His psalms and hymns would form part of the broad Jacobean church; and true to the democratizing spirit of his poetry, he deliberately chose a style that would be accessible to a wide audience, though the poems certainly lacked formal finesse. In February 1623 he achieved a remarkable coup when the king granted him a special patent to have his *Hymnes and Songs of the Church* bound in with all metrical psalm-books henceforth sold. This overruled an earlier patent which gave the Stationers' Company the exclusive right to the metrical psalter by Sternhold and Hopkins, which was used in every church. They regarded their patent as allowing them to restrict the appearance of any alternative translation.

Wither's patent was granted on the fateful day when Charles and Buckingham left for Spain, and its fortunes were henceforth bound up with the political volatilities of the reign's last years. The king made the grant shortly after Jonson's attack on Wither as a subversive populist in *Time Vindicated*. Wither later claimed that the Earl of Pembroke had helped him gain the patent, and it may be that, faced with a head-on

---

[52] Arthur M. Hind, *Engraving in Britain in the Sixteenth and Seventeenth Centuries*, ii: *The Reign of James I* (Cambridge, 1955), 248; the verses, signed 'Ge: Wi:', are not obviously Wither's in style. On the use of this portrait to evoke the spirit of the earlier Jacobean church against the Laudians in 1641, see Peter McCullough, 'Making Dead Men Speak: Laudianism, Print, and the Works of Lancelot Andrewes, 1626–1642', *Historical Journal*, 41 (1998), 401–24 (421). On Gibbons and Wither see John Harley, *Orlando Gibbons and the Gibbon Family of Musicians* (Aldershot, 1999), 67–8.

[53] The ascription of *A Paraphrase upon the Psalms of David* (London, 1615) to Sandys is Anthony Wood's, the Stationers' Court-Book entry having ascribed to Joyce Taylor; on the case for Sandys's authorship see Rabb, *Jacobean Gentleman*, 46. The printer, Thomas Snodham, also produced Browne's *Britannia's Pastorals* and Wither's *A Satyre*, *The Shepherds Hunting*, and *Songs of the Old Testament*.

collision between two poets he had patronized and whom he respected, Pembroke sought to make amends. Pembroke of course had a family interest in religious verse: his uncle and aunt, Mary and Philip Sidney, had produced the most skilful translations of the Psalms to date (Wither's friend John Davies of Hereford was the scribe of the manuscript presented to Queen Elizabeth). The death in 1619 of Mary Sidney, Countess of Pembroke, seems to have revived interest in the Sidney psalms, to which John Donne wrote a tribute in verse around this time.[54] Given those family traditions, Pembroke would have been generous indeed in favouring Wither's versions over the much more formally interesting Sidney translations; but the political spirit of the grant would not have been seen as favouring the high-flying group in the church.

That said, it nonetheless represented a decided move away from the strident literary individualism of his earlier verse, and especially in the case of the hymns, there is a sense that Wither was being bought off. He was preparing the first set of hymns from prison, and declared that he was doing so at the bidding of some churchmen; once he had his patent, he became strongly beholden to royal favour. He addressed an appeal from prison to Prince Charles, who may have helped mediate with the king; but James seems to have taken a personal interest in Wither.[55] James's generosity can be seen as a strategy of the 'kingcraft' of which he was so proud, his penchant for balancing different factions against each other. It did have the effect of largely neutralizing Wither politically in the final years of his reign. On the other hand, the award of the patent to Wither rather than to some poet more clearly identified with Laud, Neile, and their allies offered some kind of counterbalance to the high churchmen. James had a long-standing sympathy with the project of a reformed Muse, and had himself been working on his own version of the Psalms; to an extent, he now nominated Wither as a kind of poetic heir, and he did so in full awareness of his history as a figure sympathetic to Puritans. Whatever the combination of political and literary motives behind the patent, it did make it easy to present him as a traitor to godliness. The Stationers' Company, strongly hostile to the patent because of the trouble it would cause their business, started a campaign against the *Hymnes and Songs* as superstitious because they sought to give new life to the observance of saints' days and other seasonal rituals without scriptural foundation.[56] Their campaign struck a raw nerve: at the same time as Parliament was expressing concern about Wither's case it was criticizing Richard Montague's provocatively anti-Calvinist *A New Gagg*

---

[54] Allan Pritchard, 'An Unpublished Poem by George Wither', *Modern Philology*, 61 (1963), 120–1, citing Wither's *A Collection of Emblemes* (London, 1635), 196; Henry Woudhuysen, *Sir Philip Sidney and the Circulation of Manuscripts, 1558–1640* (Oxford, 1996), 38–9.

[55] Pritchard, 'An Unpublished Poem by George Wither', 120; James Doelman, *King James I and the Religious Culture of England* (Woodbridge, 2000), 146–7.

[56] The complicated history can be reconstructed from Allan Pritchard, 'George Wither's Quarrel with the Stationers: An Anonymous Reply to *The Schollers Purgatory*', *Studies in Bibliography*, 16 (1963), 27–42; Norman E. Carlson, 'Wither and the Stationers', *Studies in Bibliography*, 19 (1966), 210–15; James Doelman, 'George Wither, the Stationers Company, and the Psalter', *Studies in Philology*, 90 (1993), 74–82; and Wither's own account in *The Schollers Purgatory* (London, 1624), Spenser Society reprint, *Miscellaneous Works of George Wither*, 6 vols. (1872–8; repr. Amsterdam, 1977), i.

for the Old Goose and urging Abbot to look into it. The Stationers were trying to present Wither as part of a cohesive anti-Calvinist front, and the *Hymnes and Songs*, in
the words of a modern scholar, as 'a liturgical Trojan horse that cached ceremonial-
ism inside scripture'.[57] In defending Christmas, Wither did refer specifically to
James's 1614 proclamation urging the revival of old English hospitality. He
struck another note that would have been congenial to James in attacking apocalyptic hopes for a literal, military struggle against the Beast. An impassioned panegyric
of Elizabeth as the new Deborah, defeating the Whore of Babylon, was dropped
from the 1623 edition onwards. In the inflamed context of the 1620s, Wither was
refraining from the kind of language that would have supported war with Spain.
In the process, he was losing credit with much of his original constituency.
Interestingly, he reveals that his early admirers included a great many separatists for
whom even the relatively broad Jacobean church was too superstitious, and that they
had offered to pay him to write on their behalf. Now, reverting to a stock anti-
separatist idiom, he claimed that the tapsters, feltmakers, and all the brotherhood
of Amsterdam had scoffed at him in their conventicles and taverns.[58] Wither found
himself on the defensive on secular as well as religious issues. He liked to present his
prophetic voice as unfettered by the constraints of patronage and flattery; but his
patent put him in the position of a direct dependant on royal favour. The Stationers
were quick to seize this advantage. In the Parliament of 1624, Sandys and his allies at
last gained success in their long-standing campaign against monopolies. Wither had
supported this cause, adding an attack on monopolies to the 1622 edition of *Abuses
Stript and Whipt*. The Stationers, however, lobbied hard against Wither's patent as
an unjust monopoly, with several of their representatives, he claimed, clamouring at
the door of Parliament.[59]

Wither fought back, his anger reflecting his unease at having been manoeuvred
into a stance with which he was not comfortable. As far as he was concerned, the
Stationers were themselves defending 'one of these Monopolies that our State
abhores', and in support of this view he pointed out that the Stationers were trying
to insert a clause in the Statute of Monopolies exempting patents relating to printing. Wither petitioned the committee to remove this clause, and composed a pamphlet in his defence, *The Schollers Purgatory*. This treatise has often been seen as a
forerunner of Milton's *Areopagitica*, and it does anticipate some of Milton's anti-
monopolistic rhetoric. Wither at one point asserted a natural right of authors to the
product of their labours, though he did not dwell on this line of argument. He did,
however, challenge the whole system of licensing by the Stationers, which gave them
'the full benefit of those books, better then any Author'. He appealed to the younger
and less privileged members of the Company over the heads of its wealthy leaders. In
The Schollers Purgatory he takes on his familiar stance of the godly individual per-

[57] Clegg, *Press Censorship in Jacobean England*, 49, 197–203, 227–8.
[58] George Wither, *Hymnes and Songs of the Church* (London, 1623), 126, 195; *The Songs of the Old
Testament* (London, 1621), 15–17; *The Schollers Purgatory*, 68, 64.
[59] Doelman, 'George Wither, the Stationers Company, and the Psalter', 78–9; Wither, *The Schollers
Purgatory*, 96.

secuted by corrupt authorities, and presents the Stationers as showing a 'popish' devotion to mere human tradition in their defence of Sternhold and Hopkins. Wither, as would soon emerge, was not a natural ally of figures like Montague. His hymn to St George, for example, though singled out by his critics as especially outrageous, differed markedly from the Laudian religious vision. The cult of St George had become controversial early in the Reformation: it was based on a legend with no scriptural foundation, yet George was also patron of the courtly Order of the Garter and of the nation. Spenser, as has been seen, tried to deal with this problem through allegorization; Wither, less equivocally, claims that George is to be understood as Christ, the only appropriate patron for the English, while the dragon is the Beast in Revelation. Wither thus links English royal traditions with millennial fervour; this interpretation was to be firmly rejected by the Laudian Peter Heylyn. His versification of the Song of Songs, which the Stationers derided for its carnality, is in fact heavily allegorized in a manner that became particularly common in Puritan circles, as celebrating the union between Christ and the church, once again with apocalyptic overtones. Wither's dedication to the Visible Church was always qualified by a strong belief that all worldly institutions were inferior to the transcendent Invisible Church. For all that he had lost standing with some former admirers, Wither still commanded a significant public following; any church in which he had managed to gain a significant role would have much been closer to the Jacobean than to the Laudian church.[60]

Emboldened by strong support from King James, Wither continued to seek ways of publishing his hymns and psalms, but soon after the king's death he was deflected from this more ceremonial course into the path of immediate prophecy. In repeated self-identifications with David in his new epic, *Britain's Remembrancer*, Wither indicated how the Psalms could easily provide a model for denunciations of established religious forms, and presented his previous self-restraint as a struggle:

> While wicked men we doe remaine among,
> With David, we a while may curb the tongue;
> But, burne it will within us, til we speake,
> And forth, at last, some thundring voice will breake.

A severe outbreak of plague in the spring of 1625 had led many to flee London in panic; Wither stayed behind and felt himself divinely inspired to witness the sins that had brought down this judgement from heaven. This liminal period at the start of a new reign was when another prophet, Lady Eleanor Davies, first became inspired to her apocalyptic writings. Trying to gain favour with the new king, Wither dedicated a first draft to him, but by the time he managed to print the poem in 1628, laboriously setting the type himself, he was deeply anxious about the new reign. Presenting himself as defender of a *via media*, he criticized Calvinist theology and emergent sectarianism, and warned against using either 'Arminian' or 'Puritan' as a term of abuse.

[60] Wither, *The Schollers Purgatory*, 30, 28–9, 37, 62, 81; Joseph Loewenstein, 'Wither and Professional Work', in Arthur F. Marotti and Michael D. Bristol (eds.), *Print, Manuscript, and Performance: The Changing Relations of the Media in Early Modern England* (Columbus, Oh., 2000), 103–23; Peter Heylyn, *The Historie . . . of St. George* (London, 1631), 315–16.

His stance, however, fell far short of support of the high churchmen who were by now becoming much more rigid in their enforcement of conformity. Wither rejected any *jure divino* claims for the superiority of any one Protestant form of worship, proclaiming that he would be a presbyterian if he lived in Scotland and a democrat if he lived in Switzerland. He encouraged the fears of those who believed that the changes in religion reflected a new and dangerous openness to Popery, warning about the growth of Catholic influence at court and urging Charles that his queen must be converted to Protestantism. He contrasted the nation's strength under Elizabeth with the disastrous setbacks in defending the Protestant cause in the present. He suggested that Charles was being misled by 'instruments of Sathan', though the fault was to be laid not on the king in person but on the people's past sins.[61] Though Wither dedicated the 1628 edition to Charles, the king gave him no further patronage. When he eventually published his complete psalm translation, in 1632, it was with a dedication to Charles's sister Elizabeth. A new edition of the hymns appeared in 1641, at the beginning of the Long Parliament's campaign to reform the church, with an enthusiastic dedication to Parliament and a title, *Britain's Second Remembrancer*, that linked the hymns with his non-courtly, prophetic voice.[62] He was helping to institute an ethos for the hymn that would overcome the anxieties of earlier Calvinists, establishing the genre by the end of the century as central to the identity of English Dissenters.

Wither was not the only poet who combined hostility to Calvinism with deep unease about the politics of Charles's reign. With some stretching of the term, one might include amongst the 'Spenserians' the Scottish poet William Drummond, a great admirer of *The Faerie Queene* who remained faithful to many poetic conventions of the previous century, and who corresponded with Drayton in the English poet's last years. Drummond still more than Wither could be aligned with an Arminian tendency in the Spenserian tradition: he disliked the dogmatism of the Scottish presbyterians and hoped that a powerful monarchy would be able to permit religious toleration and the expression of different religious views. But by 1634 he was complaining at Charles's restrictions on freedom of speech and pointing out that '[n]o prince, how great soever, can abolish pens; nor will the memorials of ages be extinguished by present power'. Drummond thought that Charles should read Buchanan to remind himself of the fate reserved for tyrants.[63]

However critical Wither and Drummond might be of Calvinist orthodoxy, they

---

[61] Wither, *Britain's Remembrancer*, fos. 140ᵛ, 226ʳ–7ʳ, 165ᵛ–6ᵛ, 219ʳ–20ᵛ, 228ᵛ, 246ᵛ ff.; Esther S. Cope, *Handmaid of the Holy Spirit: Dame Eleanor Davies, Never soe Mad a Ladie* (Ann Arbor, 1992), 33 ff.

[62] George Wither, *Haleluiah; or, Britan's Second Remembrancer* (London, 1641; repr., Spenser Society, Manchester, 1879). For later developments see Sharon Achinstein, *Literature and Dissent in Milton's England* (Cambridge, forthcoming) Ch. 8.

[63] Alastair Fowler and Michael Leslie, 'Drummond's Copy of *The Fairie Queene*', *Times Literary Supplement*, 17 July 1981, 821–2; David Masson, *Drummond of Hawthornden: The Story of his Life and Writings* (London, 1873), 238–40; T. I. Rae, 'The Political Attitudes of William Drummond of Hawthornden', in G. W. S. Barrow (ed.), *The Scottish Tradition: Essays in Honour of Ronald Gordon Cant* (Edinburgh, 1974), 132–46. See now Kerrigan, *On Shakespeare and Early Modern Literature*, 152–80.

were worried that Charles's reign was turning back the clock in political and religious terms a great deal too far. To a wide body of opinion, the new priority given to ritual against preaching could only imply a planned return to Popery, a radical break with traditions that went back to the Elizabethan age and much earlier. In *The Shepheardes Calender* Spenser had praised Grindal's regime of low-church episcopacy and by his allusions to Wycliffite poetry had indicated that the demand for a church based on preaching and learning rather than ritualism and ignorance went back to the distant past. Memory of the old 'ploughman' tradition as well as of Spenser's religious allegory was still preserved amongst the Spenserians in the 1620s, as can be seen by an odd volume published in 1626, William Vaughan's *The Golden Fleece*. Vaughan had been an Essex supporter in the 1590s and had dedicated a volume of poems to him; he had also collaborated with the Puritan propagandist Thomas Scott in translating an Italian anti-Habsburg satire.[64] He had since taken up the cause of colonial exploration, and *The Golden Fleece* is essentially propaganda for the cause of colonization. But he included several allusions to the highly topical debate over predestination— the book was published soon after the York House conference at which the relative merits of Calvinism and Arminianism had been debated. Vaughan made it clear that he believed the Arminians to be in the wrong. At one point Duns Scotus, a representative of the medieval church, makes an appearance and accuses Chaucer of fomenting heresy by equating the Pope with Antichrist in his *Plowman's Tale* (Vaughan accepts the common attribution). Chaucer defends himself by pointing out that he has been anticipated in his denunciations of the Papacy by heretics like the Waldenses and Albigensians. Vaughan knew Wither, one of whose poems he alludes to.[65]

In 1626 it was still possible to publish debates over predestination, but the Arminians were gaining control of the machinery of censorship. In 1624 Richard Montague, regretting the low-church bishop Joseph Hall's laxity over censoring Calvinist controversy, had declared that 'it will never be well till we have our Inquisition'.[66] In the earlier part of Charles's reign Oxford Calvinists had a certain amount of protection since the Chancellor was the Earl of Pembroke, who had Calvinist sympathies; but late in 1628 Charles reissued the Thirty-Nine Articles with a declaration that 'curious search' about complex theological issues should be

---

[64] William Vaughan, *Poematum libellus* (London, 1598), sigs. C4ʳ–5ᵛ; Vaughan translated part of the anti-Habsburg satire *Ragguagli di Parnaso* by Traiano Boccalini, along with John Florio and (anonymously) Thomas Scott: *The New-Found Politicke* (London, 1626). On the significance of Boccalini's work see Frances A. Yates, *The Rosicrucian Enlightenment* (London, 1972), 133–9.

[65] William Vaughan, *The Golden Fleece* (London, 1626), 111 ff., 137 ff., 63; Andrew N. Wawn, 'Chaucer, Wyclif and the Court of Apollo', *English Language Notes*, 10 (1972), 15–20.

[66] Paul Christianson, *Reformers and Babylon: English Apocalyptic Visions from the Reformation to the Eve of the Civil War* (Toronto, 1978), 136 n. 11. But a book by Montague was censored in 1629; Sheila Lambert, 'Richard Montagu, Arminianism and Censorship', *Past and Present*, 124 (1989), 36–68, and Peter White, *Predestination, Policy and Polemic: Conflict and Consensus in the English Church from the Reformation to the Civil War* (Cambridge, 1992) argues that Arminians and Calvinists were treated even-handedly; I am grateful to David Como for showing me an unpublished paper which gives some striking examples of the selective character of Laudian censorship.

stopped. The Articles were extremely ambiguous and there remains much debate about their import: revisionists have claimed that the aim was not a complete shift in church policy but rather to dampen down debate over theological niceties and emphasize ecclesiastical unity. There was certainly no question of either side's favouring an absence of censorship: Calvinists were keen to use legislation against Catholic texts and also Arminian writings they considered theologically dubious. What was noticed was the way censorship was used in relation to the overall direction of policies, and there was a widespread perception that the government cracked down most harshly on Calvinists, fearing the subversive political consequences of apocalyptic zeal. In 1629, undeterred by the decree, a young Oxford poet, Samuel Austin, published a religious poem which contained 'experimentall proofes against mans free will'. Austin addressed an appeal to Browne and Drayton to turn from secular to religious themes; he would have known Browne because both men had connections with Exeter College, a centre of resistance to Arminianism.[67] In the same year another friend of Browne's, Nathaniel Carpenter, was forced to leave Oxford for publishing some anti-Arminian sermons. He entered the service of James Ussher, Bishop of Armagh, a low-church Calvinist who was to try to achieve a compromise in the Long Parliament by a scheme of 'reduced episcopacy'.[68] Ussher's secretary was another Spenserian poet, Francis Quarles, who began work in the 1630s on a series of eclogues in which he fiercely attacked the Arminians. He could not publish his anti-Laudian poems until the 1640s.[69] About this time Quarles befriended Phineas Fletcher, who had left his religious views in no doubt when he published *The Locusts* in 1627: he described the Dutch Arminians as '[a] doubtfull sect, which hang 'tween truth, lies, heaven, and hell'. The Laudians were beginning to apply the term 'Puritan' not just to presbyterians but to all Calvinists, and in a book published in 1632 Fletcher strongly condemned this practice.[70] In his last poems, probably written shortly before his death in 1628, Fulke Greville expressed his total disillusion with the corrupt visible church and implored Christ to bring time to a close:

> *Syon* lyes waste, and thy *Ierusalem*,
> O Lord, is falne to vtter desolation,
> Against thy Prophets, and thy holy men,
> The sinne hath wrought a fatall combination,
>   Prophan'd thy name, thy worship ouerthrowne,
>   And made thee liuing Lord, a God vnknowne . . .

[67] Samuel Austin, *Austins Urania* (London, 1629), sigs. A5^r ff., 81.
[68] Christopher Hill, *Intellectual Origins of the English Revolution* (Oxford, 1965), 305; Carpenter praises Browne in *Geography Delineated* (Oxford, 1625), sig. Kk4^v.
[69] Karl Josef Höltgen, *Francis Quarles, 1592–1644: Meditativer Dichter, Emblematiker, Royalist: Eine biographische und kritische Studie* (Tübingen, 1978), 60; *Francis Quarles: The Complete Works in Prose and Verse*, ed. Alexander B. Grosart, 3 vols. (1880–1; repr. Hildesheim, 1971), iii.217–20; see also Christopher Hill, 'Francis Quarles (1592–1644) and Edward Benlowes (1602–76)', in *The Collected Essays of Christopher Hill*, i: *Writing and Revolution in Seventeenth-Century England* (Brighton, 1985), 188–206 (188–97).
[70] Giles and Phineas Fletcher, *Poetical Works*, ed. Frederick S. Boas, 2 vols. (Cambridge, 1908–9), i.170; Phineas Fletcher, *The Way to Blessednes* (London, 1632), 83.

That sensuall vnsatiable vaste wombe
Of thy seene Church, thy vnseene Church disgraceth . . .

Rather, sweet *Iesus,* fill vp time and come,
To yeeld the sinne her euerlasting doome.[71]

[71] Greville, 'Caelica', no. 109, in *Poems and Dramas of Fulke Greville First Lord Brooke,* 2 vols. (Edinburgh, 1939), i.152–3, ll. 1–6, 15–16, 29–30; on dating see Ronald A. Rebholz, *The Life of Fulke Greville* (Oxford, 1971), 340, though Tom W. N. Parker, *Proportional Form in the Sonnets of the Sidney Circle* (Oxford, 1998), 90–1, argues from the date and structuring of the Warwick manuscript that the sequence was complete by 1619.

10. *The Politics of Milton's Early Poetry*

FOR Greville, the survivor from the Elizabethan era, time seemed bleakly empty. For the young Milton, however, it was full of promise. In his more confident moments he believed that he was going to be a major poet. But for a long time he was uncertain whether he should combine this vocation with the priesthood as Donne, Herbert, and the Fletchers had done. He felt unready for both poetic and religious vocations when he left Cambridge and embarked on an ambitious programme of private study. He knew, however, that this choice of the contemplative life might appear cowardly and evasive. A letter written in the early 1630s to a friend, possibly the Scots presbyterian Thomas Young, reveals his unease.[1] By any obvious standards of achievement, he acknowledges, he is wasting his time, dreaming away his years. He might already be preaching the Word; in more worldly terms, he might be pursuing a profitable career, settling down with a family, or publishing books to gain literary fame. He is painfully aware of the biblical injunction to use one's talents (Matthew 25: 14–30); but he takes heart from another parable, that of the vineyard (Matthew 20: 1–16). He is 'not taking thought of beeing late so it give advantage to be more fit, for those that were latest lost nothing when the maister of the vinyard came to give each one his hire'. His 'belatednesse' will eventually bear fruit. He sent his friend a sonnet which contrasted two kinds of time: the easy, linear progression of the 'timely-happy', of those who gain secure worldly advancement, and the more complex time of God's workings, which brings things to ripeness by more indirect means. Milton's sense of his own 'unripeness' was to persist through the 1630s; he presented his poems, with a force that was more than conventional, as things torn from him before he was properly ready. But he had an underlying conviction that when his major work did appear it would be a great one.

In his political pamphlets of the 1640s Milton viewed the development of English history in terms that mirrored his own self-development. The Visible Church, he argued, had come to be dominated by time-serving prelates while the truly godly had lived in silence and obscurity. What appeared to the apologists for the Church of England to have been its steady growth in prosperity had in fact been a process of stagnation. Milton admired Edward VI, looking back nostalgically in one of his sonnets to the days when Cheke gave him a humanist education; he felt an immediate sense of spiritual kinship when he read Bucer's Christian utopia, *De regno Christi*. But the king had died young and political difficulties had impeded the Reformation.

---

[1] *The Complete Prose Works of John Milton*, ed. Don M. Wolfe et al., 8 vols. (New Haven, 1953–82), i.319–21; bracketed references in the text will be to this edition. Sonnet VII is quoted from *The Poems of John Milton*, ed. John Carey and Alastair Fowler (London, 1968), 147–8; all quotations from Milton's poetry come from this edition.

About the reign of Elizabeth Milton had little positive to say: he admired Gr
but regarded the Elizabethan settlement as an unsatisfactory, 'luke-warm' compromise. Since then there had been a steady reaction. The bishops' obsession with tradition had prevented the 'renovating and re-ingendring Spirit of God' (*Complete
Prose Works*, i.703) from taking its course. England had been the first country to 'set
up a Standard for the recovery of *lost Truth*' but was now the last to enjoy the benefits of reformation (i.525). But the time was at last to be redeemed, the long wait of
the godly would be rewarded by 'the long-deferr'd, but much more wonderfull and
happy reformation of the *Church* in these latter dayes' (i.519). In his increasing
apocalyptic enthusiasm Milton went beyond traditional Protestant symbolism,
arguing that Truth was 'the daughter not of Time, but of Heaven' (i.639). There was
an absolute opposition between the secular realm of time and the '*datelesse* and
irrevoluble Circle of *Eternity*' (i.616). What was at hand was not a 'revolution' in the
old sense of a return to a previous state of purity but something completely without
precedent: the New Jerusalem 'without your admired linke of succession descends
from Heaven' (i.703). These ideas had already been anticipated in the early poem that
contemptuously dismissed 'envious Time', and in the fragment of 1638 reading:

> Fix here ye overdated spheres
> That wing the restless foot of time.[2]

Milton hoped in the 1640s that poetic and political expectations would converge,
that he would be able to produce a great celebration of the nation's apocalyptic renewal. His pamphlets were full of references to the traditions of prophetic
poetry—to Dante, Petrarch, *The Plowman's Tale*, and Spenser. His prose tracts were
themselves rhapsodic and linguistically inventive, but he insisted that they were not
yet his major achievement, that they were only 'abortive and foredated' (i.820). In the
end, of course, his great poem was to celebrate a lost paradise rather than a reformed
commonwealth, but the extent of his early hopes helps to explain his later disillusion.
At the height of the tumults of the 1640s, however, he did find time to bring out a
collection of his early poems, and he made prophetic claims for *Lycidas*, which, he
said, had foretold the ruin of the Anglican church.

Such claims to prophetic powers made after the event must, of course, arouse a
certain amount of scepticism. Wither was to take the Civil War as a vindication of his
own status as prophet, and he republished some of his own earlier verse which could
be held to have foretold the conflict. He was to become as firm an opponent of
Charles I as Milton, being appointed as a trustee for the dispersal of the king's property.[3] But he could hardly lay claim to lifelong consistency: a royalist took delight in
republishing sections of his earlier poetry which professed loyalty to the monarchy
and deep hostility to sectarianism.[4] Wither's views were radicalized in the course of

---

[2] Milton, *Poems*, 169, 254.
[3] Allan Pritchard, 'George Wither and the Sale of the Estate of Charles I', *Modern Philology*, 77 (1979–80), 370–81 (370 and n. 1).
[4] Anon., *Withers Remembrancer* (London, 1643). Cf. Christopher Hill, 'George Wither (1588–1667) and John Milton (1608–74)', in *The Collected Essays of Christopher Hill*, i: *Writing and Revolution*

the 1640s, and this was a very common occurrence. Recent historians have warned that it is misleading to read the polarization of the 1640s back into the 1630s. Rather than seething with pre-revolutionary ferment, it is argued, the England of that period was fundamentally tranquil, and only a tiny and unrepresentative minority cared very much about censorship or religious reaction. Certainly the religious and social radicals of the 1640s never succeeded in finding a broad political base in a country where traditionalism was still very strong, and where loyalties to local county communities were often more powerful than allegiance either to the central government or to religious ideologies. Many people were very reluctant to fight for either side in the Civil War.[5] Some critics have argued that Milton's own radicalism came very late, and have made a sharp separation between the poet of the 1630s and the Puritan of the 1640s.[6] Like Wither, Milton wrote a poem in praise of Lancelot Andrewes. As has been seen, Wither was keen to contribute his verse to the Anglican liturgy, but he did not evoke the sensual experience of ritual. In 'Il Penseroso' Milton displays a sensitivity to the 'beauty of holiness', to organ music and 'service high', not found in Wither or in any other Stuart 'Spenserian'. Even George Herbert, whose verse reflects the anti-contentious spirit, if not necessarily the theology, of Caroline Arminianism, viewed church architecture in essentially schematic, emblematic terms, without Milton's responsiveness to the sensuous qualities of religious worship.[7] It has been argued that Milton's publication of his poems in 1645 was an attempt to demonstrate his social respectability at a time when he was coming under heavy attack for the alleged democratic tendencies of his political writings.[8] After all, he declared that his denunciation of the clergy appeared in *Lycidas* 'by occasion'. Superficially at least, the 1645 edition resembles several contemporary collections of poetry with strongly royalist sympathies.[9]

There are undoubtedly discontinuities and inconsistencies in Milton's canon: there is not a simple, steadfast march towards Puritan revolution. But it is possible to

in *Seventeenth-Century England* (Brighton, 1985), 133–56. See further David Norbrook, 'Levelling Poetry: George Wither and the English Revolution, 1642–1649', *English Literary Renaissance*, 21 (1991), 217–56.

[5] J. S. Morrill, *The Revolt of the Provinces: Conservatives and Radicals in the English Civil War, 1630–1650* (London, 1976), reissued with an important review of the topic, and some qualifications, as *Revolt in the Provinces: The People of England and the Tragedy of War 1630–1648* (London, 1999). For the view of 1630s England as strongly polarized between 'court' and 'country', see P. W. Thomas, 'Two Cultures? Court and Country under Charles I', in Conrad Russell (ed.), *Origins of the English Civil War* (London, 1973), 168–93, and Christopher Hill, *Milton and the English Revolution* (London, 1977), 13–21; for one of the more temperate counter-statements, Robert Ashton, *The English Civil War: Conservatism and Revolution 1603–1649* (London, 1978), ch. 1.

[6] John Spencer Hill, *John Milton: Poet, Priest and Prophet: A Study of Divine Vocation in Milton's Poetry and Prose* (London, 1979), 44–9.

[7] Milton, *Poems*, 146; cf. Ch. 9 n. 13 above.

[8] Thomas N. Corns, 'Milton's Quest for Respectability', *Modern Language Review*, 77 (1982), 769–79.

[9] On parallels between the 1645 volume and collections by 'cavalier' poets, see Richard Helgerson, *Self-Crowned Laureates: Spenser, Jonson, Milton, and the Literary System* (Berkeley and Los Angeles, 1983), 185 ff., Warren Chernaik, 'Books as Monuments: The Politics of Consolation', *Yearbook of English Studies*, 21 (1991), 207–17, and David Norbrook, *Writing the English Republic: Poetry, Rhetoric and Politics 1627–1660* (Cambridge, 1999), 162–4.

exaggerate the discontinuities. The political tracts are of course rhetorically very different from the early poems; but they are also different from many more conventional tracts, being marked by exceptional subtlety of rhetorical strategy, modifying and subverting conventional responses.[10] Their method is indeed sometimes so oblique that their immediate political effectiveness may have been blunted. Milton's early poems use comparable strategies: they make their political points not so much by direct comment as by modification of generic expectations. The lack of explicit political statement need not be too surprising. After the dissolution of Parliament in 1629, orthodox channels of political debate were still more strictly controlled; through the 1630s ecclesiastical censorship was tightened. The period of the 'king's peace' can be seen as the most determined attempt in English history to 'aestheticize politics', to suppress articulate discussion and to try to force the realm into a harmonious pattern of ritualized submission. Advocates of a militant foreign policy continued throughout the 1630s to press for a change in direction, but had to do so by very indirect means since public discussion of foreign policy in or out of Parliament was no longer possible. Champions of British intervention in the Thirty Years War were still looking to Elizabeth of Bohemia, in her exile in the Netherlands, and even wishing that she, rather than her brother, were on the British throne.[11] The Dutch envoy complained that whenever he tried to raise urgent political and military issues the Earl of Arundel, the king's negotiator, tried to distract him by talking about pictures and galleries.[12]

There can be little doubt that substantial parts of the political nation, exhausted by the turbulence of recent years, welcomed the new peace and stability. But there were undercurrents of dissent. Charles and Laud would not have acted so firmly had they not believed that the political situation in the 1620s, under Abbot's lax regime, had been getting out of hand, that without firmer discipline radical sects would have continued to multiply until they became politically dangerous. Milton had come to political maturity in the 1620s, at a time when poets as well as radical dissenters had been growing irreverent about established authority. There were cracks in the elegant façade of religious and social uniformity, and Milton was unusually sensitive to these points of tension. His brief phase of responsiveness to Caroline aestheticized politics gave way to an increasingly emphatic politicization of aesthetics. Rather than stating his opinions explicitly he built into his poems a distrust of specious harmony

---

[10] See, for example, Joseph Anthony Wittreich, Jr., 'Milton's *Areopagitica*: Its Isocratic and Ironic Contexts', *Milton Studies*, 4 (1972), 101–15.

[11] On the 'secret whispering of some looking towardes the lady Elizabeth' see *Diary of John Rous*, ed. Mary Anne Everett Green (London, Camden Society, 1856), 19. The question of censorship has been a major focus of contention between traditional and revisionist interpretations of the period. Christopher Hill, 'Censorship and English Literature', in *Writing and Revolution in Seventeenth-Century England*, 32–71 is countered by Blair Worden, 'Literature and Political Censorship in Early Modern England', in A. C. Duke and C. A. Tamse (eds.), *Too Mighty to be Free: Censorship and the Press in Britain and the Netherlands* (Zutphen, 1987), 45–62, and by Professor Don F. McKenzie in his unpublished Lyell Lectures. See also Anthony Milton, 'Licensing, Censorship and Religious Orthodoxy in Early Stuart England', *Historical Journal*, 41 (1998), 625–52, and Sheila Lambert, 'Richard Montagu, Arminianism and Censorship', *Past and Present*, 124 (1989), 36–68. See further below, pp. 308–11.

[12] *Calendar of State Papers . . . Venice, 1636–39*, 79.

obtained at the expense of repression. In the 1640s he was to elaborate this distrust into a political theory influenced by the Florentine republicans; like the Machiavelli of the *Discourses*, he believed that an element of disorder and dissension was essential to the maintenance of liberty, that to try to achieve complete, static harmony was to invite stagnation.[13] When he used aesthetic analogies in his political works he modified their traditional associations. If building the reformed church was like carving a statue, it was necessary to acknowledge that this task was bound to produce an element of waste matter, the sects that could not be harmonized with the main church: here Milton's emphasis was on the process, the 'struggl of contrarieties', not on the finished product (i.795). When he compared the church or state to a temple, he emphasized that a building made up of human beings could never be 'united into a continuity, it can but be contiguous in this world' (ii.555). Even if he had not yet fully articulated them in his own mind, such ideas are implicit in the major works of the 1630s.

In some respects the young Milton appeared a stylistically conservative poet, remaining faithful to literary modes that were being rejected by many fashionable writers. In the political climate of the 1630s it was the poetry of the politically traditionalist Jonson and his followers that seemed most modern, most emancipated from old-fashioned Puritan pieties. Wither had responded to the pioneering role of the court in patronizing new artistic modes by attacking all literary artifice as politically suspect; but Milton's position was more complex. The Spenserian tradition by the 1630s had become worthy but dull, lacking any responsiveness to artistic innovation; and a spirit of religious and political innovation could not really be encouraged by artistic conservatism. The adventurous, experimental quality of Milton's early poetry has often been underestimated. He viewed poetic history, like political history, in apocalyptic terms: rather than envisaging a smooth, steady progression towards perfection, he sought, in his own poetry, to make the last first and the first last. He revived elements in the old prophetic tradition that were currently unfashionable. He was also willing, however, to imitate the formal experiments of more courtly writers, and to push these innovations even further, thus exposing the ultimate political conservatism behind the superficial modernity of the courtiers.

Milton's underlying commitment was to the prophetic tradition. His headmaster at St Paul's School, Alexander Gill, had been a champion of the Spenserian poets; his treatise on grammar and rhetoric featured lengthy quotations from Spenser, from other Elizabethans who had been members of the Sidney and Essex circles, and from the Jacobean Spenserians. He was a friend and admirer of Wither, whom he praised as the English Juvenal. There was only one quotation in his treatise from Ben Jonson, who pilloried both Wither and Gill in his masque *Time Vindicated*.[14] Gill's son

---

[13] On Italian influence see Blair Worden, 'Classical Republicanism and the Puritan Revolution' in Hugh Lloyd-Jones et al. (ed.), *History and Imagination: Essays in Honour of H. R. Trevor-Roper* (London, 1981), 184, 190–1, and Z. S. Fink, *The Classical Republicans* (Evanston, Ill., 1945), 90 ff.

[14] Alexander Gill, *Logonomia anglica* (1619), ed. Bror Danielsson and Arvid Gabrielson, 2 vols. (Stockholm, 1972), ii.82–3, 86, 152, 169–70, 184.

Alexander became one of Milton's closest friends; he was a fierce critic of Laud and the Stuarts, and was firmly convinced that King James's soul had gone to hell.[15] Milton does not seem to have been in contact with the older Spenserian poets, who were living in relative obscurity in the country—Wither in Kent for much of the decade, Phineas Fletcher in Norfolk, and William Browne in a 'poor cell' in Surrey. All these poets were worried by political developments in the 1630s. In court circles Spenser's poetry was being reinterpreted in rather startling ways. The cult of the Virgin Mary was being cautiously reinstated, and one anonymous pamphleteer justified it by analogy with Spenser's praise of the Virgin Queen.[16] The imagery of the Order of the Garter, which in *The Faerie Queene* was associated with anti-Habsburg militancy, had taken on radically different connotations now that Charles had returned to the policy of peace with Spain. Rubens, who had helped to negotiate the peace, painted a portrait of Charles as St George slaying the dragon. The Laudian apologist Peter Heylyn insisted that the legend of St George must be interpreted literally, not just as a political or moral allegory.[17]

Spenser's apocalyptic allegory was out of fashion in the 1630s, and so was richly mythological poetry. In his elegy for John Donne, published in 1633, Carew praised him for stripping away the pedantic weeds of pagan myth. In an early poem Milton set himself against these fashions, the 'new fangled toys, and trimming slight' of the poets of the 'strong lines', and declared his commitment to a prophetic voice, clothing his 'naked thoughts' in 'richest robes, and gayest attire'.[18] Such phrases led Leavis and his followers to declare that his attitude to language was rigid and ritualistic, that his verse lacked roots in vernacular idiom. C. S. Lewis's counter-argument that, as a Renaissance man, Milton loved ritual does not square very well with his political and religious views.[19] And recent stylistic studies have shown that claims about Milton's 'Latinate' style have been much exaggerated, that he was sensitive to the possibilities of the vernacular and was, in some respects, a linguistic nationalist.[20] But there remains a perceptible difference between Milton's 'Englishness' and that of Jonson and his followers, and Leavis was right to sense that this difference had political implications. Jonson's poems try to naturalize artifice, to give the effect of speaking with the voice of experience and common sense. In his more prophetic poems Milton seeks a self-consciously artificial idiom which will permit a critical distance from traditional assumptions. If Comus' speech to the Lady is, as Leavis argued, more concrete and vivid than the Lady's reply, it is partly because conspicuous consumption and hereditary inequality were more deeply 'rooted' in English

[15] Donald Lemen Clark, *John Milton at St Paul's School: A Study of Ancient Rhetoric in English Renaissance Education* (New York, 1948), 84–6.

[16] 'N.N.', *Maria triumphans* (London, 1635), 83; see G. F. Sensabaugh, 'A Spenser Allusion', *Times Literary Supplement*, 29 Oct. 1938, 694; Anthony Stafford, *The Femall Glory* (London, 1635), 83.

[17] Peter Heylyn, *The Historie . . . of St. George* (London, 1631), 41 ff., 315–16, cf. Roy Strong, *Van Dyck: 'Charles I on Horseback'* (London, 1972), 59–63.

[18] 'At a Vacation Exercise', *Poems*, 76–7.

[19] C. S. Lewis, *A Preface to* Paradise Lost (Oxford, 1942), 59–60.

[20] Archie Burnett, *Milton's Style: The Shorter Poems*, Paradise Regained, and Samson Agonistes (London, 1981), *passim*, Thomas N. Corns, *The Development of Milton's Prose Style* (Oxford, 1982), 70.

society than egalitarian rationalism.[21] Though he carefully studied his English predecessors Milton also acquired an unusually deep knowledge not only of classical
poetry but also of the Italian poetic tradition, with which Jonson was much less well
acquainted. At a time when Dante was out of fashion in Italy, let alone in England,
Milton made an intensive study of his poetry, which had been so much admired by
the sixteenth-century reformers.[22] On literary as well as religious issues, Milton's
first question was not how deeply a particular form or institution was rooted in
English traditions and everyday life but how well it served the cause of further
reformation.

Milton's prophetic voice first emerged in 'On the Morning of Christ's Nativity'.
His handling of the theme of the great feast-day contrasted strongly with many
contemporary poems on religious themes. Herrick and other 'cavalier' poets often
celebrated the traditional feast-days of the countryside, showing how they grew naturally out of the rhythms of agrarian life. Classical and Christian imagery were fused
to demonstrate the universal importance of ritual in religion. In the context
of Laud's insistence on traditional rituals, the poetry of popular festivities took on
a clear ideological significance. Puritans like William Prynne regarded many of the
old festivities as no more than pagan rites. Jonson had mocked such opinions in
Christmas his Masque (1616), alluding playfully to Gregory the Great, who had justified the retention of many previously pagan feast-days; he criticized the Puritans
who took exception to revelry at Christmas.[23] Milton steers clear of the rituals—and
indeed the name—of Christmas, and his poem celebrates Christ's birth as marking
the beginning of deliverance from pagan idols. He is concerned not so much with the
incarnate Christ as with the transcendental power that created the universe at the
beginning and will bend time round to its origin at the final millennial transformation of the universe. Christ's entry into history cuts through the cycle of the seasons,
which had been celebrated by the worshippers of pagan fertility-deities, and almost
makes time run back to the Creation and forward to the Apocalypse. The poem has a
cosmic scale that is lacking in most 'cavalier' lyrics. Milton is imitating Spenser's
technique in poems like *Epithalamion* and *Prothalamion*, with their multiple time-
shifts, elaborate numerological structures, and complex interplay of long and short
lines—techniques which were in turn indebted to the Italian 'canzone'. The
proportion and completeness of Milton's stanzas enacts not the good ordering of

[21] Cf. F. R. Leavis, *Revaluation: Tradition and Development in English Poetry* (London, 1936), 47–67.
On Milton's rationalism see Andrew Milner, *John Milton and the English Revolution: A Study in the
Sociology of Literature* (London, 1981), 94–137. See further John Creaser, 'Milton: The Truest of the
Sons of Ben', in Margo Swiss and David A. Kent (eds.), *Heirs of Fame: Milton and Writers of the English
Renaissance* (Lewisburg, Pa., 1995), 158–83.
[22] Irene Samuel, *Dante and Milton: The* Commedia *and* Paradise Lost (Ithaca, NY, 1966), 33; on Italian
influence generally see F. T. Prince, *The Italian Element in Milton's Verse* (Oxford, 1954). Copies of the
1568 edition of Dante, which Milton cited, were advertised by a London bookseller in 1633: Jackson
Campbell Boswell, *Dante's Fame in England: References in Printed Books 1477–1640* (Newark, Del., 1999),
197.
[23] Leah Sinanoglou Marcus, *The Politics of Mirth: Jonson, Herrick, Milton, Marvell, and the Defense of
Old Holiday Pastimes* (Chicago, 1986), 76–85, 140–68.

the existing state of society but a lost harmony which will be regained only with the apocalypse.

Milton introduces the idea of the apocalypse in the central stanza of his hymn, giving it great numerological importance. He does not predict its date; but there are signs in his early verse and prose that he was influenced by the apocalyptic enthusiasm that was gaining ground by the 1630s. A number of commentators were beginning to reconsider the idea, rejected by Bale and Foxe, that the millennium lay not in the past but the future, that Christ was going to reign for a thousand years in a renewed and transfigured world. John Stoughton prophesied 'a period of perfect harmony, both in the celestial and terrestrial worlds. The harmony of the heavenly spheres would be matched by aesthetic harmonies on the earth.' The land, he thought, would become more fruitful, mountains would regenerate precious stones in abundance, and paradise would be revealed again.[24] Joseph Mede, a Fellow of Milton's Cambridge college, was moving towards belief in a future millennium. Many Protestants who could not accept this idea were nevertheless coming to believe that a decisive defeat of Antichrist was at hand, and were encouraged to draw up ambitious programmes of educational, social and economic reform. Many reformers drew their inspiration from the writings of Francis Bacon, who had frequently used apocalyptic imagery in his writings. He believed that the fall of man had been accompanied by a fall of the imagination; the same corruption that had given rise to religious idolatry had led people to idolize erroneous mental images. The reformation of religion should therefore be accompanied by a destruction of mental idols, an apocalyptic purification of the mind, unveiling the previously hidden truths of nature. In his early writings Milton attacked the idea that Nature was declining, and called for the reformation of learning in essentially apocalyptic terms. He adapted the traditional imagery of the true and false churches—or perhaps of Book I of *The Faerie Queene*: Error could substitute its poisonous image for snow-white Truth and hence deceive even great philosophers, but the time was at hand when the disguise would be removed and Truth would be separated from its counterfeit (i.258–9).

Milton further believed that the renewal of truth would lead to a similar renewal of beauty. In a letter to his friend Charles Diodati in 1637 he wrote that he was searching for an 'idea of the beautiful . . . throughout all the shapes and forms of things' (i.326). The idea that the purification of religion would lead to the purification of poetry was implicit in the apocalyptic tradition. Bale and other writers had Protestantized the humanist attack on scholasticism, arguing that the authoritarianism of the Roman church led to the decay of learning and of poetry. George Hakewill, whose refutation of the idea of universal decay may have influenced Milton, cited Mantuan to the effect that monks and friars did not delight in verse and gave the examples of Sidney, Spenser, and Buchanan as part of his proof that a

---

[24] John Stoughton, *Felicitas ultima saeculi* (London, 1640), 272, as summarized by Charles Webster, *The Great Instauration: Science, Medicine and Reform 1626–1660* (London, 1975), 17; cf. Paul Christianson, *Reformers and Babylon: English Apocalyptic Visions from the Reformation to the Eve of the Civil War* (Toronto, 1978), 132 ff., and Katharine R. Firth, *The Apocalyptic Tradition in Reformation Britain, 1530–1645* (Oxford, 1979), 204 ff.

renewal of learning was in progress. His admirer (or plagiarist) John Jonston praised Spenser in a book which prophesied that the millennium might begin before the end of the century.[25] Such ideas were encouraging for a young prophetic poet. His verse could express in symbolic form the underlying apocalyptic implications of the reform of learning as a whole. Poets who had described the Golden Age had perhaps not been idly feigning, or looking back to the Garden of Eden, but prophesying a future millennium. The poet could not only exhort people to remember that judgement was at hand but also adumbrate the coming renewal of earth and heaven in the structure of his verse. Milton adopted a Protestantized version of the Renaissance theory that music and poetry had once been indissolubly allied, that the music of the ancients had unusual emotional power because each note was precisely adjusted in pitch and quantity to a corresponding syllable. The decline of learning in the Middle Ages had led to a neglect of words at the expense of sounds: in polyphonic church music the sacred texts were broken up and distorted. Champions of the new 'monodic' music saw themselves as overcoming this aural 'idolatry' and restoring the just relations between sound and sense. Even before his collaboration with the monodic composer Henry Lawes Milton was aiming in his poetry for a 'musicality' which was not empty mellifluousness but had precise artistic and ideological significance.[26]

But apocalyptic ideas were not viewed with enthusiasm at the Caroline court. At a time when the government was moving closer to Spain the strident identifications of the Pope with Antichrist in the Protestant tradition became somewhat embarrassing. Bacon had been careful to combine his apocalyptic rhetoric with frequent panegyrics of learned monarchs, and some of his works were published with official approval in Charles's reign. But millennialist writers considered it prudent to withhold publication. Belief in a future millennium had been associated in the previous century with popular radicalism. The theorists of the 1630s were certainly not advocating egalitarianism, but their ideas were suspect because they implied the need for Britain to take part in the general European crusade against Antichrist. The leadership of the Protestant cause had passed to Gustavus Adolphus; Joseph Mede identified his military victories with the opening of the fourth vial (Revelation 16: 8), a decisive step towards the defeat of Antichrist. In one of his eclogues Francis Quarles presented the apocalyptic hopes that Gustavus Adolphus had aroused in England and the despair caused by his death in 1632—a despair frequently compared to the emotion caused by Prince Henry's death.[27] Knevett ended the eighth book of his supplement to *The Faerie Queene* with a lament at his hero's death. Charles discouraged excessive enthusiasm for Gustavus Adolphus, however; far from defending Protestant military

---

[25]   George Hakewill, *An Apologie or Declaration of the Power and Providence of God*, 2nd edn. (London, 1630), 252–4; John Jonston, *An History of the Constancy of Nature* (London, 1657), 97 ff. (Jonston's book was first published in Latin in 1634; see Webster, *The Great Instauration*, 20 n. 40).

[26]   On the background see John Hollander, *The Untuning of the Sky: Ideas of Music in English Poetry, 1500–1700* (Princeton, 1961), 174 ff.

[27]   Christianson, *Reformers and Babylon*, 124–30; *Francis Quarles: The Complete Works in Prose and Verse*, ed. Alexander B. Grosart, 3 vols. (Edinburgh, 1880–1), iii.230–2.

influence, he closely co-operated with the Spanish navy in their campaign against the Dutch. Laud discouraged the traditional links between British and Continental Protestants and expelled foreign Protestants who did not conform to the rites of the Church of England.[28] Many apocalyptic works remained unpublished in the 1630s; the result was an explosion of millenarian publication after the collapse of censorship in the 1640s.

Not all Milton's early poems, however, remained at the high prophetic level of the Nativity hymn. He experimented with ideas and poetic forms that would have been offensive to many Puritans. A taste for the worldly pleasures celebrated in 'L'Allegro', even down to attending Jonson's plays, was not unknown in the 1630s amongst some individuals who might be classed as Puritans.[29] But the question of Milton's relationship to the Caroline court, and to the legacy of Ben Jonson, was posed in a very direct form when he was invited to write a masque for the installation of the Earl of Bridgewater as Lord President of Wales in 1634. This was to be a major state occasion. Charles was strengthening the Council for the Marches in Wales in the face of a certain amount of local opposition, and the office of Lord President carried the full weight of royal approval for the new policies. Milton seems to have gained the commission for this masque because of his contacts with the Earl's family: he had already written an entertainment in honour of the Earl's mother-in-law, the Countess of Derby, who lived not far from Milton.[30] But the Ludlow commission raised far more ideological problems than the panegyric of the Countess, a venerable survivor from the Elizabethan era. The status of the court masque as symbol of anti-Puritan policies had recently been highlighted by William Prynne's *Histrio-Mastix*, a massive attack on the public theatre which did not spare aristocratic entertainments and contained what was held to be a glancing reference to Henrietta Maria's appearing in plays and masques. Women actors, in Prynne's view, were notorious whores.[31] He saw masques and revels as part of the general order of rituals and festivities which it was the duty of reformed Christianity to eradicate. Prynne's trial, in which he was accused of fomenting regicide, took place in the summer of 1634. He was punished with the loss of his ears. Milton's friend Alexander Gill had himself

---

[28] On the severing of contacts with the Continent see H. R. Trevor-Roper, *Archbishop Laud 1573–1645*, 2nd edn. (London, 1961), 197 ff.

[29] Quarles's patron Sir Thomas Barrington, though a leading Puritan politician, supported the staging of plays and May-games: Martin Butler, *Theatre and Crisis 1632–1642* (Cambridge, 1984), 92–3. For a critique of my own and other arguments for the young Milton's radicalism see Thomas Corns, 'Milton Before "Lycidas"', in Graham Parry and Joad Raymond (eds.), *Milton and the Terms of Liberty* (Cambridge, 2002), 23–36.

[30] In my first edition I followed Cedric C. Brown in dating *Arcades* to 1634, 'Milton's *Arcades*: Context, Form, and Function', *Renaissance Drama*, NS 8 (1977), 245–74 (255), but he has since revised the dating to 1632: Cedric C. Brown, *John Milton's Aristocratic Entertainments* (Cambridge, 1985), 47. My reading of *Comus* owed a great deal to Leah Marcus's work on Jonson, and for a reading very much complementary to this one see her *The Politics of Mirth*, ch. 6.

[31] William Prynne, *Histrio-Mastix* (London, 1633), index, s.v. 'Women-Actors'. On the ways in which Prynne's attacks helped to politicize court culture, see David Howarth, *Images of Rule: Art and Politics in the English Renaissance, 1485–1649* (Houndmills, 1997), 247 ff. In the year of *Comus* the Inns of Court staged a masque, Shirley's *The Triumph of Peace*, to apologize for Prynne's misconduct; see Martin Butler, 'Politics and the Masque: *The Triumph of Peace*', *Seventeenth Century*, 2 (1987), 117–41.

almost received this punishment in 1628 for circulating obscene libels against Buckingham; and in a recent attack on Gill Jonson had expressed the wish that he should be 'whipt, Cropt, branded, slit, neck-stockt': that he should receive a punishment as severe as that meted out to Prynne.[32] Milton would have hardly seen the issue as a simple quarrel between courtly civilization and Puritan philistinism.

The politics of masque-writing in 1634 was, however, further complicated by the fact that Jonson himself had fallen from favour and launched a bitter attack on masques. He had not composed any masques in the first few years of Charles's reign, perhaps because his relations with Buckingham were strained. In 1631 he had written two masques with Inigo Jones; but the architect was no longer used to collaborating with such a demanding partner, and they quickly quarrelled. Most masque texts were from now on provided by distinctly inferior poets; and in his 'Expostulation with Inigo Jones' Jonson attacked the empty show of masques which were nothing but painting and carpentry. In an entertainment commissioned by the Earl of Newcastle in 1634 he complained that '[r]ime will undoe you, and hinder your growth, and reputation in Court'. In 1632 a letter-writer expressed surprise on learning that Ben was still alive.[33] A Puritan treatise published after Charles's execution alleged that Jonson had been exiled from court and left to starve because of the king's ingratitude.[34] Significantly, his late plays show him moving towards the political rhetoric of the 'Spenserians'. He had not shared in the Spenserians' nostalgia for the Elizabethan age in James's reign, but now he began to imitate the Elizabethans closely. At a time when new fashions in courtly pastoral were being imported from France, he wrote a self-consciously English pastoral play, *The Sad Shepherd*, in which for the first time he adopted the Spenserian archaisms which he had earlier disdained. In *A Tale of a Tub*, a play set in Elizabethan times, the audience is reminded that John Heywood, the author of interludes in Henry VIII's reign, is still alive, and in its structure the play recalls archaic dramatic and festive forms.[35]

Jonson's alienation from the court, however, was personal rather than ideological in motivation. Many of Charles's most controversial policies consisted in trying to translate into reality the political visions which had been dramatized in Jonsonian masques. Charles responded eagerly to the idea of a Britain in which political dissension had been banished and traditional social forms took on an aesthetic grace and harmony. In *Pleasure Reconciled to Virtue* Jonson had endorsed James's policy of defending rural sports; Charles had the book reissued. In *The Sad Shepherd* Jonson renewed his defence of rural traditions against Puritan attack, and rural games were

---

[32] *Ben Jonson*, ed. C. H. Herford and Percy and Evelyn Simpson, 11 vols. (Oxford, 1925–52, hereafter *H&S*), viii.410–11 (ll. 15–16).

[33] Ibid. viii.402–6, i. 92.

[34] Anon., *The None-Such Charles his Character* (London, 1651), 170. I owe this reference to Joseph Taylor.

[35] Anne Barton, 'Harking Back to Elizabeth: Ben Jonson and Caroline Nostalgia', *ELH* 48 (1981), 706–31. Martin Butler, 'Late Jonson', in Gordon McMullan and Jonathan Hope (eds.), *The Politics of Tragicomedy: Shakespeare and After* (London, 1992), 166–88, sees the late plays as closer to Newcastle's absolutism than to the politics of the Spenserian poets; for a constitutionalist reading see Julie Sanders, *Jonson's Theatrical Republics* (Houndmills, 1998), 144–79.

commemorated in a royal entertainment of 1633.[36] Like James, Charles called on the nobility to return to the country and exercise their traditional duties of hospitality; court poets celebrated this theme in poems that echoed 'To Penshurst' and 'To Sir Robert Wroth'. Jonson's celebration of the peaceful Stuart forests received new relevance in 1634 when Charles announced substantial extensions of the traditional forest boundaries. James's policy of increasing ritualism in the Scottish church, celebrated in *Pleasure Reconciled to Virtue*, was followed through by Charles; Jonson wished him good fortune on his trip to Scotland in his 1633 entertainment. Where father and son differed was not so much in goals as in tactics: Charles had a stiffer sense of his royal dignity and was much less ready to compromise at the right moment, and his gestures of royal authority succeeded in arousing political alarm without gaining him loyalty. The tactlessness with which Charles handled Scottish problems was one of the major causes of the Civil War. Such a personality, shy, fastidious, always standing on ceremony, was likely to be ill at ease with someone as abrasive as Jonson.

Despite these personal differences, however, the masque form could be said to have embodied Jonson's world-view: his belief that transcendental religious truths had to be embodied in traditional rituals, that political ideals were dangerous unless identified with personal loyalties. The end of each masque united religious and political abstractions with the persons of the courtiers. Such a world-view did imply limits on the poet's political autonomy: with what authority could he lay claim to independence of established institutions? Jonson had, in a sense, backed himself into a corner, attacking all critics of the court as seditious malcontents when in favour and finding himself impotent when out of favour. Jonson's nostalgia for the Elizabethan age superficially resembled the disillusion of the ageing Michael Drayton, whose last collection of eclogues, *The Muses Elizium* (1630), evoked the glories of that age in its title and in its 'golden' style. But even though Drayton had patched up his old quarrel with Jonson, his reservations about the masque form were more radical than his rival's. The Stuart masque offered artificial aids to the imagination; it needed elaborate machinery and spectacle to achieve its idealizing effects. In *The Muses Elizium* Drayton drew a stark contrast between the 'golden world' of his own imagination, a world evoking the glories of Elizabethan poetry, and the current state of the England of his day, ironically named 'Felicia', which had sunk into 'sordid slavery' and neglected the Muses.[37] Partly because of his inhibitions about the individual

---

[36] 'The King's Entertainment at Welbeck', *H&S*, vii.791–803. Jonson aligned himself with William Cavendish's programme of enlisting festivals against Puritan melancholy in his late entertainments, and also touched on the theme of agrarian rebellion, probably in response to the 'Western Rising' (below, n. 56), in *The Sad Shepherd*: see Julie Sanders, 'Jonson, *The Sad Shepherd*, and the North Midlands', *Ben Jonson Journal*, 6 (1999), 49–68.

[37] Drayton, *Works*, iii.321–5, v.223; on *The Muses Elizium* as a critique of the masque see Sukanta Chaudhuri, *Renaissance Pastoral and its English Developments* (Oxford, 1989), 404–5, and cf. Jean F. Brink, *Michael Drayton Revisited* (Boston, 1990), 125–7. For a different view of the later Drayton, see Thomas Cogswell, '"The Path to Elizium Lately Discovered": Drayton and the Court', *Huntington Library Quarterly*, 54 (1991), 200–33: Cogswell argues that 'the Elizium into which he escaped was Charles I's Court during the Personal Rule' and stresses his patronage connections with the Earl of Dorset, by now a

imagination, Jonson's poetry never makes such a stark contrast between the inner world of the poetry and the public world. Milton's mingling of pastoral and masquing conventions in *Comus* indicates that he ultimately had more in common with Drayton than with Jonson. And yet his attitude to Jonson's masques would have been complex, for the older poet had consistently maintained more artistic integrity than the younger masque-writers and had ensured that poetic excellence was not completely sacrificed to visual spectacle. Nor did the Spenserian tradition imply a complete rejection of masques. Certainly the Spenserians, unlike Jonson, tended to see religious truth as potentially independent of institutional embodiment: Milton was working within this tradition in 'On the Morning of Christ's Nativity', where instead of celebrating a particular court as the site of transcendent ideals he used the imagery of court masques to describe the final descent to earth of religious absolutes at the millennium. But throughout the Stuart period there had been critics of the political content of court masques who nevertheless did not reject the form itself: they wanted a 'reformation' of the masque, not its abolition. *Comus* is the most thoroughgoing 'reformation' of all; Milton both pays tribute to Jonson's art and implicitly criticizes his politics.[38]

It seems something more than a coincidence that Milton should have chosen the name of Comus for the villain of his piece—a name which posterity has transferred to the whole masque. Jonson's masques of Comus, *Pleasure Reconciled to Virtue* and *For the Honour of Wales*, were not yet in print, but Milton's collaborator Henry Lawes had probably attended Jonson's recent royal entertainments, and would have been in a position to help him in research for the Ludlow masque; if Milton knew that Jonson had written a masque with Welsh associations he would have wanted to find out about it.[39] It cannot be proved that Jonson's Comus masques were a direct model, but the general strenuous didacticism of *Comus*, and the preponderance of text over spectacle, reflect Jonson's influence rather than current courtly fashions. On the other hand, the pastoralism of Milton's masque provided at least a superficial link with the queen's dramatic tastes, with what Prynne denounced as 'scurrilous amorous

---

pillar of the court (229). However, Richard C. McCoy, 'Old English Honour in an Evil Time: Aristocratic Principle in the 1620s', in R. Malcolm Smuts (ed.), *The Stuart Court and Europe: Essays in Politics and Political Culture* (Cambridge, 1996), 133–55 (152), notes that John Reynolds presented his anti-court polemics as coming from 'Elisium'; Michelle O'Callaghan, *The 'Shepheards Nation'* (Oxford, 2000), 207–8, notes that *The Battle of Agincourt* is a 'heterogeneous and unsettling volume'.

[38] I am particularly indebted to John Creaser, '"The Present Aid of this Occasion": The Setting of *Comus*', in David Lindley (ed.), *The Court Masque* (Manchester, 1984), 111–34; see also David Norbrook, 'The Reformation of the Masque', in the same volume, 94–110. On the politics of the Caroline masque see also Kevin Sharpe, *Criticism and Compliment: The Politics of Literature in the England of Charles I* (Cambridge, 1987); Butler, 'Politics and the Masque: *The Triumph of Peace*', 117–41; 'Politics and the Masque: *Salmacida spolia*', in Thomas Healy and Jonathan Sawday (eds.), *Literature and the English Civil War* (Cambridge, 1990), 59–74; 'Reform or Reverence? The Politics of the Caroline Masque', in J. R. Mulryne and Margaret Shewring (eds.), *Theatre and Government under the Early Stuarts* (Cambridge, 1993), 118–56. Sharpe stresses the political openness of Caroline court masques while Butler has become increasingly insistent on their ideological limits.

[39] W. McClung Evans, *Henry Lawes: Musician and Friend of Poets* (New York, 1941), 31–2, 77, 97–8.

Pastorals'.[40] In these courtly pastorals, expensive scenic effects designed by Inigo Jones performed the somewhat paradoxical task of transforming the Banqueting House into a scene of rural simplicity. For one nostalgic royalist after the Civil War, pastoral drama was a symbol of the vanished culture of the Caroline era: Sir Richard Fanshawe dedicated to the young Prince of Wales his translation of Guarini's *The Faithfull Shepherd* with the claim that it presented 'a *Lantskip* of these Kingdoms . . . as well in the former flourishing, as the present distractions thereof'.[41] Milton's choice of the theme of chastity also had fashionable associations. After Buckingham's assassination and the king's rapprochement with his queen, much had been made of the married chastity of the royal couple. The Puritan Lucy Hutchinson later praised the 'temperate and chast and serious' Charles for banishing sexual excess from the court.[42] One of Sir William Davenant's masques centred on a 'Temple of Chaste Love'. But Davenant himself was sceptical about the new cult of chaste Platonic love, which easily developed, in its literary expressions, either into a blandness that had been lacking in Jonson's more robust poems and masques or into a titillating eroticism. Chastity had a special relevance to the Bridgewater family: three years earlier the Earl of Castlehaven, who had married Bridgewater's sister, had been beheaded for a series of brutal and exotic sexual crimes. Sir Henry Wotton had singled out Charles's punishment of Castlehaven as an example of the just morality he was imposing on the nation.[43] It is difficult to decide, however, whether this scandal would have made it more or less tactful for Milton to have chosen the theme of chastity. Perhaps more immediately to the point is that the leading role was to go to Lady Alice Egerton, a girl of 15; neither her sex nor her age would have made the choice of a more active central virtue appropriate. But this explanation, too, is not quite adequate: for Milton alters the conventional form of the masque to give his Lady an unusually prominent role. In his treatment of chastity he subtly revives

[40] Prynne, *Histrio-Mastix*, 253; John G. Demaray, *Milton and the Masque Tradition: The Early Poems, Arcades, and Comus* (Cambridge, Mass., 1968), notes the resemblances between *Comus* and other Caroline masques but fails to emphasize the differences.

[41] *A Critical Edition of Sir Richard Fanshawe's 1647 Translation of Giovanni Battista Guarini's Il Pastor Fido*, ed. William E. Simeone and Walter F. Staton, Jr. (Oxford, 1964), 5. On Caroline pastoral see John Harris, Stephen Orgel, and Roy Strong, *The King's Arcadia: Inigo Jones and the Stuart Court* (London, 1973).

[42] *Memoirs of the Life of Colonel Hutchinson*, ed. James Sutherland (London, 1973), 46. Cf. G. F. Sensabaugh, 'Platonic Love and the Puritan Rebellion', *Studies in Philology*, 37:3 (1940), 457–81, and 'Love Ethics in Platonic Court Drama 1625–1642', *Huntington Library Quarterly*, 1 (1937–8), 277–304. Barbara K. Lewalski, 'Milton's *Comus* and the Politics of Masquing', in David Bevington and Peter Holbrook (eds.), *The Politics of the Stuart Court Masque* (Cambridge, 1998), 296–320 (310), argues that the Lady's celebration of chastity at the height of her reply to Comus, which is not found in the Bridgewater manuscript, may have been added as a specific retort to Davenant's *The Temple of Love*, which had strong Catholic associations.

[43] Barbara Breasted, '*Comus* and the Castlehaven Scandal', *Milton Studies*, 3 (1971), 201–24; Sir Henry Wotton, *Reliquiae Wottonianae* (London, 1651), 150. Cynthia B. Herrup, *A House in Gross Disorder: Sex, Law and the 2nd Earl of Castlehaven* (New York, 1999), throws new light on this question by showing that this scandal was no mere family matter but had wide political ramifications, with those finding Castlehaven guilty of buggery including 'those most immediately dependent upon the King', while amongst those who retained doubts were several more independent figures, some of whom had opposed the forced loan (88).

some political and religious associations of that virtue which had been obscured by current fashions.

Only recently have critics recognized just how innovatory Milton was being in giving such a prominent role in a masque to a woman. Prynne's strictures against women actors were very topical in 1634. It was the Catholic queen who had encouraged play-acting by women, so that the topic was politically sensitive. The very act of giving a speaking part in a masque to any aristocrat was relatively new.[44] But Milton was not one to reject artistic innovations simply because of their unacceptable connotations; instead, he set himself to change those connotations, to make the innovation serve his own ideological purposes.[45] The parts which Henrietta Maria liked to play in court entertainments centred on concerns conventionally considered female, on love and intrigue. Lady Alice had taken part two years earlier in Aurelian Townshend's masque *Tempe Restor'd*, in which the queen and her ladies represented Beauty, while the king embodied the male principle of Heroic Virtue. Lady Alice was one of fourteen masquers representing Harmony; these ladies too were complimented for their beauty in the conventional language of love poetry. The masque arranged male and female virtues hierarchically; heroic virtue was ultimately superior because it appealed to the mind, whereas the queen embodied '*Corporeall Beauty*'. The masque presented this hierarchy of soul and body as smooth and harmonious, however: earthly magnificence became a living embodiment of the divine. At the end of the masque the evil enchantress Circe was so impressed by the splendour of the court that she abandoned her magic powers.[46]

Milton makes the relationship between virtue and physical appearance much more problematic, and challenges courtly notions of female virtue. In order to play her part effectively, Lady Alice would have had to develop qualities going far beyond the conventional aristocratic grace and deportment. She does not simply cling passively to her chastity, she justifies her position by appeal to a whole political philosophy—thus disconcerting Comus, who does not believe it to be a woman's role to think. The 'cavalier' poets had very clear and simple ideas about what women were for. But woman's conventional subordinate role was beginning to be challenged. A series of pamphlets in the second decade of the century had affirmed woman's dignity, defending Eve against the charges levelled at her by male theologians.[47] Before

---

[44]   These points are emphasized by Creaser, '"The Present Aid of this Occasion"', 117. On the feminist aspects of Caroline courtly entertainments see Erica Veevers, *Images of Love and Religion: Queen Henrietta Maria and Court Entertainments* (Cambridge, 1989).

[45]   Jennifer Chibnall, '"To That Secure Fix'd State": The Function of the Caroline Masque Form', in Lindley (ed.), *The Court Masque*, 78–93, challenges simplified notions of the 'decadence' of Caroline masques, showing their artistic inventiveness.

[46]   *The Poems and Masques of Aurelian Townshend*, ed. Cedric C. Brown (Reading, 1983), 93–108; Brown demonstrates in his edition the close links between Townshend and the Bridgewater family (54–6). Sears Jayne, 'The Subject of Milton's Ludlow *Mask*', in John S. Diekhoff (ed.), *A Maske at Ludlow: Essays on Milton's Comus* (Cleveland, 1968), 165–87, speculates on ways in which Milton may have tried to Platonize Townshend's masque, and demonstrates the Neoplatonic associations of chastity; he does not, however, consider the more directly political aspects of the masque.

[47]   See, for example, Rachel Speght, *A Mouzell for Melastomus* (London, 1617), in *The Poems and Polemics of Rachel Speght*, ed. Barbara K. Lewalski (New York, 1996), 43–90. Spenser was invoked by such

long, Puritan women in London were to be claiming a right to play a greater part in public affairs. The critical and rationalistic premisses of Milton's own thought undermined many conventional justifications for the subordination of women. This very fact may have contributed to his later defensiveness on the subject of man's superiority. At the time of writing *Comus*, however, he may have been less defensive. Woman's equality and, indeed, superiority to men had already been proclaimed in a masque performed in 1618, at the height of the Jacobean controversy over women. Six female masquers, representing chastity and other female virtues, had been urged to

> know your Strength & your own Vertues see
> which in everie Several grace
> of the mind, or of the face,
> Gives women right to have Prioritie.
> Brave Amazonian Dames
> Made no count of Mankind but
> for a fitt to be at the Rutt.
> free fier gives the brightest flames;
> Menns overawing tames
> And Pedantlike our active Spirits smother.
> Learne, Virgins, to live free;
> Alas, would it might bee,
> weomen could live & lie with one another![48]

The end of the masque did not endorse this radical separatist position but did emphasize that men and women were equal.

The tone of this masque at Cole-Orton was playful, but there may have been a certain seriousness in the play. For the six male virtues were drawn from characters in *The Faerie Queene*, and the poet may have been responding to Spenser's questioning of conventional roles. Milton too may have been encouraged to rethink the conventional imagery of sexual relations by Spenser, whom he later described as 'sage and serious' (ii.516)—the adjectives with which the Lady praises virginity. Spenser's

---

defenders of women as 'T.G.', *An Apologie for Woman-Kind* (London, 1605), sig. A4ʳ, and Daniel Tuvil, *Asylum Veneris* (London, 1616), 136–7.

[48] This Cole-Orton masque, sponsored by Sir Thomas Beaumont, not the Earl of Essex as suggested in my first edition, is printed by R. Brotanek, *Die Englischen Maskenspiele* (Vienna, 1902), 328–37. I proposed Thomas Pestell and Arthur Wilson as possible authors in 'The Reformation of the Masque', 109. Philip J. Finkelpearl, *Court and Country Politics in the Plays of Beaumont and Fletcher* (Princeton, 1990), 38 n., proposed John Fletcher as author and the suggestion is taken seriously by Gordon McMullan, *The Politics of Unease in the Plays of John Fletcher* (Amherst, Mass., 1984), 32–3, who notes that the text alludes to Francis Beaumont's masque for Princess Elizabeth, and suggests that the 'emphasis on the unexpected power of women no doubt harks back to the reign of Queen Elizabeth'. Finkelpearl has subsequently settled on Thomas Pestell as author: 'The Authorship of the Anonymous Coleorton Masque of 1618', *Notes and Queries*, 238 (1993), 224–6; in 'The Fairies' Farewell: *The Masque at Coleorton* (1618)', *Review of English Studies*, NS 46 (1995), 333–51, Finkelpearl links the masque's feminism with the cult of praise of the Countess of Huntingdon, in which John Donne had participated. Whatever the authorship, the masque is of interest in pointing to a 'Spenserian' masquing tradition within circles which retained a certain distance from the Jacobean court.

treatment of chastity had been influenced by the strong hostility to the old Catholic scheme of virtues in Protestant polemic. The chastity of monks and nuns was 'fugitive and cloister'd' (ii.515), and the artificial conditions under which it was maintained in the cloister led to hypocrisy and immorality. Bale had thundered against the falsity of the Roman cult of chastity. A century later Marvell was making similar points, rather more urbanely, in 'Upon Appleton House', where he contrasted the narrow-minded self-absorption of the nuns with Fairfax's active virtue and young Maria's learning. In *The Faerie Queene* Spenser had challenged convention by making his chief representative of Chastity an active, 'Amazonian Dame', Britomart. In *Comus* the Lady has to display her resourcefulness in unfamiliar and threatening surroundings. The Elder Brother's long speech in praise of chastity and beauty is fairly conventional in sentiment, and might almost have come from a Caroline court masque; what is extremely unusual is that his confidence in the magical power of these virtues proves to be exaggerated. The Lady's beauty and noble lineage do not make her miraculously immune. But she is given an opportunity to display her integrity and powers of argument. It could perhaps be argued that Milton is merely introducing a new set of stereotypes for ideal female behaviour; nevertheless, his rejection of courtly stereotypes is striking.

The Spenserian echoes in *Comus* are not confined to Book III. Comus in his palace with his enchanted cup is a male equivalent of Acrasia in the Bower of Bliss, and the opposition in Milton's imagery between the clear water of truth and the viscous liquid of intemperance probably owes something to Spenser's second book. Spenser's Acrasia is linked with Duessa, the wicked enchantress and antitype to the religious purity of Una. In a long tradition of apocalyptic literature, the temptations of idolatry had been represented as an enchanted cup; idolatry was defined as spiritual fornication, so that true faith became identified with chastity. In the Stuart period poets critical of the court had often drawn their imagery from Spenser's first three books. Under James the unchastity of the court had become notorious, providing a glaring contrast with the Virgin Queen who had been celebrated in a Petrarchan cult of Chastity. In his Spenserian satire *The Cuckow* Richard Niccols had shown the virgin Casta expelled first from the Bower of Bliss (James's court?) and then from Troynobantum (London?) and finally seeking refuge in Virgina (Virginia—a colony whose name recalled the Virgin Queen).[49] Other satirists drew on the imagery of Spenser's first book to signify their dislike of James's pacific foreign policy. William Browne had described the exile from court of the beautiful Aletheia in apocalyptic terms. The satirist John Day—an enemy of Jonson's—combined apocalyptic symbolism with 'faerie' legend in a satire written in the latter part of James's reign, describing how Error seduces Philosophos and his page Alethe with an enchanted cup and proceeds to entertain her captives with masques and antimasques. Time and Truth, Day implied, could not be found at court: lost time must be recovered

---

[49] Hoyt H. Hudson, 'John Hepwith's Spenserian Satire upon Buckingham: With Some Jacobean Analogues', *Huntington Library Bulletin*, 6 (1934), 39–71 (62–5).

elsewhere, with the aid of Industry.[50] By the 1630s, however, apocalyptic ideas were viewed with more suspicion than ever at court. It is significant that the most overt revival of Spenserian symbolism in court entertainments of the 1630s came in 1636, when Princess Elizabeth's sons were on a visit to England and some courtiers hoped that the king would now declare war on Spain; a character named Britomartis appeared in an entertainment debating the issue of war.[51] In the previous reign Middleton had glorified apocalyptic Truth in a pageant for Sir Thomas Myddleton, a great sponsor of Protestant propaganda and Puritan lectureships in Wales; now the lectureships were being suppressed as seditious. Milton probably knew Middleton's apocalyptic satire *A Game at Chess*. In the opening scene a Catholic priest uses love-language similar to Comus's to try to tempt the chaste and Protestant White Queen's Pawn; his phrase 'the opening eyelids of the morn' reappears, with very different connotations, in *Lycidas*.[52]

---

[50] John Day, *Peregrinatio scholastica*, *Works*, ed. A. H. Bullen, 2 vols. (London, 1881), i. On the date see M. E. Borish, 'A Second Version of John Day's *Peregrinatio scholastica*', *Modern Language Notes*, 55 (1940), 35–9. One manuscript of this work—which was too politically sensitive to be published—was dedicated to William Austin, a great admirer of Spenser and a defender of women: see his *Haec homo* (London, 1637). Jonson linked Day and Middleton together as 'base fellows' (*H&S*, i.137); both had close connections with London Puritans. In the first edition I referred to marginalia in a copy of Browne's *Britannia's Pastorals* as being Milton's, but the attribution is rejected by John T. Shawcross, entry in William B. Hunter et al. (eds.), *A Milton Encyclopaedia*, 9 vols. (Lewisburg, Pa., 1978–83), v.74.

[51] *The King and Queenes Entertainment at Richmond* (Oxford, 1636); ed. W. Bang and R. Brotanek, *Materialen zur Kunde des älteren englischen Dramas*, ii (Louvain, 1903), and see Martin Butler, 'Entertaining the Palatine Prince: Plays on Foreign Affairs 1635–1637', *English Literary Renaissance*, 13 (1983), 319–44; on Charles's apparent move towards a more militant policy about this time see R. M. Smuts, 'The Puritan Followers of Henrietta Maria in the 1630s', *English Historical Review*, 93 (1978), 26–45.

[52] On Middleton's debt to 16th-century apocalyptic drama see Jane Sherman, 'The Pawns' Allegory in Middleton's *A Game at Chess*', *Review of English Studies*, NS 29 (1978), 147–59; on Milton and apocalyptic drama see Alice-Lyle Scoufos, 'The Mysteries in Milton's *Masque*', *Milton Studies*, 6 (1974), 113–42. Further evidence could be given that Milton's audience would have been aware of differing ideological traditions in masque and drama, with specific connections to Jonson and Middleton, against Stanley Fish's dismissal of this idea, 'Milton's Career and the Career of Theory', in *There's No Such Thing as Free Speech and it's a Good Thing Too* (New York, 1994), 257–72 (261); Fish argues that Middleton's phrase was 'no doubt shared by innumerable other poets'. My 'probably' was based on a trawl of concordances then available; it is if anything strengthened by the subsequent availability of the Chadwyck-Healy *Literature Online* database, which gives the two passages in question as the only ones in the whole massive database with 'opening eyelids of the morn', other than later allusions to *Lycidas*. Work in progress by James Knowles indicates that Milton's patrons are just as likely to have been familiar with *A Game at Chess*, for the Earl of Bridgewater was a keen collector of polemical anti-Catholic writings and a manuscript of the play was in his library. This manuscript is partly authorial and partly in the hand of Ralph Crane, who had a special connection with the earl and dedicated manuscripts to him annually. The only surviving manuscript of Jonson's *Pleasure Reconciled to Virtue* is in Crane's hand. The earl's library also testified to his knowledge of the Edwardian prophetic tradition—it contained one of the most important 16th-century apocalyptic dramas, Kirchmayer's *Pammachius*, which John Bale translated. See F. P. Wilson, 'Ralph Crane, Scrivener to the King's Men', *Library*, 4th series, 7 (1926–7), 194–215 (194–20), and Scoufos, 'The Mysteries in Milton's *Masque*', 138 n. 13. There was even a local patronage connection: Sir Thomas Myddleton's son staged a masque for the earl at Chirk Castle shortly before *Comus* was performed (though the text, probably by Sir Thomas Salusbury, was certainly not Puritanical): see Cedric C. Brown, 'The Chirk Castle Entertainment of 1634', *Milton Quarterly*, 16.3 (1977), 77–86.

Comus was performed on St Michael's Day, so that apocalyptic associations would have been appropriate; the phrase 'the sun-clad power of chastity' (l. 781), added in the 1637 edition, made such echoes slightly more explicit. The scene in which the Lady wanders in a dark and threatening forest recalls the Wood of Error at the start of *The Faerie Queene*. It is also reminiscent of a more famous dark forest, in the *Inferno*; it is interesting that when Milton was later charged by an opponent with loose living he declared that his reading in Dante and Petrarch had made him love chastity. These poets also, of course, provided authority for attacks on the Papacy. The foremost opponent of the apocalyptic tradition at the Stuart court had been Ben Jonson, and while it cannot be proved that Milton knew Jonson's masque of Comus, his handling of similar imagery seems to be pointedly different. One of Jonson's aims in *Pleasure Reconciled to Virtue* had been to defend royal ecclesiastical policy against Puritan as well as Catholic attacks, at a time when the new rituals the king was trying to introduce in Scotland were being denounced as idolatrous. Jonson had made his Comus, the representative of riotous and disorderly festivity—and hence, in part, of idolatry—a relatively unformidable adversary. Hercules banished him and took back from him the cup he had 'abused'— on one allegorical level, a claim that elaborate ritual was a mere 'thing indifferent', idolatrous when abused but not intrinsically evil. Puritans feared that this argument, even if valid on a very general level, might be used to permit specific idolatrous practices to return to the church.

Milton's Comus is a much more dangerous figure than Jonson's. The reference to 'misused wine' (l. 47) may function as an allegorical reminder of the distinction between a tradition and its abuses, hence as a qualification of iconoclastic zeal; but the action of the masque emphasizes the formidable power of Comus the maker of false images, the immense danger of complacency in the face of idolatry. Comus' glass is broken but he is still on the loose at the end of the masque. If Milton did imitate Jonson's masque, he also implicitly criticized it. And in more general terms, his evocation of the apocalyptic tradition was a subtle reminder of the differences between the current cult of courtly chastity, sponsored by a Catholic queen, and older traditions. The closest he comes to a topical allusion is the Lady's indignant response to

> the sound
> Of riot, and ill-managed merriment,
> Such as the jocund flute, or gamesome pipe
> Stirs up among the loose unlettered hinds,
> When for their teeming flocks, and granges full,
> In wanton dance they praise the bounteous Pan,
> And thank the gods amiss. (ll. 170–6)

This opposition between literacy and traditional cultural forms is a characteristic Puritan emphasis. It is a distinctly odd sentiment to come from an aristocratic character in a masque, where it was more usual to find praise of the ruler in pastoral terms, as in Jonson's *Pan's Anniversary* (1620):

> *PAN* is our All, by him we breath, wee live,
> Wee move, we are.[53]

Jonson may have agreed with Newcastle that 'hinds' ought to be 'unlettered'. But the Lady's anxieties reflect the concern amongst Welsh Puritans that the Laudian regime was defending idolatrous sports at the same time as it was placing restrictions on the preaching of the Word.

Milton does not, however, reject dancing altogether. The rustics' sports turn out to be innocent; what the Lady has heard is the far more sinister sound of Comus' entourage. At the end of the masque there is dancing both by countrymen and by the Bridgewater children. But Milton, more than Jonson, and still more than current Caroline masque-writers, places the emphasis on moral struggle rather than courtly resolution. Only after Comus' rout and the Lady's release do the virtuous characters return to court; the dancing is a supplement to the main action rather than being, as in many masques, the central agent and instrument of virtue. *Comus* has often been accused of being undramatic. One answer to this charge is that masque conventions demanded the juxtaposition of moral absolutes rather than psychological realism. But most masques used spectacle to give dramatic force to the conflicts; in *Comus*, however, spectacle plays a less central part. Certainly there was scenery, and, within the limits imposed by the setting, it was probably fairly elaborate. What was original was the use Milton made of scenery. The setting for Comus' enchanted palace would have shown 'all manner of deliciousness'; but Comus, like Spenser's Archimago, is a creator of false images. He compares himself to Apollo, whose song made Daphne '[r]oot-bound' (l. 661)—organic imagery is less positive in Milton than in Jonson. The Lady must resist by an act of moral iconoclasm, refusing to be impressed by the 'magic structures' of his art. Precisely the same demand is made of the spectator. But the Lady is not even granted the power accorded to Spenser's Guyon of destroying this Bower of Bliss. Like many of Milton's Christian heroes, she is placed in a situation which is primarily one of passive resistance, a situation which is so far from conforming to standard notions of the heroic that it verges on the absurd. Immobilized in her chair, she is in a state almost as grotesque as Kent in the stocks in *King Lear*, a play that was on Milton's mind when he composed *Comus*. She can display neither the feats of strength granted to the men in conventional masques nor the courtly graces of the women.

What the Lady does have is the power of argument. She replies to Comus' speech of seduction with an indignant refutation of his arguments, attacking not only his immediate conclusions but his basic premises, his assumption that luxury and conspicuous consumption are natural. A more equitable distribution of wealth would bring society much closer to the order of nature than the traditional hierarchies. The Lady draws attention to the power of her language: she had not intended 'to have unlocked my lips' (l. 755) but her tongue must check Comus' pride. In a passage added in revision, Milton further developed the idea of the power of speech: if she really unfolded the whole mystery of virginity,

---

[53] *H&S*, vii.535, ll. 192–3.

                                    the uncontrolled worth
                    Of this pure cause would kindle my rapt spirits
                    To such a flame of sacred vehemence,
                    That dumb things would be moved to sympathize,
                    And the brute Earth would lend her nerves, and shake,
                    Till all thy magic structures reared so high,
                    Were shattered into heaps o'er thy false head. (ll. 792–8)

The word 'unfold' hints at an apocalyptic unveiling, at a destructive force which the Lady is only just able to keep in check. But she does keep it in check, for reasons which remain, on a naturalistic level, slightly unclear. Comus continues to try to make her drink; only the brothers' arrival interrupts him, and they fail to capture him. Milton undermines the confidence in human self-sufficiency normally displayed in masques: *Pleasure Reconciled to Virtue* ended with praise of virtue as a perfect quality which refines herself 'by hir owne light' (l. 341), *Comus* with an acknowledgement that virtue may be 'feeble' (l. 1021) without divine aid.

Milton's presentation of the Lady's dilemma combines intense conviction about the power of language with a sense of absurdity and impotence. Here he was revealing his own view of his situation as a prophetic poet. A self-consciously youthful writer who had taken a vow of chastity, he was aware that he would seem ridiculous in the eyes of the world. By the solitary pursuit of learning, he had recently written, 'a man cutts himselfe off from all action & becomes the most helplesse, pusilanimous & unweapon'd creature in the [world], the most unfit & unable to doe that wch all mortals most aspire to[,] either to defend & be usefull to his freinds, or to offend his enimies' (i.319). His learning almost unmanned him.[54] But he was convinced that when he did eventually publish a major work it would have a powerful effect. The commission to write the Ludlow masque gave him an opportunity to put his learning to good use, but it also involved difficult compromises. For the first major public display of his skill he had to make his mark in a form that Puritans like Prynne regarded as inherently idolatrous: for Prynne theatres and masquing-halls were little different from temples to heathen idols. Milton was well aware that the true situation was more complex: Jonson had been able to make masques into moral statements. But he had had to pay a price: he often gained least recognition from the courtiers for his most serious efforts. *Pleasure Reconciled to Virtue*, arguably his most didactic masque, had not been well received. The problem of political compromise was of course an old one: in the *Utopia* Hythlodaeus had argued that serious philosophy—by which, in this context, he meant social criticism—would never be welcome at court. More's persona had replied by comparing an austere humanist who tried to lecture princes to a figure in tragic attire interrupting a court comedy and quoting from a play which prophesied the destruction of the old unjust order and prayed for a better one. More declared that such a course would be too indecorous. But this was effectively what

[54] John T. Shawcross, 'Milton and Diodati: An Essay in Psychodynamic Meaning', *Milton Studies*, 7 (1975), 127–63, uses such statements to argue that the young Milton (the 'Lady of Christ's') had passive homosexual tendencies. Milton's sense of 'weaponlessness' may, however, have been conditioned by political more than 'psychodynamic' factors.

Milton did in *Comus*, though he skilfully kept just within the bounds of decorum. More the writer, of course, had been less timid than his persona, had given voice to Hythlodaeus as well as to counsels of moderation. Milton greatly admired More and other utopian writers like Bacon who could imagine 'better and exacter things, then were yet known, or us'd'; but he believed that conservative Laudian bishops were unable to appreciate 'the largenesse of their spirits' (i.881). At least one Caroline churchman and poet, John Donne, did in fact admire the *Utopia* and found it highly relevant to the current situation. Beside the passage where Hythlodaeus denounced monopolies and the application of political pressure to judges he wrote 'ship-monie' on his copy; where Hythlodaeus complained that the king was allowed to do all he wanted, Donne wrote 'criers up of yᵉ Kings prerogative'. But Milton would have thought that the conduct of this pillar of the Caroline church, preaching in praise of monarchy and obedience in public while he scribbled his private doubts in the margins of his books, itself exemplified the intellectually narrowing consequences of authoritarianism.[55] In *Comus* he showed that he had the courage of his convictions.

The Lady's speech, in fact, came close to shattering the very basis of the masque form: whatever its intellectual pretensions, the masque was ultimately an exercise in the very kind of conspicuous consumption she denounced. Austere criticisms were normally voiced in court entertainments only by mean-minded Puritans who failed to understand the value of magnificence. The Lady was touching on issues that were currently sensitive: in the late 1620s and early 1630s there had been extensive agrarian disturbances in south-west England in protest against illegal enclosures. A Puritan in the Forest of Dean was arrested in 1631 for inciting rebellion by preaching universal equality.[56] The government took measures against illegal enclosures and the disturbances died down; the anxieties they had raised, however, were still reflected in Davenant's masque *Britannia triumphans* (1638): Jones's designs included the figure of Jack Kett, leader of the 1549 uprising, amongst other rebels. The Lady's speech is studiedly vague and could be interpreted as compatible with aristocratic rule: she urges that 'every just man' should be given his due, which might imply distribution by geometrical rather than arithmetical proportion. She is, after

---

[55] John B. Gleason, 'Dr Donne in the Courts of Kings: A Glimpse from Marginalia', *Journal of English and Germanic Philology*, 69 (1970), 599–612 (601–2). New editions of Robinson's translation of the *Utopia* were in fact published in 1624 and 1639. The publisher, with no sense of irony, dedicated the translation to one of More's descendants, praising him for his birth and the magnificence of his estate.

[56] Eric Kerridge, 'The Revolts in Wiltshire against Charles I', *Wiltshire Archaeological and Natural History Magazine*, 57 (1958–60), 64–75; Christopher Hill, *Change and Continuity in Seventeenth-Century England* (London, 1974), 18. The lecturer in question, Peter Simon, indignantly rejected the charge of seditious speech and was released. He did admit to having preached that all were equal 'setting the Kings place and qualitie aside'. Whatever his intentions, it is possible that his parishioners missed his qualifications; the authorities were certainly jumpy about the 'western rising' of 1626–32 which spread through several parts of the midlands and west of England: Buchanan Sharp, *In Contempt of All Authority: Rural Artisans and Riot in the West of England, 1586–1660* (Berkeley and Los Angeles, 1980), 132–3 and *passim*; *Calendar of State Papers, Domestic Series, 1631–33*, 36. Like his precursor, Simon was a committed Puritan pitted against a strongly royalist 'dark corner of the land'; he became a strong supporter of Parliament during the Civil War: Ian Archer, *The History of the Haberdashers' Company* (Chichester, 1991), 80.

all, a noblewoman, and one must assume that the earl's payment of Milton for the masque did not constitute wasteful extravagance. But her insistence on government by rational principles rather than reverence for traditional aristocratic values is more in the spirit of the *Utopia* than of current court literature.

The Lady's discourse is potentially anti-hierarchical in yet another way: a woman lectures a man on how society should be governed. Denied participation in conventional forms of public discourse, some women sought an outlet in prophetic utterance. Prophecies against Laud were circulating widely in the 1630s, but for a woman to claim prophetic inspiration was regarded as doubly subversive. One such prophetess, however, would have been very much on the Bridgewater family's mind. Lady Eleanor Davies had acquired a reputation for accurate prophecy after she foretold the doom of Buckingham. Though not radical in her social views, she was fiercely anti-Laudian, and in 1633, denied an outlet for her views in print by the censorship, she went to the Netherlands and had some of her writings printed there. A poem about Belshazzar's feast described the inevitable doom that awaited this evil monarch who held drunken feasts in a 'Banqueting-house' and encouraged idolatrous Sabbath revels.[57] The parallels with Caroline masques were obvious enough and were to be gleefully pointed out by Lady Eleanor when she reprinted this poem after the king had been executed outside the Whitehall Banqueting House. When she returned from the Netherlands she was quickly arrested for circulating such propaganda, and she brought further punishment on herself by prophesying that Laud would die before the year was out. Despite such inflammatory utterances, however, she had friends amongst the great and famous; Elizabeth of Bohemia herself, who was sympathetic to the apocalyptic world-view, had pleaded her cause. Elizabeth pointed out that she was after all of noble blood. She was in fact the sister of the notorious Earl of Castlehaven, whose cause she vehemently championed in her writings. Unchastity was not the only charge that had recently been levelled against Bridgewater's relatives by marriage: there was also the offence of subversive prophecy. Lady Eleanor was still in prison when *Comus* was performed. Milton's Lady makes no explicitly feminist points—she speaks only of every just *man*—and her prophetic speech is no more a direct allusion to Lady Eleanor than the chastity theme is a direct reference to Castlehaven. The fact remains that a writer anxious to pay anodyne compliments would have steered clear of all such topics; Milton highlighted points of political, social, and religious tension. The Lady's speech with its iconoclastic philosophy threatens to disrupt the courtly framework. Milton's only other dramatic work was to be a consciously anti-theatrical tragedy, *Samson Agonistes*,

---

[57] Lady Eleanor Audeley (she also used the names of Douglas and Davies), *Strange and Wonderfull Prophesies* (London, 1649), 3: this volume reprints a poem first printed in Amsterdam in 1633. On women and prophecy see Keith Thomas, *Religion and the Decline of Magic: Studies in Popular Beliefs in Sixteenth- and Seventeenth-Century England*, rev. edn. (Harmondsworth, 1973), 162–4. The burgeoning literature on women prophets includes Phyllis Mack, *Visionary Women: Ecstatic Prophecy in Seventeenth-Century England* (Berkeley and Los Angeles, 1992) and Hilary Hinds, *God's Englishwomen: Seventeenth-Century Radical Sectarian Writing and Feminist Criticism* (Manchester, 1996); on Lady Eleanor see Esther S. Cope, *Handmaid of the Holy Spirit: Dame Eleanor Davies, Never soe Mad a Ladie* (Ann Arbor, 1992).

which allegorically denounced the idolatry and aestheticized politics of the Restoration and ended with the hero's bringing down a 'theatre' on the spectators' heads.[58]

Some critics have found the Lady's iconoclastic discourse flat and poetically uninteresting and have complained that Milton gives the better poetry to Comus. The seduction speeches are certainly given great power, putting the audience as well as the Lady to the test: Milton does not deny that poetry is capable of making evil seem beautiful. Closer reading of Comus' speeches, however, reveals the care with which Milton indicates the limitations of his ideology. There is no crude antithesis between art and bald moralization.[59] Milton was to praise Spenser as 'a better teacher than *Scotus* or *Aquinas*' (ii.516), and the context in *Areopagitica* makes it clear that one thing he valued in Spenser was his ability to try out new ideas, to step outside conventional intellectual frameworks. Philosophers like More and Bacon, who destroyed conventional idols and encouraged intellectual progress, had more in common with poets than with conservative scholastics. The second brother praises 'divine philosophy' because it is

> Not harsh, and crabbed as dull fools suppose,
> But musical as is Apollo's lute,
> And a perpetual feast of nectared sweets,
> Where no crude surfeit reigns. (ll. 475–9)

The Lady's prophetic voice is so powerful because it is informed by this musical quality. Her song moves even Comus: the 'sweet madness' of his mother's Bacchanalian music lulled the senses and the pleasure it gave was deceptive. The Lady's song does not give less pleasure but merely a different and more permanent kind, a 'sober certainty of waking bliss' (l. 262). It gives 'resounding grace to all heaven's harmonies' (l. 242): the pun which fuses divine grace with the sophisticated art of the grace-note is characteristic.[60] On this elevated plane, pleasure and virtue can be reconciled.

But Milton's masque constantly returns to the idea that the power relations of the fallen world can distort artistic pleasure, that the arts can be turned to politically dubious ends. Throughout *Comus*, music and poetry are seen as essentially independent of the court, and more closely allied with natural forces. Already in *Arcades* Milton had almost overshadowed the courtly compliment by a long speech in which the Genius of the Wood described his kinship with the harmony of nature. In *Comus* music becomes a symbol of transcendence rather than courtly splendour. But Milton's view of the relationship between art and politics is extremely complex. The Spirit's pastoral disguise links him with current Caroline masque conventions, and indeed Lawes participated in court entertainments. He was also involved with music in the royal chapel. In the Civil War he was to side with the king. At moments *Comus* verges on becoming the first English opera, an art form which had emerged at Italian

---

[58] Nicholas Jose, *Ideas of the Restoration in English Literature 1660–71* (London, 1984), ch. 8.
[59] Burnett, *Milton's Style*, 41 ff.   [60] Hollander, *The Untuning of the Sky*, 323.

courts and depended on extravagant princely subsidy.[61] But Milton, in his younger days at least, did not reject artistic innovations simply because their patronage might be suspect. It was more constructive to look for the deeper potential of these innovations, to find in them an ideological significance that their originators might not themselves have recognized.

In a poem addressed to Lawes, Edmund Waller compared medieval music to ornate stained glass: the musical elaboration obscured the sense. Lawes's music, which respected the meaning of the words, was thus iconoclastic, stripping away ritual embellishment.[62] Puritans had long valued music as more spiritual, less immediately sensual than the visual arts, and they especially valued the ability to harmonize sound with sense. As has been seen, in Milton's early poetry the reform of music had taken on apocalyptic associations. Even after he and Lawes had parted company politically, Milton was still prepared to address to him a sonnet of warm praise for his music. The concluding allusion to Dante in this sonnet very subtly plays his sense of ideological difference from his old friend against a poignant awareness of their common artistic interests. Cromwell was personally fond of music, and Lawes was to provide some music in 1656 for an entertainment by Davenant which opened the way to opera performances. As a young man he had not been associated with violently anti-Puritan circles: he had gained his position at court through the patronage of the third Earl of Pembroke, a defender of the low-church tradition and supporter of Spenserian poets; he had set to music poems by Pembroke himself, his political ally Rudyerd, and William Browne.[63] He was also renowned for settings of the Psalms. One critic has argued that the 'haemony' which grows 'in another country', obtained from a 'leathern scrip' (ll. 625 ff.), represents the Word of God: as mediator between the actors in the masque and the divine truth, Thyrsis becomes a Protestant shepherd, in the tradition of prophetic literature rather than Italianate court pastoral.[64] His skill as a pioneer counts for more than his associations with a conservative environment: this musician who 'first taught our English music' the right procedure is a worthy partner for the young Puritan poet ambitious to achieve

> What never yet was heard in tale or song
> From old, or modern bard in hall, or bower. (ll. 44–5)

It was conventional for the devisers of masques to insert some kind of compliment to their own poetic, musical, or scenic skills. But if the 'magic' that effected the masque's resolution was in an immediate sense the creation of the court artists, it was ultimately a manifestation of the power of the royal patron, and this would be made

[61] For an interesting discussion of the social basis of opera see H. G. Koenigsberger, 'Republics and Courts in Italian and European Culture in the Sixteenth and Seventeenth Centuries', *Past and Present*, 83 (1979), 32–56.

[62] *The Poems of Edmund Waller*, ed. G. Thorn Drury, 2 vols. (London, 1905), i.20. For an extensive discussion see Percy A. Scholes, *The Puritans and Music in England and New England* (Oxford, 1934).

[63] Evans, *Henry Lawes*, 32, 37, 41; for more on Milton, Lawes, and Waller, see Norbrook, *Writing the English Republic*, 160–3.

[64] Cedric C. Brown, 'The Shepherd, the Musician, and the Word in Milton's Masque', *Journal of English and Germanic Philology*, 78 (1979), 522–44; *Milton's Aristocratic Entertainments*, 104–15.

very clear. In *Comus*, however, the magic is very firmly in the hands of musician and poet. It is the Spirit who tells the brothers how to free their sister; and the aristocrats bungle the attempt. This can be put down to their youth: the masque is an educational exercise in which paternal authority is delegated to the children's tutor. But in a conventional masque the Lady's final release would have been achieved by the sudden revelation of the virtue of the courtiers or the beauty of their ladies. In *Comus*, by contrast, the Earl of Bridgewater, the representative of royal and patriarchal authority, plays no part in the resolution of the action. There are many echoes of *The Tempest*, but here it is Ariel, not the Duke of Milan, who is in charge. The Lady is saved not by heavenly courtiers descending from above but by the river-goddess Sabrina rising from below. Though she has some courtly associations—she was a British princess in legend—Sabrina is essentially an image of the beauty and harmony of nature; and hence, through the association between water and prophetic song that runs through the masque, of music and poetry. She can save the Lady only if she is 'right invoked in warbling song' together with 'adjuring verse'. Her song is a virtuoso display of Lawes's monodic art, combining sensuousness with sharpness of phonetic outline. This regenerate art is not narrowly austere—Sabrina's waters are both symbols of chastity and agents of fertility, invoked by the shepherds—but its clarity and precision distinguished it clearly from the courtly wine and viscous liquors peddled by Comus, who ridicules the idea that we should '[d]rink the clear stream' (l. 721).

The opposition between clear water and courtly 'opiate' (Trinity MS, l. 729) is developed throughout the masque, and it draws on long-established conventions in the prophetic and apocalyptic traditions. It is, essentially, a distinction between discourse corrupted by association with idolatry and injustice and discourse which is able to break free of these constraints and mirror divine truth. In *The Advancement of Learning* Bacon consistently associated reformed learning with flowing water. Milton was to develop this imagery in his political writings: 'Truth is compar'd in Scripture to a streaming fountain; if her waters flow not in a perpetuall progression, they sick'n into a muddy pool of conformity and tradition' (ii.543). Bacon argued that the 'idols' of received ideas were a prime cause of the failure to understand the secrets of nature; as the apocalyptic revelation advanced, these idols would gradually be destroyed and full harmony with nature achieved. Puritans like Cartwright had accused those Anglicans who justified ecclesiastical traditions by appeal to the order of nature of a comparable idolatry: nature was not patterned after human institutions. In *Comus* the characters' relationship to nature becomes a sign of their moral state. The masque is pervaded with the 'faerie' lore which in the Spenserian tradition had increasingly become associated with imaginative independence of the court. The Spirit can achieve perfect harmony with his surroundings through his music: his songs have often 'delayed The huddling brook'. His music can transform nature precisely because he is willing to listen to nature, to subordinate his own personality to a wider universe, so that natural and artificial sounds harmonize perfectly with each other, just as his monodic music respects, and co-operates with, the sounds and meanings of language. Comus' music rudely shatters the silence of the nocturnal landscape, whereas the Lady's song is sensitive to the atmosphere, it floats 'upon the wings of silence' and makes Silence wish 'to be never more Still to be so displaced'. Even Comus can respond to the Lady's song, and the opening of his first speech is powerfully lyrical: even evil can pay tribute to the divine order. In a similar manner, in Book I of *Paradise Lost* (ll. 781–8) Milton was to make the fallen angels suddenly dwindle in a simile comparing them to dancing elves. But when he is in his palace Comus loses his sensitivity to nature, which he sees as something to be appropriated, existing only to 'please and sate the curious taste'. Beauty is 'nature's coin', a mere exchange value. Even the silkworms are seen as labouring in 'shops' to satisfy their customers. Beneath Comus' praise of nature's fertility there is a certain fear. Apocalyptic writers like Hakewill were enthusiastically predicting a massive increase in the earth's abundance; Comus as courtier lacks a full responsiveness to the divine measure and order of the universe, he fears that without human intervention nature would be 'strangled with her waste fertility' (l. 728). She must therefore be consumed.[65]

Comus is, of course, a perverter rather than a representative of traditional aristo-cratic values; but there is a suggestion that the traditional rural and courtly rituals which were held to mirror the cosmic order in fact blunted awareness of deeper levels of cosmic harmony. To construct a truly 'natural' order, based on conformity to the divine pattern, it would be necessary to reverse the process: rather than pro-jecting conventional social hierarchies anthropomorphically on to the cosmos, and thus aestheticizing politics, it would be necessary to listen with a new attentiveness to the voice of nature. Milton was not advocating a simple primitivism: it needed effort to improve human arts to the point where they became truly natural, just as sponta-neous oratory required more effort than parroting clichés, and religious worship which did away with traditional rituals placed more demands on the congrega-tion than the 'dull Opiat' of 'the drone of one plaine Song' (i.691). Lawes's music demanded an unprecedented degree of musical skill which was itself the sign of a reawakening harmony with nature. It has been well said that *Comus* is 'a study in lis-tening'. Sabrina must 'listen and save'; in the final speech mortals are urged to '[l]ist . . . if your ears be true' (l. 996).[66] Milton's poetry does of course draw on conven-tional symbolism to describe natural processes: Sabrina's chariot is thick set with rich jewels. But the chariot and jewels paradoxically seem to stray (l. 894), wander-ing in the perpetually flowing water and in the turns of Milton's artful syntax: static artifice is set against natural process.[67]

As Milton almost defiantly proclaimed by his title, the Ludlow *Maske* adhered to the orthodox conventions of the genre. But only just: the work keeps threatening to

[65]   Cf. Ronald W. Hepburn, 'George Hakewill: The Virility of Nature', *Journal of the History of Ideas*, 16 (1955), 135–50. On Cartwright and analogies from nature see now David Norbrook, 'Rhetoric, Ideology, and the Elizabethan World Picture', in Peter Mack (ed.), *Renaissance Rhetoric* (London, 1994), 140–64.

[66]   Angus Fletcher, *The Transcendental Masque: An Essay on Milton's 'Comus'* (Ithaca, NY, 1971), 166. Cf. John D. Cox, 'Poetry and History in Milton's Country Masque', *ELH* 44 (1977), 622–40.

[67]   Burnett, *Milton's Style*, 64–5.

break out of its allotted boundaries. The end of the 1634 version was perhaps its most conventional feature, and this may be why Milton felt the need to change it before publication. Perhaps at Lawes's request, the 1634 ending was relatively simple.[68] The Spirit interrupted the courtly dancers, who were performing in front of a backdrop representing Ludlow Castle itself, in order to present the children's skill in dancing: they could emulate the 'court guise' of Mercury. After praising the children to the proud parents, and introducing a final dance, the Spirit gave a short concluding speech in praise of virtue. Mercury had made a similar speech at the end of *Pleasure Reconciled to Virtue*, calling on the masquers to re-ascend the hill of virtue. Despite this gesture of transcendence, however, this and all Stuart court masques celebrated the incarnation of divine qualities in the persons of the courtiers. King James was the god Hesperus, and the court with its beautiful ladies was the Garden of the Hesperides, a site of virtuous pleasure. In the Ludlow performance the Spirit began by descending from the Gardens of Hesperus to the masquing-hall. For the 1637 publication, however, Milton restored this passage to what was probably its position in the first draft, as part of the Spirit's concluding speech before he ascended to heaven, thus emphasizing transcendence rather than immanence. And he added two further passages which heightened the tension between the earthly and the heavenly. The Garden of Hesperus merged with the Garden of Adonis, which had been located above the normal action of Spenser's Legend of Chastity. To some extent this allusion mitigated the austerity of the masque's main action, serving as a reminder that sexual pleasure was not evil in itself. Spenser's third book had contained a prophecy of its heroine's marriage, and Milton would have shared Spenser's reservations about the traditional cult of virginity. On the other hand, his dramatization of chastity had permitted a sharp critique of aristocratic conventions. E. M. W. Tillyard argued that the oblique allusion to marriage would be appropriate to a masque: 'The setting is aristocratic; the Lady, though but young, will one day be a great lady. She must take her place in society and do what is expected of her.'[69] But Milton, in *Comus*, was not quite doing what was expected of a masque-writer; and, as it turned out, the Lady did not do what was expected of her—she did not marry until 1652.

The climactic allusions to marriage in the Spirit's speech are not references to traditional secular festivities but to the apocalyptic mystical marriage. His imagination moves 'far above' the Garden of Adonis to a heavenly realm where Psyche is united with Cupid. This myth was a conventional allegory for the union of the soul with heavenly love; it had become popular at the Caroline court. But it also had apocalyptic associations, to which Milton delicately pointed. Psyche had become a symbol of the true, Invisible Church, wandering in the wilderness; Milton's description of Psyche's labours as 'wandering' alludes to this idea and sets up an association with the earlier scene where the Lady wanders in the dark forest. But Psyche is now

[68] Parallel texts of the different versions are provided by S. E. Sprott, *John Milton: A Maske: The Earlier Versions* (Toronto, 1973).
[69] E. M. W. Tillyard, 'The Action of *Comus*', in Diekhoff (ed.), *A Maske at Ludlow*, 43–57 (54).

reunited with Cupid, the souls of the godly are with Christ.[70] The traditional epithalamic imagery with which Milton celebrated this union was in some ways a repudiation of asceticism. A famous passage in Revelation 14: 3–5, told of a heavenly song that was audible only to the undefiled; Milton was emphatically to reject the notion that this passage alluded only to virgins, as if marriage were a defilement (i.892–3). Cupid and Psyche are to have offspring, the 'blissful twins' Youth and Joy (ll. 1009–10). This masque of chastity ends with images of spiritual bliss which strongly imply that sexual joy, and the joy of poetic composition, can share its nature. But not only the births but the marriage itself will take place in the future: like Foxe's *Christus triumphans*, Milton's masque ends on a note of incompleteness. Secular time has been no more than an antimasque for the apocalyptic unmasking. Meanwhile, Comus remains on the loose, and it is essential to be vigilant in case he should attempt 'some . . . new device' (l. 940).

Despite its criticisms of aristocratic assumptions, *Comus* seems to have pleased the Bridgewater family. Milton had observed the conventional forms and his more oblique allusions were too subtle to be easily noticed. What was obvious was that this was a masque of unusual literary excellence, whose publication would therefore reflect credit on its noble patrons. And in 1637 it was published, with a dedication by Lawes to Bridgewater's heir, Viscount Brackley (the Elder Brother). But Milton added a Virgilian epigraph indicating that the work was coming to the light prematurely. Such professions were of course conventional; but Milton does seem to have felt that he had not yet found the right subject, that his verse needed to find a new direction. *Comus* represented a victory of personal integrity over public conventions, but a victory gained at the cost of extreme indirectness and of going against the grain of the form he had to use: even more than in Jonson's masques, humanist scholarship is disproportionate to the social occasion.[71] Milton did not put his name to the masque and seems to have made no effort to use his new connections to gain a place at court; he continued his programme of private study. But in 1637 he was presented with a new occasion for writing poetry, when members of his Cambridge college assembled a volume in memory of his friend Edward King, who had been drowned

---

[70] Psyche appears in Foxe's *Christus triumphans*; for the true church as Psyche cf. one of Fairfax's eclogues: Godfrey of Bulloigne: *A Critical Edition of Edward Fairfax's Translation of Tasso's Gerusalemme liberata, Together with Fairfax's Original Poems*, ed. Kathleen M. Lea and T. M. Gang (Oxford, 1981), 665–75. On this myth at court see Graham Parry, *The Golden Age Restor'd* (Manchester, 1981), 196–7.

[71] Interesting new evidence has come to light about the reception of *Comus*. In 1637 a masque of Comus was performed at Skipton in Yorkshire, the dwelling of Henry Clifford, Earl of Cumberland. The cast list makes it very unlikely that this was Milton's masque, but it does seem that the figure of Comus was a continuing focus for different ideological interpretations of the masque: Martin Butler, 'A Provincial Masque of Comus, 1636', *Renaissance Drama*, NS 17 (1986), 149–73. Clifford was a close friend of the absolutist-leaning Earl of Strafford, who was now patronizing James Shirley, author of another 1634 masque, and had also advised William Cavendish over his plans for court advancement; we might infer that the text would have offered a more positive image of Comus than Milton. A masque that seems to respond to *Comus* at a number of points was staged at Bretby in Derbyshire in 1640: a satyr exalts country simplicity over the court but is won round to the superior delights of courtly sports. The author, Sir Aston Cokayne, was a Catholic: *The Dramatic Works of Sir Aston Cokain*, ed. J. H. Maidment and W. H. Logan (Edinburgh, [1874]), 9–13.

in the Irish Sea. Though *Lycidas* opens with formulae of unwillingness, of taking up the pen before the due time, the poem is written with the assurance of someone who has at last found the proper subject. The 'sad occasion' is also 'dear', and his words are indeed 'lucky'.

But why did King's death release Milton from his impasse? He does not seem to have kept up his college friendship with King, who had gravitated towards the Laudian group at Cambridge, and whose poetry, despite Milton's claim in *Lycidas*, was unambitious and undistinguished. Death would already have been on Milton's mind before he heard that King had been drowned: his mother had recently died and the plague had struck his village. The slow maturing of his poetic gifts, his conscious deferment of worldly advancement, meant that the sudden death of a young friend would have brought home to him the fact that his own life would seem to have been effectively wasted if he were now to die. *Lycidas*, as critics have long recognized, is about Milton, and about poetry, as much as it is about Edward King. But this does not mean that the poem is narrowly egotistical, or that it is concerned with the eternal ideals of art as opposed to the transient concerns of politics. It does not mean that he saw himself as contributing to a timeless essence called 'the pastoral tradition'. But in writing *Lycidas* Milton was able to define his position in a specific tradition of prophetic poetry, and to renew and transform that tradition in the light of changed political circumstances.

Milton's awareness of alternative poetic traditions in England would have been sharpened just before he began work on *Lycidas*. For just six days after King's death, on 16 August 1637, Ben Jonson died in London. After a brief interregnum in the period immediately after Spenser's death, Jonson had effectively become poet laureate, relegating poets in the Spenserian tradition to secondary public roles. Who could now take his place? In the 1630s there seems to have been a move to formalize the post of laureate. In 'A Sessions of the Poets', probably written in the summer of 1637, Sir John Suckling surveyed the possible candidates.[72] He included Ben Jonson, but the ageing poet was by now producing little verse and was not in the public eye. Suckling went through the younger generation of poets to see which of them might be worthy of the laurel. Most of the candidates he considered were 'Cavalier' poets like Carew, Davenant, and Walter Montague, none of whom (with the possible exception of Carew) had a commitment to poetry as a vocation rather than a recreation. In his elegy for Jonson Sir Thomas Salusbury declared that his mantle had to be taken up by many poets because no individual was his equal.[73] What was taken for granted in courtly circles was that the laureate ought to come from the circle of Jonson's friends and 'sons'. Quarles's suitability for the post had been hinted at by his friend Edward Benlowes, but his earnest didacticism appealed more to London merchants than court wits.[74] When Suckling playfully awarded the laurel at the end of his poem to a

---

[72] Wayne H. Phelps, 'The Date of Ben Jonson's Death', *Notes and Queries*, 225 (1980), 146–9; *The Works of Sir John Suckling: The Non-dramatic Works*, ed. Thomas Clayton (Oxford, 1971), 71–6, 266–7; see Edmund Kemper Broadus, *The Laureateship* (Oxford, 1921), 40 ff.

[73] *H&S*, xi.485–6.

[74] See Edward Benlowes, 'Quarlëis', printed in Quarles, *Works*, i, pp. lxxix–xciv.

London alderman he took it for granted that this was absurd. Quarles's low-church views would in any case have been a political handicap. Eventually he was made Chronologer to the City of London; he was certainly more in sympathy with the mood of the city fathers than Jonson, whose term in this office had been marked by repeated disputes. In the end it was the young cavalier poet Sir William Davenant who emerged as Jonson's successor (though he does not seem to have received an official title).[75] It was natural for the 'sons of Ben' to think of poetic 'succession' as analogous to royal succession: Jonson had constantly emphasized the analogies between poet and prince, and one elegist hailed him as 'King of *English Poetry*'.[76] The name 'tribe of Ben' was a witty allusion to Revelation (7: 8), but the playfulness indicated Jonson's wariness about taking claims to prophetic power too seriously. Poetic tradition, like political tradition, was a matter of smooth continuity, with authority passing down through legitimate channels rather than being conferred by a sudden divine afflatus. Davenant's successor as laureate, John Dryden, was to crystallize these ideas in his two great poems of political and poetic 'succession', *Absalom and Achitophel* and *MacFlecknoe*, in each of which a pretender with Whiggish views is condemned as an illegitimate usurper of time-hallowed British traditions.[77]

Similar connections between literary excellence and religious conservatism were made in several of the elegies for Jonson which were published in 1638 under the title *Jonsonus Virbius*. The collection was edited by Brian Duppa, an Arminian who was Vice-Chancellor of Oxford University, and many of the contributors had links with Oxford. As has been seen, the growing Arminian influence in Oxford had disturbed some of William Browne's friends. One satirist attacked the University Arminians as 'vainglorious men' who 'stretch so farre to gett a little Laud'. Another included Duppa in a list of Oxford Arminians whom he accused of monopolizing the chief posts.[78] *Jonsonus Virbius* contained several attacks on Puritans. It should be said that not all the 'sons of Ben' were supporters of Laud. The stereotype of the 'cavaliers' created by their adversaries was often highly inaccurate. The first contributor to *Jonsonus Virbius*, Lucius Cary, Viscount Falkland, disliked Laudian as well as Puritan intolerance and was to join the critics of royal advisers at the start of the political crisis of 1640. So were three rather more flamboyant 'cavaliers', Davenant, Suckling, and Waller; but these poets were ultimately more at home in a world of courtly intrigue than with earnest political debate, and all eventually became involved in royalist conspiracies. Hostility to low-born religious enthusiasts soon outweighed

[75] Broadus, *The Laureateship*, 53–8; Mary Edmond, *Rare Sir William Davenant: Poet Laureate, Playwright, Civil War General, Restoration Theatre Manager* (Manchester, 1987), 72–4.

[76] *H&S*, xi.443, l. 6.

[77] Christopher Ricks, 'Allusion: The Poet as Heir', in R. F. Brissenden and J. C. Eade (eds.), *Studies in the Eighteenth Century*, iii. (Toronto, 1976), 209–40.

[78] Bodleian MS Eng. poet. e. 97, 31, 127–30 (quoted by permission of the Bodleian Library, Oxford); on Jonson's links with Duppa see also *The Correspondence of Bishop Brian Duppa and Sir Justinian Isham, 1650–1660*, ed. Sir Gyles Isham, *Publications of the Northamptonshire Record Society*, 17 (1951), 21–2. For a more favourable view of Duppa see Richard Ollard, *The Image of the King* (London, 1979), 41–3. In 1637 the Venetian ambassador reported that special efforts were being made by the Catholics to convert Duppa because of his influence as Prince Charles's tutor: *Calendar of State Papers . . . Venice, 1636–9*, 150.

any reservations they might have had about the king's character. During the Civil War Oxford became a centre of royalist propaganda, supervised by one of the former contributors to *Jonsonus Virbius*, Sir John Berkenhead.[79]

Many of Jonson's elegists identified excessive emotion in poetry with religious enthusiasm, and hence tried to adopt a cool and composed tone. Jonson's friend Richard Corbett had ridiculed the extravagant outpourings with which the Puritans had greeted the death of their idol Prince Henry, and elaborate funerary effusions were increasingly becoming a mark of a Puritan outlook.[80] In 1635 the Scottish presbyterian poet Sir William Mure had published a series of apocalyptic sonnets denouncing Laudian policies; he had entitled the volume *The Joy of Tears*, and his preface had urged his readers not to refrain from lamentation just because they might be taxed by the fleshly as 'greeting' (weeping) Puritans.[81] The contributors to *Jonsonus Virbius* ostentatiously restrained their weeping. In his opening poem Falkland says:

> thy *griefe* I cannot call
> A *passion*, when the ground is *rationall*.

Cary had earlier written that he had no desire to produce 'such Verse as *Quarles* makes God-all-mighty speake'.[82] Jonson himself had advised his 'son' on the right way to write an elegy. Deeply distressed at the death of Sir Henry Morison, Falkland had written an impassioned and undisciplined lament. Jonson addressed an Ode to Falkland in which he consoled him for his loss and used the poem's disciplined form to remind him that death need not be regarded as tragic, that even a short life could be regarded as perfect and beautiful. Life's

> measures are, how well
> Each syllab'e answer'd, and was form'd, how faire;
> These make the lines of life, and that's her ayre. (ll. 62–4)[83]

Jonson gave moral connotations to the terms for the different sections of the Pindaric Ode—'Turn', 'Counter-Turn', 'Stand': the poem ended in a mood of assured self-reliance—'standing' was a central concept for Neo-Stoic thinkers. The achieved form of the poem was itself a victory over death.

> Call, noble *Lucius,* then for Wine,
> And let thy lookes with gladnesse shine:
> Accept this garland [i.e. the poem], plant it on thy head[.] (ll. 75–7)

---

[79] P. W. Thomas, *Sir John Berkenhead 1617–1679: A Royalist Career in Politics and Polemics* (Oxford, 1969), 99 ff.

[80] See above, Ch. 8 n. 38; J. W. Draper, *The Funeral Elegy and the Rise of English Romanticism* (New York, 1929), 90–1; Draper assigns the change to the 1650s.

[81] Sir William Mure, *The Joy of Tears*, ed. C. Davis, Scottish Text Society, *Miscellany Volume* (Edinburgh, 1933), 159–78 (164); cf. R. D. S. Jack, 'Sir William Mure and the Covenant', *Records of the Scottish Church History Society*, 17 (1969), 1–14.

[82] *H&S*, xi.431, ll. 43–4, 400, l. 20.

[83] Ibid., viii.242–7; on this poem see Richard S. Peterson, *Imitation and Praise in the Poems of Ben Jonson* (New Haven, 1981), 195–232.

Cary implied a similar consolation in the title he chose for the elegies. Virbius was a character in the *Aeneid* (7.770–7) who descended to the underworld but was restored to life: just so, the title suggests, Jonson will rise again in his literary immortality. Most of the elegies avoid explicitly Christian imagery and accept a decorum that centres the consolation on themes common to pagans and Christians: life's brevity and the immortality of art. There is no obtrusive clash of ideologies between Christianity and classical ideas: instead the elegies suggest the underlying continuities of human experience, the importance of tradition. Cary attacked '*Puritanes* in Poesie' who scorned classical writers and tried to express their own personal grief without paying attention to literary traditions: they 'scorne the Fathers, in that art'.[84] But the 'sons of Ben' were selective in their choice of poetic 'fathers'. They placed great emphasis on craftsmanship but disliked poetry which drew too much attention to its own artifice. They were helping to hasten pastoral poetry out of fashion, finding its self-conscious tone either too pedantic or too precious, incompatible with the note of urbane directness they were trying to strike. Cary did adopt pastoral conventions for the elegy that opened *Jonsonus Virbius*, as a tribute to Jonson's unfinished *The Sad Shepherd*; but he made no effort to imitate the themes or diction of Spenserian pastoral.

At the same time as this volume of restrained and conservative elegies was being assembled at Oxford, contributions were being requested for a tribute to an obscure Cambridge don. One poet prepared elegies for both volumes, and Milton could presumably have done the same.[85] He had published a tribute to Shakespeare, and he recognized Jonson's stature. But he remained silent on Jonson's death and put all his linguistic resources into the poem for King. Whereas in *Comus* Milton had adopted a characteristically Jonsonian form and revised it, *Lycidas* marks a decisive and unambiguous commitment to the Spenserian tradition. Spenser was Milton's true poetic 'father', but it was Jonson, with his massive literary authority, who had caused a more immediate 'anxiety of influence'.[86] Milton had been struggling to avoid becoming just one more of the 'sons of Ben'; a powerful release came with his death—just as Dryden was to feel released by Milton's death. But in *Lycidas* Milton was laying claim to a literary authority that did not depend on respect for established religious institutions. The plants which the swain invokes at the beginning—laurel, myrtle, and ivy—were associated with the coronation of poets. At this time when the choice of a laureate was being considered, Milton paid tribute to the 'laureate hearse' of a King who lacked high office (several elegists made a political

---

[84]   *H&S*, xi.401, ll. 62–3.

[85]   In my first edition I confused Edward King's brother Henry, who contributed to *Justa*, with the better-known Henry King who contributed to *Jonsonus Virbius*. The Cambridge poet Clement Paman published an elegy in *Jonsonus Virbius* and an elegy for King survives in manuscript though it was apparently not completed in time for publication: Bodleian MS Rawl. poet. 147, fos. 146–7 (I am indebted to Fram Dinshaw for this reference); the poem is printed by Norman Postlethwaite and Gordon Campbell, 'Edward King, Milton's "Lycidas": Poems and Documents', *Milton Quarterly*, 28 (1994), 77–111 (92–5). However, John Cleveland did not write poems for both volumes as is often stated, the 'I. Cl' of the Jonson volume probably being James Cleyton (*H&S*, xi.428).

[86]   Cf. Harold Bloom, *The Anxiety of Influence: A Theory of Poetry* (London, 1973), 11, 27.

pun on King's name) and made a powerful critique of current poetic and political developments.

Lycidas differs radically in tone and form from the tributes to Jonson; it differs also from the poems in the Cambridge volume, which revealed a certain caution about giving free rein to prophetic passion. King's brother Henry set the tone in the first English elegy:

> No Death! I'le not examine Gods decree,
> Nor question providence, in chiding thee:[87]

Some of the Cambridge elegists did try to give an effect of strong emotion by sub-'metaphysical' conceits, but the hyperboles were so numerous that the effect was diluted. There is some evidence that *Justa Edovardo King* was planned as a whole and that Milton may have seen some of the other elegies before writing *Lycidas*. If so, he set out to distinguish himself from his contemporaries rather than subduing his own poetic voice to the tone of the whole. *Lycidas* was placed at the end of the volume; it was the longest poem, and the only eclogue, amongst the contributions in English. Far from refusing to question providence, Milton repeatedly does so. The poet's voice is never assimilated to urbane everyday speech; this enables the poem to rise to heights of prophetic zeal. But the formality of language does not permit a stately distancing and ritualizing of grief: at moments when the poem seems to be moving towards some satisfactory closure, the ritual will suddenly be exposed as a vain attempt to obscure the truth by specious beauty. The pastoral framework clearly differentiates the poem from the currently fashionable conceits and 'strong lines'; but the hyperboles are there on a more submerged level. There is an undercurrent of restless wordplay, of half-realized paradoxes—leaves which are 'shattered' (the word could mean 'scattered' but the stronger sense is there too), blind mouths, enamelled eyes sucking showers.[88] The effect is of excitement, even hysteria, only just contained. The disruptions of the rhyme-scheme reinforce this effect. Milton builds up expectations of formal completion which are then disrupted: for example, there are moments (ll. 130–8, 163 ff.) when the poem seems to be about to fall into *ottava rima* stanzas, but not until the very last eight lines are these expectations fulfilled. Milton could have found precedents in the Spenserian tradition for such experiments, in Bryskett's pastoral elegy for Sidney and in some of Daniel's poems. Some critics have drawn analogies with the 'mannerist' art fashionable at Italian courts, in which a conspicuous asymmetry was played against an underlying order; Alastair Fowler

---

[87] *Justa Edovardo King Naufrago* (Cambridge, 1638), sig. F2ʳ. The English elegies are conveniently reproduced in Joseph A. Wittreich, *Visionary Poetics* (San Marino, Calif., 1979), 279 ff., and the volume as a whole, ed. Edward Le Comte, in *Milton Quarterly*, 35 (2001), 125–225. On numerological unity in the collection see Alastair Fowler, '"To Shepherd's Ear": The Form of Milton's *Lycidas*', in Alastair Fowler (ed.), *Silent Poetry: Essays in Numerological Analysis* (London, 1970), 170–84 (171, 181 n. 6), and on *Lycidas* as a critique of the other poems, Wittreich, 89 ff. One elegist compared King to Virbius (*Justa Edovardo King*, sig. E4ʳ).

[88] John Creaser, '*Lycidas*: The Power of Art', *Essays and Studies*, NS 34 (1981), 123–47 (134–5). Cf. Ellen Zetzel Lambert, *Placing Sorrow: A Study of the Pastoral Elegy Convention from Theocritus to Milton* (Chapel Hill, NC, 1976), 155 ff.

has detected an elaborate numerological structure in the poem, despite its apparent irregularity.[89] But even if this structure does enact some underlying analogy with the cosmic order, the point of the poem is to show how unconsoling the order of nature is in the face of death and the corruptions of the church. Milton's experiments in rhyme go beyond anything attempted by the Italian poets he imitated, such as Della Casa and Tasso.[90] It is as if he were trying to produce not an imitation of more recent courtly writers but an impression of the kind of poetry that might have been written in Italy had the prophetic tradition not been stifled by the Counter-Reformation (Della Casa and Tasso had both had problems with the Inquisition). There is a toughness in *Lycidas* that is closer to Dante, who was disdained by many Italian courtiers for his uncouthness, than to fashionable pastoralists.

Analogies have been made between the structure of *Lycidas* and the Pindaric structure of 'turn', 'counter-turn' and 'stand'; but Milton's 'turns' and 'returns' are far more violent than in Jonson's Cary-Morison Ode.[91] The final 'stand' offers a kind of formal resolution, but the distancing by the narratorial voice places this stanza outside the framework of the poem as a whole and creates an asymmetrical effect. If the poem 'stands' on a point of ideological resolution, this is to be found not at the end but in the allusion to Christ's walking on the waters, a state of miraculous and paradoxical poise anticipating Christ's 'standing' on the pinnacle in *Paradise Regained*.

The elegies in *Jonsonus Virbius*—and most of those in *Justa Edovardo King*—indicate the growing hegemony of the closed couplet as dominant metrical form, a development which Jonson had strongly influenced. This form was to become for the Augustans a symbol of political as well as poetic order; and within five years of the composition of *Lycidas* Sir John Denham was to make these analogies explicit in 'Cooper's Hill'. Here the couplet signifies the balance and harmony of the constitution, and it disciplines excessive enthusiasm in poetic imagination in much the same way as traditional political and religious forms curb Puritan enthusiasm. In *Lycidas* movements towards a closed couplet are constantly disrupted. A temporary resolution is reached at the end of Phoebus' speech:

> As he pronounces lastly on each deed,
> Of so much fame in heaven accept thy meed. (ll. 83–4)

This consolation already distances the poem from the emphasis on earthly fame to be found in many Jonsonian elegies; but in the context of the poem's formal unevenness, the couplet appears too facile to offer a convincing resolution, and the poet's questions continue. Jonson had claimed that a short life could be seen as a harmonious poem; in *Lycidas* life and death constantly evade harmonious patterns. The immortality given to Virbius is radically insufficient.

Milton's choice of the pastoral convention itself ran counter to current fashions.

---

[89] Fowler, ' "To Shepherd's Ear" '; on the rhyme-scheme see also Wittreich, *Visionary Poetics*, 167–84, who shows some previously unsuspected regularities.

[90] Prince, *The Italian Element in Milton's Verse*, 71–88.

[91] On Milton and Pindar see Clay Hunt's valuable study Lycidas *and the Italian Critics* (New Haven, 1979), 71, 85 ff., 139–40.

It is necessary, of course, to distinguish between different kinds of pastoral. The 'Arcadian' pastoral of Sannazaro and Tasso was in vogue in some court circles, though the 'sons of Ben' had little time for the fashion. In *Lycidas*, as in *Comus*, Milton indicates the dangers of escapism in this tradition. The long 'flower' passage (ll. 132–51), in which the poet tries to divert his thoughts after the terror of St Peter's speech, may be felt to go on slightly too long, as if the poet were desperately trying to shut out unpleasant realities. And at l. 153 he concedes that he has been dallying with 'false surmise', that no amount of pastoral embroidery can conceal the fact that King's corpse has been washed away to sea. Milton's pastoralism is less courtly than humanist and didactic, in the tradition of the eclogues of Petrarch, Mantuan, and Spenser. The allegorical eclogue was already passing from fashion by the 1630s. For poets trying to achieve a more colloquial speaking voice, the genre seemed too elaborate and also too pedantic. After *Lycidas* no really important allegorical eclogues were produced in England until Shelley's *Adonais*. When Dr Johnson attacked the poem for its pedantry he probably sensed a connection between Milton's militant humanism and his political radicalism. He refused to conceal his erudition for the sake of social propriety. The artifice of his allegory is never naturalized: Milton makes it very clear that there is a dissociation between surface level and deeper meaning, between Lycidas and his friend battening their flocks with the dew of night and the activity of reading or discussing poetry. The rising and setting of the sun had become a stock symbol of life's transience and appeared frequently in the Oxford and Cambridge elegies; but in *Lycidas* the sun rises and sets three times, each time on a slightly different symbolic level. The juxtaposition of classical mythology with Christian symbolism had become standard in Renaissance eclogues but Jonson had always tried to avoid any violent clashes; his verse implies the smooth continuity of human experience from classical to Christian eras. Milton makes the discontinuities as conspicuous as possible.

Self-conscious display of learning was, of course, appropriate in a volume of Cambridge elegies, and there is in *Lycidas* a level of academic wit. The description of Camus as 'footing slow' (l. 103) plays on the etymological sense of 'pedantic'. But this pun is immediately succeeded by the ferocious urgency of St Peter's speech; none of the other elegies has a comparable range of tones. Milton is not simply parading classical learning or engaging in literary jokes; his classical allusions are politically pointed. His most important classical model was Virgil's tenth eclogue, but he departs conspicuously from his original. Virgil's poem is a lament for Gallus, who is dying of unrequited love. The highly politicized commentaries of Renaissance humanists assumed that this 'love' was at least in part political, that what Gallus really lacked was courtly favour. In *The Shepheardes Calender* Spenser had contrasted the difficult and unequal 'love' of courtly relationships with more mutual friendships; in *Lycidas* Milton revises his classical model to make his hero someone who repudiated love both in erotic and political senses, who never sought courtly advancement and found fulfilment instead in personal friendships.[92] Several elegists

[92] J. Martin Evans, 'Lycidas, Daphnis, and Gallus', in John Carey (ed.), *English Renaissance Studies Presented to Dame Helen Gardner* (Oxford, 1980), 228–44.

pointed the contrast between this humble King and King Gustavus Adolphus of Sweden, whose death had occasioned many poems in England. As in *Comus*, Milton distinguishes his version of pastoral from more courtly forms by emphasizing the chastity of his protagonist. Like Sabrina, King is a chaste figure who has suffered death by water; as in *Comus*, clear water becomes a symbol of temperance and of poetry. Both *Comus* and *Lycidas* present images of fulfilment not on earth but in participation in the mystical marriage, the 'unexpressive nuptial song'. Lycidas is one of those chaste individuals who alone can hear the new song of Revelation 14: 3.

If *Lycidas* affirms the value of the academic as opposed to the courtly life, this is only to be expected in an elegy for a college fellow. But the fact that Milton was contributing to a Cambridge volume had political significance in itself. Cambridge had special associations with the Spenserian tradition. The very first collection of elegies printed there had inaugurated the cult of Sir Philip Sidney. Spenser, who had studied at Cambridge, wrote a pastoral elegy for Sidney, though it was not published until later. The Spenserian tradition at Cambridge had been continued by the Fletchers, who had contributed poems in Spenserian verse forms to university anthologies. Contributors to a collection of elegies for Sir Edward Lewkenor, a leading presbyterian from East Anglia and a relative of Quarles, had used Spenserian forms and diction.[93] In 1633 Phineas Fletcher had published a collection of his father's poems which included a Latin elegy for a drowned friend, spoken by Lycidas, and an allegorical eclogue on British learning which narrated the myth of Sabrina.[94] Milton may have read this poem and certainly drew in *Lycidas* on the store of Cambridge mythology to which Fletcher had alluded. At the beginning of Fletcher's eclogue Lycidas, who has been grazing his flocks near Cambridge, asks Camus to tell of his origins. Camus explains that learning in Britain can be traced back to King Druis and his son Bardus. Cambridge was founded before the birth of Christ, by Britons who were carrying on the tradition of the Druids. Like John Bale, one of Fletcher's possible sources, he followed British learning back to a time before the hegemony of the Roman church, when poets were also prophets and there was no corrupt ecclesiastical hierarchy. Milton subscribed to the patriotic myth that the Druids had made England 'the Cathedrall of Philosophy to *France*' (ii.231, cf. ii.551–2). King had been drowned near Anglesey, the Druids' traditional home, and Milton refers to them and to Camus. In the Caroline period the Druids did not always receive favourable mention: Inigo Jones argued that Stonehenge could not possibly have been built by them as was sometimes believed, for such skill in architecture could have been attained only in an age of peace and strong authority—that is, under the rule of the Romans, the forerunners of the glory of the Stuarts.[95] Druids who appeared in Caroline entertainments were associated with a primitive uncouthness and martial zeal that had

[93]   *Threnodia in obitum D. Edovardi Lewkenor* (London, 1606), 1–6, 35–6, 39–48.

[94]   Giles Fletcher, *De literis antiquae Britanniae* (Cambridge, 1633); Warren B. Austin, 'Milton's *Lycidas* and Two Latin Elegies by Giles Fletcher, the Elder', *Studies in Philology*, 44 (1947), 41–55. On Cambridge allusions in *Lycidas* see further David Shelley Berkeley, *Inwrought with Figures Dim: A Reading of Milton's* Lycidas (The Hague, 1974), 85–112.

[95]   Parry, *The Golden Age Restor'd*, 155–8.

now been transcended.[96] But the Druids' proud independence appealed to the poet Dudley North, who argued in 1640 that Charles should pattern the English religious order on the presbyterian islands of Jersey and Guernsey just as ancient British rulers derived their religion from Anglesey.[97] Milton's allusion to the Druids is much less specific but it does provide one of the many links in the poem between the roles of poet and priest and helps to link *Lycidas* with the apocalyptic Protestant view of British cultural history. The poem thus forms a bridge between the sixteenth-century gospellers and those Whig oppositionists in the eighteenth century who associated the Druids with political liberty and poetic independence.[98]

As Phineas Fletcher indignantly pointed out in 1632, the low-church tradition, which in his mind was associated with Spenserian poetry, was now being denounced as seditious 'Puritanism'. Resistance to Laudianism had, however, been stronger at Cambridge than at Oxford. The Chancellor, the Earl of Holland, tended to side with the Calvinists against Laud, who postponed a visitation to enforce conformity in 1635. But tighter controls were being imposed, and in 1637 the satirist John Bastwicke, reviving the irreverent satire of the Marprelate tracts, imagined the Archbishop advancing on the universities 'with a rod in his hand . . . to whip those naughty scholars, that will not learne well their lesson of conformity'.[99] By the time Milton wrote *Lycidas*, Bastwicke was in prison and his ears had been cut off. Of course, Laud had supporters at Cambridge, and King seems to have been amongst them. One contributor to *Justa Edovardo King* invoked Spenser to attack dissenting iconoclasts, equating them with the 'blatant beast'.[100] In *Lycidas* Milton recalled a very different element in the Spenserian tradition, the strong suspicion of clerical authoritarianism.

The anxieties felt by Cambridge Calvinists were shared elsewhere in the country. There had been some hopes in 1635–6 that the king might be persuaded to summon a Parliament and take a more militant stand against the Spanish, but in 1637 he was still co-operating with the Spanish navy. The ascendancy of the high-church party was revealed in June 1637 by the arrest of Bishop John Williams, one of Laud's enemies and a defender of the Calvinist tradition. Williams was not arrested for directly political reasons and his character was far from austere—he was no Archbishop Grindal—but his arrest increased the general resemblances between the political

---

[96] See the Richmond entertainment of 1636 and Carew's *Coelum britannicum*, ll. 904 ff.

[97] Dudley North, *A Forest of Varieties* (London, 1645), 236.

[98] e.g. Thomson, 'Liberty', iv.630, and Collins, 'Ode to Liberty', ll. 64–144. On theories about the Druids see A. L. Owen, *The Famous Druids* (Oxford, 1962); Christine Gerrard, *The Patriot Opposition to Walpole: Politics, Poetry, and National Myth, 1725–1742* (Oxford, 1994), 136–47, finds a discontinuity between favourable views of the Druids in some Renaissance texts and the patriots of the 1720s and 1730s.

[99] *The Letany of John Bastwicke* (London, 1637), 6; Trevor-Roper, *Archbishop Laud*, 205–10.

[100] *Justa Edovardo King*, sig. H2ʳ. In the first edition I assumed rather too easily that King's relationship with Milton would not have been personally important; though their political and religious views were evidently diverging, they had many friends in common, and his sister Dorothy had Puritan sympathies and was to marry the reformer John Dury. For new information on King see Postlethwaite and Campbell, 'Edward King, Milton's "Lycidas": Poems and Documents', 77–81. Lawrence Lipking, 'The Genius of the Shore: Lycidas, Alamastor, and the Poetics of Nationalism', *PMLA* 111 (1996), 205–21 (208), argues that King's Irish connections would have particularly fuelled Milton's Puritan imagination.

conjuncture in 1637 and the situation when Spenser published *The Shepheardes Calender*. Ecclesiastical reaction seemed to be in danger of stifling the voice of Protestant prophecy. The savage punishment of Prynne, Bastwicke, and Burton had disturbed even people who were not particularly sympathetic to religious dissent. A Star Chamber decree of July 1637 had introduced sweeping new restrictions in an attempt to block loopholes in the censorship laws.[101] Foxe's *Acts and Monuments* had chronicled the attempts of Catholic bishops to suppress godly preachers; now it had 'almost come to be a prohibited *book*' (i.679). Fulke Greville's treatise on religion, with its derogatory remarks about bishops, had been cut from his collected poems; his highly oblique protests against the Caroline regime by means of Tacitean lectures had been quickly stopped. The collected poems of George Herbert, which appeared in 1633, also ran into difficulties: the censor took exception to lines in 'The Church Militant' which implied that persecution might lead the godly to seek refuge in America, that religion stood on tip-toe in England. In 1636 Samuel Ward, a Puritan controversialist, answered accusations of religious extremism by declaring that he was not as 'melancholy' (i.e. Puritan) as the person who wrote that religion stood on tip-toe in the land.[102] William Drummond had complained about censorship in Scotland. Sir William Mure had lamented in his apocalyptic sonnets that

> The mouth of godly *Zephanie* is bard,
> Because the truth in honestie hee showeth.[103]

His poems had to appear anonymously, with a gibe at the Laudian censorship: 'Published with the most gratious licence and priviledge of GOD Almightie'. Quarles was unable to publish his ecclesiastical eclogues. By 1638 Weckherlin considered that it would be dangerous for him to publish some sonnets attacking the Roman church. Dudley North criticized the 'castrations, expurgings and expurgatories' of the censors.[104] William Browne published nothing in the 1630s, but his opinion of what was happening was revealed in 1640 when he wrote an excited letter to Sir Benjamin Rudyerd in praise of a speech he had made in the Long Parliament. Rudyerd had denounced those who abused all the godly as 'Puritans'; Browne wrote that his speech had been infused with 'the spirit which inspired the Reformation and the genius which dictated the Magna Charta'.[105]

In this climate of increasing dislike of censorship, the apparent digressiveness of the most explicitly polemical passage in the poem, St Peter's attack on the clergy, takes on a particular significance. Milton marked off this passage both in the 1645

[101] Frederick Seaton Siebert, *Freedom of the Press in England, 1476–1776* (Urbana, Ill., 1952), 142 ff.; Franklin B. Williams, Jr., 'The Laudian Imprimatur', *Library*, 5th series, 15 (1960), 96–104; Christianson, *Reformers and Babylon*, 136 ff.

[102] *The Works of George Herbert*, ed. F. E. Hutchinson (Oxford, 1941), 196, ll. 235, 546–7; *Calendar of State Papers, Domestic Series, 1635–6*, p. xiv.

[103] Mure, *The Joy of Tears*, 168.

[104] Forster, *Weckherlin*, 83, 113; shortly after making this complaint Weckherlin, who had served as a licenser for news pamphlets, lost his position: Anthony B. Thompson, 'Licensing the Press: The Career of G. R. Weckherlin during the Personal Rule of Charles I', *Historical Journal*, 41 (1998), 653–78 (675); North, *A Forest of Varieties*, 62.

[105] William Browne, *Poems*, ed. G. Goodwin, 2 vols. (London, 1894), i, p. xxv.

rubric—'by occasion'—and by internal stylistic pointers: the speech threatens to break the poem's frame, to shrink the pastoral streams. On a rhetorical level the speech is in a strict sense digressive: the aim of the poem is to mourn Edward King. But the way in which Milton chose to mourn his friend was politically charged; in writing an elegy for someone who was both poet and priest he was led to ask questions about the state of the church as well as about poetry. Even if he had not included Peter's speech the poem would still be highly political. And this speech is carefully worked into the poem's structure. It is prepared for by Phoebus' speech, which likewise raises the style to a higher level; St Peter's final 'smite no more' takes up the opening 'Yet once more' and will be echoed in the triumphant 'weep no more' (l. 182). But by making Peter's speech stand out from its immediate context Milton is able to give the effect of truth bursting through censorship—an idea that was highly charged in 1637–8. Earlier in the poem there is an image of the blind Fury as a censor, cutting off the existence of a poet who hoped to 'burst out into sudden blaze'. Milton was to use this phrase in *Animadversions* to describe the collapse of censorship: 'aggreev'd, and long persecuted Truth . . . burst out with some efficacy of words . . . after such an injurious strangle of silence' (i.669). St Peter's speech is a reminder that language can not only 'build the lofty rhyme', that it can have destructive as well as creative force. At the beginning of the poem the swain's words 'shatter' the leaves (l. 5). St Peter's speech is the equivalent of the Lady's speech in *Comus* which threatens to 'shatter' the enchanter's 'magic structures'. The attack on the clergy gains in impact from its very abruptness, from the poet's signalling that had it continued any longer it would have completely shrunk the pastoral streams, would have broken out of the genre of the pastoral elegy just as the Lady's speech would have broken the generic boundaries of the masque.

A concern with the power of language and of music unites the different charges made by 'the pilot of the Galilean lake' (l. 109). The major allegations were conventional to the tradition of anti-ecclesiastical pastoral; Quarles made similar charges in *The Shepheardes Oracles*. But Milton gives the indictment an exceptional unity, concision, and intensity. St Peter's complaint is vague enough to have evaded the Laudian censorship, but he hints at more than he says. The attack on shepherds who 'scramble at the shearers' feast' reflects the stock complaint that the Laudian bishops cared only about personal advancement. 'Blind mouths' (l. 119), Milton's brilliant pun on the etymologies of 'bishop' (person who sees) and 'pastor' (person who feeds), accuses the bishops of failing to encourage the preaching of the Word and hence of encouraging ignorance and superstition. The Laudians argued that simple people were incapable of benefiting from the austerely intellectual atmosphere of Calvinist worship, that they needed the aid of ritual. Milton later wrote that to justify the suppression of Puritan lectureships on this basis was to put out the people's eyes and then complain that they were irredeemably blind (i.933). The figure of the blind mouths leads on to a further indictment of their incompetence at preaching, couched in musical terms: their songs grate on their scrannel pipes. The idolatry rife amongst the people is symbolized by the sheep-rot, by a grotesque swelling of wind that corresponds to the bishops' corrupt music. While the bishops' mouths are blind, the throat of the 'grim wolf' gapes to devour his prey (l. 128). The wolf is clearly one of the Jesuits who were making converts at court, but his 'privy paw' implies consummate dissimulation and recalls the old Protestant satiric convention of the Anglican foxes who were wolves in disguise. The crucial factor is that nothing is said, that prophetic voices are being silenced.

The culminating image of this passage is the 'two-handed engine at the door' (l. 130). An enormous amount of critical effort has gone into finding a precise referent for this 'dark conceit'. But its most likely referent is yet another rhetorical figure, the two-edged sword of Revelation 1: 16 and 19: 15, which was commonly interpreted in the apocalyptic tradition as referring to the immense power of the prophetic Word. The threatening, almost surreal character of Milton's 'two-handed engine' recalls the illustrations in Bale's *Image of Both Churches* and in many Protestant New Testaments of Christ standing with his arms apart and the two-edged sword issuing from his mouth.[106] In this sense the trope is self-referential: its menacing indeterminacy, designed to inspire awe and repentance, embodies, as well as referring to, what Milton later called the 'quick and pearcing' force of the Christian message (i.827). Christ's 'reforming Spirit', wrote Milton, mounts a 'sudden assault' on human traditions (i.704). Earlier in the 1630s he had felt himself to be 'unweapon'd', but *Lycidas* reflects a growing confidence in his linguistic powers. He is also assimilating more fully than ever before the legacy of the Continental as well as English traditions of prophetic poetry. The combination of the extremely elliptical and the matter-of-fact in the phrase 'that two-handed engine' is reminiscent of Dante, whose presence can be felt at several points in *Lycidas*. In *Paradiso* ix St Peter vehemently denounces ecclesiastical corruption; and in *Paradiso* xxix Beatrice complains that preachers are telling idle stories instead of heeding Christ's injunction to go forth with the shield and lances of the Word. Flacius had reproduced these passages in his catalogue of testimonies to the spirit of reform, which had opened with a lengthy discussion of St Peter's humility: he would never have interpreted the keys offered to him by Christ (Matthew 16: 18–19) as supreme temporal authority or abused the sword of the Spirit to fight for a temporal kingdom. Later Protestant writers like Duplessis-Mornay had popularized not only Dante's attacks on Papal pretensions in the *De monarchia* but also the polemical passages in the *Paradiso* ix and xxix, which embarrassed Catholic censors. At the time he wrote *Lycidas* Milton had been doing some research into Papal censorship of the *De monarchia* (i.438). Such censorship, he believed, was ineffectual: his own allusion to Dante showed that the prophetic voices of preaching and poetry could never be completely silenced. Retribution, says St Peter, stands 'at the door'. This allusion to Revelation (3: 20) indicates that the apocalypse cannot be long deferred: in 1641 Milton was confidently to proclaim that 'thy Kingdome is now at hand, and thou standing at the dore' (i.707). Milton leaves it for history to give a full explication of his 'two-handed engine', to reveal precisely what

---

[106] Illustrated by John N. King, *English Reformation Literature* (Princeton, 1982), plate 9. For a brief summary of interpretations of the 'two-handed engine' see *Poems*, ed. Carey and Fowler, 238–9, and *John Milton: Complete Shorter Poems*, ed. John Carey, 2nd edn. (Harlow, 1997), 242–3.

political form the triumph of the Word will take. Commentaries on Revelation themselves conceded that the process of interpretation was progressive and in some sense bound up with political action: to effect a decisive defeat of the forces of Antichrist would be to translate one of St John's prophecies into reality, to reach a new understanding of the text. Echoes of Revelation become more explicit in the later sections of *Lycidas*. The speaker invokes St Michael just before the consolation, and the vision of Lycidas in heaven draws heavily on apocalyptic prophecies. The cry that 'there shall be no more tears' (Revelation 7: 17, 21: 4) provides the ultimate authority for the injunction to 'weep no more'. At the start of the poem the speaker is locked in the cycle of natural recurrence—'yet once more'—but by the end he has had a vision of the ending of time, and the word 'once' has taken on connotations of finality. In Hebrews 12: 26–7 St Paul writes that 'once more' promises God's apocalyptic judgement.[107] The phrase modulates into 'no more', which is at once consoling for the elect and threatening to the unregenerate.

St Peter's speech is a call for religious reform; but how radical, in 1637, did Milton want those reforms to be? The 1645 rubric seems to claim that he had already anticipated the complete destruction of episcopacy; and some critics have found indications of a radically separatist programme in the poem's allegory. The ship was a traditional emblem of the Visible Church, and King's shipwreck may, on one reading of the poem, represent the corruption of the Laudian church: King can be saved from ecclesiastical shipwreck only by the direct intervention of Christ who walked the waves. On this reading the 'pilot' must be not St Peter, the first Bishop of Rome, but Christ, the only true head of the Invisible Church of the faithful, who is described as carrying keys in Revelation 1: 18.[108] But the allusions to the mitre and the keys make St Peter a more likely attribution; and there are significant qualifications in Milton's rhetoric.[109] The 'pilot' condemns 'such as' are greedy, thus implying that the church is not entirely irredeemable. His complaint that nothing is said at court about the growing influence of Jesuit proselytizing, the 'grim wolf with privy paw' (l. 128), was modified by Milton between November 1637 and the first publication of the poem in 1638: Laud had taken some steps against the Jesuits, and 'nothing said' was amended to 'little said'. A frontal attack on episcopacy would in any case have made little sense in 1637–8, at a time when opposition to Arminianism and to other aspects of royal policy was bringing together a broad front of political forces which were united in hostility to Laud but not in more specific religious programmes. Neither Prynne nor the majority of Puritans were at this stage completely opposed to episcopacy; on the other hand, Prynne was ready to co-operate politically with radical anti-episcopalians like Leighton and Bastwicke. Only after the collapse of Anglican authority was it to be fully revealed how much the unity of 'Puritanism'

---

[107] On these apocalyptic echoes see Wittreich, *Visionary Poetics*, 137 ff.

[108] Berkeley, *Inwrought with Figures Dim*, 73 ff., 197–8. Interestingly, the contrasts between Christ and Peter, and between different kinds of ecclesiastical vessel, are developed by Mure: see *The Works of Sir William Mure of Rowallan*, ed. William Tough, 2 vols. (Edinburgh, Scottish Text Society, 1898), i.305, and *The Joy of Tears*, 177.

[109] Contrast Bastwicke's satire of the ecclesiastical keys in *The Letany*, 4.

had been an illusion created by common hostility to Laud.[110] For his part, Milton was trying to speak with the authority of a whole tradition of prophetic poetry which went back to an era before the Reformation; and the more recent 'Spenserian' tradition had been sympathetic to low-church episcopacy on the Grindalian model. That he still had hopes of possible reform within the existing structures is indicated by his plans, after he had finished *Lycidas*, for an epic poem about King Arthur: such a poem would have implied panegyric of the Stuarts. As recently as 1636 there had been hopes that Charles might revert to more militantly Protestant domestic and foreign policies. *Lycidas* rises to epic tones at the point where Milton describes St Michael's Mount—a stronghold associated with the angel of apocalypse—looking towards the Spanish garrison at Bayona. In legend King Arthur had defeated a Spanish giant at St Michael's Mount.[111]

But such allegiance to the monarchy and to episcopacy was in Milton's case very much conditional on the king's pursuit of godly policies. In *Lycidas* the transforming authority of the divine Word has priority over all secular traditions. Whenever we date Milton's final rejection of any compromise with traditional Anglicanism, it can be argued that the poetry of the 1630s already constituted an emotional preparation for this decision. Milton was certainly not one to lag behind contemporary opinion. He was moved to publish his first pamphlet, *Of Reformation*, at a time when some kind of compromise, the 'reduced episcopacy' advocated by Ussher and supported by Quarles, seemed to be likely to prevail. Milton fiercely attacked such lukewarm compromises and urged the need for a radical break with the past. He was soon to become disillusioned with many features of the presbyterian programme, but in 1641 it provided the most immediately practicable means of achieving radical change. England must reject merely national traditions and bring herself in line with the 'best reformed churches' on the Continent. And that pressure was already being felt when Milton wrote *Lycidas*. In July 1637 Laud's attempts to impose a new prayer book on the Scots had provoked riots in Edinburgh which were to develop into a full-scale rebellion. Charles's attempts to aestheticize politics foundered on the intensely politicized and rationalistic culture created by the Scottish Reformation. Already in the summer of King's death the Venetian ambassador was writing that Laud feared that this rebellion would spread to England: the English people 'no less than the Scots seem greedy for an opportunity to extricate themselves from the yoke to which they are being subjected insensibly, little by little'.[112] Certainly there was considerable sympathy in England for the Scottish stand: Weckherlin was to support the rebels and regarded the English bishops as little better than 'papists'.[113] It did not

[110] Nicholas Tyacke, 'Puritanism, Arminianism, and Counter-Revolution', in Russell (ed.), *The Origins of the English Civil War*, 135, 141–2. On Prynne's links with Bastwicke, and strategies for circumventing the censorship, see Stephen Foster, *Notes from the Caroline Underground: Alexander Leighton, the Puritan Triumvirate, and the Laudian Reaction to Nonconformity* (Hamden, Conn., 1978), 46–7.

[111] Hunt, *Lycidas and the Italian Critics*, 142–4; Berkeley, *Inwrought with Figures Dim*, 70.

[112] *Calendar of State Papers . . . Venice, 1636–9*, 273.

[113] Forster, *Weckherlin*, 98–9. For more on Weckherlin and on contacts between England and Scotland at this time see 'Afterword', nn. 104, 106.

necessarily require supernatural gifts to believe that though Laud was now at the height of his power, his fall might be at hand. God the master-dramatist would bring low the mighty and exalt the humble, just as Lycidas, though 'sunk low', had 'mounted high', just as the humble pastoral form had become in the hands of prophetic poets a vehicle for divine discourse.

Lycidas is not a call for revolution, but its tone is not exactly cautious and moderate. Milton's political outlook at this time can usefully be contrasted with the response to current events of another poet, William Drummond. A literary conservative, and admirer of the Spenserian poets, Drummond also published a pastoral elegy in 1638. As has been seen, he disliked Laud's policies and supported religious toleration. But he was extremely worried by the growing force of radical Protestant opinion in Scotland, rightly fearing that it would unleash forces as intolerant as Laud's reaction. Moreover, Drummond was socially conservative, afraid that Protestant zeal might overthrow the social hierarchy. Whereas Milton had revised and revalued the tradition of Spenserian pastoral, Drummond was content simply to preserve the tradition; and a similar conservatism informed his social thought. In his pamphlet 'Irene', written in 1638, he warned the nobility who were leading the Scottish rebellion that '[t]he climactericke and period of the monarchicall Governmentes of Europe is not yet come, and when, or if ever, it shall come, yee who are Nobles shall perish with it'. Turning to the people, he urged them: 'Questione not the thrones of Kinges, revive not your old equalityes of Nature.'[114] This was of course a quotation from the climactic scene in Greville's *Mustapha*, where the priest backs down after wanting to incite the people to revolution:

> Question these Thrones of Tyrants;
> Reuiue your old equalities of Nature[.][115]

Before long, sections of the people were indeed to be demanding the revival of their old equalities, and radical questioning was to pass from Tacitist closet drama to uncensored pamphlets addressed to the general public. The prospect of such an event terrified Drummond. Milton, however, was to welcome the ferment of questioning and debate in *Areopagitica*, and *Lycidas* fuels, rather than quelling, the apocalyptic excitement that was soon to shatter the old order. About the time he wrote *Lycidas* Milton entered in his commonplace book a quotation from Sulpicius Severus: 'the name of kings has always been hateful to free peoples' (i.440).

But *Lycidas* is not merely a destructive poem, a prophecy of doom. Milton's apocalyptic hopes involved not just the reformation of a reactionary church but also a renewal of all the arts, including the art of poetry. As in *Comus*, the prophetic voice of judgement is counterbalanced by visions of a new kind of harmony with nature.

---

[114] *William Drummond of Hawthornden: Poems and Prose*, ed. Robert H. MacDonald (Edinburgh, 1976), 182–3. On Milton's interest in Drummond see Hill, *Milton and the English Revolution*, 490.

[115] Greville, *Mustapha*, v.iii.92–3. A reference to 'voluntarye servitude' in the next sentence of Drummond's pamphlet indicates that he recognized the affinities between Greville and La Boétie. For some interesting political annotations to Greville's works in the 1630s, see G. V. Akrigg, 'The Curious Marginalia of Charles, Second Lord Stanhope', in James G. McManaway et al. (eds.), *Joseph Quincy Adams Memorial Studies* (Washington, 1948), 785–801.

The fact that the bishops' songs are 'lean and flashy' implies the possibility of a newer, more ample and resonant kind of poetry. A radical change in political conditions would permit the release of the full potential of the English literary tradition. In *Of Reformation* Milton set his own, open and inventive style against the 'fantastick, and declamatory flashes' admired by the Laudian bishops (i.568). In *Lycidas* as in *Comus*, new developments in poetic style are symbolized by music and by clear water. When he called the work a 'monody' Milton was not only using a technical term for a particular kind of elegy but also alluding to the new music that revived a long-lost harmony with nature. This secular music is itself an echo of the apocalyptic music which Milton had already described in 'On the Morning of Christ's Nativity': he describes heaven in musical terms, making Lycidas hear the 'unexpressive nuptial song' (l. 176) while the saints 'sing, and singing in their glory move' (l. 180). The fluid syntax (possibly echoing *Paradiso* xxxi.4–5) makes song and action interchangeable. The 'other streams' of the heavenly waters are shadowed on earth by the Muses' streams, and the heavenly harmony is adumbrated by the harmony with nature which Lycidas' musical skill permitted: like Orpheus, he made the trees fan 'their joyous leaves to thy soft lays'. The imagery of Arcadian pastoral can be 'false' if it is used simply to aestheticize, to block out awareness of pressing political and religious concerns; but it can also provide a vision of an apocalyptically redeemed secular existence.[116] *Lycidas* ends not with doom and terror but with the swain's joyful song; his pipe with its 'tender stops' almost comes to life itself under the power of his Orphic song. His song is not insipidly Arcadian: it has confronted the realities of death and judgement. But it has gained a new energy from this confrontation; it leads him on to 'pastures new'. Milton's early poetry is radical not only in its explicit political comments but in its underlying visionary utopianism. The joy of poetic composition is bound up with the exercise of the political imagination. The early poems in fact heralded a period of unprecedented utopian speculation.

The swain's song is solitary, however; his audience is only the 'oaks and rills' (l. 186). He is 'uncouth', a word which in its sense of 'clumsy' enacts a conventional pastoral gesture of humility but which has a slightly more pointed implication: he is reviving the harsh language of religious prophecy which bland courtiers find too indecorous. In its other sense of 'unknown', the word is also allusive: 'uncouth' was the opening word of E.K.'s preface to *The Shepheardes Calender*, which declared that this new poet was as yet 'regarded but of few' but would soon be universally known. Milton signed *Lycidas* only with his initials; he was even more obscure than the modest Edward King. But at the end of the poem the swain energetically and confidently twitches his 'mantle blue'. Blue was a colour of hope: while the swain may lack the courtly laurel, he has earned the right to wear the mantle of prophecy.[117] His lay is 'Doric', simple and pastoral; but the multiple musical puns in the conclusion or

---

[116] Hunt, *Lycidas and the Italian Critics*, provides an excellent account of Milton's debt to, and revaluation of, the Italian court pastoralists. His point that there is no such thing as a single, undifferentiated 'pastoral tradition' (33) is worth reiterating.

[117] Fowler, ' "To Shepherd's Ear" ', 174.

'commiato' help to evoke also the 'Dorian' mode, which was stately and heroic. Milton has raised the humble pastoral genre to a new level of dignity and intensity; the last is coming first.[118] Milton's originality was not a matter of superficial innovation: true originality required a deep understanding of the poetry of the past. But he used conventional forms in highly innovative ways. Eclogues normally ended on a note of pathos as night approached. Phineas Fletcher, one of the less inventive of the Spenserian poets, ended canto vi of *The Purple Island* on such a note: the last stanza contains the words 'stealing', 'softly', 'creeps', 'unmask', 'evening', 'drouzie', 'rest', 'falling'. The only positive note comes with the last two lines:

> To morrow shall ye feast in pastures new,
> And with the rising Sunne banquet on pearled dew.[119]

Milton's conclusion linked him with his Spenserian predecessors: 'Tomorrow to fresh woods, and pastures new.' But these words strike a much more positive note because of the energetic and youthful tone of the 'commiato' as a whole: 'tender', 'various', 'eager', 'warbling', 'rose', 'twitched'. There is no need to refer the 'pastures new' too specifically to Milton's Italian tour—though he was to find a more sympathetic audience there than in England. More generally, the phrase indicated the responsiveness to artistic and political experimentation which the whole poem had demonstrated, and which was to make him welcome the Puritan revolution so enthusiastically. Milton believed that his own radicalism, however much it might go against the grain of recent political traditions, was a logical extension of the insights of the greatest European and English poets.

---

[118] Hunt, Lycidas *and the Italian Critics*, 93–4, 151–2, 168–70.

[119] Giles and Phineas Fletcher, *Poetical Works*, ed. Frederick S. Boas, 2 vols. (Cambridge, 1908–9), ii.86. The figure of new pastures for new poetic topics can in fact be traced back to the classical period: see E. R. Curtius, *European Literature and the Latin Middle Ages*, trans. Willard R. Trask (London, 1953), 86. It is the context which makes Milton's ending genuinely original. For a different reading of the Spenser–Milton relationship see Annabel Patterson, 'Couples, Canons, and the Uncouth: Spenser-and-Milton', in *Reading Between the Lines* (Madison, 1993), 36–56.

Afterword 2002

THIS book was intended to stimulate new research and to raise new questions; it is gratifying how many of those questions have received fuller answers since 1984, though much still remains to be done. At the same time, many areas which I largely or entirely neglected have started to receive a lot of attention. There are methodological reasons for these different developments, and I shall discuss these in section I below. Some readers may want to start with section II, which surveys recent work and proposes some new lines of enquiry; but the underlying paradigms deserve some general attention.

I

Poetry and Politics in the English Renaissance was an attempt to unite literary and historical studies. Interdisciplinary work of this kind is fraught with difficulties, which can perhaps be illuminated by the perspective of nearly two decades. I hoped that the book would be taken seriously by historians as well as literary critics, and this hope has on the whole been realized. Some literary scholars, indeed, have assumed that I actually am a historian by training. This is not always taken as a positive feature. Some readers have felt that I went too far in the direction of history, and neglected the kinds of close reading expected of a literary critic. It is true that the book is sceptical of rigid boundaries between poetic or metaphorical language and all other forms of discourse, and aims at a certain strategic suspicion of the imagination; yet it is also, as will emerge below, intended as a defence of poetry. In the final chapter I tried to offer a reading of *Lycidas* as close as ideally I would like all such readings to be, but such a procedure would have been quite impossible for all texts discussed in a book that was fundamentally a survey. As for the historical emphasis, in many respects the book is much closer to a traditional literary history than has become fashionable, in so far as I constantly set poems against their generic precursors, finding a linguistic and political dialogue moving through history, rather than setting literary texts immediately against quite different contemporary forms of social life.

That emphasis on the details of literary history and on a diachronic narrative, however, has seemed to other critics to represent a retrograde move at a time when theorists have turned so strongly against traditional historical modes. In his manifesto for a 'new historicism', Stephen Greenblatt indicated his own accommodation with the theoretical turn by sharply distinguishing his method from an older historicism which was theoretically uninformed and unaware of the interpretative stakes at issue in any historical narrative.[1] My own work does not identify itself with such a

---

[1] Stephen Greenblatt, 'Introduction', *The Power of Forms in the English Renaissance* (Norman, Okla., 1982), 2–6.

sharp opposition between old and new historicisms; with the result that it has often proved hard to categorize. Stanley Fish has aligned me with an outmoded positivism, with its belief that 'basic interpretive questions can be settled by finding the right (self-interpreting) materials' and failure to understand that history 'is a discipline, an intellectual praxis, and not a thing'. When he remarked that *Poetry and Politics in the English Renaissance* was 'a book cited almost reverentially by those of the historical persuasion', he did not intend it as a compliment.[2]

That kind of sharp opposition, between a Dark Ages of simple-minded positivism and a Golden Age of theoretical progress—a moment of inexorable 'post'ness, whether labelled poststructuralist or postmodern—has become taken for granted in much current discussion. It represents a mentality of a kind my book aimed to contest: a tendency to divide history into a series of hermetically sealed epochs, each with its own discourse. I was less concerned to oppose old to new historicisms than to locate opposing radical and conservative traditions of analysis going back to the early modern period itself, and to suggest that the polemics of the early modern period are still inescapably present in today's debates. For the currently dominant divisions between old and new lead to some serious misreading of historical debates, with the assumption that before the new historicism, all historians did was innocently to transcribe data without any awareness that their work might have ideological or political implications.[3] This results in a curious blindness to the fact that the historiography of early modern England has been a fierce arena of ideological charge and counter-charge for many years—arguably, indeed, since the Civil War itself. *Poetry and Politics in the English Renaissance* was involved in those debates (and, indeed, not received all that reverentially by some historians I disagreed with); Fish simply edits that polemical element out of the book when he presents it as a random accumulation of facts. Fish himself, I am sure, knows perfectly well that more is at stake; but we do sometimes find in recent criticism the phenomenon of critics who sincerely believe that Michel Foucault was the first person to point out that literature might be political, and who use historians as radically different as Kevin Sharpe and Christopher Hill as unproblematic 'sources', with no awareness of the debates in which their work has been enmeshed. Whatever the faults of historians reared on the Communist Party Historians' Group, unawareness of political implications was not one of them.[4]

---

[2] Stanley Fish, 'Milton's Career and the Career of Theory', in *There's No Such Thing as Free Speech and it's a Good Thing Too* (New York, 1994), 257–72 (262), *Surprised by Sin: The Reader in* Paradise Lost (1967; 2nd edn., Cambridge, Mass., 1997), p. lxii.

[3] For detailed refutation of that point, see Robin Headlam Wells, Glenn Burgess, and Rowland Wymer, 'Introduction', *Neo-Historicism: Studies in Renaissance Literature, History and Politics* (Woodbridge, 2000), 1–28. In so far as the specifically new element is supposed to be a revolt against positivism, René Wellek, 'The Revolt against Positivism in Recent European Literary Scholarship', in *Concepts of Criticism*, ed. Stephen G. Nichols, Jr. (New Haven, 1963), 256–81, traces the phenomenon back as far as Dilthey, in the 1880s.

[4] For a recent study that highlights political aspects of historiography see James Holstun, *Ehud's Dagger: Class Struggle in the English Revolution* (London, 2000). David Cressy, 'Foucault, Stone, Shakespeare and Social History', *English Literary Renaissance*, 21 (1991), 121–33, remarks on literary scholars' tendency to take particular historians as authorities; though I do not quite share his confidence that newer history is always better.

To some extent, this problem reflects disciplinary protocols: more strongly grounded in positivist traditions, historians are more concerned to subordinate whatever polemical aims they have to a marshalling of concrete evidence that can be appealed to across ideological dividing-lines. On a purely anecdotal level, it has long been my experience that historians tend to be much more sharply aware of the ideological stakes of their work than literary critics, and that the degree of political insight is not necessarily commensurate to the amount of space one takes up in proclaiming allegiances. The problem also reflects a transatlantic gap: the study of British history within the United Kingdom has been politicized in very specific ways that seem harder to understand elsewhere. One reason is that the political agendas have been substantially different. At the risk, of course, of the most monstrous simplification, in Britain considerations of class have been an ever-present concern, and questions of individual rights have often been subordinated to a preoccupation with social and political inequalities and to addressing them through collective or institutional action. In more recent years, though different forms of socialist policy have been steadily eroded, there has been a renewed interest in constitutional changes that would reform the neo-feudal institutions perpetuating social inequalities. In proposals for constitutional reform, Enlightenment-based models including American republicanism have attracted attention. In the United States, a polity founded on Enlightenment principles, there has been much more emphasis on the violence done by universality and abstract equality, on the exclusions from that constitutional model in its repression of different gender and ethnic identities. It is not surprising that the new historicism, with its anti-Enlightenment positions and its strong interest in questions of identity, subjectivity, and representation, should have taken off so quickly in the United States. In the process, however, the Continental theoretical models, with their sharp critiques of false universalizing or 'essentializing', have themselves tended to become decontextualized, often cited as authorities by critics who show little interest in their original linguistic and social milieux. Compared with the newer models, my own book's concern with a rationalist model of political debate and constitutional change, and with some traditions of Marxist history, will have seemed old-fashioned. In Britain in 1984, the emergence of the new historicism could look like a conservative development, while across the Atlantic it tended to be greeted as a radical break with an old conservatism. Those transatlantic differences help to explain why both views might have an element of truth; though of course neither side of the Atlantic has ever had a monopoly of any critical school or political position. (And I must ask the indulgence of other parts of the English-speaking world in focusing only on this particular relationship.)

At this distance in time, it may be hard to recall the British political climate in 1984, when contests between a collectivist socialist tradition and a newly aggressive neoliberalism were nearing a climax and debates on the left on their visions of the past and the future had a particular—one might say apocalyptic—intensity. Contending superpowers made the threat of nuclear war a very present one. If the Orwellian date conjured up fears of the worst dangers of totalitarianism, there was also widespread anxiety across a broad political spectrum about the Thatcherite challenge to a political culture that valued the public and the collective. The fact that the book emerged from its original publishers looking as if it had been hand-set by members of a small, amateur collective, though it inconvenienced readers, seemed not wholly inappropriate to its spirit, and I did not lament the absence of glossy pictures of members of the royal family. The book's subject matter, of course, was a long way from immediate political practice, and it aimed at an independent, or perhaps idiosyncratic, line in British cultural politics; but it did hope to stimulate the political imagination by recovering the range and boldness of early modern political verse and prose.

Contemporary British poetry and historiography often seemed lacking in such a perspective. The then-dominant currents of English poetry, I believed, suffered from a narrowing concern with the immediacies of personal experience, a lack of historical and political perspective; while more explicitly political and polemical verse often seemed a long way short of the formal and stylistic brilliance of so much Renaissance writing. In bringing to the fore a prophetic and Spenserian tradition, one that connected with the major Romantic poets, I was trying to redirect attention to forms of poetry that aimed to move outside direct experience and to defamiliarize the present. (Shelley's *Defence of Poetry* and *A Philosophical View of Reform* are strong if implicit influences; as are the exciting contextual works on Romantic poetry and on continuities between Renaissance and Romanticism by such critics as Marilyn Butler, Stuart Curran, and Joseph Wittreich.)[5] In analysing Milton's reworking of masque conventions in *Comus* I had in mind more recent experiments in political music and drama, such as the then-fashionable political adaptations of operas, and the translations and adaptations of Tony Harrison, a poet whose reworkings of earlier dramatic conventions themselves drew on Shelley's readings of the early modern period.[6] Another contemporary poet, Tom Paulin, drew heavily on the book in the introduction to his anthology of political verse.[7]

In historiography, the mid-1980s saw perhaps the high tide of a movement that has been termed 'revisionism'. This was a challenge to long-current versions of sixteenth- and seventeenth-century history. The historiography of early modern England had long been dominated by the revolution of the mid-seventeenth century. In the Whig tradition, it is true, 1688 was the real 'Glorious Revolution' and the tumult and regicide of the mid-century were a distressing aberration. The Whig version had long overshadowed the interpretation of republicans like John Milton and Edmund Ludlow for whom the establishment of a republic in 1649 had been a high

---

[5] Cf. Marilyn Butler, *Romantics, Rebels and Reactionaries: English Literature and its Background 1760–1830* (Oxford, 1981); Stuart Curran, *Shelley's 'Annus Mirabilis': The Maturing of an Epic Vision* (San Marino, Calif., 1975); Joseph Anthony Wittreich, Jr., *Visionary Poetics: Milton's Tradition and his Legacy* (San Marino, Calif., 1979).

[6] My essay 'The Reformation of the Masque', in David Lindley (ed.), *The Court Masque* (Manchester, 1984), 94–110 (94–5), cites as a parallel for Milton's strategy in *Comus* Shelley's insertion of commentary on Shirley's 1634 masque *The Triumph of Peace* in his tragedy *Charles the First*; Harrison found the same passage useful, with interestingly parallel political purposes: Tony Harrison, *The Trackers of Oxyrhyncus* (London, 1990), pp. xiv–v.

[7] Tom Paulin, *The Faber Book of Political Verse* (London, 1986).

point of national liberty. But historians sympathetic to dissenting religion, notably the great Victorian scholar S. R. Gardiner, had shown admiration for the 'Puritan revolution'. More recently, Marxist historians had identified the Puritan revolution with a social revolution, a decisive point in the transition from feudalism to capitalism. There had emerged what might be called a 'Popular Front' consensus, though with differing emphases on constitutional, religious, and socio-economic factors: the liberal Lawrence Stone and the Marxist Christopher Hill might differ widely on the causes of the English Revolution but they agreed that it had marked a very important milestone in world history. Hill was also formidably widely read in the period's literature and ready to draw on poetry and drama in his portrayal of a society in conflict. He represented a tradition of humanist Marxism which tended to see poetry as offering a utopian perspective beyond an existing social order.[8]

In the 1970s, such interpretations began to be sharply challenged by scholars like Conrad Russell and John Morrill.[9] This challenge was in part a response to the opening up of many new archival sources which any responsible account of the period had to incorporate. Though it was cast as a return to objectivity after years of political bias, however, the polemic of the revisionist challenge in many ways paralleled the neoliberal attack on the post-war political consensus. Older analyses of early modern England as riven by major social, economic, and cultural divisions were dismissed, and any attempt to relate English history to some wider narrative of political change and revolution was rejected as anachronistic or teleological. As David Cannadine has put it, the revisionists had a stake in showing that 'less happened, less dramatically, than was once thought'.[10] An extensive literature was devoted simply to castigating Hill's errors. And not the least of those errors, it appeared, was his readiness to rely on literary evidence, which tended to be viewed as unsound and subjective. The revisionists gave priority to what they considered the hardest forms of positive evidence, administrative and legal documents, and were strongly suspicious of what seemed softer evidence, such as more abstract political theory and above all such untidy and extravagant areas as poetry and drama. There were always significant exceptions, notably Blair Worden, a leading political historian with a very strong interest in literature; though in Worden's case there often seemed a tension between the literary interests and the revisionist conclusions. The dismissiveness with which revisionists greeted Margot Heinemann's *Puritanism and Theatre*, a bold if uneven book which charted connections between literary and political 'oppositions' in the Jacobean period and drew attention to a whole body of plays that had been almost entirely

---

[8] Cf. Lawrence Stone, *The Causes of the English Revolution 1529–1642* (London, 1972), and Alastair MacLachlan, *The Rise and Fall of Revolutionary England: An Essay on the Fabrication of Seventeenth-Century History* (London, 1996).

[9] Conrad Russell (ed.), *The Origins of the English Civil War* (London, 1973) offers a good introduction to the early stages of revisionism; the title, if not the explicit polemic, of his *The Causes of the English Civil War* (Oxford, 1990) indicates an extended riposte to Stone. See also John Morrill's new edition of his 1976 *The Revolt of the Provinces*, *Revolt in the Provinces: The People of England and the Tragedy of War 1630–1648* (London, 1999).

[10] David Cannadine, 'British History: Past, Present and Future', *Past and Present*, 116 (1987), 169–91 (183).

neglected by literary critics, seemed designed to warn off any critic with the temerity to suggest that literary evidence might weight against revisionist truths.[11]

I was publishing in the face of such a climate, with some anxiety about the likely reception but a firm belief that it was impossible to square revisionist interpretations with the immense imaginative and political openness of the period's poetic texts. And sceptical though I was about some of the revisionists' conclusions, for the literary historian there was a refreshing quality in the turn from very broad sociological generalizations to the detailed analysis of political agency in the light of previously neglected archival sources. This was an era in which the prestige of abstract theorizing was at its height and the humdrum activities of bibliographers and other literary scholars, already given a secondary status by the New Criticism, were if anything falling still lower in academic status. Reflecting that mentality, Stanley Fish reports that he finds the repeated brandishing of new documents a mere Satanic, positivistic noise, in its 'randomness and openness to surprise'.[12] I was starting on the contrary to find the a priori assumptions of contemporary theory depressingly closed and unsurprising, and to take particular pleasure in archival surprises, believing that they could have large-scale implications; I was as yet a novice in that kind of exploration, but a younger generation of scholars and critics has been able to give much greater definition to many areas the book was trying to open up. Revisionist scholarship helped to indicate many resources as yet little used by literary scholars, and had the revisionists not existed, it would have been necessary to invent them to tighten and reinvigorate tired arguments; if on occasion in the skirmishing below I may seem to have invented straw men, I have tried to be faithful to specific arguments, which it has been galvanizing to engage with. The task I set myself, then, was to respond to revisionist analysis with a literary history that stood a chance of being taken seriously as history; that task was also embraced in two other books that appeared in the same year, Martin Butler's *Theatre and Crisis* and Annabel Patterson's *Censorship and Interpretation*.[13] (Patterson, as a British-born critic based in the United States, has long spanned the transatlantic divide I have discussed, which helps to account for the specificities of her work.)

Articulating one's methodology for such a project, however, had become more problematic in the face of recent theoretical developments. My book was also responding to a very different critique of the old historiographical 'Popular Front', mounted with the same polemical energy from Perry Anderson, Tom Nairn, and their followers on the far left as the revisionists were mustering from the right. Rejecting romanticized views of a proud English radical tradition, they emphasized the backwardness of English theoretical speculation and political practice, caught, as they saw it, between a crude empiricism and a reactionary organicism. Where Hill saw the 'bourgeois revolution' of the mid-seventeenth century as launching England

[11] Margot Heinemann, *Puritanism and Theatre: Thomas Middleton and Opposition Drama under the Early Stuarts* (Cambridge, 1980).

[12] Fish, *Surprised by Sin*, p. lxii.

[13] Martin Butler, *Theatre and Crisis 1632–1642* (Cambridge, 1984); Annabel Patterson, *Censorship and Interpretation* (Madison, 1984).

towards modernity, even as it defeated more radical alternatives, Anderson and Nairn found that England was still locked within an archaic constitutional and political structure that belied its claims to modernity. Nairn considers the term 'bourgeois revolution' to be 'over-flattering' to the deeply conservative republicans of the mid-seventeenth century.[14] Though their evaluation was very different, their analysis of English political culture as deep-seatedly hierarchical and backward-looking had many affinities with J. C. D. Clark's arch-revisionist portrayal of a traditionalist order surviving with little challenge down to 1832.[15]

As a corrective to English parochialism the new theorists had a salutary force; and through the work of Tom Nairn their work helped to galvanize the reappraisals of the status of 'Britain' that have attracted so much attention more recently in theory and in political practice. My book's concern to link specifically English elements in poetry to a common, international humanist culture with a rationalist rather than traditionalist emphasis is in line with the new theorists' programme. As an explanation of how political change could occur and had occurred, and of the role of literature in that process, the new theoretical history was less satisfactory. The most influential theoretical model, Louis Althusser, retained a traditional Marxist appeal to an objective 'science', but his scorn for empiricism and positivism derived force from successive waves of anti-humanist theory—Heideggerian, structuralist, Lacanian, Foucauldian. All these theories insisted on the dominance of ideological or linguistic structures over the agents who believed themselves to be exploiting them for individual utterance. The Althusserians attacked figures like Hill, E. P. Thompson, and Raymond Williams for being contaminated by 'essentialist humanism' or, worse still, 'liberal humanism'. Their interest in literature was seen as part of an ideology that gave human creativity and agency the centre of the historical stage, whereas in fact 'biological men are only the *supports* or bearers of the guises (*Charaktermasken*) assigned to them by the structure of relations in the social formation'.[16] This ideology was at once illusory and desperately difficult to resist beyond a tiny theoretical vanguard. In the favourite Althusserian analysis, literature was an 'ideological state apparatus', functioning to contain resistance.[17] That particular claim seemed to me to involve a high degree of resistance to empiricism: it was advanced most vigorously at a time when Margaret Thatcher's government was showing more inclination to close down English departments than to bolster them in defence of its ideological authority. Literature has always been hard to tie down to the

---

[14] Tom Nairn, *The Enchanted Glass: Britain and its Monarchy* (London, 1988), 151 ff.; Perry Anderson, 'Components of the National Culture', in *English Questions* (London, 1992), 48–104.

[15] J. C. D. Clark, *English Society 1688–1832: Ideology, Social Structure and Political Practice during the Ancien Regime* (Cambridge, 1985).

[16] Ben Brewster, 'Glossary', in Louis Althusser and Étienne Balibar, *Reading Capital*, trans. Ben Brewster (London, 1970), 320. For different stages of the debate see E. P. Thompson, 'The Peculiarities of the English', in *The Poverty of Theory and Other Essays* (London, 1978), 35–91; Perry Anderson, *Arguments within English Marxism* (London, 1980), *In the Tracks of Historical Materialism* (London, 1983).

[17] For an analysis of English studies in these terms, see Terry Eagleton, *Literary Theory: An Introduction* (Oxford, 1983), ch. 1.

precise needs of a government, and the same, I believed, applied to the early modern period. Thomas Hobbes had placed a large part of the blame for the Civil War on humanist scholarship's admiration for republican Rome. To the extent that the book constitutes a defence of poetry, it is a response to that line of argument.

These debates between revisionists, liberals, and different shades of Marxism were fiercely contested. It is notable that what has since become seen as the major feature of any new historicism, a radical critique of empiricism, took only a secondary role in the discossions. What gave them such urgency was a sense that their stakes bore not only on the past but on the constraints the past might lay on, or the incentives it might give to, action in the present. Long before Hill gave the debates over the English Revolution a Marxist inflection, British historiography had been polemically engaged to the extent of virtually fighting the Civil War anew in each generation. The debates between Hill, Hugh Trevor-Roper, and Lawrence Stone on the role of the gentry clearly involved large claims about the validity of liberalism, Marxism, and their critics.[18] There was also, however, a consensus that such claims could be tested in ways that were open to public scrutiny and debate.

By this stage, however, it was already clear that one current within Althusserianism was pushing towards a far more radical epistemological position, rejecting not just the narrower forms of positivism as manifested by the revisionist historians but any claim to a grounding for historical knowledge outside the interpreter's own position. The emphasis on the overriding power of the structures of power and ideology was hard to square with the belief that it might ever be possible to think oneself enough outside a given discourse to encounter some empirically verifiable truth; and the claims of 'science' were hard to sustain. The Althusserians' militant anti-positivism had always been in an unstable equilibrium with the elements of dogmatic Marxism. (On one level, a scorn for the empirical meant that it was possible to safeguard the true faith without being disturbed by counter-evidence, though at a considerable long-term cost.) Their views had overlapped on epistemological questions with thinkers from a very different perspective, from Nietzschean critics of Enlightenment notions of individuality. The choice of 'humanism' as a term for the central evil to be eliminated follows Martin Heidegger's *Letter on Humanism* (1947), where this apparently arcane topic also took on political dimensions. Western civilization, Heidegger argued, had gone wrong because it had proceeded with a concept of man as a fixed, timeless, metaphysical essence, and the Renaissance had marked a decisive turning point towards an ever more abstract and essentialist conception of man. In this elegiac presentation, Heidegger blamed modernity's closed world of representation for the recent devastation of Europe, while absolving the counter-modern radicalism of the Nazi Party, of which he had been an initially enthusiastic member and which he conspicuously failed to repudiate now.[19] There was some overlap between Heidegger's very negative portrayal of the

[18] MacLachlan, *The Rise and Fall of Revolutionary England*.
[19] *Letter on Humanism*, trans. Frank A. Capuzzi in collaboration with J. Glenn Gray, in *Martin Heidegger: Basic Writings*, ed. David Farrer Krell (New York, 1977), 189–242.

Enlightenment from the right and Horkheimer and Adorno's critique from the left in their *Dialectic of Enlightenment*, which was also becoming influential.[20]

In the writings of Michel Foucault, whose Nietzschean anti-humanism provided the central theoretical basis for the new historicism, these currents from right and left converged. And they soon transformed interpretations of early modern literature. Stephen Greenblatt published his manifesto essay for a 'new historicism' and his *Renaissance Self-Fashioning* in 1980. Greenblatt himself always remained ambivalent towards anti-humanist theory, giving his work a particular internal dynamic. This is one of the strengths of his writings but has the odd consequence that the figure who more than anyone is taken to epitomize the 'new historicism' often eludes generalizations about it.[21] The force and elegance of his writings puts most of his critics, the present writer included, to shame, and *Renaissance Self-Fashioning* remains much the most compelling study of the period; but its followers are often more schematic. Much writing that falls under the 'new historicist' label has been more unambiguously committed to a Foucauldian programme.[22] In what follows I shall be dealing with an ideal type which individual critics would find a simplification; but I shall try to show in section II that the paradigms have often worked in consistent ways.

Catherine Gallagher has argued that Foucault's popularity derived logically from developments in the American New Left, where his radical questioning of conventional forms of representation worked with a widespread reaction against the vanguardism of the Old Left and its stiffness in responding to emerging movements more open to searching explorations of questions of gender and identity. This response was certainly not universal: in a memorable debate back in 1971, Foucault, declaring that 'I will be a little Nietzschean', ridiculed any notion of a human nature or 'ideal justice' and insisted that one 'makes war to win, not because it is just', while Noam Chomsky urged on him the need for a 'vision of a future just society', appealing to universal concepts derived from the Enlightenment.[23] Many others, however, found such 'humanism' stale, and in the postmodern reconfiguration of the intellectual world Chomsky has become positioned as a conservative. Foucault's break with Marxism, with positivism, with an entire bourgeois order of representation, seemed a welcome liberation, a way of escaping from older forms of social determinism: now, rather than seeing literature as reflecting economic developments, one could dismiss such analysis as appealing to an outmoded version of 'reality', and insist that

[20] Max Horkheimer and Theodor Adorno, *Dialectic of Enlightenment* (1947), trans. John Cumming (London, 1972).

[21] Stephen Greenblatt, *Renaissance Self-Fashioning from More to Shakespeare* (Chicago, 1980). Catherine Gallagher and Stephen Greenblatt, *Practicing New Historicism* (Chicago, 2000), 54–66, draw a not entirely convincing analogy between the work of Thompson and Williams and the new historicist interest in the anecdote; they concede, however, that Thompson 'clung to a humanist faith in historical understanding throughout his career' (56).

[22] In the vanguard was Jonathan Goldberg, with his *James I and the Politics of Literature: Jonson, Shakespeare, Donne and their Contemporaries* (Baltimore,1983).

[23] Catherine Gallagher, 'Marxism and the New Historicism', in H. Aram Veeser (ed.), *The New Historicism* (New York, 1989), 37–48; Fons Elder (ed.), *Reflexive Water: The Basic Concerns of Mankind* (London, 1974), 172–80.

signifiers or poems were as 'material' as anything else. If 'cultural materialism' is an oxymoron that implies some kind of tension between the component parts, the new historicists preferred chiasmic formulations which eliminated any distinction: 'the real is as imagined as the imaginary . . . All power is invested in fictions, and fictions are potent.'[24]

There were certainly equivalent movements in Britain, where there was a shared response to Foucault's sardonic inversions of many conventional liberal pieties and his interest in 'others' marginalized by Enlightenment discourse—the insane, the irrational, the sexually 'deviant', the criminal. From his insistence on the links between power and sexuality there has emerged a huge body of historiographical and critical work. These were not topics one could find discussed in the pages of the British revisionist historians—though they had been broached in Hill's more recent work, such as *The World Turned Upside Down*, and he was to champion this new work. The Old Left, however, in its commitment to a universalizing discourse, had tended to place issues of gender in a secondary position. Foucault was to have a major influence on the English 'cultural materialists', such as Jonathan Dollimore, whose *Radical Tragedy* was also published in 1984, and Alan Sinfield.[25] Their nomenclature indicated an attempt to find some kind of synthesis with the 'humanist' Marxism of Raymond Williams, and some kind of attempt to hold 'culture' in tension with a 'material' reality.

Perhaps rather more in Britain than in the United States, however, there was also concern about the tendency for this new 'materialism' to lose its historical anchorings. The vogue for Foucault could be seen as one of many enthusiastic returns to Nietzsche whose effects on European intellectual and political life over the past century had been strongly equivocal. Only a generation earlier, many of those who took the elimination of positivism and 'humanism' from intellectual life as their major goal had been found on the far right. This is not to equate epistemological with political positions in any simple way: in the long history of revolts against positivism one can find a broad range of political positions, from Collingwood to Croce to Heidegger. Nevertheless, in such cases as the revelation of Paul de Man's early fascist affiliations, what was striking was the complete stupefaction shown by a critical community attuned to an unhistorical, decontextualized opposition between an old, repressive positivism and an emancipatory Nietzscheanism. Perhaps in part because that history was a little closer to home, in Britain there was more resistance to different forms of poststructuralism on political grounds. There was also a suspicion that the Foucauldian attack on vanguards and representation, the all-embracing suspicion of power, might chime with a more traditional American hostility to the state.

---

[24] Goldberg, *James I and the Politics of Literature*, 33, 177; cf. my review, 'Absolute Revision', *English*, 33 (1984), 251–63.

[25] Christopher Hill, *The World Turned Upside Down: Radical Ideas during the English Revolution* (London, 1972); Jonathan Dollimore, *Radical Tragedy: Religion, Ideology and Power in the Drama of Shakespeare and his Contemporaries*, 2nd edn. (New York, 1989); Alan Sinfield, *Faultlines: Cultural Materialism and the Politics of Dissident Reading* (Oxford, 1992); for my own critique of the cultural materialists see my review of a number of Shakespeare books, *London Review of Books*, 7:13 (1985), 3–5.

There were, of course, many Foucaults—the last thing he aimed at was a 'humanist' coherence. With the discrediting of argument through empirical evidence, argument by authority was becoming more important, and Foucault was emerging as something like a medieval 'auctoritas', providing respectability for statements ranging from the truly adventurous to the utterly banal. Some elements in his work pointed to a relatively traditional, positivist archival scholarship, others were very close to Althusserian Marxism, but at other points his tone seemed reminiscent of conservative moments in Nietzsche and Heidegger in their rhetoric of a contemptuous intellectual aristocracy. Those 'humanists' on the left who had been opposed to Althusser were unlikely to find more appeal in an Althusser with the Marxism left out—this latter point being also, of course, disquieting to many Althusserians.[26] Many British feminists preferred to focus on questions of labour and economics which seemed to be sidestepped in the Foucauldian emphasis on representations. (As so often, of course, similar debates did take place on both sides of the Atlantic, with some American scholars criticizing the new historicism for suppressing the memory of recent and older moments of feminist agency.[27])

The new critiques of representation and reflection had the merit of tackling questions of literary language and form that had often been slighted in political and historical criticism. And yet the course chosen, while apparently gaining a greater centrality for literary texts in the social process, had its own limitations. By insisting so strongly that apparently literary categories such as 'theatricality' were also integral to political and religious life, the new historicism avoided marginalizing the aesthetic, but at the risk of projecting literary categories too easily on to political processes which might resist them. The belief in an extra-textual 'reality' need not involve denying the specificities of literary genre and language—it may indeed produce an added respect for those qualities as being, indeed, specific. If this latter approach may always risk over-politicizing aesthetics, the former risks aestheticizing politics; steering the right course is never an easy one. More generally, the confidence that textuality could explain everything led to the loss of a certain hard-nosed aware-

---

[26] Criticisms of Foucault's pan-textualism can be found in Edward Said, *The World, the Text, and the Critic* (London, 1983), ch. 9, and are hinted at in Frank Lentricchia, *After the New Criticism* (London, 1980), 188–210, who nonetheless chooses Foucault as the way ahead for criticism, 349–51; contrast Terry Eagleton's much sharper verdict that 'Foucault's political pronouncements have rarely been less than ambiguous and, on occasions, fatuous': 'The Idealism of American Criticism', *New Left Review*, 127 (1981), 53–65 (58), a judgement to which Lentricchia himself moves closer in 'Foucault's Legacy—a New Hitoricism', in Veeser (ed.), *The New Historicism*, 231–42. For earlier critiques from differing perspectives which seem to have made little impact on critics of Renaissance literature, see also Anderson, *In the Tracks of Historical Materialism*, Peter Dews, 'Power and Subjectivity in Foucault', *New Left Review*, 144 (Mar.–Apr. 1984), 72–9, repr. in *Logics of Disintegration: Post-Structuralist Thought and the Claims of Critical Theory* (London, 1987), ch. 5, and Gillian Rose, *Dialectic of Nihilism: Post-Structuralism and Law* (Oxford, 1984), ch. 9. On earlier traditions of Nietzschean politics in the study of the Renaissance see David Norbrook, 'Life and Death of Renaissance Man', *Raritan*, 8:4 (Spring 1989), 89–110, and 'The Emperor's New Body? Richard II, Ernst Kantorowicz, and the Politics of Shakespeare Criticism', *Textual Practice*, 10 (1996), 329–57; see also Holstun, *Ehud's Dagger*, ch. 3.

[27] Cf. Carol Thomas Neely, 'Constructing the Subject: Feminist Practice and New Historicist Discourses', *English Literary Renaissance*, 18 (1988), 5–18.

ness of the constraints on language and action that had been second nature to an older variety of 'materialism'.

Of the different forms of agency traditionally offered for change, class and economic determinants tended under Foucauldian influence to be dismissed with the old Marxist baggage, while individual forms of agency were equally questioned in a remorseless assault on the 'humanist' category of the individual or author. The favoured term was 'subject', a term coloured by structuralist linguistics, with its emphasis on the 'I' as an effect of language rather than an agent. Language increasingly came to seem the central or even the only determinant in the historical process, and language was analysed as a rigorously synchronic system, with the overall *langue* regulating any individual *parole*. Within a given system, there was little room for explaining any form of conflict or change; mutations would occur at certain times without evident explanation or continuing agency. Attempts have since that point been made to refine the model: for Louis Adrian Montrose, a critic much concerned with cultural conflict, subjectification is equivocal, 'it shapes individuals as . . . initiators of action' even as it '*subjects them to* . . . social networks and cultural codes'.[28] Just where this all-powerful 'it' is located remains obscure, however; and the moments of agency that 'it' is pleased to allow are seen as possible only through contradiction, in fleeting liminal glimpses, so that the base-line for what counts as critical thought is set very low, and the possibilities of collective work for change on a coherent ideological basis remain obscure.

The result of this attenuation of agency has been a 'historicism' of a very particular kind. The label had been used by Sir Karl Popper to attack Marxist and other theories of history that produced deterministic grand narratives of historical change. The new historicism, to this degree in line with Popper, tends to insist that all forms of knowledge are radically bound up with a specific historical context: so much so that it is in principle impossible to produce the kind of transcontextual laws posited by the other kind of historicism. Stephen Greenblatt has indeed included in his genealogy of the 'new historicism' theorists of the Romantic counter-Enlightenment like J. G. Herder, who insisted on the irreducible particularities of local cultures and specific periods, which are then to be analysed synchronically, in terms of the inner unity of a given epoch—one basis for later theories of the organic community.[29] This kind of insistence on the otherness of the past also had its impact on the understanding of contemporary intellectual history, which again tended to be seen in terms of abrupt shifts from 'old' to 'new' paradigms, with the old becoming very quickly bankrupt and devoid of further interest, rather than as dialogues responding in changing ways and with varying degrees of depth to continuing social, economic, and political pressures. The insistence that we can never transcend our time can instil a salutary sense of limitation, but the danger is that it

---

[28] Louis Adrian Montrose, *The Purpose of Playing: Shakespeare and the Cultural Poetics of the Elizabethan Theatre* (Chicago, 1996), 16; cf. Catherine Belsey, *The Subject of Tragedy* (London, 1985).
[29] Gallagher and Greenblatt, *Practicing New Historicism*, 5–9 (7).

can allow intellectual life to become complacently self-enclosed. We can never speak with the dead as we can with the living; but with patience, much is possible.

From the perspective of the historiographical debates in which I had been involved, Foucault and the new historicism looked to have a lot in common with the revisionists. To some extent, this perception reflected my own parochial biases. There was no opening towards queer theory or postcolonial criticism in the writings of Conrad Russell, and revisionist historians tended to be deeply suspicious of literary, or any, theory. In a representative attack, Sir Geoffrey Elton spoke of the 'virus' emanating from literary circles and warned against the 'cancerous radiation that comes from the forehead of Derrida and Foucault', authors whom this champion of the empirical method was ready to denounce without showing the slightest sign of having read them.[30] Elton's empiricism was as far removed as could be from the deep-rooted hostility to positivism and empiricism that characterized both the new historicism and, to a large degree, cultural materialism.

In terms of its ideological impact, however, revisionism often seemed not so much a full-blooded defence of the naked facts against theorizing as a selective interpretation, sometimes pushed into some quite abstract logic-chopping, with a conservative slant. Foucault encouraged a frontal assault on Enlightenment 'grand narratives' and on a history based on individual agency; the revisionists concentrated in detail on individual action and often presented themselves as returning to a traditional narrative history against the kind of interpretative sociological history associated with Hill. In practice, however, their work often focused on structural constraints on agency rather than on narrative.[31] In a sense, revisionist narrative always has to be ironic and anti-climactic, since it is designed to puncture old grand narratives of the English as struggling heroically for freedom or bourgeois revolution; the characteristic strategy of revisionist history has been to read against the grain of such narratives, breaking them down into discrete moments which it would be inappropriately teleological to connect with each other. In this tendency towards an analysis of synchronic moments rather than historical progression, revisionism shares intellectual affinities with the new historicism. In the same manner as new historicists insist that power works through discourses rather than individuals, the revisionist historian Glenn Burgess has argued that apparent contradictions and conflicts in the early modern political discourses are to be explained by the existence of discrete political 'languages', part of the patchwork of different institutional discourses in an *ancien régime* which lacked the post-Enlightenment quest to generalization and universalization.[32] Despite what have become ritualized attacks by critics on E. M. W. Tillyard's static and frozen account of *The Elizabethan World Picture*, the new models of early modern society have seemed strikingly reminiscent of

[30]   G. R. Elton, *Return to Essentials: Some Reflections on the Present State of Historical Study* (Cambridge, 1991), 26, 41.
[31]   Peter Lake, 'Review Article' on Conrad Russell, *Huntington Library Quarterly*, 57 (1997), 167–97 (169).
[32]   Glenn Burgess, *The Politics of the Ancient Constitution: An Introduction to English Political Thought, 1603–1642* (Basingstoke, 1992), 116 ff.

Tillyard.[33] The poststructuralist rejection of binary oppositions, of a split between the representer and the represented, can be invoked by revisionists against the idea that there might be profound social or political divisions in a social formation. Such a view, it has been claimed, would make us 'marginalise other contemporary positions' instead of leading to the appropriate 'decentred vision'.[34] In emphasizing such positions, Kevin Sharpe has to some extent abandoned an earlier fight for revisionist victory, urging instead in the manner of postmodern pluralism that we celebrate different views without trying to 'privilege' one interpretation as better grounded in the evidence than the other. In practice, however, this genial pluralism benefits a revisionist position, in being able to say farewell to all grand narratives.

At the time of writing *Poetry and Politics in the English Renaissance*, it was possible to foresee enough of these developments to think it urgent to try to clear a space for a different kind of literary history. On one level it would have been very easy to contest revisionist and other interpretations by dismissing them as empiricist; but such a victory would ultimately have been a Pyrrhic one, ceding the empirical ground unnecessarily. In 1984 the revisionists were indeed at a high point; but in the intervening years, many of their interpretations have been effectively contested on their own archival grounds, and revealed as having been subject to the kinds of polemical blind spots or evasions of which they accused their opponents.[35] Whatever Hill's limitations, he had read far more of the literature of the period than any other historian and probably than any other literary critic, and at a basic level of data-assembling, he was the most serious of all empiricists in grounding his generalizations about the culture. It cannot be said that the new researches have decisively changed the historians' preexisting interpretive dispositions. What such work can accomplish is to keep those dispositions under the constant necessity of engaging with a stream of new evidence and thus prevent them from hardening into completely closed circles—or what postmodernism more optimistically terms 'interpretive communities'. In response to the theorists, meanwhile, it seemed necessary on historical and political grounds to challenge what was coming to be a routine opposition between an old, conservative positivism and a new, progressive theory.

[33] David Norbrook, 'Rhetoric, Ideology, and the Elizabethan World Picture', in Peter Mack (ed.), *Renaissance Rhetoric* (London, 1994), 140–64, responding in part to Kevin Sharpe, 'A Commonwealth of Meanings', *Politics and Ideas in Early Stuart England* (London, 1989), 3–71. Jonathan Gil Harris, *Foreign Bodies and the Body Politic: Discourses of Social Pathology in Early Modern England* (Cambridge, 1998), 1–18, argues for the influence on the new historicism of functionalist sociology, in which opposition is seen as an external, alien force, and the parallels between such models and the conservative early modern models described by Tillyard. On the tendency of new theories of the subject to reinforce comparably static views of the Middle Ages, see David Aers, 'A Whisper in the Ear of Early Modernists; or, Reflections on Literary Critics Writing the "History of the Subject"', in Aers (ed.), *Culture and History, 1350–1600: Essays on English Communities, Identities and Writing* (Detroit, 1992), 177–202.

[34] Holstun, *Ehud's Dagger*, 13, notes the affinities between revisionists' and postmodernists' 'short work with binaries'; Kevin Sharpe and Peter Lake, 'Introduction', *Culture and Politics in Early Stuart England* (London, 1994), 1–20 (19). This is an admirably ecumenical work of collaboration between a strong anti-revisionist and an emergent post-revisionist, and it is at some risk of lapsing into humanist conceptions of 'authorship' that I speculate that this formulation may owe more to Sharpe.

[35] For a useful overview see the collection of essays edited by Richard Cust and Ann Hughes, *The English Civil War* (London, 1997).

I cannot claim that the book mounted those challenges in a comprehensive way, but it attempted to find a way forward by synthesizing different currents in historical and theoretical work. In beginning a book on English poetry with the Latin prose of More's *Utopia*, I was weighting its analysis towards the vigorous current of research into classical republicanism that had been inaugurated for early modern England by J. G. A. Pocock and Quentin Skinner. In their own way, these scholars were revisionists, arguing that social explanations of the English Revolution had greatly simplified the internal complexities of intellectual arguments. On the other hand, against many revisionists they strongly believed that ideological debates and divisions had played a significant part in the historical process. And they drew attention to the importance within those debates of classical republics as a benchmark for contemporary politics: not necessarily as a direct political model but as a source of norms which could be translated into the very different terms of early modern English institutions. That process of translation was important: the literary and political elites were encouraged to be able to think, and write, in Latin, in a language that was open to political values very different from those of the court, and the gap between those worlds was a space for writing and imagining that revisionist historians were reluctant to acknowledge. Since 1984, there has been an abundance of work on the impact of republican ideas. Skinner has continued to explore the intersection of classical and modern ideas of liberty; Markku Peltonen has offered a history of humanist political theory which overlaps in many ways with my own book.[36] Patrick Collinson has provocatively argued that Elizabethan England was a 'monarchical republic', with active citizens contained within the shell of subjecthood. In a study of officeholding, Mark Goldie has continued the theme of the 'unacknowledged republic'.[37] For these scholars, the republic of 1649 may not have been the economically driven 'bourgeois revolution' of Marxist interpretations, but neither was it the cataclysmic aberration from an older unified order portrayed by the revisionists and by some new historicists: rather, it was an exceptional development of tendencies already strong throughout the culture—a culture which was shaped by citizens rather than simply shaping subjects.

For the student of literary history, this current of historiography is especially interesting in making connections between language and politics, in emphasizing the high priority given by humanist education to the use of rhetoric in the active life, and also the deep suspicion within that tradition of any apparent attempt to crack down on public speech inappropriately. In theoretical terms, this emphasis on active speech offers a helpful counter to contemporary anti-humanist theory. In 1984, it was difficult to argue for the importance of understanding authorial intention, with the New Critics' attacks on the 'intentional fallacy' having gained a new lease of life

---

[36] Quentin Skinner, *Liberty before Liberalism* (Cambridge, 1998); Markku Peltonen, *Classical Humanism and Republicanism in English Political Thought 1570–1640* (Cambridge, 1995).

[37] Patrick Collinson, '*De republica Anglorum*' and 'The Monarchical Republic of Queen Elizabeth I', in *Elizabethan Essays* (London, 1994), 1–29, 31–58; Mark Goldie, 'The Unacknowledged Republic: Officeholding in Early Modern England', in Tim Harris (ed.), *The Politics of the Excluded, c.1500–1850* (Basingstoke, 2001), 153–94.

from recent proclamations of the death of the author. Support could be found in Skinner, whose project of setting political debates in historical contexts had led him to a 'linguistic turn' parallel to but distinct from that of poststructuralism, drawing not on structuralist linguistics but on pragmatics or speech-act theory. To understand a text, we need to analyse not only its cognitive content, considered as timeless truths, but the kinds of 'illocutionary act' the author was performing in publishing it: which positions she or he was attacking, how she or he was intervening in a contemporary context of debate. The history of political thought is thus reconceived as one part of the history of political action. It is also part of the history of reading: the study of the recovery of classical republican texts is also the study of their deployment in early modern debates. And by the same token, the modern historian charting the course of early modern republicanism is also involved in a series of contemporary debates which carry ideological significance today.

In this kind of analysis, authorial intention is important, but it is conceived in social, intersubjective terms, rather than as a singular isolated will. My book is certainly concerned to contest the kind of literary criticism which would abstract a writer's poems into a timeless canon of texts that speak only to each other or to other poems. I have tried to set individual poems in the context not of a single writer's development but of a shared political project; rather than accepting a choice between an isolated, totally autonomous author and the decentred subject of poststructuralist theory, I explore the ways in which authorial agency can connect with broader political agencies without being dissolved into the culture as a whole. La Boétie exemplifies a current in humanism for which individuality, in the sense of a deviation from the common good for the sake of private reward, was the lure used by princes against liberty. More's imaginative vision of Utopia was an extrapolation from a common humanist discourse which did not fit easily with his religious commitments. Greville's acutely self-critical discourse, which can seem to work at odds with authorial intention, needs to be understood against the wider background of later sixteenth-century Tacitism. The clustering of activity by the Spenserian poets around the 1614 Parliament, for example, becomes apparent only when moving beyond narratives of individual authors. Intention is clarified by situating a text in relation to a sequence of interventions in debates. As Skinner has observed of his version of speech-act theory, 'the approach I am sketching leaves the traditional figure of the author in extremely poor health'.[38]

Indeed, if pushed in one direction this approach to collective authorship may converge with a Foucauldian radical historicism and discursive determinism—as in some of the work of revisionists like Sharpe and Burgess.[39] The specific character of this linguistic turn, however, gives it an inherent emphasis on the possibilities of dialogue and change. Modern pragmatics, indeed, can be regarded as a rethinking of

---

[38] James Tully (ed.), *Meaning and Context: Quentin Skinner and his Critics* (Princeton, 1988), 276.
[39] There has been a remarkable shift between Skinner's dismissal of Foucault and poststructuralist philosophy as being merely 'interesting to connoisseurs of the more decadent forms of individualism' (ibid. 272) and his more recent declaration that he has been 'much influenced' by Foucault's *The Archaeology of Knowledge* (*Liberty before Liberalism*, 112 n).

classical rhetoric, which was central to the practice of classical republics and their early modern admirers. Here we encounter a sense of the term 'humanism' related to, yet significantly contrasting with Heidegger's: the *studia humanitatis*, the revival of classical learning and in particular of the arts of language. Logic was increasingly dethroned from its central place in the medieval arts curriculum, the *trivium*, by rhetoric, the effective of use of language for public argument and enquiry. Humanist education centred on the possibility of arguing *in utramque partem*, on the possibility and pedagogical value of finding counter-arguments for any proposition, however commonplace and apparently incontrovertible.

The humanist movement can be aligned with different sides in current theoretical debates. In so far as the humanists valued rhetoric over metaphysics, local and concrete argument over abstraction, and hence emphasized that language was not just a medium of thought but what shaped thought, they can be aligned with various critiques of modernity. Derrida's ludic mode has points in common with the Renaissance humanist valuation of wordplay as a response to the linguistic insensitivity of Aristotelian philosophy. Heidegger can be seen as reclaiming the legacy of Renaissance 'humanism' even while applying that particular term to designate the revival of logic and metaphysics in the seventeenth century.[40] Such a line of argument informed McLuhan's doctoral thesis on Thomas Nashe, whose assumptions underlie his later work on the media: for McLuhan, Nashe's attack on Puritans is linked with his defence of a traditional mentality centred on rhetoric and an oral culture.[41] A conservative humanist tradition can certainly be traced down to figures like Swift and Pope. Yet Nashe's adversary Gabriel Harvey, as was seen in Chapter 3, was both aggressively modern and very definitely a humanist; if humanist 'philosophy' is not that of Descartes and Locke, neither does it involve a systematic embrace of tradition.[42] In valuing the process of debate, humanism produced a critical pressure against institutions which might impede that process. Many of its canonical texts, notably the writings of Tacitus, presented monarchical government, with its monopoly of power, as a blight on independent thought and an enemy of rhetoric. In the early modern period, similar arguments were brought to bear against other institutions which exercised control over discourse, from the church to, for the more radical, the legal, medical, and other professions. The humanist emphasis on the practical use of language involved an eager exploitation of the printing press, the newest medium of communication.

[40] Ernesto Grassi, *Heidegger and the Question of Renaissance Humanism: Four Studies* (Binghamton, NY, 1983). For all their differences, connections can also be traced with the neoconservative classicizing of Leo Strauss.

[41] Marshall McLuhan, 'The Place of Thomas Nashe in the Learning of his Time' (Ph.D. thesis, Cambridge, 1943).

[42] For surveys of humanist political thought, see J. H. Burns (ed.), *The Cambridge History of Political Thought 1450–1700* (Cambridge, 1991), Part I. On humanist interest in probable argument rather than the scholastic syllogism see Lisa Jardine, 'Humanistic Logic', in Charles B. Schmitt (ed.), *The Cambridge History of Renaissance Philosophy* (Cambridge, 1988), 173–98, and on the implications for literature, Lorna Hutson, *The Usurer's Daughter: Male Friendship and Fictions of Women in Sixteenth-Century England* (London, 1994).

Humanist ideas were an important component in the pressure for what Jürgen Habermas has termed the 'bourgeois public sphere', a space for rational debate and critique independent of traditional, hierarchical monopolies of discourse. Habermas dates the emergence of this sphere in England to the early eighteenth century, with a securely based parliamentary government, the foundation of the Bank of England, and the breakdown of the old licensing system. In the highly uneven development of early modern England, however, strong pressures towards a political public sphere can be traced much earlier.[43] Habermas's project can be seen as a rethinking of classical republican ideals in the context of new media and economic conditions. Habermas claims that the rationality built into language permits a utopian moment in each speech-act, a pressure towards less exclusive communication in an ideal speech situation. His history of the bourgeois public sphere is anchored in a sociological, and in some ways classically Marxist, causal explanation through economic forces, but is still able to find a utopian moment in the opening from older restrictions on discourse. He has continued to claim that his history of the public sphere stands or falls on empirical grounds, but his historical work is only one moment in a more general theoretical engagement with the critiques of the Enlightenment found both in Horkheimer and Adorno and in Heidegger. In the neo-Heideggerianism of the Foucauldians and poststructuralists he found openings to a neoconservatism— though the conservative label is one that his critics have applied to him.[44] Habermas certainly drew attention to problematic aspects of Heidegger's political legacy long before they were discussed by literary theorists. For Heidegger, what was wrong with modernity was 'the peculiar dictatorship of the public realm'. This phrase may have been one of the provocations behind Habermas's very different conception of the public realm—Habermas has emphasized his perturbation at the political disingenuousness of the *Letter on Humanism*.[45] Though Habermas, like Horkheimer and Adorno, does consider the modern public sphere to be deeply flawed, in a history of its long-term development he found potential as well as containment.

In revisionist terms, this approach stands as unacceptably teleological, and certainly Whiggish. And it needs a lot of caution and refinement in being brought to bear on the early modern period.[46] Nonetheless, it has proved heuristically valuable, and in rewriting Chapter 8 I have alluded more explicitly to his ideas. His model encourages us to locate pressures towards a wider political community, contesting top-down models in which monarch and court set the ideological agenda. In

---

[43] Jürgen Habermas, *The Structural Transformation of the Public Sphere: An Inquiry into a Category of Bourgeois Society* (1967), trans. Thomas Burger with the assistance of Frederick Lawrence (Cambridge, Mass., 1989).

[44] Jürgen Habermas, *The Philosophical Discourse of Modernity: Twelve Lectures* (1985), trans. Frederick G. Lawrence (Cambridge, Mass., 1987).

[45] Heidegger, *Letter on Humanism*, 197; *Autonomy and Solidarity: Interviews with Jürgen Habermas*, ed. Peter Dews (London, 1986), 159, 195–7.

[46] For critiques see David Zaret, 'Religion, Science and Printing in the Public Spheres in Seventeenth-Century England', in Craig Calhoun (ed.), *Habermas and the Public Sphere* (Cambridge, Mass., 1992), 212–35, and Joad Raymond, 'The Newspaper, Public Opinion, and the Public Sphere in the Seventeenth Century', in Raymond (ed.), *News, Newspapers and Society in Early Modern Britain* (London, 1999), 109–40.

insisting on the dialogical character of language, Habermas prompts us to look for opposing viewpoints rather than to assume that such viewpoints cannot have existed, and such an approach leads to a useful scepticism toward any generalization about a uniform 'culture'. It is also part of Habermas's argument, however, that critical or oppositional views are likely to encounter material obstacles; the historiographical implication is that they will be less well preserved and hence need extra effort in unteasing them.[47] This is not a point that is new to Christopher Hill, who has mischievously cited William Blake's claim that '[n]othing can be more contemptible than to suppose Public RECORDS to be True'. The official and administrative documents on which revisionists tend to rely, he points out, 'convey what ruling persons wanted to believe, not necessarily what actually happened'.[48]

Hill is here endorsing a healthy and concrete scepticism about archival survival, rather than an all-embracing postmodern scepticism about the possibility of any separation between power and knowledge. The implication is that our interpretations should be historical, in the sense of locating a text in a context, but not historicist, in the sense of defining each historical epoch as a self-contained, synchronically coherent unit. Stanley Fish assumes that the 'master rule' of all historical criticism is 'always historicize'; but as has been seen, the Foucauldian model of historicism is far from my own, and if I am proposing any master rule it is 'always contextualize', with the assumption that specific contexts always have universal resonances.[49] Political views which are strongly asserted generally have the aim of confuting an opposing position; often, however, oppositional texts are less likely to be preserved in archives, and, even to understand the orthodoxy of an age, it is necessary to be able to imagine heterodoxy. History does not move in a smooth linear progression; certain views may be dominant for a time and almost erase the traces of counter-views. It is all the more important to be sensitive to the short-term and long-term operations of ideological conflict and change. David Wootton has pointed out that while we have a word for 'anachronism', we need and lack a word—he suggests 'parachronism'—for an equal and opposite error, which 'blindly insists that current events have yet to occur'. The latter is a particular pitfall in dealing with a time of rapid change when the horizons of future possibility are suddenly open.[50] By the same token, there are grounds for scepticism about the concept of 'ideology', if it is taken to imply a single world-view so dominant that nobody could think outside it; though structures of political and economic power do very often function to obstruct oppositional thought. I have taken some pleasure over the years in drawing attention to documents which the conventional understanding insisted could not have existed, from the text of a court

[47] David Greetham, 'The Cultural Poetics of Archival Exclusion', *Studies in the Literary Imagination*, 32 (1999), 1–28 (writing himself, in fact, from a strongly postmodern viewpoint; I owe this reference to Bill Sherman).

[48] William Blake, *Poetry and Prose*, ed. Geoffrey Keynes (Oxford, 1966), 392, cited by Christopher Hill, *Milton and the English Revolution* (London, 1977), 69; *A Nation of Change and Continuity: Radical Politics, Religion and Literature in Seventeenth-Century England* (London, 1990), 196.

[49] Fish, 'Milton's Career and the Career of Theory', 259.

[50] David Wootton, 'Leveller Democracy and the Puritan Revolution', in Burns (ed.), *The Cambridge History of Political Thought 1450–1700*, 412–42 (417).

masque opposing the official Jacobean line to an epic poem by a female republican.[51] Reading historically need not imply a drastic narrowing of the intellectual horizons.

II

Many of the ideological passions of my book's original context have dissipated in the ensuing years. Large bodies of literary history and scholarship in a fairly traditional mould have been proceeding quietly in many parts of the world, relatively independent of theoretical perturbations. Historians speak of 'post-revisionism', or no longer speak of revisionism at all. Literary scholars with a strongly theoretical bent, informed by the new turn to the material culture of the book, are becoming engaged in animated dialogues with bibliographers of the most positivist cast. In surveying work on poetry and politics since 1984, these tendencies to synthesis can often be seen, and I offer many of the remarks below as a contribution to that process. If I have nonetheless thought it important to highlight the earlier differences, it is out of a lingering concern that terminology and issues which once carried a very serious ideological and emotional charge may become routinized into a predictable professional jargon. In more recent work, some of the earlier debates are still very much present, albeit sometimes in an attenuated form.

Since 1984 there has been much new work in four areas to which I gave severely restricted attention: gender; national identity; religion and especially Catholicism; and questions relating to the social circulation of texts—censorship, manuscript circulation, the history of reading. All these gaps may be considered inherent in the book's methodology, in a focus on public debate and public agency that leaves little space for the subjective element. In the traditional grand narratives of modernity, the realm of politics has been considered in abstract and universal terms; in the postmodern critique of modernity, more and more attention has been paid to the repressions involved in effacing different forms of specific and discrete identity. Much work since 1984 has focused on the politics of identity rather than the politics of Parliament and the state; in dislodging the author, critics have paid attention to the multiple means by which texts reached the public. In this turn to a politics of identity, however, there has often been a tension between postmodern theory with its radical critique of any 'essentialist' model of subjectivity, and a tendency to view politics in terms of a coalition of different identity constituencies. If the old grand narratives suppressed identities, the new anti-narratives sometimes reify them. And the tendency for a convergence between certain revisionist and new historicist emphases reveals itself at a number of points. In the longer term, it is to be hoped that these different perspectives can find a more nuanced mutual accommodation.

Before turning to these questions, a few words should be said about the contingencies of the book's history, which account for some of its gaps and emphases. It was based on my doctoral thesis, which took a detailed study of the patronage and

[51] Norbrook, 'Rhetoric, Ideology, and the Elizabethan World Picture', 140–64; '*The Masque of Truth*: Court Entertainments and International Protestant Politics in the Early Stuart Period', *Seventeenth Century*, 1 (1986), 81–110; Lucy Hutchinson, *Order and Disorder*, ed. David Norbrook (Oxford, 2001).

politics of masques, pageantry, and other occasional poetry as a point of departure for a study of political poetry in the reigns of Elizabeth and James. By the time the thesis was completed, I was becoming eager to move on to different terrain. The final chapter is in a sense a prologue to my book on the poetry of the English Revolution, *Writing the English Republic* (1999), whose first chapter revisits the 1630s. As a result of this shift of direction, in some ways the book underplays the specific political significance of the world of the court. Since 1984 there has been much important historical work on the apparently private world of the monarch's immediate circle; as revisionists have played down the role of Parliament, so the significance of other forms of offering counsel to the monarch has gained new attention. Access to the monarch's Privy Chamber was a crucial avenue of political influence, and under some circumstances could be as important as membership of the Privy Council. These names indicate the blurring between public and private matters that was inherent in the institution of monarchy. Presenting a gift or a poem to the monarch was in its own limited sense as much of a public act as printing a political pamphlet. New historicist critics have been strongly interested in these aspects of the poetic world, while there has been important scholarly work by Steven W. May and many others.[52] A new edition of Nichols's editions of the progresses of Elizabeth I and James I—the staple sources of my thesis—is now under way.[53] Much remains to be done. By the time I was working on the book, however, I was becoming rather impatient with the tendency of the latest new historicist criticism to focus on the court as centre of power. Frances Yates's important work on the iconography of monarchy was becoming used rather uncritically, to the point where portraits of Queen Elizabeth that would only have been seen by a very small elite were presented as if they were the key to the nation's collective unconscious.[54] A few years later, I found it quite a struggle to publish an anthology of Renaissance verse which did not have a picture of Queen Elizabeth on the cover. I wished to shift the emphasis towards a broader conception of the public world.

It could be argued that the book's title was inappropriate to the new project. Since 1984 there has been growing disquiet with the label 'Renaissance', and a preference for the more neutral—though hardly less teleological—'early modern'. As it emerged in later nineteenth-century literary history of England, 'Renaissance' implied a distinct preference for certain kinds of courtly verse; poetry on public themes, ballads, and other satirical verse were relegated to lesser categories, and in

---

[52] Frank Whigham, *Ambition and Privilege: The Social Tropes of Elizabethan Courtesy Theory* (Berkeley and Los Angeles, 1984); David Starkey (ed.), *The English Court: From the Wars of the Roses to the Civil War* (London, 1987); Jason Scott-Warren, *Sir John Harington and the Book as Gift* (Oxford, 2001); Patricia Fumerton, *Cultural Aesthetics: Renaissance Literature and the Practice of Social Ornament* (Chicago, 1991); Steven W. May, *The Elizabethan Courtier Poets: The Poems and their Contexts* (Columbia, Mo., 1991); Catherine Bates, *The Rhetoric of Courtship in Elizabethan Language and Literature* (Cambridge, 1992).

[53] John Nichols (ed.), *The Progresses and Public Processions of Queen Elizabeth* (London, 1788–1805 and 1823); *The Progresses, Processions, and Magnificent Festivities of King James I*, 4 vols. (London, 1828); a new edition is to be produced by the John Nichols Project, University of Warwick, under the general direction of Dr Margaret Shewring.

[54] See, for example, Christopher Pye, *The Regal Phantasm: Shakespeare and the Politics of Spectacle* (London, 1990).

many ways the study of public poetry still suffers from the disproportionate focus of scholarly and editorial labour on courtly verse.[55] The term 'Renaissance' does, however, have the merit of drawing attention to the historical consciousness of the humanist project, the attempt to recover and re-create the literature of a far-distant epoch, in the process gaining critical perspective on the present.

That most tired of clichés, 'Renaissance man', has recently been receiving especially sharp scrutiny, with the period's glorification of masculine virtue seen as at once restricting masculine sexuality and depending upon the suppression of a female Other. My book does touch on these questions in its readings of Spenser and of Fulke Greville, but in rewriting today it would be necessary to take account of a much larger body of criticism and theoretical reflection. The characteristic new historicist mode has been to insist on the radical otherness of early modern models of gender. Following Thomas Laqueur's widely influential book, it has become almost axiomatic that for the early modern period with its 'one-sex model', the distinction between male and female was believed to be so fragile and arbitrary that unexpected mutations of gender were a distinct possibility.[56] Following Foucault and Alan Bray, scholars of homoerotic desire have affirmed what has been termed a 'neo-inventionism', holding the early modern period to be so different from ours that there can be no transhistorical category of 'the homosexual'. While there was strong aversion to sodomy, placed in the statute book in 1533 as a capital offence, that term was a wide and diffuse one, while same-sex friendship between males with a strong erotic component did not arouse any particular shock. These strongly anti-empiricist models have tended to focus attention on the dominant languages and discourses that constructed gendered subjects, with less interest in specific forms of agency.[57]

In the case of heterosexual women, the focus on discourses and identity formation may lead to an overemphasis on the period's conservatism. One current of criticism has started from the conduct manuals that insisted women should be chaste, silent, and obedient, and has concluded that women who did speak or write must have been seen as deviant, a threat to the symbolic order and productive of endless male anxiety. The manuals also insisted that the public realm should be confined to males, while females should remain private; for women to take an interest in political affairs would therefore have been anathema. We are thus presented with a female equivalent of the Tillyardian Elizabethan World Picture, a world in which any behaviour other than obedience is effectively unthinkable.[58]

---

[55] *The Penguin Book of Renaissance Verse*, selected and introduced by David Norbrook, ed. Henry Woudhuysen (London, 1992), pp. xxi–xxvi.

[56] Thomas Laqueur, *Making Sex: Body and Gender from the Greeks to Freud* (Cambridge, Mass., 1990); the evidence advanced is, however, rather limited, see Lorna Hutson, 'On Not Being Deceived: Rhetoric and the Body in *Twelfth Night*', *Texas Studies in Literature and Language*, 38 (1996), 140–74, and Jane Sharp, *The Midwives Book*, ed. Elaine Hobby (New York, 1999), pp. xxviii–xxix.

[57] Alan Bray, *Homosexuality in Renaissance England* (London, 1982); Joseph Cady, ' "Masculine Love", Renaissance Writing, and the "New Invention" of Homosexuality', in Claude J. Summers (ed.), *Homosexuality in Renaissance England* (New York, 1992), 9–40.

[58] Patricia Parker, *Literary Fat Ladies: Rhetoric, Gender, Property* (London, 1987), ch. 6, offers a highly suggestive reinterpretation of the Tillyardian 'world picture' in rhetorical terms, but in emphasizing fear

As other scholars have been showing, however, it is rash to assume that all women meekly allowed themselves to be subjected to the dominant discourse—or that the dominant discourse was so uniform. Resisting a more recent orthodoxy, many feminist scholars have argued that the emphasis on all subjectivity as illusory and constructed elides the very specific social differences between males and females. While those differences were firmly based, they were not quite as uniform as is suggested by a focus on representation rather than practice. In the English Renaissance the public life may very broadly have been gendered male; but to overemphasize that point is to neglect the many women who actively concerned themselves with public issues. Recent work on women and the law, for example, shows ways in which it was possible to circumvent some of the rigid restrictions on female agency imposed by the common law through a recourse to Chancery.[59] As for access to making the law, the official position was confidently stated in the standard Stuart treatise on women and the law: 'Women have no voyce in Parliament, they make no Lawes, they consent to none, they abrogate none.'[60] And yet women did not always accept this view; some of them did vote in parliamentary elections. Though this privilege was normally confined to widows of men of high rank, in the fiercely contested 1641 election, on the eve of the Civil War, large numbers of women caused concern by turning up for the polls. We have an interesting record by the Puritan politician and scholar Sir Simonds D'Ewes (who makes a fleeting appearance above at p. 209). D'Ewes may have been particularly interested because of his long-standing contacts with a pioneering woman intellectual. He was a friend of Bathsua Reynolds, who had published a precocious volume of Latin verse in 1616, campaigned actively for women's education in the 1640s, and much later in her life was to publish one of the most eloquent defences of that cause. She and D'Ewes were both correspondents of the noted Dutch scholar Anna Maria van Schurman. Remarkably, D'Ewes decided that the women's votes were perfectly legal; but it is sad to relate that he went on to conclude they should not be counted since it was dishonourable for a woman to vote.[61] The seventeenth century saw a steady pressure to change the old chequerboard of different franchises and electoral privileges into more clearly codified rights, and though this process was far from complete it did result in a more systematic exclusion of women from parliamentary elections. The history of that earlier participation was uncovered by feminist scholars of the late nineteenth century as part of their campaign for women's suffrage, and then again forgotten over a long period when 'high' political history excluded questions of gender. A narrowly historicist reading would be able to offer many sophisticated explanations of why those women of 1641 could not have

---

of female disorder in Puttenham, 108–10, omits to mention that Puttenham is offering his rhetorical manual to show ladies how to write poetry (cf. pp. 63–4, 70–1, above).

[59] Maria L. Cioni, *Women and the Law in Elizabethan England with Particular Reference to the Court of Chancery* (New York, 1985).

[60] T.E., *The Lawes Resolution of Womens Rights* (London, 1642; facsimile, Amsterdam, 1972), 6.

[61] Derek Hirst, *The Representative of the People? Voters and Voting in England under the Early Stuarts* (Cambridge, 1975), 18–19; Frances Teague, *Bathsua Makin, Woman of Learning* (Lewisburg, Pa., 1998); Sara Mendelson and Patricia Crawford, *Women in Early Modern England* (Oxford, 1998), 396 ff.

existed; a dialogical reading will help us to ask, within the limited evidence available, why they did.[62]

Women poets were in the vanguard of humanist and Protestant politics. In my 1984 Introduction I arguably gave an unduly bleak account of the attitudes of humanists towards female education. It is true that the humanists emphasized the role of education as preparing for the active life, and that women were excluded from most of the public professions. Some humanists, nevertheless, pressed for at least modest education for women, while fathers eager to arrange prestigious marriages came to feel that their daughters should at least be able to meet educated suitors on the same ground. Henry VIII's unusually high turnover of queens was a vivid reminder that you never quite knew when your daughter might be raised to high rank; and though courts were the centres for female education, it is becoming increasingly clear that literary interests and abilities were diffused more widely. The aristocratic Surrey's apocalyptic sonnet against London (p. 41) was remodelled by Anne Askew in her bold stand against the church, while a woman of considerably humbler origins, Anne Lock, was the first English poet to compose a Protestant sonnet sequence.[63] In his quest for a native English prophetic tradition, John Bale looked back to earlier women writers and sought to cast Elizabeth in the same mould.[64] Bale's hero the Duke of Somerset was ready to take up avant-garde cultural positions in relation to female education: his three daughters published a joint volume of elegies for Marguerite of Navarre, whose *Mirror of a Sinful Soul* had been translated by Elizabeth and published, probably under Bale's auspices, in 1548.[65]

Elizabeth's own accomplishments as a humanist still need fuller exploration. The latest edition of her works, while valuably opening up her devotional writings and her letters, fails to include her extensive translations in prose and verse, ranging across the humanist canon—Plutarch, Cicero, Horace, Seneca, and also Boethius.[66] It is almost as if the Renaissance stereotypes are being perpetuated in inversion: entering the 'masculine' sphere of learning is not what is now expected of a woman writer. As Kevin Sharpe has observed, it is striking that Elizabeth should have translated Horace's *Ars poetica* in the late 1590s, when poets' involvement in political debates was prompting heightened censorship, and Horace appeared on stage in Jonson's *Poetaster* as a figure of the responsible poet.[67] Around the same time she

[62] Charlotte Carmichael Stopes, *British Freewomen: Their Historical Privilege* (London, 1894), a book that needs reprinting.

[63] W. A. Sessions, *Henry Howard: The Poet Earl of Surrey. A Life* (Oxford, 1999), 354–7; *The Collected Works of Anne Vaughan Lock*, ed. Susan M. Felch (Tempe, Ariz., 1999), 62–71.

[64] Jennifer Summit, *Lost Property: The Woman Writer and English Literary History, 1380–1589* (Chicago, 2000), 138–61.

[65] Patricia Demers, 'The Seymour Sisters: Elegizing Female Attachment', *Sixteenth Century Journal*, 30 (1999), 343–65.

[66] *Elizabeth I: Collected Works*, ed. Leah S. Marcus, Janel Mueller, and Mary Beth Rose (Chicago, 2000). But see Susan Bassnett, *Elizabeth I: A Feminist Perspective* (Oxford, 1988), 57.

[67] Kevin Sharpe, 'The King's Writ: Royal Authors and Royal Authority in Early Modern England', in Kevin Sharpe and Peter Lake (eds.), *Culture and Politics in Early Stuart England* (London, 1994), 117–38 (119–23).

translated Plutarch's essay 'On Curiosity', which rebukes prying and prurience, from subjects over-curious about mysteries of state to men looking through windows to catch intimate glimpses of women. These were very much concerns of Elizabeth towards the end of her reign—they are the issues dramatized in the Actaeon episode of Spenser's *Mutabilitie Cantos* (above, pp. 135–6). Her late translation of Boethius' *Consolation of Philosophy* (above, pp. 137–8) can be seen as a return to the mid-Tudor imagery of an unpredictable Fortune, and in a sense a retreat from the humanist idealization of civic activism. But in the extensive critical literature on Elizabeth's construction by her poets as a new incarnation of Petrarch's Laura, proper attention has yet to be paid to the fact that she seems herself to have inaugurated this association by becoming the first English translator from Petrarch's *Triumphs* (above, pp. 137–8). She was followed in this path by Mary Sidney, who has been emerging from the shadow of her brother Philip in recent scholarship. Her dedication of her and Philip's psalm translations to Elizabeth, in which she writes as poet to fellow poet as well as subject to prince, is one of the richest of the poems addressed to the queen.[68]

James I, whose mother had herself composed poetry, showed scant sympathy for female learning. For students of gender, it is the male homoerotic element of his courtly culture that is attracting attention. This is an area revisionist historians have tended to play down, since the leading evidence for the king's own sexual predilections comes from the 'Whig' tradition, which had handed down a body of scurrilous polemic—some of which has been considered too shocking to print down to the present day. More generally, revisionists have rejected claims that the king's love for favourites like Somerset and Buckingham reflected a political dotage, arguing that he retained his shrewdness in balancing factions to the end. There is a lot of evidence for that view, and it has understandably commended itself also to historians of gay or queer subject-formations who are alert to the prejudices involved in those satires.[69]

As Michael B. Young has argued, however, we can reject the satirists' assumptions and still find problems with the 'new constructionism'. However uncertain we must remain about the precise nature of his sexual practices, there was a widespread belief that the king did have sexual relations with his favourites, and this aroused a strongly negative reaction. That reaction, Young argues, was coloured by some specifically early modern discourses, notably the republican and Puritan association between manliness and a readiness to wage war; assaults on James's sexuality were most vociferous when James was trying to hold the line against interventions in the Thirty Years War. (It is worth recalling, however, that masculinity was not equated with military activity under all circumstances: many of the same people who championed war with Spain in 1624 were strongly hostile to Charles's taking up arms against the Scots in 1639–40.) More generally, courtly environments were arguably more open to less

---

[68] *The Collected Works of Mary Sidney Herbert, Countess of Pembroke*, ed. Margaret Hannay, Noel Kinnamon, and Michael G. Brennan, 2 vols. (Oxford, 1998), i.102–4.

[69] Roger Lockyer, *James VI and I* (London, 1998), 12; Alan Bray, 'Homosexuality and Male Friendship', in Jonathan Goldberg (ed.), *Queering the Renaissance* (Durham, 1994), 40–61 (54). David M. Bergeron, *James I and Letters of Homoerotic Desire* (Iowa City, 1999), argues that the letters between James and Buckingham do have a specifically sexual element.

rigid concepts of masculinity, while radical Protestantism from Bale onwards had a particular animus against what it saw as the perverted male sexuality encouraged by Catholic institutions. James's later sexuality can be read as a defiance not only of Buchanan's monarchomachical views but of the rigid sexual morality imposed by the Kirk.

At the same time, as Alan Stewart has pointed out, humanist pedagogues like Buchanan might generate the kinds of sexual associations they set themselves to suppress through their rigid regimes of corporal punishment. After all, in reviving the classics, humanists were reviving texts with very different attitudes towards masculine desire, and the literature of the 1590s reveals imaginative experimentation that cannot easily be encompassed within the terms either of the old religion or of the radical Protestants for whom Catholicism was a byword for sexual irregularity.[70] We might ask, for example, whether the circle of the Earl of Southampton, who became a leading opponent of absolutism, was not in fact more hospitable to homoerotic relationships than James's court. The friendship between Montaigne and La Boétie had strong political implications, as I argued in Chapter 6 in relation to Fulke Greville; more could be done to ask whether those connotations extended to the politics of gender. In this context remarkably little attention has been paid by scholars of English literature to Marie de Gournay, one of the earliest French feminists, who edited Montaigne's *Essays* and presented her intellectual friendship with him as a counterpart to his earlier friendship with La Boétie. Though John Florio omitted her strongly feminist preface from his translation of Montaigne, he mentioned her and dedicated each book to prominent women in the Southampton and Essex circles. Whether there was a long-term influence here on the ideals of same-sex friendship in later writers like Katherine Philips is a topic for further exploration. It has been argued that there was a 'queer' element in the politicized friendships of the Jacobean Spenserian poets.[71]

There was a considerable overlap between Jacobean 'oppositional' poetry and the court of Queen Anne. Whatever the masculine ethos of James's court, his wife maintained a household which itself became a centre for patronage and included many former members of the Essex circle. In Chapter 8 I glanced briefly at the queen's patronage of Samuel Daniel at a time when he was displaced by Jonson as leading author of the king's masques; more recent research suggests that the masques she patronized had a distinctive character, sometimes with a feminist aspect.[72] Though

[70] Michael B. Young, *King James and the History of Homosexuality* (New York, 2000); Alan Stewart, *Close Readers: Humanism and Sodomy in Early Modern England* (Princeton, 1997); Bruce R. Smith, *Homosexual Desire in Shakespeare's England: A Cultural Poetics* (Chicago, 1991).

[71] Montaigne, *Essays*, i.28, 'Of Friendship', ii.17, 'Of Presumption'; trans. John Florio (London, 1603), sig. A2^r; Marie de Gournay, *Preface to the 'Essays' of Montaigne*, trans. Richard Hillman and Colette Quesnel (Tempe, Ariz., 1998); Rictor Norton, 'The Homosexual Pastoral Tradition 4: The School of Spenser', online at *http://www.infopt.demon.co.uk/pastor04.htm*. On Florio in relation to eroticized friendships between women, see Jonathan Goldberg, *Desiring Women Writing: English Renaissance Examples* (Stanford, Calif., 1997), 75 ff.; on Lanyer see 16–41.

[72] Barbara K. Lewalski, *Writing Women in Jacobean England* (Cambridge, Mass., 1993), ch. 1; Leeds Barroll, *Anna of Denmark, Queen of England: A Cultural Biography* (Philadelphia, 2001), chs. 3–4.

Anne, as a Catholic, would not have offered the same kind of political alternative for Puritans as Prince Henry, the poems of Aemilia Lanyer indicate that the queen's circle of learned ladies engaged in biblical discussions that cut across confessional lines. Amongst those ladies was Lady Mary Wroth, niece of Philip and Mary Sidney. Though emphasis on gender identity alone has led some critics to emphasize her poetry's subjectivity and inwardness, she continued Sidneian political traditions, aligning herself in some respects with the disaffected 'Spenserian' poets.[73] Lanyer herself has attracted a lot of attention, and the traditional history of the country-house poem has been transformed with the recognition that her 'The Description of Cookham', rather than Jonson's 'To Penshurst', may have founded the Stuart genre.[74] Elizabeth Carey is another writer whose works make the traditional canon look different. Her *Tragedy of Mariam* was one of those highly politicized closet dramas, like Fulke Greville's *Mustapha*, admired by the Spenserian John Davies of Hereford; her *History of the Life, Reign and Death of Edward II* belongs to the genre of highly politicized historiography, with a Catholic slant.[75]

The genre of prophecy, and women's particular contributions to it, have received much more attention since I briefly discussed Lady Eleanor Davies in relation to Milton (pp. 246–7). Her first husband, Sir John Davies, had been the author of *Orchestra*, one of the key texts used by Tillyard to demonstrate the Elizabethan World Picture; Lady Eleanor caused a sensation by accurately predicting his death, thus making her own distinctive contribution to the demise of that world picture. Lady Eleanor is remarkable for the persistence with which from the very beginning of Charles's reign she mounted a campaign of prophetic menace—anticipating the much larger emergence of female prophecy with the breakdown of religious controls in the 1640s. Recent work is revealing further activity by female religious dissenters during the 1630s, and doubtless more will come to light.[76] All these women may be taken as exceptions, but scholarship is bringing still more such cases to light, and there must come a point when one asks what rule they prove.

If the early modern subject, on the anti-humanist conception, needed to enforce rigid gender rules, it also needed to assert itself by projecting aggressively outward on to an Other. The links between subjectivity and empire have been much developed in criticism since 1984, especially with the parallel growth of postcolonial theory. Here is a rich field for enquiry, and an opportunity for putting early modern texts into much broader contexts. The different venues of commercial expansion,

[73] Rosalind Smith, 'Lady Mary Wroth's *Pamphilia to Amphilanthus*: The Politics of Withdrawal', *English Literary Renaissance*, 30 (2000), 408–31.

[74] *The Poems of Aemilia Lanyer: Salve Deus Rex Judaeorum*, ed. Susanne Woods (New York, 1993); Marshall Grossman (ed.), *Aemilia Lanyer: Gender, Genre, and the Canon* (Lexington, Mass., 1998).

[75] Elizabeth Cary, Lady Falkland, *The Tragedy of Mariam the Fair Queen of Jewry*, ed. Barry Weller and Margaret W. Ferguson (Berkeley and Los Angeles, 1994); Diane Purkiss (ed.), *Renaissance Women: The Plays of Elizabeth Cary, the Poems of Aemilia Lanyer* (London, 1994).

[76] Esther S. Cope, *Handmaid of the Holy Spirit: Dame Eleanor Davies, Never soe Mad a Ladie* (Ann Arbor, 1992), 41–4; David R. Como, 'Women, Prophecy and Authority in Early Stuart Puritanism', *Huntington Library Quarterly*, 61 (1999–2000), 203–22; see the verse by Jane Hawkins in Jane Stevenson and Peter Davidson (eds.), *Early Modern Women Poets (1520–1700): An Anthology* (Oxford, 2001), 226–7.

westward to the New World, southward to Africa, and eastward to the Islamic world, raised very different issues and have received uneven attention. There has been an understandable tendency for the centre of gravity to be tilted westward, with the Mediterranean island of *The Tempest* dragged ever further into the Atlantic; but more and more work is being done on other areas where economic contact brought with it new kinds of cultural exchange or domination.[77] One topic that seems in danger of being underexplored is the specific question of English interpretations of different political systems, as opposed to ethnic categories. We learn much of general, stereotyped responses to the Other; but some of the writings accessible in the period did have a great deal to say about questions of government and state structure. For example, John Pory was an experienced commentator on English politics; how far did his edition of Leo Africanus, and Leo's own text, bring classical or other discourses of politics to bear on their reading of African kingdoms?[78] Greville's *Mustapha* and *Alaham* may have elements of topical allegory but they are also reflections on specifically Islamic institutions.

The self–Other model is also not well equipped for dealing with internal divisions over the question of empire. Though More's Utopians engage in colonization, there was a strong radical humanist tradition of opposition to empire, and in his poetry, highly influential in England, George Buchanan launched 'one of the most thorough-going attacks on the emerging notion of empire ever to be undertaken in the sixteenth century'.[79] Samuel Daniel was another eloquent critic of foreign empire.[80] His contemporary Francis Bacon has become the paradigmatic figure for establishing a connection between modern empirical philosophy and colonial and patriarchal violence, given his use of the imagery of masculine conquest of a female nature. Here as often there has been a continuity between older and newer forms of attack on positivism. In 1967 Stanley Fish wrote that the 'entire scientific program . . . is from one point of view a wilful refusal to face up to' the insight into human error originally transmitted in the doctrine of Original Sin; today, early modern

[77] For a survey see Ivo Kamps and Jyotsna G. Singh, *Travel Knowledge: European 'Discoveries' in the Early Modern Period* (New York, 2001); for eastward contacts see, for example, Nabil Matar, *Turks, Moors, and Englishmen in the Age of Discovery* (New York, 1999) and Lisa Jardine, *Worldly Goods: A New History of the Renaissance* (London, 1996). Peter Hulme and William H. Sherman (eds.), The Tempest *and its Travels* (London, 2000) presents a very wide range of geographical contexts for Shakespeare's play.

[78] Kim F. Hall, *Things of Darkness: Economies of Race and Gender in Early Modern England* (Ithaca, NY, 1995), 28–44 and Jonathan Burton, ' "A Most Wily Bird": Leo Africanus, Othello and the Trafficking in Difference', in Ania Loomba and Martin Orkin (eds.), *Post-Colonial Shakespeares* (London, 1998), 43–63, open up this question; more generally, see Andrew Hadfield, *Literature, Travel, and Colonial Writing in the English Renaissance 1545–1625* (Oxford, 1998). For a fascinating example of religious controversies in Ethiopia serving not as an Other but as a direct parallel to contemporary theological debates in Europe, see Jane O. Newman, ' "Race", Religion, and the Law: Rhetorics of Sameness and Difference in the Work of Hugo Grotius', in Victoria Kahn and Lorna Hutson (eds.), *Rhetoric and the Law in Early Modern Europe* (New Haven, 2001), 285–317.

[79] David Armitage, 'Literature and Empire', in Nicholas Canny and Alain Lowe (eds.), *The Origins of Empire: British Overseas Enterprise to the Close of the Seventeenth Century* (Oxford, 1998), 99–123 (113–17, 110), and see further his *The Ideological Origins of the British Empire* (Cambridge, 2000); *George Buchanan: The Political Poetry*, ed. Paul J. McGinnis and Arthur H. Williamson (Edinburgh, 1995), 12–24 (12).

[80] 'To Prince Henrie', *Samuel Daniel: The Brotherton Manuscript. A Study in Authorship*, ed. John Pitcher (Leeds, 1981), 131–7.

science continues to be indicted as the agent of a fall into evil, though Derrida and Foucault are more likely to be invoked than St Augustine. However, this argument is often conducted highly selectively. Readings of Bacon's imagery have relied too easily on inadequate translations of Latin texts; meanwhile, more attention needs to be paid to the evidence that his own sexuality was aligned with, and certainly his persuasive rhetoric had to address itself to, the masculinist and perhaps homoerotic ethos of James's court: Bacon was hardly the stock representative of conventional virility. His utopian society in *The New Atlantis*, with its idealization of male friendship yet rejection of 'masculine love', its toleration for Jews, though for Jews close to a Christian position, and its specific rejection of overseas conquests, implies a more conflicted figure than is sometimes assumed. Such conflicts are the less surprising if we concede some truth to Hill's portrait of Bacon as a figure whose interests linked him with the citizen culture of London quite as much as with the court. Bacon and others were certainly ready to support both war and overseas expansion—but it is important that there were others for whom such expansion does not seem to have been an essential component of their symbolic order.[81]

Frances Yates long ago demonstrated that the ideas of empire that most concerned the Elizabethans connoted the dominance of England over other parts of the British Isles, though Spenser and other visionaries might hope for an extension to the New World.[82] Limiting the idea of empire to the British Isles does not, of course, exclude questions of colonization and political subjection. Recent historiography has paid more and more attention to the 'British question', to the complex interrelations between England, Ireland, and Scotland in the early modern period. The union of 1603 which established 'Great Britain and Ireland' as an entity was never ratified by Parliament, where there was persistent anxiety about excessive Scottish influence. John Hoskyns's prophecies of a massacre of Scots were a major factor in the breakup of the 1614 Parliament. 'Whig' evaluations of James I have arguably been coloured by English prejudices, from those of contemporary observers to those of later historians too ready to interpret cultural differences between Scotland and England as evidence of the king's uncouthness or pedantry. There are good grounds for tracing the physical attributes contemporaries found so repulsive to medical factors.[83] As a half-Scot, I could be accused of having fallen victim to internal colonization by my English half, and my book certainly fails to do justice to James's interest

---

[81] Fish, *Surprised by Sin*, 126–7; Francis Bacon, 'The Advancement of Learning' *and* 'The New Atlantis', ed. Arthur Johnston (Oxford, 1974), 236, 234, 227–8; Cady, ' "Masculine Love" ', 14–21; Evelyn Fox Keller, *Reflections on Gender and Science* (New Haven, 1985), 33–42; Sarah Hutton, 'The Riddle of the Sphinx: Francis Bacon and the Emblems of Science', in Lynette Hunter and Sarah Hutton (eds.), *Women, Science and Medicine 1500–1700* (Stroud, 1997), 7–28; Michèle Le Dœuff, *Le Sexe du savoir* (Paris, 1998), 238–53; Peter Pesic, 'Wrestling with Proteus: Frances Bacon and the "Torture" of Nature', *Isis*, 90 (1999), 81–94; Graham Hammill, 'The Epistemology of Expurgation: Bacon and *The Masculine Birth of Time*', in Goldberg (ed.), *Queering the Renaissance*, 236–52; Christopher Hill, *Intellectual Origins of the English Revolution* (Oxford, 1965), ch. 3. On the tension between the pacific demands of philosophy and the martial demands of civic greatness in Bacon, see Peltonen, *Classical Humanism and Republicanism in English Political Thought*, 206–7.

[82] Frances A. Yates, *Astraea: The Imperial Theme in the Sixteenth Century* (London, 1975).

[83] A. W. Beasley, 'The Disability of James VI and I', *The Seventeenth Century*, 10 (1995), 151–62.

in poetry, both as practitioner and as patron. Work by Jonathan Goldberg, Kevin Sharpe, James Doelman, and others is redressing the balance, but there is much more to be done.[84]

As in many other cases, however, focusing on a politics of identity may lose sight of other political stakes. James himself pales in poetic stature beside his tutor George Buchanan, whose writings likewise have been much neglected by historians of English literature. James reacted very sharply against Buchanan's constitutionalist humanism, and his act in calling in Ralegh's *History of the World* for its censure of princes had a Scottish precedent in his censorship of Buchanan's *History of Scotland*. In 1622 James had a nightmare in which Buchanan foretold his death, indicating how much of a continuing presence that formidable writer remained for him.[85] As Arthur H. Williamson has shown, many Scots intellectuals had reservations about the particular version of the Union sponsored by James which in some ways mirrored the English opposition. Andrew Melville, Buchanan's successor as the leading Scots neo-Latin poet, began work on an epic poem, 'Gathelus', which would have celebrated James and Prince Henry as leading a unified Britain against the Antichristian Spanish Empire. As in later periods, Scots found it easier to invest in the idea of Britain than the English did, but Melville's anti-Spanish agenda and his strong Protestantism could find echoes south of the Border.[86] James's record in the encouragement of Scottish verse was uneven. In 1606, when Melville composed a bitter epigram attacking the English church, he was called before the Council and soon afterwards thrown in the Tower for three years without trial.[87] Melville ended his days in exile in the Huguenot outpost of Sedan, whence another leading Scots Latinist, Arthur Johnston, published a series of eloquent poems appealing—unsuccessfully, of course—for the king to intervene in the Palatinate.[88] Differences between James and his critics cannot be tied down neatly to issues of national identity.

Relations between England and Ireland raised very different kinds of problem. The island's status in the early modern period was and remains a matter of hot debate. An Act of 1541 established it as a separate kingdom; Spenser and other 'new English' settlers were involved in new colonial plantations whose sponsors also had an interest in expansion to the New World. Ireland's ambiguous status as kingdom or colony continues to preoccupy historians. In postcolonial theory, the familiar

[84] Goldberg, *James I and the Politics of Literature*; Sharpe, 'The King's Writ'; James Doelman, *King James I and the Religious Culture of England* (Woodbridge, 2000). For a caveat about attribution of poems to James, see Curtis Perry, 'Royal Authorship and Problems of Manuscript Attribution in the Poems of King James VI and I', *Notes and Queries*, 244 (1999), 243–4.

[85] *Calendar of State Papers . . . Venice, 1621–3*, 444; see also David Norbrook, '*Macbeth* and the Politics of Historiography', in Kevin Sharpe and Steven Zwicker (eds.), *Politics of Discourse* (Berkeley and Los Angeles, 1987), 78–116 (80–93).

[86] Arthur H. Williamson, 'Patterns of British Identity: "Britain" and its Rivals in the Sixteenth and Seventeenth Centuries', in Glenn Burgess (ed.), *The New British History: Founding a Modern State 1603–1715* (London, 1990), 138–73 (138–9); Buchanan, *The Political Poetry*, 284–97.

[87] Doelman, *King James I and the Religious Culture of England*, 65–72.

[88] *Querelae Saravictonis et Biomeae* and *Nicrina ad Heroas Anglos*, in *Musa Latina Aberdonensis: Arthur Johnston*, ed. Sir William Duguid Geddes, 2 vols., New Spalding Club (Aberdeen, 1892–5), i.53–75.

paradigms readily establish themselves, with the Irish functioning as the Other to be repressed by the colonizing early modern subject. One result is that Spenser has come into a new prominence. The Irish episodes in *The Faerie Queene*, and the *View of the Present State of Ireland*, were long regarded as embarrassing lapses; under the stimulus of Stephen Greenblatt's *Renaissance Self-Fashioning* they have effectively moved to the centre of critical work on Spenser. At the cost, perhaps, of a new distortion of focus; but the new work has tended to confirm the readings above, indicating Spenser's links with an innovative, even quasi-republican, humanism. The new focus on the *View* has called attention to unresolved problems about its text and even its authorship, and hence to the urgent need for a new edition.[89]

In continuing this line of work, care will be needed in applying postcolonial categories to the early modern period (as indeed it is in relation to any period). Postcolonial theory has relentlessly contested any form of ethnic 'essentialism', insisting that all identities are artificial—indeed arbitrary—constructs; but as in other areas, the tendency to analyse identity in terms of binary oppositions has often made it hard to break free of some rigid categorizations. Early modern colonialism did not share the same kind of racist ideology as its nineteenth-century variety; in a careful survey, Colin Kidd concludes that ethnic identity had 'a secondary place in political argument'. This does not mean that he offers a benign account of the period's injustices; he finds, however, that the 'horrors of ethnic hatred and paranoia coexisted with confused ethnic classification'.[90] Much current analysis of representations of Ireland, however, has conformed to a pattern analysed by Aijaz Ahmad, in which common historical processes become split into an opposition between a modern Western Self and a homogenized Other, a label which brings together very different cultural and political traditions.[91] When one critic writes that if 'in one sense English power called Ireland into being, in another sense Ireland was not really there at all', he is referring to complexities of definition; and yet it can appear that the relentless insistence on the constructedness of identity and the external world at the expense of empirical reality has led critics into replicating older blindnesses.[92] Spenser is repeatedly denounced for projecting his own anxieties on to the Irish and failing to understand their culture, but the voluminous body of literature on Spenser and Ireland is only beginning to edge us any closer to such an understanding. This may be in part because the main agenda of much postmodernist criticism is less to

[89] Greenblatt, *Renaissance Self-Fashioning*, 184–92; Jean R. Brink, 'Appropriating the Author of *The Faerie Queene*: The Attribution of the *View of the Present State of Ireland* and *A Brief Note of Ireland* to Edmund Spenser', in Peter E. Medine and Joseph Wittreich (eds.), *Sounding of Things Done: Essays in Early Modern Literature in Honor of S. K. Heninger Jr.* (Newark Del., 1997), 93–136; a new edition is in progress from Oxford University Press; for an overview see Andrew Hadfield, *Edmund Spenser's Irish Experience: Wilde Fruit and Salvage Soyl* (Oxford, 1997).

[90] Colin Kidd, *British Identities before Nationalism: Ethnicity and Nationhood in the Atlantic World 1600–1800* (Cambridge, 1999), 287, 151.

[91] Aijaz Ahmad, *In Theory: Classes, Nations, Literatures* (London, 1992), *passim*.

[92] David J. Baker, 'Off the Map: Charting Uncertainty in Renaissance Ireland', in Brendan Bradshaw, Andrew Hadfield, and Willy Maley (eds.), *Representing Ireland: Literature and the Origins of Conflict, 1534–1660* (Cambridge, 1993), 76–92 (82).

understand different cultures than to discredit Enlightenment 'humanism' through its allegedly inevitable association with violence.

There were indeed many English champions of a militant colonial role in Ireland, culminating in the repressive policies during the Interregnum. But there were opposing counsels on that role within England, while amongst different groups within Ireland there was significant resistance through legal and other means, culminating in the Catholic Confederacy of the 1640s, the closest to an independent government before the twentieth century. Research into these complexities is in progress, but it has not always come from postmodernist paradigms. Indeed, one of the fullest accounts of the relations between England and different factions in Ireland in the seventeenth century remains the grand narrative of S. R. Gardiner (1829–1902), which represents everything to which postmodern theory is opposed. Gardiner's Nonconformist conscience reinforced a very strong positivist concern for rigorous documentary accuracy; yet his history was also informed by his liberal sympathy with pressures towards Irish home rule.[93] More recently, critics working from within Ireland on Irish sources, in conjunction with a revivification of contemporary poetry in Irish, have been exploring the archives. J. G. A. Pocock's call for an analysis of the interaction between different parts of the 'Atlantic archipelago' has inspired a large corpus of 'new British history' which has been opening up all kinds of complex interrelations between differing confessional and cultural identities. Such an approach may be open to the objection of reinscribing Irish questions as British ones, but it does reveal the limitations of exploring politics simply through questions of identity. Irish bardic poetry has often been seen as subsisting in a timeless, backward-looking cultural purity, a view that can offer satisfaction both to hardline Irish republicans and to modernizers concerned to show the benefits of English rule. Recent research, however, suggests that the bards were adapting in complex ways to the changing political situations, and moreover that there was a considerable degree of cultural hybridization in Irish verse from non-bardic contexts.[94] Irish verse by women is starting to be recovered.[95] Back in 1916 Robin Flower declared that the bards could 'be avenged upon Edmund Spenser' if it were recognized how much more resourceful Irish-language love poetry had become by the early sixteenth century than the English lyric, and to prove his point translated two of Wyatt's lyrics into

[93] Samuel Rawson Gardiner, *History of England, 1603–1640*, 10 vols. (London, 1883–4), continued in *History of the Great Civil War* (1886–91), reissued with introduction by Christopher Hill, 4 vols. (London, 1987); *History of the Commonwealth and Protectorate* (1895–1901), reissued, 4 vols. (London, 1988–9); J. S. A. Adamson, 'Eminent Victorians: S. R. Gardiner and the Liberal as Hero', *Historical Journal*, 33 (1990), 641–57.

[94] Marc Caball, *Poets and Politics: Reaction and Continuity in Irish Poetry, 1558–1625* (Cork, 1998); Breandan O'Buachalla, 'James our True King: The Ideology of Irish Royalism in the Seventeenth Century', in D. George Boyce, Robert Eccleshall, and Vincent Geoghegan (eds.), *Political Thought in Ireland since the Seventeenth Century* (London, 1993), 7–35; Mícheál Mac Craith, 'Gaelic Ireland and the Renaissance', in Glanmor Williams and Robert Owen Jones (eds.), *The Celts and the Renaissance: Tradition and Innovation* (Cardiff, 1990), 57–90 (I owe this reference to Patricia Palmer).

[95] Stevenson and Davidson (eds.), *Early Modern Women Poets (1520–1700)*, pp. xlv–xlvi.

Irish.[96] For the bards to be avenged upon Spenser, in that poetic sense, learning to read Irish would need to acquire at least a modicum of the cultural capital to be derived from denouncing Spenser for his failure to do so.[97]

The effect of the new attention to Scottish and Irish contexts has sometimes been to heighten the rigidity of English identity by contrast. On one kind of revisionist analysis, the prime cause of the Civil War was the failure of Charles's policies in Scotland, which upset the balance between the Three Kingdoms.[98] This emphasis on an external cause makes it possible to insist on an English political culture that was still unified rather than sharply divided. In new historicist analysis, while there may be less confidence that the unity actually existed, the assumption tends to be that the early modern English were obsessively anxious about preserving their symbolic bodies from any violation or contagion. That there was a strengthening sense of English identity is certainly important, and offers a corrective to those historians who see nationhood in a modern sense as emerging only with the populist movements of the post-1789 era. The best studies, however, have been open to the complexities of different conceptions of identity. As its title indicates, Richard Helgerson's ambitious *Forms of Nationhood* emphasizes the intellectual ferment in which differing religious and social perspectives were brought to bear on the concept of Englishness, and his analysis of an emergent sense of national identity in distinction from monarchical allegiance overlaps with my own reading of the Spenserian poets. Helgerson writes that 'self-estrangement was . . . the fundamental condition of national self-representation', a comment with which I would agree, while also arguing that the period's writers may have had good reasons for wanting to hold on to such self-estrangement, like La Boétie imagining himself as a Venetian (above, p. 27).[99]

For in developing a political self-consciousness independent of the monarchy, the English might identify themselves as 'patriots', a term that always retained a universalizing element from its classical origins, as a form of public responsibility that respected particular institutions but was generally valid.[100] The Scots were especially prone to this universalizing mode of patriotism because the limited currency of their vernacular encouraged them to turn to Latin verse and prose, but a comparable ten-

[96] Thomas F. O'Rahilly (ed.), *Dánta Grádha: An Anthology of Irish Love Poetry* (Dublin, 1916), pp. xvii–xx; Mac Craith, 'Gaelic Ireland and the Renaissance', 62, notes that Flower omitted this passage from the new edition which appeared in 1926, 'in the heady early days of the Irish Free State'. He discusses the role of Old English writers in mediating between Irish, English, and Latin literary traditions, with imitations of Ovid appearing in Irish and English verse (63–70).

[97] For studies that do encourage an awareness of the Irish language see Richard A. McCabe, 'Edmund Spenser, Poet of Exile', *Proceedings of the British Academy*, 88 (1993), 73–104 and Patricia Palmer, *Language and Conquest in Early Modern Ireland: English Renaissance Literature and Elizabethan Imperial Expansion* (Cambridge, 2001).

[98] Cf. Russell, *The Causes of the English Civil War*, 29.

[99] Richard Helgerson, *Forms of Nationhood: The Elizabethan Writing of England* (Chicago, 1992), 107–47, 16. For further discussion of the Spenserians and nationhood see Claire McEachern, *The Poetics of English Nationhood, 1590–1612* (Cambridge, 1996), ch. 4, and Michelle O'Callaghan, *'The Shepheards Nation': Jacobean Spenserians and Early Stuart Political Culture, 1612–1625* (Oxford, 2000), 21 ff.

[100] Roland Knowles, 'The "All-Atoning Name": The Word *Patriot* in Seventeenth-Century England', *Modern Language Review*, 96 (2001), 624–43, shows that the word by no means always had a politically specific sense in the early modern period but does chart some antitheses between patriots and courtiers.

dency can be found in England. Sidney's admiration for George Buchanan spoke to his participation in an international, Latinate humanist republic of letters. In beginning the book with More's *Utopia*, I was concerned to emphasize humanist universalism, the extent to which the vernacular might sometimes seem strange and barbaric, rather than a comforting expression of identity. The period's neo-Latin poetry remains seriously underexplored, skewing our sense of English relations with the Continent. One of the best-known poets of English origin in this period was Jane Weston, who lived in Prague and published exclusively in Latin but nonetheless maintained English contacts. (However, her presentation to James I of a poem which declared that he had been elected by his people may help to explain why the king failed to invite her home—quite apart from his general distaste for learned women.[101]) Thomas May, best known in England through Andrew Marvell's satire as a drunken debauchee, had a European reputation in his time as author of a neo-Latin continuation of Lucan's republican *Pharsalia*.[102] While Continental readers took an interest in English Latinity, middle-level officials in English towns were eagerly translating Continental texts on civic humanism, including republican constitutions.[103] In religious terms, emphasis on an 'Anglican' tradition—itself an anachronistic label—has tended to deflect attention from the Puritans' propensity to identify themselves not with a national church but with an international Invisible Church of the godly.

Only such tendencies can help to explain the moments of enthusiasm for Anglo-Scottish union under Edward VI and the close ties between English and Scots Protestants in the late 1630s. Recent work has shown how a flood of Scottish publications was making a pronounced impact in England from the summer of 1638; some of them were published or reprinted in Amsterdam. The same Amsterdam press was used by John Lilburne, who was co-ordinating propaganda for Prynne, Burton, and Bastwicke and was quickly to come to the fore during the 1640s as a Puritan and subsequently a Leveller pamphleteer. A Protestant public sphere was emerging that transcended English, and British, boundaries.[104] 'You are wise,' wrote the Earl of Dorset to the Earl of Middlesex in 1639, 'and know how much liberty and puritanism rayne in the populace of this people and my masters the Hollanders are fitt instruments to promise both.' During the 1650s serious proposals were made for a political union with the Netherlands. As Jonathan Scott has forcefully pointed out, the 'Glorious Revolution' of 1688, in which the English acquiesced to an invasion by a Dutch monarch, was the culmination of a long process of close political links with

---

[101] Elizabeth Jane Weston, *Collected Writings*, ed. and trans. Donald Cheney and Brenda M. Hosington (Toronto, 2000), 171–3.

[102] David Norbrook, *Writing the English Republic* (Cambridge, 1999), 80–1.

[103] Peltonen, *Classical Humanism and Republicanism in English Political Thought*, chs. 1–2.

[104] Joseph Black, ' "Pikes and Protestations": Scottish Texts in England, 1639–40', *Publishing History*, 42 (1997), 5–19; Joad Raymond, *Pamphlets and Pamphleteering in Early Modern Britain* (Cambridge, forthcoming), ch. 5; Alastair Bellany, 'Ritual Subversion and the Literary Underground, 1603–42', in Harris (ed.), *The Politics of the Excluded, c.1500–1850*, 99–124 (111–16). See also Dagmar Freist, *Governed by Opinion: Politics, Religion and the Dynamics of Communication in Stuart London 1637–45* (London, 1997).

the Netherlands.[105] One aspect of my first edition that has been less taken up than I would have wished has been this international dimension. A major inspiration behind *Poetry and Politics* was Frances Yates's insistence on the contacts between courtly cultures in different parts of Europe. I was keen to connect English and German literary histories by drawing attention to Georg Rudolf Weckherlin, who played a significant role in German poetry but was also closely involved in English politics, and was to be succeeded by Milton as secretary for foreign affairs to Parliament.[106] As long as criticism is preoccupied with the English concern for inviolate bodies, however, such connections will be neglected.

This emphasis on international Protestantism illustrates a third area in which this book shows symptomatic omissions: religion. If it was ever possible to imagine a historical process in which religion gradually and inevitably gave way to secularization, recent events on the world stage have made such a position very hard to sustain, and the early modern preoccupation with reconciling confessional and constitutional demands can have a contemporary ring. It is only quite recently that there has been a sustained attempt to rethink the old grand narrative in which Protestantism was the force of inevitable progress, Catholicism merely regressive. My book concentrates on a tradition with strong confessional allegiances, and to that extent remains largely within the grand narrative. Deeply embedded in English Whig and liberal traditions, that narrative also informed the writings of Marxists like Hill and Thompson. In his riposte to Anderson and Nairn, Thompson objected that their paradigms failed to account for the role of Protestant religion as a force of political agency in England.[107] And it is arguable that Althusser's and Foucault's accounts of the state apparatus were heavily influenced by the French experience of a strongly dominant official church, while in Thompson's attack on Althusser there resounds something of the rhetoric of the Dissenter outraged at the very idea of a national church. As sharply critical as the Althusserian analysis could be of the repressive role of religion, it worked within the assumption that significant dissent was extremely difficult for the subject to achieve. It has been a common complaint about the new historicism that it lacked attention to religion. Stephen Greenblatt has certainly been trying to respond to that charge in his recent writing, and he has of course been much concerned with aspects of religion from an early phase. There are parallels, however, between Althusserian analysis and the ambivalence in Greenblatt's treatment of religion, which has tended to focus on the church, and on a church whose theatricality or magic exercises a balefully compelling influence on even the most resistant. There is certainly grounding for such an analysis in the period, as in the writings of La Boétie,

---

[105] Charles J. Phillips, *History of the Sackville Family*, 2 vols. (London, 1930), i.334; Jonathan Scott, *England's Troubles: Seventeenth-Century English Political Instability in a European Context* (Cambridge, 2000).

[106] For a recent study of his significance in England see Anthony B. Thompson, 'Licensing the Press: The Career of G. R. Weckherlin during the Personal Rule of Charles I', *Historical Journal*, 41 (1998), 653–78; see further my *Writing the English Republic*, 183, 292.

[107] Thompson, 'The Peculiarities of the English', 58.

on which Greenblatt draws in his latest book.[108] What tends to be missing from such a view of religion, with its focus on the public and liturgical aspects, is the critical and individualistic potential of strong religious conviction. My own approach can certainly be accused of going to the opposite extreme. I have tried, for example, to say a little more in Chapter 9 about Wither's evident interest in the liturgy, despite his claims to a non-institutional, prophetic voice.

Since 1984 there has been an opening to different views from either the state-apparatus or the dissenting models. With the general discrediting of all such progressive 'grand narratives' in recent years, literary and historical scholarship has been keen to counter Protestant bias and to take a fresh look at Catholic culture in early modern Britain.[109] In works like Eamon Duffy's eloquent *The Stripping of the Altars*, the Reformation emerges as an imposition by a narrow ruling elite, with no right to speak for a 'people' amongst whom devotion for the older ways was strong. Alison Shell and other scholars have been trying to write Catholic texts back into the larger literary histories of the period.[110] The limitations of *Poetry and Politics* certainly appear in such a perspective: Robert Southwell and Richard Crashaw, the two leading Catholic poets of the age, receive no mention whatever. My account of Mary's reign fails to note the significance of the multiple publications of translations of Virgil in that reign, in what looks like a conscious alignment between the Rome of humanist literary culture and the Rome of religious allegiance.[111] Any full account of the politics of women writers would need to pay attention to the major revival of courtly Catholicism in the 1620s and 1630s.[112]

Such gaps reflect the fact that the book was conceived as a polemic against a literary history which did have an Anglo-Catholic, if not specifically a Roman Catholic, bias. At a somewhat different level, I was certainly swayed by my reservations about an analysis of Irish history then current on the British left, in which a rather romanticized model of Irish republicanism led to sharp antitheses between the dour, bodiless rationalism of the entire Protestant tradition and the romantic corporeality of Irish identity. I was interested in Tom Paulin's attempts to rehabilitate aspects of the Enlightenment radical tradition in an Irish as well as English context, and remain deeply interested in the very complex ideological mutations of republican ideology

[108] Richard Strier, *Resistant Structures: Particularity, Radicalism, and Renaissance Texts* (Chicago, 1995), 74, notes in the new historicism 'a great difficulty seeing in the Reformation any positive content'. On La Boétie see Stephen Greenblatt, *Hamlet in Purgatory* (Princeton, 2001), 12–13, and cf. Ch. 6 above.

[109] Edwin Jones, *The English Nation: The Great Myth* (Thrupp, 1998); Norman Davies, *The Isles: A History* (London, 1999).

[110] Eamon Duffy, *The Stripping of the Altars: Traditional Religion in England, 1400–1580* (New Haven, 1994); Alison Shell, *Catholicism, Controversy and the English Literary Imagination, 1558–1660* (Cambridge, 1999); A. D. Cousins, *The Catholic Religious Poets from Southwell to Crashaw: A Critical History* (London, 1991).

[111] Donna B. Hamilton, 'Re-engineering Virgil: *The Tempest* and the Printed English *Aeneid*', in Hulme and Sherman (eds.), The Tempest *and its Travels*, 114–20.

[112] Erica Veevers, *Images of Love and Religion: Queen Henrietta Maria and Court Entertainments* (Cambridge, 1989).

across the confessional divides.[113] More recently, postmodern binaries have risked reinstating new forms of identity politics, with Catholic identity seen as one more of the Others repressed by modernity, rather than as engaged in a continuing interplay between different forms of tradition and modernity.

Shell, Hamilton, and others have been sensitive to the political nuances. English writers who chose or retained loyalty to Rome were often involved in very complex relations to the state, ranging from a strong sense of commitment to existing political institutions to radical critique, and these positions do not easily lend themselves to the homogenizing tendencies of identity analysis. It was already clear from Quentin Skinner's *Foundations of Modern Political Thought* that theories of resistance to unconstitutional and ungodly rulers often emerged from Catholic milieux even though they were sometimes taken up by Protestants. Hence, indeed, the otherwise baffling claim by presbyterians during the English Revolution and afterwards that more radical Protestant groups were really in league with the Jesuits. The cult of Anglo-Saxon liberties, often seen as a specifically Protestant construction, was invoked by Catholic apologists.[114] The Catholicism of the young John Donne brought him in contact with the legacy of the radical humanism of the *Utopia*.[115] Similar considerations apply to Jonson: his political sympathies were arguably more complex than is suggested in Chapter 7, 'red' and 'black' Tacitism being extremely difficult to disentangle.[116] Brief mention is made in Chapter 5 of Essex's cultivating Catholic as well as militant Protestant support, and Shell has discovered a particularly remarkable instance: in 1595 a Catholic priest, Thomas Wright, composed imprese for Essex for the queen's Accession Day tournament.[117] Further research may even uncover cases as extraordinary as the plans of the pioneering atomist Nicholas Hill for establishing a utopian republic on Lundy Island.[118] Contrary to some of the generalizations of Ong and McLuhan, for whom print culture was associated with the destructive, homogenizing effects of modernity and Catholicism with an older oral culture, English Catholics proved resourceful in exploiting the new media.[119] All this being said, attention still needs to be paid to the view of those Protestants for whom the likeliest outcome of a Catholic restoration would have been in practice a strengthening of

[113] Tom Paulin, *Writing to the Minute: Selected Critical Essays 1980–1996* (London, 1996), 1–100; Norbrook, *Writing the English Republic*, 245–50. Cf. Terry Eagleton, 'The Poetry of Radical Republicanism', *New Left Review*, 158 (1986), 123–8.

[114] *The Foundations of Modern Political Thought*, 2 vols. (Cambridge, 1978), ii.320 ff.; Donna B. Hamilton, 'Catholic Use of Anglo-Saxon Precedents, 1565–1625: Thomas Stapleton, Nicholas Harpsfield, Robert Persons, Richard Verstegan, Richard Broughton and Others', *Recusant History* (forthcoming).

[115] David Norbrook, 'The Monarchy of Wit and the Republic of Letters: Donne's Politics', in Katharine Maus and Elizabeth Harvey (eds.), *Soliciting Interpretation: Literary Theory and Seventeenth-Century English Poetry* (Chicago, 1990), 3–36 (7–10).

[116] Blair Worden, 'Ben Jonson among the Historians', in Sharpe and Lake (eds.), *Culture and Politics in Early Stuart England*, 67–90; Julie Sanders, *Jonson's Theatrical Republics* (Houndmills, 1998).

[117] Shell, *Catholicism, Controversy and the English Literary Imagination*, 125–33.

[118] Hugh Trevor-Roper, *Catholics, Anglicans and Puritans: Seventeenth-Century Essays* (London, 1987), 1–39.

[119] Alexandra Walsham, '"Domme Preachers": Post-Reformation English Catholicism and the Culture of Print', *Past and Present*, 168 (2000), 72–123.

international absolutist politics: such a view is open to debate, but it need not be considered exclusively as a projection from a paranoid identity construction.

The book's polemics against Leavisite and Anglican criticism undoubtedly led to distortions through omission, helping to account for its scant treatment of the tradition of metaphysical verse by poets aligned with the Church of England—above all George Herbert and the post-conversion Donne. My concern was explicitly with poetry directly concerned with public occasions, but I did make assumptions about these poets' political stance that have now been widely questioned. In reacting so strongly against the canonization of the metaphysical lyric by the Leavisites and the New Critics, I neglected significant political nuances. It has become clear that the 'Anglo-Catholic' tradition that was so important to T. S. Eliot was to a considerable degree an invention of the nineteenth century, and that neither Donne nor Herbert would have fitted quite easily into the Church of Archbishop Laud.[120] By now, indeed, critics, myself included, tend to be vying with each other to show that their chosen poet is even less high church than other contemporaries, and it may be that the pendulum has swung about as far as it can before there is again talk of an Anglican poetic tradition. There are signs of a renewed interest in redefining such a tradition.[121] I have tried to rectify some of my omissions in the footnotes.

A fourth main area in which there has been an immense amount of new work since my book was published is the history of print and manuscript culture. Here there has been a certain convergence between different methodologies. Though new historicists have come at the 'materiality of the text' from a distinct perspective, they have drawn on the formidable and growing body of positivist scholarship made possible by such resources as the online *English Short-Title Catalogue* and Peter Beal's magnificent catalogues of literary manuscripts.[122] Once again, however, different theoretical perspectives will produce different views of the period. The case of censorship is a striking example, where there has been a certain convergence between new historicist and revisionist views, with both agreeing that there was a radical difference between early modern ideas and what we today condemn as censorship. For revisionists, this is an important question because they often rely for their arguments about the basic uniformity of the early modern mentality on the shortage of concrete evidence of oppositional views. Christopher Hill's essay on 'Censorship and English Literature', often taken as the revisionists' target, claimed that such evidence is not more widely found because of a widespread practice of censorship which inhibited the overt expression of radical views. I have drawn on, and to some extent added to, the cases instanced by Hill.[123] Revisionists have countered by a kind of 'salami

---

[120] Daniel W. Doerksen, *Conforming to the Word: Herbert, Donne, and the English Church before Laud* (Lewisburg, Pa., 1997). See also Ch. 8 n. 15, above.

[121] Debora Kuller Shuger, *The Renaissance Bible: Scholarship, Sacrifice, and Subjectivity* (Berkeley, 1994); Ramie Targoff, *Common Prayer: The Language of Public Devotion in Early Modern England* (Chicago, 2001).

[122] Peter Beal (ed.), *Index of English Literary Manuscripts*, vols. i (1450–1625) and ii (1625–1700) (London, 1980–7).

[123] Christopher Hill, 'Censorship and English Literature', in *Writing and Revolution in Seventeenth-Century England*, 32–71.

tactics', in which specific cases are redefined as not censorship but something quite different. Glenn Burgess has argued that many apparent manifestations of censorship 'manifest nothing much at all': the Stationers' Company called in books because of threats to their profits, not because of political differences; noblemen had critics imprisoned because of the thinness of their skins. When James had books burned, as he did Pareus' commentary on Romans during the Bohemian crisis, he was not threatening free speech but staging a demonstration for the benefit of foreign ambassadors. For the censors, 'it was not *ideas* that were the problem, but ideas deemed likely to have actual political consequences'—a situation that early modern humanists might not have found so reassuring. Blair Worden similarly insists that the role of such censorship as did exist was 'to forestall not criticism but disorder'. Greville's burning of his own tragedy of Antony and Cleopatra, which must be considered a major loss to Elizabethan literature, was a response less to state repression than to jealous political enemies who might have smeared him with false charges of sedition (though Greville's assumption that such smears would be believed by the authorities is itself worth noting). The bishops' ban on satires in 1599, it has been argued, was concerned with pornography, not politics.[124] Debora Shuger has amplified the case that what concerned the early modern authorities was not political censorship but the anti-Christian offence of slander. From her perspective, my suggestion that Northampton had political motives in imprisoning Wither and other critics would look like an anachronistic projection of modern concerns, the earl in this radically different world being motivated purely by the need to defend Christian charity.[125] The imprisonment of Andrew Melville in the Tower for three years for an offensive epigram does not register in revisionist discussions of censorship; as deficient in Christianity as he may have been, commentators throughout Europe assumed a political motive in his punishment.

For many literary critics, meanwhile, a central theoretical point of reference has been Foucault's rejection of traditional models of censorship according to which power acts on an autonomous process of free thought. Such a model implies a humanist notion of an independent agent or author, whereas for Foucault there can be no such thought outside discourses of power. To that extent, oppositional thought is not just empirically but necessarily impossible, or at least deeply problematic. Following Foucault's Nietzschean ironies at the expense of liberal humanitarianism, Foucauldian critics have emphasized the ways in which the early modern state rejected any individualistic sense that the body was one's own, as in such punishments as chopping off Stubbs's hand or Prynne's ears. Still less was one's mind one's

---

[124] Blair Worden, 'Literature and Political Censorship in Early Modern England', in A. C. Duke and C. A. Tamse (eds.), *Too Mighty to be free: Censorship and the Press in Britain and the Netherlands* (Zutphen, 1987), 45–62 (48); Glenn Burgess, *Absolute Monarchy and the Stuart Constitution* (New Haven, 1996), 7–12; Cyndia Susan Clegg, *Press Censorship in Elizabethan England* (Cambridge, 1997), 213; on political and other factors see Richard A. McCabe, '"Right Puisante and Terrible Priests": The Role of the Anglican Church in Elizabethan State Censorship', in Andrew Hadfield (ed.), *Literature and Censorship in Renaissance England* (Houndmills, 2001), 75–94.

[125] Debora Shuger, 'Civility and Censorship in Early Modern England', in Robert C. Post (ed.), *Censorship and Silencing: Practices of Cultural Regulation* (Los Angeles, 1998), 89–110.

own, retreating to some autonomous sphere: modern notions of intellectual property or individual authorship were quite unknown. Moreover, traditional models of censorship, we are told, rest on an illegitimate, positivist distinction between physical force and coercion on the one hand and ideas and language on the other. 'However horrible, the meaning of bodily mutilation', writes Richard Burt, 'was nevertheless itself always open to interpretation.'[126]

These critiques have had the merit of forcing us to be clearer about our terms. Shuger does well to remind us of the savage vituperation that accompanied what in the editing of Whig historians may sound as the sober and purely rational demands of the Parliamentarians. Hill certainly did reify 'the censorship' into too fixed and absolute a category. At a number of points my own book does paint too simple a picture of writers pitted against the state, perhaps giving the impression that 'oppositional' figures were struggling for an end to censorship. This is clearly not the case: the more radical Protestants were likely to be the more insistent on the need to seize and burn Catholic books, and in the debates between Arminians and Calvinists in the 1620s, the issue was which side's books would be suppressed, not whether the press should be wholly free. In a recent survey of Jacobean censorship, Cyndia Susan Clegg provides an admirable wealth of detailed historical material, and some corrections to my own narrative. I played down the extent to which George Wither had aligned himself with the king against the Stationers by the end of the reign over the publication of his *Hymnes and Songs*. In telling this story, Clegg highlights the dangers of too rigid an adherence to the model of censorship as a purely external and restrictive force: Wither is offered a space to speak by one Jacobean authority, denied it by another, and himself works to suppress writings he disapproves of.

I have tried to complicate my account of Wither in the new edition; but I remain unpersuaded by some of Clegg's general assumptions and conclusions. She cites Sharpe on the need to understand early modern culture outside positivist assumptions, which involves recognizing the degree to which discourses, texts, and performances are 'the only "reality" that can be known by humans'. One implication of this assumption is that censorship, to 'the degree that it participates in royal authority, is as much a fiction as royal authority—one that may be made to serve multiple cultural ends and that may be subjected to interpretation, appropriation, and resistance'. In her account of the Spenserians' response to the events of 1614, the poets used the fiction of censorship to

serve their ulterior motives as effectively as Northampton had in his imprisonment of Wither. As Northampton used Wither to illustrate the danger a meeting of parliament could pose, so the poets could use the trope of censorship to illustrate courtiers' presumptions.[127]

---

[126] Michel Foucault, 'Two Lectures', in Colin Gordon (ed.), *Power/Knowledge: Selected Interviews and Other Writings 1972–1977* (Brighton, 1980), 78–108; Francis Barker, *The Tremulous Private Body: Essays in Subjection* (London, 1984); Richard Burt, *Licensed by Authority: Ben Jonson and the Discourses of Censorship* (Ithaca, NY, 1993), 69; cf. Holstun, *Ehud's Dagger*, 47–50. On changing conceptions of poetic authorship see Kevin Pask, *The Emergence of the English Author: Scripting the Life of the Poet in Early Modern England* (Cambridge, 1996).

[127] Cyndia Susan Clegg, *Press Censorship in Jacobean England* (Cambridge, 2001), 49, 197–203, 227–8, 5, 15, 116; see also her *Press Censorship in Elizabethan England* (Cambridge, 1997).

The difference between the jailer and the jailed here is neutralized by the rhetorical figure of chiasmus. I am more than happy to insist that texts do constitute acts with real-world consequences, but the effect of this levelling of distinctions is, I think, seriously to distort the balance of power. Clegg takes me to task for implying that there was 'a repressive system of controls'. I am not sure that I put it quite so directly, but there certainly are many entries in my index under 'censorship'. Some of them may be disputable cases, but often there is more evidence than I was able to provide in the first edition. In response to my statement that William Goddard's *A Satirycall Dialogue*, a book containing a bitter anti-courtly satire in the wake of the Overbury affair, was printed abroad because of censorship, Clegg shows that there is no specific evidence of an overseas printing, and suggests that it was misleading to imply that its contents were 'dangerous'. She may well be right to correct the imprint given by the *Short-Title Catalogue*; but her argument that censorship cannot be involved is hard to square with the fact that the three leaves containing the satire in question have been cut out of one of the few surviving copies. To suggest censorship, or at least self-censorship, does not seem an outrageous stretching of the facts. Moreover, the content of the poem, with mutual charges of murder between king and nobility leading to the outbreak of a civil war, is odd evidence to advance for the case that I was exaggerating fears of civil war.[128]

Nonetheless, control of the press was certainly very far from absolute. Jacobean England was not a police state, and the contending authorities that had sway over different forms of spoken and written utterance often reflected different factional and ideological allegiances. The portion of printed output that was censored was very small, and there was a remarkable intellectual range in what did get into print. Just how we interpret these points, however, remains open to discussion. It could be argued that this was a fundamentally deferential society in which the authorities saw little need to enforce conformist views that were spontaneously held. Or we could see the monarchy, under James and especially under Charles, trying to contain pressures towards a public sphere which would undermine traditional unities in church and state, the former being much cannier in recognizing that the process had already gone far enough to be handled with great care. What emerges from the many cases of poets' protesting against imprisonment, or merely licensing, is a consistent resentment at being treated like children, or perhaps like subjects rather than citizens. When John Davies of Hereford objects to the 'chaplaines allowed to allow Books', echoing Juvenal's 'Quis custodiet ipsos custodes?' (*Satires*, 6.347; cf. Ch. 8 n. 45 above), he is reflecting a widespread sense of writerly self-respect, a sense which Wither and Milton were to articulate more fully in their tracts on printing, but which can be traced back at least to the early days of the printed 'republic of letters' in the sixteenth century—and which could on occasion cut across confessional boundaries,

---

[128] Clegg, *Press Censorship in Jacobean England*, 116; Hoyt H. Hudson, 'John Hepwith's Spenserian Satire upon Buckingham: With Some Jacobean Analogues', *Huntington Library Bulletin*, 6 (1934), 39–71 (58 n.): the signatures (F2–4) containing 'the Owles Araygnement' have been removed from the Huntington copy. Some highly pornographic passages earlier in the book seem not to have posed quite the same problem.

Davies being a Catholic who identified strongly with the militant Protestant Wither. (Davies's is one of many cases which Hill mentioned in his notorious essay on censorship, and which are routinely passed over in silence by his critics.) We need a fuller study of the rhetoric of protests against censorship, and of its possible classical models. For as so often in the early modern period, a study that focuses purely on administrative mechanisms will miss important aspects of cultural meaning. Roman literature provided ample case-studies of the processes by which the emperors had gradually restricted freedom of speech; Greek literature provided a rich lexicon for different forms of verbal freedom. La Boétie and Greville are striking examples of self-consciousness about the parallels with their own times, which led them to see current political mechanisms through darkly suspicious spectacles. In my revised discussion of the literature of 1614, I have tried to show how those larger meanings play across different media, resulting in a strong awareness of and response to a phenomenon we can legitimately call censorship, even if contemporaries did not have a catch-all word.

To speak of a writerly self-respect is to imply that authors did exist in this period. Much recent work has been devoted to denying their existence, or at least to dating their emergence very late. As argued above, the concept of authorship indeed demands careful analysis; but the characteristic process of erecting a large and categorical distinction between old and new forms of authorship is in the end less fruitful than being open to the very different forms of individual or collaborative authorship that may reflect different social, political, and economic contexts in any period. For example, the recent, and welcome, revival of interest in early modern manuscripts has been seized on by critics eager to find a radically pre-modern form of authorship. The manuscript ethos is seen as the antithesis of the coolness and modernity of print as analysed by McLuhan.[129] In some respects, this new emphasis on manuscript culture parallels revisionist historiography, which has criticized Hill for relying so heavily on printed texts, implying that the heart of the period is to be found in archival documents and in private letters exchanged between aristocratic patrons and clients. Manuscript verse may seem a classic instance where language speaks the subject rather than vice versa: in verse miscellanies, poems often circulated anonymously and their transcribers felt free to adapt poems to their own purposes. Manuscript transmission can be aligned with a discrete 'manuscript culture' in which modern senses of authorial agency were far less significant than in print. This backward-looking element can be linked with the political conservatism of manuscript culture, with its largely royalist and Anglican weighting.[130] Jonathan Goldberg, bringing together Derrida and Foucault in his analysis, strongly resists any attempt to link scribal culture with an idealized, traditional oral culture, but is

---

[129] Arthur F. Marotti, *Manuscript, Print, and the English Renaissance Lyric* (Ithaca, NY, 1995); Harold Love, *Scribal Publication in Seventeenth-Century England* (Oxford, 1993), reissued as *The Culture and Commerce of Texts: Scribal Publication in Seventeenth-Century England* (Amherst, Mass., 1998); Peter Beal, *In Praise of Scribes: Manuscripts and their Makers in Seventeenth Century England* (Oxford, 1998); the serial *English Manuscript Studies, 1100–1700* is a mine of information on this topic.

[130] Marotti, *Manuscript, Print, and the English Renaissance Lyric*, 137, 207, 125.

even more sharply opposed to any idealization of an emergent print public sphere: the new print technology is 'not . . . one more episode in how we all become more rational, scientific, individualized, and democratic' but 'a technology that goes hand-in-hand with the ideological formations of the Elizabethan state'.[131]

Discipline and constraint there certainly was; but that antithesis offers us a more absolute choice than is either theoretically or empirically necessary. There is indeed, as Marotti argues, a huge body of interesting, anonymous verse which has escaped critical notice because it cannot be tied to a specific author. But if we elide questions of authorial agency altogether we shall risk burying evidence of unusual variations on the dominant cultural code, for example work by women writers: the poems of Anne Southwell, for example, formed part of a series of literary exchanges which were marked by very specific gender interests.[132] As Margaret Ezell has so persuasively shown, manuscript circulation was a means by which women could undertake the relatively avant-garde activity of circulating literary work while evading censures against immodesty.[133] While the early stage of revisionist historians' turn to the archives concentrated on official records which tended to present ideological consensus, it is emerging more and more that the world of manuscripts provides fascinating evidence of previously unsuspected forms of political agency, from extensive writings by women to satires and polemics to petitions. These writers seem to have been strongly resistant to some aspects at least of the state's disciplining. Harold Love—concentrating, it is true, on a later period—writes of 'a natural tendency for scribally published texts to be oppositional'.[134] Certainly some of the most daring political poetry of the period was confined to manuscript—notably the satires against Cecil and James I and the eulogies of Buckingham's assassin John Felton.[135] Such 'underground' verse can indeed be very hard to identify with a single author— evading responsibility for authorship was a major means of diminishing the danger of punishment. But the authors of the Felton poems frequently protest against the silencing of truth, to the extent that they seem to be protesting against their own medium and longing for the opportunity of speaking more publicly: as James Holstun has put it, in 'the relatively anonymous space of the streets and the circulated manuscript, they engage in something like a repressed republican *conversazione civile*'.[136] This burgeoning 'underground' verse, much of which never reached print and is still difficult of access today, is hard to fit under the stock revisionist response

[131] Jonathan Goldberg, *Writing Matter: From the Hands of the English Renaissance* (Stanford, Calif., 1990), 27.

[132] *The Southwell-Sibthorpe Commonplace Book: Folger Ms. V.b. 198*, ed. Jean Klene (Tempe, Ariz., 1997); Louise Schleiner, *Tudor and Stuart Women Writers* (Bloomington, Ind., 1994), 113–22.

[133] Margaret J. M. Ezell, *The Patriarch's Wife: Literary Evidence and the History of the Family* (Chapel Hill, NC, 1987).

[134] Love, *Scribal Publication in Seventeenth-Century England*, 185.

[135] Pauline Croft, 'The Reputation of Robert Cecil: Libels, Political Opinion, and Popular Awareness in the Early Seventeenth Century', *Transactions of the Royal Historical Society*, 6 (1991), 43–69; Alastair Bellany, ' "Rayling Rhymes and Vaunting Verse": Libellous Politics in Early Stuart England', in Sharpe and Lake (eds.), *Culture and Politics in Early Stuart England*, 285–310; Holstun, *Ehud's Dagger*, 158–65, 177–86.

[136] Holstun, *Ehud's Dagger*, 165.

to allegations of censorship: that the writing was so dull that stationers held back from purely economic motives.[137]

In such cases of sustained campaigns mounted through verse, we need to go beyond the binaries of fixed, stable print identity and fluid manuscript identity, and to look for patterns of collective agency. Such patterns can, of course, be found in print as well as manuscript texts, as Michelle O'Callaghan shows in her study of the Jacobean Spenserian poets. Manuscript and print were different media in which the period's writers explored the possibilities of a public sphere.[138] And that public sphere extended to the international republic of letters. However metaphorical the term 'republic' in that phrase, it did imply a sense of empowerment, of common citizenship, that could be appealed to against the subjecthood of local restrictions.[139] It is fascinating that one of the earliest English uses of the phrase should have come from Sir Henry Wotton, who commented on the basis of his diplomatic knowledge of the Venetian republic that the Parliamentarians of 1614 acted as if they were citizens rather than subjects.[140] How far that communal self-identity affected English writers' sense of themselves is a topic still needing more exploration.

The less one believes in the agency of authors in the period, the more emphasis one will tend to put on patronage.[141] It is true and important that a patron–client relationship remained a very significant mode of literary production, with writers ready to produce texts to be circulated on behalf of a patron, anonymously or under the patron's name. (Equivalent relationships, after all, are not unknown in today's political world.) Revisionist historians, emulating Sir Lewis Namier's analysis of the politics of the mid-eighteenth century, have placed much emphasis on the significance of patronage and clientage as opposed to political ideology. The result is a top-down model of political culture, with the writer as a transmission-belt for the intrigues of the leaders at court. Such models militate against any attempt to link poets with some kind of coherent 'opposition'. Perhaps the most problematic part of the book is the attempt to give two different narratives of the early part of James's reign, from the point of view of Jonson as court poet and then of the Spenserian 'opposition'. Some

---

[137] Thomas Cogswell, 'Underground Verse and the Transformation of Early Stuart Political Culture', in Susan D. Amussen and Mark A. Kishlansky (eds.), *Political Culture and Cultural Politics in Early Modern Europe* (Manchester, 1995), 277–300.

[138] O'Callaghan, *The 'Shepheards Nation'*, 3–7 and *passim*. Cf. Douglas Bruster, 'The Structural Transformation of Print in Late Elizabethan England', in Arthur F. Marotti and Michael D. Bristol (eds.), *Print, Manuscript, and Performance: The Changing Relations of the Media in Early Modern England* (Columbus, Oh., 2000), 49–89.

[139] Norbrook, 'The Monarchy of Wit and the Republic of Letters'; Paul Dibon, 'Communication in the Respublica literaria', *Respublica litterarum: Studies in the Classical Tradition*, 1 (1978), 43–56; Marc Fumaroli, 'La République des lettres redécouverte', in Marta Fattori (ed.), *Il vocabolario della république des lettres: Terminologia filosofica e storia della filosofia. Problemi di metodo* (Florence, 1997), 41–56; Peter Miller, *Peiresc's Europe: Learning and Virtue in the Seventeenth Century* (New Haven, 2000).

[140] Sir Henry Wotton was using the phrase in the 1590s: *Life and Letters of Sir Henry Wotton*, ed. Logan Pearsall Smith, 2 vols. (Oxford, 1907), ii.312; cf. David Colclough, '"Better Becoming a Senate of Venice": Freedom of Speech and the Addled Parliament', in Stephen Clucas and Rosalind Davies (eds.), *1614: Year of Crisis. Studies in Jacobean History and Literature* (Aldershot, 2002).

[141] For a survey of the topic see Cedric C. Brown (ed.), *Patronage, Politics, and Literary Traditions in England, 1558–1658* (Detroit, 1993).

readers have objected that this turns into ideological differences what was merely a dispute between 'ins' and 'outs'; and they can point to the fact that Jonson seems to move closer to the Spenserians when he is losing court favour. Similarly, Middleton's *A Game at Chess* has been read as the dramatist's responding to a commision from Charles and Buckingham rather than some kind of autonomous oppositional gesture.[142] The new edition of Middleton's works currently in process will certainly complicate Heinemann's picture of a straightforwardly oppositional writer. As indeed I pointed out myself, there was certainly nothing like a modern political opposition, and I reflected long on whether to structure the book in this way; but I was fortified by the support of the publisher's reader for the first edition, Frances Yates, and I continue to believe that doing so is in fact less distorting than breaking the period up into an endless series of local, fragmented factional disputes. Such disputes existed, and at times like the 1614 Parliament their effects are so intricate that it is hard not to get completely lost. But there are reasons why writers gravitate to certain patrons, and they can do so to influence them as much as to follow their directives. Patronage and ideology are far from mutually exclusive. In a classic analysis of the politics of the 1730s, Quentin Skinner countered the Namierite tendency to reduce debates about principles to manoeuvres for patronage and interest. Even if it could be shown that a politican adopted a particular political rhetoric with the motive of gaining power, this did not mean that the issues being debated between him and his opponents could be simply reduced to a struggle for power. Having professed a position in public, he would find readers ready to hold him to it and perhaps to develop in directions he would not himself have expected.[143] There is still a need, as Paul Hammer observes in his biography of Essex, to 'put the mind back into our understanding of Elizabethan culture'.[144] For the Jacobean period, recent studies of figures like Sandys and Southampton have found significant ideological continuity. My own accounts of the policies of Protector Somerset under Edward VI, of the Essex circle in the 1590s, of the Jacobean opposition, and of Milton in relation to the opposition in the 1630s, take for granted the significance of ideological debate.

The death of the author, current theory reminds us, is the birth of the reader. The recent revival in the history of reading has partly been a response to anti-humanist theory, directing our attention away from authorial agency; but in practice it has opened up new areas in which writers and readers were involved in actively changing the political world. Spenser's and Sidney's friend Gabriel Harvey, who receives some attention in Chapters 3 and 5 below, appears in a now-classic article by Lisa Jardine and Anthony Grafton along with a book-wheel, a mechanism by which a scholar

---

[142]   See the differing views referenced at Ch. 9 n. 17.

[143]   Quentin Skinner, 'The Principles and Practice of Opposition: The Case of Bolingbroke versus Walpole', in Neil McKendrick (ed.), *Historical Perspectives: Studies in English Thought and Society in Honour of J. H. Plumb* (London, 1974), 93–128.

[144]   Paul E. J. Hammer, *The Polarisation of Elizabethan Politics: The Political Career of Robert Devereux, 2nd Earl of Essex, 1585–1597* (Cambridge, 1999), p. xii.

could easily keep several books open and available for consultation at the same time.[145] Whether or not Harvey actually owned such a contrivance, it indicates his humanist habits of reading, darting quickly from text to text in order to form aphorisms that could then be applied to the current political situation. Such a mode of reading did indeed imply scant respect for authorial presence—though we should bear in mind that figures like Sidney were in fact strongly interested in Aristotelian ideas of literary unity. When it came to practical politics, however, the fragmentary 'sentence' was important. Leading aristocrats and statesmen often employed humanists like Harvey to read with—or for—them. Harvey guided Sidney through Livy, an author whose zeal for liberty made him appeal to early modern republicans. Harvey's own views were hardly republican, but the enthusiasm for studying such texts, and the insistence that they were relevant to current politics, does help to explain Hobbes's later comment that humanist studies were a major cause of the English Revolution.[146] Work by William Sherman, Lisa Jardine, Alan Stewart, and others continues to illuminate these sensitive areas where ideological debate intersected with political patronage.[147] And a study of Sir William Drake by Kevin Sharpe has led him radically to modify his earlier claims about the restricted and consensual character of early Stuart political discourse, revealing how far the imagination could range.[148]

*

It will perhaps be clear from the above discussion why I decided not to rewrite the book: it would never have ended, so hard have I found it to rein in even an Afterword. So many exciting avenues remain to be explored, and I can only hope to have encouraged others to press further. At this distance in time, some of the transatlantic and other methodological divisions discussed at the beginning have arguably diminished. This is partly a product of political change, with the steady expansion of an international economic order which has brought the United Kingdom in some ways closer to the United States, and greater awareness in a multiethnic Britain of the difficulty of sustaining older ideas of cultural homogeneity. Today a confrontation with different forms of colonial legacy is a common concern, necessarily engaging many questions of identity that were little explored in Britain a couple of decades ago. Whether some older questions about general norms of social and political justice have been slighted in the process remains open to debate. I hope to have suggested some ways in which older and newer critical approaches

---

[145] Lisa Jardine and Anthony Grafton, '"Studied for Action": How Gabriel Harvey Read his Livy', *Past and Present*, 129 (1990), 30–78 (46–51).

[146] Cf. Ch. 8 n. 70.

[147] William H. Sherman, *John Dee: The Politics of Reading and Writing in the English Renaissance* (Amherst, Mass., 1995); Lisa Jardine and Alan Stewart, *Hostage to Fortune: The Troubled Life of Francis Bacon* (London, 1998).

[148] Kevin Sharpe, *Reading Revolutions: The Politics of Reading in Early Modern England* (New Haven, 2000).

might come into dialogue, while continuing to believe that a long time-scale may be helpful as a counterweight to intellectual fashion. More practically, I hope the book will continue to provide a useful way into a literature and a historical epoch of inexhaustible richness.

Further Reading

IT sometimes seems as if everyone in Renaissance England wrote poetry. Very many did, much of it has survived, and a lot of it is worth reading. A large quantity of this verse concerned politics in some sense. To gain access to this profusion is not always easy. Anthologies tend to concentrate on love lyrics, though *The Penguin Book of Renaissance Verse*, selected and introduced by David Norbrook, ed. Henry Woudhuysen (London, 1992), tries to give a good weighting to political verse. Jane Stevenson and Peter Davidson (eds.), *Early Modern Women Poets (1520–1700): An Anthology* (Oxford, 2001), is an outstanding introduction to a very wide range of poets. The works of the major writers give crucial insight into the age's politics and are available in numerous editions. There are excellent selections of Sidney's writings by Katherine Duncan-Jones (Oxford, 1989) and of Jonson's by Ian Donaldson (Oxford, 1985); the Longman edition of *The Faerie Queene*, ed. A. C. Hamilton (London, 1967) provides a lot of guidance, as does the edition of *Edmund Spenser: The Shorter Poems* by Richard A. McCabe (Harmondsworth, 1999). The edition of *The Complete English Poems of John Donne* by C. A. Patrides (London, 1985) is very well annotated. For Milton, *The Complete Shorter Poems*, 2nd edn., ed. John Carey (London, 1997) is highly recommended. There are selections from Fulke Greville by Thom Gunn (London, 1968), with an excellent introduction, by Joan Rees (London, 1973), and by Neil Powell (London, 1990). *Elizabeth I: Collected Works*, ed. Leah S. Marcus, Janel Mueller, and Mary Beth Rose (Chicago, 2000) provides a monarch's-eye view of poetry and politics.

For less canonical texts, resources are fewer. There is an anthology of *Court Masques: Jacobean and Caroline Entertainments, 1605–1640*, ed. David Lindley (Oxford, 1995). For the Jacobean 'Spenserians', there are William B. Hunter, Jr. (ed.), *The English Spenserians: The Poetry of Giles Fletcher, George Wither, Michael Drayton, Phineas Fletcher and Henry More* (Salt Lake City, 1977) and James Doelman (ed.), *Early Stuart Pastoral* (Toronto, 1999). Wither's longer poems are available through the Victorian Spenser Society facsimiles, and reprints made during the 1960s. A lot of otherwise obscure poetry was edited with immense enthusiasm, if some inaccuracy, by the industrious Victorian clergyman A. B. Grosart. Much of the most outspoken, and some of the best, satirical verse circulated only in manuscript, and those poems that have found their way into print have often been liable to bowdlerization by editors, so that there is a pressing need for an anthology of Elizabethan and Stuart satirical verse, and in the longer term for a sixteenth-century or early-Stuart equivalent of the *Poems on Affairs of State* series for the post-1660 epoch. *Poems and Songs Relating to George Villiers, Duke of Buckingham*, ed. F. W. Fairholt (London, Percy Society, 1850) provides one starting point, and the articles referenced in Chapters 8 and 9 provide extensive quotations.

For those with access to subscribing libraries, the *Early English Books Online* series, or its microfilm equivalent, makes it possible to explore a huge quantity of neglected political verse without the need for editorial intervention. Steven W. May's forthcoming *First-Line Index of Elizabethan Verse* will provide an index opening up a lot of previously uncharted political verse. *The New Cambridge Bibliography of English Literature*, i, ed. George Watson (Cambridge, 1974) offers a very comprehensive guide to poetry.

The footnotes to individual chapters effectively provide reading lists for specific topics, so I shall confine myself to a selection of general and introductory works. Of the traditional literary histories, C. S. Lewis, *English Literature in the Sixteenth Century: Excluding Drama* (Oxford, 1954) remains a *tour de force* of readable erudition; for the latter part of the period see Douglas Bush, *English Literature in the Earlier Seventeenth Century, 1600–1660* (Oxford, 1945). Stephen Greenblatt, *Renaissance Self-Fashioning from More to Shakespeare* (Chicago, 1980) remains the best example of more recent 'new historicist' criticism, compellingly written and argued. For excellent examples of a different form of historical criticism, see Annabel Patterson, *Reading Between the Lines* (Madison, 1993). Recent general surveys include Arthur F. Kinney (ed.), *The Cambridge Companion to English Literature, 1500–1600* (Cambridge, 1993) and Thomas N. Corns (ed.), *The Cambridge Companion to English Poetry, Donne to Marvell* (Cambridge, 1999). Steven W. May, *The Elizabethan Courtier Poets: The Poems and their Contexts* (Columbia, Mo., 1991) gives a valuable introduction to the conventions and contexts of courtly verse. C. V. Wedgwood, *Poetry and Politics under the Stuarts* (Cambridge, 1960) remains a useful survey; for a more recent introduction to public poetry in the later part of the period see Gerald Hammond, *Fleeting Things: English Poets and Poems, 1616–1660* (Cambridge, Mass., 1990). Joanna Martindale, *English Humanism: Wyatt to Cowley* (London, 1985) is a useful anthology of humanist writings with historical commentary.

R. Malcolm Smuts, *Culture and Power in England, 1585–1685* (New York, 1999) provides an up-to-date synthesis of political, literary, and cultural history, with a courtly focus. For general histories, see for the sixteenth century John Guy, *Tudor England* (Oxford, 1988), Penry Williams, *The Later Tudors: England 1547–1603* (Oxford, 1995), and Susan Brigden, *New Worlds, Lost Worlds* (London, 2000); for the seventeenth century, Derek Hirst, *England in Conflict, 1603–1660: Kingdom, Community, Commonwealth* (London, 1999); Christopher Hill, *The Century of Revolution, 1603–1714* (London, 1980) is still an excellent introduction. Valuable collections of recent historical debates can be found in John Guy (ed.), *The Tudor Monarchy* (London, 1997) and Richard Cust and Ann Hughes, *The English Civil War* (London, 1997).

On early modern political theory, David Wootton (ed.), *Divine Right and Democracy: An Anthology of Political Writing in Early Stuart England* (Harmondsworth, 1986) provides not only an excellent selection of political prose, including texts from the Jacobean period, but incisive commentary.

On historiography, Alastair MacLachlan, *The Rise and Fall of Revolutionary*

England: An Essay on the Fabrication of Seventeenth-Century History (London, 1996) gives a detailed (and, as its title suggests, critical) account of Marxist interpretations of the English Revolution; for a defence, see James Holstun, *Ehud's Dagger: Class Struggle in the English Revolution* (London, 2000), chs. 2–4. R. C. Richardson, *The Debate on the English Revolution Revisited*, 3rd edn. (London, 1998) offers a more general survey.

Index